THE ITALIAN SOCIALIST MOVEMENT

I: ORIGINS (1860-1882)

by

RICHARD HOSTETTER

D. VAN NOSTRAND COMPANY, INC.

PRINCETON, NEW JERSEY

TORONTO   LONDON

NEW YORK

D. VAN NOSTRAND COMPANY, INC.
120 Alexander St., Princeton, New Jersey (*Principal office*)
257 Fourth Avenue, New York 10, New York

D. VAN NOSTRAND COMPANY, LTD.
358, Kensington High Street, London, W.14, England

D. VAN NOSTRAND COMPANY (Canada), LTD.
25 Hollinger Road, Toronto 16, Canada

Published simultaneously in Canada by
D. VAN NOSTRAND COMPANY (Canada), LTD.

Library of Congress Catalogue Card No. 58-13833

PRINTED IN THE UNITED STATES OF AMERICA

To Eugenia

Preface

THIS volume tries to illuminate the origins of a political movement that today commands the voting loyalty of a huge and vital segment of the Italian nation. The mass political organizations headed by Pietro Nenni and Palmiro Togliatti, whatever their points of difference, share a basic premise: that the struggle to gain control of the Italian state and create a socialist society must be based, not on a mere alliance between organized labor and political socialism, but on their fusion into an articulated class organism capable of exerting the maximum political and economic pressure on the existing system. If the student of Italian socialism uses this premise as his criterion in fixing the origins of the movement, his point of departure must be the decade of the 1880's, when the two essential elements of the formula made their appearance: a political socialist party and a modern industrial workers' movement. The former was a direct consequence of the electoral law of 1882 which, by quadrupling the Italian electorate, opened up the possibility of sending socialists into the Chamber of Deputies. There was a workers' movement prior to 1880, but it had neither organic bonds nor a wage-earning class of factory workers at its base; only in the third decade of national unity did the Italian economy reach that stage of industrialization necessary to the organization of a modern labor movement. The effort to achieve the confluence of these two elements, socialism and organized labor, bore fruit at the Genoa Congress of 1892, which founded the Italian Workers' Party, the direct lineal forebear of the modern Italian Socialist Party, the indirect antecedent of the present-day Italian Communist and Social Democratic organizations. In what sense, then, can a discussion of the period antedating the rise of a socialist political party and an organized industrial proletariat lay claim to clarifying the origins of the modern Italian socialist movement?

The socialist experience during the first two decades of national unity defined very clearly the limits, both ideological and methodological, within which Italian socialism had to proceed if it would become a living political force among the masses whose welfare it claimed as its central concern. The controlling assumptions, both as to methods and goals, of the labor and socialist leaders who, in the late 1880's, gave the Italian socialist movement its modern form, were a direct derivative of two decades of socialist activity and discussion aimed at "emancipating the proletariat." Definition as to socialist methods was particularly sharp by 1880, for previous experience had included a true socialist movement, "true" in the sense that it, too, had proposed the material salvation of the common man through class struggle. Though this movement never gained mass support, though it was weighted down with prejudices against the state and political action, with a stubborn predilection for conspiratorial and insurrectional methods, though it was inescapably doomed by the emergence after 1880 of possibilities for more realistic and practical approaches to the socialist goal, those responsible for the exploitation of these new opportunities were, in the main, men either drawn from the ranks of that earlier movement or men whose appreciation of more modern methods was heightened and confirmed precisely because they had witnessed—and, in some cases, fought—the inadequacies of the old.

The creation of the Italian Workers' Party in 1892 presupposed the existence of a partially enfranchised industrial proletariat and a tradition of political socialism, but the dynamic factor that brought these two elements together was an appreciation of the inferences to be drawn from the experience of the antecedent generation of socialists. The Italian socialist movement of the late nineteenth century was no denial of the past, no creation *ex novo*, however complete the liquidation of old methods and forms of organization, but an organic progression from an earlier experimental epoch, full of false starts, ideological confusion, and dissension. Concerning itself with this slow process of clarification occurring during the twenty years following Cavour's forging of the Italian nation-state, the present volume is no "prehistory" of the modern Italian socialist movement, but an effort to summarize the experience that helped produce its characteristic premises.

Given the vastness of bibliographical resources in the field of Italian socialism, the present discussion claims neither completeness nor thorough originality of interpretation. It is presented as a critical exploitation of the pertinent, serious monographs by Italian scholars, supplemented by source materials—newspapers, magazines, pamphlets, memoirs, correspondence, congress proceedings, etc.—in all cases where modern monographic treatments either do not exist or differ appreciably in their conclusions.

The subject matter covered and its chronological presentation parallel, to a great extent, those of the first three volumes of Professor Aldo Romano's projected nine-volume *Storia del Movimento Socialista in*

*Italia**—evidence of my conviction that the author succeeded brilliantly in his announced intent "di ordinare e qualificare il vasto materiale esistente," that his indispensable volumes are, indeed, a "pilot-research" for students in the field. In many instances, however, the conclusions and interpretations of the present volume contrast substantially with those of Professor Romano—a consequence, partly, of differing canons of historical analysis. No one more than Professor Romano, I might add, has encouraged my belief that a "definitive" history of the complex phenomenon of Italian socialism will be written—if at all—only when the topic has been subjected to a far greater catholicity of approach than has characterized socialist historiography since the Second World War. From this belief stemmed the study here presented, which contributes in a small way, I trust, to the current effort to clarify the genesis of the Italian socialist movement. For his eloquent insistence on the need for further independent analysis, as well as for many evenings of amicable dissension, always stimulating, always informative, I am heavily indebted to Professor Romano.

To Professor Gastone Manacorda, Professor Franco Della Peruta, and to Doctor Luciano Cafagna, I am grateful for the opportunity to test my conclusions against their expert knowledge of the historiographical problems abounding in the field of post-Risorgimento social history. To Doctor Giuseppe Del Bo, Director of the Biblioteca G. G. Feltrinelli of Milan, go my thanks for facilitating my use of that institution's uniquely valuable collection of materials on Italian socialist and labor history. Doctor Luigi Cremascoli made very pleasant several days spent in the library in his charge, the Biblioteca Comunale of Lodi. At the Biblioteca Braidense of Milan, the Biblioteca Nazionale of Rome, and the Biblioteca di Storia Moderna e Contemporanea of Rome, I found cordial cooperation, especially at the last named, where Dottoressa Vilia Visone, Piero Valente, and Ennio Bozzetti proved unfailingly helpful.

My entire research effort in Italy, culminating in the publication of this book, was made possible by generous grants from Brown University of Providence, Rhode Island and the Catherwood Foundation of Bryn Mawr, Pennsylvania. To the Board of Directors at each institution, and especially to President Barnaby C. Keeney of Brown University and Mr. Cummins Catherwood, goes my deepest appreciation.

---

* Vols. I-III published by Fratelli Bocca Editori, 1954-55, Rome.

RICHARD HOSTETTER

Rome, Italy
June, 1958

Contents

I

The Social Question and the
Making of Italy

NATIONAL UNITY AND THE PARTY OF ACTION

THE national unity formalized by proclamation of the Kingdom of Italy in the spring of 1861 seriously undermined the Party of Action (*Partito d'Azione*), that loose alliance of republicans whose activist impulses were personified by Giuseppe Garibaldi and whose democratic aspirations had their spokesman in Giuseppe Mazzini. Of those who reconciled themselves to the monarchical solution imposed by Camillo Cavour, some did so because their republicanism had been of such consistency that it could survive only so long as there was a reasonable hope that unity could and would come under republican auspices. Prior to 1859, there was a basis for optimism, for almost up to the eve of the actual unification, the policies of the Savoyard monarchy rarely suggested Victor Emmanuel and his prime minister as protagonists of national unity. As late as 1856 Cavour ridiculed the idea as a "joke" (*corbelleria*).[1] Piedmontese policy was dynastic, not national.[2] Under the circumstances, Italian republicans could feel that their cause was the wave of the future, the more so given their assumption that the ideals of *la patria* and political democracy under a republic guaranteed the popular support they considered indispensable to the making of Italy. Cavour exploded this myth. Those patriots whose republicanism depended on the indi-

[1] Letter to Rattazzi, Apr. 12, 1856, in Emile Ollivier, *L'Empire libéral* (Paris, 1895-1911), IV, 596.
[2] Cavour and the monarchy ". . . believed very late in the unity of the fatherland, when events, under the pressure of an irresistible logic, imposed themselves even on the narrow conceptions of a policy of expansion . . ." Mario Missiroli, *La monarchia socialista* (Bologna, 1922), p. 63. Cf., also, Cesare Cantù, *Della indipendenza italiana. Cronistoria* (Turin, 1872-76), p. 559.

1

visibility of the binomial, unity and republic, made their peace with the monarchy when the Piedmontese prime minister brusquely ruptured the integrity of their formula.

Even republicans whose faith might have weathered the *Partito d'Azione*'s loss of the unity plank could justify defection by pointing to the failure of the party's political and social platform to muster the popular support needed to forestall unification under the monarchy. The vision of political democracy, obviously, had nowhere near the propulsive power among the common people that it had for the militants of the party, in the main, petty bourgeois professionals and intellectuals. Nor had the social democratic elements of the republican propaganda sufficed to attract a mass following. "Democracy" had been defined as far more than the realization of civil rights; the republic would also promote the material well-being of the plebes. But republican leaders, in whom the patriotic passion was paramount, had to reject a priori any idea of preaching a class movement, a proletarian action combining social revolution with expulsion of the foreigner. Carlo Pisacane's argument in this sense remained, prior to 1860, a purely individual recommendation. The bulk of republican propaganda in the social field promised improvement of the material status of the masses as a *consequence* of an Italian republic, not as an integral aspect of the unification process itself, and certainly not as a condition for national independence. French doctrines of social revolution had their echoes in the peninsula, but after 1848, and more especially after Louis Napoleon's *coup d'état* of December 1851, all segments of the patriotic movement, monarchists and republicans alike, formed a *union sacrée*, a tacit but effective common front, against the spread of such ideas. Thus, to many of the republicans accepting the solution of 1860, the social no less than the political content of the Mazzinian doctrine had demonstrated its lack of popular appeal. Unwilling to pretend that national unity had not dealt the republican idea a mortal blow, unable to accept social radicalism as an alternative to the new solution, the only refuge for these men was the parliamentary Left or political anonymity.

Of the republicans whose political convictions kept the Party of Action in existence as the anti-constitutional current of the Left, most saw the terms of their problem as essentially unchanged. Though Cavour had reduced their unity plank to the demand for Rome and the Veneto, it was still enough to justify their claim that opposing the monarchy on the institutional question was no proof of their lack of patriotism. The ethical appeal of republicanism suffered very little, given the undemocratic political aspects of the new regime. For men whose political beliefs reflected an intimate attachment to the moral values of democracy, the practical implications of Cavour's victory must have suggested no more than a revision of tactics, not of principles.

And a change of tactics there was, for until 1866 Mazzini declared a temporary truce with the monarchy to the extent that he abated his efforts to subvert the regime through republican insurrection, even to the extent that he briefly negotiated with the monarchy for republican collaboration in the liberation of the Veneto. Also tending to neutralize the vigor of the Party of Action's opposition role in the immediate post-unification period was the fact that the new state embodied a key element in Mazzini's political formula: administrative centralization, the logical corollary of his emphasis on the necessity of making "Italians." The unitary structure of the new kingdom made it no inconsistency at all that Mazzini was reluctant to agitate for a disruption of monarchical political centralization while the system was engaged in its initial efforts to perpetuate and strengthen itself. The criticism that Mazzini conceived his republic as a monarchy without a monarch touches a crucial aspect of the republican position in the immediate post-unity years.[3]

If the great majority of those republicans whose convictions weathered the events of 1859-60 clung to the view that the "Italian problem" was essentially that of completing territorial unification under a democratic republic, there were those who demanded, in the name of greater realism, a broader definition of "democracy" than that advanced by Mazzini. Patriots and republicans no less than Mazzini himself, convinced of the profound sense of *italianità* among the masses, they generally agreed with the prevailing assumption that the ideals of national unity and political democracy were elements necessary to the success of republican propaganda among the common people. Like Mazzini, they continued to believe, too, in the practicality of a popular initiative to complete Italy's territorial unification. Yet it was precisely the question of whether such a popular initiative could be stimulated without a redefinition of the democratic goal that sired an internal conflict among republicans which, by its intrinsic nature, could not be confined within the limits of a discussion of tactics alone.

The record of the recent past had much to say, in fact, about popular

[3] For an elaboration of this point, Emilio Sereni, *Il capitalismo nelle campagne* (1860-1900) (Turin: Einaudi, 1947), pp. 85 ff. In 1853, Mazzini wrote that "After foreign domination, . . . federalism [is] the greatest plague that can descend on Italy: foreign domination contests our [national] life for a little while longer; federalism would cover it with impotence and condemn it to a slow, inglorious death from its birth." "Agli Italiani," Mar., 1853, *Edizione nazionale degli scritti di Giuseppe Mazzini. Scritti editi ed inediti* (Imola, 1906 ff.), LI, 39-40. This collection is cited below as *S.E.I.*; the volume numbers indicated refer to those for the entire collection, not to those of the several individual series (*Epistolario, Appendice Epistolario, Letteratura, Politica*).

patriotic initiatives. The people had not expelled the Austrians in 1848; the Roman Republic, with far from negligible popular assistance, had not kept the French out of Rome in 1849. Nor did the welcome accorded Garibaldi's Red Shirts by the populations of the *Mezzogiorno* (South) obscure the fact that his success owed much to ill-led, disorganized, inept Bourbon opposition, to nonintervention by Paris and London, and to Cavour's tacit connivance. Even this enterprise had its finale in a political transaction violating the sentiments of the "liberated" southerners. Most devastating of all: Cavour had accomplished more in two years than had popular agitation, plotting, and tumult in decades. That popular patriotism had facilitated his work, that republican militants had helped create a climate of opinion essential to his success, could not obscure the fact that, in the milieu of the mid-nineteenth-century state system, the diplomatic, military, and administrative resources at Cavour's disposal, intelligently organized and applied, proved a practical means of fulfilling quickly—and with a minimum of bloodletting—the nationalist aspirations awakened half a century earlier.

The logic of the republicans' situation of 1860 underlined the need to identify the error that had vitiated their efforts to make the unity struggle a movement of the *Popolo*. It was partly out of this analysis of the past that a small but vocal segment of them came to a thesis purporting to be both an explanation of past failure and the key to cancelling Cavour's victory on the institutional question. In a word, they advanced the idea of a "second revolution." Their assumption: that a republic can come only out of a thoroughgoing social transformation. It was in this sense that the "democracy" of the republic was to be broadened.

This orientation was not born solely out of republican reaction to the crowded events of 1859-60. It was new only in that it made explicit an idea that had found some nourishment ever since 1848.[4] In their thinking and propaganda, Italian republicans could not have avoided the socioeconomic implications of a "democratic" republic—Mazzini himself openly recognized them. Even had republicans ignored the issue on an abstract level, they could not have discounted the red thread of social radicalism running through the popular uprisings of 1848, the clamorous "Five Days" in Milan, and the riots and disorders in Tuscany, the Puglia, and the Campania. And abroad, the June Days in revolutionary Paris even more forcefully established in the minds of Italian democrats an unforgettable connection between popular political revolution and the economic aspirations of the people manning the barricades.

That these events produced no significantly increased emphasis on the

---

[4] See, for example, Luigi Bulferetti, *Socialismo Risorgimentale* (Turin: Einaudi, 1949).

social aspects of the republican program, prior to 1859-60, underlined the all-important difference: France existed, Italy was yet to be made. The foreigner, not the Italian bourgeoisie, was the primary obstacle to the republic. In the republican version of a democratic state, Italians, as free citizens of a free Italy, would enjoy economic and social justice, but not as the "proletarian" bulk of the nation, not as a distinct social class with unique economic interests. To have advanced a social program depending for its logical coherence on demonstrating a conflict of vital interests between the masses, however preponderant numerically, and propertied Italians, however small a fraction of the nation, would have reduced to a shambles the republican argument that the sacred duty of the Italian was to fight the occupying foreigner, not compatriots. Mazzini's own social program was not posited on the class-struggle thesis; for him, the poverty of Italy's masses, deemed a consequence of political disunity, argued the priority of the patriotic objective.

Until Cavour denied republicans the luxury of equating unity with the republic there was no real quarrel with this view of the problem. Only then did those republicans, in whom the 1848 movement had created inconclusive and vague, but nonetheless real, doubts about Mazzini's subordination of social to political demands, begin to formulate a coherent criticism of that policy. Now the republic seemed almost as distant as the popular social benefits it was supposed to produce. Cavour, in cutting much of the ground out from under the republican unity program, established the conditions for open discussion of an issue germinating within the ranks of Italian democracy for more than a decade. No longer lost in the clamor of competing patriotic programs, propaganda, and action that pretended to deny its importance—if not its existence—as an Italian problem, the social question could now demand attention. In the context of a united Italy, it was no longer an abstract or subsidiary problem, in these men's opinion, but a vital issue the lineaments of which could be seen whole for the first time, thanks to the fact that the central and passionately political aspiration of the preceding decades had been so richly served, which in turn, it might be noted in passing, released the intellectual energy needed to sustain the social critique of the new regime.

The new current of republican opinion, however, reflected no substitution of patriotic loyalties; they simply assumed a new content. In unified Italy the social question had become an "Italian" problem. As such, its identification by Italian democrats, as well as their search for its solution, proceeded under the same spiritual impulse motivating their previous revolutionary careers: love of la patria. The new state was seen as a betrayal of the "nation," the product of a revolution imposed from above in the political interests of the monarchy and its relative handful of supporters—less than 2 per cent of the population, if the right to vote be taken as the measure. But the crux of the criticism lay deeper: that Cavour had not only created a politically undemocratic state reflecting his personal political and social philosophy, but a state institutionalizing the economic interests of but a small part of the nation, the upper middle-class industrial and commercial aristocracy. In this sense the nation had been "betrayed," in this patriotic nexus the social critique of the new order had its true and intimate genesis.

CAVOUR AND THE BOURGEOIS ALLIANCE

By the republicans' criterion, the political shortcomings of the Cavourian state were so transparent as to make them of dubious value to a criticism seeking to justify itself as an insight into the sources of the system's character. The Senate was not the elective body Cavour himself had favored in 1848, for its members were named by the Crown, and its powers enabled it to frustrate every deliberation of the "popular" representative Chamber of Deputies, itself chosen by a highly restricted electorate,[5] so restricted by a property-tax qualification that the argument of historical necessity, so often adduced to defend it, is more specious than relevant. The deputies, with few exceptions, owed their seats to the possessing classes of Italian society.[6] Only northern Italy, with its higher economic level, had anything approaching popular representation, while the southern provinces averaged only one elector to every thirty-eight inhabitants. The military conscription system put the burden of service almost exclusively on the poorest classes. A tax system, including the ubiquitous salt levy, bore heavily on the poverty-ridden *contadini* (peasants) of the southern regions, to whom a money tax must have seemed a grim joke being played on them by their new masters in Turin.

Above all, the political structure of the new Kingdom of Italy reflected Cavour's success in extending the politically conservative system embodied in the Piedmontese *Statuto* of 1848. His doing so derived partly from his deep personal loyalty to the House of Savoy and the monarchical principle, but it was in his rigid and constant hostility toward the idea of popular participation in the making of Italy that he revealed his prejudice against applying the democratic principle to state and society. His formula, Risorgimento historians agree, lay in "diplomatizing" the na-

[5] By the electoral law of 1860 only 1.92 per cent of the population was enfranchised; by 1874 the electorate had grown to only 2.10 per cent of the total population.
[6] "The political class, in the sense of politically active groups, was furnished by plutocratic groups in the first decades of unity . . ." Giacomo Perticone, "Movimenti sociali e partiti politici nell'Italia contemporanea," in *Questioni di storia del Risorgimento e dell'unità d'Italia*, ed. by Ettore Rota (Milan: Marzorati, 1951), p. 554. This volume is cited below as *Questioni*.

tional revolution, removing it from the context of a patriotic mass movement and manipulating it in the dynastic interests of the monarchy by diplomatic and—as an extension of the diplomatic—military means. His was a complete denial of the spirit of popular revolution that republicans had so assiduously sought to keep alive after 1848. It is indicative that Garibaldi's audacious attack on the Kingdom of the Two Sicilies, the only territory won by a genuinely popular revolutionary force, gravely worried the Piedmontese statesman until the Hero of the Thousand surrendered his conquests in the name of "Italy and Victor Emmanuel."

At least two practical considerations help explain Cavour's use of diplomacy and war, rather than a stimulation of a mass revolt against the foreigner, as the means of forging a united Italy. Certainly the 1848 failure of a popular initiative encouraged no sponsorship of such a crusade for national liberation. Nor could a realistic appraisal of the Sardinian kingdom's strengths and weaknesses in relation to the European diplomatic constellation have suggested reliance on popular tumult in preference to diplomacy and war. Cavour had to deal with a conservative, monarchical Europe. But may he not also have feared the eventual price of popular assistance might prove excessive? Might not the Italian state have to be made synonymous with the nation—the nation to which the republicans were preaching democracy as the fruit of political unity?

The social implications of such a solution, no less than the political, could not have been lost on a man who for years was neither ignorant of, nor insensitive to, the social problems of his day.[7] Prior to the revolutionary movements of 1848, though firmly opposing anything that might disturb the social order, he considered it

> . . . a strict duty of society to consecrate part of the riches which are being accumulated . . . to the improvement of the moral and material conditions of the lower classes. . . . Let us see to it that all our fellow citizens, rich and poor, the poor more than the rich, participate in the benefits of advancing civilization, of increasing wealth, and we shall have resolved pacifically, in a Christian manner, the great social problem that others pretend to be able to resolve with tremendous subversions and frightening ruination.[8]

The events in France of 1848 brought him to rank the social problem first among those confronting the age:

[7] For full-length views of Cavour's social philosophy, see Antonio Fossati, *Il pensiero e la politica sociale di Camillo Cavour* (Turin, 1932); Adolfo Omodeo, *L'opera politica del conte di Cavour* (2d ed.; Florence: La Nuova Italia, 1945).

[8] Introductory article in the first issue of his newspaper, *Risorgimento*, Dec. 15, 1847.

The revolution in France of '48 has had the merit, if no other, of bringing a great truth into the full light of day: that is, that the greatest problems that an age is called upon to solve are no longer political, but social problems; that well above the questions in regard to the various forms of government stand those that reflect the economic structure of society. This truth . . . is now made so clear and indisputable by the tumults of the piazzas, by the wars of the streets, that anyone not smitten by intellectual blindness is compelled to recognize its very great importance.[9]

Cavour's concern for the economic condition of the common man, however, never pushed him to the conclusion that the working classes had the right to improve their lot through political action, far too advanced a view to expect from any statesman of the time. The 1848 movement in Paris, precisely such an attempt, had found in Cavour a critic who, already alarmed at the ideas of Louis Blanc and Blanqui, as well as those of the German "communists," considered such popular revolution a threat to the foundations of civilization. General Cavaignac's bloody suppression of the Parisian workers he deemed a matter of "saving the social order from an absolute destruction, of maintaining intact the sacrosanct principles of family and property, threatened by socialism and anarchy; of preserving modern civilization from an invasion of barbarians. And it is not a matter of France alone . . ."[10]

Of course it was not a matter of France alone, and the June Days stimulated a decisive turn toward social conservatism among moderates in Italy as well as abroad. After 1848 Italian republicans, including Mazzini,[11] had to defend themselves against charges of socialism, communism, and anarchism. The specter of social revolution haunting the European ruling classes after 1848 must have bulwarked Cavour, too, in his decision to "diplomatize" the Italian unity movement, to rule out popular support on the grounds that it might prejudice the creation of the socially conservative regime to which his personal social philosophy, perhaps as much as practical requirements, impelled him.[12]

[9] "Sul discorso proemiale del corso di Economia politica del Prof. Ferrara, 1849," A. Perrone, *Idee economiche del Conte di Cavour* (Turin, 1887), pp. 129-30.

[10] *Risorgimento*, June 30, 1848. *Cf.*, also, his letter to G. Corio of June 27, 1848, in E. Visconti, *comp.*, *Cavour agricoltore. Lettere inedite a G. Corio* (Florence, 1913), p. 230.

[11] "Whether the accusation comes from pontifical encyclicals or from venal newspapers, we shall be able to reply: you lie, knowing you lie." *S.E.I.*, XXXIV, 236.

[12] For documentation of the fear of communism and socialism in Italy during the decade, 1850-60, see Gastone Manacorda, "Lo spettro del comunismo nel Risorgimento," in the "Quaderni" of *Rinascita*, No. 2 (1951); Bulferetti, *op. cit.*, Appendix D, pp. 345-63; Gaetano Salvemini, *Mazzini* (4th ed.; Florence, 1925), Appendix: "La paura del socialismo fra il 1847 e il 1860"; Nello Rosselli, *Carlo Pisacane nel risorgimento italiano* (2d ed.; Genoa, 1936), pp. 148-74.

The conservative principle continued in full force after the death of Cavour in the summer of 1861, for the Piedmontese prime minister merely personified a socio-economic viewpoint pervading fairly generally the upper bourgeoisie, who had backed Cavour's policies in the full consciousness that he was detaching the "Italian problem" from the context in which Mazzini had sought to fix it: that of a general democratic revolution in Europe. These were the effective rulers of the new Italy, tenacious in their resolve to consolidate the state as a classically liberal, but socially conservative, institution. To them the "Italian problem" had no significant social content, not because they ignored or were indifferent to the poverty of millions of their countrymen, but because they could conceive that problem only within the limits of an as yet untested assumption: that its solution was implicit in the new economic freedom attending national unity.

If the pre-unity preoccupation with the patriotic objective impeded a clear identification of the social question by republicans, the same was true for the economically dominant classes of Italian society, the more so because the Italian industrial and commercial aristocracy had but recently acquired its own character as a distinct segment of society with a clearly defined set of economic interests. The development was very retarded, compared to that of the French and British bourgeoisie, who had long before gained the upper hand over the old landed aristocracy and disciplined their monarchies into a frank and unblushing tutelage of their class interests. In Italy the impetus was not given until the Napoleonic intrusion smashed the quasi-feudal pattern of economic relations and released the latent productive energies of the peninsula. Napoleon's policy may have made northern Italy an economic colony of the French Empire,[13] but the French also abolished ancient privileges and feudal corporative remnants, introduced the Napoleonic Code and new commercial and financial law, improved communications, introduced some machinery to industry, and stimulated—if but temporarily— a more rapid circulation of capital and a greater velocity in the exchange of goods. French taxes were in part returned to the Italian economy in the form of contracts for military supplies, wages, and other benefits. These were all economic developments favoring the rise of a modern bourgeois class, in itself one of the objectives of the revolution that had sired the French conqueror.[14]

[13] The thesis of Eugène Tarlé, *Le blocus continental et le Royaume d'Italie* (Paris, 1928).

[14] Antonio Fossati, *Lavoro e produzione in Italia dalla metà del secolo XVIII alla seconda guerra mondiale* (Turin: Giappichelli, 1951), pp. 53-59; *cf.*, also, the same author's essay, "Problemi economici e finanziari del Risorgimento e dell'Unità d'Italia," in *Questioni*, pp. 707-80; Roberto Tremelloni, *Storia dell'industria italiana contemporanea*, Vol. I: "Dalla fine del Settecento all'Unità italiana" (Turin: Einaudi, 1947), pp. 46-89.

Perhaps more significant, in this connection, than the impetus given by money-making opportunities in commerce, banking, and manufacturing, was the breaking up of the landed wealth of the old privileged patrician classes, both lay and ecclesiastical. Heavy French taxation of these groups forced them to sell the only possession capable of providing the necessary tribute: their landed estates. With so much land on the market simultaneously, prices were low enough that businessmen, professional people, and even well-to-do peasants were able to acquire the properties piecemeal.[15] This common acquisition of real estate greatly consolidated the position of the Italian middle class.

The disappearance of the Napoleonic system saw Italy revert to a patchwork of customs regimes, systems of weights and measures, transportation complexes, etc. In many respects the Restoration meant retrogression,[16] yet in the three decades after Napoleon there was a general technical advance in transportation and means of production, Italians broadened their economic as well as their cultural experiences, education was more widely diffused, labor became increasingly specialized, and petty industry tended to separate itself from agriculture. All these developments were definite evidence of a profound transformation in the economic structure of the peninsula, a set of changes no amount of political reaction in the various states could prevent. Actually, insofar as these changes were an expression of middle-class activity, the rulers of the Italian states had good reason to encourage, not hinder, them, since it was precisely these economic tendencies that enabled the new business aristocrats to increase the royal revenues while augmenting their own material fortunes. It was an atmosphere, in short, in which a self-conscious class of Italian entrepreneurs aimed for the same type of dominant position in society that their French and British counterparts had conquered for themselves long before.

Unlike the position of the French and British businessman, though, that of the Italian bourgeois was inextricably enmeshed with the broader program of national unification, for only in national unity could that class —especially its upper stratum—satisfy its natural need for economic expansion. Free exchange of goods, services, and capital between all parts of the peninsula; a coordinated transportation and communications system; a single system of customs, weights and measures, currency, and administrative law; a chance to compete on the international market; protection against foreign competition—all presupposed an Italian

---

[15] The church, particularly, suffered from this French-sponsored "land-grab." For details, Nello Quilici, La borghesia italiana; origini, sviluppo e insufficienza (2d ed.; n.p.: I.S.P.I., 1942), pp. 137 ff.

[16] For a documentation of the retrograde aspects of this period, see Fossati, Lavoro e produzione in Italia, pp. 67 ff.

state.[17] The desire for economic unity inevitably made champions of political unity out of the Turinese industrialist, the Milanese merchant, and the Genoese banker.

The nexus between the unitary program and the economic benefits they could derive from unification was perceived but slowly by the Italian business classes. In the northern regions the identification was made more quickly, since this area had already passed from a paternalistic rural regime to a rudimentary industrial economy, thus facilitating the development of a politically active middle class. In the case of Lombardy, the success of the unitary gospel among the Milanese bourgeoisie has been ascribed to the ambition of this group to establish an industrial and commercial domination over the other regions of the peninsula. In the case of the Piedmontese businessmen and industrialists, national unity promised salvation from Lombard competition and even the possibility of nudging the Lombards out of their leading position.[18] The bourgeoisie of the *Mezzogiorno*, on the other hand, were the very last to see their economic welfare in national unity.[19] As the leaders of the southern liberal movement in 1848, they wanted a constitution guaranteeing their own predominance in the government and agrarian legislation confirming their position as landowners. But their political aspiration was local, not unitarian and national.[20] Even the nationalist spirit that appeared in the south on the eve of Garibaldi's expedition has been described as "a true and proper improvisation," having no roots in the preceding decade.[21]

Though he did not intend his words as an appeal to the economic cupidity of a single class, Cavour himself was apparently more aware than the Italian bourgeoisie of the close relation between national unity and the only kind of economic progress that could strengthen that class. In the introductory article appearing in the first issue of his newspaper, *Risorgimento* (December 15, 1847), he clearly suggested the path to be

[17] "Younger, less prejudiced, more dynamic than the former dominant classes, sprung from the struggling nuclei of the Napoleonic neo-bourgeoisie, free from every caste prejudice and superstition," the Italian middle class of the post-Napoleonic period tended to give the national cause "a connotation of economic expansion, as well as of moral redemption." Quilici, *op. cit.*, p. 146. For a balanced discussion of the economic forces contributing to Italian unity, see the essay by Ettore Rota, "Spiritualità ed economismo nel Risorgimento italiano," in *Questioni*, pp. 217-58.

[18] Ettore Rota, *L'Austria in Lombardia e il partito democratico cisalpino* (Milan, 1913).

[19] See Domenico DeMarco, "Le classi sociali nell'età del Risorgimento. La nuova borghesia industriale e commerciale del regno di Napoli," in *Orientamenti per la storia d'Italia nel Risorgimento* (Bari: Laterza, 1952), pp. 87 ff.

[20] A. Anzilotti, *Movimenti e contrasti per l'unità italiana* (Bari: Laterza, 1930), p. 239.

[21] Ruggero Moscati, "Il Mezzogiorno nel Risorgimento italiano," in *Questioni*, pp. 285-86.

followed: "The political *risorgimento* of the nation is never detached from its economic *risorgimento*. . . . The conditions of the two progressions are identical."

Though only a minority of the Italian middle class understood the ineluctability of unification, that minority was politically powerful enough to impose a solution of the national problem that represented an indisputable tutelage of bourgeois economic interests—again excluding the entrepreneurs of the *Mezzogiorno*. In this sense, certainly, the unification of 1860 was a uniquely bourgeois triumph, even though the fact was not, perhaps, immediately apparent to all its beneficiaries.[22]

This institutionalizing, in a political sense, of the interests of the dominant bourgeoisie found its rationale among those patriotic intellectuals who drew from the events of 1848 the conviction that the *Risorgimento* must henceforth proceed on the basis of a sound conservative and monarchist policy, as distinguished from those in whom 1848 reinforced a determination that unity should be completed by a defense à outrance of the original democratic ideals. It was the former group that lent the necessary intellectual support to the alliance between Cavour and the new bourgeois aristocracy.[23] To some extent, Mazzini himself was responsible for this. After 1848, he began to re-evaluate his sympathies for the utopian socialism of Saint-Simon, and by the time dictatorship descended on France in December 1851, he felt compelled to make a blanket indictment of French socialism and the materialism at its core. When an unadulterated democrat like Mazzini raised doubts as to the ethical validity of socialist ideals, to which most bourgeois ideologians in Italy attributed the horrors of Parisian class struggle in 1848, it is not surprising that many of the country's intellectual leaders and the upper bourgeoisie whose social and political philosophy they had come to reflect should support a resolution of the national problem that would substitute the gentle arts of diplomacy and the disciplined campaigns of a professional army for popular insurrection. It was to their great good fortune, of course, that the European diplomatic milieu of the 1850's was peculiarly adapted to Cavour's particular talents in realizing the kind of Italy both he and they wanted.

[22] The study of economic factors in the Risorgimento is still in its initial phase, but for a classic example of the argument for the primacy of material considerations, almost entirely excluding ideological factors, see Arnaldo Agnelli, "L'indipendenza italiana dal punto di vista economico," in *Rendiconto del Reale Istituto Lombardo di Scienze e Lettere* (Milan, 1913), p. 757; and the same author's "Il fattore economico nella formazione dell'Unità italiana," *Risorgimento Italiano*, Yr. VI, Nos. 2-3 (Mar.-Apr., May-June, 1913), 253-78, 471-88.

[23] For an elaboration of this thesis, Aldo Romano, *Storia del movimento socialista in Italia*, Vol. I: "L'Unificazione nazionale e il problema sociale (1861-1870)" (Rome: Bocca, 1954), pp. 19 ff. This work is referred to below as *Storia*.

THE MEZZOGIORNO AND NATIONAL UNITY

The first coherent criticism of the solution of 1860 from a social point of view took the form of a protest against the administrative centralization of the hugely expanded Piedmontese political system. The federalist complaint, closely interwoven with advanced positions on the social question, found its most articulate expression in Naples,[24] the intellectual center of the *Mezzogiorno,* not surprising in that the former Kingdom of the Two Sicilies, with its unique political, economic, social, and cultural legacy, presented the most serious assimilation problem for the new national government. The differences between north and south and the problems arising therefrom are properly the concern of a massive historical literature, so they need not detain us here, but it may be well to summarize the central problem, in the words of an agent of the Turin government, Diomede Pantaleoni, as he reported his on-the-spot findings to Marco Minghetti, Minister of Interior in 1861:

> A *unitary* party does not exist in Naples; I would dare to affirm that there are not *twenty* individuals who want [national] unity and these are [returned] *émigrés* or those who have been given posts by the [Turin] government. It was the hatred of the middle classes for the Bourbons, the admiration for Garibaldi, his prestige, that made the revolution. . . . Will the people want to be governed by Turin and the local government here to be destroyed? One would have to be insane to think so. . . .[25]

On October 18, 1860, there appeared in Naples a newspaper called *Il Popolo d'Italia,* edited by Agostino Bertani, Aurelio Saffi, Filippo De Boni, and other republicans who thought they had detected the inner weakness of the Cavourian solution of the national problem. In the first issue, they argued that "the exaggerated administrative concentration" of the new Italy represented a direct challenge to the liberty of *la patria.* The government should represent "the instincts, desires, and needs of the people" and in the close articulation of the one with the other "the element of the working class must be the very first element." In the new epoch opened by national unity, the "people" would occupy the same position as had the bourgeoise in the era now in its wane. The new Italy must have

---

[24] For a description of the democratic circle in Naples during the decade prior to unification, see G. Lazzaro, *Memorie sulla rivoluzione dell'Italia meridionale dal 1848 al 7 settembre 1860* (Naples, 1867), and M. Mazziotti, *La reazione borbonica nel Regno di Napoli* (Rome, 1912).

[25] Franco Della Peruta, "Contributo alla storia della questione meridionale. Cinque lettere inedite di Diomede Pantaleoni, 1861," *Società,* Yr. VI, No. 1 (March, 1950), 69-94.

. . . that baptism of social morality without which every revolution is a lie and, after a certain period, is condemned to die. Every revolution that does not considerably broaden the circle of social coexistence, that does not morally and materially improve the condition of the many, is a profoundly immoral work or one whose principle is falsified. . . .[26]

Or, again, in the issue of October 31: "every revolution is a problem of improving the moral and material conditions of the people or it is a deception."

A significant aspect of these laments lay in the new emphasis on the *right* of the people to an improvement of their material condition, a far cry from Mazzini's notion that it could be achieved only through increasing awareness and performance of their social *duties*. The writers for *Il Popolo d'Italia*, moreover, put the "people," understood as distinct from the bourgeoisie, at the very center of the social order they felt should emerge from a united Italy. There is no suggestion of class struggle in this position, no hint that the working classes should fight their way to this central position at the expense of the middle classes, but these intellectuals were preaching a radicalism to the left of Mazzini, who never conceived his ideal social structure in any terms but those of an amalgamation or fusion of classes. In fact, in the sense intended here, Mazzini refused to recognize classes *per se*, preferring to view all Italians as a single moral entity whose *italianità* is the point of departure in erecting an equitable society.

The men of *Il Popolo d'Italia*, using the Turin government as their whipping boy, brought the idealism of Mazzini under fire, too, even though by indirection. Far from Mazzini's anti-materialism was the affirmation, in the November 12, 1860, issue, that "abstract truths, . . . generous aspirations . . . [and] liberty of speech" can not move the masses. The state that looks after the material interests of the people is invincible; the government that abuses or neglects them is inevitably destroyed by revolution. The implications of this position, in terms of its imminent socialism, are apparent. Though there is no explicit reference to class struggle, the right of revolution is based on a government's neglect of the material interests of the masses, considered as separate from those of the bourgeoisie.

That the new national government in Turin, rather than the bourgeoisie as an economic class, appeared as the immediate target of criticism was merely the consequence of its position as the central, overriding fact of the time, but the writers of *Il Popolo d'Italia* made it very clear that Turin's centralizing policies were most to be condemned on social and

[26] Issue of Oct. 18, 1860.

economic grounds. All the faults of the Bourbons were admitted, yet the poorer classes of the former kingdom had somehow found the wherewithal to keep themselves alive, albeit miserably. But now the Turin government's apparent indifference toward the mounting cost of living and increasing unemployment offered no hope.

Though much of the bitterness stemmed from economic stresses and strains implicit in the government's colossal problem of integrating, economically and politically, the newly acquired *Mezzogiorno* with the rest of the Italian kingdom, though presumably the criticism would lose its force once the initial shock of uniting two such disparate economies were overcome, the principles of a new and vital critique had been enunciated. Whether the criticism elaborated by the men of *Il Popolo d'Italia* would reach its logical extreme, i.e., become truly socialist in its analysis and conclusions, would depend in great part—perhaps even entirely—on whether the government could reconcile the peoples of the *Mezzogiorno* to a centralized administration and, at the same time, resolve the economic difficulties which the southerners believed a consequence of rigid centralization.

A veteran student of the Neapolitan situation in those years has pointed out that the problem of local autonomy in the south, as expressed by *Il Popolo d'Italia*, was of particular importance to the bourgeoisie of the area.[27] The government functionaries, the professional people, the merchants, and the proprietors of the former Bourbon kingdom had constituted the directive class in southern society, exercising their directive functions through participation in local administration. The centralist policies of the new national government, by greatly diminishing the powers of the municipality, sorely disillusioned these bourgeois, whose support of the political revolution had stemmed, as Pantaleoni observed, from hatred of the Bourbons and admiration for Garibaldi, not from any consuming affection for the House of Savoy and the example of the Piedmontese state. The criticism in the columns of *Il Popolo d'Italia* echoed this discontent.

By the eve of Garibaldi's Sicilian expedition, there had developed a close interdependence between middle-class political authority and that group's position of economic preponderance. It followed, then, that any deprivation by the Turin government of this local political power could not fail to disrupt the economic as well as the political conditions under which the south's middle class had found itself enjoying a directive role. The widespread reference in the *Mezzogiorno* to the "royal conquest" was due far more to the sensation that unity had brought a deterioration of general economic conditions and that "things were better" under the

[27] Romano, *Storia*, I, 47-48.

Bourbons, than to wounded regional pride, to Bourbon propaganda, or to resentment of Piedmontese bureaucrats with little comprehension of and much disdain for the newly acquired southern populations. However bad the old regime, it had achieved a certain stability in an economic sense; now that stability was destroyed, and the climate was one of uncertainty and flux, inevitable under the circumstances.[28]

It was not, however, a matter of climate alone, for the economic flowering expected from political unity, an expectation not confined to the south, failed to materialize; in fact, economic conditions temporarily worsened. In the south food prices were going up, along with unemployment. The region's embryonic industries immediately felt the devastating effects of northern competition when customs barriers were eliminated. The national government, burdened with a war debt and the necessity of greatly increased expenditures for the administration and economic development of the new territory, instituted a fiscal regime that seemed oppressive to the southerners, long accustomed to the relatively modest exactions of the Bourbons.[29]

The Turin government's financial policies and the general economic pressures had far more damaging effects on the bourgeoisie of the *Mezzogiorno* than on the middle class in the north. In Lombardy and Piedmont one can speak of upper and middle bourgeoisie as well as *petit bourgeois*, thanks to the higher degree of industrialization and commercial activity. In general, the upper and middle bourgeoisie in the north were sufficiently well entrenched, in an economic and financial sense, to withstand the impact of the temporary economic imbalances implicit in the unification process.

In the *Mezzogiorno* the majority of the middle class might be described, from a strictly economic viewpoint, as petty bourgeois. Aside from the ownership and exploitation of land—which in the south represented no quick way to make a fortune, considering the almost total lack of mechanization and the general infertility of the soil—there was simply no way for this majority to improve its material condition and achieve those gradations of middle-class society characterizing the class in the north. Commercial, industrial, and professional opportunity was at an absolute minimum, where it existed at all.

That the social critique of the new Italian state had its origins in the south, then, is no more surprising than the fact that it originated with

---

[28] The intimate flavor of this atmosphere is communicated in the Pantaleoni report reproduced by Paolo Alatri, "Le condizioni dell'Italia meridionale in un rapporto di Diomede Pantaleoni a Marco Minghetti, 1861," *Movimento Operaio*, Yr. V, Nos. 5-6 (Sept.-Dec., 1953), 750-92.

[29] For the impact of unification on southern economic conditions, G. Carano-Donvito, *L'economia meridionale prima e dopo il Risorgimento* (Florence, 1928).

lower middle-class intellectuals. From what other group could the complaint arise? There was no factory proletariat, nor even a diffused class of artisans. The huge majority of the southern population consisted, on the one hand, of an amorphous peasant mass, illiterate, stagnant, ignorant, poverty-ridden, opposed to change and susceptible to reactionary propaganda, be it clerical or Bourbon in origin; on the other, of the *lazzaroni* (urban poor), living from hand to mouth, steeped in vice, capable of the greatest excesses of mob violence and cynical torpor.

To what extent the low estate, as such, of the poorer classes in the south stimulated the moral indignation of the writers of *Il Popolo d'Italia* is difficult to guess. Even if their criticism of the new order derived essentially from a sentiment of outraged and frustrated republicanism, from an awareness that the system impinged on petty bourgeois economic and political prerogatives and opportunities, or even from a resentment that they and their kind had been excluded from the work of consolidating the state, their talents unexploited in the service of Italy— even allowing such motivations does not deny that their emphasis on the material interests of "the people" carried an implicit appeal for an alliance between the masses and petty-bourgeois intellectuals who considered themselves *déclassés*, politically and socially dispossessed. In the identification of their material interests with those of the humble classes, they were tacitly laying claim to the role of legitimate spokesmen of popular needs and aspirations. It was not the first time it had happened in Italy, but what mattered now was that political disunity no longer guaranteed containment of such a tendency within the limits of a single city or region. Naples and the *Mezzogiorno* had no monopoly on poverty and disgruntled petty-bourgeois intellectuals.

SOCIAL REVOLUTION AND PATRIOTISM:
CARLO PISACANE

Considered separately, the incipiently socialist ideas appearing in the articles of *Il Popolo d'Italia* constituted no novelty. Centering a new order on the working classes; the tutelage of popular material interests as the criterion of sound and just government; improvement of the material and moral conditions of the masses as the essential sanction of revolution; the *rights* of the people, as distinct from the bourgeoisie, to this betterment; material interests as the prime mover of the masses— all these concepts had found expression at one time or another in the pre-unity period. Mazzini himself had come close to accepting some of them in his writings addressed to the working classes of Italy. Still, the *pattern* was unique, the more so in that this particular set of social postulates was integrated with a protest against political centralization.

In brief, the social revolutionary content of a federalist critique argues a certain maturity of synthesis that, in turn, suggests no improvised reaction to the "royal conquest," but a reiteration—with allowances for a new political situation—of a previous formulation.

To the extent that the ideas expressed in *Il Popolo d'Italia* can be attributed to a single source, they derived from Carlo Pisacane (1818-57), who but three years earlier had died leading a military expedition against the Bourbons.[30] Scion of a noble Neapolitan family and a career officer in the royal army, Pisacane spurned both career and social position in 1847 when he fled the country with a wealthy landowner's wife of whom he was enamoured. His name leapt into prominence two years later when Mazzini named him chief-of-staff of the Roman republican army. In the period of enforced inactivity following the French occupation of Rome, Pisacane found the time and inclination for an intensive reading program that included history, eighteenth-century Italian philosophers, and contemporary social thinkers, with particular attention to Proudhon. In addition to maintaining a voluminous correspondence, especially with Carlo Cattaneo, the Milanese federalist writer and economist, Pisacane wrote a military history of the campaigns of 1848-49 called *La guerra combattuta in Italia negli anni 1848-49,*[31] a four-volume *Saggi storici, politici, militari sull'Italia* (published posthumously in 1858-60)[32] and his famous *Testamento politico,*[33] hurriedly composed on the eve of the Sapri expedition as a justification of that ill-fated adventure.

Though traces of the thought of Giambattista Vico, Gaetano Filangieri, Mario Pagano, and Gian Domenico Romagnosi are to be found in

[30] For an introduction to Pisacanian bibliography, see G. A. Belloni, "Bibliografia di Carlo Pisacane," *Rassegna Storica del Risorgimento,* Yr. XVI, Fasc. 1 (Jan.-Mar., 1929), 253-59. In addition to the biography by Nello Rosselli, cited above, see L. Fabbri, *Carlo Pisacane. La vita, le opere, l'azione rivoluzionaria* (Rome, Florence, 1904); P. Orlando, *Pisacane* (Rome, 1935); Vincenzo Mazzei, *Il socialismo nazionale di Carlo Pisacane* (Rome: Ediz. Italiane, 1943); Oreste Mosca, *Vita di Pisacane* (Rome: Atlante, 1953); Robert Michels, "Der patriotische Sozialismus oder sozialistische Patriotismus bei Carlo Pisacane," in Carl Grünberg, *ed., Archiv für die Geschichte des Sozialismus und der Arbeiterbewegung* (Leipzig, 1914), IV, 222-42. Pisacane's correspondence has been collected and edited by Aldo Romano, *Epistolario* (Rome: Dante Alighieri, 1937). For the Sapri expedition, Paolo Emilio Bilotti, *La spedizione di Sapri* (Salerno, 1907); L. Pollini, *La tragica spedizione di Sapri* (Milan, 1935); G. Racioppi, *La spedizione di Carlo Pisacane a Sapri con documenti inediti* (Naples, 1863).
[31] The latest edition published in Genoa, Tipografia Andrea Moretti, 1951. 372 pp.
[32] The first two volumes were published in 1858 by the Stabilimento Tipografico Nazionale (Genoa); the third and fourth volumes in 1860 by the Tipografia Agnelli of Milan. Subsequent references to this work are taken from the modern edition by Aldo Romano, *Saggi storici-politici-militari sull'Italia* (Milan, Rome: Edizioni Avanti!, 1957), 4 vols.
[33] *Testamento politico di Carlo Pisacane con l'aggiunta di alcuni cenni biografici* (Ancona, 1880), 15 pp.

Pisacane's writings, the chief influences were those of contemporary writers: Cattaneo, Proudhon, and, most of all, Giuseppe Ferrari, the author of *La federazione repubblicana* and *Filosofia della rivoluzione,* both published in 1851.[34] From this catholic array of ideological tendencies, Pisacane produced, in the third volume of his *Saggi,* a message to his fellow Italians that led the late Carlo Morandi to this final judgment of the man's work: "The binomial, social revolution and political liberty, as the premise of the national risorgimento, is the peculiar trait of Pisacane, his title of nobility, the motif that assures . . . the validity and interest of his position." [35] It is in Pisacane's definitions of social revolution and political liberty, however, that a far greater uniqueness comes to light.

Pisacane was the first Italian socialist to break with the assumption that French Jacobinism and Babeufism were the only legitimate wellsprings of socialist ideology. Doing so required real intellectual intrepidity, for the Italian utopianists of the preceding half-century, from Filippo Buonarroti, the War Commissioner in Liguria in 1794-95 under the French, to Giuseppe Ferrari, had been thoroughly hypnotized by French precedents. The Jacobin egalitarianism of Buonarroti, Guglielmo Cerise, and Antonio Ranza was frankly French in origin, and even Vincenzo Russo, who found his point of departure in Italian Jusnaturalism during the period of the French Revolution, had to fall back on Rousseau in criticizing riches and luxury as the source of popular oppression, poverty, and vice.[36] Of all the leaders of Italian socialist thought prior to the unification, Ferrari was regarded as the interpreter *par excellence* of the French socialist tradition, especially that being established by Proudhon. The failure of the unity effort of 1848-49 convinced Ferrari that nationalist hopes should no longer reside in the House of Savoy. In a letter to Cattaneo in September 1850 and a year later in his *La federazione repubblicana,* he argued that the Italian national movement had to be reoriented in conformity with the latest revolutionary ideologies prevalent in France, i.e., become socialist. Moreover, the Italian revolutionaries had to provoke French armed intervention as the only sure guarantee of success in the making of a united Italy.[37]

Though deploring Ferrari's francophilism, Pisacane accepted his con-

---

[34] On Ferrari, see Bruno Brunello, *Il Pensiero di Giuseppe Ferrari* (Rome: Dante Alighieri, 1933); A. Ferrari, *Giuseppe Ferrari* (Genoa, 1914); and the excellent essay by Alessandro Levi, "Il pensiero politico di Giuseppe Ferrari," *Nuova Rivista Storica,* Yr. XV, Nos. 3-4, 5-6 (May-Aug., Sept.-Dec., 1931), 217-58, 365-97.

[35] *I partiti politici nella storia d'Italia* (Florence: Le Monnier, 1945), p. 24.

[36] For a summary of the socialism of Buonarroti, Ranza, Cerise, and Russo, see Leo Valiani, *Storia del movimento socialista,* Vol. I: "L'Epoca della Prima Internazionale" (Florence: La Nuova Italia, 1951), pp. 94 ff.

[37] Rosselli, *op. cit.,* p. 190.

clusion that in Italy two revolutions must erupt simultaneously: the democratic national revolution—conceived by Ferrari as federalist rather than unitary—and the social revolution, "a natural, spontaneous, and irresistible act" of the masses, who must "arise by themselves, select and nominate their chiefs." [38] Ferrari was right, according to Pisacane, in identifying the error of 1848-49 as assaulting the political forms of despotism without overthrowing the despotic economic constitution. Insurrection of the masses would never truly liberate Italy unless radical social reforms were undertaken at the same time. Beyond this point, however, Pisacane and Ferrari parted company.

In the Neapolitan's opinion, Ferrari had neither an appreciation of the need for a modern army and a national military leadership nor sufficient faith in the ability of the Italians to liberate themselves. In a letter to Cattaneo, written just after he had read Ferrari's *La federazione repubblicana*, Pisacane agreed with Ferrari "in believing Italy can hope for salvation through socialism; but . . . if the socialist party is formed, . . . Italy will not undergo the military dictatorship of France and perhaps would even be able to take the initiative." [39] A month later he wrote: "by admitting a powerful concept [socialism] as the mover of the masses, Italy can go it alone [*far da sè*]." [40] Ferrari and the other pro-French socialists in Italy "indicate France as our protectress, as the source of our future welfare, and preach fraternity with her: a manifest absurdity," since it could only mean dependence, not liberty. [41] As between France and Italy, the latter is much closer to social revolution. [42] French armies are not needed; socialist ideas, adopted by Italians, would bring national unity.

Louis Napoleon's *coup d'état* in 1851 was only one more reason for Pisacane to deny French socialist doctrines as the key to Italy's redemption. Napoleon III's dictatorship "makes me fear sometimes that France is in a period of decadence. Would it be possible?! France, the laboratory of all the ideas of present progress? The France that a little more than a half-century ago achieved such a great revolution?" If Bonaparte were overthrown, "we approach the only just and secure form of government: the anarchy of Proudhon." [43]

Spurning the ready-made French theories of social revolution even while praising Proudhon's anarchy, Pisacane claimed to have derived his

[38] As quoted by Valiani, *op. cit.*, I, 102.
[39] Letter of May 22, 1851. *Cf.*, also, Pisacane's letter to Cattaneo of July 31, 1851, in *Epistolario*, pp. 120-21, 128-30.
[40] *Epistolario*, pp. 123-24.
[41] *Saggi*, III, 157.
[42] *Ibid.*, III, 135-55.
[43] Letter of Dec. 15, 1851, to Cattaneo, *Epistolario*, pp. 133-35.

national socialist formulas from an analysis of the past. Like Marx, he saw history as the product of economic determinism and expounded both a rudimentary "law of capitalist concentration" and a theory of surplus value. Forty centuries of history prove that "the economic reason, in society, dominates the political; therefore, without reforming the former, it is useless to reform the latter." Wealth tends to concentrate in the hands of the few at the expense of the many, for "the misery of the worker increases *with the growth of social wealth and the net product of industry*." [44] By producing more cheaply, large capitalistic enterprises eliminate competition; social wealth increases while the number of those who possess it diminishes.[45] Pisacane explained this phenomenon in essentially Marxian terms:

> The capitalist who pays eight [units] of wages to every worker who produces ten, not only steals two from each of them, but even steals their collective power [read Marx's "labor power"], that power through which the simultaneous action of a hundred persons is superior to the successive action of all the men on earth; that power through which the product is increased beyond measure, that power which generates capital.[46]

Marxian analogies in Pisacane's thinking were sheer coincidence, so far as his biographers have discovered,[47] but the anarchist principles embraced by the Hero of Sapri were inspired by Proudhon. For Pisacane, the chief source of all social evil lay in the institution of private property.[48] The "monstrous right of property," by increasing poverty, leads to decadence and social dissolution and perverts all reforms to the detriment of the poor. Like a line from Proudhon is Pisacane's demand: *"The fruit of one's own labor guaranteed;* all other property not only abolished but denounced by the law like theft, . . . the destruction of him who usurps." [49] The state, too, blocked the path to human felicity. "Society, constituted in its real and necessary relationships, excludes every idea of government," unnecessary and useless, both as a corrector of customs and as a guarantor of the social pact. In the past, perhaps, the state had a regulatory and moderating function, but today "the tendency is toward simplification, the ultimate goal of which is anarchy, where the human intellect will be appeased." [50] Along with property and the state, religion,

[44] *Saggi*, III, 47. Italics P's. *Cf.*, also, *ibid.*, III, 48, 114-15.
[45] *Ibid.*, III, 46-47. Italics P's.
[46] *Ibid.*, III, 59-60.
[47] Mazzei writes that Pisacane, notwithstanding his stay in London from November, 1849, to June, 1850, knew neither Marx nor his writings. *Op. cit.*, p. 117, note 2; see also, Rosselli, *op. cit.*, pp. 102 ff.
[48] *Saggi*, III, 43.
[49] *Ibid.*, III, 120-21.
[50] *Ibid.*, III, 126.

in its current institutionalized form at least, would have to go, for it is "an effect of ignorance and terror" and wholly at the service of the state. The new society should be irreligious, since religion can not survive in a modern society aware that superhuman powers do not exist. Today "men associate with one another, certainly not to pray and suffer, but to lend each other neighborly assistance, to acquire, by working, greater prosperity and to fight; the aspiration of socialism is not to ascend into heaven, but to enjoy the earth." [51]

The popular notion that human association involves some sacrifice of personal liberty by the individual, in Pisacane's opinion, is nonsense. In fact, wrote he, putting all of society's facilities at the disposal of the individual would further "development of his physical and moral faculties and put him in a position to recognize his own attitudes and decide on how to use his own abilities." [52] But liberty of the individual can not exist without equality, and by equality Pisacane meant economic egalitarianism. Patriotism, freedom of the person, of thought, of the press, are meaningless to the poor, who, through ignorance, neither think nor read.[53] Those who would unite Italy with the help of the people must be able to demonstrate that expelling the foreigner and realizing the Italian nation mean social and economic reform, the creation of a materially equitable society.

This is not to say that Pisacane saw the process of unity only as the occasion, the excuse, for social revolution. The patriot never flinched in his loyalty to the principle of nationality as an intrinsically precious ideal, but he gave it a far different content than did Mazzini by relating it to his peculiarly Proudhonist libertarianism. "Liberty can not exist without nationality," [54] but further, both liberty and equality are "indispensable conditions of nationality, which, in turn, contains them, as the sun contains light and heat." [55] Thus, national unity won under a league of Italian princes or a single dynasty, or even under a capitalist republic, would be an illusion. The belief that liberty is an inevitable consequence of national independence, regardless of under whose auspices it is won, is a "fatal error," for it is precisely what "drove us back into slavery in '48." [56] No one dynasty is preferable to any other, for there is no nationality under monarchy, only despotism, the negation of nationality.[57] The liberal monarchy of Victor Emmanuel was actually more harmful to

[51] Saggi, III, 65, 72, 75.
[52] Ibid., III, 105.
[53] Ibid., III, 62.
[54] Ibid., III, 104.
[55] Ibid., III, 107.
[56] Ibid., III, 97.
[57] Ibid., III, 85-86, 97-99.

Italy than that of the Bourbons, "because the one deadens passions and the other arouses them." [58]

For a Mazzini, revolutionary action found its sanction in the idea inspiring it; for a Pisacane, the deed fathers the idea, it justifies itself through its consequences, not its premises.

> The propaganda of the idea is a chimera, . . . the education of the people is an absurdity. Ideas result from deeds, not the latter from the former, and the people will not be free when they are educated, but will be educated when they are free. The only work a citizen can undertake for the good of the country is that of cooperating with the material revolution; therefore, conspiracies, plots, attempts, etc. are that series of deeds by which Italy proceeds towards her goal.[59]

Here lay the most indelible legacy of all for a post-Risorgimento generation of socialists, for whom Italy's goal was no longer linked to political unity, but wholly comprised in the material revolution. Their formula, "the propaganda of deeds," understood in the Pisacanian sense of "conspiracies, plots, and attempts," legitimized their claim, twenty-one years after his death, that he was "our glory, . . . the Nestor of Italian revolutionary socialists." [60]

The *propaganda dei fatti* (propaganda of deeds)—in Pisacane, as in the leaders of Italy's pioneer socialist movement, the guiding principle— was based on an essentially romantic assumption. Pisacane rested his whole case for the Italian national liberation on an assumed spontaneous voluntarism of the population, apparently convinced that a mass intuition of his socialist principles would suffice to give a truly socialist content to the patriotic revolution. His ill-fated attack on the Bourbon kingdom would provide the spark, the clamorous adventure of an elite band of revolutionaries that would inspire popular revolt. The *Mezzogiorno's* peasants needed only a dramatic example to turn them into social revolutionaries whose uprising would create Italy, for Pisacane was "convinced that in the South the moral revolution exists, . . . that a vigorous impulse can push them into action. . . . To have arrived at the point of debarkation . . . is, for me, the victory, even should I have to perish on the scaffold." [61] And with this parting message, all the pretensions of the

---

[58] Letter to Giuseppe Fanelli, Aug. 24, 1856, in *Epistolario*, pp. 259-63. Nor had he changed his mind when he penned his Political Testament: "I . . . believe that the constitutional regime of Piedmont is more harmful to Italy than the tyranny of Francis II."

[59] *Testamento Politico*.

[60] Editorial introduction to Pisacane's *Testamento Politico*, published in *L'Avvenire* (Modena), June 8, 1878, as part of a series of articles on "Socialismo in Italia" by A. Pistolesi.

[61] *Testamento Politico*.

Saggi as a scientific analysis of past and present societies from the stand-point of economic determinism, all of Pisacane's talk of "the immutable laws of natural facts," went by the board. The pace had to be forced by the fanatical voluntarism of an intrepid few.[62] Nor did the southern *contadini*, as represented by the hysterical, terror-stricken villagers who finished off Pisacane and his friends in the hills around Sanza, regard the invaders as social liberators, nor even as Italian patriots, but as wild-eyed brigands and cutthroats.[63] His whole furious, star-crossed action, intended as an inspiring blow for *patria* and socialism, caused only a passing ripple of attention in the peninsula—and this because of the quixotic audacity of the enterprise.

CONCLUSION

His social philosophy aside, Pisacane must be classified—if his thought belongs to any single "school" of Risorgimento writers—as a federalist. From a patriotic social revolution he would construct a free federation of communes, "governed" by a democratically elected national congress, whose authority would be restricted to those areas involving the common interests. It would not be a government, but "a center in which the nation is balanced, . . . a vigilant guardian of the national pact."[64] Given the ubiquitous influence of Carlo Cattaneo's federalist writings on the Italian Left, it would certainly strain the argument to sustain that the anti-centralist critique of the writers of *Il Popolo d'Italia* reflected a direct Pisacanian influence. The federalism of the Hero of Sapri was hardly original—notwithstanding its extremism—and probably owed its inspiration to the correspondence with Cattaneo, who had elaborated his federalist conclusions long before Pisacane gave any serious attention to the problem of how to organize, politically, a unified Italian nation. Besides, at least one of the *redattori* (editors) of *Il Popolo d'Italia*, Filippo De Boni, was very much a disciple of Cattaneo.[65]

Still, the real novelty of the articles appearing during the early 1860's in the Neapolitan newspaper, as previously indicated, lay in the close

[62] For an elaboration of this contradiction between Pisacane's determinism and his romantic voluntarism, as revealed in his *Testamento Politico*, see Rosselli, *op. cit.*, pp. 283 ff.

[63] "The Sapri expedition is interesting as an index of the reaction, in part instinctive and in part cultivated by the Bourbons, that the people opposed to socialist theories." Antonio Monti, "Guerra regia e guerra di popolo nel Risorgimento," in *Questioni*, p. 191.

[64] For Pisacane's decalogue of principles governing his envisaged economic and political order, *Saggi*, III, 128-33; for the attributes of the national congress, pp. 229-32; for the formal constitution, in detail, of his communal society, pp. 232-36.

[65] Romano, *Storia*, I, 41, note 46.

coupling of the federalist lament with advanced positions on the social question, to the left of Mazzini and even more advanced—to the extent that he saw the problem as one of social transformation—than Cattaneo, whose federalism, after all, derived essentially from the analysis of an economist. It was the *combination* of socialist premises with the plea for communal autonomy that appears an echo of Pisacane's thinking—and perhaps it was no accident that the first of the federalist-socialist articles in *Il Popolo d'Italia* coincided with the publication of the third volume of Pisacane's *Saggi*, the one containing his extended justification of social revolution and a federalist solution of Italy's political problem.[66] Nor is it irrelevant, in this connection, that three of the men writing for the Neapolitan social democratic organ in the early 1860's—Carlo and Raffaele Mileti, Attanasio Dramis—were collaborators of Pisacane in the Sapri attempt.[67]

Il Popolo d'Italia continued its criticism of the monarchical regime for the next several years without attaining status as the intellectual nucleus of a current of socialist opposition, to say nothing of political organization. Nor did the name of Pisacane, in those years, evoke the image of a "Nestor of revolutionary socialists." For the vast majority of republicans, radical no less than moderate, his central appeal, his significance to posterity, was contained, not in the pages of *La guerra combattuta* or his *Saggi*, but in the ardent generosity of his self-immolation on the altar of *la patria*. For them, his memory was enshrined with those of the Cairoli brothers, Agesilao Milano, Felice Orsini, and the rest of that numerous company whose heroic exits gave so much emotional content to the Risorgimento.

It was far too early for Pisacane's ideas on social revolution and the echo they found in *Il Popolo d'Italia* to make any major breach in the ranks of Italian republicanism. To bring to maturation such a criticism, more was needed than the impulse imparted by a handful of intellectuals in Naples, whose generically socialist assumptions were, in effect, little more than a by-product of political objections to the status quo. The new monarchical state had to demonstrate its capacity to consolidate itself before any significant number of republicans would be willing to concede the inutility of centering their opposition on the institutional question. And so long as there was Italian territory still to be made a part of the nation, the dream of completing unity under republican auspices was never completely dispelled. In the meantime, criticism of the Italian

[66] Beginning with the second issue, *Il Popolo d'Italia* carried an advertisement of the *Saggi*.

[67] Romano, *Storia*, I, 137-38.

social system by radical democrats never implied that changing the pattern of relations between possessing classes and masses must precede, not follow, unity under a republic. In this respect no sector of republican opinion was yet ready to accept Pisacane's formula. That of Giuseppe Mazzini still held the field.

II

The Piedmontese and Mazzinian
Labor Traditions

THE PIEDMONTESE SOCIETIES OF MUTUAL AID

To Andrea Giannelli, his good friend in Florence, Giuseppe Mazzini wrote on November 24, 1860:

> Help the trend toward the mutual aid societies. Form them wherever you can. If others create them, place our workers in them, so that the National Idea is inserted, so that they are not reduced to a mere fact of material interest. They will be created in the south at any time and, once founded, they will seek contact with yours [of the center and north], so that later a strong league of the people can be formed.[1]

Thus Mazzini launched a serious campaign to harness the workers' mutual aid societies of the peninsula to the political program of the Party of Action. This effort was suggested by the existence of a workers' movement representing the national projection of an associative movement begun in Piedmont several years earlier. As of 1860 the new national organization of mutual aid societies reflected the social and political outlook governing the development of the Piedmontese associations. The chances of molding the workers' movement into an effective republican political instrument would largely depend on the degree to which the "Piedmontese" orientation lent itself to the pursuance of Mazzinian objectives. This complex of relations between the workers' movement and the apostle of *italianità*, moreover, helps explain a major peculiarity of the original Italian socialist movement: its almost complete separation from the ambient of organized labor.

The workers' mutual aid societies (*società operaie di mutuo soccorso*)

[1] *S.E.I.*, LXX, 197.

27

of Mazzini's time, like the medieval corporations of arts and crafts, exercised and defended the crafts, guarding their traditions and helping their members in the face of misfortune. In spirit and purpose, in organization and results obtained, however, the mid-nineteenth century societies incorporated important differences. Unlike the medieval associations, the modern mutual aid societies had definite rules defining the conditions of financial aid. Members were helped in case of sickness or unemployment, education and training opportunities were developed, and funeral expenses were generally covered. Instead of the patriarchal jurisdiction and rather paternal procedure of the older bodies, the modern societies ran their own affairs, usually making their decisions on the basis of direct and universal suffrage. The clearest break with organizations of the traditional type lay in the modern societies' essentially associative character and in the basic assumption behind the fact of association: that the members could improve their moral and material conditions *by their own efforts*, depending upon neither secular nor ecclesiastical authority.[2]

Statistics on the mutual aid societies furnished by the Italian Ministry of Agriculture, Industry, and Commerce in 1864,[3] approximately comprehensive, reported thirty-two workers' societies founded in the various Italian states, exclusive of Piedmont, before 1850; twenty-seven more between 1850 and 1859. Of the total of fifty-nine (still excluding Piedmont), ten were in Lombardy, ten in the Papal States, nine in Tuscany, and two in Sicily. Prior to national unification, any efforts to federate these scattered workers' associations would have failed from the start.

In the kingdom of Piedmont-Sardinia, on the other hand, one can speak of a true workers' movement before 1859-60. Here, after 1848, the freedom of association and assembly permitted by the *Statuto* of Charles Albert compensated, in terms of hastening the development of a workers' movement, for Lombardy's more intense industrialization and Tuscany's greater proportion of artisans. The statistics of 1864 reveal an instantaneous blossoming of workers' associations after 1848. Prior to the *Statuto*, there were only twelve workers' societies in the kingdom, but between 1850 and 1853, the more liberal atmosphere of Piedmont encouraged the creation of eighty-five new associations. All were simple

[2] For the organization and functions of the societies, see Enrico Martuscielli, *Le società di mutuo soccorso e cooperative* (Florence, 1876), pp. 155-209; E. Fano, *Della Carità preventiva e dell'ordinamento delle Società di Mutuo Soccorso in Italia* (Milan, 1868); Rinaldo Rigola, *Storia del movimento operaio italiano* (Milan: Editoriale Domus, 1947), pp. 9-22.

[3] *Statistica del Regno d'Italia, Società di Mutuo Soccorso, Anno 1862; per cura del Ministro di Agricoltura, Industria e Commercio* (Turin, 1864). Figures in this publication indicate only those societies which, though created before 1850, were still in existence in 1862.

mutual aid organizations, save the Turin typographers' society, founded in 1848 as a resistance group to prevent wage cuts. All were dedicated, too, to cooperation with the established political and social order and to acceptance of the moderate leadership of middle-class professional men who, for various reasons, including a humanitarian impulse, encouraged the development of the mutual aid societies. Moreover, monarchist sentiment among the Piedmontese workers and artisans was very strong during the entire decade of the 1850's.[4]

Illustrative of how the liberals supporting Cavour's modernization of the Sardinian state managed to keep the workers away from political affairs in the face of efforts by Mazzinian republicans, concentrated in Liguria, to make the societies of mutual aid true and proper political organizations was the series of Piedmontese workers' congresses held between 1853 and 1859. Throughout, the moderates held that politics would falsify the purposes of the societies: "benefiting" and "moralizing" the working classes. All the Jacobin arts of the Mazzinians could not bring the societies into the political arena.

The first attempt to associate the Piedmontese mutual aid societies was made in October 1850,[5] but it was not until 1853 that Stefano Boldrini, a Vigevano lawyer, and his brother Vincenzo, convoked the first of a numbered series of formal congresses.[6] At the Asti Congress (October 17-19, 1853), twenty-seven of the Piedmontese and Ligurian mutual aid societies were represented. The tone of the proceedings was most unmilitant; political discussion, even by implication, was avoided,

---

[4] For a documentation of Piedmontese working-class monarchical sympathies, see Anonymous [Giuseppe Boitani], Le società operaie di Torino e del Piemonte. Sunto storico dal 1850 al 1865 (Rome, 1883).

[5] Giovanni Giolito, "Sviluppo industriale e forme di associazione operaia in Pinerolo nella prima metà dell'Ottocento," Movimento Operaio, Yr. V, No. 1 (Jan.-Feb., 1953), 5-55, reproduces, in an "Appendice documentaria," the essential documents in this development. For a more detailed discussion, Giantommaso Beccaria, Storia delle società di mutuo soccorso d'Europa dalla loro origine fino ai tempi nostri (Turin, 1867), II. 3-36.

[6] The proceedings of the first four of these congresses (Asti, 1853; Alessandria, 1854; Genoa, 1855; Vigevano, 1856) are contained in Movimento Operaio, Yr. II, Nos. 11-12, 13 (Aug.-Nov., 1950), 314-24, 385-97; Yr. III, Nos. 14, 15-16, 17-18 (Jan.-Sept., 1951), 450-72, 534-47, 647-72. These are cited below with the name of the congress and the Movimento Operaio pagination. Other sources: Mauro Macchi, "Le associazioni operaie di mutuo soccorso," Rivista Contemporanea, XXVIII (Mar., 1862); Anonimo [Giuseppe Boitani], op. cit.; Beccaria, op. cit.; Stefano Boldrini, Brevi Cenni intorno ai congressi generali degli operai (Florence, 1861); and several north Italian newspapers which carried, during the congress sessions, summaries of the proceedings: L'Italia e Popolo (Genoa), La Gazzetta di Genova, Il Vessillo della Libertà (Vercelli), La Gazzetta Piemontese (Turin). By far the best account to date is that of Gastone Manacorda, Il movimento operaio italiano attraverso i suoi congressi. Dalle origini alla formazione del Partito Socialista (1853-1892) (Rome: Ediz. Rinascita, 1953).

except on one occasion: when the news reached the congress that a crowd in Turin, protesting the current food scarcity, had milled about in a *piazza* on October 18 and thrown stones at Cavour's windows, the Asti delegates immediately registered "high disapproval of such manifestations," a stand that gave the pro-government press a chance to boast of worker loyalty to the regime.[7] Stefano Boldrini reminded the societies of their indebtedness to the Piedmontese *Statuto* for the privilege of freely assembling and discussing their opinions. Though he warned against admitting any government influence, as a threat to their independence, he also put them on their guard against "extraneous and disintegrative" ideological penetrations.[8]

The effects of a cholera epidemic and a deteriorating food supply on the workers of Piedmont gave a tone of greater urgency to the deliberations of the next congress (Alessandria, November 10-12, 1854), but the delegates overwhelmingly rejected a proposal that Parliament be asked to take "energetic measures" to meet the food crisis. The justification was advanced that these matters were the concern of the government and any "interference" by the societies would prejudice their development and independence and distract them from their real purpose of mutual aid and instruction. Besides, the function of the congresses was "to study the moral and material needs" of the societies and to provide for them by their own efforts, "without prejudicing the rights and attributes of others."[9] It was a convenient formula with which to avoid commitments in questions considered essentially political in nature.

Rejected, too, was a plea that a common statute for all the participating associations be drawn up. A general set of regulations binding on all associations, the majority held, would impair the autonomy of each and "involve all the faults of centralization without bringing any of its advantages."[10] Within narrow limits, though, the need of some systemization of their activities was recognized. A committee was named to collect the questions to be discussed at the next congress and to formulate the agenda, "giving the preference to those subjects they think are the most urgent and useful in the interests of the Workers' Societies." A professor, two lawyers, and a cavalry general were among the six persons named to determine what was most useful and urgent to the workers.[11]

In approving a petition to the Chamber of Deputies for elementary technical schooling, the Alessandria delegates claimed it as their right

[7] "Asti," pp. 316-17.
[8] *Ibid.*, p. 323.
[9] "Alessandria," p. 391.
[10] *Ibid.*, p. 395.
[11] *Ibid.*, pp. 388, 390.

to have and the legislators' duty to provide but explained that the education of the workers

> . . . is not only the way to halt so much poverty, but [it] is necessary to the happiness and tranquillity of every social class. When the Worker is educated . . . he will be better off, that is, he will have purchasing power and will no longer covet the luxuries of the possessing classes. Educate the Worker and you will dissipate all the specters of the socialist school.[12]

It was another way of describing the "extraneous and disintegrative" forces Stefano Boldrini had mentioned at Asti the year before.

The Genoa Congress of November 23-25, 1855, in approving a *Regolamento dei Congressi delle Società Operaie* (Regulations of the Workers' Societies' Congresses), demonstrated that so long as the congresses were held in Piedmont, the associations had no intention of establishing an organic unity among themselves. The statute merely required annual congresses and denied any executive powers to the coordinating committee. The congresses should limit themselves to "the promotion of the moral and material well-being of the working class through instruction and mutual aid; the propagation of useful knowledge of social and private economy relative to the condition of the industrial and working classes"; and putting together "the practical knowledge of the different Societies in order to use it in the general interest." [13]

Subsequent efforts to create a unity based on something more than the annual congresses came to nothing. At the Vigevano Congress (October 10-12, 1856) no enthusiasm could be mustered for a suggestion that the societies hold provincial as well as national congresses.[14] At the fifth congress (Voghera, September 10-12, 1857), the priest, Don Giovanni Capurro, and Agostino Depretis proposed that a uniform set of regulations, based on the existing statutes of the individual societies, be drawn up and applied to all associations. The proposal was turned down, but Vincenzo Boldrini convinced the delegates of the need to create provincial committees to promote the implementation of general congress decisions.[15] A very loose confederation was proposed at the Vercelli Congress (October 2-4, 1858), but a uniform set of regulations and a pact of confederation were declared unacceptable, again thanks

[12] "Alessandria," p. 397.
[13] "Genova," p. 460.
[14] "Vigevano," pp. 651-52.
[15] *Sunto degli atti del Congresso generale delle associazioni operaie dello Stato, tenutosi il 10, 11, 12 settembre 1857 in Voghera* (Voghera, 1857), pp. 16-18. Hereafter cited as *Sunto . . . 1857 . . . Voghera.*

to the Boldrini brothers.[16] With no federal pact, no common regulations, no official organ, nor even the increased sense of cohesion that might have resulted from the system of reciprocal assistance to migrant workers— which had been functioning poorly in practice[17]—the Piedmontese societies remained until the founding of the Kingdom of Italy without the organic bonds that might have enabled them to promote their members' economic interests vis-à-vis their employers.

The reluctance to develop organizational strength probably stemmed from the old fear that a tightly knit and centralized organization would alienate associations extremely sensitive about their independence. It may have reflected a fear, too, that any appearance of solidarity might elicit unwelcome government attention. In fact, some of the conservatives at the Genoa meeting apparently felt that the best way to avoid such attention was to ask the government to grant the societies juridical recognition as beneficent institutions, a development that would have made illegal any activity other than functions of assistance. The Boldrini brothers scotched the move by pointing out that the societies needed no governmental authorization, since their existence was justified by "natural law and the special dispositions of the *Statuto*" and their goal nothing more than "the brotherly exchange of [financial] assistance provided from the earnings of the individual workers." [18]

One of the major hurdles, certainly, to the development of the mutual aid societies as militant protagonists of working-class interests lay in their unwillingness to exclude members of the bourgeois professional classes. On the eve of the Genoa Congress, a Piedmontese newspaper, *L'Osservatore Tortonese*, argued that the societies should be represented at the congresses by bona fide workingmen familiar with the needs and desires of their class, rather than by lawyers, doctors, and other professional men who, though excellent orators and genuinely interested in the plight of the workers, had little first-hand acquaintance with proletarian living conditions and mentality.[19] The recommendation was timely in that the number of bourgeois professionals in the societies made the term "workers'" societies a gross misnomer. Most of the societies admitted, as honorary members, lower middle-class professionals, required to pay dues but not entitled to the financial benefits extended to the regular

[16] *Sunto degli atti del sesto Congresso generale delle associazioni operaie dello Stato, tenutosi il 2, 3, 4 ottobre 1858 in Vercelli* (Vercelli, 1859), p. 32. Hereafter cited as *Sunto . . . 1858 . . . Vercelli.*

[17] This was a matter of serious concern at the 1859 congress. *Sunto degli atti del 7° Congresso generale delle associazioni operaie dello Stato, tenutosi il 22, 23, 24 ottobre 1859 in Novi* (Novi, 1860), p. 27. Cited below as *Sunto . . . 1859 . . . Novi.*

[18] "Genova," pp. 465-66.

[19] Reprinted by *L'Italia e Popolo* (Genoa), Nov. 22, 1855.

working-class members, a condition giving the former almost the status of patrons.[20] They directed the societies and congresses and provided the personnel, in the main, for the permanent committees acting between congresses, to say nothing of outnumbering greatly the manual workers and artisans at the annual meetings.[21] Their hegemony derived from their major role as founders of the individual societies, from their less straitened financial condition—which let them leave their work to attend the congresses—and from their superior education. Many were conscious of their anomalous position in workers' societies, fully realizing that if the associations developed into a genuinely popular—i.e., working-class— and autonomous movement, their prevalence in the leadership would pose a real problem.

At the Genoa Congress it was suggested that the title of honorary member be abolished and this category of persons given the rights and duties of regular members. One delegate observed that having honorary members who paid dues without participating in the benefits might make bosses of them, a threat to the societies' independence. Another said that "the Societies of mutual aid are Societies of Workers and . . . must be independent of the administration of the lawyers, doctors, priests, proprietors, and other possessors of the earth." Vincenzo Boldrini, a lawyer himself, warned against the growing tendency of society to separate into distinct classes and, to smooth things over, proposed that regular members administer the societies while honorary members be allowed a deliberative voice in their governing bodies. No decision was reached.

The *Regolamento* (Article 5) adopted at Genoa tried to meet the problem by requiring that at least one of the two members a society sent to a congress be a regular member.[22] This provision was vitiated in practice by the inability of regular members to absent themselves from their jobs and pay for their lodging and meals while attending a congress. Two years later at Voghera Vincenzo Boldrini vainly proposed abolition of the distinction between honorary and regular members by retaining practicing professionals and excluding those living on incomes derived from sources other than their professions.[23]

The same resistance to defining the interests of the workers as a class was implicit in the opposition to organizing the mutual aid societies

[20] Martuscielli, *op. cit.*, pp. 161-62.
[21] No statistics on the number of honorary members in the Piedmontese societies are available, but the ratio of one to every eleven regular members indicated in the previously cited *Statistica* for 1862 (p. xiii) may suggest the ratio of the previous decade.
[22] "Genova," pp. 456, 460, 468.
[23] *Sunto . . . 1857 . . . Voghera*, p. 19.

on a craft or trade-union basis and to even considering the principle of worker resistance to the employer as a means of securing shorter working hours, higher wages, and better working conditions generally.[24] Though a working day of thirteen to fourteen hours was not uncommon in the Piedmontese textile mills, though female and child labor was completely unprotected by law,[25] the delegates of the mutual aid societies were not even certain that it would be "useful and appropriate" to discuss maximum working hours for "the more fatiguing and deleterious work." At the Vercelli Congress of 1858, Vincenzo Boldrini favored legislation to eliminate deplorable working conditions in the rice fields and textile mills of Piedmont, but he believed that only public indignation—which would take time to stimulate—could force its passage. The mutual aid societies could only try to extend their own ethics of brotherly love and honesty to the entrepreneurs. Though a committee to study working conditions was projected, it was stipulated that any action by the societies arising from such a study should impinge on neither "the competence of the government nor the rights of private interests." [26]

Awareness of abuse of the workingman never manifested itself in anything more than broadly humanitarian protests, such as that of Giovanni Mollino, president of the Voghera society: "From the cry of Spartacus to the roar from the Paris barricades, there has been a continuous protest against the injustice dominating the earth." [27] The remedy was improving the "moral and intellectual status of the workers," not giving them a revolutionary education, for Mollino went on to condemn revolutionary violence and subversive doctrines. Neither the ideas of the communists nor other "exaggerations" of the kind, the fruit of "turbulent and fantastic minds," could bring happiness to the workers.[28]

Mollino could not have been too worried, since in all probability the working-class members would have refused support to any directive group urging a socialist recommendation for the solution of workers' problems. This is not to say that socialist and communist ideas had no currency in Piedmont or that no attempts were made to win the workers over to socialist tenets.[29] After the shock of 1848-49 the word "socialism" appeared frequently in the press, thanks principally to French develop-

[24] Sunto . . . 1858 . . . Vercelli, p. 6.
[25] For an analysis of the available statistics on the prevailing material conditions of the workers and artisans, see Ch. III, Nello Rosselli, Mazzini e Bakounine; 12 anni di movimento operaio in Italia (1860-1872) (Turin, 1927).
[26] Sunto . . . 1858 . . . Vercelli, pp. 17 ff.
[27] Sunto . . . 1857 . . . Voghera, p. 6.
[28] Loc. cit.
[29] See the chapter entitled "Piemonte socialista," by Rosselli, Carlo Pisacane nel risorgimento italiano, pp. 148-74.

ments, and there were some spontaneous strikes, agitations, and invasions of several large estates inspired by food shortages, increased living costs, unemployment, and the age-old land hunger of the peasantry. There was even the nucleus of a socialist press. In 1851 the Genoa Workers' Association, through its official organ, *Il Giornale del Povero*, preached social no less than political revolution, though the goals were limited to higher living standards for the workers, producers' cooperatives, direct taxation of the well-to-do, and public works. In Turin after 1854, *La Ragione* ("Reason"), edited by Ausonio Franchi, an unfrocked priest, urged a rationalist, anticlerical, reformist socialism of the French type, directed attention to social questions long neglected by the classical economists and suggested that Italian socialists be more specific and concrete in their propaganda if they would win a popular following.[30] Yet, as one student of this "socialism" has pointed out, the impressive documentation of socialist thought during the period is no proof that it was reflected in practice, however inflammatory its language.[31] Moreover, the intellectual preparation of the Italian workers of the pre-unity era, as Rosselli notes, was too low to support more complex and effective forms of workers' organizations, "more fruitful methods of struggle" than those represented by the mutual aid societies. Considering the "ignorance and poverty which oppressed our working classes at that time," even the limited success of these associations is surprising.[32]

The efforts of the clerical-reactionary press to put flesh and blood on the red specter and the government charges, after the Genoa disorders attending the failure of Pisacane's Sapri venture, that the mutual aid societies nourished subversive forces were completely without basis in fact. More likely, such charges mirrored fear, not of socialism or communism, but of any movement of ideas even remotely suggesting a departure from the role assigned labor by Cavour. As long as moderates like the Boldrinis and Depretis headed the congress movement, the mutual aid societies would stand as firm bulwarks, in the lower reaches of Piedmontese society, of the existing social and economic system.

On the national question the societies showed no lack of patriotic sentiment, though they displayed an immense reluctance to commit themselves to anything more than generic professions of *italianità*, another testimonial to their tenacity in staying clear of issues extraneous to mutual assistance. In opening the Genoa Congress, Fortunato Assalino probably expressed a majority attitude:

[30] See Luigi Bulferetti's analysis of the "socialism" of *La Ragione*'s collaborators in his *Socialismo risorgimentale*, Appendix D, pp. 359-63.

[31] See the discussion of this point in the essay on social movements by Giacomo Perticone, in *Questioni*, pp. 545-83.

[32] *Mazzini e Bakounine*, pp. 38-39.

> Since the cult of *la Patria* must be the religion of every day
> and every hour for the worker, I hope that the meeting of the
> workers of a single province will soon be transformed into an
> assembly of all the workers of the tormented Italian Fatherland.
> When there can be convened, alongside the people of Turin, the
> still more unfortunate proletariat of the Roman States and
> Naples, degraded by ignorance and poverty, on that day, hav-
> ing again become men and citizens of a great, free, powerful
> Fatherland, we shall finally be able to inaugurate, in the in-
> toxication of triumph, the Congress of the Workers with the holy
> cry of *Viva l'Italia!*[33]

Concrete cooperation with the patriotic effort, however, did not live
up to the promise of such ringing pronouncements. The Vercelli Congress in 1858 spurned contact with the National Society, the propaganda
organization founded in August 1857 by Giorgio Pallavicino, Giuseppe
La Farina, and Garibaldi, to preach Italian unity through Piedmont and
the House of Savoy.[34] Even in October 1859, with the whole peninsula
in a patriotic ferment, many delegates to the Novi Congress refused to
affirm that the mutual aid societies should become involved in politics,
however sanctioned by the cause of *la patria*. When the question arose
of subscribing to a fund for the purchase of a million rifles, suggested by
Garibaldi,[35] Stefano Boldrini objected to the move as a political action
and urged the congress to make no formal statement concerning the
matter. By this late date not even the mutual aid societies could resist
the intoxication of the impulse towards unity; Boldrini was overruled.

For the Piedmontese moderates, national unity was a mixed blessing,
rupturing, as it did, the pattern of near unanimity characterizing past
deliberations. The Novi Congress (October 22-24, 1859) was the last
gathering permitted to concern itself with the interests of a small,
homogeneous community of artisans and workers whose expectations
seemed confined to the formula of mutual aid and instruction. The union
of Piedmont with Lombardy and the central states brought the intrusion
of new ideas, issues, and goals, representing the views of highly divergent
groups of workers in the newly acquired territories. The abjuration of
politics, collaboration with the entrepreneur class, the refusal to transform the mutual aid societies into instruments for winning higher wages,
shorter working hours, and better living conditions—these dicta of the

---

[33] "Genova," p. 452.
[34] *Sunto . . . 1858 . . . Vercelli*, p. 36.
[35] Domenico Ciampoli, *comp., Scritti politici e militari, ricordi e pensieri inediti*
[di Garibaldi] (Rome: Enrico Voghera, n.d.), p. 125. Cited henceforth as Ciampoli,
op. cit.

Piedmontese moderates could not avoid attack by the workers' representatives of Lombardy, where a more advanced industrialism lent greater militancy to the conflicts between workers and employers.

The tendency to break out of the moderate Piedmontese mold announced itself at the Milan Congress (October 26-28, 1860), attended by 109 delegates, representing 64 societies in Piedmont, Liguria, Lombardy, the Emilia, and Tuscany.[36] Significantly, the proposals of the Milanese delegates sharply contrasted with the agenda items of the Piedmontese congresses: the strike question, organization of the workers by trades and crafts, sanitary conditions in the factories, arbitration of labor-management disputes, and the like. Earlier congresses dealt summarily with this kind of topics—when they appeared on the agenda at all.[37]

Not the question of organizing economic pressure on employers, but that of political activity by the societies threatened to rupture the Milan Congress. Francesco Franchini, an aggressive democrat, and Franco Mistrali, a Milanese newspaperman, proposed, to the dismay of the Piedmontese delegates, that the government be asked to provide free railway fare for delegates to the workers' congresses so that the "effective" members (i.e., the bona fide workingmen) could attend, and that the societies demand universal suffrage in national and local elections. Until the workers had the vote, Franchini reasoned, their representatives were entitled to the same free rail transportation once a year to the workers' congresses as that afforded deputies to the national legislature. Refusal by the government, added Mistrali, would constitute a hostile act toward the people.

Led once more by the Boldrini brothers, moderates insisted that urging "political acts" would ruin the congress movement and arouse dissensions inimical to the real interests of the workers. To avert a rupture of the congress, Riccardo Sineo advanced a substitute proposal that won approval on the basis of its innocuous wording: "The Congress expressed the desire that the electoral law be reformed so that the working class can have its just part in the naming of deputies." A two-thirds majority carried the motion, but many Piedmontese abstained, thus emphasizing their opinion of the resolution as irrelevant to a workers' congress.

As a milestone in the development of the Italian labor movement, the Milan Congress was of singular importance, for

[36] The previously cited *Statistica* for 1862 gives the following regional distribution of mutual aid societies created in 1860: Lombardy, fourteen; Piedmont, ten; Emilia, six; Tuscany, three; Umbria, one. Here again was a reflection of the extension of liberty of association to the new territories.

[37] For the Milan Congress proceedings, *Sunto degli atti dell'VIII Congresso generale delle società operaie italiane, tenutosi il 26, 27, 28 ottobre 1860 in Milano* (Milan, 1861).

. . . in substance, [it] had only begun to uncover some of the
most serious and complex issues in the labor world: there the
Piedmontese had come into contact with a more modern social
reality and, therefore, richer in contradictions and ferment. And
if their concepts still prevailed, the peril had been clearly defined
that they could not hope to dominate the whole of the Italian
workers' movement. The political fight over universal suffrage
had been only the first warning of a great battle.[38]

MORALITY AND THE SOCIAL PROBLEM:
MAZZINI

Immersion, in itself, of the Piedmontese workers' movement into the
broader stream of Italian national labor issues and experiences was of no
great moment to Giuseppe Mazzini. The new emphasis on political action
was a promising tendency, but the fact that such concern centered on
the question of a vote for the workingman was no proof of republican
sympathies. Stimulating a rupture with the nonpolitical tradition of the
Piedmontese societies was essential, but this alone would not orient the
now national congress movement toward the goal of an Italian republic.
To turn the workers into republican activists, a social reform platform
reflecting a realistic analysis of their material wants and needs would be
more to the point. Mazzini was supremely confident that his own social
formulas had precisely such a foundation. Was this objectively true, or
was his certainty based on a highly subjective view of the realities of the
social problem? The answer lies in his definition of the "social revolution"
that his republic would inaugurate.

The notion of organizing the Italian working classes as the backbone of
national revolution dated back to the beginning of Mazzini's republican
apostolate. In 1834 he had defined the terms of "warfare between the
people and tyranny" by equating a "league of proletarians" with an
"anti-Austrian brotherhood." [39] Throughout his long career the principle
was never modified: revolutionary action by the masses finds its sanction
in serving the interests of the national community, not those of a single
class. Within the limits of this patriotic imperative, nonetheless, the
rationale of Mazzini's view of society and its economic problems was
extraordinarily complex.

Salvemini claimed that four-fifths of Mazzini's social philosophy was
Saint-Simonist in origin.[40] If so, the remaining fifth clearly distinguished

[38] Manacorda, *Il movimento operaio italiano*, p. 47.
[39] *S.E.I.*, X, 25.
[40] *Mazzini*, p. 154. As of 1846-47, Mazzini considered Saint-Simonism "dead, buried,
and forgotten," even though it had been "the most advanced manifestation of the
spirit of new things that breathes through the era, . . . the boldest and most sincere

him from the humanitarian—or, in Marx's term, "utopian"—socialists of
the pre-1848 period. Certainly the similarities proved no more than that
the pre-1848 socialists had many ideas in common with nonsocialist
democrats, not surprising in that the doctrines of all of them had a
common root in the humanitarian revolutionary philosophy of the
eighteenth-century Enlightenment and the early decades of the nineteenth
century. All sought the essence of democracy. For Mazzini it was to be
found in a harmony between the principles of liberty and authority, of
the freedom of the individual and the legitimate demands of the collective
whole. Without association, liberty begets anarchy; without liberty,
association generates tyranny. To find the just balance, man must rise
above his baser appetites and educate himself to accept the restrictions
on his personal liberty implicit in the moral principles of "mission" and
"duty." The divine goal of life is virtue, and anything that blocks or
impedes its pursuit gives no true happiness and betrays the real nature
of man.

With this quasi-theosophical view of life, Mazzini could not agree with
the utopian socialists, who substituted the principles of utility and self-
interest. They assumed that human happiness, their avowed objective,
was to be had from the satisfaction of material and physical appetites.
Since neither the assumption nor the goal corresponded to man's true
nature and divine purpose, according to Mazzini, the utopians either
"destroyed individuality in aiming at social happiness," like the Saint-
Simonists; or "suppressed the potent idea of society, of the mission of
power, by aiming at the happiness of the individual," like the Fourierists;
or denied both the individual and society, like the communists (and here
Mazzini meant Babeuf and his latter-day disciples), who would organize
society "upon a fixed immutable model, after the manner of bees and
beavers, . . . upon the foundation of absolute equality, so that nothing
remains for power to do, save to repeat continually a series of identical
acts, nothing for the individual, except to maintain the productive activity
of the soil." [41]

For Proudhon, the "Mephistopheles of Democracy," [42] Mazzini reserved
a special damnation because, in his opinion, Proudhon had more completely corrupted the socialist idea with the poison of materialism than
had Babeuf, Saint-Simon, and Fourier:

> Anarchy entered the field. One man, armed with a tremendous
> logic put at the service of a false principle, [a man who]

attempt ever made hitherto to realize in practice the fundamental principle of
Bentham's idea to organize a society from the point of view of *utility*. *S.E.I.*, XXXIV,
160-61.

[41] *S.E.I.*, XXXIV, 206-07.

[42] *Ibid.*, XLVI, 182.

dominated weak minds through an unrestrained audacity and language vulgarly clear and incisive, diffused a somber light over that anarchy and adopted it as the supreme formula of his labors. Proudhon, substantially antisocialist in any case, summarized in himself all the phases of the orgy of French socialism. . . . The principal reason for this anarchist deviation of socialism is materialism. . . .[43]

Mazzini's identification of materialism as the spawning ground of "deviation" from authentically socialist doctrine strongly suggests that he, too, considered himself a socialist, even though he did not choose to call himself such, given the fact that in the popular mind it was becoming —if it had not already become—associated with materialist principles. His generic definition of socialism amounted to this: "abolition of the proletariat, emancipation of the workers from the tyranny of capital concentrated in a small number of individuals; division of the product, or of the value that issues from it, according to the work accomplished." [44] Concretely, his socialism consisted of "substituting . . . free Association for the unrestricted competition of individuals"; State control of credit; a single, direct tax on all income above that required for subsistence; free and equal primary education for all. These reforms, he wrote in 1852, he had preached for more than twenty years; they were all included in "that ancient word, Republic, for which our fathers died and which is good enough for me." [45] A few months later, he called himself a socialist by means of this circumlocution: "we are not communists, nor levellers, nor hostile to property, nor socialists in the sense given to that word by the systematic sectarians of a nearby country." [46]

Alexander Herzen, the great Russian revolutionary, called Mazzini a socialist in the days before socialism.[47] He was probably referring to Mazzini's radical democracy, but even if he meant by "socialism" the system implicit in the Communist Manifesto, the generalization applies to the extent that Mazzini's social philosophy contrasted far less with Marxism than with the systems of the French utopians. Mazzini and Marx had more in common than condemnation of Proudhon as a deviationist, notwithstanding the fundamental antithesis between Mazzini's idealism and the historical materialism of the philosopher of Treves.

[43] S.E.I., XLVI, 257.
[44] Ibid., XLVI, 247.
[45] Ibid., XLVI, 208.
[46] Manifesto of the Italian National Committee, Jan. 31, 1852, ibid., XLVI, 185.
[47] Memoirs (New York, 1924-25), III, 112. On Mazzini's "socialism," the following have contributed monographs: G. Bertacchi, Giovanni Bacci, Eugenio Florian, Giuseppe Guccia, F. Mormino-Penna, Napoleone Colajanni, and O. Zuccarini.

Like the authors of the *Manifesto*, Mazzini identified the principal new element of history as the growing, beneficent, social, and political power of the working classes, implied in what he called "the vast social idea, . . . the glory and mission of the epoch, . . . the emancipation of the men of labor, the benediction for all, the [full] *cup for all*." [48] Resolution of the social question in this sense is "inevitable to all peoples, in fact, the only thing that matters." [49] History was a struggle between oppressors and oppressed: the patriciate had broken monarchical despotism; the bourgeoisie had ended the privileges of the blooded nobility; now the time was at hand for the "people of labor" to end those of the "proprietary and capitalist bourgeoisie." Society now consisted of only two classes of men: "the exclusive possessors of the elements of all labor, land, credit, or capital" and those "deprived of everything but their arms, . . . forced to spend twelve or fourteen hours of the day in an almost exclusively manual labor, . . . broken by poverty, tormented by the precariousness of employment and the insufficiency of wages." [50] From this injustice derived the necessity of action, a revolution simultaneously resolving the political and social problems.

That every great revolution, generally speaking, is social, that "it inevitably modifies social relations and the division of social wealth," did not satisfy Mazzini's demand that revolutions requiring supporting action by the masses satisfy "the just needs" of the latter. "A revolution is holy when it has as its intent the progress of the millions; it is a crime any time the goal proposed is the interest of a minority, of a caste, of a monopoly." [51] Proletarians, as a class, have a unique set of needs arising from their radically different economic condition. If the satisfaction of these needs can be summed up in the necessity of social revolution, why should the workers support a merely political upheaval, "why should they labor to provide for needs they do not feel?" Merely political remedies do not suffice. [52]

The Italian workingman's mistake was to have fought for the political program of the middle class without demanding satisfaction of his own social aspirations; he had fought "as a man, as a citizen, not as a worker." On the few occasions when the workers advanced their claims, they did so as individuals, not as a class, with the consequence that proletarian interests were lost in the clamor of realizing middle-class objectives. The mistake must not be repeated. "The approaching revolution will have to do for the *proletarian*, for the popular classes, for the men of

[48] *S.E.I.*, XLVI, 208.
[49] Letter to the editor of *Italia e Popolo*, 1856, *S.E.I.*, IX, 208-09.
[50] *Ibid.*, XXV, 111-12.
[51] "Condizioni e Avvenire dell'Europa" (1852), *ibid.*, XLVI, 245-46.
[52] *Ibid.*, XXV, 116.

Labor, what past revolutions did for the . . . middle classes, for the men of capital." [53]

For Mazzini, as for Marx, the first step toward proletarian emancipation was the creation of class consciousness and class organization:

> . . . the millions who invoke a better social order [must] express their needs. . . . The workers need to consult with one another in order to know and calculate their own strength, to agree on the remedies that can put an end to their ills, to gather together the necessary means to express them. . . .
>
> When the workers, organized, strong with uniform convictions, closely bound together in unity of will, militate in the National Association, not only as citizens, but as workers, they will no longer have to feel deluded in their just hopes and to see revolutions consummated in questions of merely political form for the benefit of a single class. . . .
>
> [To the workers:] United into one body, *who* can betray you? You have fought up to now for the program of the other classes; put yours forward today and announce collectively that you will not fight if not for that. . . . Believe us. He who uses different language with you either deceives himself or deceives you.[54]

Though proletarian unity in a "National Association" is a far cry from the spirit of the *Manifesto*'s final plea for the workers of the world to unite, though Mazzini was certain that "the social question can be resolved . . . more or less within the confines of a single people," that "it is an internal question for each of them," [55] Marx and Engels, too, conceded that "in form the struggle of the proletariat with the bourgeoisie is at first a national struggle. The proletariat of each country must . . . first settle matters with its own bourgeoisie." [56]

Nor was Mazzini very far from the Marxian analysis in seeing the moral justification of private property in its being the consequence of labor. It must be "the sign of the quantity of labor with which the individual has transformed, developed, and increased the productive forces of nature." [57] The real evil is not private property itself, but the way in which it is used to buttress tyranny and perpetuate poverty. Though Mazzini would restrict the state to administering a few enterprises, such as the railroads, the great bulk of economic activity would be carried on by producers' and consumers' cooperatives, which, in effect, would own all capital in common. Very little inalienable private property would exist outside

---

[53] *S.E.I.*, XLVI, 186.
[54] *Ibid.*, XXV, 112-14, 120.
[55] *Ibid.*, XLVI, 246.
[56] *Communist Manifesto.*
[57] *S.E.I.*, XXXIV, 235-38. *Cf.*, also, "Agli operai italiani," *ibid.*, XCII, 305-15.

the cooperatives, and in this respect Mazzini's economic associations, collectively considered, constituted for all practical purposes a socialist state.

Beyond this point, analogies between Marxism and the social philosophy of Mazzini break down for want of agreement as to the nature of man himself. Like the utopians before him, Marx equated human happiness with the satisfaction of material needs, thus arriving at the logic of the class struggle. Mazzini, too, wanted human happiness but saw its advent only as the product of a moralizing process, not of a full stomach. Marx demanded the elimination of poverty as a right, the exercise of which opened the path to moral improvment, among other benefits; Mazzini insisted that workers should seek and obtain material betterment "as a means, not as an end; seek it out of a sense of *duty*, not only of right; seek it to make yourselves *better*, not only to make yourselves *materially* happy." [58] That amelioration of the workers' material lot is essential did not make it an end in itself:

> Material improvements are essential, and we will fight to achieve them, but not because being well fed and housed is all that matters, but because the consciousness of your dignity and your moral development can not be attained as long as you are . . . in a continual duel with poverty. . . . Your material condition must be changed so that you can develop morally; you need to work less to be able to devote some hours of your day to the progress of your mind; you need a compensation for labor that enables you to accumulate savings, to quiet your mind about the future [and], above all, to purify you of any feelings of reaction, any vindictive impulse, any unjust thought toward those who are unjust toward you. [59]

The spirit of concord, not vendetta, informed Mazzini's social dynamic. His view of the historical process as a conflict between dominators and dominated; his identification of two distinct classes in contemporary society, proletarians and bourgeoisie, each with its own peculiar needs and aspirations; his emphasis on the need of proletarian class consciousness and organization; his insistence that social transformation would help men attain virtue—all these positions did not lead Mazzini to accept the principle of class struggle. The general reason is to be found in the mystical aspect of his interpretation of history, for he saw the significance

---

[58] Pisacane called Mazzini's concept of the duty to be virtuous "nothing more than the Gospel's dream of brotherhood" and ironically suggested that if, as Mazzini believed, this sentiment of duty is to be found in every heart, then the Austrians must have it, too, in which case they should be expected to go home and stage their own revolution and let the Italians alone. *Saggi*, III, 164.

[59] "Dei Doveri dell'Uomo" (new edition of 1860), *S.E.I.*, LXIX, 18-19.

of centuries of struggle between rulers and ruled as a gradual progress of the principle of human association. The fact that monarchical despotism was overthrown by the nobility, that, in turn, the latter was replaced by the bourgeoisie, meant that each succeeding epoch adds new and positive elements to the social synthesis achieved by the preceding one. The competitive and divisive propulsions of mankind are gradually attenuated as perception of the necessity of virtue as the key to realizing the divine design takes root in men's consciousness. To speed the universalization of this perception is not a matter of free choice for the individual, but a duty, the obligation to further in every possible way the application of the associative principle. To accept this duty rules out, on the part of the worker, "any feeling of reaction, any vindictive impulse, any unjust thought" toward the classes standing above him on the economic ladder. There is no place for class struggle, which Mazzini feared would transform the social question into a controversy concerned only with material interests.

Even had Mazzini been willing to accept class struggle in theory, he would not have considered it applicable to Italian conditions:

> In Italy . . . the social question does not carry with it threats of unjust subversions or anarchy. In those regions there boils no profound hatred between class and class, [there is] no exaggerated, abnormal development of concentrated industry, no agglomeration of poverty that demands the urgent application of instantaneous remedies, no [necessity for] the introduction of rash systems or solutions.[60]

Implicit in Mazzini's analysis was a refusal to recognize that under certain conditions maldistribution of wealth produces divergent class interests and struggle, just as Marx refused to admit that, at times, insuring propitious conditions for production causes class interests to converge. In Mazzini's case, however, the refusal was due in great part to the peculiar way in which he conceived one of his favorite terms: *Popolo*. As Salvemini has indicated,[61] Mazzini rarely had a factory proletariat in mind when applying this expression to Italy, an obvious consequence of the country's low level of industrialization in mid-century. Nor did Mazzini mean the agricultural "proletariat" of the peninsula, by far the most numerous working-class element. His was a constantly cavalier attitude toward the problems of the countryside, and, though he urged in a general way more equitable relations between landlords and *contadini*, his action programs never envisaged the participation of rural proletarians on a major scale. When Mazzini referred to "our workers"

[60] S.E.I., XLVI, 250.
[61] *Mazzini*, p. 173.

and the foundation of a "league of the people" in the letter quoted at the beginning of this chapter, when it is said that in 1860 he began his campaign to insert the workers of Italy into the national revolution, it must be understood that by "workers" and the "people" he meant chiefly the country's petty bourgeois and artisan classes. Bound by such a definition, convinced that the "law of moral progress" subordinates the economic fact and social inequities to the point of guaranteeing the advent of a society composed only of "workers," [62] Mazzini could not hinge his social action formula on conflicting economic interests and their derivative of class struggle.

Unresolved, nonetheless, is the curious paradox of Mazzini, the advocate of violence in the war on absolutist principles, the foreign occupiers, the papacy, and the Mazzini opposed to social insurrectionism, the man who would build social justice through gradual, pacific, moral suasion while creating Italy by fire and sword—and even the dagger. When he spoke of the necessity of an insurrection having at once a political and social character, he envisaged no internecine conflict among Italians, for such a revolution required "that the best, or the majority of the men composing [the possessing classes], sympathize with the expression of [workers'] needs and understand the necessity of getting together to satisfy them in harmony; . . . otherwise revolutions would be reduced to civil wars in which the outcome, whatever else it may be, whoever the victor, is always a question of strength and substitutes one tyranny for another.[63] To realize all "reasonable" aspirations of the working class:

> . . . is not a matter of violently destroying, abolishing, or transferring the wealth of one class to another; it is a matter of enlarging the circle of consumption, of consequently augmenting the products, of giving a larger share of them to those who produce, of opening up a broad road for the worker to acquire wealth and property, of assuring that every man who demonstrates willingness, ability, morality, finds capital and a way to work freely.[64]

With class struggle ruled out, how can the dominant classes be brought to sympathize with the workers' needs, to work out a solution in harmony? Mazzini's answer: educate them to it.

> Preach Duty to the men of the classes above you and, to the extent possible, fulfill your own duties; preach virtue, sacrifice, love, and be virtuous and ready for sacrifice and love. Coura-

[62] S.E.I., XXV, 110-11.
[63] Ibid., XXV, 112-13.
[64] Ibid., XLVI, 247.

geously express your needs and ideas, but without anger, without aggressiveness, without threatening; the most potent threat . . . is firmness, not heated language.[65]

The comfortable classes know the facts of material misery but do not *feel* them; those who have not suffered are inclined either to see poverty as a regrettable necessity of the social order or to leave its cure to future generations.

> The difficulty is not in convincing them, but in shaking them out of their inertia, in inducing them . . . to *act,* to associate and fraternize with you in order to win the social organization that will put an end, as much as the conditions of Humanity permit, to your ills and terrors. Now this is the work of faith, of faith in the mission that God has given to the human creature here on Earth, in the responsibility that weighs on all those who do not fulfill it. . . .[66]

In this *mystique* ends the logic of Mazzini's quest for a solution to the social problem: the dominant classes must be persuaded to change a system Mazzini himself recognizes as the product of their own secular egotism; to improve his condition, the worker must educate himself and his social superiors, but his educative capacity depends on improving his condition. Mazzini admitted that it was as "absurd" to tell men compelled to work fourteen to sixteen hours a day to educate themselves as it was to preach the gospel of love to those "who meet only the cold calculations of speculators and the tyrannies of capitalist legislators." [67] A logical resolution of the contradiction would have required Mazzini to contravene "God's design for Humanity," and this he could not do, however strongly —and spontaneously—his conscience rebelled against the injustices of society.[68]

CONCLUSION

By the time Mazzini set his hand to organizing Italian workers as the popular support of his drive for a republic, the word "socialism" in Italy, as in the rest of Europe, no longer implied economic democracy

[65] *S.E.I.,* LXIX, 22.
[66] *Ibid.,* LXIX, 20.
[67] *Ibid.,* XLVI, 250.
[68] In Pisacane's view, Mazzini's failure to resolve the contradiction reflected either ignorance or hypocrisy: ". . . to speak of more equitable conditions between peasant and landowner, between capitalists and workers, admits only two cases: either [Mazzini] believes it possible to resolve the social problem without abolishing property, in which case he has not deeply studied existing society; or [he] speaks this way so as not to intimidate the proprietors, in which case he is dissembling; this is not [the attitude] of a revolutionary." Letter to Dall'Ongaro, Oct. 30, 1851, in Emilio del Cerro, *Fra le quinte della storia* (2d ed.; Turin, 1903), p. 209.

based on the principle of association between capital and labor. Between the formulations of Saint-Simon, Fourier, and Robert Owen and the unification of Italy, Marx and Engels had written the *Communist Manifesto* and, more immediately important, the violence of class warfare in Paris in 1848 and the reverberations of the French upheaval elsewhere in Europe marked the opening of a time of troubles for Mazzinianism as a popular dogma. The events of 1848-49 destroyed many people's faith in the humanitarian nationalism so eloquently urged by Mazzini, as well as by other Europeans like Herder; they ushered in an era of religious scepticism, materialism, positivism, voluntarism (popularly misinterpreted as a sanction of the uninhibited expression of urges and interests), and *Realpolitik,* which, for the social radical, meant that a more equitable society would not emerge from goodness or the love of justice, but from the application of political methods: power and calculation. For a man who believed in God's design for mankind, in the compelling force of the Idea, in moral discipline, in duty, it was a discouraging atmosphere. By the same token, it was an atmosphere peculiarly conducive to the growth of really revolutionary socialism, the socialism of the class struggle, of Marx and Proudhon.

After Louis Napoleon clamped his dictatorship on France in 1851, Mazzini initiated in earnest the antisocialist campaign that was truncated only by his death two decades later. The immediate fault lay with the French socialists, he wrote, in that they had frightened the bourgeoisie into the arms of the dictator: "Hatred for the *coup d'état,* but no pity for the socialists!"[69] In his "Discorsi agli amici d'Italia" (February 1852), in the subsequent manifestos of his Italian National Committee, and in the pages of his newly published *Doveri della Democrazia* (*Duties of Democracy,* March 1852),[70] Mazzini broadened his attack into a merciless indictment of the French socialists.

He granted that they had given the European intellect a much needed jolt, focused public attention on social and economic problems that might otherwise have been ignored, promoted an examination of working-class conditions, "bared the suffering hidden in a system founded on caste and monopoly," and forced the bourgeoisie to such "absurd and ferocious" resistance that its days as a governing caste were numbered.[71] Conceding this, Mazzini delivered himself of a *"J'accuse"* justifying the other half of Herzen's estimate of Mazzini as a socialist in the days before socialism: that the Genoese apostle "became its enemy as soon

[69] Jessie White Mario, *Della vita di Giuseppe Mazzini* (Milan, 1886), pp. 349-50, 357-58.
[70] S.E.I., XLVI, 177-204, 207-14.
[71] *Ibid.,* XLVI, 252-53.

as socialism changed from a generic tendency into a new revolutionary force." [72] In his *Duties of Democracy,* Mazzini wrote:

I accuse the socialists . . . of having falsified, mutilated, diminished that great [social] thought with absolute systems that simultaneously usurp the liberty of the individual, the sovereignty of the country, and the continuity of progress. . . . I accuse them of having rashly thrown into the arena, in the name of their miserable individual, positive solutions of the problem of human life before life itself can be manifested in the fullness of aspirations and capacity that belong to it under the impulse of those electric currents called revolutions. I accuse them of the silly pretense of drawing . . . from their narrow or infirm minds the organic concept that can only emerge from the confluence of all human faculties stimulated into action; of having substituted the solitary *I* for the collective European *we,* of having spoken in the name of Saint-Simon, Fourier, Cabet . . . , while it was important to forget the prophets for the benefit of the continuous revolution and to write in front of the Temple—*God is God, and Humanity is his Prophet.* I accuse them of having cancelled man in favor of the *sectarian;* the free intellect in favor of the formula; the concept of Life in favor of a single manifestation of life; of having assumed the name of communists, communionists, communitarians, . . . instead of calling themselves republican men, democrats of the XIX century; of having invented the harmful distinctions between socialists and republicans; between socialists and revolutionaries. I accuse them of having always preferred . . . *I am,* when we all should have been saying *we are;* of having consecrated all the power of the intellect to [men's] fighting and devouring each other, to destroying in the heart of the people all faith in any authority of men or things; of having generated . . . the dissolvent, Mephistophelian genius of Proudhon, who denies [all authorities]: God, Society, Government, and sets up Irony to reign over the Void. I accuse them of having dried up the springs of faith, animalized man, pushed the worker toward bourgeois egotism, by concentrating the general attention almost exclusively on the problem of the materially useful . . . , by selecting as a *principle* the physical betterment of the individual, which can only be a consequence of his moral betterment. I accuse them of having repeated with Bentham and Volney: *life is the search for happiness,* instead of repeating with all those who produced the great transformations in the world: *life is a mission, the fulfillment of a duty.* I accuse them of having brought others to believe that a people can regenerate itself by becoming fat; of having substituted for the

[72] *Memoirs,* III, 112.

problem of humanity a problem *of the kitchen of humanity;* of having said: *to each according to his ability, to each according to his needs,* instead of loudly proclaiming . . . : *to each according to his love, to each according to his sacrifices.* I accuse them of having . . . weakened and cancelled, to the extent it was in them, the sentiment of Nationality; of having pretended that . . . Humanity can proceed while suppressing the only organization that renders action possible. . . .[73]

Thus, long before he tried to muster the workers of Italy behind his republican program, to convince them that it held the best guarantee of their own moral and material improvement, Mazzini had established himself as a doctrinaire antisocialist. True, his social platform was not the explicit point at issue in Mazzini's relations with the workers' movement during the early 1860's. He saw as his first task that of overcoming the movement's reticence to lend itself to political activity. The problem was far from simple: where the Piedmontese tradition rejected political action as irrelevant to the needs of the working class, the radicals who found their opportunity in the new national scope of the workers' societies did not exclude politics, as shown by the fight over the suffrage question at the Milan Congress, but in going beyond the simple formula of mutual aid and instruction, in raising the question of strikes, the arbitration of labor-management disputes, and trade-union organization, they argued, in effect, the superiority of a nonpolitical method: resistance on the economic plane, syndical organization and tactics. Their premise was clearly non-Mazzinian: that worker unity was primarily important as the condition of successful struggle against the employer class. Implicit, then, in Mazzini's effort to persuade the workers' societies that proletarian well-being lay at the end of the republican rainbow was a test of the realism of his central plea that harmony, concord between the classes, be accepted as the animating principle of the workers' quest for social justice.

[73] *S.E.I.,* XLVI, 208-10.

III

Mazzini and the Italian Labor Movement (1860-1864)

THE QUESTION OF POLITICAL ACTION BY LABOR: CONGRESS OF FLORENCE (1861)

EXTENSION of the Piedmontese *Statuto* to the newly incorporated regions removed the barriers to the proliferation of the mutual aid societies. Forty-nine new workers' associations appeared in 1861: four in Piedmont, eleven in Lombardy, three in Liguria, five in the Emilia, fourteen in Tuscany, four in the Marches, five in Umbria, one each in the Abruzzi and Puglia, two in Sicily.[1] Some of these societies, from their inception, had objectives that went far beyond the simple function of mutual assistance, while others were organized in such a way as to guarantee a large membership from the beginning. The Workers' Society of Naples, for example, had 2,860 members by the end of 1861, organized by trades.[2]

Mazzini's immediate problem was to unite these burgeoning societies to provide a wide and coherent base for antimonarchical opposition. The Genoa *Regolamento* of 1855, lacking federative provisions and affording no organizational discipline through a governing hierarchy, was patently inadequate. To fill the need, the Florentine Artisans' Brotherhood, created in February 1861 and headed by Giuseppe Dolfi, Andrea Giannelli, Giuseppe Mazzoni (the last, along with Francesco Guerrazzi and Giuseppe Montanelli, had formed the triumvirate of the provisional Tuscan government in 1849), all friends of Mazzini, developed a draft statute of a national organization.[3]

[1] *Cf.*, the previously cited *Statistica* for 1862.
[2] *La Nuova Europa* (Florence), Nov. 23, 1861.
[3] The idea of using the statute of the Florentine Artisans' Brotherhood as the constitutional basis for a national organization originated with Giuseppe Dolfi. Elio Conti, "Lettere inedite di Giuseppe Mazzini a Giuseppe Dolfi," *Rassegna Storica del Risorgi-*

The scheme provided for an intricate hierarchy extending from the individual local "college" of those practicing the same trade, through "Artisans' Communes," regional organizations under a "primate," to a national "Grand Council," headed by an executive triumvirate.[4] Carlo Cattaneo, asked for his opinion, objected to the artificiality of such centralization and suggested a simpler structure and more local autonomy to allow for the variation in the needs and economic conditions of each region. He noted, in passing, that although the statute required members to be authentic practicing artisans and workers, the signatories of the document were mostly lawyers, doctors, and professors.[5] For his part, Garibaldi, named "Great Well-Deserving Primate," found nothing but praise for the efforts of the Florentines "to make themselves the initiators and apostles of a fraternal spirit between all the artisans of Italy." [6]

By June 1861, the Florentine Artisans' Brotherhood, confident of Mazzini's support, circularized the Italian workers' societies, announcing the hope that, when their Ninth Congress met in Florence in September, a pact of national unity could be ratified on the basis of the statute of the Florentine Brotherhood, thus realizing the "potent unity" of *Italia Artigiana* ("Artisan Italy").[7] Though arguments between Mazzinians and non-Mazzinians (the latter led by Giuseppe Montanelli) within the Florentine Brotherhood itself actually diminished the prospects of a congress acceptance of the Florentine formula, Mazzini was confident that the forthcoming congress would be dominated by his followers and that a national organization would result.[8] In a letter to the Workers' Society of Bologna, he defended the right of the workers' organizations and their congresses to concern themselves with politics, underlined the necessity of demanding universal suffrage, and urged the Bolognese to work for a

---

mento, Yr. XXXVI, Nos. 3-4 (July-Dec., 1949), 164-65, 167-68. For the history of the Florentine Artisans' Brotherhood, Luigi Minuti, *Il Comune artigiano di Firenze della Fratellanza artigiana d'Italia. Cenni storici* (Florence, 1911); Andrea Giannelli, *Cenni autobiografici e ricordi politici* (Milan, 1925), pp. 360-63, note 3; Elio Conti, *Le origini del socialismo a Firenze (1860-1880)* (Rome: Edizioni Rinascita, 1950), pp. 57-67. This volume is cited below as Conti, *O.S.F.*

[4] *Capitoli di una Fratellanza Artigiana preceduti dal Rapporto della Commissione incaricata della revisione dei medesimi ed illustrati dal bilancio centenario* (Florence, 1861). A curious combination of historical influences is reflected in the titles used: masters, grand masters, priors, primates, decurions, centurions, censors, triumvirs, directors, sub-directors, delegates.

[5] Carlo Cattaneo, *"Scritti politici ed epistolario* (Florence, 1892-1901), III, 23 ff.

[6] Giuseppe Garibaldi, *Scritti e discorsi politici e militari. Edizione Nazionale. A cura della Reale Commissione* (Bologna: Cappelli, 1937), IV, 398-99; Ciampoli, *op. cit.,* p. 227.

[7] *La Nuova Europa,* June 21, 1861.

[8] *Lettere di G. Mazzini ad A. Giannelli* (Prato, 1882-92), pp. 178-80. This correspondence is included in Andrea Giannelli's previously cited *Cenni autobiografici,* pp. 360-63, 368-74, and in the *Epistolario* of the *S.E.I.*

national organization which, when formed, would signify the foundation of "the league of the People." The congress should elect a commission (composed, of course, of Mazzini's men) to draw up a national statute; the Florentine Artisans' draft might well serve as a model. Then, "if God lets me live beyond the redemption of Venice and Rome, my whole life will be consecrated to the development of the interests [of the workers' societies], which are the interests of Italy." [9]

Two weeks before the Ninth Congress convened, Mazzini was still trying to guarantee in advance the success of his national organization. On September 11, he wrote his friend, Dolfi: "I have written and am writing for the Artisans' Brotherhood. From Genoa I have a . . . promise [to support the statute] and I hope to have the same from elsewhere." [10] He reserved the right, nonetheless, to make revisions of detail in the Florentine model. Two days later he informed Giannelli that he would send secretly the bases of a statute and suggested the names of three reliable persons whom the congress might elect as a drafting commission, men who could be trusted to accept Mazzini's version or write a constitution consistent with his principles. He declared himself satisfied with the preparatory work and optimistic about the outcome of the congress.[11]

The moderates, after their hard experience at the Milan Congress the year before, were naturally put on their guard by Mazzini's preparatory activity. Again conservatism centered in Piedmont, where Giuseppe Boitani, the secretary of the Turin Workers' Society, headed opposition to the idea of a unified organization and the introduction of politics, which he was sure centralized control would entail.[12] The strongest weapon in the hands of the Piedmontese societies was Articles VII and XI of the 1855 *Regolamento*, which required the Permanent Commission, in arranging the agenda, to give priority to those themes it considered "most urgent and useful in the interest of the workers' societies." The Commission was now besieged by the moderate societies to place political questions last on the agenda. They need not have been overly exercised, for out of slightly more than a hundred queries received,[13] only eleven were political in nature (ten had to do with the suffrage question, the other with the attitude the societies should assume in the event Sardinia were eventually ceded to France), but, because the Piedmontese societies

[9] Letter of Aug. 14, 1861, *S.E.I.*, LXIX, 385-88.

[10] Conti, "Lettere inedite . . . ," pp. 164, 167-68.

[11] *S.E.I.*, LXXI, 351; *Lettere di G. Mazzini ad A. Giannelli*, p. 183.

[12] For the instructions given to the delegates of the Turin Society on the attitude they were to assume at the Florence Congress, *Gazzetta del Popolo* (Turin), Oct. 5, 1861.

[13] For the complete list, *La Nuova Europa*, Sept. 22, 1861.

had threatened to shun the congress if political topics were included in the agenda, the offending questions were dropped.[14]

Despite the clear majority the Piedmontese were to have at the congress, they submitted very few questions for discussion, probably fearing that the Mazzinians would politicize any topic suggested. The Mazzinians and their friends, on the other hand, packed the agenda with questions which, if reflected in resolutions, would have provided a fairly comprehensive picture of how the Italian workers' movement, at that stage of its development, proposed to deal with the more important problems confronting the workingman. They asked for discussion of such matters as the creation of labor arbitration boards, workers' credit banks, and producers' cooperatives; collective action by the workers' societies for higher wages and shorter working hours; the need for legislation concerning child labor in the factories; subsidies for the unemployed; a government investigation of working conditions throughout the country; the creation of special workers' schools; the problem of honorary members; and the founding of an official newspaper.

Represented at the Congress of Florence (September 27-29, 1861) were 124 workers' societies, over half (67) of which were from Piedmont; 16 from Liguria, 16 from Lombardy, and the remainder from Tuscany, Emilia, Umbria, Lazio, Naples, and Sardinia.[15] Two hundred and five delegates were present. Though the Piedmontese and Ligurians had a clear majority, not all were doctrinaire opponents of political activity; some—including the pioneer, Stefano Boldrini—formed a center group whose desire to continue the congress movement superseded their objections to politics.

With political questions eliminated from the agenda, it seemed that the moderates had only to block the Mazzinians' drive for a pact of national federation to keep the workers' movement directed along the traditional path of mutual assistance, pure and simple. On the sidelines, La Nazione, Florentine Liberal daily, supported the moderates by praising the Permanent Commission for keeping politics off the agenda, proving thereby that it understood "how useless as well as harmful it would have been to follow the advice Mazzini gave the Society of Bologna." [16]

[14] Rosselli, Mazzini e Bakounine, p. 74.

[15] For the Congress of Florence: Atti del nono congresso generale tenuto a Firenze delle società degli artigiani d'Italia nei giorni 27, 28, 29 settembre 1861 (Florence, 1861); Stefano Boldrini, Brevi cenni sul congresso IX, in Firenze, e sull'adunanza del 10 novembre in Asti (Vigevano, 1861); La Nuova Europa, Sept. 26-Oct. 5, 1861. The best secondary treatments are Manacorda, Il movimento operaio italiano, pp. 48-55; Rosselli, Mazzini e Bakounine, pp. 76-84.

[16] Issue of Sept. 26, 1861.

The hopes of *La Nazione* and the moderates proved illusory, for the first session of the Florence Congress barely had time to elect Garibaldi president *in absentia* when the delegates of Cagliari and Sassari asked whether the Italian workers' societies would take a stand against the cession of Sardinia to France, rumored to be under consideration by the Turin government. The query caused an uproar among the moderates, but Vincenzo Boldrini asked for debate on the question so as to clarify once and for all whether politics were a legitimate concern of the congresses. Workers had the duty to interest themselves in politics, said Boldrini, but their congresses should not be turned into political gatherings. The effect of this statement, conciliatory in intent, was decisively neutralized when one of the Sardinians retorted that the cession of his island to Louis Napoleon was not a political matter at all but concerned precisely the mutual aid principle, since it was a question of preventing the transition of "brothers from liberty to slavery." In the face of a growing tumult in the hall, he demanded that the congress at least go on record as considering anyone proposing the cession of Sardinia a traitor to *la patria*.

Francesco Guerrazzi, ex-Triumvir of Tuscany, argued that it is impossible to separate the worker from the citizen; the former, no less than the voter, has the duty to concern himself with the affairs of his own country. Nor can the political and economic questions be separated.

> If the worker concerns himself only with the material aspects of the economy, he will form absolute ideas, abstractly good, but wicked, even subversive, in application. . . . Alienate the people from the study of politics and they shall turn on us with passion, . . . they will turn to the politics of excess, at times erroneous, absurd, and ferocious. Our adversaries are sowing revolution . . . and bitter days for themselves and *la Patria*.

To put a period to the debate, Montanelli proposed an innocuous resolution, approved by 74-30 after the Piedmontese walked out in protest: "The Assembly declares that political questions are not extraneous to its institutions and recognizes that, at times, they are useful to their growth and consolidation." [17] If the 205 delegates attending the Congress represented the sentiments of Italy's workers' movement, two-thirds of its membership had yet to recognize political action as relevant to advancing labor's cause.

With what was now almost a rump congress, discussion of universal suffrage and a national organization of the workers' societies proceeded harmoniously, though debate on the latter, under the circumstances, must have seemed academic to the men aspiring to include all Italian

[17] *Atti . . . 1861 . . . Firenze*, p. 35.

workers in their politically oriented federation. A vote for the working-man found its most eloquent advocate in Francesco Savi, prominent Ligurian friend of Mazzini. Universal suffrage was not only a matter of equity; without it, the bourgeois legislators could never be expected to introduce measures promoting labor's interests. The worker, no less than the educator, the businessman, the industrialist, represents a social necessity deserving of parliamentary representation. To those objecting that the franchise should be limited to educated citizens, Savi replied: "the swimmer learns only by throwing himself into the water." Nor would giving workers the vote exacerbate class conflict, for social harmony depended on national unity, not denying the franchise to proletarians.[18] On this sound Mazzinian note, the Congress, now reduced to little more than a gathering of the apostle's followers, adopted his *Duties of Man* as the textbook for the education of the workers and elected a committee to recommend how unification of the societies, universal suffrage, and compulsory, secularized education—deemed essential to "the complete redemption of the common people"—might be obtained.[19]

Though many of the traditional remedies were suggested in the discussion of the several agenda items concerning strictly labor problems, the delegates betrayed a real appreciation of the need to confront squarely some of the issues in labor-management relations. Guerrazzi, for example, pointed out that strikes and the "disastrous cleavages" between capital and labor were becoming entirely "too frequent an evil." If these conflicts were to be kept within harmonious limits, said he, the workers' societies would have to take a stand.[20] The resolution voted under such prompting, though far from belligerent, sharply contrasted with the innocuous tenor of previous congress pronouncements, which usually recommended no more than further study. The wage question was described as urgent; strikes and other violent means of putting pressure on employers were condemned as disastrous to the workers' welfare, which could only be guaranteed through the growth of the societies. Meanwhile, boards of "honest and upright men," chosen from the societies and the "friends of the workingman," should try to obtain "equitable and Christian" provisions covering salary increases and reduction of working hours and to demand the abrogation of those articles of the Penal Code prohibiting workers' coalitions.

Thus the Florence Congress, at the price of schism within the ranks, had established the right of the congresses and societies to concern themselves with politics; universal suffrage was made an official demand;

[18] *Ibid.*, pp. 42-45.
[19] *Ibid.*, pp. 47, 67.
[20] *Ibid.*, pp. 64-65.

organizational unity on a national scale was put under the study of an official committee; and a clear attitude had been assumed in favor of higher wages, shorter hours, and arbitration boards. The congress, however, had moved no closer to making the projected national organization an authentic workers' association, for out of the fifteen men elected to the new Permanent Commission (including Garibaldi, Dolfi, Savi, Guerrazzi, and Montanelli) only three were workingmen. And though the congress decisions were a clear victory for Mazzini, the problem remained of persuading the dissident societies to adhere to those decisions. The national unification of labor was still a hope, not a reality.

The echoes had scarcely died down in the meeting hall when the polemic between moderates and Mazzinians exploded in the press. *La Nazione*, on September 31, carried a protest, signed by forty-four delegates of moderate Piedmontese, Ligurian, and Lombard societies, denouncing the Montanelli resolution, which sought "to introduce a political principle into the mutual aid societies that clashes . . . with the true, unique, and great principle animating the Societies, . . . that of mutual assistance, instruction, education, love of labor." The Florentine Artisans' Brotherhood was blamed for the turn of events. In a "Proclamation Motivated by the Protest of the Deputies of Piedmont, Lombardy, Emilia, against the Ninth Congress held in Florence," the organization was called a sect dedicated to agitation and disorder and a scandalous affront to the good sense of the Tuscans. The moderates had gone to Florence under the impression that all delegates were subjects of Victor Emmanuel, but at the congress they had discovered they were "in the Kingdom of the Idea, in the Empire of the Apostle of systematic revolt against the Government, in the furnace of the national disasters of '48 and '49." [21] On October 3, *La Nazione* printed a protest of the Turin Workers' Society against the Florence deliberations, including the verdict that universal suffrage would be harmful to the country and the workers, "useful only to reactionaries and political agitators."

Even within the Florentine Artisans' Brotherhood itself sixty-odd members resigned in protest against the Mazzinian program, declaring they preferred a society that could offer certain guarantees against "sectarian purposes and personal ambitions." [22] Another Tuscan society, the masons of Livorno, inserted a provision in their constitution prohibiting political action or discussion, which makes the artisan "lazy and arrogant." [23]

The Mazzinians, of course, did not endure these diatribes in silence. In a manifesto the Florentine Artisans' Brotherhood suggested that it was

[21] *La Nazione*, Oct. 2, 1861.
[22] *Ibid.*, Oct. 9, 1861.
[23] *Statuto della Società degli Artigiani muratori di Livorno* (Livorno, 1861).

not the principle of political discussion by the workers' societies that disturbed the moderates, but the fact that more and more associations were joining the parties of opposition. After all, jibed the Mazzinians, those who, at the Florence Congress, objected to politics in the societies were precisely the gentlemen who, at the Vercelli Congress of 1858, had voted for affiliating with the National Society, which was nothing if not political. Free political discussion, wrote the Florentines, is a time-honored means of providing for the moral and material improvement of the working classes. Reverting to the sweeping quasi-mysticism of Mazzini himself, they defined "the politics of the workingman" as "the solemn manifestation of the popular conscience that instills strength and vigor in the great soul of the people, the cult of the fatherland, the incitement to the conquest and exercise of those sacred rights and austere duties without which the populace becomes a 'thing,' passive and inert." [24]

Nor did the polemic limit itself to the single issue of politics in the societies. The whole broad Mazzinian program was brought under venomous attack by the moderates and the pro-government press. La Nazione, on October 13, admonished all honest men to demonstrate that the "entire program of the Party of Action, captained by Mazzini," aimed at the undoing of Italy by provoking internal strife and foreign wars. It was well to be on guard against the agents of Austria and Cardinal Antonelli, but one must not forget "the socialists [sic] of Mazzini, the usurpers of the red shirts." Counterattacking, the Milanese organ of the Mazzinians, L'Unità Italiana, interpreted the fact that most of the dissident societies were Piedmontese as one more proof that Piedmont put itself ahead of Italy. The Italian workers must choose between Mazzini and the moderates, who pretend that only material interests concern the worker and "never dare to complain if the government leads the country to perdition." [25]

Inevitably, the verbal tilting soon expressed itself concretely. Boitani and his Turin Society, on October 6, called for a meeting at Asti of all dissident societies, to be held on November 10, declaring the Florence Congress "null and illegal" and lamenting that the delegates at the rump Florentine meeting were not workers, but mostly "lawyers, journalists, novelists, or marchesi [marquises]—a strange accusation, considering the source.[26] Thanks to the Boldrini brothers and Mauro Macchi, opposed to such an intransigent stand, the Turin Society agreed to issue, along with the Asti association, another circular of convocation on October 24,

---

[24] The manifesto was issued on October 6 and published three days later by La Nazione.
[25] Oct. 1, 1861.
[26] Gazzetta del Popolo, Oct. 8, 1861; La Nazione, Oct. 10, 1861.

which considerably toned down the acerbity of the initial call for a counter-congress. In this document the purpose of the projected congress at Asti was described as gathering together "under the old banner of mutual assistance" the societies that had been thrown into confusion at Florence by "the strife of political passions." [27] Even Boitani agreed to go along with the conciliatory gesture.

Probably more in anger than amusement, the Mazzinians ridiculed the Asti meeting as the "Astian *Sonderbund*." [28] Their chieftain in far-off London, however, cautioned them to "continue without becoming irritated. Leave the Piedmontese societies to themselves. Unite as many societies as you can. Little by little, you shall see the dissident societies come back, one by one." [29] In a letter to the workers of Parma, Mazzini assured them that the dissidents were deluding themselves in thinking they could improve the people's material conditions by ignoring politics. They were unconsciously condemning the workers' associations to the fate of "blind and mechanical instruments of production." [30]

Notwithstanding the efforts of Mazzini and his followers to sabotage the Asti meeting, many non-Piedmontese societies participated.[31] Out of the 106 societies represented, 22 were from Emilia, Liguria, Tuscany, Lombardy, and Naples. Even so, consciousness of their numerical superiority did not prevent the Asti delegates from trying to steal the Mazzinians' thunder by wrapping themselves in the tricolor. Of the two questions put to the congress, one was intended to show that the patriotism of the workers did not depend on introducing politics into the mutual aid societies. In the pertinent resolution, the congress stated that, although the discussion of politics was not the purpose of the societies and though self-preservation and the workers' welfare dictated abstention from politics, there is no doubt that "the Worker can . . . be both a good citizen and a good patriot." There was some sentiment for discontinuing the congresses, a view stemming from the militant tenor of the discussions at the Milan and Florence congresses, but the Boldrinis and Mauro Macchi persuaded the Asti group to mandate a committee to discuss a reconciliation with the Permanent Commission elected at Florence. This gesture was somewhat prejudiced, however, by the express instructions of the Asti delegates that the same committee convoke the *Ninth* Congress of

[27] *La Nazione*, Oct. 29, 1861.

[28] An allusion to the separatist league founded in 1845 by the seven Catholic cantons of Switzerland to fight federal unification.

[29] Mazzini to Dolfi, Nov. 14, 1861, in Conti, "Lettere inedite . . . ," p. 169.

[30] Oct. 25, 1861. *Lettere alle Società operaie scritte nel decennio 1861-71* (Genoa, 1875), pp. 8-9; S.E.I., LXIX, 388-91.

[31] For the Asti Congress proceedings: *Sunto degli atti del Congresso generale delle società operaie italiane tenutosi il 10 e 11 novembre 1861 in Asti* (Asti, n.d.); cf., also, Stefano Boldrini, *Brevi cenni sul Congresso IX*.

the mutual aid societies, i.e., invalidate the Florence Congress, if the Permanent Commission did not accept the resolutions of the Asti meeting.

Yet by July 1862, the negotiations between the Florence and Asti committees produced a peace treaty, by which the Asti faction recognized the validity of the Florence deliberations and promised to come to the *Tenth* Congress of the societies. The Asti meeting had not intended, with its resolution, to exclude politics absolutely—so ran the document—and since the Montanelli motion of Florence was recognized as consistent with the Genoa *Regolamento* of 1855, the peacemakers decided to accept the Florence resolution as the basis for determining which questions were to be accepted for discussion by future congresses.[32] It was a slender reed, indeed, on which to base the future harmony of the Italian workers' movement, for the Montanelli motion was as much an argument for keeping politics out of the workers' congresses and societies as for continuing discussion of political matters, as intended by its authors in the first instance.

The equivocal aspects of the situation discouraged not at all the man whose principles were at the root of the dissension. Mazzini's letters to the Italian societies were as optimistic as ever about the possibility of uniting the associations. To his friends, Savi, Mazzoni, and Franchini, he outlined a statute for a national workers' organization and advised his followers in the peninsula not only to take advantage of the lack of any real rival for control of the workers' movement but to begin thinking in terms of the Italian movement stimulating a European-wide action by republican-minded workingmen.[33]

Nor did Mazzini entertain the possibility that the workingman he wanted to bind into a national organization might not be stimulated by the fervid abstractions he used in his propaganda: Humanity, National Mission, Moral Law. Against any proletarian demand for immediate economic improvement, Mazzini offered Italian labor the stern duty of forwarding the acquisition of Rome and Venetia. "Once Italy is made into a Nation," he wrote on November 19, 1861, to the workers' society of Reggio, "you shall have to resolve . . . the vital question of your moral, intellectual, and economic improvement." [34]

THE PARMA AND NAPLES CONGRESSES

Mazzini's insistence on the completion of national unity under a republic as the precondition for resolving the "vital question" of Italy's working classes was consistent with his premises, but this made it no more palat-

[32] *La Nuova Europa*, July 26, 1862.
[33] *S.E.I.*, LXXII, 104-07.
[34] *Ibid.*, LXIX, 392-94.

able to the mutual aid societies. There is some evidence that the indoctrination efforts of the Party of Action were not entirely lost on the Italian workers, especially in the Lombard industrial centers,[35] but hinging the effort almost entirely on the national question, on the republicans' chances of "making Italy into a Nation" by their own endeavors, ignored the logical inferences to be drawn from the political developments of 1862.

On March 3 the Ricasoli government was replaced by that of Urbano Rattazzi, a change hailed by the Party of Action as the dawn of an era of government sympathy for its activities. And so it seemed—for a few weeks. Rattazzi openly favored the Party of Action, encouraged Garibaldi to go into Lombardy and begin recruitment of volunteers for a raid on Venetia and tolerated, without the usual police reprisals, demonstrations in the larger cities of Italy and a lively press campaign demanding the fulfillment of national unity. A week after Rattazzi became premier, the *Società Emancipatrice*, dedicated to the unity cause, was founded and soon became the focal point of the patriotic agitation. Workers' societies of both the Mazzinian and nonpolitical variety joined the organization, and, under this patriotic stimulus, the negotiations for an accord between the Asti *giunta* (committee) and the Florence Permanent Commission moved rapidly ahead.

Early in May the honeymoon between Rattazzi and the *Partito d'Azione* was brusquely broken off by the premier, who, worried about the international repercussions of Garibaldi's resolute preparations for adding the conquest of Venetia to his laurels, had the hero's eager volunteers arrested and sent Garibaldi off to Caprera to meditate on the inconstancy of prime ministers and kings. The Emancipation Society was put under close police surveillance, and the many workers' societies affiliated with the organization became the objects of official suspicion. Garibaldi, never one for sustained meditation, soon left his island retirement and, on arriving in Palermo, immediately began gathering volunteers for a march on the Eternal City: "*Roma o la morte!*" Young Italians flowed southward, drawn by the magic of the hero's name. Rattazzi's government, now thoroughly frightened by the forces it had itself conjured up from the populace, decreed the suspension of the right of association and on August 20, 1862, dissolved the *Società Emancipatrice* and all its affiliated associations. Nine days later at Aspromonte, Garibaldi's volunteers fell apart before the government regulars of General Cialdini, their leader wounded and some of their number hanged as deserters from the army of Victor Emmanuel. Under the circumstances, the Permanent Commission

[35] *Rerum Scriptorum* [Gaetano Salvemini], *I partiti politici milanesi nel secolo XIX* (Milan, 1899), pp. 169 ff.

elected at Florence decided it was impossible to hold a general congress of the workers' societies in October, as anticipated.

From the Mazzinian point of view, the decision of the Permanent Commission was politically more than justified, for the dissolution of the societies affiliated with the Emancipation Society worked a much greater hardship on the Mazzinian associations than on those of moderate persuasion—the former, given the objectives of the agitations of 1862, had been much more active in the unity manifestations. The August 20 decision and Aspromonte were pointed to by the moderates as the fruit of involving the societies in political questions, of subordinating the workingmen's interests to partisan political ends.

The practical inference drawn by many societies which had not affiliated with the Emancipation Society was that they could ill afford to take the path recommended by Mazzini. Nor could there be much doubt that of the ninety-three new societies founded in 1862,[36] those appearing after August favored the nonpolitical ideal of the moderates. In 1862 Lombardy, as in 1861, led Piedmont in the number of new societies founded,[37] but this was cold comfort to the Mazzinians, since the Piedmont-Liguria area still had a comfortable lead over the Lombards in relative strength. As of the end of 1862, there were 4.95 societies and 1,043 members in Piedmont-Liguria for every 100,000 inhabitants, 2.71 and 769 in Lombardy.[38] Tuscany more than made up for the difference, but here the strongest and most influential of Mazzinian societies, the *Fratellanza Artigiana*, had been forced by the government action of August to suspend its activity.[39] In absolute figures, the Piedmontese preponderance at the beginning of 1863 was even more suggestive of continuing moderate influence on the organized workers' movement: of the 445 Italian mutual aid societies indicated by the official *Statistica* of 1862, Piedmont had 165 to Lombardy's 83. Detracting to some extent from the significance of these figures, however, is their lack of completeness; many societies, especially the Mazzinian, chose to ignore the government compiler's request for data, a natural enough silence on the part of associations which, since August, were considered subversive. Yet the very fear that advised this silence also counseled a much less vigorous—and, therefore, less effective

---

[36] *Statistica . . . 1862.*

[37] For the year 1861: Lombardy, eleven; Piedmont, three; for 1862: Lombardy nineteen; Piedmont, fourteen.

[38] Martuscielli, *Le società di mutuo soccorso e cooperative*, p. 193.

[39] Minuti, *op. cit.*, p. 44. Almost from its inception, the Florentine Brotherhood had been active in the patriotic campaign. In July, 1861, for example, the association created a special fund to further agitation for Rome and Venetia, supported by regular, though voluntary, contributions from its members. *La Nuova Europa*, July 13, 1861.

—dissemination of Mazzinian propaganda aimed at the workingman.

One other datum of the 1862 *Statistica* records a fact that could not have pleased Mazzini's lieutenants in their struggle for control of the Italian workers' movement: the burgeoning of societies organized, not as mixed associations, but as trade-unions, a type of organization described by an official report of 1863 as conducive to "interests . . . other than those having to do with assistance to the sick and the infirm." [40] As Rosselli indicates, these "other interests" were strikes, resistance funds, autonomous organization, liberation from every control by bourgeois intellectuals, and "all those forms of struggle which prove themselves adequate in achieving economic improvements," [41] all of which interests came before the issue of how and under whose auspices the national unification was to be completed. The government figures show a total of 121 such societies, most centered in Lombardy and the Emilia. It is difficult to imagine these societies being attracted by Mazzinian propaganda lamenting "the dangerous antagonism" between capital and labor, reflected in strikes, which causes the worker "to lose his whole concept of order, his entire love of labor." [42]

In the light of these developments, the Asti *giunta*'s acceptance of the Florence resolution permitting political discussion at the congresses, though compromising the previously intransigent nonpolitical position of the moderates, afforded no real satisfaction to the Mazzinians. The Permanent Commission and the Asti committee, meeting in Genoa on September 13, 1863, decided to include political questions on the agenda of the imminent Parma Congress, but to place them at the bottom of the list.[43] This gesture settled nothing, for each faction, in the month preceding the congress, maneuvered vigorously to insure its maximum program: the moderates, to sabotage the meeting in advance; the Mazzinians, to create a national federation. The moderate organs, the *Gazzetta del Popolo* of Turin and the *Gazzetta di Parma*, backed by the government press, urged the societies to abstain from the congress. Many of them heeded the call. Others, like the powerful Turin Workers' Society, decided to go to the Parma Congress but instructed their delegates, notwithstanding the moderating efforts of Mauro Macchi and the Boldrini brothers, to withdraw if political questions were raised.[44] For their part, the Mazzinians were advised by their chief to "exhaust pacifically" the

[40] Fano, *Della carità preventiva e dell'ordinamento delle Società di mutuo soccorso in Italia*, pp. 190-91.

[41] *Mazzini e Bakounine*, pp. 103-04.

[42] *Fede e Avvenire* (Milan), Apr. 21, 1863.

[43] Circular in *L'Unità Italiana*, Sept. 26, 1863.

[44] *Gazzetta del Popolo*, Sept. 6, 27, Oct. 5, 12, 1863; *Gazzetta di Parma*, Sept. 30, 1863; *Il Dovere* (Genoa), Oct. 17, 1863.

items on the agenda, but to elect on the fourth day of the congress a permanent "central directorate" to write a constitution for a national organization. "You may be certain that the Societies, one by one, will feel the need of joining the Confederation." [45]

As a representation of the collectivity of Italian mutual aid societies and trade-unions, the Congress of Parma, meeting on October 9, 1863, was a failure from the start. The 115 delegates represented only 60 societies, that is, about one-eighth of the country's associations. If those whose representatives withdrew during the sessions of the congress are deducted, Mazzini's slight influence on the Italian workers' movement may be appreciated.

The tenor of the Parma proceedings was almost predictable in advance.[46] The delegate of the moderate society in Parma proposed the exclusion of political questions but was hissed into withdrawing his proposal and his person from the hall. A query put by the delegate of the Artisans' Brotherhood of Lucca regarding the causes and cure of unemployment was not even deemed worthy of discussion. Instruction of the rural worker, "in order to emancipate the peasant from priestly influence and to spread the spirit of association in the countryside," was put into a resolution. An official newspaper, to be called *Il Giornale delle Associazioni Operaie Italiane*, was projected. Only two really important questions were discussed at length: the foundation of a workers' credit bank and unification of the societies. Carlo Cattaneo, along with two others, was commissioned to study the technical aspects of creating a bank for workingmen. Guerrazzi, Savi, and Gaspare Stampa urged unification vigorously enough to secure acceptance of a federative pact between the associations, the central executive function to be exercised by the Permanent Commission, but maximum autonomy to be retained by the affiliated societies, who could accept or reject a uniform *regolamento*. Among the handful of opponents to this proposal was the founder of the congress movement, Stefano Boldrini, who, having cast his vote, withdrew, vowing he would have nothing more to do with the congresses.

At the very conclusion of the meeting, someone suggested that official greetings be sent to Mazzini who, "to the shame of the reaction, languishes in exile." When the moderates—there were still a few of them—roared disapproval, a conciliatory delegate tried to smooth things over with the sophistry that the communication should be addressed to Mazzini, the "worker of the mind," not the "political man." Again there

[45] Mazzini to Dolfi, Sept. 27, 1863, reproduced by Conti, "Lettere inedite . . . ," pp. 173-74.

[46] For the congress proceedings, see the running accounts in *La Gazzetta di Parma, La Nazione, L'Unità Italiana*; for secondary treatments, Manacorda, *Il movimento operaio italiano*, pp. 59-62; Rosselli, *Mazzini e Bakounine*, pp. 111-14.

were objections, so the presiding officer dissolved the congress and sent off the address in the name of the presidency.[47]

Thus, the Tenth Congress made a shambles of all hopes of effective unity among the mutual aid societies. Even the patient Mauro Macchi, who, with the Boldrinis, had provided a link between moderates and Mazzinians, resigned his post on the Permanent Commission, thus leaving only five members in that organ, three Mazzinians (Savi, Astengo, Cannonieri), one a Garibaldian (Asproni). In the wake of the congress, the Turin Workers' Society, with its thousands of members, refused to recognize the authority of the Permanent Commission elected at Parma and abjured all future general congresses "so long as they are not better oriented in the true interests of the working classes." [48] The withdrawal of the moderates left the Mazzinians in control, a pyrrhic victory in that there remained precious little to control.

The Permanent Commission busied itself, nonetheless, with the tasks assigned it by the Parma Congress. On January 3, 1864, it brought out the first issue of the *Giornale delle Associazioni Operaie Italiane* in Genoa, with Francesco Savi as editor-in-chief. Despite its excellent coverage of the mutual aid societies and labor generally, the paper was poorly supported by the workers and in July, 1866, had to cease publication, a casualty of the war with Austria.

The constitutional project, on the other hand, dragged along for months, a delay not shortened by Mazzini's running criticism of and impatience with the Commission's efforts.[49] The work of the group might have been greatly simplified if its members had not had to wrestle with the problem of how to incorporate Mazzini's religious and moral abstractions into a constitution for a national workers' organization. The harassed Commission had three points of departure in composing the statute: the constitution of the Florentine Artisans' Brotherhood, with its ridiculously complicated organizational apparatus; a draft submitted by Mazzini himself after the Parma Congress, in which the preamble premised a belief in God, a moral law demanding the moral, intellectual, and economic progress of all, and the associative principle, while the text summarized his religious, political, and social ideas; and a project by Cattaneo, delineating in simple, concrete language a very decentralized federation, allowing for regional differences in the capacities, needs, and aspirations of the peninsula's societies.[50]

[47] The address was published in *L'Unità Italiana*, Oct. 24, 1863.

[48] Manacorda, *Il movimento operaio italiano*, p. 62.

[49] "Why should a labor of ten days be protracted for months?" *L'Unità Italiana*, Apr. 16, 1864; *cf.*, also, his letter to the Artisans' Brotherhood of Lugo, June 21, 1864, in the same newspaper, issue of July 16, 1864; *S.E.I.*, LXXXIII, 285-86.

[50] For a comparison of the Cattaneo and Mazzini versions, Rosselli, *Mazzini e Bakounine*, pp. 118-20.

The Permanent Commission's final draft, completed in June 1864, known as the "Act of Brotherhood of the Italian Workers' Societies," [51] had some of the essentials of the master's blueprint. Gone were the preconditions of belief in God and moral law, but the moral, intellectual, and economic progress of the working classes remained the objective, to be attained through the association of "all the capacities and existing forces in that class." Cattaneo's safeguards of sectional autonomy were incorporated; Mazzini's original requirement of an explicit expression of nationalist faith was watered down to "promoting . . . the greatness and prosperity of *la patria*." Where Mazzini had proposed "legal agitation," the final draft spoke of "petitions to be sent to the parliament" in favor of workers' rights and interests. The organizational structure was relatively simple: in place of the Permanent Commission, a five-man central council elected by the annual congresses and operating as three sections, corresponding to the moral, intellectual, and material purposes of the Brotherhood; a regional committee in the capital city of every Italian region. The chief novelty of the scheme, as against the Genoa *Regolamento* of 1855, lay, aside from the proclaimed principles, in the greater degree of centralized organization. This statutory innovation, however, was never realized.

It was primarily for the purpose of discussing and approving the Act of Brotherhood that the Naples (Eleventh) Congress was convoked for October 25, 1864.[52] No appreciable objections were raised to the document, since there were only fifty-seven societies represented (less than one-tenth of the Italian total), of which twelve were from Naples itself. The great majority of the delegates, of course, were Mazzinians and Garibaldians. This probably accounts for the scant attention paid to extremely vital questions submitted for discussion: demands for the compilation of statistics on wages in industry and agriculture, agitation for the elimination of night work and arbitrary firings, and the exclusive hiring of Italian workers for all public works.

For republican activists, these were bland issues, indeed, compared to the recent developments on the national scene. Only a few weeks before (September 15), Victor Emmanuel had signed the September Convention with the French, promising not to attack Rome nor allow anyone else (read Garibaldi) to do so. The French had promised to withdraw their troops from the city within two years, but the Pope was to be permitted

---

[51] For the final draft, *Il Giornale delle Associazioni Operaie* (Genoa), July 3, 1864; also reproduced in *Il Proletario* (Florence), Oct. 8, 1865.

[52] For the Naples Congress proceedings: *Atti del congresso XI delle Associazioni Operaie italiane tenuto in Napoli il 25, 26 e 27 ottobre 1864* (Naples, 1865); *Il Giornale delle Associazioni Operaie*, Nov. 6, 1864; *Il Popolo d'Italia* (Naples), Oct. 25-28, 1864; Manacorda, *Il movimento operaio italiano*, pp. 62-65.

to organize a defense force. The national capital was to be moved to Florence from Turin. In less than a week the details of this "secret" protocol leaked out, for on September 20-22, the Turinese arose in protest, a gesture costing the lives of almost two dozen citizens, the victims of army repression. To further complicate matters, an anti-Austrian insurrection had erupted in the Friulian area, fomented by Mazzinians. Preoccupation with events of such importance to the sacred cause of national unity obviously precluded serious attention to the agenda of the Naples Congress by the followers of Garibaldi and Mazzini.

The Congress of Naples marked the beginning of a long hiatus in the Mazzinian drive to organize the Italian workers' movement behind the republican program. Francesco Savi, the most active member of the Central Council, died early in 1865, and for the rest of the year no progress was made in implementing the Act of Brotherhood, other than securing the adherence of a few more societies to its provisions. The congresses were put off from year to year, in 1865 because of a cholera epidemic, in 1866 because of the war with Austria.[53] After the monarchy's acquisition of Venetia, Mazzini and the *Partito d'Azione* dedicated themselves to a program of unflagging war on the Vatican and preparation for a republican revolution. Rome was the center of all their calculations. In September 1866, Mazzini organized his Universal Republican Alliance for the hard campaign ahead.[54] The awkward figure cut by the monarchy in the Mentana affair of 1867 and the economic unrest of 1868-69 probably strengthened the appeal of Mazzinian propaganda, but again the primary purpose of that propaganda was nationalist, not social, except insofar as criticism of the social order served to strengthen republican nationalism. Furthermore, his objectives required, in Mazzini's view, the sympathies of the Italian middle class as much as those of the workingmen. "War on capital, abolition of [private] property, hostility toward the bourgeoisie, . . . terror and vendetta, all these are an unhealthy cry."[55] The goal was a republican constituent assembly, in a liberated Rome; then, and only then, reforms would be made, and these but gradually. The cloth was being cut to fit the class for whom it was intended.

CONCLUSION

Paradoxically, Mazzini's failure to organize the Italian workers behind his political program contributed to the appearance of a socialist move-

[53] For the Central Council's circular, postponing the 1865 convention, see *Il Proletario*, Oct. 8, 1865.

[54] For the manifesto of the Republican Alliance, S.E.I., LXXXVI, 25-46.

[55] Mazzini, *L'Iniziativa* (Rome, 1887), pp. 18 ff. These articles are reproduced in S.E.I., XCII, 3-29.

ment in the peninsula. The question of whether or not the workers' societies, as such, should interest themselves in political affairs became a dead issue, principally because the organizers and leaders of the associations concluded that the day-to-day struggle for higher wages, shorter hours, and better working conditions could best be served through syndical organization and direct economic pressure on the employer class. Moreover, the highly restricted suffrage of the Italian political system ruled out a political party of labor, geared to the peculiar needs of electoral and parliamentary tactics and strategy. Cattaneo pointed out, too, that Mazzini's effort to force an overt recognition of politics as a prime concern of the mutual aid societies was pointless, for "a great association of workers will always be a political force; but it will be much less so the more it professes the desire to be one." [56]

However pointless Mazzini's effort in a constructive sense, it demonstrated among other things that the Italian working class, under the prevailing low level of industrialization, was not ready to seek satisfaction of its needs through political action, through a labor party, and certainly not inclined to see its only salvation in letting Mazzini educate it to the urgency of Rome, the Veneto, and the Italian Republic. In effect, Mazzini's failure encouraged the search among Italian radicals for an apolitical—even antipolitical, as it developed—method of applying the power of proletarian numbers to the task of overthrowing the existing social and political system. Rejecting the syndicalist alternative as too slow, as conceiving the struggle within too narrow limits, they found themselves moving toward the Pisacanian premise: that redemption of the Italian nation lay in direct action, in the "propaganda of deeds" that would simultaneously resolve both the institutional and social questions, not in the Mazzinian sense, but through class warfare.

The protracted arguments between Mazzinians and moderates over the question of political discussion and action by the workers' societies ended in no more than a shallow victory for the former, since a large majority of the mutual aid societies showed no tendency to adopt the program of the Act of Brotherhood. Unfortunately for the Mazzinian cause, however, this was but a small part of the price that had to be paid for the privilege of insisting on a political program whose rationale depended on the acceptance of Mazzini's quasi-religious assumptions. And by 1864 there were a good many Italian radicals who, in the name of freedom of conscience, openly questioned these assumptions. The hostility was stimulated and nourished, in great part, by the appearance of a vogue of positivism among Italian democrats during the 1860's, manifesting

[56] Letter to Agostino Bertani, Feb. 24, 1864, *Scritti politici ed epistolario*, III, 34.

itself in numerous freethinkers' societies which, as Mazzini had cause to lament, were at once atheist, materialist, and libertarian.[57] The general tendency was toward an assertion of the individual conscience against the confining influence of religious tenets, be they sponsored by the Genoese apostle or the Roman pontiff. The coincidence in time of this tendency and the Mazzinians' peak involvement with the workers' movement was to cause Mazzini's program for the worker to be subjected by the more radical democrats to the test of positivist, materialist criteria, free of any abstract, ethical assumptions. In that Mazzinianism was found wanting in this analysis, many republicans, especially those who were in more immediate contact with the economic and social problems of the common people, drew the conclusion that if popular support were required, social renovation would have to be given a higher priority by the Party of Action. In this negative sense, too, Mazzini involuntarily lent an impulse to the rise of a socialist movement.

Nor was Mazzini's role as a contributor to the genesis of a socialist movement limited to that of arousing opposition to his principles, for at least one of them exercised a very positive influence on the fortunes of socialism in the peninsula. If the pioneers of Italian socialism rejected Mazzini's religious mysticism in choosing the socialist path to the left, part of the reason is to be found in their having learned well a primary teaching of the master: the historical necessity of greater social and political power for the common man, in Europe as well as in Italy, in itself one of the basic assumptions behind Mazzini's vision of collective humanity and progress. He wanted a unification of the forces of labor in Italy, but more than this, he insisted that building this unity should, in itself, "constitute an initiative among the European working classes." [58] In attaching a cosmopolitan significance to his followers' attempts to organize the Italian workers, Mazzini, in effect, had helped prepare a favorable reaction among Italian radicals to the institutionalization of proletarian internationalism that was the International Workingmen's Association, founded in September 1864.

The shadow of the Great Exile lay fully athwart the rostrum when Gennaro Bovio, the representative of the Trani Workers' Society, asked the Congress of Naples whether there was any possibility of convoking an international congress among the workers' associations of various

---

[57] In 1869 he vowed to the Countess Marie d'Agoult that he would gladly give half the remainder of his life to be able to write two books: one on the French Revolution of 1789 and the other on the religious question, against the Comtists, the materialists, the atheists, the "dilettantes" like Renan, the "artists of brutality" like Taine, the Proudhonists, etc. "They mislead democracy and ruin the future." Letter of July 19, 1869, *S.E.I.*, LXXXVIII, 107-08.
[58] *S.E.I.*, LXXI, 104-07.

countries to provide for their mutual needs through a common statute favoring "that moral unity among nations and peoples which is the most sublime inspiration of our century." [59] Ideologically, it was the point of meeting between Mazzinianism and modern socialism; in its practical consequences, it marked the point of separation.

[59] *Atti . . . 1864 . . . Napoli,* pp. 35-36.

IV

Bakunin in Italy (January 1864 to September 1866)

MAZZINI AND THE CREATION OF THE FIRST INTERNATIONAL

UNDER the column heading of "Miscellany," the *Giornale delle Associazioni Operaie* of October 9, 1864, carried a brief notice: "The other evening there was a meeting of workers in Saint Martin's Hall [London]. . . . It was decided that it would be convenient to create committees in all the principal cities of Europe; the idea was proposed of convoking in Belgium next year a general workers' congress; a resolution was voted which took these two proposals as the basis of an international alliance [of industrial workers]." These few lines were probably the first public reference in Italy to the International Workingmen's Association. Given the I.W.A.'s objective of associating European proletarians, the initiative could not have been ignored by Mazzini or his followers in Italy.

The Naples Congress had been informed, probably through Mazzini or one of his intermediaries, of the historic gathering in St. Martin's Hall. Though the statute of the new association was not approved until four days after the Naples Congress dispersed, several delegates—Savi, Asproni, and Giuseppe Fanelli—made speeches praising the new initiative, and the congress decided to send a representative—if the money could be found to cover his expenses—to the first I.W.A. congress, scheduled for Brussels in the spring of 1865.[1] The resolution may well have been inspired by the fact that, so far as its authors knew at the time, the new organization was to be governed by the principles of Giuseppe Mazzini, not those set out in Karl Marx's "Inaugural Address."

Through two of his agents in London, Major Louis Wolff and G. P.

---

[1] *Atti . . . 1864 . . . Napoli*, pp. 36 ff.

Fontana, representatives of the London Italian Workers' Society, Mazzini almost succeeded in having his own principles incorporated into the constitution of the First International.[2] Fully briefed by his master, Wolff attended the September 28 meeting and, as a member of the subcommittee entrusted with drawing up a constitution for the association, persuaded the committee to approve a declaration that the goal of the International was the promotion of "the moral, intellectual, and material progress of the European working classes," read the Act of Brotherhood of the Italian societies, and proposed it as the basis of a constitution for the International. The sub-committee passed the Mazzinian scheme to the main committee. Marx, a member of this committee, made the mistake of not attending its October 12 sitting. After suggesting only minor additions and revisions of the Act of Brotherhood, this group ordered the subcommittee to draw up a final draft.

When the full committee met again on October 18, Mazzini's man, Wolff, had already left to attend the Naples Congress,[3] but Marx, informed of developments in the meantime, was very much in evidence. "I was really alarmed," he wrote a few days later to Engels, "when I head the good Le Lubez . . . read a useless, wordy, poorly written and absolutely infantile preamble, that pretended to be a declaration of principles, in which Mazzini could be perceived at every point, encrusted with loose scraps of French socialism. . . . [The proposal] aimed at the impossible, a kind of central direction (naturally with Mazzini behind it) of the European working class."[4] Though voting in favor of the subcommittee's proposal, Marx had himself delegated to "improve the form [of it] here and there." His "formal" revision effectively demolished the Mazzinian influence in the statute. He rewrote the preamble, reduced the forty articles to ten, wrote an entirely new address to the workers, and, as a conciliatory gesture toward the English and French supporters of the original proposal, left in two Mazzinian sentences pertaining to truth, justice, morality, duties and rights, including

[2] For details, Valiani, *op. cit.*, I, 120-22. For details of the Mazzini-Marx feud, see A. Luzio's essay in the volume, *Carlo Alberto e Mazzini* (Turin, 1923), pp. 435-62; and G. Ambrosini, *Marx, Mazzini e l'Internazionale socialista* (Campobasso, 1917).

[3] Wolff had told the I.W.A. General Council on October 12 that he was going to Naples to sound out the representatives of the Italian workers' societies in regard to the International. He never reached Naples, however, and when he returned to London in February, 1865, he said he had been jailed in Alessandria. Rosselli, *Mazzini e Bakounine*, p. 124. On the rather equivocal figure of Wolff, see S.E.I., *Epistolario, ad nomen;* G. Castellani, *Eroi Garibaldini* (Milan, 1931), pp. 242 ff.; and U. Barengo's treatment of the question of whether Wolff was in the pay of Napoleon III, in *Vicende mazziniane e garibaldine nelle carte dei Carabinieri Reali* (Rome: Ediz. del Museo Storico dell'Arma, 1942), pp. 175-88.

[4] Letter of Nov. 4, 1864, in *Marx/Engels Gesamtausgabe. Dritte Abteilung: Briefwechsel* (Berlin, 1929-31), III, 197-98. This work is cited below as *Briefwechsel*.

the motto: "No duty without a right; no right without a duty." These references, he told Engels, could do no damage, since they were diffused through the context of the whole document.[5] Even so, in the "Inaugural Address" Marx omitted any reference to truth, justice, and duty. On November 1, 1864, the Marxian texts were approved.[6]

Mazzini did not immediately concede Marx's victory. Within a month of the acceptance of Marx's revision of the statute, eight London Italians were sitting on the General Council and on December 13, 1864, the Italian Workingmen's Society of London (about 350 members), with a manifesto extolling practically all of Mazzini's social tenets, joined the International *en masse*. By the spring of 1865, though, Wolff and the Italians had resigned from the General Council and, though it did not cause him to order the Italian Workingmen's Society to withdraw from the I.W.A., Mazzini was furious when the Society circulated an Italian translation of Marx's "Inaugural Address" that ignored Mazzini's censorship of several passages, especially those condemning the middle class.[7] Marx could justifiably exult,[8] for it marked the end of the Italian prophet's direct involvement with the First International. Nor did Marx choose to rest on his laurels, for on April 11, 1865, he wrote Engels that he intended to carry the battle against Mazzini into the Italian peninsula through the person of Michael Bakunin, then in Florence.[9] But the facts proved him only half-right, for the Russian agitator's activities in Italy damaged the cause of Marxian socialism quite as much as that of Mazzini.

BAKUNIN IN FLORENCE

Michael Bakunin, the legendary hero of the Dresden uprisings against Prussian authority in May 1849, arrived in Florence on January 26, 1864.[10]

[5] *Briefwechsel*, III, 198.

[6] Reproduced by James Guillaume, *L'Internationale; Documents et Souvenirs* (1864-1878) (Paris, 1905-10), I, 11-21 (this volume is cited below as Guillaume, *I.D.S.*); Marx, *Indirizzo inaugurale dell'Associazione Internazionale dei Lavoratori* (Rome, 1901).

[7] Rosselli, *Mazzini e Bakounine*, pp. 147-50; Marx to Engels, Feb. 15, 1865, *Briefwechsel*, III, 246.

[8] "Mazzini is rather disgusted that his people are subscribing to [the Inaugural Address], but *il faut faire bonne mine à mauvais jeu*." Letter to Engels, Nov. 7, 1864, *ibid.*, III, 202.

[9] *Ibid.*, III, 259.

[10] Still the standard life of Bakunin is Max Nettlau's three-volume work, *Michael Bakunin, eine Biographie* (London, 1896-1900). For Bakunin's stay in Italy, see the same author's *Bakunin e l'Internazionale in Italia dal 1864 al 1872* (Geneva, 1928). The bulk of Bakunin's writings have been published in French, *Oeuvres*, ed. by James Guillaume (Paris, 1907-13), 6 vols.; in German, *Gesammelte Werke*, ed. by Max Nettlau (Berlin, 1921-24), 3 vols.; in Spanish, *Obras completas de Miguel Bakunin*, ed. by Nettlau (Buenos Aires, 1924-29), 5 vols.; and in Russian, *M. A. Bakunin. Sobranie socinenij i pisem, 1828-1876 pod redakciej i s primečanijami Ju. M.*

By then his conspiratorial activity, his stentorian threats to arouse the Slav peoples for the overthrow of Romanov and Habsburg tyranny, capped by over a decade in tsarist prisons, had established the Russian agitator as an authentic *enfant terrible* in the mid-century world of revolutionary conspiracy. After an around-the-world flight from Siberia, Bakunin reached London late in 1861 and immediately began plotting the liberation of the Slavs, "my *idée fixe* after 1846, . . . my specialty after 1848-49." [11] Since he envisaged the Latin countries imitating the Slavs' initiative in revolting against their royal masters, the Russian established an early contact with Mazzini in London, though the latter made it clear, according to Bakunin's testimony, that he could not be interested in furthering an agrarian revolt in Italy: "At this time, there is nothing to be done in the countryside; the revolution will first have to be made exclusively in the cities." [12]

Garibaldi, whose revolutionary fame Bakunin had encountered even in far-off Irkutsk,[13] was also eagerly approached, through correspondence. Arguing that Italy, "because of its situation, interests, and relative youth, is a real friend of the Slavs" and that "we [Slavs and Italians] are natural enemies of the Germans," Bakunin conjured up a glowing picture of the hero of two worlds leading his Italian volunteers, flanked by legions of Czechs, Slovaks, Croatians, and Serbs, to a victorious assault on the Habsburgs. "I know . . . that there are many young men who would be ready to desert [the Austrian armies] if they were sure of finding in Italy not only an asylum but a welcome into the Italian legions." [14] But by the summer of 1862 Garibaldi was too busy preparing, from Palermo, the attempt on Rome that ended in disaster at Aspromonte. His concern for the Balkan Slavs and Hungarians under Turkish and Austrian domination

---

Steklova [Collected works and letters, 1828-1876, ed. and annotated by J. M. Steklova] (Moscow, 1934-35). The latter work goes only to 1861. The most exhaustive biographies of Bakunin by Soviet scholars are those of V. Polonskij and J. M. Steklov; for French readers, there are biographies by M. De Préadeau and H. Isvolsky; in German, by F. Brupbacher; in Italian, by Kaminski; in English, by E. H. Carr.

[11] *Correspondence de Michel Bakounine. Lettres à Herzen et à Ogareff* (*1860-1874*), *publiées avec préface et annotations par* M. Dragomanov, translated by M. Stromberg (Paris, 1896), p. 122 (cited below as Dragomanov, *Correspondence*).

[12] *S.E.I.*, LXXII, 167 ff.; LXXIII, 62; Rosselli, *Mazzini e Bakounine*, p. 184.

[13] "The fame of Garibaldi extended as far as the Siberian peasants, who used to call him Garibaldoff." Nettlau, *Errico Malatesta, vita e pensieri* (New York [1922]), p. 5. In a letter to Garibaldi of Jan. 31, 1862, Bakunin wrote: "If you could have seen, as I did, the passionate enthusiasm of the whole town of Irkutsk, capital of eastern Siberia, at the news of your expedition into Sicily and of your triumphal march across the possessions of the mad King of Naples, you would have said, as I did, that there is no longer space or frontiers." Pier Carlo Masini and Gianni Bosio, "Bakunin, Garibaldi e gli affari slavi, 1862-1863," *Movimento Operaio*, Yr. IV, No. 1 (Jan.-Feb., 1952), 81.

[14] *Ibid.*, p. 87.

was limited to issuing two appeals for them to support the current insurrection of the Serbs and Montenegrins.[15]

The earliest indication that Bakunin intended to go to Italy is his letter of late June 1862 to Aurelio Saffi, a friend of Mazzini whom the Russian probably met during Saffi's brief stay in London in the spring of that year. Bakunin wanted to know what progress, if any, had been made toward a "real *entente* and union between Italy, the Magyars, and Slavs," and assured Saffi that he would come to Italy in September, presumably to further such a revolutionary understanding by propaganda activity. He excluded the possibility of settling in Italy because, "having been put at the head of the Russian Secret Societies, I must remain in London to concert my action with that of my friends of the *Cloche*." [16] Mazzini, on August 23, confirmed Bakunin's intention to go to Italy when he wrote his friends in Genoa that Bakunin—"a good man"—would probably be in Genoa soon to talk with Maurizio Quadrio, one of Mazzini's Ligurian lieutenants.[17]

The Aspromonte fiasco (August 29, 1862) frustrated Bakunin's plans for an Italian trip, and when the Polish insurrection broke out in January 1863, he dashed off to Stockholm in a vain attempt to promote a Finnish uprising against the Tsar. In October he returned to London, resumed his contacts with the Italian *émigrés*, and again laid plans to go to Italy.[18] His reasons for going are indicated in a letter of introduction (October 29, 1863) to Agostino Bertani from Saffi: "He is coming to Italy to seek an interval of repose in order to finish his memoirs . . . [and] to organize an agency for the transmission to Constantinople of the publications of the Russian Typography in London." [19] Saffi obliged the Russian with letters of introduction to republican circles in Turin and Milan.[20] To his Genoese friend, Federico Campanella, Mazzini wrote on November 12 asking that Bakunin and his wife be welcomed by "our people" in Genoa[21] and on the following day warmly recommended "a friend of mine" to the Mazzinian faithful in Florence.[22]

[15] For the appeals of July 23 and 26, Ciampoli, *op. cit.*, pp. 274-77.

[16] G. Quagliotti, *Aurelio Saffi, contributo alla storia del mazzinianesimo* (Rome: Ediz. Italiane, 1944), pp. 155-56. *Cloche* refers to Herzen's newspaper, *Kolokol* (the Bell), which voiced the demands of Herzen's London group of Russian revolutionaries for the abolition of serfdom in Russia.

[17] *S.E.I.*, LXXIII, 76.

[18] Tsarist agents in Stockholm had been informed late in September that Bakunin intended to go to Florence. Nettlau, *Bakunin e l'Internazionale in Italia*, p. 11. This volume is cited henceforth as Nettlau, *B.I.I.*

[19] Alessandro Levi, *La filosofia politica di Giuseppe Mazzini* (2d ed.; Bologna, 1922), pp. 190 ff.

[20] Nettlau, *B.I.I.*, pp. 11-12.

[21] *S.E.I.*, LXXVI, 187.

[22] Letter to Dolfi, Nov. 13, 1863, Conti, "Lettere inedite di Giuseppe Mazzini a Giuseppe Dolfi," p. 175.

Thus, when Bakunin arrived in Florence late in January 1864, these introductions and his own colorful past opened the doors of the Florentine democrats.[23] If any further recommendation had been needed, it was forthcoming when Garibaldi, after receiving Bakunin's courtesy visit shortly after the Russian's arrival in Italy, wrote to Dolfi recommending "our Bakunin, whose name honors the democrats of the whole world." [24] Under the circumstances, Bakunin's rapid enlargement of his Florentine circle of acquaintances is not surprising: Giuseppe Dolfi, the Florentine *capo-popolo;* Giuseppe Mazzoni, the former triumvir of the Tuscan revolution; Andrea Giannelli, Mazzini's first adjutant in Florence; Lodovico Frapolli, veteran of 1848-49 and a Garibaldian volunteer; Alberto Mario, fellow conspirator in Pisacane's Sapri expedition and seasoned combatant in the struggles of the Risorgimento; and Antonio Martinati, professor and journalist, active collaborator with the Roman committee of Mazzini's Italian National Association—these men soon became a part of the bohemian circle around Bakunin's samovar. Prominent foreign exiles of the city, too, were drawn into the salon of the gregarious Russian agitator: Ludmilla Assing, the German poetess, now fully absorbed in Italian politics after having fled Germany and the pen war she had waged against the Prussian court; the Russian Leon Metchnikov, member of Garibaldi's Red Shirts; Count Francis Pulsky, a former leader of the Hungarian independence movement; the Spanish trio of Fernando Garrido, E. Ruiz-Pons, and Leonardo Sanchez Deus, general and friend of Garibaldi.[25]

So far as the Italians were concerned, Bakunin's apparent good standing with Mazzini was enough to keep them coming to hear the giant Russian discourse at length on his grand schemes for a general uprising of the Slavs and to tell him of their hopes for a projected Garibaldian action in the Veneto.[26] Andrea Giannelli, probably a bit ruefully, recalled thirty-one years later that among the Florentine republicans Bakunin "made much of his friendship with Mazzini, highly praising his political qualities, so much so that he succeeded in gaining our sympathies." Looking back over the years, Giannelli assured Bakunin's biographer, Nettlau, that the Russian managed "to gather around himself some initiates of the Mazzinian party, lovers of novelty. But it was a very minor

[23] For details of Bakunin's stay in Florence, Conti, *O.S.F.*, pp. 69-83; and the same author's article, "Michele Bakunin; alcuni documenti relativi al soggiorno fiorentino (1864-1865)," *Movimento Operaio,* Yr. II, Nos. 5-6 (Feb.-Mar., 1950), 121-30.

[24] Letter of Jan. 2, 1864, as cited by Conti, "Michele Bakunin . . . ," p. 122. While on Caprera, Bakunin also collected letters of introduction from Garibaldi to Giorgio Asproni and Carlo Gambuzzi in Naples. Nettlau, *B.I.I.*, p. 50.

[25] For particulars on these political refugees, as revealed by the Florentine police files, see Conti, *O.S.F.*, pp. 70-71.

[26] See, for example, Bakunin's letter of Mar. 4, 1862, to Herzen, in Dragomanov, *Correspondence,* pp. 194-203.

thing, to which Bakunin himself attached very little importance." [27]

There were doubtless several generic points of agreement between the Florentine republicans and the Russian: a vaguely defined aspiration for political and social reform, anticlericalism, and a common belief in the principle of national self-determination. Rosselli asserts that Bakunin used this limited area of agreement as a point of departure in trying to persuade his Italian acquaintances to accept a matured anarchist formula: catastrophic social revolution, based on the immediate stimulation of class conflict; international organization of the working class; rejection of authority in any form; and the application of federalist principles to the whole of human society.[28] As Romano demonstrates, however, Bakunin did not reach a fully developed anarchist formulation until after his Italian sojourn, and Rosselli's attribution of an anarchist doctrine to the Russian while in Florence is based on the evidence of his post-1868 writings.[29]

Bakunin's correspondence with his friends in London, Alexander Herzen and Ogarev, in the spring of 1864, reveals that he was primarily concerned with promoting a revolutionary penetration of Russia from the south.[30] When he first arrived in Italy, he had tried, through persons presented to him by Agostino Bertani, to establish conspiratorial contacts inside Russia by using the commercial shipping route from Genoa through Constantinople to Odessa.[31] After Garibaldi returned to Caprera (May 9, 1864) from a visit to London, he and his collaborators fleetingly considered a Balkan expedition, beginning with a landing on the Dalmatian coast and eventually developing into an anti-Austrian action in Galicia, but Bakunin was completely extraneous to the plan.[32] The Russian cer-

---

[27] Nettlau, *Michael Bakunin; eine Biographie*, I, 174-75, and note 1166. "He personally loved Giuseppe Mazzini, esteeming him for his intellectual and moral qualities. But he did not at all share his political, economic, and especially his religious ideas. From this [derived] the continuous arguments between us, verbal arguments and nothing else, because, very essentially, Bakunin was above all a revolutionary . . ." Giannelli, *Cenni autobiografici*, p. 443, note 1.

[28] *Mazzini e Bakounine*, pp. 165-67, 170-71.

[29] *Storia*, I, 126, note 92. See also Romano's discussion of Bakunin's pre-1864 political development, in *ibid.*, I, 93-119.

[30] Dragomanov, *Correspondence*, pp. 196 ff.

[31] Nettlau, *B.I.I.*, pp. 11 ff.; *cf.*, also, Bakunin's letter to Herzen and Ogarev, Mar. 4, 1864, Dragomanov, *Correspondence*, pp. 194-96.

[32] The record indicates only two contacts between Bakunin and Garibaldi in the period between the Russian's visit to Caprera in January, 1864, and August of that year, when Bakunin left Italy for Sweden. On Feb. 11, 1864, Bakunin sent "tanti saluti al generale" through Dolfi-Guerzoni and on Mar. 18 he invited himself and a visiting Swedish friend, August Blanche, to Caprera for the purpose of indulging the Swede's desire "to shake the hand of the great liberator" and "to unite the Swedish democracy with the democracy of all Europe, through you and in your person." The visit did not occur, however, since Garibaldi left Caprera for London on Mar. 22 and did not return until May 9, 1864. Pier Carlo Masini, "La visita di

tainly appreciated the possible connection between Italian action against the Austrians and tsarist Russia's efforts to contain the Polish insurrection, but he retained the status of an observer, pure and simple, of the development of Italian republican schemes for the completion of national unity. In this spirit, he reported to Herzen on March 4, 1864, that the *Partito d'Azione* was reconciling its directives from Mazzini in London and Garibaldi on Caprera so as to act in concert:

> It seems that an attempt at insurrection will be made in the province of Venetia . . . in the hope of inducing the government and the army to make war against Austria. . . . Everywhere [in Italy] one is confronted by legitimate demands and a movement in which the Napoleonic venom is mixed. At the same time one feels that the electricity is accumulating in the air and that the atmosphere is becoming more and more charged: the hurricane is imminent. Perhaps the explosion will come later, but it seems to me that the ebb tide is finished and that the high tide is beginning.[33]

Bakunin's concern here, furthermore, is with the European situation as a whole, rather than its particularly Italian aspects. Police spies, keeping a close check on the Florentine republicans' discussions, reported the topics touched upon as the approaching European war, the "cooperation of all for the undoing of the old Europe, . . . the alliance of peoples against the tyrants, . . . the complete triumph of the democratic principle, . . . the urgent need of renovating European public law." [34] The tone was democratic and republican, not socialist or anarchist. Beyond these few references, there is nothing to suggest the precise political orientation of Bakunin in the spring of 1864, a lack legitimizing the conclusion that, whatever schemes lay at the back of the agitator's restless imagination, he gave no impulse at this time to the development of a specifically socialist attitude among these Florentine adherents of Mazzini.

The first revelation that Bakunin attempted to organize his Florentine associates to speed the advent of the social "hurricane" concerns his second stay in Florence between late November 1864 and June 1865. In the summer of 1864 he left Florence for a holiday in Antignano with Giannelli and in August he revisited Sweden, where he convinced himself that the Polish cause was hopeless. On his way back to Italy, he stopped off in London, where, in early November, he renewed his

---

Bakunin a Garibaldi," *Movimento Operaio*, Yr. IV, No. 3 (May-June, 1952), 480; Conti, "Michele Bakunin," pp. 123-24.

[33] Dragomanov, *Correspondence*, pp. 198-200.

[34] Conti, *O.S.F.*, pp. 71-72.

acquaintance with Marx, whom he had last seen sixteen years before. Their antecedent relations were anything but conducive to a cordial reunion,[35] but the meeting came off in friendly enough fashion, perhaps due to Marx's calculation that Bakunin might prove useful, both as a propagator of the International, founded only a few weeks before, and as the German's *longa manus* in carrying Marx's feud with Mazzini into the apostle's home territory.

Disappointingly little is known about the content of the conversation of November 3 between the two revolutionaries. For his part, Marx reported to Engels that Bakunin, "after the failure of the Polish story, will now take part only in socialist movements. . . . I must say that I like him much better than before . . . On the whole, he is one of the few persons whom . . . I find not oriented toward the past, but toward the future." [36] Bakunin's recollection of the meeting reveals nothing concerning a commitment to confine his efforts to forwarding socialism, but he makes it clear that Marx had taken the initiative toward a reconciliation:

> He swore that he had never acted against me, either in words or in deeds; that, on the contrary, he had always nourished toward me a sincere friendship and a great respect. I knew he was not telling the truth, but I had never really maintained any resentment. . . . I knew he had had a big part in the foundation of the International: I had read the Address he had written, . . . an important, serious and profound manifesto, like everything that comes from his pen when he is not engaged in a personal polemic.[37]

[35] Bakunin's 1847 assessment of Marx and Engels: "they continue in their habitual evil. Vanity, roguery, loud noises and blustering in theory and pusillanimity in practice; dissertations on life and action and complete absence of life and action; repugnant coquetries with illiterate and naif workers . . . they are bourgeois from head to foot. In a word, bestiality and falsehood, and nothing else." Letter to Herwegh, quoted by Giovanni Domanico (*Le Vagre*), *L'Internazionale, dalla sua fondazione al Congresso di Chaux-de-Fonds (1880), con note e documenti, 1864-1870* (Florence, 1911), p. 87, note 1. In 1848, Marx, as Paris correspondent of the *Neue Rheinische Zeitung*, reported in the July 6 issue that Georges Sand had documents to prove that Bakunin was a tsarist agent. Sand flatly denied the veracity of the story, but Marx did not conclusively accept this vindication of Bakunin. In February, 1849, Marx warned, in connection with Bakunin's *Appeal to the Slavs*, that though "Bakunin is our friend," this "should not keep us from subjecting his brochure to criticism" (*Neue Rheinische Zeitung*, Feb. 14, 1849). Favorable comment on Bakunin did not come until after the Russian's participation in the Dresden insurrection of May, 1849. Then, wrote Marx, the Dresden insurrectionaries had found "a competent and cold-blooded chief in the Russian refugee, Michael Bakunin" ("On Revolution and Counter-Revolution in Germany," *New York Daily Tribune*, Oct. 2, 1852), cited by Domanico, *op. cit.*, pp. 89-90, notes 1, 2.

[36] "Im Ganzen ist er einer der wenigen Leute, die ich nach 16 Jahren nicht zurück, sondern weiter entwickelt finde." Letter of Nov. 4, 1864, *Briefwechsel*, III, 199.

[37] Guillaume, *I.D.S.*, I, 292, note.

Whether Marx gave Bakunin any specific commission to stimulate opposition to Mazzini when he returned to Italy is uncertain, but such an hypothesis is suggested by the far from cordial tenor of the Marx-Mazzini relationship during the early months following the founding of the First International. The Marx-Engels correspondence from November 1864 through the spring of 1865 reflects the bitterness of the struggle between the Marxian and Mazzinian currents within the General Council of the I.W.A.,[38] and at one point Engels wanted to enter into "a union with persons who at least represent their class . . . Especially good [would be] the influence on the Italians: in this way there is a chance that the *Dio e Popolo* [influence] among the workers would be ended, which would be completely unexpected by the *bravo* Giuseppe." [39] A specifically concerted project to sabotage Mazzini's influence in Florence seems implicit, at least, in Marx's assurance to Engels in April that "I shall put some countermines against . . . Mazzini through Bakunin." [40] That Marx considered Bakunin subject to direction from London seems the obvious inference, further supported by the fact that between Bakunin's departure from London in early November and February 7, 1865, Marx wrote three letters to Bakunin,[41] the content of which is not known, but Marx's having written in itself suggests that he was following up on whatever agreement he had made with the Russian on November 3.

If Bakunin hatched such an agreement with Marx, he seemed in no hurry, once back in Florence, to carry out his end of the bargain. He was tardy in answering Marx's letters, and by February 7 he could report, as his only concrete achievement, the sending of a copy of the "Address of the International Committee" to Garibaldi, "according to your wish." He lamented the lack of money in Italy for propaganda purposes, the scepticism and fatigue of Italians "demoralized by the complete fiasco and errors" of the Party of Action, and averred that "only socialist propaganda, impassioned, energetic, and logical," could redeem the situation in a democratic sense. To build an organization founded on the "sole cult of labor" would require "beginning entirely from the beginning" and the process would be a slow one. The elements for such an organization were plentiful in Italy, but much *pazienza* was needed.[42]

[38] *Briefwechsel*, III, 200, 202, 246, 248, 259.
[39] Engels to Marx, Nov. 7, 1864, *ibid.*, III, 200.
[40] Marx to Engels, Apr. 11, 1865, *ibid.*, III, 259.
[41] Bakunin to Marx, Feb. 7, 1865: "*Carissimo*—You have formally the right to be angry with me, for I left your second letter without a reply and I delayed until today to answer the third." N. Rjasanoff, "Bakuniniana," in Grünberg, ed., *Archiv für die Geschichte des Sozialismus und der Arbeiterbewegung*, V (1915), 187; Nettlau, *B.I.I.*, p. 38.
[42] Rjasanoff, "Bakuniniana," pp. 187-88.

If he had to depend on such reports as to what Bakunin was doing in Florence, Marx was grossly deceived—deliberately so, if the subsequent course of Bakunin-Marx relations is the test. The Russian agitator, in the spring of 1865, was in fact deeply immersed in conspiratorial activity, but not such as to advance the cause of the International Workingmen's Association. Unfortunately, direct testimony concerning this activity comes from a single source and leaves many questions unanswered. Furthermore, the witness, one Angiolo De Gubernatis, a young professor of Sanskrit at the Institute of Higher Studies in Florence, gave his testimony many years after the event in the spirit of explaining away a fleeting and foolish enthusiasm of his youth.[43] Still, to the extent that De Gubernatis' account is not at all inconsistent with the general pattern of Bakunin's temperament and conspiratorial habits, there is no reason to reject its essentials. Bakunin's fertile imagination, it appears, was already at work on the scheme for an international alliance of social revolutionaries that was eventually to split the First International wide open.

De Gubernatis met Bakunin late in January 1865 at the home of the aristocratic Hungarian revolutionary, Francis Pulsky. After a brief catechization of the young professor as to his views on Mazzinianism, republicanism, and the goals of society, Bakunin enthusiastically accepted De Gubernatis as "one of ours" by inviting him to join an international secret society, whose conspiratorial channels, he confided, extended from Florence to Geneva, Paris and London. The fascinated young pedant was assured that "the social revolution will break out very soon." His impressionable spirit completely captivated—or, in De Gubernatis' metaphor, "enveloped in the coils of the great serpent"—the new recruit dashed off a poem, La Sociale, intended to be set to music and serve as "the Marseillaise of the new revolution," and resigned his teaching post in order to preach the gospel of the imminent social cataclysm in the surrounding countryside. Bakunin insisted on the greatest secrecy concerning the mysterious Apparat (organization of disciplined militants), shared a secret code with the new proselyte, and arranged for his formal catechization by Giuseppe Mazzoni in the home of Giuseppe Dolfi—this in order to determine his fitness and willingness to make any sacrifice for the social revolution.[44]

Disillusionment came quickly. When De Gubernatis went into the field to preach "the socialism of Christ and St. Francis," he was sorely

[43] See De Gubernatis' autobiographical preface to his Dizionario biografico degli scrittori contemporanei (Florence, 1897), pp. xxi-xxv; and his Fibra, pagine di ricordi (Rome, 1900), pp. 211-60.
[44] Ibid., pp. 223, 226.

tried in his new-found faith by the indignant refusal of a stoneworker—an ex-Garibaldian—to enroll in a society headed by unidentified persons. The quondam professor was further shaken by discussions among the brethren of such questions as whether, in order to help finance the social revolution, it would be legitimate to assassinate postal couriers carrying large sums of money; whether traitors to the cause should be liquidated by poisoning or by provoking them into duels.[45] The climax came at a meeting held shortly after Bakunin had outraged the disciple's concepts of Fatherland, Ideal, and Conscience. Confronting a group of about thirty comrades, gathered to honor an illustrious fellow conspirator, the French geographer, Elisée Reclus,[46] De Gubernatis denounced the society as an organization "intent on evil" and, amidst general stupefaction, took his leave of the group. His "proud discourse," De Gubernatis wrote later, proved the impulse that caused the society to disband shortly thereafter.[47]

Was the clandestine society, as Bakunin described it to De Gubernatis, a fact or merely a product of the Russian's heated imagination? There is no proof that Bakunin headed a revolutionary apparatus on an international scale, nor even one confined to the modest limits of the refugee salons of Florence. De Gubernatis' catechization by Mazzoni implies the ritual of an established conspiracy with a definite program, but by the test of visible results, the society was a paper organization at most. De Gubernatis referred to a membership of about thirty persons, but many —perhaps most—were drawn from the Slav, Hungarian, and Spanish refugee colony of Florence, a bohemian clique all too susceptible to fantastic and irresponsible revolutionary schemes, however gossamer their content. As for Italian adherents, the number must have been small indeed, perhaps no more than the handful of young republicans avid for novelty to whom Giannelli referred three decades later. Of the prominent Mazzinians succumbing temporarily to the persuasive blandishments of the Russian, only Antonio Martinati was to reappear as a philo-socialist.[48]

[45] *Ibid.*, pp. 233-34.

[46] In 1893, while visiting Florence, Reclus recalled the details of his 1865 visit to that city and established, to the satisfaction of an Italian historian of the First International, that he and Bakunin had hatched an "International Brotherhood" during the Russian's stopover in Paris in the fall of 1864. See Domanico, *L'Internazionale*, Appendix III, pp. 184-85.

[47] *Fibra*, pp. 237-38. For Bakunin's later low estimate of De Gubernatis, see his letter to Fanelli, May 29, 1867, in Nettlau, *B.I.I.*, pp. 114 ff.

[48] After leaving Florence, Bakunin continued a cordial correspondence with Giannelli and Dolfi, though differing with them "as to the revolutionary program." Giannelli, *Cenni autobiografici*, p. 443, note. Dolfi was written off by Bakunin in December, 1868, as having adopted "une politique de mirage à courte vue, d'expédients et d'expéditions *della gioventù borghese e fuori del popolo* qui ont mené votre belle *Italia* au point où elle se trouve à présent" ("a shortsighted policy of self-deception, of

In short, there is no trace of any organizational continuity between the nebulous cabal in which De Gubernatis found himself involved and the International Brotherhood that was to appear in 1866.[49]

If his efforts to weld the Florentine republicans into an effective social revolutionary nucleus were without practical issue, Bakunin was equally unsuccessful in exercising any appreciable influence on their thinking in regard to the social question. Only one manifestation of a tendentially socialist point of view among Bakunin's friends in Florence has been adduced to suggest that the Russian made an impression in this respect: the publication, shortly after Bakunin left Florence for the *Mezzogiorno*, of Niccolò Lo Savio's weekly newspaper, *Il Proletario*, champion of certain socialist principles and styling itself an "economic-socialist newspaper for the workers' democracy."[50] This, plus the fact that Lo Savio, a young Neapolitan lawyer who had moved to Florence in 1859, was a member of Bakunin's Florentine circle of acquaintances, has bred the assumption that the Russian agitator was responsible for the tenor of *Il Proletario*'s articles.[51] Bakunin conceivably contributed in some small way to the ideological development of the young Mazzinian, but Lo Savio's social radicalism was well rooted long before the Russian had a chance to talk to him.

Like some other leaders of the Florentine Artisans' Brotherhood, Lo Savio had drawn the twin conclusions from the government's suppression of the *Società Emancipatrice* (August 20, 1862) and its affiliated workers' societies, including the *Fratellanza Artigiana*, that the regime would not permit the insertion of the working classes in Italian political life and that the problems inherent in worker-employer relations were not only urgent but required, in their discussion, a more peremptory tone than that sanctioned by Mazzinian doctrine. In this sense he had already distinguished himself from the orthodox Mazzinians by the time Bakunin

---

expedients, and expeditions *of bourgeois youth, extraneous to the people,* that have led your beautiful *Italia* to her present condition"). Gino Cerrito and Pier Carlo Masini, "Quattro lettere di Bakunin a G. Mazzoni," *Movimento Operaio,* Yr. III, Nos. 17-18 (June-Sept., 1951), 621. Correspondence with Mazzoni was not resumed until August 3, 1868, when Bakunin asked him to come to the Bern Congress of the League for Peace and Liberty in September. *Ibid.,* pp. 617-23.

[49] The documents on the basis of which Domanico (*L'Internazionale,* pp. 184 ff.) put the founding of the International Brotherhood "early in 1864" are held by Romano to have originated in 1866, i.e., after Bakunin moved from Florence to Sorrento. *Storia,* I, 154-55.

[50] On the masthead appeared this brief catechism: "What is Capital? *Everything.* What is Labor? *Nothing.* What will Capital be [in the future]? *Nothing.* What will Labor be? *Everything.*"

[51] *Cf.,* Alfredo Angiolini, *Cinquant'anni di socialismo in Italia* (Florence, 1903), pp. 70-71; and, apparently taking his cue from Angiolini, Rosselli, *Mazzini e Bakounine,* p. 178.

arrived in Florence. As early as February 1863 he evinced an appreciation
of the need for a redivision of land among the peasants and said it was
intolerable to him that one-third of mankind works to maintain the
other two-thirds in sloth. The themes of his articles in *Il Dovere* and
La Nuova Europa in the spring and summer of 1863 reveal his conviction that the social question needed immediate attention: the necessity of workers' organizations, a rudimentary theory of surplus value, and
the division of society into a class of capitalists and a class of workers.
If one consumes, one must produce, so, in order to establish an equilibrium in social relations, the workers must be all, the capitalist nothing.[52]

The articles of Lo Savio in *Il Proletario*, beginning on August 20, 1865
(two months after Bakunin's departure), were most probably a deepen-
ing of these earlier convictions, the result of an independent analysis of
the Italian social and economic milieu. In fact, the ideas expressed in
the columns of this newspaper were much closer to a precise socialist
formulation than any documented attitude on Bakunin's part while in
Florence. The abstract quality of the Russian's social revolutionism at
this time had little in common with the specific and concrete qualities
of Lo Savio's writings. The ex-lawyer, in the first issue of *Il Proletario*,
defined precisely his concept of class, associating with the wage earners
in his workers' democracy small proprietors, industrialists, and merchants,
whose interests were distinct from, and opposed to, those of the "industrial and mercantile aristocracy." The proletariat must acquire "the
consciousness of all that concerns its true welfare" and advance themselves materially by their own efforts: "It is useless . . . , workers, to
nourish the hope that others will come to rescue you in your sufferings:
it is time to come out of this intellectual chaos, this antagonism, this
struggle that slowly devours you; a path must be chosen and your well-
being provided for by yourselves." The ultimate objective: "a real,
rational, effective equality" in the material condition of all.

Lo Savio consistently put economic problems above political questions
and denied Mazzini's subordination of the social question to the achievement of national unity—a sophism, he wrote, foisted off on the workers
to distract them from pursuit of their vital interests.[53] In this connection,
Il Proletario significantly ignored the nation-wide clamor in 1865 for a
war against Austria. There is an echo of Proudhon, too, in Lo Savio's
well-defined tendency toward political abstentionism:

> . . . the people look with indifference at this dark fog of elec-
> toral intrigues. . . . [They] know that the Parliament of the
> Bourgeoisie is not their Parliament, that their spirit does not

[52] For a summary of these articles, Conti, *O.S.F.*, pp. 84-85.
[53] *Il Proletario*, Oct. 22, 1865.

enter that Assembly, that its members . . . can not define the national question as [the people] conceive it, indissolubly conjoined to the political and social question, because [the legislators'] *caste* interests are perfectly opposed to the collective interests of the proletariat. Hence the people do not get excited one way or another about the elections. . . .[54]

Still, Lo Savio never reached the one affirmation needed to qualify him as a modern socialist: that the principle of class struggle is the logical inference of opposed class interests. The masthead formula of *Il Proletario*—capital is nothing, labor everything—meant simply that everyone should be a worker, a producer. Every citizen should be simultaneously—and to the same degree—"capitalist, worker, and scientist or artist;" otherwise, "you inevitably create castes, inequality, poverty." [55] Social equality is not reached through violence and the confiscation of private property. "The socialists are not despoilers." [56] To emancipate themselves, proletarians must organize workers' cooperatives and mutual aid societies; there must be a reciprocal exchange of products, i.e., the union of capital and labor in the same hands, thus safeguarding the principle of private property.[57] In this respect, Lo Savio never really broke out of the matrix of Mazzinian social democracy. "For us, socialism is not a system; it is a protest." [58]

The short-lived phenomenon of *Il Proletario*,[59] nonetheless, testified to impatience among the younger Mazzinians with the apostle's unshakeable resolve to keep the national and institutional questions as the focal points of agitation at a time when economic conditions, coupled with a short-sighted government policy of repression designed to keep the workers' societies out of politics, suggested to them broadening of the democratic struggle against the status quo to the social terrain. With or without Bakunin, the crisis of Mazzinianism was developing, however modestly, in answer to broad social and economic exigencies to which the Russian was completely extraneous. Nothing about his activity or his thinking in Florence, to the extent that we know it, suggests that he understood, on a necessarily intimate level, the complex nature of a problem peculiar to Italian democrats and the Italian milieu. Bakunin himself documented his incapacity to see in the protests of Lo Savio and radical Mazzinians like him a sign of new vigor, portent of a crisis that was to establish the

[54] "La questione sociale e le elezioni politiche," *Il Proletario*, Oct. 22, 1865.
[55] August 20, 1865.
[56] Issue of Dec. 3, 1865.
[57] Issues of Aug. 20, Dec. 3, 1865.
[58] Issue of Aug. 20, 1865.
[59] Publication stopped with the twenty-first issue, Jan. 7, 1866, because of financial difficulties.

premises for a socialist movement. Early in November 1865, just a few weeks after leaving Florence, he judged Italian democracy "a melancholy thing," in "a state of prostration, of stagnation difficult to describe, and of chronic and perpetual misapprehension." [60] Given Bakunin's high-flying dreams of world revolution, the slow and barely perceptible evolution of a socialist point of view in Italy must, indeed, have seemed of little moment, if he discerned these first faint stirrings at all.[61] Nor, for that matter, was Bakunin ever to forsake his own concept of a grand social cataclysm based on the very elements he charged to the account of the "stagnant and prostrate" Italian democracy: "sentiments, instincts and . . . bravura airs." [62]

BAKUNIN IN NAPLES (JUNE 1865 TO OCTOBER 1866)

When Bakunin arrived in the Naples area in June 1865, he encountered an important difference between the radical republicans of the Parthenopian city and those he had left in Florence. In the former Kingdom of the Two Sicilies, the economic stresses of the post-unity years, the glaring need of agrarian reform, and the unwelcome administrative centralization of the national government had stimulated an even livelier hostility in the republican camp than that expressed by *Il Popolo d'Italia* in 1860-61. Like their Tuscan colleagues, the Neapolitan republicans were intensely committed to the cause of a united *patria*, to bringing Rome and the Veneto into the national fold, but their desire to unhorse the Sabauda monarchy was inspired, to a much greater extent, by social injustices they deemed a direct consequence of the Piedmontese "conquest." This, in itself, enabled Bakunin to encourage among some of his Neapolitan friends a desertion of certain Mazzinian social principles and to this extent he fulfilled the function of "undermining Mazzini" earlier envisaged for him by Marx. On the Apostle's social doctrine he was to lavish all his powers of devastating invective and ridicule and by the time he left Naples in August 1867, his Neapolitan associates represented the first

[60] Fragment of a letter to Ludmilla Assing, Nov. 5, 1865, published by Ettore Zoccoli, *L'Anarchia, gli agitatori, le idee, i fatti* (Milan, Turin, 1907 [actually 1906]), p. 110.
[61] The socialism preached by Lo Savio was not confined to the narrow ambient of Florence. In the Sept. 17, 1865, issue of *Il Proletario*, Osvaldo Gnocchi-Viani (1837-1917), still a fervent Mazzinian but destined to prominence in the early Italian socialist movement, contributed a letter auguring the promising future of European socialism. The proof of the strength of the socialist idea lay in the fact that the possessing classes took such extraordinary precautionary measures against it. On Gnocchi-Viani, see P. Mantovani, *ed., Vita ed opere di O. Gnocchi-Viani* (Verona: Mondadori, 1948); "Fatti e figure del movimento sociale italiano. Osvaldo Gnocchi-Viani," *Nord-Sud*, Yr. II, No. 8 (May 15, 1946), 18-19.
[62] Zoccoli, *op. cit.*, p. 110.

cohesive group of Mazzinian republicans to adopt a set of unequivocally socialist principles. It was a demonstration, with some qualifications, of the agitator's own dictum that to destroy is to create, for the advent of socialism in Italy required, among other things, at least a partial destruction of the Mazzinian ideological edifice.

Bakunin had not intended his stay in the south to be prolonged for over two years. On October 8, 1865, he anticipated remaining in Naples for only three more months and as late as March 23, 1866, he told his friends Herzen and Ogarev that he would leave Italy for Switzerland before summer.[63] Until the spring of 1866, therefore, whatever held Bakunin in Naples, aside from inexpensive living and agreeable climate, was apparently of such a nature as not to require, in his opinion, an extended stay. In turn, one may infer that the Russian agitator, during the first ten months of his residence in Naples, did not become involved in any serious organizational activity in the name of socialism.

As in Florence, Bakunin quickly established contact with the leading figures of the local democracy. Giorgio Asproni, editor of *Il Popolo d'Italia*, "a superior man of intelligence, heart, and character," [64] was among the first, though there is no indication that the Russian, with his anti-Mazzinian sentiments, made any significant impression on the thinking of this elderly disciple of the Great Exile. In the young Carlo Gambuzzi (1837-1902), ex-journalist, veteran of Aspromonte, now a promising lawyer, the quasi-legendary newcomer aroused an immediate enthusiasm, though again causing no noticeable weakening of Gambuzzi's doctrinal loyalty to Mazzini. In addition to Asproni and Gambuzzi, another member of the staff of *Il Popolo d'Italia*, Attanasio Dramis, was presented to Bakunin on his arrival. Of the twelve years between 1848 and 1860, Dramis had spent eight in jail for his revolutionary activity, but had been released in time to participate in Garibaldi's enterprises. In the Neapolitan ambient his reputation was further enhanced by his collaboration in the 1857 conspiracy of Carlo Pisacane.[65]

Through these initial acquaintances, Bakunin, during his summer in Sorrento, just outside Naples, met other republican radicals. Most important of the lot, as a future collaborator, was the Neapolitan, Giuseppe Fanelli (1826-77), who had started his revolutionary career in a

---

[63] Dragomanov, *Correspondence*, pp. 204, 208; Zoccoli, *op. cit.*, p. 110.

[64] Letter of Bakunin to De Gubernatis, Aug. 8, 1865, Conti, "Michele Bakunin . . . ," pp. 128-29.

[65] On Gambuzzi's background, see *In memoria di Carlo Gambuzzi nel trigesimo della morte* (Naples, 1902). On Dramis (1829-1911), see Antonio Lucarelli, "Attanasio Dramis," *Movimento Operaio*, Yr. II, Nos. 7-8 (Apr.-May, 1950), 181-87; and, by the same author, the biographical article in *Archivio storico per la Calabria e la Lucania*, Yr. XIX, Fasc. 3 (1950), 133-48.

creditably valorous manner in the movements of 1848-49 in Lombardy and Rome, but, as secretary of the Secret Revolutionary Committee of Naples in 1857, he had failed miserably in preparing the Neapolitan uprising that was to have greeted Pisacane and his band when they landed at Sapri. He returned from exile in time to partially redeem his reputation by fighting with Garibaldi's Thousand Red Shirts, and in November 1865, shortly after Bakunin arrived in Naples, he was elected to the national legislature. To prove an active Bakuninist, too, was Saverio Friscia, Sicilian-born, ex-divinity student, now a homeopathic physician. A deputy to the Sicilian parliament of 1848, he had served on Mazzini's National Committee during the 1850's in Paris. After returning from exile in 1860, he was elected to the Chamber of Deputies in 1861 and 1865. As a thirty-third-degree Mason, Friscia exercised a considerable influence among the Sicilian lodges.[66] Friends and co-conspirators of Pisacane, the Calabrian brothers, Carlo and Raffaele Mileti, were now active as writers for *Il Popolo d'Italia*. Of the remainder of Bakunin's acquaintances in Naples during his first year in the area, only the young lawyer, Alberto Tucci, was to become a Bakuninist militant.[67]

Bakunin's international reputation as a social revolutionary, his vigorous personality, and his conspiratorial airs undoubtedly impressed the younger Neapolitan democrats, but his ideological influence was negligible, if it existed at all, during the early months of his stay. He found

[66] On Fanelli's part in the Pisacane conspiracy, see the extensive references, *ad nomen*, in Pisacane's *Epistolario;* Rosselli, *Carlo Pisacane;* Racioppi, *La spedizione di Carlo Pisacane;* and Luigi De Monte, *Cronaca del Comitato Segreto di Napoli sulla spedizione di Sapri* (Naples, 1877). For the subsequent period of Fanelli's life, which ended in a Neapolitan rest home for lunatics in January, 1877, see Carlo Gambuzzi, *Sulla tomba di Giuseppe Fanelli* (Naples, 1877); Antonio Lucarelli, *Giuseppe Fanelli nella storia del Risorgimento e del socialismo italiano* (Trani: Vecchi, 1952); C. Teofilato, "Fanelli dalla Giovane Italia all'Internazionale," *Pensiero e Volontà* (Rome) Aug. 1, 1925 ff.; Errico Malatesta, "G. Fanelli, ricordi personali," *ibid.*, Sept. 16, 1925.

On Friscia (1818-86), see Francesco Guardione, *Saverio Friscia. Articoli. Pensieri. Giudizi. Ricordi* (2d ed.; Naples, 1913); Antonio Riggio, *Per Saverio Friscia, nella solenne commemorazione celebrata il 28 febbraio in Girgenti* (Girgenti, 1886); Gino Cerrito, "Saverio Friscia nel primo periodo di attività dell'Internazionale in Sicilia," *Movimento Operaio*, Yr. V, No. 3 (May-June, 1953), 464-73. "Fecund and imaginative speaker, Fanelli; sober and calm speaker, Friscia; both of them manifesting such a sincere, profound, communicative conviction that it had the effect of gusts of wind on us, that attacked and scattered the clouds that still deceived so many young minds, in order to let us see new skies and horizons, more limpid and beautiful." Thus, Osvaldo Gnocchi-Viani, *Ricordi d'un internazionalista in Italia* (2d ed.; Milan, 1910), p. 121.

[67] On the Mileti brothers, see, *ad nomen*, Pisacane's *Epistolario*, and V. Visalli, *I calabresi nel Risorgimento italiano* (Turin: Tarizzo, n.d.); Domanico, *op. cit.*, pp. 190-91, note 2. Little information on Tucci is available, other than that presented by Nettlau, *B.I.I.*, *ad nomen*, based apparently on a Tucci-Nettlau conversation in 1899.

these men beginning to question the tenets of Mazzini even while—as in the case of Friscia—cooperating in the plans of the Party of Action for the winning of Venetia and Rome.[68] Mazzini's binomial, God and People, was already losing its appeal for these men, with no help from Bakunin. Attanasio Dramis rejected the offer to head the Mazzinian Sacred Falange in the southern provinces because "the Mazzinian formula seemed to me to have run its course. In my opinion, it needed to be renovated with the new democratic formula of the social question, since it no longer seemed possible . . . that the popular masses, cruelly deceived by exclusively political movements, would follow such a program." [69]

The tone of *Il Popolo d'Italia* in the second half of 1865 reflected the same issue, stated in terms of an appeal to Mazzini to shift from his strictly political formulation of the national problem and his traditionally Christian moral philosophy, as it limited his view of the social problem, to the new lay religion of Free Thought, based on the wedding of classical humanism and the new scientific materialism.[70] Nor was the problem posed as one of inaugurating socialism: the word was often mentioned and *Il Popolo d'Italia* devoted much space to the "workers' movement," but, as in the case of Lo Savio's *Il Proletario*, class struggle was never implied. These democrats were simply asking, not that Mazzini forget about his political program of national redemption, but that he see it in the same way Pisacane had viewed the matter: in terms of a concurrent social transformation.

In a short-lived newspaper, *Libertà e Lavoro*, which began publication on September 2, 1865,[71] the growing tension between orthodox and radical Mazzinians was further documented. Pressing problems of the workers were discussed in its columns: child labor, the emancipation of women, illiteracy, emigration, rent levels, etc., but more indicative of a sense of urgency in regard to the social question were articles by some of the younger contributors which, though departing from Mazzinian premises, arrived at conclusions unacceptable to the orthodox followers of Mazzini: the rejection of parliamentarism and the ballot in favor of revolution as the only effective means of bettering the workers' social and economic conditions, adherence to the First International as an

[68] See, for example, the Mazzini-Friscia letters of July 23 and Dec. 4, 1865, and Mazzini's letter to Felice Dagnino of Feb. 8, 1866, in *S.E.I.*, LXXXI, 22-26, 256-58, 299-300.

[69] Lucarelli, "Attanasio Dramis," p. 185.

[70] For a definition of the new non-Mazzinian synthesis, see the issue of Sept. 22, 1865.

[71] Of the contributors, only Pier Vincenzo De Luca, Raffaele Mileti, and Concetto Procaccini were in contact with Bakunin, so far as is known. Romano, *Storia*, I, 138-39. The paper had to stop publication on June 23, 1866.

organization that could promote "the sacred and inviolable rights" of labor.[72]

Nor was the criticism of political and administrative centralization, so vigorously moved in the pages of *Il Popolo d'Italia* in 1861, neglected by the Neapolitan democrats. Like an echo of Pisacane was the speech delivered by Carlo Gambuzzi on February 11, 1866, before a public meeting called to protest heavy taxes. Gambuzzi lamented political and administrative centralization as a policy entailing a financial disequilibrium that bore heavily on the masses. Tax money is used, said he, to support a "parasitic bureaucracy," a national army that the government refuses to use to acquire Rome and Venetia, police forces guaranteeing the security of the government rather than that of the people, and, finally, public instruction that could be handled better and more cheaply on the local level. Gambuzzi's solution: a popular militia, communal responsibility for police and education. "The economic weakness of Italy resides in the political system . . . ; our program is political and administrative decentralization. Our banner is: Long live liberty." [73]

If the Neapolitan democrats, including those in close touch with Bakunin, first in Sorrento and later in Naples, were preoccupied in 1865 and early 1866 with the unity question and the socio-economic problems of the young Italian kingdom, the Russian revolutionary seems to have been relatively indifferent to the ferment. Rather than reflecting a concern with the immediate and concrete issues confronting these men, Bakunin's writings—almost the sole evidence of his interests during this period—betray a certain detachment from Italian political developments and a considerable disdain for the efforts of Italian democracy.[74] His propaganda of the pen during these months was directed against very general targets. In a series of five articles written over the signature of "Un francese" for *Il Popolo d'Italia* in late September and October 1865,[75] the Russian attacked the concepts of religion and the state as bastions of bourgeois morality, argued for complete liberty as the basis of the political, social, industrial, and moral order, and from this position arrived at a generic statement of the federalist principle so concretely defined by Gambuzzi in the February 11 speech:

> Every true organization of human Society, while devoutly respecting individual and local liberties as the *sine qua non*

[72] Romano, *Storia*, I, 175-78; *cf.*, also, Valiani, *Storia del movimento socialista*, I, 114.

[73] *Il Popolo d'Italia*, Feb. 13, 1866.

[74] See his letters of Nov. 5, 25, 1865, to Ludmilla Assing, reproduced by Romano, *Storia*, I, 145-46, notes 54-55.

[75] Reproduced in *ibid.*, I, 341-53.

condition of universal liberty, must proceed, not from top to bottom, nor from the center to the circumference, but from the bottom to the top and from the circumference to the center.

The socialism of these articles, too, was stated in only the broadest of terms. Labor is "the greatest glory, the unique sign of dignity and nobility for the man who, in becoming a creator, . . . transforms the world and makes it over in his own image." Without labor there is neither honor, dignity, right, liberty, nor humanity for man. "Labor alone produces wealth." If labor does not organize, its efforts will be impotent and sterile, and the workers will be condemning themselves to poverty.

Probably the most significant aspect of these articles, from the standpoint of Bakunin's own ideological development, was his argument against any compromise with those who call themselves democrats but refuse to draw the inference that liberty is meant to operate for the masses as well as for the bourgeoisie and the aristocracy. Democratic transformation, social no less than political, can be achieved only by unmasking the false democrats and letting the hard core of intransigent fighters for liberty lead the way. Uncompromising faith in democracy is essential; numbers are not. After all, Bakunin reminded his readers, the Christian religion needed only twelve apostles to conquer the world, "and they conquered it . . . because of the heroic *madness*, the absolute, indomitable, intractable character of their faith in the omnipotence of their principle and because, disdaining deception and cleverness, they waged open war, without transactions or concessions, on all the opposed religions and even on those only differing with theirs." Here, in a few words, was an anticipation of the guiding principle of Bakunin's later revolutionary activity in the peninsula: that an heroic elite, with a single-minded faith in the libertarian ideal, can carry the day for socialism by the very intransigence of their credo and by a spontaneous mass intuition of its validity.

It is at this point, along with Bakunin's generically antistatist and anticentralist views, that the Russian agitator began to find a common ideological ground with Neapolitan democrats, to whom the doctrines of Pisacane and Cattaneo had a peculiar applicability to the problems of the *Mezzogiorno*. To speak of Bakunin influencing his Neapolitan friends toward anarcho-socialism at this point would be premature, in that their laments against political centralization, their awareness of the urgency of the social problem and their approval of Pisacane's ideas antedated by far the Russian's appearance on the Neapolitan scene. On the other hand, to say that Bakunin was now beginning to feel the influence of the Neapolitan ambient is to argue a much greater intellectual intimacy and *rapport* between him and the Neapolitan democrats than the record will sustain.[76] In a very real sense, the problem of who influenced whom does not arise until the ideas of Bakunin and those of his handful of associates in the *Mezzogiorno* converged into a single, consistent, coherent program of political action, backed by deeds. This criterion can not be applied to Bakunin's first several months in Naples.

THE INTERNATIONAL REVOLUTIONARY FRATERNITY

On July 19, 1866, Bakunin, in a long letter to Herzen and Ogarev, related that for the preceding three years his "sole occupation was to organize a secret international socialist society," the program of which he was sending to Herzen:

> Certainly you will find in it many useless details, but remember that I wrote this program while in an Italian milieu where, alas, social ideas are still little known. Besides, I had to struggle enormously, especially against the so-called national ideas and passions, against that detestable theory of bourgeois patriotism spread by Mazzini and Garibaldi. But, after a painful labor of three consecutive years, I have managed to obtain some practical results.
>
> At present, we have adherents in Sweden, Norway, Denmark, England, Belgium, France, Spain, and Italy. We also have some Polish friends and we even count some Russians among us. The majority of the Mazzinian organizations of southern Italy, of the Sacred Falange, have come over to us. In southern Italy, especially, the little people [*le bas peuple*] are coming to us *en masse*, and it is not the raw material that we lack, but rather the educated and intelligent men who act honestly and who are capable of giving a form to this raw material. The job to be done is enormous; the obstacles to be surmounted are innumerable; we absolutely lack pecuniary resources. But despite everything, . . . we move forward every day.[77]

How much was truth, how much fantasy? Bakunin could well have been thinking, on his arrival in Florence two and a half years before, of some vaguely defined international social revolutionary organization. De Gubernatis' testimony indicates that much, but, as already noted, whatever energy Bakunin expended in this direction had no perceptible consequences. His epistolary contact with social revolutionary friends in the capitals of Western Europe does not prove the existence of an actual

---

[76] In fact, the editors of *Il Popolo d'Italia* made it quite clear that they did not share the views expressed in the articles of "Un francese." "We hesitated for a moment to give [the article] publicity in our columns" because "We believe in God . . ." Issue of Sept. 22, 1865.

[77] Dragomanov, *Correspondence*, pp. 215-16.

international association with an agreed-upon program. Nor were the lower classes of the *Mezzogiorno* and/or the Mazzinian organizations of the area "coming over" to Bakunin and his friends. What the Russian probably meant was that he had begun to detect a loosening of republican loyalties to Mazzini and a growing hostility toward the government under the impulse of adverse economic conditions. That this discontent was manifesting itself in an actual political movement under Bakunin's control, permeated with his own ideas, was sheer wishful thinking on his part.

What, then, were the "practical results" to which Bakunin referred in his letter to Herzen? Substantially, three facts alone emerge from the inadequate documentation of Bakunin's organizational activity during this period: (*a*) that by mid-1866 he had worked out a formal blueprint for a vast and intricately organized "International Fraternity"; (*b*) that he and his Neapolitan intimates had written a parallel constitution and program for the Italian branch of the Fraternity; (*c*) that several sections of the Italian branch existed in Sicily, while a "central committee" composed of Bakunin's friends held forth in Naples itself. Put together, these facts do not at all support Bakunin's boast that his efforts had broken the back of the Mazzinian organizations in southern Italy and provoked a tidal wave of adhesions to his program among the "little people."

In addition to the program of the International Fraternity,[78] there exist copies of two documents pertaining to the Italian branch of the association: (*a*) the program as applied to local Italian conditions, entitled "*Società per la Rivoluzione Democratica Sociale;*" (*b*) a fourteen-page pamphlet entitled "*Società dei Legionari della Rivoluzione Sociale Italiana,*" describing administrative organization, rules of procedure, countersigns and passwords, correspondence code, discipline, dues, and recruitment.[79]

The documents pertaining to the International Fraternity describe an elaborately organized clandestine association, a "great international revolutionary undertaking." Under the rubric of the "International Family" are included a council, a constituent assembly, and a central committee (*Giunta*). Detailed norms governed the methods of revolutionary action, the raising of funds, countering police surveillance, the maintenance of discipline, and, finally, the expulsion and punishment of

[78] Reproduced in its entirety by Nettlau, *Michael Bakunin, eine Biographie,* I, 209-33, and republished in Bakunin's *Gesammelte Werke,* III, 7-61.

[79] Museo del Risorgimento di Roma, Envelope 427, fasc. 6/20 and 6/22. Reproduced by Nettlau, *Michael Bakunin, eine Biographie,* I, 204 ff.; and, in part, by Romano, *Storia,* I, 155-56, note 68; Domanico, *op. cit.,* pp. 191-92; Nettlau, *B.I.I.,* pp. 61-64; Zoccoli, *op. cit.,* p. 99, note 2.

traitors. The profession of faith required of all applicants for admission to the society reveals the association's platform: atheist, federalist (communal autonomy, federation of communes in the nation), anti-authoritarian (intellectually, morally, politically, economically, and socially), antistatist (since liberty and the state are incompatible), libertarian-nationalist (every nation must fully respect the liberty of other nations), socialist "in the full meaning of the word" (labor is "the sole generator of wealth and must be the unique basis of human right and the economic organization of society"), revolutionary (social revolution can not be effected by pacific means).

The Italian branch's "supreme direction" resided in a "central committee," the peninsula was divided into sections, each of which was directed by a "general staff" named by the central committee. The program itself is more succinctly stated but parallels that of the international society in most particulars: abolition of divine, diplomatic, and historic law, as well as existing public and private law; renunciation of the idea of "national preponderance"; liberty of the individual in the commune; liberty of the communes and their free federation in the province and the nation; political equality for all; abolition of every personal and real privilege; emancipation of labor from capital; the only property: "the instruments of labor to him who works; the land to him who cultivates it"; and free federation of the nations. "Any insurrectional action or movement that does not conform to the abovementioned propositions we shall consider *reactionary*. . . ." The preamble of the document suggests a continuity of the criticism of Cavour's national revolution voiced by the Neapolitan democrats ever since 1861 in *Il Popolo d'Italia*. The recent political revolutions of the different European peoples have not prevailed against the European state system because the nationalist principles inspiring them prohibited elimination of the "vice" of the system: "the great *national centers* with their sovereigns, clergy, army, nobility, and bureaucracy."

Given Bakunin's personal association with the Neapolitan democrats, the Russian's plans for a secret organization must have had their active collaboration, at least in drafting the Italian program. Obviously Bakunin and they had found an area of general agreement with respect to a platform for social revolution, but the physical manifestations of the organization were few indeed. Saverio Friscia involved himself in some highly obscure organizational activity on behalf of the society during the weeks, possibly months, preceding the outbreak of the Italian war against Austria. By mid-July 1866 his efforts among the Masonic lodges of Sicily had produced several sections of the Bakuninist society on the island, but of these only those in Palermo and Sciacca (Friscia's home town) are positively identified.[80] In Naples there existed a central committee manned presumably by Fanelli, Gambuzzi, Raffaele Mileti, Tucci, and Dramis, and possibly others of Bakunin's intimate circle,[81] but the record is silent as to the existence of sections in Naples or elsewhere on the mainland.[82] Even the Sicilian success was abortive, for only the day before Bakunin penned his optimistic letter to Herzen and Ogarev, the "general staff" of the Bakuninist society in Palermo issued this decree to the Sicilian sections of the brotherhood:

> In the name of the C.[entral] C.[ommittee] of the It[alian] Soc[iety for the] D.[emocratic] S.[ocial] R.[evolution], we declare you released of any obligation and from any oath taken. We declare illegal and immoral any group which, in not observing the present injunction, wants to continue to exist and we leave to it all the responsibility and consequences.[83]

The issue so abruptly frustrating Bakunin's modest organizational success was precisely the "detestable theory of bourgeois patriotism" and its appeal to Mazzinian republicans, who, so long as Italian unity was incomplete, could never give a really serious loyalty to a program recommending the substitution of "the so-called principle of nationality [by] the much greater and comprehensive principle of liberty"—understood in the antistatist and anti-nationalist sense intended by Bakunin. The Russian had yet to establish his doctrinal leadership of these men, to whom the social revolution in Italy should never be divorced from the national revolution personified by Mazzini. Making a united Italy should be used as an opportunity for social upheaval, as Pisacane had taught, but, in the clinch, consistency as social revolutionaries would have to be sacrificed on the altar of patriotism. Bakunin, the stateless, the wanderer denied physical and spiritual contact with his native soil, was in no position to appreciate the force of the central idea of the *Risorgimento* among his Neapolitan friends. From this inability flowed a vital

---

[80] *Cf.*, Gino Cerrito, "Saverio Friscia . . . ," p. 464, note 2; p. 465.

[81] The assumption seems reasonable in view of these men's subsequently close cooperation with Bakunin. Domanico claims that Vincenzo Luci, a veteran Garibaldian Red Shirt, and Beniamino De Rosa, seasoned anti-Bourbon conspirator, were also members of this intimate circle. *L'Internazionale*, p. 190, note 2; p. 191, note 1.

[82] In a memorial of the Neapolitan federation of the anarchist International, ten years later (July 2, 1876), reference is made to a Neapolitan "circle of revolutionary socialists" dating from 1866. *Bulletin de la Fédération Jurassienne* (Locle, Switzerland), July 16, 1876. This newspaper, on the files of which Guillaume based most of his three-volume history of the International, is cited henceforth as the Jura *Bulletin*.

[83] Nettlau, *B.I.I.*, p. 69.

frustration of his schemes for creating a revolutionary nucleus in Italy—
until the red-white-green tricolor flew over the Campidoglio.

The war against Austria of 1866 occasioned the first revelation of this
ideological chasm between Bakunin and his associates. The Russian's
position was clear enough. Three months before the conflict began he saw
the imminent struggle as an attempt by the Italian government to escape
the consequences of domestic difficulties and opined that Garibaldi was
playing the government's game with his patriotic program. "Garibaldi
is letting himself be seduced for the tenth time and is becoming . . . an
instrument for deceiving the people. . . . Our personal role will be that
of spectators." [84] When the war he anticipated broke out in mid-July,
Bakunin saw in both Mazzini and Garibaldi betrayers of the Italian
popular cause, in that they had compromised with the government and
the privileged classes, justifying support of the conflict by pleading the
necessity of "ceding to the sovereign will of the people." Errant nonsense,
wrote the Russian: "They ceded to the bourgeois minority that arrogated
to itself the right to speak in the name of the people, who remain indifferent to all the twists and turns of politics." [85]

Apparently, too, the directives of the central committee of the secret
Fraternity had demanded opposition to the Austrian war, for, after having
issued the decree of dissolution to the Sicilian sections, the Palermo
"general staff," in notifying the Naples *Giunta* of this move, elaborated
a critique of that body's insistence on interpreting the principle of
nationality in a way that disapproved the war for complete national
unity:

> You marvel that we could reprove you for *individualism* and
> you want to prove . . . that Nationality . . . must *be based on
> the free sovereign will of its own elements;* and is not the *free
> sovereignty* of the *elements* the same as individualism? If you
> give *sovereignty* to the *elements,* i.e., to the *individuals,* you
> elevate the individual into a social reason, and the social
> synthesis becomes a vain name, without substance. . . .
>
> In regard to the question of fact, that is, the one of the present
> war, you see very well that since condemnation of it issues
> logically from your program, so, naturally and logically, the con-
> trary issues from ours.[86]

One might explain the defection of the Sicilian sections of Bakunin's
society in terms of the Russian's lack of direct personal contact, but
Gambuzzi, Fanelli, and Raffaele Mileti, all intimates of Bakunin and

[84] Dragomanov, *Correspondence,* pp. 210-11.
[85] Letter of July 19, 1866, *ibid.,* p. 234.
[86] Nettlau, *B.I.I.,* pp. 67-69.

probably members of the Neapolitan *Giunta* as well, immediately volunteered to fight the Austrians at the side of Garibaldi. Fanelli's participation in the war was explained as an attempt to redeem himself for his failure in the Pisacane conspiracy of 1857; Gambuzzi claimed that he himself had felt morally obliged to fight because of his relations with the revolutionary committee for freeing Rome and the Veneto.[87] Bakunin, Gambuzzi told the Russian's biographer, recognized this justification privately but condemned participation from the standpoint of principle.[88] Of the three volunteers, Gambuzzi apparently felt under a compulsion to reconcile his patriotism with his position as a lieutenant on Bakunin's "general staff." The method chosen—making propaganda for the secret Fraternity among the Garibaldian volunteers—was not appreciated by the Russian, whose sarcasm permeates a letter of the Neapolitan *Giunta* in answering Gambuzzi's report of the failure of his recruiting efforts.[89] Fanelli, Mileti, and Gambuzzi were to return to Naples immediately. Since Gambuzzi's letter was shot through with pessimism concerning Italian military prospects—the Austrians had defeated the Italians on land (Custozza) and sea (Lissa)—the central committee adopted an I-told-you-so tone. Gambuzzi's sad experience "will bind you to us in an indissoluble manner" in the future.

The withdrawal of Austria from the Veneto—as provided by the Armistice of Cormons of August 12—"has created a magnificent situation for us," for now the Mazzinians and Garibaldians can no longer use the excuse of foreigners in Italy "to postpone social and domestic questions and those of liberty." Custozza, Lissa, and General Cialdini's "harlequinades" have destroyed the militarism in Italy that threatened liberty. Any attempt by the Garibaldian volunteers to stir up an armed popular insurrection would only play into the hands of the government, which, unsure of itself after the frustrating military adventure, would welcome the chance to strengthen its position by using the regular army and police to suppress a revolution. Even were the government defeated by "our so-called democracy," who would save Italy from the reaction of Europe? Gambuzzi should return to Naples, for

> . . . you have already satisfied your military honor, your political position, in brief, your individuality.
>
> Furthermore, our friends think your immediate repatriation is

[87] Gambuzzi had been an active promoter of the Neapolitan "Central Committee of the southern provinces of Italy," an arm of the *Associazione dei Comitati di Provvedimento per Roma e Venezia*, headed by Garibaldi, Nettlau, *B.I.I.*, p. 50.

[88] *Ibid.*, p. 74.

[89] For the letter, *ibid.*, pp. 70-74. It was both unsigned and undated, but written about Sept. 9, 1866, since it refers to "the conclusion of the armistice [Cormons, Aug. 12] four weeks ago."

not only opportune and useful, but even necessary. . . . We can not describe to you in words the effects the disillusionment has produced in everyone; threats and fiery proposals are on everyone's lips. This is certainly the most propitious moment for our affairs, especially since the false democracy (*semper idem*) is trying to reform its ranks from the top.

CONCLUSION

Thus the outcome of the Austrian war, morally discrediting the monarchy without seriously jeopardizing its existence, was an unexpected dividend in Bakunin's campaign to sabotage Mazzinian influence in southern Italy. In addition to the sense of humiliation deriving from an inglorious military campaign and from Louis Napoleon's role in the transfer of the Veneto to Italian sovereignty, it was painfully obvious that neither Mazzini nor Garibaldi had succeeded, for all their feverish advance planning, in bringing Italian republicanism one iota closer to realization. Mazzini, aware of the extent of his followers' disillusionment and goaded by the First International's threat to recruit Europe's republican workers to the cause of socialism, founded his Universal Republican Alliance on September 1, 1866, to counteract I.W.A. influence and reaffirm the priority of republicanism over socialist aspirations.[90] This was the probable basis of the Neapolitan *Giunta*'s reference of a few days later to "the false democracy . . . trying to reform its ranks from the top."

In Naples, Bakunin's circle now gathered new adherents from the ranks of the local Mazzinians, among whom was the tailor, Stefano Caporusso, very active in a local workers' society, president of another, the Mazzinian Humanitarian Workers' Society of Naples, and soon to prove a key figure in the work of socialist propaganda among the city's plebes.[91]

More indicative of the dilemma in which the apostle's intransigently political program placed the Neapolitan republican radicals was Fanelli's visit to Mazzini in Lugano in the early fall of 1866. Armed with a declaration signed by Dramis and Raffaele Mileti, Fanelli pleaded with Mazzini to put aside the religious question and direct his energies and attention toward social problems. Mazzini remained adamant and reportedly treated Fanelli like a schoolboy.[92] The episode testifies to the reluctance of Fanelli and his friends to turn their backs on Mazzini as the logical leader of the social transformation they deemed possible within the framework of the national unification movement, by this time reduced to

[90] Marx had been worried about Mazzinian influence in the Council and was taking countermeasures. See his letters to Engels of Mar. 24, May 17, 1866, *Briefwechsel*, III, 316-17, 334. For the manifesto of the Alliance, *S.E.I.*, LXXXVI, 25-46.

[91] *Cf.*, Romano, *Storia*, I, 87, 139 (note 36), 141 (note 43), 161.

[92] Nettlau, *B.I.I.*, p. 55.

the problem of uniting Rome with Italy. At the very moment when Bakunin seemed to have been completely vindicated in his opposition to the Austrian war, these Neapolitan democrats closest to him felt compelled to make one last desperate gesture of loyalty to the man who personified the national ideal. Yet, the gesture had been made and rejected; Bakunin could legitimately expect to reap the harvest of his friends' disillusionment.

By the fall of 1866, then, the situation seemed ripe for Bakunin to emerge as the ideological mentor of the south's disaffected republicans. Mazzini had apparently said his last word on the question of giving the national unity movement a social revolutionary content. Even in terms of realizing the final goal—Rome—the Mazzinian program, for the moment, appeared discredited, while Garibaldi, whose campaign in the Tyrol had been something less than lustrous, lowered his own stock with republican patriots when he made his terse reply, "I obey," to the monarchist government's order to withdraw his volunteers from Austrian territory. Republican hopes of a popular unity movement were at a low ebb, indeed. In this atmosphere of severe moral depression, Bakunin may well have assumed that "the detestable theory of bourgeois patriotism" no longer barred the way to complete acceptance of his libertarian doctrines.

V

Bakunin in Italy (October 1866 to August 1867) and the International Alliance of Socialist Democracy

"LA SITUAZIONE ITALIANA"

A PROPAGANDA leaflet of two pages of fine print, published clandestinely in Naples in October 1866 and entitled *La Situazione Italiana*,[1] gives the full flavor of the dissatisfaction of Bakunin's Neapolitan clique with the Mazzinian program and the equivocal position of Garibaldi in his relations with the monarchist government. In a tactical sense, the piece was probably intended to harass Mazzini's attempt to reorder his frustrated followers' ranks. If so, its effectiveness was not apparent, but as both a portrayal of a state of mind on the verge of embracing a full-fledged socialism and a coherent expression of anti-Mazzinianism based on social revolutionary assumptions, the document has a vital indicative importance.

Alberto Tucci told Bakunin's biographer that he had written the pamphlet after having consulted the Russian, who "reviewed the text."[2] Bakunin, referring to a subsequent propaganda leaflet of the same title, described it as "the complete refutation of the policy of Mazzini and Garibaldi, in still clearer and more violent terms *than I applied to it in the first number.*"[3] In one vital respect, however, the content of *La Situazione* denies the Russian's authorship: the social revolutionism of the piece is imbedded in the general context of a fervent and unrelenting concern for national unity as envisaged by Carlo Pisacane.

---

[1] Reproduced in its entirety by Nettlau, *B.I.I.*, pp. 77-93.
[2] *Ibid.*, p. 77.
[3] Letter of May 7, 1867, Dragomanov, *Correspondence*, p. 249. Italics supplied.

After a summary criticism of the works and ideas of both the dynastic legitimists of the pre-1860 period and the constitutional unitarians of the post-unity era (who have compromised with outmoded and reactionary ideals in the name of *praticismo politico*), the writer(s) of *La Situazione* turned to "the errors and contradictions" of Mazzini's program, not, however, without a preliminary appreciation of his success in arousing Italy from her "dream of death" and conquering "the tired, sad lethargy of so many centuries." Why, then, the small effect of Mazzini's teachings, their loss of appeal, the desertion of so many of his followers? According to *La Situazione*, these are but the consequences of his program:

> *Italy, a power of the first rank in Europe, legitimate and first-born heir of God's designs in the initiation of a Great Mission, which is the future of Humanity; God and People, that is, God and the moral law emanating from him as the sole and unique Sovereignty; the inspirations of the Chaste Genius as the sole and unique Apostolate of this Sovereignty.* Because of this principle of national greatness and national mission, Mazzini, in constituting himself an Apostle . . . of a faith in God and a statesman, could not be really revolutionary; because of this principle, the *people* of his formula have always been no more than an attractive and resonant word; he has always wanted the *People for Italy* and not *Italy for the People*.

Mazzini's conviction that the solution of social problems requires a centuries-long process forces him into alliance with social conservatives, to the point of making pacts with kings. From this stems the inefficacy of his republican action and the demoralization of his party:

> Mazzini wanted what the Monarchy has already partially achieved and claims that it wants to carry to completion: the unity of Italy and her historic greatness. The sole difference between them is the public form, with all the consequences it entails. In the fundamental constitutive principles, these two political forms are in entire agreement, given the common basis that sustains them. For the People this difference is substantially nothing; perhaps [it] is only in name, since if the president is substituted for the king, it amounts to the same thing.

Liberty and justice are only empty words in the Mazzinian program, for in a unified and powerfully centralized Italy all the elements of tyranny against which humanity has fought for centuries would be preserved: God, the state and socio-economic injustices, the negations of reason, liberty, and justice. Actually the great majority of the Italian nation opposes the Mazzinian solution: "only the bourgeois youth, most of whom are educated in the spirit of traditions and History, inspired by the classical grandeurs of the Country, strongly aspire to the reconstruction of these old glories." Alone, this group can not hope to undo the work of centuries; the more so in that it has lost its easiest means of organization in *Garibaldinismo.* "The magic influence" once exercised by the Red Shirt hero has vanished; his name "will no longer arouse a quiver from one end of the peninsula to the other, nor be capable . . . of raising in arms a whole population knowing neither the why nor the where."

As the sword of Mazzinianism, Garibaldianism had to break with Mazzini when he refused to accept the monarchy. Then, with no ideology of its own, it went from bad to worse, ending up in the dishonorable and lethal embrace of the monarchy. It descended from revolutionism to revolutionary militarism and, finally, to outright militarism. As an example of valor, as the apotheosis of abnegation and a fine source of patriotic legend, it still lives, but as a party it is finished, going to the tomb without a struggle or protest. With his program of "Italy and Victor Emmanuel," Garibaldi, the hero of Marsala and Calatafimi, of the Thousand Red Shirts, has tricked the people. They will no longer follow the once-worshipped captain.

Only one force, "potent, invincible, hitherto inert and unknown," can create a great and free Italy: *"the real Italian people,"* the millions of workers and peasants whose interests have been sacrificed in the political revolutions of militarists and bourgeoisie:

> This majority, by which we mean solely and uniquely *the People,* has none of the rights given the bourgeoisie by a series of revolutions; not political liberty, since social conditions constitute an illusory exercise of it; not equality before the law, since it is contradicted and destroyed by the inequality of fact; not well-being, since its labor is absorbed by capital and materials, since it has had to pay for the greatness or unity of the centralist State, which is a need of the bourgeoisie; not, finally, either renown or history, since it is pushed ever more into the darkness of ignorance, where the lying protectorate of the privileged castes is seeking it out to deceive it anew.
>
> During and after every revolution the People have always . . . *suffered and paid.* . . . They have paid for everything they do, for going and coming, buying and selling, drinking, eating, breathing, warming themselves in the Sun, getting born, dying. *They have paid for permission to work! !*

This popular force can be enlisted in the cause of Italian freedom, greatness, and happiness only if the rallying cry be justice, which in the popular mind means:

> *. . . true, complete, positive emancipation, intellectual, moral, political, economic, and social; this lever is: the conquest of liberty and well-being of each and all in his own commune, in his own Province, in the entire Nation.*
>
> Then only will the people fight their first and last battle, . . . and they will win because on the one side of their banner is written, labor, that is, the mover of humanity, on the other, bread and liberty, the all-powerful, imprescriptible rights of all men.

Three "secular tyrannies" must be exorcised: the church, the centralized state and social privileges. The first oppresses the conscience and violates collective and individual liberty; the second must be dissolved by destroying its constituent elements: the monarchy, militarism, and bureaucracy. Under the mask of constitutionalism and parliamentary procedure, the monarchies have not really changed, for they still exercise rights and privileges without commensurate duties. *La Situazione* draws the revolutionary inference:

> By the strength of your cry alone, oh people, bring down these crowned vampires, from your infested slums break into the great gilded halls of their superb palaces, rest in the shade of their gardens, drinking the water of their fountains . . . everything is yours, because it is the sweat of your brows, the work of your hands, of which they have robbed you.

Social privileges are defined as "the injustice of society toward the working and peasant classes, the disproportion between labor and wages and the slavery of labor." These conditions can not long endure, since the workers are in the majority. "Let us stir up, then, the terrible revolutions in which *neither men nor things* . . . would be respected; let us today call justice what the working people would deliberately claim by force tomorrow: the *emancipation of labor from capital and material*." In terms of its doctrinal maturity, the socialism of *La Situazione* was crudely defined:

> Without labor, material is inert and unproductive, without labor the golden cows produce no gold; therefore, neither capital nor material is the creator of what exists in humanity; it is labor. Justice . . . , since we want liberty for everyone, but we cry out: *equality,* and by this we mean *we want labor to be the basis of society, and no one to have the right to live on the labor of others* . . .
>
> We do not need to develop these ideas; they are easy [to understand] and obvious. . . . Those who do not understand them . . . will never understand them. . . .

We have faith only in the revolution made by the People for their positive and complete emancipation; a Revolution that will make Italy a free republic of free communes in the free Nation— freely united among themselves.

Thus *La Situazione*. In defining the *vero Popolo Italiano* as "millions of workers and peasants," in affirming the conflict of class interests, in concluding that violent revolution is needed, that the proletariat must emancipate itself, the pamphlet clearly departs from Mazzini's pattern of class collaboration and pacific, gradual resolution of the social problem. Where Lo Savio's *Il Proletario*, though treating some aspects of the social question with greater sophistication, stayed within the limits of Mazzinian social philosophy by abjuring class struggle, *La Situazione*, despite its more roughly defined premises, made a clean break with Mazzini's formula.

THE LIBERTY AND JUSTICE ASSOCIATION

Where did Bakunin fit into this evolution toward a socialist point of view among his Neapolitan associates? Whether he wrote all or part of *La Situazione*—or merely "reviewed the text"—the conclusion is inescapable that up to a certain point the ideas of the Russian and his Italian coterie were of a piece. Certainly an identification is apparent in the anticlericalism, the anticentralist, federalist, and social revolutionary tenor of *La Situazione*. From Bakunin's side, this identification has been explained in terms of Bakunin's having found in Naples and in the *Mezzogiorno* generally a set of conditions strikingly similar to those in the Russia from which he had drawn his original revolutionary premises: little industry; a pressing peasant problem, still viewed with a high degree of romantic extremism; agrarian revolution and administrative decentralization as popular panaceas; a strong illuministic and humanitarian tradition; the same egalitarian concept of the social solution; and a common—though indirect in both cases—ideological antecedent in Proudhonism.[4]

That Bakunin and his Italian collaborators shared the libertarian, revolutionary ideas expressed in *La Situazione* argues no intellectual stimulation by the Russian. From the Italians' side, the point of view can be accounted for by external impulses, operating independently of Bakunin: dissatisfaction with Mazzini, with the government's domestic and foreign policies, with the increasingly apparent futility of *Garibaldinismo*, and with the economic situation generally. And on the level of ideas, the radical Neapolitan republicans already had, in Pisacane's

[4] Romano, *Storia*, I, 188-89.

synthesis, an indigenous social revolutionary formula that fully embraces the essential arguments of *La Situazione*. Fanelli, Gambuzzi, Tucci, and Dramis, after much intellectual travail, had arrived at modern socialism, but Bakunin was far more a witness—albeit a vociferous one—to that journey than its guide and inspiration.

Nor, during the remainder of Bakunin's stay in the Naples area, did these Neapolitan democrats, who willingly enough collaborated with Bakunin in discussing and planning the creation of a secret International Fraternity, of a Society of Legionaries of the Italian Social Revolution, evince any interest in rupturing the nexus between Italian unity and social revolution, so dramatically advocated by Pisacane, so ridiculed by Bakunin. The proof lies in the record of their activity in 1867, revolving around their creation and propagation of the Liberty and Justice Association.[5]

In the issue of March 5, 1867, *Il Popolo d'Italia* informed its readers that the *Libertà e Giustizia* Association, meeting in extraordinary session on February 27 under the presidency of Saverio Friscia, had unanimously adopted an electoral manifesto in anticipation of the scheduled March 20 parliamentary elections. Because the Chamber of Deputies had been dissolved in the midst of a "frightening economic, financial, industrial, agricultural, commercial, political, and religious situation," the voters of the Naples area were exhorted to use the Association's program as a guide in selecting their new deputies, as a "touchstone to test the liberalism of the candidates." Specifically, the program demanded:[6]

1. Universal suffrage
2. The right of electors to recall any representative losing their confidence
3. A senate with a fixed term of office, elected by the provincial councils
4. Absolute separation of judicial from executive powers and election of magistrates by the provincial councils and the senate
5. Ministerial responsibility to the legislature
6. Freedom of the press, association, and public meeting
7. Absolute religious freedom
8. Restitution of church properties to the communes
9. A single direct income tax in place of the current system of direct and indirect levies

[5] The following summary discussion of the *Libertà e Giustizia* Association is based on the *Storia* (I, 189-214) of Professor Romano, who, in my opinion, has conclusively demolished the thesis of Nettlau (*B.I.I.*, pp. 100-12) and Rosselli (*Mazzini e Bakounine*, pp. 197-200) that the Association and its program were directly inspired by Bakunin.

[6] For the program, Nettlau, *B.I.I.*, pp. 101-06; Romano, *Storia*, I, 355-60.

10. A national policy consistent with the principles of justice and liberty, the sentiment of national dignity and solidarity with other nations on the basis of liberty. Above all, a policy free of Napoleon III's designs, "to whose chariot we have thus far been yoked"
11. Abolition of the standing army and creation of a national militia
12. Abolition of the state bureaucracy
13. Administrative autonomy for the communes and provinces
14. Election by the communes, on the basis of universal suffrage, of their own authorities; election by provincial councils, composed of delegates of the communes, of all provincial authorities, senators, and judicial officers
15. Abolition of the gendarmerie and national police, with the provincial and communal authorities assuming responsibility for public security
16. Abolition of all "useless" ministries (e.g., agriculture, commerce, cults, and public instruction) and assumption of their functions by provincial and communal authorities
17. Liberty of education; no state interference in public or private education; free, compulsory education for both sexes; provincial and communal administration of all schools above the primary level
18. Abolition of all privileged banks and the creation of legal safeguards for the liberty of all

The document was signed by fifteen Neapolitan republicans, all members of Bakunin's intimate circle. Friscia signed as president of the Association, Attanasio Dramis as secretary, while Fanelli, Gambuzzi, and Raffaele Mileti appeared as members of the directive committee, along with the Neapolitan democrats who had joined Bakunin's group after the Austrian war.

After the parliamentary elections the group decided to continue its propaganda for "the political and social redemption of the multitudes" and, in a formal reorganization of April 3, 1867, the directive committee was reduced to three men: Friscia (president), with Gambuzzi and Dramis as his assistants. An official newspaper was projected, and within a few days the *questore* (chief of police) of Naples, who followed closely the activities of the Association, transmitted to his superiors the printed program of the projected journal. Written by Pier Vincenzo De Luca, the document was a verbose criticism of existing parties and institutions and promised more to come:

Departing from the principle that all institutions must be for the people and that true government is that which emanates from direct and free suffrage of the people, we shall examine all those institutions, not only in respect to the extent to which they can be modified or suppressed, to which they benefit or harm the people and the reign of liberty and justice, but we shall also denounce all their abuses and reveal their sores.[7]

If this program—if such it may be called—revealed nothing of the activity of the Liberty and Justice Association, the *questore* was not misled in the least. His reports to the prefect during the spring and summer of 1867 describe, not a propaganda campaign against the social and political system, but a feverish clandestine preparation for the liberation of Rome.[8] The Liberty and Justice Association cooperated with the Neapolitan subcenter for the freeing of the Eternal City; it tried to reach an understanding with Garibaldi in the matter; it put out feelers to Giuseppe Dolfi in Florence in an attempt to extend its net of antipapal conspiracy to Tuscany; and Fanelli himself was indicated as the chief of one of the armed bands scheduled to invade the Papal State from the south. In short, the goals, political orientation, and activity of the Association were in clear contrast with Bakunin's program, and its members, obviously, were giving little attention to the Russian's pet project, the development of his International Fraternity.

The men of *Libertà e Giustizia* did formulate an official program in mid-August 1867, when there appeared the first issue of their weekly organ, bearing the same title as the Association itself, but it was a substantial repetition of the electoral manifesto published by *Il Popolo d'Italia* in early March. Only one demand had been added:

> Emancipation of labor, by means of proletarian instruction and association, from the conditions of servitude in which it is held by the despotism of land and capital.[9]

As Romano has demonstrated, the ideological premises, the general analysis of the social structure, and even the details of the Liberty and Justice program are exactly identical to those contained in the third volume of Pisacane's *Saggi*.[10] Even the formula of emancipating labor

[7] Romano, *Storia*, I, 361-63.

[8] *Ibid.*, I, 192-96.

[9] For the program, as it appeared in the first issue of *Libertà e Giustizia, ibid.*, I, 364-66.

[10] See Romano's detailed comparison of the two texts, in *Storia*, I, 201-05. In arguing against a Bakuninist influence in the *Libertà e Giustizia* circle, Romano writes: "But when this nucleus was constituted, Bakunin was not in Naples, but . . . on the island of Ischia; and when it had its most important manifestations and published [its] newspaper, he had already left Italy, or was preparing to leave" (*ibid.*, I, 189). I can not agree, since: (1) the August program Romano uses for comparison with the Pisacanian texts was identical, save the single point indicated

through instruction and association, at first glance a mere echo of Mazzini's hoary recommendation to the workers, was conceived in the social revolutionary sense intended by Pisacane. In the first issue of *Libertà e Giustizia,* an article defined the concept of workers' association. The Italian worker must expect no help from priests, government, capitalists, bankers, or landlords:

> The secret of your redemption lies in your own hands, in labor; the capital and credit necessary to labor lie in your numbers, in the [workers] associations.
>
> Do not allow the associations to be merely negative or passive, like the so-called [associations] of mutual aid, which might better be termed disgraces.
>
> They must be essentially positive and active, they must be transformed into cooperative associations of production, consumption and labor credit; [they must] unite among themselves with a free bond, in Italy and abroad.[11]

It was a recommendation of workers' associations in the special form conceived by Pisacane: aggressively active, understood essentially as a social pact, freely entered into by all. It was also a clear surmounting of the mutualistic concept of the Piedmontese workers' societies, of Lo Savio's *Il Proletario,* of the Mazzinian *Fratellanza Artigiana.* Of symbolic significance, too, was *Libertà e Giustizia*'s statement of adherence to the First International, the first such on the part of any Italian organization.[12]

In addition to the implicit departure from Mazzini's principles contained in the Liberty and Justice program, an explicit condemnation of

---

above, with the electoral manifesto issued in late February; (2) the Liberty and Justice Association was formed on February 27, or earlier, and was reorganized on April 3; (3) the newspaper, *Libertà e Giustizia,* was projected and issued its program in early April; (4) Bakunin did not leave Naples for Ischia (only sixteen kilometers outside Naples in any case) until late August (*Storia,* I, 164). In my opinion, the scarce influence of Bakunin on the thinking of the Liberty and Justice group finds its proof in the patriotic spirit of its program, not in whether the Russian was living in Naples or on Ischia long after the program was initially published as an electoral manifesto.

[11] Issue of Aug. 17, 1867, as quoted by Romano, *Storia,* I, 200.

[12] *Loc. cit.* In the Aug. 31 issue, the paper printed the London General Council's *Address* concerning the imminent Lausanne Congress of the I.W.A., and in the Oct. 27, 1867, issue there appeared under the title, "Il Socialismo in Europa," an excerpt from the preface of *Das Kapital,* sent by the author himself. "We are happy to make known to our readers an excerpt that we take from the preface kindly sent us by the author." This points to a direct contact between the Liberty and Justice group and Marx, but Romano has found no corollary evidence in this regard. In any case, the Liberty and Justice Association was free to apply for membership in the I.W.A. and failed to do so.

his party appeared in the August 24 issue of *Libertà e Giustizia*.[13]
With greater clarity and maturity, the editorialist developed the anti-
Mazzinian theme along the lines already established by Gambuzzi's
speech of February 11, 1866, and by *La Situazione*:

> The equivocation of the program, the emptiness and abstractness
> of [the Mazzinian] republic, the continual political transactions
> of Mazzini, always generated among his followers an uncon-
> sciousness of principle, uncertainty in action, pusillanimous
> attempts, sterile efforts and incessant desertions. Without a firm
> concept in mind, with their hearts closed to the popular spirit,
> . . . the Mazzinians did not form and shall never form a serious
> and powerful party, preferring to lend their strength to the inane
> mysteries of conspiracy rather than to the omnipotent arm of
> the people. The immortal victims produced by this party are to
> be counted by the tens, the perjured and the traitorous by the
> hundreds.

Significantly, the Liberty and Justice program denied neither the
national unity already achieved, nor the goal of Rome, nor the concept
of *patria*. The implied attitude toward the state was Pisacanian, in that
the Martyr of Sapri, though genuinely anarchist in his conviction that
the state must be destroyed,[14] had postponed this necessity—by the
terms in which he defined the process of national political unity—beyond
the creation of an Italian national state. Bakunin, by this stage of his
doctrinal development, could never have encouraged tolerance of the
state on the grounds that it was indispensable to the political organization and social regeneration of the nation. The Russian's influence on the
Liberty and Justice Association is unmistakably denied.

Nor could Bakunin have lent his *imprimatur* to the analysis contained
in an unfinished essay by Carlo Gambuzzi on the necessity of constituting
the Italian state on a federalist basis:

> To constitute the State on the indestructible basis of liberty in
> all its forms—political, religious, and economic—is the new task
> to be assumed by European democracy. From this point of view,
> a strictly democratic party has never existed in Italy up to now.
> This title can not be claimed by the Mazzinian school, which,
> preoccupied with the first two terms of the problem, neglects

---

[13] Bakunin's sole contribution to his friends' newspaper was an essay on "The
Slav Question" (Aug. 31, Sept. 7, 1867) and another called "Essence of Religion"
(Nov. 3, 24, Dec. 1, 1867), neither of which can be identified as a reflection of
the thinking of the Liberty and Justice members. Marx thought he detected Bakunin's
hand in an anti-Mazzinian article in the Aug. 24, 1867, issue. Letter to Engels, Sept.
4, 1867, *Briefwechsel*, III, 418.

[14] *Saggi*, III, 121-27.

entirely the third and most important. Today only one young and spirited party appears on the political scene and inaugurates true Italian democracy by inscribing on its banner: *federal and social Republic*.[15]

Gambuzzi's language could not have been plainer: his republic, however federalist and social, was still a state, a compromise with the principle of authority. In Gambuzzi the concession was inescapable, for any political structure erected in the name of the Italian nation required a degree of central authority, without which the nation would remain a complete abstraction. The Neapolitan socialists wanted a flesh-and-blood Italy, as well as the state authority needed to make it a reality. Bakunin, whose libertarianism was free of the nationalist compulsion, had no such theoretical problem.

In the fall of 1867 the practical consequences of this different point of view were more than apparent. Bakunin left the Naples area in late August or early September of that year to attend the Geneva congress for peace, an international pacifist meeting held on September 9-12.[16] The Geneva conclave offered the Russian a podium from which to expose his social credo to an international audience and the mooted idea of organizing a permanent "League for Peace and Liberty" promised an ideal instrument for the diffusion of Bakuninist ideas. In the presence of Garibaldi, Victor Hugo, Edgar Quinet, John Stuart Mill, and other pacifist leaders, Bakunin developed his arguments against the centralized state *and* the spirit of nationality. In support of the Russian's federalist position, Carlo Gambuzzi then read, in the name of the Neapolitan Liberty and Justice Association, an address arguing that peace is impossible without religious, economic, political, and scientific liberty and, since this kind of liberty can not be won under "the existing systems of centralization, exclusiveness, and national rivalry," it is necessary to eliminate all "privileged, monopolistic, and violent institutions," *including the state* and "the plutocracy dependent upon it." [17]

Was the Liberty and Justice Association's talk of "eliminating the state" an implied contradiction of Gambuzzi's earlier plea for constituting it? Where Bakunin had spoken of federalism in terms of war on "bourgeois"

[15] For the entire text, Romano, *Storia*, I, 385-87.

[16] The prefect of Naples considered Bakunin "the promoter and head of the [subversive] movement in Sicily . . . and southern Italy generally." The Russian was also under suspicion as a counterfeiter. Dragomanov, *Correspondence*, letters to Herzen and Ogarev, May 23, June 23, 1867, pp. 254-58, 265-73. Cf., also, Nettlau, *B.I.I.*, pp. 113 ff.

[17] For the proceedings of the Geneva Congress, Guillaume, *I.D.S.*, I, 41-55; Nettlau, *B.I.I.*, pp. 111-12, 116-17; Zoccoli, *L'Anarchia*, p. 372, note 2. The deliberation of the Liberty and Justice directive group, read by Gambuzzi, was reported in the Sept. 29, 1867, issue of *Libertà e Giustizia*.

nationalism, the Neapolitan Association's message condemned, not the national spirit per se, but aggressive and competitive exaggerations of it. The state to be eliminated was the existing Italian state; in effect, the "federal and socialist republic" was to be *substituted* for the bourgeois state. Again Italian socialism used the Pisacanian formula to stay within the patriotic orbit.

The definitive proof of this non-Bakuninist orientation lay in Gambuzzi's and Fanelli's involvement in Garibaldi's preparations for the capture of Rome which resulted in the Mentana expedition of early November.[18] Bakunin, compelled *faire bonne mine à mauvais jeu* if he did not want to risk losing these two close collaborators, made a tactical retreat on October 12 when he wrote Gambuzzi from Geneva:

> . . . all that you have done, you have done well—and all the decisions you made were well taken. There are moments and dispositions common to a whole country in which it becomes both impossible and harmful to abstain. At present, Italy is in precisely such a condition—I have always recognized that in the midst of the general paralysis that seems to have struck your country, one living fact remained—it was the question of the pope, of the Catholic religion and of Rome, which you have the mission to resolve, not only for yourselves, but also for the whole civilized world.—Therefore, do that which your good inclination inspires you to do, but in the midst of the chaos and tumult produced by the new events, do not forget our alliance, which must supersede them.[19]

In another letter of October 25 (only a few days before Garibaldi's defeat at Mentana), Bakunin extended his admonition to Fanelli as well:

> . . . all that you have done, all that you propose to do, fine. And now my advice, dear friends, is this—unless Garibaldi, finally recognizing that he has followed a mistaken path since 1858, . . . finally decides to raise the banner of revolution without conditions, without subterfuges and senseless chatter—of which I do not believe him capable—abstain from, and renounce decisively any collaboration. You have already done so much to show the blindest and most malevolent that you lack neither good will nor courage. . . . Therefore, withdraw from the lists . . . and gather the fruits of the intellectual and moral consistency you have demonstrated in this affair. Do not let yourselves be shot by some pontifical brigand or poisoned by an agent of Cialdini. Save yourselves for better days and these will not be long in coming to console you for your present

[18] Rosselli, *Mazzini e Bakounine*, p. 207.
[19] Nettlau, *B.I.I.*, pp. 118-19.

fiasco, which is by no means due to you. Study the horizon, the hurricane threatens to erupt everywhere; therefore, have patience, furl your sails and prepare for it.[20]

While Gambuzzi and Fanelli openly demonstrated their disagreement with Bakunin's antinationalist principle, other members of the Russian's Neapolitan circle—Dramis, Raffaele Mileti, Friscia—erred, from Bakunin's point of view, in another direction: they were doing nothing to advance the cause of the secret International Fraternity, which in itself suggests that their acceptance of some of his preachings was due more to the personal persuasive powers of the Russian than to the intrinsic attractiveness of his revolutionary philosophy. In any case, Bakunin's lament underscores the frustration of whatever plans for organized action he had hatched with these socialist but patriotic republicans:

> . . . I pray you to write me more often and ask our friends to write to me. . . . Why does De Luca not send me [*Libertà e Giustizia*]? . . . . and why does [Carlo] Mileti not send me the *Popolo* [*d'Italia*]? *Attanasio* [Dramis]! *you are asleep! for shame! it is time to get up and make a man of yourself again!* . . . . *And the very dear homeopathic Doctor* [Friscia], *so full of good will and passivity? As always?—is he, too, asleep?* [21]

In the letter of October 25, Raffaele Mileti was indicted, while Dramis suffered still another scolding, despite certain financial difficulties he seemed to be undergoing:

> . . . tell [Dramis] for me that within a few days of the time financial lacks no longer weigh on him, I [shall] expect news of his resurrrection—otherwise, I shall really bury him in my mind, in my heart, and shall nourish only disdain for him. The word is hard, I know, but it is sincere. . . . As for Raffaele [Mileti], tell him for me, too, that he has acted like a delinquent in betraying in your regard the laws of *solidarity* and *mutuality*.[22]

The net significance of Bakunin's sojourn in the Naples area? To the extent that his revolutionary philosophy paralleled that of Pisacane and Proudhon, he doubtless confirmed and strengthened—by dint of his dialectical vigor, powerful personality, and revolutionary reputation—the libertarian-socialist tendencies that had begun to develop among radical republicans well before his own arrival in Naples. As for organizational activity for socialist ends, the Russian had little effect. In this regard, probably the most meaningful aspect of his Neapolitan experience was

[20] Nettlau, *B.I.I.*, pp. 119-21.
[21] *Ibid.*, p. 119
[22] *Ibid.*, p. 120.

that it provided him with the insight into Italian revolutionary mentality that enabled him, four years later, to exercise a decisive influence on the development of the Italian socialist movement. In 1867, however, that insight did not serve his purposes, for his Italian friends' concern for the nation and its unity remained the premise of their social revolutionary thinking.

BAKUNIN AND THE LEAGUE FOR PEACE AND LIBERTY

In the Swiss environment, Bakunin's hopes of stimulating a social revolutionary organization into action were born anew.[23] In the League for Peace and Liberty, organized at the Geneva peace congress in September, he saw a promising medium for imposing his libertarian credo on European democrats. With no apparent further concern for the development of his secret International Fraternity, he lustily turned to the task of inserting himself and his cronies among the revolutionary exiles into the directive organs of the League, "an optimum thing," as he described it to Gambuzzi, "which promises to proceed with a breadth of ideas." [24]

By the early summer of 1868 Bakunin was sitting on the Central Committee of the League,[25] urging its acceptance of libertarian socialist principles, notwithstanding the predominantly bourgeois orientation of the organization. At a meeting of the Central Committee, May 31 to June 1, Bakunin persuaded the group to adopt, among others, this principle for consideration by the League congress scheduled to convene in Bern on September 21, 1868: "That the present economic system must be radically changed, if we wish to arrive at an equitable partition of wealth, labor, leisure, and education, the essential condition for the emancipation of the working classes and the abolition of the proletariat." [26]

Bakunin then sought a working *entente* between the International Workingmen's Association and the League for Peace and Liberty, fully appreciating the rapidly increasing prestige of the I.W.A. and the fact that if he could swing the League over to socialism, the former organization, as a going enterprise on behalf of the workers, would prove a natural ally. He personally joined the Geneva section of the I.W.A. and secured

[23] He had intended, after the Geneva peace congress, to return to Italy, settling either in Milan or Venice, but finally chose to remain in Vevey, near the eastern end of Lake Geneva. Nettlau, *B.I.I.*, pp. 117-19.

[24] *Ibid.*, p. 121. He did not, however, neglect his polemic against Mazzini and the apostle's concept of a strongly centralized state. For Bakunin's anti-Mazzinian writings of the winter of 1867-68, *ibid.*, pp. 122-24.

[25] Zoccoli, *op. cit.*, p. 372; Guillaume, *I.D.S.*, I, 71.

[26] Nettlau, *B.I.I.*, p. 124; Guillaume, *I.D.S.*, I, 71.

the promise of Charles Perron, an influential member of the section, to urge a formal alliance between the League and the International at the Brussels Congress of the latter association, scheduled for September 6-13, 1868. On the Russian's insistence, the League invited the delegates of the Brussels Congress to attend its own Bern Congress, while Bakunin himself sent a "fraternal" greeting to the Brussels meeting.[27] Finally, in order to have a trusted observer at these proceedings, he arranged for Saverio Friscia to attend in the name of the *Figli del Lavoro* of Catania, a group which, though unrecognized by the I.W.A. General Council, had declared its adherence to the Brussels Congress.[28]

Whether Bakunin, in this attempted *rapprochement* with the First International, was initiating a long-range plan to capture the I.W.A. for himself is still open to question, but there is no doubt that Marx, ever on the alert against possible rivals for the leadership of the International, considered the organization his and Engels' personal machine and had his doubts about the role of Bakunin on the stage of European revolutionism. As early as September 11, 1867, he had exulted over the progress of the International in these terms:

> Things are moving. In the imminent revolution, which is perhaps closer than it seems, we have (that is, you and I) this potent *engine* in our hands. Compare this with the results of Mazzini, etc., for approximately the last thirty years. Furthermore, without financial means! [Compare this] with the intrigues of the Proudhonists in Paris, of Mazzini in Italy and of the ambitious Odger, Cremer, Potter in London, with the Schulze-Del[itsch group] and the Lassallians in Germany! We can be content! [29]

In connection with Bakunin's appearance at the first congress for peace at Geneva, Marx commented to Engels, in a letter of October 4, 1867, that "The Russians, naturally, have set up the Congress . . . and for this purpose they sent their well worn-out agent Bakunin." [30]

Bakunin's hopes for a League-I.W.A. *entente* were momentarily dampened by a Brussels Congress resolution asserting that the League had no *raison d'être*, since the I.W.A. was already performing the same function. The League was invited to join the International by having its members enroll, as individuals, in the various sections of the I.W.A. The delegates to the Brussels Congress were permitted to attend the League's

[27] Rosselli, *Mazzini e Bakounine*, p. 221; Guillaume, *I.D.S.*, I, 71-72.

[28] Tullio Martello, *Storia dell'Internazionale dalla sua origine al Congresso dell'Aja* (Padua, Naples, 1873), pp. 53-54, note. Friscia arrived too late to take part in the proceedings; the only representative for Italy at the Brussels Congress was Eugène Dupont, of the London General Council. Nettlau, *B.I.I.*, p. 126.

[29] *Briefwechsel*, III, 420.

[30] *Ibid.*, III, 428.

congress in Bern, but only if they took with them the resolutions of the
I.W.A. congresses and discussed them at Bern on their own personal
responsibility. In Bern, the League leadership reproached Bakunin for
the overture that had led to the International's mortifying refusal to
recognize even the League's right to exist.[31]

Undaunted, Bakunin continued his efforts to turn the League into an
effective socialist organization. To Gustav Vogt, president of the League,
he explained his insistence on cooperation with the International. To
recognize "the great economic and social principles" of the I.W.A. is
not to make the League a satellite of the International. Social principles
are the exclusive property of no single group or individual and no one,
either from above or below, "has the right to keep us from speaking,
from organizing, and from acting in the name of these principles." In
any case, the Brussels decision "must not be considered by us as an
expression of the sentiments of the mass of workers represented [at
Brussels], but as [an expression] of defiance, or even . . . malice on the
part of a certain coterie, the center of which [read Marx] you have
doubtless guessed as well as I."

The Brussels decision, termed an "impertinence" and a "flagrant injustice" by Bakunin, must not lead the League to underrate the "immense
and useful significance" of the International:

> It is . . . the greatest event of our day; if we ourselves are
> sincere democrats, we must not only desire that the [Interna-
> tional] eventually embrace all the workers' associations of
> Europe and America, but we must cooperate with it completely,
> for today it alone constitutes the true revolutionary power that
> must change the face of the world. We can and must render a
> great service to the cause of socialist democracy and to the
> [International] itself by posing and preparing the questions, and
> thus clarifying the political path that must be followed to arrive
> at a complete solution of the social question itself.

The League, argued Bakunin, should accept the following fundamental
principles: "the economic equalization of all classes and individuals . . . ;
the abolition of hereditary property, the appropriation of all instruments
of labor by the universal federation of workers' associations, a federation
in which all the existing States and political institutions founded on the
individual and hereditary ownership of capital and land must be submerged." These, wrote Bakunin, are the principles of the International.
Refusing them, the League would not only be useless, but "harmful and

[31] Guillaume, I.D.S., I, 67, 72.

reactionary." The workers would then be justified in rejecting and even fighting the association.[32]

Actually, Bakunin's personal interpretation of the International's doctrinal positions, as of September 1868, was highly arbitrary, for the Brussels Congress had not yet clarified its attitude toward the collectivization of landed property and the instruments of production;[33] nothing had been said about the abolition of inheritance, nor had the socialists at Brussels made any reference to a "universal federation of workers' organizations." Finally, Bakunin's choice of the expression, "economic equalization of classes"—cited by some historians as proof that Bakunin's theory was counterrevolutionary on the grounds that true socialism aims at the *abolition* of classes[34]—was a poor description of the International's official attitude on the subject. On this last point, however, Bakunin himself met the objection in these words: "I want the suppression of classes economically and socially as well as politically. . . . This is what we mean by . . . the equalization of classes. It might have been better, perhaps, to say the suppression of classes, the unification of society by the abolition of economic and social inequality. But we also demanded the equalization of individuals, and it is this, especially, that subjects us all to the fulminations of our adversaries' indignant eloquence." [35]

Whatever the doctrinal discrepancies between Bakunin and the masters of the First International, the libertarian socialism the Russian proposed at the Bern Congress of the League for Peace and Liberty was enough to horrify the liberal bourgeois majority. He asked for debate on the question of how to achieve the economic and social equalization of classes, the precondition for the attainment of peace and liberty.[36] In defending himself against the charge of communism, he succinctly indicted that system as the negation of individual freedom:

> I am not a communist at all, for communism concentrates and causes all the powers of society to be absorbed by the State, because it leads necessarily to the centralization of property in

[32] For Bakunin's letter to Vogt, Guillaume, *I.D.S.*, I, 72-74.

[33] There was enough equivocation on both these points, however, that Bakunin's mistaken interpretation need not be construed as a wilful distortion. *Cf., ibid.*, III, 66.

[34] As a particularly vigorous example, see Romano's discussion of this point, designed to indict the counterrevolutionary "poison of Bakuninism." *Storia*, I, 236-37.

[35] Guillaume, *I.D.S.*, I, 74, note 1.

[36] *Ibid.*, I, 74-79, for the proceedings. As a preliminary to his own personal intervention at the Congress, Bakunin had Gambuzzi read a long report on the political situation in Italy and present a resolution in favor of European federalism based on the principle of the "autonomy of the communes in each province and of the latter in every nation." Marc de Préadeau, *Michel Bakounine* (Paris, 1912), pp. 126 ff.

the hands of the State, while I want the abolition of the State—
the radical extirpation of that principle of authority and control
by the State, which, under the pretext of moralizing and civilizing men, has up to the present enslaved, oppressed, exploited,
and depraved them. I want the organization of society and
collective or social property from the bottom up, through free
association, and not from the top down by means of whatever
authority. Wanting the abolition of the State, I want the abolition
of individually inherited property, which is only an institution
of the State, a very consequence of the principle of the State.
This is the sense in which I am a collectivist and not at all a
communist.[37]

When Bakunin found no majority support of these views, he and his
friends withdrew in protest:

Considering that the majority of the members of the Congress
for Peace and Liberty have passionately and explicitly expressed
themselves against the *economic and social equalization of
classes and individuals,* and that any program and any political
action that does not have as a goal the realization of this principle could not be accepted by socialist democrats, that is, by
conscientious and logical friends of peace and liberty, the under-
signed believe it their duty to separate from the League.[38]

Seven Italians attended the Bern Congress, including Fanelli, Gambuzzi, Tucci, and Friscia. Of the eighteen signatures affixed to the
withdrawal declaration only three were those of Italians: Fanelli, Tucci,
and Friscia. Gambuzzi, for reasons not apparent from the record,
remained as a member of the League, for the time being at least.[39] If this
signified a difference between him and Bakunin, it did not last long,
for within a matter of weeks Gambuzzi was again on the scene as the
Russian's key agent in Italy.

THE INTERNATIONAL ALLIANCE OF SOCIALIST
DEMOCRACY AND THE I.W.A.

With the help of his handful of Russian, Polish, Swiss, French, German,
and Italian friends, Bakunin forthwith founded his famous International
Alliance of Socialist Democracy.[40] At the outset the group declared itself

---

[37] Guillaume, *I.D.S.,* I, 75.

[38] *Loc. cit.*

[39] *Ibid.,* I, 75-76; Nettlau, *B.I.I.,* p. 124

[40] The original name of the organization, "International Alliance of Social Democracy," was later changed because the term, "social democracy," smelled too much of
the German Social Democratic Party, the heart and soul, in Bakunin's view, of
"authoritarian communism."

a branch of the First International and accepted its statutes. Bakunin headed its executive group, the Central Bureau. At the constituent meeting the Italians and some of the French members argued for complete independence from the I.W.A., but Bakunin overcame this current by pointing out the possibility of an undesirable rivalry between the Alliance and the International. John Becker, ex-Garibaldian colonel, was accordingly instructed to ask the London General Council for admission of the new association *en bloc* into the I.W.A.[41]

The program of the Alliance was much more radical than that of the International.[42] In its militant atheism and its demand for the collectivization of all instruments of production, for suppresson of the right of inheritance, for the abolition of national states in favor of a "universal union of free associations, agricultural and industrial"; for the political, economic, and social equalization of classes and individuals, the program far exceeded the most advanced positions of the International at the time. Even so, this constituted no technical obstacle to acceptance of the Alliance by the London General Council, for Article I of the I.W.A. statutes defined as eligible for admission "all workers' societies aspiring to the same goal, to wit: mutual assistance, the progress and complete emancipation of the working class." True, the Alliance was by no means a collection of "workers'" societies, but Marx and Engels could hardly have objected on *that* ground.

The work of promoting this public association was entrusted by Bakunin to his collaborators of the still existent but apparently dormant International Fraternity, the secret society the Russian had launched during his stay in Naples. Fanelli, by now no hesitant assistant, was sent off to Spain to organize sections of the Alliance among the revolutionary groups that had but recently engineered the expulsion of Queen Isabella.[43] Tucci was put to work writing another clandestine revolutionary pamphlet, *La Situazione #2,* addressed to the Italians, full of the well-worn diatribes against Garibaldi and Mazzini.[44] For Gambuzzi, now back in Italy, Bakunin had urgent and plentiful advice: "Get to work, dear

---

[41] For details on the founding of the Alliance, Guillaume, *I.D.S.*, I, 76-79; Nettlau, "Bakunin und die Internationale in Italien bis zum Herbst 1872," pp. 292-93.

[42] For the program, Guillaume, *I.D.S.*, I, 132-33; Domanico, *L'Internazionale*, p. 131.

[43] On Fanelli's Spanish activities, see Nettlau, *B.I.I.*, pp. 147-53; by the same author, "Bakunin und die Internationale in Spanien 1868-1873," in *Archiv für die Geschichte des Sozialismus und der Arbeiterbewegung*, IV (1914), 248-52; Lucarelli, *Giuseppe Fanelli*, pp. 104-12.

[44] Reproduced by Nettlau, *B.I.I.*, pp. 132-46. Tucci broke off relations with both Bakunin and Gambuzzi shortly afterward. Nettlau does not indicate the source of this defection. Tucci's refusal to undertake the propaganda mission to Spain that was later assigned to Fanelli could have been a contributing factor to the dissension. Cf., *ibid.*, pp. 131, 148 .

friend, as soon as you receive the program and official regulations [of the Alliance]." As members of the Italian National Committee of the Alliance, Bakunin suggested, in addition to Gambuzzi: Friscia, Dramis, Raffaele Mileti, and Giuseppe Mazzoni of Florence, with whom the Russian had resumed correspondence shortly before.[45] Five days later (November 7) Gambuzzi was urged to study well both the rules of the secret International Fraternity and the overt Alliance—"and do not depart from them." Again the Russian indicated his candidates for the Italian committee and, as a first step, suggested that Gambuzzi, Mileti, and Friscia organize an office in Naples without the help of Dramis, "if Attanasio prefers to remain in a shameful passivity." Again, on November 10: "Work, work, and make the others work. . . . You and Fanelli have been admitted as members of the International [section] of Geneva." In Geneva, Bakunin and his Swiss lieutenants, Guillaume and Schwitzgue-bel, founded a newspaper to propagate the libertarian program, L'Egalité, with Gambuzzi and Tucci as correspondents for Italy.[46]

Bakunin's intense organizational activity of this period was premised on the Alliance's admission into the First International. Whether his ultimate intent was to oust Marx from the leadership of the international socialist movement or to add real strength to the socialist cause in general, Bakunin had to recognize that the International was first in the field, with a consequently large following among European socialists and workers. On December 12, 1868, John Zagorsky, secretary of the central office of the Alliance, urged Gambuzzi not to forget that "our Alliance will never really be useful until it is genuinely fused with the International Workingmen's Association; that . . . its principal purpose, its reason to be . . . is to propagate and spread everywhere this great and

[45] Ibid., pp. 153-54. On Aug. 3, 1868, Bakunin had invited Mazzoni to attend the Bern Congress of the League for Peace and Liberty. Mazzoni did not appear, but after the creation of the Alliance, Bakunin, apparently desperate for agents in Tuscany, sent Mazzoni the program of the Alliance and informed his Florentine correspondent that he and Berti-Calura (also of Florence) had been presented as candidates for membership in the Geneva section of the International. On Feb. 14, 1869, both Mazzoni and Berti-Calura became members of the I.W.A., but neither proved active in the cause and continued their contacts with the Mazzinians. Bakunin's final judgment on Mazzoni (Mar., 1872): "Giuseppe Mazzoni, of Prato, called the Cato of Tuscany, the friend of Alberto Mario, and both are regional federalists, each in his own manner." Cerrito and Masini, "Quattro lettere di Bakunin a G. Mazzoni," pp. 619-22; Nettlau, B.I.I., p. 198, note.

[46] Guillaume, I.D.S., I, 102; Nettlau, B.I.I., pp. 154-55. Friscia was not brought into the I.W.A. until Feb. 14, 1869. Ibid., p. 198, note 2. L'Egalité ceased to be a Bakuninist organ early in January, 1870, as a consequence of a difference of opinion among the editors. The Bakuninists, Charles Perron, Robin, and others resigned, leaving the paper in the hands of John Phillip Becker and the Russian, N. I. Utin. Guillaume, I.D.S., I, 270-71.

salutary Association." [47] On December 22 Bakunin even tried personal blandishment on the formidably suspicious Marx:

> I am [your friend] more than ever, dear Marx, for more than ever I have come to understand how you were right in following and in inviting us to march on the great road of economic revolution. . . . I am now doing what you began to do . . . more than twenty years ago. Since the solemn and public adieux that I addressed to the bourgeois of the Congress of Bern, I have known no other society, no other milieu than the world of the workers. My fatherland now is the International, of which you are one of the principal founders. You see, therefore, dear friend, that I am your disciple and I am proud of being one. [48]

On the very day Bakunin composed this siren song—Marx called it an *entrée sentimentale*—the International's General Council unanimously rejected the Alliance request for admission to the I.W.A. and declared null and void those articles in the Alliance statute pertaining to its relations with the International. [49] Reading the Alliance program prompted Marx to aver that he had never encountered anything "more pious" and to conclude that "Siberia, his belly, and the young Pole [Bakunin's wife, Antonia Kwiatkowska] have made a perfect ox of Bakunin." [50] As for the Alliance itself, Marx argued that if it had the same goals as the International, it was superfluous; if it was actually a rival organization, as he suspected, admitting it to the I.W.A. was impossible. Besides, a second international group would weaken and disorganize the first and set a bad precedent. [51]

When apprised of the London Council's decision, some members of the Alliance's central bureau in Geneva proposed ignoring the I.W.A. and continuing independently, but Bakunin and Charles Perron successfully pleaded the necessity of coming to an agreement with the General Council. Perron was commissioned to propose to the General Council the dissolution of the Alliance and its central Bureau, in return for recognition, as regularly constituted sections of the I.W.A., of the Alliance sections already founded in Switzerland, Spain, and Italy. On these conditions the central bureau promised to advise the Alliance sections to

[47] Nettlau, *B.I.I.*, p. 155

[48] Domanico, *op. cit.*, pp. 136 ff.; Guillaume, *I.D.S.*, I, 103. Romano cites Bakunin's letter as "the precise, inconfutable documentation of the double game played by the Russian adventurer and of his moral and political ambiguity." *Storia,* I, 242.

[49] Guillaume, *I.D.S.*, I, 102-04.

[50] Letter to Engels, Dec. 18, 1868, *Briefwechsel,* IV, 143. "Sibirien, der Bauch und die junge Polin haben den Bakunin zum perfekten Ochsen gemacht."

[51] Zoccoli, *op. cit.*, p. 376, note; Guillaume, *I.D.S.*, I, 102-04.

eliminate from their constitutions anything contrary to the statutes of the First International.[52]

While the London Council pondered the Alliance offer, Bakunin himself resigned from the central directory of the secret International Fraternity, from the central bureau of the Alliance and from "all public affairs" of the latter organization, vowing to "take no part, either direct or indirect, in the affairs of these societies until the next [I.W.A.] Congress."[53] Shortly afterward, an undated circular announced the dissolution of the International Fraternity, indicating as the chief reason the fact that Élie Reclus and Aristide Rey were making "bourgeois socialist" propaganda in Spain, thus undercutting the missionary work there of Fanelli, one of the "faithful brothers."[54] Actually, dissolution of the Fraternity meant little more than the rupture of Bakunin's vague personal ties with men like the Reclus brothers, Benoît Malon, Aristide Rey, Valerien Mroczkowski, and Nicholas Joukovsky, probably the sole substance of the Russian's mysterious international secret society in the first instance. Moreover, the organizational framework for propagating Bakunin's libertarian socialism was to continue in the Alliance of Socialist Democracy, despite the formal dissolution of that association's central bureau.[55]

It was the London General Council itself that established the arrangement giving Bakunin, for the first time in his long and adventurous career, the kind of organizational support needed to develop an undreamed-of influence over the international socialist movement in Italy and, to a lesser extent, in France, Spain, Switzerland, and Belgium. On March 20, 1869, the Council agreed to admit the Alliance sections as regularly constituted sections of the International. The Alliance program presented no obstacle, Marx and his friends had concluded, for both it and the I.W.A. program aimed at the complete emancipation of the working classes; besides, "It is outside the functions of the General Council to make the critical examination of the program of the Alliance."[56]

---

[52] Guillaume, *I.D.S.*, I, 109-10.

[53] *Ibid.*, I, 120.

[54] Nettlau, *B.I.I.*, pp. 148, 277; Guillaume, *I.D.S.*, I, 131.

[55] For Bakunin's denial that he continued the Alliance on a clandestine basis, i.e., as a continuation of the "dissolved" International Fraternity, see his "Rapport sur l'Alliance," in *Oeuvres*, VI, 186-89. For Marx's proof that Bakunin never dissolved his clandestine organization, see the formidable indictment he presented to the Hague Congress of 1872 in mustering his case for the expulsion of the overt Alliance from the I.W.A. *L'Alleanza della Democrazia Socialista e l'Associazione Internazionale dei Lavoratori* (Rome, 1901).

[56] Guillaume, *I.D.S.*, I, 140-41. By no means did this signify that Marx had dropped his reservations; in fact, he would have preferred a Council refusal of the Alliance application: "It would have been a great deal nicer for us if the [Bakuninists] had kept to themselves their 'innumerable legions' in France, Spain, and Italy." Still,

Immediately on receiving the London communication, the central bureau of the Alliance asked all its dependent groups to reorganize as regular sections of the I.W.A., but to retain their program. The Geneva section substituted "abolition of classes" for "political, economic, and social equalization of classes and individuals." On May 1 its directive committee, which included Bakunin, was elected; in June the central bureau announced its own dissolution. On July 28 the secretary-general of the London General Council announced that body's unanimous acceptance of Bakunin's Geneva group as a section of the First International.[57] From this point forward, Bakunin could advance the cause of his libertarian socialism within the organized European socialist movement under the cloak of legitimacy conferred by Marx and his friends.

From the Italian point of view, the identification of Bakunin and his group with the First International was of cardinal importance, for it meant that the international socialist movement was to penetrate the peninsula under the sponsorship of a small clique of agitators and organizers closely bound by personal ties to the Russian revolutionary and sharing with him a body of socialist doctrine deriving, not from the *Communist Manifesto* or *Das Kapital*, but from Proudhon and Pisacane, as edited and revised by Bakunin. In delaying the debut of "scientific socialism" in Italy by more than a decade, this, from the Marxists' point of view, was a calamity.

---

admitting the Alliance would mean that the Bakuninists had to send the General Council a complete roster of Alliance sections, and this "will particularly disturb those gentlemen." Letter to Engels, Mar. 5, 1869, *Briefwechsel*, IV, 164-65.

[57] Guillaume, *I.D.S.*, I, 141, 181; *cf.*, also, Zoccoli, *L'Anarchia*, p. 376, note 1.

VI

Italy and the First International
(1866-1870)

THE WORKERS' SOCIETIES AND
INTERNATIONAL SOCIALISM

BENOÎT MALON, the French socialist who broke with Bakunin's International Fraternity early in 1869, wrote fifteen years later that Bakunin's relations with the Liberty and Justice Association in Naples served "to put the Italian socialist movement in the hands" of the Russian agitator.[1] Aside from the fact that the Liberty and Justice group hardly represented an "Italian socialist movement," Malon erred in that Bakunin did not establish any control over the movement until several years after the Neapolitan association passed out of existence. In 1869 and 1870 the Russian's effective contacts with his former clique of Neapolitan intimates were almost limited to Carlo Gambuzzi and Saverio Friscia. Fanelli returned to Italy in March, 1869, after many laments that Bakunin had failed to keep him in operating funds during his propaganda mission to Madrid, and for more than a year he nursed his grudge against the Russian, interesting himself hardly at all in propagating the International in the peninsula. Dramis was no longer active, preferring to remain in what Bakunin called his "shameful passivity," and Tucci followed suit after his break with Bakunin and Gambuzzi late in 1868.[2] As for Friscia and Gambuzzi, their efforts to establish the I.W.A. in Italy encountered a set of circumstances that would have frustrated the labors of dozens of socialist militants far more active than Bakunin's brace of henchmen.

Italy's embryonic industrialism precluded the concentration of large numbers of workers that would encourage a consciousness of common

---

[1] "L'Internationale," *La Nouvelle Revue*, XXVI (Jan.-Feb., 1884), 751.
[2] Nettlau, *B.I.I.*, pp. 152, 157, 161-62.

economic interests. There were literally hundreds of workers' mutual aid societies—573 in 1867, 771 in 1869[3]—but the vast majority of their members were artisans, not industrial workers in the modern socialist sense; as such, they could not be expected to have the same reaction to socialist doctrines as the factory workers of the industrialized regions of France, Belgium, and Germany. Marx, too, touched on another aspect of the situation when, in March 1869, he reserved a sneer for the "revolutionary" workers' movement of Italy, "where the workers . . . are the tail of Mazzini." [4] Certainly Marx was right in regarding the Italian workers' societies as unrevolutionary, for even those associations with a policy of syndical resistance to the employer class saw their problem as one of wringing concessions on wages, working hours, and conditions within the framework of the existing system, not challenging the wage system itself. And if willingness to wage political warfare on the possessing classes as exploiters of the masses be taken as the criterion of social revolutionism, the record reveals no trace of such an impulse among the workers' societies. To the extent that Mazzini had convinced a minority of the associations to adopt his program for the republic, there was a degree of revolutionary spirit, politically motivated, but its manifestations carried no social revolutionary implications.

Marx's generalization erred, rather, in not making a distinction between two distinct groups of Italian workers' societies: the majority, disinterested in the institutional question and/or social revolution because they considered both to be extraneous and even harmful to the purposes of their associations, and the Mazzinian minority, with perhaps vague ideas about harnessing the motive power of social revolution to a republican movement, but definitely indifferent, if not hostile, to the socialist argument that proletarian welfare must be pursued through class struggle. The first category may be considered as beyond the power of the socialist idea to penetrate, at least until Italian industrialization reached the stage where the workers could be persuaded that their material condition was a direct consequence of the capitalist system of production. As of 1869-70, the lineaments of that system, thanks to its immaturity, were seen "as through a glass darkly," perhaps intuited but hardly identified as *the* obstacle to the terrestrial felicity of proletarians. The second category, the Mazzinian associations, fully justified the description Marx intended as an epithet. Until the political and social program of Mazzini, the spiritual father of the Italian Left for almost forty years, revealed itself as impractical, his hold over the minds and imaginations of Italian republicans —be they simple artisans or young intellectuals sincerely concerned for

[3] Rosselli, *Mazzini e Bakounine*, p. 249.
[4] Letter to Engels, Mar. 14, 1869, *Briefwechsel*, IV, 168.

their lot—might be shaken but not broken by the impact of a materialist doctrine. No better proof is needed than that during the period 1865-70 several political, economic, and social developments in the peninsula favoring defection to socialism failed to produce more than the merest handful of bona fide socialist organizations by the time Italian unity was completed with the capture of Rome.

The frustration at Mentana (November 19, 1867) of Garibaldi's attempt to capture Rome must have disillusioned many radical young republicans with Mazzinian agitations and Garibaldi's ineffectual enterprises. As Rosselli observed,[5] their discontent was aggravated by the fact that all apparent paths to direct action for a republic were being closed to them; the heroic era was drawing to a close, and they were being denied an historic function. A psychological impulse was given toward acceptance of the notion that perhaps a republic might never be won after all, except in the context of social revolution. The concept of revolution in a strictly national and political sense began to lose its appeal in the face of a rapidly maturing international revolutionary force incarnated in the International Workingmen's Association.

Secondly, Mazzini, in neglecting to follow up on his pre-1864 attempts to mold the Italian workers' societies into a republican political force, gave them no organizational solidarity with which to resist efforts to introduce a socialist orientation. The Genoa *Consociazione,* the most vigorous of the workers' groups adhering to the Mazzinian Pact of Brotherhood, chafed at the inaction of the movement after the Naples Congress and would have called a congress of the societies of northern Italy in 1867, had the preparations attending Garibaldi's Mentana venture not intervened. In September 1868, on the initiative of the same group, a congress of Ligurian societies was convened. Gaspare Stampa and Quirico Filopanti, members of the central council elected at Naples in 1864, turned in their resignations, while assuring the congress that the other three members of the council would be willing to accept its decisions. The Ligurian delegates, in turn, named both Stampa and Filopanti to a commission, along with five Ligurian representatives, whose function was to convoke the long overdue Twelfth Congress. Since, in effect, this new commission supplanted the old central council, Stampa and his colleagues were bound by the Naples decision of 1864 that the next congress be held in Palermo, which meant in turn that a general meeting in Genoa, the only practical locale for such a gathering, was out of the question—unless the commission wished to appear as seceders from the sovereignty of the Naples Congress. The net result: no general con-

[5] *Mazzini e Bakounine,* pp. 207-08.

gress was held in 1869 and in the following year the capture of Rome consumed the attention of all.[6]

Nor did Mazzini make any particular effort, aside from his customary propaganda against materialism, to block contact between the workers' societies and the First International. Professor Savi, editor of the official organ of the Italian associations, *Il Giornale delle Associazioni Operaie,* Gaspare Stampa, and Giuseppe Fanelli, then to be counted a Mazzinian, albeit a wavering one, planned to attend the first I.W.A. congress, scheduled for Brussels in the fall of 1865, but the gathering was put off until the following year.[7] In Florence, Niccolò Lo Savio urged the Italian workers' societies to join the International, to have themselves represented on the General Council in London. How, he wanted to know, can the social revolution be initiated in Italy without "concluding a pact of solid union among all the sons of labor"?[8] On March 18, 1866, the *Giornale* announced that it was in touch with the section in Geneva. On March 30 Stampa, in the name of the central council elected at Naples in 1864, hailed the work of the International and assured its leaders that "the aspirations and purposes of our pact [of Brotherhood] are the same as yours [*sic*], except that yours is more extensive and promises a more potent life." The Italian workers' societies, wrote Stampa, "give you the most complete declaration of adherence to your program and we ask you . . . to gladden us with your fraternal contacts."[9] Three weeks later the *Giornale* called the International "the emblem of universal brotherhood."[10] The following week, L. D. Canessa, Savi's successor as editor of the newspaper, asked Hermann Jung, secretary for Switzerland on the London General Council, to send him the statutes of the I.W.A., "because I want to organize a section [of the International] in Genoa."[11]

The war against Austria kept the Italian societies from sending delegates to the Geneva Congress of 1866,[12] and it also occasioned a sharpening of the General Council's hostility toward Mazzini. On June 26 the secretary for Italy on the Council, Giacomo Traini, resigned in high

---

[6] For the organizational activity of the Mazzinian workers' societies between 1864 and 1870, see Manacorda, *Il movimento operaio italiano,* pp. 65-67.

[7] Valiani, *Storia del movimento socialista,* I, 116.

[8] *Il Proletario,* Nov. 12, 1865.

[9] *Der Vorbote* (Geneva), 1866, as quoted by Valiani, *op. cit.,* I, 116.

[10] Issue of Apr. 22, 1866.

[11] Nettlau, *B.I.I.,* p. 125. Jung replied, but on May 26 Canessa wrote that he was no longer editor of the *Giornale* and was about to join Garibaldi "for the liberty of Venice." *Loc. cit.*

[12] The I.W.A. congress at Geneva, however, received two letters of adherence from Italy; one from the central committee of the workers' societies of Lombardy, another from the committee of representatives of forty-four Italian workers' associations, with its headquarters in Genoa. Guillaume, *I.D.S.,* I, 26.

dudgeon because he took exception to an article written by Paul La-
fargue, French member of the Council, in which the Frenchman had
taken Mazzini and Garibaldi to task for supporting a war that allied Italy
with autocratic Prussia. Traini protested that both the Italian leaders were
"good socialists." Stoking the fire, the General Council voted an address
to the workers of the Continent, expressing the hope that the Italians
could win Venetia without the Prussian help condoned by Mazzini.[13]
Mazzini's Universal Republican Alliance was seen by Marx as a weapon
intended for use against the socialist International,[14] but if this was
Mazzini's purpose he was singularly ineffective in pursuing it.

At the International's Lausanne Congress in 1867, Gaspare Stampa,
representing the central committee of the Milanese workers' associations,
and the Marquis Sebastiano Tanari, delegated by workers' societies in
Bologna and Bazzano, were the sole Italian delegates present.[15] Stampa
said he personally adhered to the International and hoped he might
persuade his sponsoring societies in Milan to do the same; Tanari extended personal greetings, but no formal adhesion of his sponsoring
groups. Even Canessa's promise of the year before to organize a Genoa
section had come to nothing, for the report of the General Council to the
Lausanne conclave indicated that no dues had been received from Italy.[16]
Perhaps to offset this poor showing, Stampa reported the strength of the
Italian workers' movement as at least 600 societies, counting 1,000,000
members, while his own Milanese confederation, said he, consisted of
30 societies with a total membership of 30,000 and a capital of 120,000
francs. Unimpressed, the congress delegates decided that "for the sake of
decorum" Stampa would have to be "a little more exact" in his statistics.[17]

At the I.W.A. congress of Brussels in 1868, as already noted, Italy
was represented only by Eugène Dupont, of the London General Council.
In May 1869, Dupont wrote Gambuzzi that he was in touch with Canessa
in Genoa,[18] but again this contact did not produce a Ligurian section of
the I.W.A. Stefano Caporusso attended the Basel Congress in 1869 but
remained throughout the proceedings a creature of Bakunin. His mandate,
furthermore, had been given by a Neapolitan section that had its origins

---

[13] Rosselli, *Mazzini e Bakounine*, p. 195, and note 2; *cf.*, also, Nettlau, *B.I.I.*, pp. 378-79.

[14] See Marx's reference to the "International Republican Committee," the group that planned the Universal Republican Alliance. Letter to Engels, May 17, 1866, *Briefwechsel*, III, 334.

[15] Charles Guillaume referred to them as "Tanari, of Bologna, the socialist marquis, and Gaspare Stampa, of Milan, *un beau vieillard, doux comme un enfant.*" *I.D.S.*, I, 40.

[16] Nettlau, *B.I.I.*, pp. 126-27.

[17] Martello, *Storia dell'Internazionale*, p. 40, note; Valiani, *op. cit.*, I, 131-32.

[18] Nettlau, *B.I.I.*, p. 128.

completely outside the influence of Mazzini. Finally, it might be noted that the Ligurian workers' societies, always a stronghold of Mazzinian influence, were maintaining as late as 1870 no more than platonic contacts with international socialism and still refusing to join the I.W.A. The central committee of the Genoa *Consociazione* sent a message of fraternal solidarity to the Neapolitan section of the International when the latter organization encountered police persecution in February 1870,[19] and in October of the same year Saverio Friscia's I.W.A. section in Sciacca was trying, with no success, to recruit the Ligurian societies into the International.[20]

In these sporadic and almost casual contacts between the Italian workers' societies and the international socialist movement, Mazzini saw no threat to his own influence over the former. He gave a measure of attention to firming up his relations with the workers' movement, but always in terms of strengthening his republican insurrectionary *Apparat*. Nor would he even implicitly concede that the program of international socialism might appear far more relevant, in the minds of the workers, than his own insistence on the subordination of social questions to the problem of erecting an Italian republic. "I am convinced that the popular element has been heretofore neglected by our people," he wrote the Swiss Committee of his Republican Alliance on May 28, 1868; fraternal contacts must be established with workers' nuclei.[21] The socialist International offered no real obstacle to his plan:

> The International Association, good in concept, is dominated a little too much by a certain Marx, a German, a little Proudhon, a dissolver, a hater, who speaks only of the war of class against class. . . . [The I.W.A.] can not lead to a great deal. Correspondence of sympathy, but without commiting ourselves in matters that will take time and money from our workers.[22]

Italian workers, rather than letting themselves become involved in schemes for social renewal, should work for the advent of the republic by "seeking every opportunity to fraternize with the soldier. The army is more than disposed" toward a republican revolution.[23]

Nor were individual defections to socialism considered more than minor nuisances, temporary aberrations that should not occasion the diversion of much republican energy. Caporusso's attendance at the Basel Congress

[19] *Il Monitore di Bologna*, Sept. 11, 1871, as cited by Rosselli, *Mazzini e Bakounine*, p. 270, note.
[20] *L'Unità Italiana*, Oct. 27, 1870.
[21] *S.E.I.*, LXXXVII, 94.
[22] Letter to Federico Campanella, Nov. 14, 1868, *ibid.*, LXXXVII, 206 ff.
[23] *Ibid.*, LXVI, 204.

elicited Mazzini's passing advice to Maurizio Quadrio that the strayed sheep needed a mere "catechization" to bring him back into the fold. If the workers of Caporusso's Neapolitan organization "expect any improvement of their condition from the foolish chatter at [Basel], they are in trouble." [24] Giuseppe Mazzoni's temporary flirting with socialism in the same period brought only a disgusted snort from Mazzini: "What the devil Mazz[oni] means by a social revolution, I do not know. If they can do it, let them. I am content to make a republican one." [25]

THE MACINATO REVOLT

The economic disturbances and manifestations of social unrest in the late 1860's hardly justified Mazzini's air of innocence as to what Mazzoni meant by social revolution. In practically every region of the peninsula economic protest by the masses found expression in violence which, if it did not add up to social revolution, at least forced the representatives of the ruling classes to admit—with unmistakable conviction—that in the situation were "the latent germs of a social question." [26] Perhaps Mazzini, too, might have conceded the social revolutionary implications of these evidences of class conflict if his attention had not been so irrevocably riveted on Rome and the republic.

The financial drain of the Austrian war was still keenly felt, 1867 proved a bad harvest year, food costs soared, a cholera epidemic took thousands of lives, brigandage rapidly increased in the *Mezzogiorno*, and the winter of 1867 was one of the hardest in years, for severe and extensive storms blockaded thousands of hungry peasant families in their homes. Attempting to balance the budget, the government cut down expenses, devalued the currency—which had immediately painful effects on foreign trade—and increased the tax on real property to 16.25 per cent, on fluid wealth to 8 per cent. Salaried employees and wage earners found their standard of living seriously jeopardized.

Early in 1868 a desperate government presented a tax measure to the parliament that promised considerable relief to the national budget: in effect, a capitation tax bearing on the entire population.[27] The government proposed levying an impost an all cereal grains as they were brought in for milling. For the city workers, the effect of such a tax would be greatly diminished in that the original levy would be covered, in part, by the various middlemen involved between the mill and the consumer. In

[24] S.E.I., LXXXVIII, 188.
[25] Letter to Federico Campanella, Mar. 11, 1870, *ibid.*, LXXXIX, 37-38.
[26] Rosselli, *Mazzini e Bakounine*, p. 246.
[27] For details, A. Plebano, *Storia della finanza italiana dalla costituzione del regno alla fine del secolo XIX* (Turin, 1899), I, 240 ff.

the countryside, where money was scarce, the tax represented near disaster for the *contadino,* required to pay the levy on the grain he brought in for milling, in many instances the sole and entire product of his farm. Workers' societies in the urban centers and the opposition newspapers, but even more the provincial press, closer to the agrarian dissatisfaction, lent all possible support to the deputies of the parliamentary Left in their fight against passage of the measure.[28] Francesco Crispi described the levy as "a progressive tax, not in proportion to wealth, but in proportion to poverty. It affects bread, the staff of life, . . . which constitutes nine-tenths of the poor man's food and only one-tenth . . . on the table of the rich man." [29] In the midst of the clamor, Mazzini, never swerving from his concept of revolution based on the idealistic force of his own republicanism, observed: "the growing poverty and the milling tax, if approved, . . . will increase discontent; but material reasons have caused disturbances, never Revolutions." [30]

Mazzini had no sooner penned these lines when a whole series of extremely serious strikes in Italy threatened to give him the lie. Early in April, arsenal workers in Turin, railroad employees in Piedmont, and the workers in the tobacco factories went out on strike; in mid-April a two-day general strike, the first in Italy, resulted in arrests and the dissolution of political and workers' organizations. In Milan, Pistoia, Livorno, Pavia, Sordevole, and other centers the wave of protest against low wages and living conditions rolled on. *La Nazione,* in Florence, speculated on the possibility that the International Workingmen's Association was behind the Bologna general strike and urged its readers to decide whether, "within the folds of political questions, there might not be hidden a more terrible one, . . . which must inexorably be resolved, under pain of catastrophe . . . : the social question." [31]

It was the peasants of the Emilia-Romagna region who dramatically demonstrated how painful the catastrophe might be. The milling tax, approved by the legislature in May 1868, was put into effect at the end of December. Spontaneously, without a trace of concerted preparation, the enraged peasants and *braccianti* (agricultural day-laborers) of the

---

[28] For a summary of adverse press comment, Rosselli, *Mazzini e Bakounine,* pp. 215-20; for parliamentary comment, Saverio Cilibrizzi, *Storia parlamentare politica e diplomatica d'Italia da Novara a Vittorio Veneto* (Naples: Tosi Editore, 1939 ff.), I, 545-48.

[29] Speech of Mar. 18, 1868, Francesco Crispi, *Discorsi parlamentari* (Rome, 1915), I, 584 ff. Subsequent developments fully sustained Crispi's characterization, for in 1873 the revenue from the *macinato* tax was highest where peasant poverty was at a maximum. See Epicarmo Corbino, *Annali dell' economia italiana* (Città di Castello: Soc. Tip. Leonardo da Vinci, 1933-38), II, 284, note 1.

[30] Letter to Andrea Giannelli, Mar. 31, 1868, *S.E.I.,* LXXXVII, 27-28.

[31] Issue of Apr. 16, 1868.

provinces of Bologna, Parma, and Reggio Emilia, armed themselves with ancient muskets, pitchforks, clubs, scythes, plowshares, and pruning hooks, demonstrated in front of municipal buildings, broke the devices on the mills that counted the revolutions of the machinery (determining the tax imposed), forced some authorities to approve the free milling of grain and, in a few cases, burned official records and sacked the homes of rich citizens.[32] Some of the demonstrators even began barricades to fend off the forces of public order. Once the uprising had started, scattered republican and clerical supporters—strange bedfellows—added encouragement and, in some localities, a measure of guidance, hopeful that the days of the Sabauda monarchy were numbered. Through it all, though, the city workers remained passive, and by mid-February 1869 royal troops and *carabinieri*, energetically commanded by General Raffaele Cadorna, had the situation firmly in hand. The cost, according to the statistics appearing in various newspapers: 257 persons killed, 1,099 wounded and 3,788 arrested.

Mazzini was certainly justified in refusing to interpret these events as a manifestation of socialism among the Italian peasants; on the other hand, the nearest he came to drawing a class-interest inference from the affair was his judgment that "The *macinato* [milling tax] draws the peasants closer to us; they must be cultivated and [the word] must be passed among them that the first decrees of the republic would be: abolition of the milling tax; diminution by half, preparatory to total abolition, of the duty on salt; abolition of conscription."[33]

THE NEAPOLITAN I.W.A. SECTION

However unrealistic Mazzini's notion that adding a few concrete promises to his social program would help "sell" his republic to the peasants, however tardy his efforts to increase his influence over the Italian workers' movement, he can hardly be blamed for holding a low opinion of the force of international socialism and the socialist idea in Italy. More than the fact that the *macinato* revolt and the strikes betrayed no socialist influence among the urban and rural populations, the extremely sparse success of the socialist movement prior to 1871, in terms of I.W.A. sections in being, justified Mazzini's refusal to become alarmed. During this period, the

---

[32] For details and a discussion of republican and clerical participation, Rosselli, *Mazzini e Bakounine*, pp. 229-48. For an insight into how the movement looked to the man who suppressed it, L. Cadorna, *Il generale Raffaele Cadorna nel Risorgimento italiano* (Milan, 1922), pp. 317 ff.

[33] Letter to Carlotta Benettini, Jan. 13, 1869, S.E.I., LXXXVII, 257-58. For his part, Bakunin qualified the agrarian disorders as an indication of the "natural, revolutionary socialism of the Italian peasants." *Oeuvres*, IV, 37; Nettlau, *B.I.I.*, p. 185.

existence of less than half a dozen sections can be documented. In September, 1868, a section existed in Catania, Sicily, the *Figli del Lavoro*, presumably founded by Saverio Friscia, delegated by the group to represent it at the I.W.A. congress in Brussels.[34] Friscia is also reputed to have established another in Sciacca (Sicily) at about the same time, but in view of the lack of any supporting evidence, this group may have amounted to nothing more than a revived section of Bakunin's secret International Fraternity.[35] The most important International socialist nucleus in Italy, that of Naples, was in an extremely stagnant condition by September, 1870, its membership depleted and its leadership discredited. Its history prior to this date is illustrative of the diverse and often conflicting influences attending the introduction of the international socialist movement in the peninsula.

In May 1868, a nucleus of tailors and hat workers broke away from the long-established workingmen's association of Naples and declared itself a section of the I.W.A. Stefano Caporusso, who had joined Bakunin's circle while the Russian was still resident in Naples, was named president and it was he, in all probability, who inspired its declaration of adherence to the International.[36] In August of the same year the group advised the London General Council that it wished to be represented at the forthcoming Brussels Congress.[37] Both this nucleus and the Catania section became inactive during the fall of 1868, for on January 20, 1869, Eugène Dupont, in the name of the General Council in London, wrote a Neapolitan socialist leader—probably Gambuzzi—that the General Council had received no news from Italy since the Congress of Brussels. "It is urgent to establish a regular correspondence with the General Council and you must understand the necessity of it."[38]

On January 31, 1869, the Neapolitan section of the I.W.A. was officially constituted—or reconstituted—under the presidency of Caporusso, but the real organizer of the move was Carlo Gambuzzi, who seems to have had Caporusso completely under his thumb.[39] If the activity and orienta-

[34] Rosselli, *Mazzini e Bakounine*, p. 221. The *Figli del Lavoro* society reverted to orthodox Mazzinianism in 1871 and expelled its internationalist president. Cerrito, "Saverio Friscia," p. 468, note 16.

[35] Rosselli, *Mazzini e Bakounine*, p. 221; Salvatore Carbone, *Le origini del socialismo in Sicilia* (Rome: Ediz. Italiane, 1947), p. 42. Friscia is credited with the reorganization of an International Fraternity section in Sciacca and the creation of another in Syracuse in the course of 1867. Angiolini, *Cinquant'anni di socialismo in Italia*, p. 75; A. Bertolini, "Cenno sul socialismo in Italia," in Giovanni Rae, *Il socialismo contemporaneo* (2d ed.; Florence, 1895), p. xc.

[36] Romano, *Storia*, I, 301, note 21.

[37] "Dupont has received a mandate from Naples to represent the local branch." Marx to Engels, Aug. 29, 1868, *Briefwechsel*, IV, 87.

[38] Nettlau, *B.I.I.*, pp. 127-28.

[39] *Il Popolo d'Italia*, Feb. 18, 1869. See, also, Martello, *L'Internazionale*, p. 92; Rosselli, *Mazzini e Bakounine*, pp. 258-59, note 2; Nettlau, *B.I.I.*, pp. 168-69.

tion of this section are to be judged a reflection of those of its animating spirit, the organization certainly did not live up to its avowed intention of furnishing the "provisional central section" of the International in Italy.[40] Not the furtherance of socialism, but republican insurrection was the goal of Gambuzzi's efforts in the late winter and spring of 1869; nor did he hesitate to use his position as the most prominent representative of international socialism in Naples to advance the cause of purely political opposition to the Sabauda monarchy—and this in alliance with representatives of the Bourbons!

Painstakingly following the leads provided by one confession after another in March 1869, the Neapolitan police uncovered a conspiratorial complex in the area that included members of Mazzini's central committee for the southern provinces (an arm of his Republican Alliance); army subalterns; military prisoners on Capri; the secretary of the local Masonic lodge; two members of a prominent pro-Bourbon family, ex-Colonel Marino Caracciolo and the Countess Giulia Cicala-Cacciolo; and, finally, Naples' contribution to international socialism, Gambuzzi and Caporusso.[41] The latter, at one stage in the conspiracy, had reached the point of planning, with the Countess and the ex-colonel, the organization of the workers of the local naval arsenal as supporters of the projected insurrection. Despite their documented participation in the machination, neither Gambuzzi nor Caporusso was jailed—a commentary, perhaps, on their slight stature as dangerous subversives in the eyes of the local police. The whole affair proved, beyond a shadow of doubt, that both agitators were still most unclear about the difference between socialist and Mazzinian objectives.[42]

Bakunin, to whom these "deviations" had become a familiar burden, suggested to his chief agent in Italy that political insurrections and patriotic conspiracies be left to those "who do not understand" socialist principles (sic)! Still, he resigned himself to further relapses by Gambuzzi: "If, after having conscientiously and deliberately reflected, you decide it is necessary to undertake [an insurrection] of any kind, tell yourself clearly that it will not succeed if you base it only on the [bourgeoisie] and if you do not, above all, have [the welfare of the people] as its object." [43]

[40] "Desolating" was Bakunin's description of the new society's program. Letter to Gambuzzi, Feb. 11, 1869, Nettlau, B.I.I., p. 157.

[41] For details of this plot, Romano, Storia, I, 316-23.

[42] Some of the Neapolitan Mazzinian leaders were just as confused. See the comparison made by Romano between an article in L'Italia Nuova (Mazzinian journal of Naples) and La Situazione No. 2, in Storia, I, 324-25.

[43] Nettlau, B.I.I., p. 158. In the fall of 1869, Friscia, too, was among those who, by Bakunin's standards, did not understand socialist principles, for he was involved, according to the police, with the Mazzinians and the Party of Action in preparing the armed occupation of the Pontifical State. Cerrito, "Saverio Friscia," p. 471.

Whether the result of Bakunin's proddings or of Gambuzzi's temporary disillusionment with the most recent failure of republican conspiracy, the Neapolitan section began to assume some of its responsibilities as the "provisional center" of the International in Italy. In May, 1869, the group issued a manifesto to Italian workers, one of the first public evidences of the I.W.A. in the peninsula:

> We have united in the number of twelve hundred Neapolitan workers to form the Neapolitan section of the International. . . . Brothers of the other provinces of Italy, come and augment our ranks. Let us unite with our brothers of the entire world . . . through the pact of the International. . . . So long as we remain divided or poorly associated, we shall not conquer. It alone is capable of improving our economic and moral conditions, it alone can emancipate us once and for all from the power of the privileged classes. . . . Do not delay, therefore, we await your adherence with ardent impatience. Will you remain deaf to our appeal? We do not believe so.[44]

Did this promising start reflect the influence of Bakunin? Not at all. The Russian, anticipating the need of personal support for his forthcoming polemic with the Marxist faction on the General Council, pleaded with Gambuzzi to drum up Italian representatives to attend the fourth I.W.A. congress, to be held in Basel on September 6-12, 1869:

> It is absolutely necessary that your sections send their delegates. It would be highly important . . . that you yourself come, with [Fanelli] if it is possible, unless he is definitely dead to us. . . . It is important that as many Italians as possible come—and all good ones, our men. It is absolutely necessary that one of your sections of the [I.W.A.], not of the Alliance, name me as their delegate. . . . How many [sections] have you? Only one? The smallest section can send a delegate, even if [it] is composed of only 20, of 10 members. In case you can improvise one: any workers' association, even if previously constituted, provided it declares its adherence to the Statutes of the International and sends 10 cents for each member, is legally a section of the International. . . . Do well and as soon as possible—time presses. I have waited too long for a slightly detailed statistic on your sections of the International and on your group of the Alliance.[45]

Aside from proving that the Neapolitan section of the International had no direct relations with Bakunin in mid-1869, the document attests to

[44] Rosselli, *Mazzini e Bakounine*, pp. 259-60.
[45] Nettlau, *B.I.I.*, pp. 162-63.

Bakunin's belief in the existence of a Neapolitan "section" of his Alliance, an inner circle functioning on the basis of the Russian's libertarian program. The latter assumption corresponded, actually, more to Bakunin's desires than to the facts. On the membership rolls of the Geneva section of the Alliance were the names of several Italians recommended by Gambuzzi and Friscia as trustworthy brothers in the secret network: Friscia had nominated Calogero Cienio of Sicily; Gambuzzi had sponsored several Neapolitan democrats: Luigi Chiapparo, Raffaele Mileti, Attanasio Dramis, Giuseppe Tivoli, Carmelo Palladino, Giuseppe Bramante, and Stefano Caporusso. Friscia, Gambuzzi, and Fanelli were inscribed on the Geneva list as "founders" of the local Alliance.[46] Since all, save Friscia and Cienio, were normally resident in Naples, this group apparently constituted the "Alliance section" mentioned by Bakunin. Yet, as of the summer of 1869, only the names of Gambuzzi, Caporusso, and Friscia appear in the record of socialist activity in the *Mezzogiorno*. Such activity, furthermore, seems to have been but tenuously associated, at most, with Bakunin. For all practical purposes, the Russian's influence in the peninsula was limited to three men, two of whom, so far as is known, were not even in direct contact with Bakunin, while the third, Gambuzzi, pursued a course of action that reflected little concern for either Bakunin or the program of the secret Alliance.

At the Congress of Basel, Bakunin had a mandate from a mechanics' society in Naples, contrived for him by Gambuzzi, but in his first test of strength with the Marxist faction, the Russian had but one Italian among his supporters, Caporusso, Italy's sole representative at the congress. Neither Gambuzzi, Friscia, nor Fanelli had responded to the Russian's bugle call to the imminent war on Marx and his friends.[47] As for Caporusso, Bakunin had at least the consolation of seeing him vote the straight Bakuninist line on every resolution. Otherwise, Caporusso's personal intervention at the congress was of little moment.[48]

On November 5, 1869, the Neapolitan section brought out its long heralded official newspaper, *L'Eguaglianza* ("Equality"), edited by one Michelangelo Statuti, an ex-cleric and relative of Caporusso. Despite its announced intention of concerning itself exclusively with "the cause of labor and the economic, social, and political interests of the working class," the paper was socialist only in name. Its editor was convinced, for example, that strikes had the sole merit of developing a spirit of solidarity

[46] Nettlau. *B.I.I.*, p. 164.

[47] Fanelli had a mandate from "some workers' associations of Florence," but, because of illness, did not go to Basel. Nettlau, *B.I.I.*, p. 165; Rosselli, *Mazzini e Bakounine*, p. 262.

[48] For the Congress proceedings, *Verhandlungen des IV Kongresses des Internationalen Arbeiterbundes in Basel* (Basel, 1869).

among the workers.[49] From the socialist point of view, the paper's suppression by the police in February 1870 was no great loss.

With no help from *L'Eguaglianza,* the Neapolitan section made rapid strides numerically. Caporusso told the Basel Congress in September that its membership was six hundred. In mid-November, a strike by some leather workers belonging to the section was settled to the satisfaction of both employer and strikers by the intervention of the section's leadership. Membership immediately increased in the wake of this impressive performance, and by early 1870 a strength of 3,710 dues-paying members was noted by the attentive local police.[50] At Castellamare di Stabia, the huge shipbuilding center just outside Naples, another section soon appeared and within a matter of weeks counted five hundred members. By this time, too, Saverio Friscia's isolated activity in Sicily had apparently produced four I.W.A. sections in Sciacca, Girgenti, Caltanissetta, and Catania.[51]

However modest these beginnings of a socialist-oriented workers' movement, in agrarian Italy they provoked the prefect of Naples into the conviction that it was his duty to "make every effort to find the legal way to break them up and put the protagonists to flight."[52] The opportunity came early in February, 1870, when another leather workers' strike involved the local I.W.A. section in an active supporting role in connection with the creation of a resistance fund to sustain the strikers' families. Because the section was "threatening to become a powerful instrument in the hands of political agitators" (in the words of the prefect), the police arrested Caporusso, Gambuzzi, and three other ringleaders. All were jailed for a month, except Gambuzzi, who, "though he had been the real inspirer and organizer of the international society, was able to maneuver in such a way as to make all the legal responsibility fall on Caporusso" and the other arrestees.[53]

Since the police could not legally suppress the section itself, its vice-president, the carpenter Cristiano Tucci, was persuaded—and/or paid?—to reorganize the group, excluding all who were not "honest workers, alien to politics." To facilitate his collaborator's task the prefect induced the mayor of Naples to grant the section the use of a former convent for

[49] On *L'Eguaglianza,* Robert Michels, *Il proletariato e la borghesia nel movimento socialista italiano* (Turin, 1908), pp. 30-32; Romano, *Storia,* I, 329-30; Rosselli, *Mazzini e Bakounine,* p. 266.

[50] Romano, *Storia,* I, 330-32; Nettlau, *Errico Malatesta,* p. 47.

[51] So reported by Cerrito ("Saverio Friscia," p. 470), but his sources, Rosselli (*Mazzini e Bakounine,* pp. 221, 267), Nettlau (*B.I.I.,* p. 156) and Domanico (*L'Internazionale,* p. 114), agree on neither the sections involved nor the dates of their origin.

[52] Romano, *Storia,* I, 331-32.

[53] Rosselli, *Mazzini e Bakounine,* pp. 268-69.

the meeting called to elect Tucci to the presidency. Not at all deceived, the members on July 10, 1870, expelled him as a spy, traitor "and worse," elected Antonio Giustiniani as their head. Caporusso, "the model workingman," shared Tucci's fate, condemned for slander and highly illicit forays into the resistance fund for which he had so vigorously solicited contributions to the support of strikers' families.[54]

CONCLUSION

By the outbreak of the Franco-Prussian War, which put the capstone on the process of Italian unity, neither Marx nor Bakunin had reason for optimism about the progress of socialism in the peninsula. No serious socialist organization existed. The Neapolitan section was completely demoralized;[55] the few sections in Sicily had contacts with neither Bakunin nor the London General Council, and to all appearances, Friscia's personal, but necessarily sporadic, ministrations were all that kept them going.[56] On an ideological level, there was no appreciable trace of Bakuninist penetration and certainly none of Marxian socialism. For all practical purposes, the generic manifestations of a socialist tendency appearing in Lo Savio's Il Proletario and the Liberty and Justice Association had been isolated and unfruitful phenomena. With respect to the split shaping up between Marxist and Bakuninist factions in the International, there was certainly no awareness among Italian democrats of the doctrinal issues involved, since the first external expression of this conflict had but recently appeared at the Congress of Basel, and the struggle did not reach clearly defined proportions until a year later.[57] Bakunin, nonetheless, was to affront the fray in the Italian theater with the advantage of having established himself, in the eyes of socialist militants like Friscia, Gambuzzi, and Fanelli, as the internationally recognized champion of a libertarian socialism appearing far more relevant to the solution of Italian social problems than what was soon to be termed the "authoritarian" socialism of Marx and the General Council.

[54] Romano, Storia, I, 334-36; Rosselli, Mazzini e Bakounine, pp. 269-70, note 2.

[55] Bakunin to Gambuzzi, July 4, 1870: "Is there still a section in Naples? In what condition is it? Might it have fallen into the hands of intriguers? . . . But, in the name of Heaven, don't sleep." Nettlau, B.I.I., p. 172. Cf., also, Cafiero's letter to Engels, June 28, 1871, ibid., pp. 173, 220-21.

[56] Friscia was still a member of the Chamber of Deputies and in no position to give constant attention to these sections.

[57] On Feb. 10, 1870, Marx decided on open war against the Bakuninists. "The armistice is now finished between us, for he knows that on the occasion of the recent Geneva events [i.e., the creation of the Bakuninist Alliance] I vigorously attacked and denounced him." Briefwechsel, IV, 275. On Mar. 28, Marx laid down the first barrage in his famous Confidentielle Mittheilung to Ludwig Kügelmann, warning the German socialists against Bakunin's "counterrevolutionary" intrigues and maneuvers. It is reproduced by Guillaume, I.D.S., I, 292-98, and was published first by Die Neue Zeit, July 12, 1902.

As of 1870, Mazzinianism, not the Marx-Bakunin polemic, remained the primary obstacle in the path of Italian socialism. So long as the question of Italian unity remained open, so long as Mazzini and Garibaldi could arouse patriotic fervor in Italian republicans by promising and scheming for the acquisition of Rome in the name of the Italian popular republic, the future leaders of Italian socialism would never give themselves wholly to a doctrine holding the completion of political unity to be extraneous and subordinate to subverting capitalism, not only in Italy, but in the world.[58]

This consideration probably played little, if any, part in the orientation of the common worker in Italy, but many workers' societies had, by mid-1870, begun to develop the resistance concept in their relations with employers, a clear preliminary to acceptance of modern socialism's central doctrine, the class struggle. In the event, Mazzini's neglect of the workers' movement, his failure to impose either his republicanism or his social views on the workers' movement, certainly raised no barrier to the penetration of socialist ideology. In this regard Mazzini was coasting, in the spring and summer of 1870, on the strength of his personal prestige —considerable, but not enough to justify his apparent conviction that it made superfluous a social program with direct appeal to the Italian workingman. Socialism was in its infancy in Italy, as Bakunin observed in September 1870,[59] not because—as the Russian claimed—Italian workers were blinded to their own material interests by Mazzini's patriotic and republican propaganda ("they speak of marching on Rome as if the stones of the Colosseum and the Vatican must give them liberty, well-being, and bread"), but because nothing was offered them other than Mazzini's republican program, which, with its merely incidental promise of material improvement, could not achieve passionate adherence among the masses. On the eve of the monarchy's completion of national unity, Mazzini's appeals to the workers still pretended that social injustice and a republic are mutually exclusive terms.[60]

As the program of the anticonstitutional Left, Mazzinianism was in a crisis on the verge of resolution, a crisis in part encouraged by the intransigence of Mazzini's social doctrine and political program, in part provoked by the impact of materialism, now reaching flood tide among the

---

[58] True to form, Gambuzzi wanted to enlist with Garibaldi in the French Republic's war against the Prussians. Bakunin, of course, urged him to remain in Italy. "If we succeed, you shall have much to do in your country, and we shall give you all the necessary means to act." Letter to Gambuzzi, Oct. 15, 1870, Nettlau, *B.I.I.*, pp. 187-88.

[59] *Oeuvres*, IV, 32-37; Nettlau, *B.I.I.*, p. 184.

[60] See his appeal of May, 1870, for popular participation in the movement for a republic, in *L'Iniziativa* (Rome, 1887); *S.E.I.*, XCII, 3-29. See also, "Ai Republicani d'Italia," *ibid.*, XCII, 66.

petty bourgeois intellectuals, whose loyalty Mazzini needed to give substance to his dream. Ironically enough, international socialism, such a minor factor in bringing matters to a head, was to emerge as the chief beneficiary. This, in turn, was due neither to Bakunin and his handful of radical friends in the peninsula nor to the even less influential London General Council, but, as had happened many times before in crucial moments of the *Risorgimento,* to the influence of external events—in this case, the Paris Commune. With justice, Andrea Costa, the patron saint of modern Italian socialism, could say from the vantage point of several years later: "Before the Commune of Paris . . . the International did not exist in Italy."[61]

[61] Association Internationale des Travailleurs, *Compte-rendu officiel du Sixième Congrès Général de l'Association Internationale des Travailleurs, tenu à Génève du 1ᵉʳ au 6 septembre 1873* (Locle, 1874), p. 32.

VII

Mazzini and the Paris Commune (March to August 1871)

THE COMMUNE'S INITIAL IMPACT ON ITALIAN RADICAL REPUBLICANS

GIUSEPPE MAZZINI seemed to be recognizing that his work was done when, as a prisoner in the fortress of Gaeta in the fall of 1870, he penned this comment on the Savoyard monarchy's completion of Italian unity by the capture of Rome: "And Italy, my Italy, the Italy as I preached it? The Italy of our dreams? Italy, the great, the beautiful, the moral Italy of my soul? . . . I believed I had evoked the soul of Italy and I see only its cadaver in front of me." [1] Even the final step in the unification of the fatherland had been denied Mazzini and the "popular initiative" on which he had rested his hopes. For decades Mazzinian republicanism had offered itself as the most efficient instrument for making Italy, yet in September 1870, the Italian army finished the task at the cost of 40 dead, 150 wounded and the angry but ineffectual denunciations of Pius IX. To all appearances, the fortunes of the Party of Action were irretrievably lost.

Yet Mazzini, immediately after his release from Gaeta, once more laid plans for republican agitation, unconvinced that the loss of the national unity plank in his program had seriously undermined his crusade for a republic. [2] In the event, he was spared disillusionment on this score by a completely unforeseen development, the violent episode of the Paris Commune. The reaction of the Italian republican Left to the events in

---

[1] S.E.I., XC, 49. Yet, "Mazzini had won: very far from his ideals and predispositions in so many respects, the Italy that had arisen was . . . his Italy, one bound together in a single organism and not federally articulated." Federico Chabod, *Storia della politica estera italiana dal 1870 al 1896*, I, *Le Premesse* (Bari: Laterza, 1951), 209.

[2] See his letter to Giannelli, Oct. 10, 1870, in Giannelli, *Cenni autobiografici*, p. 545; and Mazzini's famous circular, "To My Republican Brothers," Nov. 5, 1870, S.E.I., XCII, 79.

Paris between March 18 and May 25, 1871, completely altered, to Mazzini's disadvantage, the terms of his struggle for an Italian republic. Not the monarchy's capture of Rome, but open class warfare in Paris, with all its implications for the European social order, brought the Mazzinian party into the crisis from which it never recovered.

The interest of the Italian public in the Franco-Prussian War went beyond the capture of Rome on September 20. Since Napoleon III, in concluding the September Convention of 1864, had guaranteed papal possession of Rome, the Italians had regarded the French government as a prime obstacle in the path of unification. On September 6, 1870, only two weeks before Rome fell to Victor Emmanuel's *bersaglieri*, Jules Favre, head of the French provisional government in Paris, assured the Italian ambassador that the fall of the Second Empire had nullified the September Convention,[3] but even after Italian troops entered the Eternal City, French republicans appeared almost as upset by the red-white-green tricolor over the city as Louis Napoleon would have been. Whether the new French Republic would try restoring the Pope's temporal position appeared to depend on the outcome of its conflict with Prussia.

Of more immediate interest to the great mass of Italians was Garibaldi's participation in the war against the Germans.[4] The warrior hero led an army of forty thousand men, including hundreds of Italian volunteers, through a mid-winter campaign in the Vosges Mountains, featuring a military action at Dijon which, though entirely ineffectual, lived up to the audacity of his earlier enterprises. Subsequently elected a deputy to the Bordeaux Assembly by four of France's *départements*, he was denied his seat by this body on the grounds that he had not renounced his Italian citizenship. After the Franco-Prussian armistice, the Savoyard monarchy intensified the interest—and disgust—of Italians by agreeing to the Bordeaux government's proposal that Italian volunteers who had fought under Garibaldi's command be treated as criminals, deserving of an amnesty, of course, but nonetheless guilty of the "crime" of fighting abroad without an authorization![5]

Against this backdrop, the advent of the Paris Commune on March 18, 1871, suddenly threw French affairs into an entirely new focus for Italians of all classes. In some, the war of class against class aroused horror and disgust, in others, a keen sympathy for the Communards, depending mostly on the social status of the individual observer. Reactionaries,

[3] Cilibrizzi, *Storia parlamentare, politica e diplomatica d'Italia*, I, 590.

[4] For Garibaldi's role in the Franco-Prussian War, see Ph. J. Bordone, *Garibaldi et l'armée des Vosges* (Paris, 1871). For that of the Italian volunteers, Jessie White Mario, *I Garibaldini in Francia* (Rome, 1871).

[5] Valiani, *Storia del movimento socialista*, I, 190.

Moderates, the constitutional Left, republicans, and socialists agreed on one thing alone: that the future of western civilization was hinged on the outcome of the Paris Commune's experiment with popular government. All parties accepted the fiction that the Commune was a true socialist enterprise engineered by the International Workingmen's Association.[6] The variety of ideological tendencies represented by the Commune's leadership was lost on the Italian press and its readers; the full spectrum of political opinion on the French Left, from Jacobinism, through social democracy and revolutionary socialism, to anarchism, was seen as a cohesive manifestation of but one power: the First International. Any sober analysis of the Commune's real meaning by either Right or Left was precluded by the terror aroused in the middle and upper classes and the social radicals' appreciation of this effect.

The conservative press unanimously indicted the Communards as madmen, devoid of love of *patria,* intent on overthrowing the social order for selfish ends. The Red Terror today grips France; tomorrow it will be Italy's turn.[7] Writing in *Nuova Antologia,* Ruggiero Bonghi was scandalized by the appearance of a "new fact": that instead of two nations going to war to make themselves more powerful and vigorous, "one of the social classes [is] attempting, for its own profit, to break down the natural hierarchy of all and, by taking from the other [classes] the post that they occupied for centuries, it is seeking to usurp it for itself." [8] Catholic organs, disgruntled by the recent destruction of the papacy's temporal power, adopted an apocalyptic tone. France was undergoing the scourge of God for having lacked faith, for harboring atheistic and masonic tendencies. Italy, too, must soon pay for offending God in taking Rome, for its anticlericalism. Unable to resist the opportunity to slap the despoilers of the church, a writer for *Civiltà Cattolica* even tried to establish an identity between local liberals and socialism by arguing that the Communards were the logical offspring of liberalism's poisonous teachings.[9] For their part, the constitutional democratic papers drew

[6] Marx and the I.W.A.'s General Council naturally stressed the notion that the Commune was a "proletarian revolution." Karl Marx and Friedrich Engels, *Il Partito e l'Internazionale,* tr. by Palmiro Togliatti (Rome: Ediz. Rinascita, 1948), pp. 169, 181, 207-08.

[7] The government "must . . . take preventive measures with an energetic hand if it does not want some of our large cities to become . . . a pallid imitation of the Parisian Commune." *La Perseveranza* (Milan), Apr. 26, 1871. For more diffuse treatments of the Italian press reaction to the Commune, see Rosselli, *Mazzini e Bakounine,* pp. 279-98; Romano, *Storia,* II, 33-60.

[8] "Rassegna Politica," XVIII, Fasc. 6 (June 1, 1871), 468 ff. His three articles against the Commune, written for the Apr. 1, May 1, and June 1, 1871, issues of *Nuova Antologia,* are contained in his *Nove anni di storia di Europa nel commento d'un italiano, 1866-1874,* a cura di Maria Sandirocco (Milan: Garzanti, 1938-42), II, 465-78, 479-89, 491-501.

[9] Series VIII, Vol. II (Apr. 22, 1871), 257 ff.

the moral that more attention would have to be given to the needs of the working classes. The moderate republican press found itself in the uncomfortable necessity of deploring the intemperance of the Commune while denying it as a trait implicit in republicanism. Excommunication of the socialists had to accompany praise for what were considered the nobler aspects of the Parisian experiment.[10] Given the almost universal impression that the Commune was a socialist enterprise, the position smelled of casuistry.

No such dilemma confronted the radical republicans. Though none dared extoll the profligacies of the beleaguered Communards, papers like the *Gazzettino Rosa* of Milan (directed by Achille Bizzoni,[11] a veteran of the Vosges campaign), *La Favilla* of Mantua, *Il Presente* of Parma, *Il Romagnolo* of Ravenna, and *La Plebe* of Lodi, frankly hailed the Commune as the harbinger of European democracy and damned the government of Thiers.[12] The Paris revolutionaries were represented as heroes in a battle against foreign oppression and internal reaction, brothers in the universal struggle for true democracy. From the republican International Democratic Society of Florence, on April 12, went an "Address to the Citizens of the Commune of Paris,"[13] expressing the warmest sympathy:

> Paris . . . is fighting, against the egotism of the earth's privileged, the great battle for liberty and the emancipation of the proletariat. . . . Whether you are conquered or victorious, yours . . . will be the banner of the future. . . . Your principle of social revolution will soon be . . . the regulating principle of modern societies.

Two of the six signers of the address, Luigi Castellazzo and Ettore Socci, had but recently returned from the fighting in the Vosges.

In Milan *Il Gazzettino Rosa* led the pro-Commune chorus. The writing corps of this newspaper was composed of militant young Garibaldians, described many years later as "a flying squadron of pioneers who, having divided in two the celebrated formula of *God and People,* had appropriated for their own use and consumption only the second part and, as for the first, disinterested themselves completely."[14] On receiving the

[10] Rosselli, *Mazzini e Bakounine,* pp. 282-84.

[11] On Bizzoni, see Francesco Giarelli, *Vent'anni di giornalismo* (*1868-1888*) (Codogno, 1896), pp. 71 ff. He, too, was a veteran of Garibaldi's campaigns in the Trentino (1866) and the Agro Romano (1867).

[12] For representative articles, see *La Plebe,* Apr. 18, 20; *Il Romagnolo,* Mar. 29; *La Favilla,* Apr. 28, 1871.

[13] *La Favilla* (Mantua), Apr. 18; *Il Gazzettino Rosa,* Apr. 22, 1871.

[14] Francesco Giarelli's description, in Paolo Barduzzi, *ed., Felice Cavallotti; nella vita, nella politica, nell'arte* (Milan, Palermo, 1898), pp. 34-35.

first news of the Paris insurrection, the *Gazzettino Rosa* hailed "with profound joy the courageous and very noble initiative of generous Paris." Vincenzo Pezza, under the pen name of *Burbero*, warned Italy's privileged that the same revolutionary force inspiring the Communards was also operative among the common people of Italy, "the unknown X." The question of liberty against priests, privilege and superstition now being debated and acted upon in Paris must sooner or later come up for consideration in Italy.[15] By April 18, Pezza was seeing the French situation in terms of a struggle between the forces of Light and Darkness, Good and Evil:

> Between the Commune of Paris and the Versailles Assembly there is as much distance as there is between liberty and despotism, between love of fatherland and lust for power, between generosity and egotism, between the democratic sentiment of fraternity and the instinct of usurpation and the ferocious tyranny of privilege, between the might of right and the right of might, between courage and cowardice, between love and hate, between the heart and the mind.

As the encircling forces of MacMahon slowly strangled the Paris Commune, Bizzoni, now getting into the fray, admitted the hopelessness of resistance but warned that "a terrible tomorrow awaits us." The "iniquitous work" of the "parricides who intrigue with the foreigner and enlist his arm to plunge the assassin's sword into the breast of the fatherland" will soon be dealt with by "the avenging Nemesis of the people." Then the conscience of mankind "will salute with joy the triumph of true democracy." [16]

With the bloody extirpation of the Commune late in May, the Italian leftist press interpreted the victory of the French bourgeoisie, not as the reaction's final triumph, but as the beginning of a new and universal struggle against human inequality. The social republic falls, wrote Enrico Bignami in *La Plebe*, only to arise again, stronger and holier. The idea survives and spreads. "The disaster of Paris is the misfortune of democracy all over the world." But Paris would be avenged: "after the injustice of kings, the justice of the peoples." [17] From Milan, Bizzoni, too, wrote of retribution: "the time of sentimental and poetic policy is past; now that of the policy of compensation has come; the example of poor France serves us as a lesson and we shall know how to profit from it." [18] *Il*

---

[15] Mar. 21, Apr. 1, 14, 1871.
[16] *Il Gazzettino Rosa*, May 20, 1871.
[17] Issue of May 23, 1871; *cf.*, also, the issues of May 27, 31, 1871.
[18] *Il Gazzettino Rosa*, May 27, 1871. See, also, Bizzoni's editorial in the May 20, 1871, issue.

Romagnolo inferred a lesson for the Party of Action: "The Commune has not fallen: it is in the mind and heart of the proletariat of all Europe . . . The republican party of Italy, an essentially political party, today feels for the first time the need of broadening the confines within which it narrowly progressed and hopes to become a scientific party." [19] For Antonio Riggio, editor of Sicily's *L'Eguaglianza,* the Commune was but the prelude to universal social revolution:

> What must be, shall be; . . . The horrors of the Versaillese do not frighten us; the mourning of the Parisians, if it wrenches our soul, does not discomfort us. The good will succor the victims, the strong will look after avenging them. What must be, shall be. The prodigies of the Commune in the meantime have made inevitable and urgent the solution of the social problem.[20]

In the early summer of 1871 sentiments such as these, accompanied by declarations of solidarity with the victims of French republican proscription, by renewed affirmations of anticlericalism by rapidly multiplying freethinking societies, expressed the emotional impact of the life and death of the Paris Commune on radical republican circles. Perhaps the phenomenon was partly due to Italian republicans' reticence to give monarchists and clericals the satisfaction of seeing them discomfited by the failure of the French experiment they had so ardently espoused, but the fundamental determinant was the interpretation of the Commune, not so much as a practical formula of immediate action, but as a forceful argument for giving social revolutionary content to a republican movement aspiring to mass support. Coming at the precise moment when Italian republicans were thoroughly disillusioned by the monarchical conclusion of the *Risorgimento,* the novelty of the revolutionary orientation so dramatically affirmed by the Commune could not fail to have a decisive impact on these men. The change in the thinking of many was probably epitomized by the articles of the Lodi physician, Dr. Carlo Arrigoni, in the columns of *Il Gazzettino Rosa.* Writing under the *nom de plume* of *Semplicione,* Arrigoni on March 19 was certain that Italian republicans abhorred "communist utopias" as deviations from the struggle for the republic, but on June 8 he lamented that Mazzini and Victor Hugo, in opposing the Commune, had proved themselves incapable of understanding the conditions that make popular revolution necessary. "What we expect, and what a few but resolute people will perhaps very soon initiate, is internal, economic and social revolution."

Implicit in this point of view was a denial of Mazzini's thesis that social change must come gradually, pacifically and without setting class

[19] Issue of June 12, 1871.
[20] Issue of July 16, 1871.

against class, yet Vincenzo Pezza, eloquent admirer of the Commune as a noble attempt to "redeem labor from the tyranny of capital," insisted that the Italian revolution could only be political[21] and apparently thought restating Mazzini's social objectives in sufficiently militant language eliminated the discordance between extreme methods and moderate goals:

> We do not want to destroy property, we even want to respect it. We do not want material leveling, we want moral leveling. We want the emancipation of labor, not the abolition of labor. We want to demand rights, not to destroy duty. . . .
>
> We want the participation of labor in capital. We want labor equitably paid. We want the hindrances to intelligence removed and the way paved to social betterment.
>
> We want a new order of things that sanctions the rights of each and protects them with the fulfillment of the duties of all. We want a society where being good patriots is not a cause for persecution, where being an honest citizen is not a disgrace.
>
> We want a government which, by continuously retempering itself in the popular will, feels the nobility and responsibility of its mission: be it educational in essence, be it a code of morality and a tribunal of justice. We want human dignity upheld, the generous instincts still in the people encouraged. We want a society and a government in which a man is proud of himself and his qualities as a citizen.[22]

Such evidences of loyalty to Mazzini's social program could not long endure in a generation of young republicans denied "the stimulating nourishment of the conspiracies and expeditions of volunteers for the completion of National Unity, that nourishment which . . . educated it to high aspirations and noble works." [23] For these frustrated young intellectuals, international socialism, the presumed sponsor of the strikingly novel insurrection of the Parisians, promised a cause worthy of dedicated effort, social justice. To them, Mazzini's political program was hopelessly compromised by the monarchy's completion of unity, his social program by its lack of militancy. Even his religious aspirations seemed irrelevant —if not reactionary—to youths being fed a diet of anticlericalism and atheism by the freethinking societies.[24] Andrea Costa, himself one of the

---

[21] *Il Gazzettino Rosa*, May 14, 1871.

[22] *Ibid.*, June 12, 1871.

[23] Thus a witness to the crisis, Osvaldo Gnocchi-Viani, *Ricordi d'un internazionalista*, p. 119.

[24] Mazzini "became obdurate on the religious question, without realizing that on that path, in those years, no one would have followed him, and he did not understand that there was something good and exploitable, even for idealistic ends,

socialist recruits of that year of travail among Italian republican youth, described its spiritual crisis in these words:

> By raging against the fallen Commune and by attributing the fall of France mostly to materialistic theories, Mazzini . . . alienated the most ardent and generous of youth, grown up on the new science. It was on the corpse of the Commune, fecund in its ruins, that the struggle was engaged between the old spirit and the new: and it was from the blood of the massacred Communards that the omens were drawn.
>
> Remember '71 and '72? How we fearfully waited for the news from Paris—how we sought the statutes of that potent *International Association*—how we anxiously read what the very newspapers of the adversaries wrote about it? The rapidity with which the new spirit was propagated in Italy was marvellous. . . . We threw ourselves into the movement, compelled much more by the desire to break with a past that oppressed us and did not correspond . . . to our aspirations than by conscious reflection on what we wanted. We felt that the future was there: time would determine by which ideas we would be inspired.[25]

THE MAZZINIAN CRITIQUE

Had the Commune occurred fifteen years earlier, Mazzini's indictment of it would have been no less severe than the diatribes he loosed against it in 1871, but the effect on young republicans would have been far different. When the civil war broke out in Paris, Italian republican youth, accustomed to materialist propaganda, faced with the *fait accompli* of monarchist unification, spurred by a desire "to break with the past," was in no mood to accept criticism of a phenomenon that appeared to open new prospects for revolutionary action. And though, as Costa observed, there was little "conscious reflection on what we wanted," Mazzini's stand in the summer of 1871 seemed both an anachronism and an attempt to prejudice, if not block, the search for a new *Weltanschauung*. The bitter chagrin of radical republicans was the more intense because Mazzini, in the polemic waged in his newly created organ, *La Roma del Popolo*,[26] moved from clear hostility toward the bourgeois government of the French republic and neutrality toward the Commune to thundering de-

---

in that wave of materialism that made him furious and, at times, unjust . . ." Carlo Morandi, *La Sinistra al potere e altri saggi* (Florence: Barbera, 1944), p. 292.

[25] *Bagliori di socialismo. Cenni storici* (Florence, 1900), pp. 7-8.

[26] The first issue of this weekly newspaper, projected in late Nov., 1870 (Giannelli, *Cenni autobiografici*, p. 546) appeared on Mar. 1, 1871, under the direction of Giuseppe Petroni, close friend of Mazzini and survivor of almost two decades in papal prisons (Aug. 1853—Sept. 1870). For the program of *La Roma del Popolo*, see *S.E.I.*, XCII, 85-115, "Agli Italiani."

nunciations of the latter and a tacit alliance with the forces of conservatism. Actually, the shift mirrored neither a betrayal of his own principles nor uncertainty about his own criteria of judgment; it simply meant that Mazzini only gradually recognized that the Commune, in its deeds and intentions, epitomized the forces of materialism he had decried from the very beginning of his decades-long apostolate. But this made the end result no more palatable to radical republicans.

In the first of his articles dealing directly with the events in Paris,[27] Mazzini plastered the federalism of the Commune's program as a gross immorality. Broadly applied, it promised "exaggerations of the federalist spirit, fatal to any moral unity, collective action, everything that makes a Nation great and helpful to Humanity." The fault of provoking the insurrection, however, lay with the Versailles Assembly: it had voted the dismemberment of France; it had given executive power to Adolphe Thiers, who reflected the essential ideas of Bonapartism and the pretensions of the Orleanists; it had retained Louis Napoleon's generals; it had refused to meet in republican-oriented Paris. If the more intelligent men of proved republican faith had taken over the direction of the Paris Central Committee from the "unknowns," the Commune could have been kept on the right path; the civil war, especially tragic in the face of foreign invasion, would have been avoided.

Italy's official press need not fear similar disturbances in the peninsula,

> . . . where the ascendent movement of the working class is developing miraculously, unalterably temperate and pacific. Where the men of labor have spilled no blood other than their own in the cause of the *Patria's* Independence and Unity? Where the sectarian socialist systems of France and elsewhere have found no visible followers? Where the Apostolate of the [workers'] Associations bases all its acts on the holy idea of Duty and says nothing . . . of the *right* that arises from the fulfillment of that Duty? Where the agitations, if there were agitations among the Workers, were always motivated by the sense of violated Italian honor and the betrayal of the greatness of the Fatherland, never by the improvement of their own economic condition? . . . The artisans of our cities, miserable and afflicted as they often are, do not pass to thoughts of violence or unjust changes. . . . Lissa, Custoza, irritate their minds much more than the frequent imbalance between wages and the necessities of life; the servile policy followed by our ministers and the transactions

---

[27] "The Artisan Classes," *La Roma del Popolo*, Apr. 12, 19, 1871; S.E.I., XCII, 173-89. The Mar. 19, 1871, program of the Commune is reproduced in *La Favilla*, Apr. 28, 1871.

with the Pope that profane Rome arouse more anger in them than the unfair division of a production that is impossible without them.

The "deviations and exaggerations" in France are the fruit of the indifference of the comfortable classes and their refusal to share the benefits of the political and economic program the common people had helped them achieve. "Abandoned and disillusioned, the artisan class [of Paris] followed whichever agitators, republican or dictatorial, offered it the broadest hopes and promises." In Italy growing proletarian strength threatens no other classes; in fact, emancipation of the Italian worker "will give . . . a new element of life to the moral progress of the effete generations, a new guarantee of strength to our political development, a new impulse to production."

In his article of April 26, "The Commune of France," Mazzini still blamed the Paris insurrection on the National Assembly and admitted that the Communard movement, in deriving from a just claim, would leave a praiseworthy legacy to the future: "the lesson of how a people *can*, even alone and without the prestige of illustrious names, raise and order itself." But since the Paris uprising was inopportune, without a previously fixed program, corrupted by "a purely negative element educated by the old sectarian socialism," forsaken by brilliant French republican leaders, it found itself enmeshed in the consequences of "dominating materialism" and adopted a program which, if applied to the whole of France, would take the country back to the Middle Ages and remove all hopes of resurrection.

The program to which Mazzini referred was a statement by the government of the Commune in early April: "France will no longer be Empire or Republic, one and indivisible: it will form a federation, not of little States or provinces, but of *free cities* bound together only to the extent that they concede the most absolute decentralization and local government." [28] That program, wrote Mazzini, is derived from "the materialist system" that erects the individual as a source of all sovereignty. The practical consequences could never be condoned by the Apostle of Nationality:

> Politically, that system leads to the indefinite dismemberment of *authority*, to the exclusive recognition of sovereignty in the smallest local collective entity; and therefore to the absolute negation of the Nation and to the absurd proposition that the Commune, more than the Nation, has the secret, the inspiration of the national life and right. . . . [Such a league of] inde-

[28] *Journal officiel de la Comune,* as cited by S.E.I., XCII, 98. *Cf.,* also, *La Perseveranza,* Apr. 26, 1871.

pendent and sovereign Communes would destroy everything that makes the national idea sacred.

Now Mazzini was less certain that Italian republicans were immune to the contagion of the Commune. Italians were too prone to sympathize with every protest, too impressed by the courage with which the Communards defended their movement, too imitative of other people, too ready to confuse "a concept of local liberty . . . with the concept that must . . . guide the progressive development of the Nation," too susceptible to dangerous ideas:

> Today there is too much of the rebel in us, too little of the apostle. And the banner of insurrection fascinates us wherever it arises and for whatever reason. We have endured so much from the actual governments that any protest against an existing power assumes for us a semblance of the holy exercise of liberty, of the demand for the right of insurrection against the immobility to which we were condemned for centuries. Every audacious affirmation finds an echo in the minds of our youth, not because it is maturely scrutinized or because it enunciates a hitherto unknown part of the Truth, but because it is audacious: every bold resolution, every flash of exceptional warlike courage in support of that boldness, transforms man into a hero for us.

Praise the Parisians for their republicanism, he counseled his countrymen; salute their quick formation of a popular militia and government; but "deplore and cast out the retrograde and immoral program, . . . fatally chosen by the insurrection."

When he wrote his piece for the May 3 issue of *La Roma del Popolo,* Mazzini had read the April 19 *Manifesto of the Paris Commune,* in which the program of extreme municipal sovereignty was spelled out in terms that prompted Mazzini to detail its dire political, economic, and moral consequences. He still "deplored" the actions of the Commune and "censured" those of the Versailles Assembly, but the former was beginning to appear the gerater threat to the mental health of Italian republicans: "the sacred idea of National Unity" was being weakened among them by their unslaked thirst for liberty, by the scarcity of serious studies, by the "wretched habit of imitating the foreigner," and by the false system of government. "The Republic, as it is understood by the Commune, is not ours."

A series of questions put to Mazzini by a pro-International newspaper in Naples caused him to shift his attack on May 24 to the socialist International. The opinions of the central committee of the I.W.A. in London, wrote Mazzini, err in tending "to separate the social from the political question." The charge, in itself, was an error on Mazzini's part, for he was reading into the official program of the International the doctrine which thus far Bakunin could only hope to make I.W.A. orthodoxy. The Russian and Marx were only beginning to find the kernel of their doctrinal disagreement in the question of whether political action was relevant to resolving the social question. Marx, the effective boss of the I.W.A.'s governing body, was no protagonist, of course, of the "error" Mazzini laid at the door of the General Council.[29]

The same unfamiliarity with official I.W.A. doctrine is apparent in Mazzini's charge that the men of the General Council were attempting "to eliminate from the minds of the men of Labor the sacred idea of God, . . . *Patria*, . . . educative Authority." Mazzini hit his intended mark only when he ascribed to the International's leadership the intention of "inaugurating an unhealthy war between *labor* and *capital*." Driven toward "empty and sterile cosmopolitanism, negation, and impotent anger because it was ill founded," the program of the International opposes progress, hinders republican victory in Europe, leads the "good but pliable instincts" of the people into fatal errors, and wastes much energy in vain endeavors that might actually improve the condition of the artisan classes if properly applied. Let those Italians who favor the International join with the Mazzinians "to conquer the indispensable elements for the unity of the Nation: only then, if the conquest does not give the desired fruits, will they have the right to protest."

The violent death of the Commune, the killing of hostages, the burning of public buildings by the Communards, and the equally insensate, savage vengeance meted out by the triumphant forces of the Versailles Assembly shocked Mazzini into writing a lengthy essay for the June issues of *La Roma del Popolo*,[30] in which he traced the cause of those sanguine events all the way back to the materialism of various French philosophers of the Enlightenment. Significantly, he did not transfer the "guilt" of socialism to Marx, but ended his summary of the influences that "perverted" the moral sense of the French with Saint-Simon and Fourier, "petitioning for money" to put their doctrines into practice, and Proudhon, "abolishing

---

[29] Mazzini's notion that the federalism of the Commune and the antipolitical doctrines of Bakunin represented the official I.W.A. program probably derived from his experience with French socialism, encountered in 1848-49 and the following decade. In this sense, his attacks on International socialism in 1871 merely continued his long-standing feud with the only socialist doctrines with which he was really familiar, i.e., those of Proudhon and Blanqui, not of Marx. As the jealous custodians of Internationalist orthodoxy, Marx and Engels were among the first to resent Mazzini's unfounded assumption that Bakuninist libertarianism was the official gospel of the First International, or at least that part of the organization under the direct control and influence of the London General Council. See Engels' letter of Dec. 5, 1871, *La Roma del Popolo*, Dec. 21, 1871; and in *S.E.I.*, XCIII, 176.

[30] June 7, 21, 28, 1871, "Il Comune e l'Assemblea."

God in favor of Force." By inference, the principles of Marx had not really registered on Mazzini's consciousness as the "scientific" application of materialism to social problems.

To Mazzini, materialism was a French phenomenon and the source of French corruption. His alarm at its influence among Italian young people was now visibly augmented. "Today, unfortunately, the tendencies instilled by materialist systems are leading many of our young men into a blind adoration of physical courage, of the *external* fact, unrelated to the origin or the *goal* sought, that threatens to substitute a new *militarism* in the classical style." For the Italian victims of this materialist disorientation, Mazzini had this advice: "Do not recall from foreign examples remembrances of a terror that has defamed liberty or the names of men who have changed the concept of love into a concept of hate and, with this mutation, paved the way to new tyrannies. . . . Put aside France and her false doctrines."

For Mazzini, the glorification of the Paris insurrection by young Italian republicans reflected a corruption, an impoverishment of their ideals, the same loss of a moral sense that had led the Parisian workers to revolt. It followed that Mazzini would never accept the argument of many Italian republicans that the Commune, by focusing the attention of the civilized world on the social question, had in fact inaugurated a new era in which the material needs and hopes of the common man could no longer be regarded as of minor consequence to the continued integrity of bourgeois society. Mazzini had explicitly denied this thesis early in May when he wrote that the program of the Commune *"will not inaugurate a new political era; it is not the end of the old world,* but the ultimate consequence of the ancient principle of *individualism,* the ultimate logical deduction of the materialism of a School that completed its mission with the fall of the first [French] Empire, and it is incapable of initiating a new [world]." [31]

That this increasingly dogmatic rejection of the Commune and all its works was alienating a growing number of his followers mattered little to Mazzini. He was ready to pursue his crusade against the engulfing tide of materialism whatever the cost:

> If, because we are republicans, we . . . have to accept the absurd, retrograde, politically immoral concept of a republic newly founded in Paris . . . , it is better to throw down the pen and remain silent. If, because some youngsters like to deny the entire tradition of Humanity, to call Science the more or less accurate description of organic phenomena and the negation of the cause of those phenomena, to call themselves atheists and

[31] *La Roma del Popolo,* May 3, 1871.

enemies of all religion because they do not believe in the present one, we must not speak of religious philosophy and [if we must] infer the mission and fate of our fatherland from the fortuitous concourse of the atoms or from a certain number of passive combinations of a given quantity of matter, it is better to let chance and matter operate in their wisdom and limit ourselves to registering—and respecting—events.[32]

On July 13 Mazzini returned to his attack on the International and its governing group.[33] In his summary of the "principles promoted by the Chiefs and influential men" of the International under the rubrics of: (1) negation of God, (2) denial of nationality, and (3) hostility toward private property, he again betrayed his unfamiliarity with the explicit positions of the *Inaugural Address* of Marx, the statutes, and the resolutions of the International congresses, for the official doctrines of the I.W.A. included neither atheism, antinationalism, nor a clear-cut rejection of the principle of private property.[34] In judging the weaknesses of the International's organizational pretensions, however, Mazzini's analysis had real prophetic value:

> This Association . . . is directed by a Council, the soul of which is Karl Marx, a German, a man of acute genius, but, like that of Proudhon, dissolvent, of a dominating temperament, jealous of the influence of others, without strong philosophical or religious beliefs and, I fear, moved more by anger, even if just, than by love in his heart. The Council, composed of men belonging to different countries, in which the conditions of the people are different, can have no unity of positive conception of existing evils and possible remedies, but must inevitably conclude . . . in simple negations.
>
> A nucleus of individuals that assumes to govern directly a vast multitude of men, different in nationality, tendencies, political condition, economic interests, and means of action, will finish by not functioning at all or it will have to function tyrannically. . . .
>
> No force is capable of enduring if it is not based on Truth and Justice. The *International* is condemned to be dismembered; and

---

[32] "Il Comune e l'Assemblea."

[33] "Agli Operai Italiani."

[34] Mazzini's intuition of the International's implicit atheism, however, was unerring, even though he did not have the following statement of Engels to document his charge: "As for the religious question, we can not speak of it officially, except when the priests provoke us into doing so, but you will perceive the spirit of atheism in all our publications and, furthermore, we do not admit any society that has the slightest religious allusion in its statutes." Letter to Cafiero, July 28, 1871, Romano, *Storia*, II, 318.

in England, the headquarters of the Center, the dismemberment has already begun.

In an arrangement like that of the [International] true unity can not exist and I know of sections located in lands distant from the Center that are in complete ignorance of its tendencies: they know they belong to a European Association that has as a *goal* the emancipation of the Working classes and nothing else. The *official* acts of the Center up to now were rare and not well known.

The sincerity of Mazzini's moral objections to the Commune and the International is not denied by the fact that his opposition had a practical purpose. He was perfectly aware that if the Italian bourgeoisie ever established republicanism and the Commune as cause and effect, his hopes of weaning that class to his republican objective would be permanently frustrated. This is what prompted him to remind his followers that "In Italy, every imprudence, every manifestation in favor of those guilty of these acts [in Paris] suffices to arouse suspicions and fear in the middle class that only favor the Government." [35] For the same reason he assured this class that his program of "emancipating" the Italian worker would be painless, that it

. . . would not involve serious sacrifices by anyone and would increase the sources of production to the benefit of all. A system of taxes that would leave inviolate the necessities of life; a system of Banks that would establish *local* and *special* credit [for workers' organizations]; a system of farm settlement [*colonizzazione*] applied to the four million . . . hectars of land hitherto uncultivated in Italy; a few aids and facilitations given to the method of [workers'] Association that aims at uniting *capital* and *labor* in the same hands; some institutions tending to constitute fair arbitrational decisions between the Workers and the present holders of capital—these would suffice to guarantee the pacific triumph of the emancipating movement, without the least disturbance of existing economic conditions.[36]

Even more indicative of the practical inferences Mazzini drew from the sudden prominence lent the socialist International by the experience of the Paris Commune was his equally sudden decision to renew his courtship of the Italian labor movement. Addressing himself directly "To the Italian Workers" in the issue of July 13, he recalled that the Pact of Fraternity had been accepted by "the majority of the Societies in one

[35] "Il Comune e l'Assemblea." The monarchist press is "frightening people away from us with what they call the inevitable consequences of the Republic." Letter to Caroline Stansfield, May, 1871, S.E.I., XCI, 63-69.
[36] *La Roma del Popolo*, Apr. 19, 1871.

of your Congresses," but it remained "a dead letter, useless, forgotten, through an error committed in the formation of the Directive Authority." The time had come to resuscitate the bond:

> Why do you not hasten to meet in Rome in a Congress and there attain a new baptism of your Fraternity? Perhaps, in addition to the immense advantage to you, you would remind . . . Italy that from Rome must issue another and broader Pact, the *National Pact*, the definition of our future life, without which Rome and Italy are empty names.

The master had issued a new strategic directive: on August 14 the Ligurian Permanent Commission published a circular convoking the Twelfth Congress of the Italian Workers' Societies, to be held in Rome on November 1, 1871.[37]

REPUBLICAN "INTERNATIONALISM" (SUMMER 1871)

Mazzini's sacerdotal thunders against the Commune and the International generated bewilderment and considerable indignation among radical republicans. Part of the reason was that the Moderate press welcomed an unexpected ally in damning the Communards: thus, *La Nazione* of Florence, "We are happy . . . that the head of the republican party has also felt the duty of protesting against the excesses of Paris. . . . *It pleased us that Mr. Mazzini wrote as he did.*" [38] In the columns of *Il Gazzettino Rosa*, Vincenzo Pezza bitterly noted that Mazzini's position was being exploited by the monarchists for their own advantage,[39] that Italian republican sympathy for the Commune did not entail approval of its methods. "We do not defend the socialist theories of the men of the Commune and their acts as legislators; we do not want to discuss [them] because it is impossible to form an exact idea of the conditions the people of Paris were experiencing. We can not understand [them] here in Milan, where property is well divided and a certain prosperity is reflected even in the lower classes" (June 4). And a few weeks later: "We are materialists, but we do not make a political school of materialism" (June 30). The atheism of the Communards insufficiently explained to Pezza the refusal of Mazzini, the living assertion of the doctrine of permanent insurrection, to see in the Commune the idea of a democratic revolution to emancipate the people.[40]

On July 18 *La Favilla*, influential republican organ of Mantua, entered

[37] *La Roma del Popolo*, Aug. 24, 1871.
[38] July 10, 1871.
[39] Aug. 28, Sept. 9, 1871.
[40] Aug. 14, 16, 1871.

the lists against Mazzini. In a highly sarcastic piece, Paride Suzzara-Verdi waxed indignant over Mazzini's refusal to concede moral value to any formula but his own. Those who believe in the International are "bastards and thieves, a priori, because they do not believe in the a priori God of Giuseppe Mazzini." They treat him with respect and benevolence; why, then, should Mazzini not admit *their* right to differ in regard to religion? "He who takes an a priori system as a point of departure . . . forms a catafalque of vacuity that falls at the first breeze. To sustain it, he is forced to reject the profane who might be capable of a sacrilegious gust of wind. Herein lies the intolerance of Mazzini."[41]

For many radical republican newspapers, singing the praises of the International was the logical corollary to criticism of Mazzini's stand. In fact, prior to September 1871, three new journals made support of the I.W.A. their primary theme: *L'Internazionale* of Naples; *Il Proletario Italiano,* issued on July 2 as the organ of a newly created Turin workers' society; *L'Eguaglianza* of Girgenti, appearing on July 16 under the editorship of Antonio Riggio, one of the signers of the April 12 Florentine International Democratic Society's address of solidarity with the Paris Commune. In adition to *Il Gazzettino Rosa, La Favilla, Il Presente, Il Romagnolo,* and *La Plebe,* other previously established republican newspapers came over to a pro-International point of view: *Il Ciceruacchio* of Rome ("What . . . is this potent society of the sons of labor that makes the monarchs of Europe tremble on their thrones? . . . . It is a social problem, a thousand times rejected and always reborn more formidable and tenacious than ever, that knocks at the door of the future"),[42] *L'Apostolato* of Catania (the I.W.A. wants "to found the government of Liberty, Fraternity, and Equality, . . . to unite all men in a single family in order that each be given his due"),[43] *La Fenice* (Legnago), *L'Asino* (Alessandrino), *Il Diavolo Rosa* (Rome), *La Libertà* (Pavia).

If the pro-International sentiments of these newspapers reflected the attitude of many republican societies in the peninsula, these associations were nonetheless unready to take the one step needed to seal a rupture with Mazzini and the Party of Action. Of the hundreds of democratic societies in the peninsula in the summer of 1871, there were only three regularly constituted sections of the First International—in Naples, Sciacca, and Girgenti—and these originated independently of the furor created by the Paris Commune and Mazzini's excommunication of its

[41] See also, Suzzara-Verdi's defense of the International against Mazzini's charges of July 13, in *La Favilla,* Aug. 13, 1871; and his article, "Il sistema di Mazzini e la morale," in the Aug. 1 issue.

[42] *Il Gazzettino Rosa,* Aug. 3, 1871, in reprinting the Roman paper's article, commented: *Repetita juvant.*

[43] Rosselli, *Mazzini e Bakounine,* pp. 301-02, note.

Italian defenders. Dissatisfaction with Mazzini's position was plentiful enough, but, aside from the press reaction just reviewed, it manifested itself in the formulation of social democratic, not socialist, programs, only slightly more radical—or less cautious—than Mazzini's recommendations for social reform. Expressions of atheism and anticlericalism marked their only real incompatibility with Mazzinian dogma, but even these owed their adoption to factors quite unrelated, in the main, to the issues posed by the Commune and/or the International. No more than a handful of Italian republicans was ready to embrace the socialist alternative, partly because they were even more confused than Mazzini as to the International's program and partly because the forty-year apostolate of the Genoese had produced an almost indelible legacy of indifference to any doctrine that did not put the nation in a central position. The intellectual climate of the Risorgimento was not exorcised by the breaching of the Porta Pia. In the summer of 1871 the momentum of forces tending toward a definitive split in the Mazzinian party was clearly perceptible, but that rupture was still in the making.[44]

The episode of the Florentine International Democratic Society illustrates the variety of influences at work within almost any given republican association and the inability of socialism to establish a clear hegemony at this time.[45] The group was organized in November 1870 by Francesco Piccini, Grand Master of the Artisans' Brotherhood, Salvatore Battaglia, Antonio Riggio, and Antonio Martinati. Of these four founding spirits, Piccini was an orthodox Mazzinian; Battaglia called himself partly Mazzinian, partly Internationalist: "From Mazzini and the International I accept the true and the good as I find it"; Riggio and Martinati were well along in their transition to socialism. The mixture of Garibaldianism, socialism, freemasonry, and atheism personified by Luigi Castellazzo, president of the society, caused Battaglia to characterize him as a "potpourri."[46] The heterodoxy of the rank and file might be inferred from the fact that the membership of about a hundred was recruited from local freethinking, veteran, and artisan associations.

The Florentine society's purpose, according to the police, was "to stimulate youth into action by preparing the terrain for the triumph of

[44] The hesitancy to burn any bridges was voiced by Il Romagnolo (June 18): "To be a materialist or a rationalist . . . , to be or not to be a socialist, does not keep individuals with disparate scientific opinions from belonging to the republican party." On July 2, Il Romagnolo was still addressing La Roma del Popolo in conciliatory tones.

[45] Except as noted, data on this organization is drawn from Conti, O.S.F., pp. 116-20.

[46] A socialist's evaluation of Castellazzo: "atheist in religion, . . . socialist republican in politics." Cafiero to Engels, June 12, 1871, Nettlau, B.I.I., p. 195.

the universal republic and for the practical implementation of socialism."
And in mid-May 1871 when a young Pugliese with an evangelical gleam
in his eye appeared on the scene, one Carlo Cafiero, fresh out of London
with a mandate from the I.W.A.'s General Council to organize Internationalist sections in Italy, he was not only amicably received, but elected
corresponding secretary of the association.[47]

Yet the Florentine organization became neither a section of the
International, nor even a socialist circle. It was an uneasy mixture of
Florentine democrats associated in protest against the status quo and
apparently little else. The group did have an ambitious plan, in the
spring of 1871, for a congress of all Italian democrats "to coordinate in
common agreement their efforts for the improvement of the welfare of
the proletarian class, and thus bring into being as soon as possible a
republic based on justice," and the police, at least, understood the intent
of the scheme as anti-Mazzinian.[48] Made privy to the project, Carlo
Cafiero registered immediate enthusiasm and began dreaming of transforming the congress into a constituent assembly for a national federation
of Internationalist sections.[49]

The whole structure collapsed on June 20, 1871, much to the relief of
Giannelli, Piccini, and the other Mazzinians, when the police dissolved
the Society and confiscated its files on the grounds that the group was too
sympathetic to the principles of the Paris Commune, "the declared enemy
of every Government and the subverter of all social order." [50] Relieved of
the embarrassment of formal association with republicans poisoned by the
socialist heresy, the Mazzinians tried setting up a society dedicated exclusively to the republican program of their *duce,* but the radicals anticipated them by forming the "Social Democratic Union" in July, with
a program stated in generic enough terms that practically all shades of
democrats in Florence could join with a clear conscience.[51] Interminable
arguments and schisms featured the life of this association, with neither
the Mazzinians nor the pro-Internationalists achieving supremacy. Not
until the following year did Ettore Socci, Battaglia, Lorenzo Piccioli-
Poggiali, Francesco Natta, and Gaetano Grassi—all prominent in the
new organization—emerge as committed agents of the International in the

[47] Cafiero to Engels, June 12, 1871, Rosselli, *Mazzini e Bakounine,* p. 305.
[48] Romano, *Storia,* II, 86, note 14.
[49] Nettlau, *B.I.I.,* p. 219.
[50] Rosselli (*Mazzini e Bakounine,* p. 303) dates the dissolution of the Society
as "early May," though he ascribes the police action to the Society's "Address to the
Survivors of the Commune," obviously not written until after the Commune collapsed
on May 25. The association's headquarters were raided on June 20. *La Plebe,* June
22; *La Favilla,* June 25, 1871.
[51] *L'Eguaglianza,* July 16, 1871; Conti, *O.S.F.,* pp. 117-18.

region. Meanwhile, to secure agreement on a single program in that swirling intellectual ambient was, in Socci's words, "a work of Sisyphus." [52] International socialism had yet to put down roots on the banks of the Arno.

THE "SOCIALISM" OF GARIBALDI

No less than Mazzini, Giuseppe Garibaldi contributed to the ideological confusion besetting the Party of Action in the spring and summer of 1871. The perennially activist Red Shirt leader, unlike the philosopher-agitator Mazzini, had no highly refined political and social criteria with which to assess the Paris Commune and the socialist International. Back on the island of Caprera, thoroughly disillusioned and humiliated by the government's attitude toward his role in the Franco-Prussian War, angry with the spinelessness of the French republican government that had folded under pressure from Bismarck, Garibaldi firmly sided with the Commune against the bourgeois politicians at Versailles.[53] No student of the day-to-day developments in Paris, he simply equated the Commune with the cause of humanitarian virtue besieged by the forces of greed, reaction, and oppression. The Parisians were fighting out of a sentiment of justice and human dignity, he wrote his friends in Nice on May 2.[54] Though he begged out when offered the command of the National Guard in Paris—on the grounds that it would be a useless sacrifice of his person—he deplored the fall of the Commune in highly indignant terms.[55]

Garibaldi's sympathy for the Commune and the pro-International position resulting from it enormously contributed to the I.W.A.'s popularity among Italian republican youth. In the face of the increasingly obvious futility of Mazzinian schemes for republican insurrection, there persisted, with undiminished force, a desire for action, motivated by a vague aspiration to give substance to the humanitarian ideals that had pervaded the *Risorgimento*. With the capture of Rome, the republicans lacked a myth, "a distant and perhaps unattainable horizon toward which to move." [56] Following Garibaldi into the winter campaign in the Vosges only partially satisfied the activist compulsion, but it also riveted the image of the brooding warrior on Caprera as the protagonist qualified to

[52] *Un anno alle Murate* (Pitigliano, 1898), x.

[53] Rosselli, *Mazzini e Bakounine*, pp. 295 ff.; Giuseppe Fonterossi, *Garibaldi e l'Internazionale* (Rome, 1933), p. 6.

[54] *Epistolario di Giuseppe Garibaldi, con documenti e lettere inedite (1836-1882).* Compiled and annotated by Enrico Emilio Ximenes (Milan, 1885), I, 376-77 (this volume is cited below as Ximenes, *comp., Epistolario*); *La Favilla*, May 7, 1871.

[55] Michels, *Il proletariato e la borghesia nel movimento socialista italiano*, p. 40. Garibaldi wanted to fight with the Communards only if they opposed the Germans, not fellow Frenchmen. Fonterossi, *op. cit.*, p. 6.

[56] Morandi, *La Sinistra al potere*, p. 291.

lead young republicans in a crusade against the status quo, not by preaching duty and morality from the serene heights of the philosopher, but by setting the example of a man of action in the thick of the fray. That the picture no longer corresponded to Garibaldi's potentialities mattered little, for this was the new myth, determining the actions and thinking of a generation too young to have experienced the exaltation of shooting papal, Bourbon, and Habsburg troops in the name of Italy. Thus, when Garibaldi fell victim to the cliché that sympathy for the martyrs of the Commune entailed praise of the socialist International, the popularity of the latter was insured among his less mature worshippers.

By 1871 another current of thought among Italian republicans was becoming identified with the Hero of the Thousand. Ever since the early 1860's, rationalist circles and atheist associations had been multiplying steadily, stimulated by such external influences as the diffusion of Darwin's *Origin of Species,* the positivist doctrines of Comte, Spencer's social Darwinism, the polemic inaugurated by Strauss's *Life of Jesus,* and Feuerbach's *Essence of Christianity.* In 1871 atheism was in high fashion among radical republicans. It had a definite political aspect in that its devotees enlarged their concept of freedom from religious authority into a protest against political authority as well.[57] Garibaldi's inveterate hostility toward the Catholic clergy and its institutions, intensified by the emergence of the Roman Question after September 1870, readily personalized the essentially romantic critique of the Italian freethinkers, though its chief literary outlet was Luigi Stefanoni, Garibaldian editor of the Florentine weekly, *Il Libero Pensiero, Giornale dei Razionalisti,* and president of the local Society of Free Thought.[58]

For Stefanoni, rationalism had a socialist function, for he defined it as the method by which "the worker can deduce his rights. . . . Reason is . . . the cardinal principle from which all the consequences must be deduced; otherwise, they will always be founded on sand." [59] Such subtleties were probably lost on Garibaldi, but his public sanctification of the mushrooming atheistic societies, whose pronunciamentos reflected Stefanoni's identification of rationalism as the methodology of socialism, reinforced substantially, if indirectly, the pro-socialist current in the Party of Action. The effect was the greater, coming precisely when Mazzini was

---

[57] "We do not believe in any Divinity and . . . we necessarily do not admit the principle of authority, because a people must be free to establish what it wants, not to observe what an imaginary God has established through his prophets"—thus, *Il Romagnolo,* Sept. 9, 1871, in defining its basic dissent with the "politico-philosophical principles of Mazzini."

[58] On Stefanoni, see Conti, *O.S.F.,* pp. 110 ff.; Romano, *Storia,* II, 132. Stefanoni was the translator of Feuerbach, Büchner, Herzen, and Fontanelle.

[59] Letter of Stefanoni to Erminio Pescatori, *Il Libero Pensiero,* Feb. 15, 1872.

laying down his heaviest barrage against materialism and the anti-religiosity corrupting Italian youth.[60]

If the activist predilections of young republicans and their addiction to the "new science" had the effect of lining them up behind Garibaldi in his support of the socialist International, the general's pro-International stand, too, had a mixed derivation. One aspect was the fact that ever since 1848, disagreement over political methods and objectives had been poisoning the relations of the two republican chiefs. The Mentana episode of 1867 brought the schism fully into the open; with Garibaldi attributing to Mazzini a great share of the blame for its failure.[61] The rift has been attributed to Mazzini's resentment of Garibaldi's ambition to guide Italian democracy without benefit of training or natural aptitude for the job and to Garibaldi's impatience with Mazzini's authoritarianism, coupled with scorn for his *modus operandi* and program.[62] Whatever the cause, their opposed reactions to the Paris Commune irrevocably confirmed the split, much to the chagrin of Italian democrats, denied their hope for a perfect agreement between the "arm" and the "mind" of the Risorgimento.

Garibaldi's desire to manifest a certain degree of independence of Mazzini only partly explains his pro-International reaction,[63] for he also wanted to see the common man liberated from need, and he sincerely, if naively, believed that all men of good will could be united under the same banner, be they Mazzinians, Masons, freethinkers, revolutionary, or evolutionary socialists, or even constitutional democrats. Programmatic and methodological differences could be painlessly resolved if all men adopted the reign of human virtue as their goal. Many of the fundamental doctrines of International socialism he deemed "exaggerations," and its primary assumption, the class struggle, he did not understand or, if he had, would have rejected. His entire defense of the International

[60] Garibaldi's anticlericalism was deeply resented by the Mazzinians when he identified it with the International, thus implying that Mazzini and his followers were "soft" on priests. Giuseppe Petroni tried to straighten the record: "Given the fact that the illustrious General Garibaldi's adherence to the *International* authorizes any foreigner unacquainted with Italian affairs to believe that only this Association is opposed to priests and privileges, I, the last of the unitary-Republican Party, must declare that . . . it does not seem to me that I endured eighteen years of prison and refused the amnesty of the pope in order to support *priests and privileges*. And I believe that all my brothers in faith can say as much." *La Roma del Popolo*, Sept. 14; *La Favilla*, Nov. 1, 1871.

[61] Fonterossi, *op. cit.*, pp. 3 ff. On the pre-1867 differences between the two men, see G. Bandini, "Contrasti tra garibaldini e mazziniani all'inizio del 1862," *Camicia Rossa*, Yr. XIII, Nos. 11-12 (1937); G. Curatolo, *Mazzini e Garibaldi* (Milan, 1928).

[62] Rosselli, *Mazzini e Bakounine*, pp. 297-98.

[63] Mazzini: "Garib[aldi] would not support the International if I had written in favor of it." *S.E.I.*, XCI, 220.

beginning in the late summer of 1871 was based on his consistent mis-reading of the nature and purposes of the movement. The I.W.A., in Garibaldi's view, was nothing more than an international humanitarian undertaken to end the material enslavement of the downtrodden.

In this oversimplified conception is to be found the essential reason for Garibaldi's much publicized support of the socialist International; from this faulty generalization stemmed much of the confusion among Italian republicans that led them to call themselves socialists, to organize sections of the I.W.A., to name Marx, Bakunin, and Garibaldi as honorary triumvirs of a single association, and to believe, with Garibaldi, that the International was "the sun of the future."[64] This is why the self-proclaimed exponents of *Garibaldinismo,* in the late summer of 1871, initiated a movement for a national congress of Italian democrats in the hope of reconciling the Mazzinian and Garibaldian wings of the Party of Action.

The growing schism between the two segments of the republican party was nowhere more clearly revealed than in the Romagna and the Emilia, where, thanks to recent papal rule, antireligious and anticlerical sentiments were particularly vivacious. Early in June, 1871, Celso Ceretti, veteran of many Garibaldian campaigns and an especially devoted admirer of the general, founded in Mirandola a "Republican and Anti-Catholic Association."[65] Garibaldi gave his immediate blessing: "I hope you intend to combat despotism and the priest: the goal, therefore, is holy and I am with you for life."[66] In Mantua there appeared another Garibaldian association, the Society of Young Democracy, proposing the "association of capital with labor, . . . the moral and material emancipa-tion of the proletariat, oppressed today by priests and capitalists."[67] The Mirandola and Mantuan organizations, joined by a society of veterans in Verona, and with the full approval of Garibaldi, issued a circular on August 25 inviting all Italian democratic societies to attend a general congress to discuss the possibility of forming a single national organiza-tion to achieve greater unity of action.[68]

Invited by Ceretti to support the August 25 initiative, Mazzini refused on the grounds that the projected congress, exposing many conflicting

[64] "The International is the sun of the future that dazzles and which obscurantism and privilege would like to throw into the tomb." The famous passage occurs in the general's letter to Celso Ceretti, Sept. 22, 1872. *Il Gazzettino Rosa,* Oct. 5, 1872.

[65] For its Statuto, *La Favilla,* June 10, 1871. On Ceretti (1844-1909), a key figure in the pioneer socialist movement, see Renato Zangheri, "Celso Ceretti e la crisi delle formazioni democratiche del Risorgimento," *Fatti e Teorie,* XI-XII (1950), 34-39.

[66] *La Favilla,* July 4, 1871.

[67] For the Society's program, *ibid.,* Aug. 22, 1871.

[68] *Ibid.,* Aug. 29; *L'Eguaglianza,* Sept. 5, 10, 1871.

points of view, would disillusion the Italian middle classes as to the unity of the republican program.

> Ten programs would emerge, nine of which will frighten [the middle classes] more than ever. Some will speak of abolishing God: we would be forced to protest. Others will sing the praises of the International and the Parisian Commune; and those who sympathize with us will declare they want to have nothing to do with it. . . . Remember what I say to you: The Congress, if it meets, will benefit the enemy.[69]

Mazzini privately assured his good friend, Sarah Nathan, that the congress would be "an awesome mess," what with Garibaldi and his "anti-priest monomania," the freethinkers, the Internationalists, etc.[70]

To the accompaniment, then, of Mazzini's ridicule, the Garibaldians forthwith set their sights on establishing a unity among themselves which, given the growing unpopularity of Mazzini's anti-International polemic among his followers, promised to attract the dissidents to the banner of the Red Shirt hero. In the whole forthcoming effort, socialism remained but a peripheral issue, because the Garibaldians, taking their cue from their hero, understood the socialism of the International as a merely generic set of principles that could easily be adapted to the exigencies of their struggle with the Mazzinians for control of the democratic movement. Garibaldi's directive was clear enough; on August 29 he wrote to Lodovico Nabruzzi, editor of *Il Romagnolo*: "Dear friends, the *International* is that most numerous part of society that suffers in the presence of the privileged few. We must, therefore, be with the *International*, and *if there are some defects in it, we must correct them.*" [71] Suzzara-Verdi, in commenting on his idol's message, drew the necessary conclusion: that Garibaldians might profitably borrow the term "International" for their own political purposes, that the I.W.A. program was outdated, merely suggestive, and ready to be made over in the image of Garibaldi's amorphous, humanitarian formulas.[72] In this sense, the hero of Calatafimi was responsible for his followers' impetuous and often unreflective adherence to the international socialist movement.

In this notion that the International's program was still open for discussion and revision lay an important element in the birth of the Italian socialist movement. Its clever exploitation by Michael Bakunin enabled

[69] *S.E.I.*, XCI, 173 ff.

[70] *Ibid.*, XCI, 171.

[71] *Il Romagnolo*, Sept. 9, 1871. Italics mine. Practically every pro-International organ in Italy reprinted the letter immediately: *Il Gazzettino Rosa*, Sept. 11; *La Favilla*, Sept. 12; *La Plebe*, Sept. 12; *Il Proletario Italiano*, Sept. 14; *L'Eguaglianza*, Sept. 17.

[72] *La Favilla*, Sept. 12. In the same vein, *La Plebe*, Aug. 3, 1871.

him to muster sympathy for his own program and establish himself as the acknowledged mentor of the primitive socialist school in the peninsula. For their part, the Garibaldian societies of the Emilia-Romagna region simply took seriously the first article of the I.W.A. statutes: that admission to the International was open to all organizations dedicated to mutual assistance, the progress and complete emancipation of the working classes, a definition covering even Garibaldi's broad vision of the meaning of socialism. Even Friedrich Engels, a month before he became secretary for Italy on the London General Council, encouraged Italian republicans in this misconception when he wrote his agent in the peninsula: "We have people of every kind in our Association, communists, Proudhonists, unionists, trade-unionists, Bakuninists, etc. . . . When the Association becomes a sect, it is lost. Our strength consists of the breadth with which the first rule is interpreted, that is, that all men who aim at the complete emancipation of the working classes are admitted." [73]

There was no hypocrisy, *rebus sic stantibus*, in the Garibaldians' styling themselves socialists and Internationalists, however prominent in their calculations their political rivalry with the Mazzinians. As of August, 1871, they had no way of knowing that both terms would soon require a far more exact definition of their social objectives than that to be deduced from Garibaldi's insistence that all men are brothers.

[73] Letter to Cafiero, July 1, 1871, Romano, *Storia*, II, 309.

VIII

The Paris Commune and Italian
Socialism (Summer 1871)

CARLO CAFIERO AND THE NEAPOLITAN
I.W.A. SECTION

WHILE Mazzini fulminated against the International and planned a congress of workers' societies to immunize them against the socialist virus, while Garibaldi and his followers lauded the I.W.A. and, in its name, planned to wrest control of Italian democracy from the Mazzinians, the governing group of the International Workingmen's Association in London made a slow start in exploiting the widespread sympathy for socialism occasioned by the Paris Commune and its suppression. By mid-August, 1871, the Italian International was still limited to the *Mezzogiorno,* and even here there existed fewer self-proclaimed sections of the International than in 1869.

Naples was still the center of the movement, thanks to Carlo Cafiero, the General Council's sole active agent in the peninsula prior to September, 1871.[1] Scion of a rich landowning family of Barletta (Apulia), Cafiero studied law at the University of Naples and entered the diplomatic service, but soon gave it up to go abroad for the study of economics, the social sciences, and modern languages. After a brief sojourn in Paris,

[1] On Cafiero (1846-92), see the excellent bibliography by P. C. Masini and Gianni Bosio, "Bibliografia generale di Carlo Cafiero," *Movimento Operaio,* Yr. III, Nos. 17-18 (June-Sept., 1951), 701-10; and, *ad nomen,* the general works, already cited, of Rosselli, Nettlau, Angiolini, Romano, Guillaume, Zoccoli, and Conti. For the Cafiero-Engels correspondence, see Gianni Bosio, ed., "Carteggio da e per l'Italia (1871-1895) di Marx-Engels," *Movimento Operaio,* Yrs. I, II, Nos. 1-8 (Oct., 1949—April, May, 1950); Romano, *Storia,* II, 308-21.

Peter Kropotkin described Cafiero as "an idealist of the highest and purest type; he spent a considerable fortune in the service of our cause and never worried later what he would have to eat on the morrow." *Autour d'une vie* (2d ed.; Paris, 1902), p. 405.

Cafiero moved to London. Here in 1870 at the age of twenty-four, he came to know Marx, Engels, and several other directors of the I.W.A., who persuaded him to dedicate himself to the redemption of the working-man. Accepting Engels' proposal that he organize I.W.A. sections in Italy, armed with a letter of introduction to Carlo Gambuzzi in Naples, the now inspired socialist returned to Italy to put his keen intelligence and fat patrimony at the service of the London General Council.[2]

Arriving in Florence in mid-May 1871, Cafiero talked Luigi Castellazzo, president of the local International Democratic Society, into some kind of declaration of loyalty to the socialist International, though Castellazzo, as noted above, was unable—or unwilling—to convert his association into a regular section of the International.[3] The two men corresponded for the next several months, but the relationship gave the General Council no foothold in Florence.[4]

After a brief holiday in Barletta, Cafiero headed for Naples, the scene of his student days, to test his organizing talents. "I hope for much from Naples: my old student and journalist friends, the existence for the past several years of a firmly socialist newspaper and the appearance of some others of the same color indicate to me a certainly propitious terrain."[5] On the scene, his letter of introduction to Gambuzzi and an early en-counter with Carmelo Palladino, a radical young lawyer and fellow Apulian, gave him an *entrée* into local democratic circles, composed for the most part, as Cafiero reported to Engels on June 28, of "poor school teachers, unhappy journalists, modest students," among whom he found "friends of merit, ideas, and education."[6] Reconstructing a Neapolitan section, after the scandalous conduct of local socialist leaders in the wake

[2] Nettlau, *B.I.I.*, pp. 218-19; Romano, *Storia*, II, 85.

[3] Engels, on Cafiero's recommendation, agreed to open correspondence with Castellazzo and after the dissolution of the International Democratic Society sent propaganda material via Cafiero, so as not to compromise Castellazzo. The effort was wasted, for the new Social Democratic Union, as noted previously, did not become an I.W.A. section, and its constitution said nothing of the International. Nettlau, *B.I.I.*, pp. 197-98; Engels' letters to Cafiero, July 1, 16, 1871, Romano, *Storia*, II, 308-14.

[4] The minutes of the London General Council meetings did not mention Florence, but the *Eastern Post* of London reported I.W.A. progress in Italy, "especially in Florence and Naples." Nettlau, *B.I.I.*, p. 195. The item was probably based on Engels' contact with Castellazzo via Cafiero. The latter informed Engels that Castellazzo had written him on June 17 that in Florence "We are going under full sail . . . ; the associates increase in number from day to day in truly marvelous proportions." *Ibid.*, p. 196.

[5] Letter to Engels, June 12, 1871, *ibid.*, p. 219. The newspaper was probably *L'Internazionale*.

[6] *Ibid.*, p. 178. For the letter of June 28, *ibid.*, pp. 173, 220-21. On Palladino (1842-96), whose name had appeared on the membership roll of the Genevan section of Bakunin's Alliance (see above, p. 134), see Antonio Lucarelli, *Carmelo Palladino. Nuovo contributo alla storia della Prima Internazionale*, reprinted from *Umanità Nuova*, Yr. XXIX, Nos. 36-39 (Rome, 1939).

of the government dissolution of the section in January 1870, meant beginning from scratch. "Here in Naples I found the most complete decay." Nothing was to be hoped for from Caporusso, now completely discredited, while the other socialist sympathizers had to be won over gradually. The great mass of workers in Naples was submerged in indescribable conditions of poverty, ignorance, and superstition; a shocking moral *malaise* pervaded the whole *Mezzogiorno,* inevitable consequence of Bourbon misrule. In another two weeks, however, Cafiero saw a glimmer of hope in the situation: "A handful of decisive and convinced men has always remained and has never ceased to meet in the midst of misfortunes. . . . Now it can not even be said that they have organized themselves, but there is a president, Giustiniani, a worker, who is good, and a handful of excellent workers, two medical students, some young lawyers, etc." [7]

One of the convinced socialists of this group was an eighteen-year-old medical student destined to be the leader of Italian anarcho-socialism during the succeeding six decades. Like Cafiero, Errico Malatesta had been educated in a religious school as a child, but, according to his memoirs, his heart was "turned to ice" when in the winter of 1868-69 he paused in his studies to contemplate the plight of the poor: "I thought of the Gracchi and Spartacus, and I realized that my soul was that of a tribune and rebel." [8] As a student at the University of Naples, he acquired a reputation for fiery republicanism and was suspended from his studies as the result of a brawl—presumably political in origin. His transition from orthodox republicanism to socialism was the outcome of his own impatience with Mazzini's social formulas and of numerous café conversations with his lawyer friend, Carmelo Palladino. [9]

The work of reconstruction undertaken by the triumvirate of Cafiero, Palladino, and Malatesta moved slowly; by mid-July 1871 the section counted no more than 268 effective members, [10] a far cry from the membership of approximately 3,000 on the rolls in January, 1870. Nonetheless, the efforts of Cafiero and his group were enough to focus Mazzini's attention on socialist progress in Naples and caused him to send some personal emissaries to Naples early in July. As Cafiero reported it to Engels, they met "a reception that their obdurate, sectarian intolerance merited." [11] This is probably what accounted for Mazzini's reference to

[7] Nettlau, *B.I.I.,* p. 176.

[8] Nettlau, *Errico Malatesta. Vita e Pensieri* (New York [1922]), p. 14. The most recent biography of Malatesta (1844-1932) is by Armando Borghi, *Errico Malatesta* (Milan: Ist. Editoriale Italiano, 1947).

[9] Nettlau, *B.I.I.,* p. 176; Lucarelli, *Carmelo Palladino,* p. 4.

[10] Romano, *Storia,* II, 106.

[11] Nettlau, *B.I.I.,* p. 225.

Naples in his July 13 article in *La Roma del Popolo*: "If there is a city among ours in which the International has found adherents, it is the one —I do not name it, but it is known to you—where the workers' element is most mute, most opposed to any vitality of progress."

On a propaganda level, Cafiero's opposition to Mazzini in the name of international socialism had no perceptible influence outside his immediate circle in the summer of 1871. His sole effort as a pamphleteer was abortive. Engels, on July 16, sent Cafiero a summary of the July 3 session of the General Council, in which that body had decided to publish its indictment of Mazzini's erstwhile secretary, Major Louis Wolff, as a former spy in the pay of Napoleon III's secret police.[12] Later, after having read Mazzini's first formal condemnation of the International and its program, published in *La Roma del Popolo* on July 13, Engels wrote Cafiero a long refutation of Mazzini's charges, suggesting that Cafiero publish it, along with the Council's condemnation of Wolff. Early in August, Cafiero drafted a pamphlet as suggested—but never got around to publishing the piece.[13]

As a clarification of his own thinking in regard to Mazzini's hostility toward the socialist movement ("the poor old man can not understand that his time is past"[14]), Cafiero's editorial effort may have had some value, but it can not be adduced—as it is by an historian of the movement —as proof that Engels and Marx initiated the anti-Mazzinian polemic in the peninsula.[15] After all, any of the pro-Communard and/or pro-International editorials of papers like *La Favilla* and *Il Gazzettino Rosa*, written prior to Mazzini's first formal indictment of the I.W.A. on July 13,[16] were "anti-Mazzinian" in the sense that Mazzini attacked the International as early as May 24 ("All'*Internazionale* di Napoli") and began to criticize the Commune as early as April 12 ("Le classi artigiane"). An unpublished manuscript among the personal papers of a lone

[12] Romano, *Storia*, II, 314. Mazzini had been informed of Wolff's treason early in April, 1871. His relations with Wolff had long since been broken off. S.E.I., XCI, 14 ff.

[13] Romano, *Storia*, II, 315-21, 325-29. Romano puts the piece under the rubric: "Federico Engels e Carlo Cafiero: Abbozzo di un opuscolo contro Mazzini." The idea of an anti-Mazzinian pamphlet by the Neapolitan socialists did not originate with Engels, but Cafiero. As early as July 12, Cafiero wrote Engels that "a reply is being organized here, with emphasis on that which concerns Naples particularly; but we all hope that the General Council will also make its voice heard." Nettlau, B.I.I., p. 224.

[14] *Ibid.*, p. 219.

[15] Romano offers the document as proof that Rosselli and Nettlau erred in crediting Bakunin with being the first to inaugurate the anti-Mazzinian campaign. *Storia*, II, 102-03.

[16] See *La Favilla*, Apr. 27; *Il Gazzettino Rosa*, Apr. 1, 14, 18, 20, May 20, 23, 27, 29, June 12, 1871.

Neapolitan agitator was no significant contribution to the anti-Mazzinian polemic then raging, however trenchant its contents, however ghost-written by Marx's *alter ego*.[17] Besides, on the very day Engels penned his attack on Mazzini, a socialist figure of far greater renown than Engels' green recruit finished the first of a series of powerfully effective and widely published essays designed to destroy Mazzini's credit among Italian radicals.[18] Michael Bakunin, certainly, was inserting himself in an already existing debate. So was Engels.

THE CAFIERO-ENGELS CORRESPONDENCE

Engels' target in the summer of 1871, so far as Italian affairs were concerned, was not Mazzini at all, but Bakunin. In his correspondence with Cafiero in July, Engels assiduously tried to discredit the Russian, while feeling out the strength of the agitator's ideas among the Neapolitan associates of Cafiero. In fact, Cafiero himself, in some of his reports to London, seemed to have been touched by the egalitarian virus. Engels, therefore, had to handle the problem gingerly, as is apparent from the following paraphrased summary of the correspondence:

(1) *Cafiero to Engels, June 28:*[19] A "Genevan current" [i.e., Bakuninist] exists in Naples. Would it not be well for "the friends of Geneva" to be told that they are performing "no act of social utility" in assuming a guiding role that properly belongs to the London General Council?

(2) *Engels to Cafiero, July 1-3*[20] (in reply to Cafiero's letter from Barletta of June 12): Bakuninism is a mixture of communism and Proudhonism. He is a political abstentionist because he does not wish to recognize the state. He believes all political acts "authoritarian." The I.W.A. accepts all societies desiring the emancipation of the proletariat, but the Bakuninists are not satisfied with the freedom they have under this rule; they claim that the General Council is composed of reactionaries and that the I.W.A. program lacks definition. Atheism and materialism— which he learned from us Germans—he wants made mandatory; so, too, with abolition of inheritance and the state. Marx and I are "just as

---

[17] Luigi Stefanoni, to whom Cafiero sent the anti-Mazzinian passages of Engels' letter, published them in the Aug. 31 issue of *Il Libero Pensiero* and *La Favilla* reprinted on Sept. 7. Bakunin's reply to Mazzini, on the other hand, was published as a supplement to the Aug. 16 issue of *Il Gazzettino Rosa.*

[18] "Risposta d'un Internazionale a Giuseppe Mazzini," begun by Bakunin on July 25 and completed on the 28th. Nettlau, *B.I.I.*, p. 246; Guillaume, *I.D.S.*, II, 173. Despite its "ideological poverty," Romano grants that it made a "great impression" among fervent socialists, wavering Mazzinians, and dissatisfied Garibaldians, and that it accelerated the process of disintegration within the republican party. *Storia*, II, 155.

[19] Nettlau, *B.I.I.*, p. 221.

[20] Romano, *Storia*, II, 308-11.

good and veteran atheists and materialists as Bakunin." We know that inheritance is nonsense, but we do not believe its abolition eliminates all evils. "Abolition of the state" is an old German philosophical phrase that we used to employ when we were simple youths. But putting these ideas into our program would lose members for the I.W.A. and divide European proletarians, which is precisely the effect Bakuninist action is having. If we can acquire sections in Italy free of this "special fanaticism," our work would be greatly benefited.

(3) *Cafiero to Engels, July 12-16:*[21] Bakunin has some friends in Naples who share many of his principles, but not a sect or party that differs with the principles of the General Council. The Bakuninist tendency in Naples is due to the fact that letters directed to the General Council were never answered, probably because they were inadequately addressed. Moreover, none of our people have ever been to London; many have visited Switzerland. Nonetheless, we still have a "handful of decisive and convinced men," such as Giustiniani, Palladino, and Gambuzzi, "one of our most competent." I agree with you in rejecting any sectarian principle, and I like the broadness of Article I of the I.W.A. statute. But to avoid difficulties, why not (a) forbid sections to have relations with non-I.W.A. organizations, even if these are composed of individual I.W.A. members, and (b) let each I.W.A. section decide for itself how to implement its own principles?

> None of the members of the International with whom I have talked in Italy demand that those principles of atheism, materialism, abolition of the right of inheritance, etc., be transcribed into so many articles of our social pact; to the contrary, they are opposed to it with all their might; but, on the other hand, they are very tenacious in wanting to bring all the members of their section to that order of ideas. . . .
>
> I can assure you that our men in Italy, without belonging to any special sect, firmly desire the end of all the present *disorder* of things and the principle of the social *order* which, to be such, must be based on *equality.*

They are tired of abstractions and want something concrete. They do not pretend to dictate "this or that plan of social organization," but they certainly want an end to inequality. I urge the General Council to send me "some manifestations of sympathy for the line of conduct followed by our men in Naples in the *rational* inculcation of those principles which, if untranslatable into articles of faith because they are contrary to our tendencies and the spirit of our Association, are finding indefatigable propagators in the persons of well-deserving proletarians." A statement

[21] Nettlau, *B.I.I.*, pp. 221-23.

by the General Council stressing "practical principles" would forestall any misunderstanding, which, if allowed to grow, could result in "an open rupture" at a future general congress.

(4) *Engels to Cafiero, July 16*[22] (in answer to Cafiero's letter of June 28): It would be much better if you can find elements in Naples or other cities who "have nothing in common with this Genevan current." These men will always be a sect inside the I.W.A., even if not openly. If they stay in the organization, it will not be for long, for the questions will arise again that will lead to their expulsion. We have the proofs that they are trying to form an International distinct from the I.W.A., but neither the General Council nor the general congress will permit any violation of our rules.[23]

(5) *Engels to Cafiero, July 28*[24] (in reply to Cafiero's letter of July 12): We are glad to know that Naples has no Bakuninists. We thought otherwise, because the Swiss Bakuninists always said so. Since we had no reply from Naples to our letters, we assumed this was so. You are right in saying that the I.W.A. must limit itself to the simple, explicit affirmation of Article I of the statute. If not developed, it would remain a "mere negation." We are constantly seeking to develop this principle in General Council discussions, but the Bakuninists are always trying to impose their program on the Association and to compete with it while remaining inside. [Here Engels reviewed the background of the General Council's decision of December 22, 1869, rejecting the application for membership in the I.W.A. of Bakunin's Alliance of Socialist Democracy.] We were always tolerant of other views, provided their proponents refrained from trying to undermine the Association and to impose their program on us. [Engels here cited the General Council decision of March 1869 admitting the Bakuninist Alliance on the grounds that its goal was consistent with Article I of the statute.] I cite this to prove to you how unfounded are the charges that the General Council has never gone beyond a rigid interpretation of Article I; in fact, we want nothing more ardently than discussions of these theoretical points. In our congresses, Bakunin and his friends have participated very little in such discussions. The Council is entitled to go beyond the official program of the I.W.A. "to the extent that circumstances justify doing so." It can not recognize any section's right to challenge its interpretation of the statutes and to proclaim as official things that are not in the rules of the Association. Your friends in Naples want something concrete; they want equality of

[22] Romano, *Storia*, II, 312-14.
[23] Marx and Engels were about to announce the London Conference of September, 1871, which was to disavow the Bakuninist Jura federation,
[24] Romano, *Storia*, II, 315-21.

social classes instead of inequality. Very well, we are ready to do more. The whole General Council wants the total abolition of social classes:

> We must liberate ourselves from the rural proprietors and the capitalists by guiding the associated classes of the workers of the land and industry to possess themselves of all the means of production: land, implements, machines, raw materials, and whatever else is needed to sustain life during the time necessary to production. With this, inequality will have to cease. And to realize this, we must have the political supremacy of the proletariat. I believe that this is sufficiently concrete for the friends of Naples. . . .

It is apparent from this exchange that Cafiero's associates in Naples had not taken sides in the Bakunin-Marx controversy. The question had not even been publicly posed as yet, and so long as the General Council did not openly excommunicate Bakunin and his friends of the Swiss Jura, Italian socialists other than Cafiero and Bakunin's few correspondents were not directly involved and could hardly have had any clear idea of the power struggle between the leaders of the orthodox and libertarian segments of the International. On the other hand, the libertarian ideas of Bakunin, per se, unquestionably had some currency in the Neapolitan section, and there is more evidence than Cafiero's letters to Engels to testify to its existence.

Carlo Gambuzzi, Bakunin's sole correspondent in the Naples area, probably did not play a major role in the rebuilding of the section during the spring and summer of 1871. He was far too involved in using his influence among the communal authorities to secure a contract for the building of an aqueduct by a local construction firm and a brace of English engineers, a shady piece of business netting Gambuzzi something like 400,000 *lire* in fees.[25] By August 16 the Neapolitan *questore* was sure that Gambuzzi was "losing ground and prestige for having demonstrated so little concern in looking after the interests of the International since he has bettered his financial condition." Nonetheless, Cafiero's reference to Gambuzzi as "one of our most competent men" and the *questore's* description of the section's president, Giustiniani, as "a passive instrument in the hands of Gambuzzi" suggest that Bakunin's Neapolitan correspondent was still a sufficiently prestigious figure to keep alive the "Genevan current" of ideas among Neapolitan socialists.[26]

[25] For details of this affair, *ibid.*, II, 89-92. It was due to this windfall, presumably, that Gambuzzi was able to contribute many hundreds of francs to help Bakunin cover his personal expenses in 1871. Guillaume, *I.D.S.*, II, 132-33, 146.

[26] Romano, *Storia*, II, 107-08. *Questore* to prefect, July 21, 1871: "Recent information . . . indicates as beyond question that this city is the center of the Italian Section of the International League. The president of the Central Council of the

Other wisps of evidence, too, indicate continuing Bakuninist influence. Alberto Tucci, another of the Russian's former associates, attended the meetings of the Neapolitan section, and there is no strong reason to think that the author of *La Situazione No. 1* had turned his back on libertarian ideas merely because he had broken off personal contact with the Russian agitator. Cafiero's two closest collaborators, Palladino and Malatesta, were subscribers to the Bakuninist newspaper in Geneva, *Solidarité*. On July 31 the *questore* bemoaned the fact that the local I.W.A. section was no longer limiting itself to "suborning workers only, but is reported to be distributing gratis very pernicious newspapers, pamphlets, and leaflets among the middle class" and university students. Forni's bibliography of subversive literature on the loose consisted of two pieces by Adhemar Schwitzguebel and Albert Richard, both cronies of Bakunin in Switzerland, and another entitled "Socialist Propaganda: Letters to a Frenchman," from the pen of Bakunin himself. Nor can the probability be denied that at least some of the two hundred copies of Bakunin's *L'Empire knouto-germanique et la Révolution sociale*, which were sent into Italy by Charles Guillaume, high mogul of the Swiss anarchist press, and which contained the Russian's first public attack on Marx, found their way into the hands of the Neapolitan Internationalists.[27]

The Neapolitan police, however, torpedoed any possibility that either Marxian socialism or the Bakuninist heresy would establish itself as the guiding gospel of the local section. On August 14 the Minister of Interior, alarmed by police reports on the strength, influence, and purposes of the section, decreed its dissolution; on the 18th, the prefect of Naples prohibited further meetings; and on the 20th, police invaded the meeting hall of the section, seized its files, and searched the homes of its leaders for compromising material, including Cafiero's living quarters. This young radical's precaution of depositing Engels' letters with a lady friend from Barletta was unavailing, for the police, again proving the efficiency of their informant system, marched straight to the house in Piazza Cavour and found the Engels letters on the person of the accommodating widow. The several residences in Florence maintained by Bakunin's now affluent agent, Gambuzzi, yielded another sizable batch of socialist propaganda material, a letter from Saverio Friscia, and an imposing list of names

---

Section is the lawyer, Carlo Gambuzzi, who shows himself more cautious than in the past . . . , and [its] vice-president is the lawyer, Carmelo Palladino." *Ibid.*, II, 107. Does this report prove the unreliability of the *questore*'s informants or, in view of Cafiero's failure to corroborate this intelligence in his correspondence with Engels, does it mean Gambuzzi was actually performing a clandestine service for Bakunin's secret Alliance, hidden even from Cafiero?

[27] Nettlau, *B.I.I.*, pp. 176, 178, 190; Romano, *Storia*, II, 107. On this propaganda effort of Bakunin, see Guillaume, *I.D.S.*, II, 130-33, 148-50.

of individuals throughout the southern provinces of Italy, which the police—probably erroneously—assumed to be an I.W.A. membership roll.[28]

Cafiero, Gambuzzi, Palladino, Malatesta, and other prominent figures of the section were indicted for inciting contempt of, and discontent with, constitutional institutions by making speeches in public gatherings.[29] They were never brought to trial, however, and Cafiero, after spending five days in jail, was released pending payment of a 2000-*lire* fine. Though the whole affair undoubtedly aroused further sympathy for the International Workingmen's Association, the fact remained that the only Italian section in which Engels and the General Council could claim any direct influence had disappeared. Moreover, Carlo Cafiero, the General Council's sole agent in the peninsula, planned to resume his studies in Germany as soon as his expected trial was concluded.[30]

THE SICILIAN AND TURIN SECTIONS

In the summer of 1871 there were other Internationalist nuclei in Italy, of course, but none of them was a direct reflection of the organizational activity of either Bakunin or the General Council. In the *Mezzogiorno* the Castellamare di Stabia and the Catania sections had disappeared in the wake of the January 1870 dissolution of the Neapolitan organization.[31] The section in Sciacca continued, but if its orientation is to be judged from an article written by its founder, Saverio Friscia, for the August 6 issue of *L'Eguaglianza*, the break from Mazzinianism had by no means been effected. Addressing himself to Mazzini, "the man who first taught me to pronounce the holy name of Italy with emotion," Friscia advanced a remarkable thesis: that Mazzini's social principles were substantially those of the socialist International and, in many respects, even more radical! The principles Friscia identified with the I.W.A. were those of Bakunin (anti-authoritarianism, anti-nationalism, federation of communes etc.), but in his opinion this was no obstacle to collaboration with the man who was engaged in a *guerre à outrance* with materialism, if only Mazzini remained true to himself:

> Maestro! Why, after forty years of ineffable suffering, of magnanimous actions, of indomitable constancy, do you align your-

[28] *La Plebe*, Aug. 22; *La Perseveranza*, Aug. 24; *La Favilla*, Aug. 26, Sept. 1, 1871. For more extensive discussions, see Nettlau, *B.I.I.*, pp. 225 ff.; Romano, *Storia*, II, 108-15; Rosselli, *Mazzini e Bakounine*, pp. 306-08.

[29] The section itself, in the ministerial decree of dissolution, was defined "a permanent offense to the laws and fundamental institutions of the nation, as well as an obvious danger to public order." *La Perseveranza*, Aug. 24, 1871.

[30] Cafiero letter to Engels, Sept. 10, 1871, Nettlau, *B.I.I.*, p. 227.

[31] Rosselli, *Mazzini e Bakounine*, p. 305.

self with the enemies of those who learned from you to love *la patria* and humanity; with the enemies of those who, at your signal, fearlessly defied the cannon and the gallows? Why, after forty years of an incomparable apostolate, . . . do you seek to deny yourself and let your banner fall into the hands of your enemies without a struggle? Italian youth is with you, the workers of the world love you and admire you, but do not give them the indescribable pain of having to fight the last battles for the redemption of the plebe without the direction and support of the old standard-bearer of liberty.

In Girgenti an Internationalist section was founded early in 1871, probably by friends of Friscia, and its program announcing the imminent publication of an official weekly newspaper, *L'Eguaglianza,* contained suggestively anarchist affirmations.[32] On June 11 the section approved an address "To the Vanquished of the Commune" and ten days later began collecting relief funds for the Communard refugees.[33] On July 16, Antonio Riggio brought out the first issue of *L'Eguaglianza.* Nettlau, in noting that Friscia collaborated with this "most clearly libertarian newspaper," implies a cause and effect relationship, but the first issue reported the proceedings of the anti-Bakuninist Romand congress in Switzerland, introducing the *compte-rendu* with a sarcastic reference to "dime-a-dozen wiseacres" (*barbassori a dieci al quattrino*) who demand a "religious abstention from politics." In the same issue (August 6) containing Friscia's defense of libertarian socialist principles—minus, it is true, that of political abstentionism—Riggio, apropos of the Girgenti communal elections, reaffirmed his conviction that political abstention is "a very serious error." The trend of the Girgenti section was apparently in the direction of the Marxist position on political action by the proletariat, but it was not until October 10 that Engels established direct contact with Riggio.[34]

The equivocation as to guiding principles among the "socialists" of Florence, Naples, Sciacca, and Girgenti was exceeded only by the ambiguity prevailing in Turin. Here, the organizer of a self-avowed Internationalist section was a twenty-six-year-old individual with a very obscure past, one Carlo Terzaghi, whose curious activities in the name of socialism were to prove the source of much bewilderment among Internationalists and the Italian republican Left generally. In the late

[32] Nettlau, *B.I.I.,* p. 192.

[33] For the address, *La Plebe,* June 27; *L'Eguaglianza,* July 16, 1871.

[34] Nettlau, *B.I.I.,* p. 237. Riggio in 1875: "In 1871 I created a Girgenti section of the International which, after a few months, died of anaemia, not to arise again." *Ibid.,* pp. 192-93.

spring or early summer of 1871, Terzaghi organized a local factory workers' group, and on July 2 he founded the semi-weekly *Il Proletario Italiano*, "dedicated to the sons of the people" in the name of free thought, legal equality, labor, and fraternal love.[35] The newspaper almost immediately joined the ranks of the anti-Mazzinian, pro-Internationalist organs. In its August 6, 13, and 20 issues, Mazzini's program was criticized and contrasted with that of the International. Between the two, "we are with the International. *Mazzinianism divides us, the International unites us.*"[36] For the July 23 issue, Carlo Laplace, a workingman friend of Terzaghi, penned a rousing declaration of adherence to the I.W.A., and in the July 27 number Terzaghi published a eulogy of "Carlo Max [*sic*], Supreme Chief of the International." On August 20 a piece by Bakunin himself was recommended. The whole mélange of tendencies was applauded by Garibaldi, for on August 29 he gave his blessing to Terzaghi's orientation with one of his laconic *sur le mêlée* pronouncements: "The International wants all men brothers, not priests, and the end of privilege. I naturally sympathize with it."[37] Thus encouraged, Terzaghi was soon to make his bid for the title of Turin's No. 1 Internationalist. Ironically enough, Engels and Bakunin, no less than Garibaldi, were to support his claim.

The prospects for the spread of the socialist International in Italy by the end of August 1871 were promising, but in the whole of the peninsula and Sicily, only Girgenti and Sciacca had I.W.A. sections, neither of which had any direct contacts with the London General Council. Pro-International sentiment pervaded the Italian republican Left, but the effort to channel it into the creation of a nation-wide network of I.W.A. sections had yet to be made. This was to be one of the primary concerns of Friedrich Engels, named the General Council's corresponding secretary for Italy early in August, and of Michael Bakunin. The imminent struggle between these two champions of Marxian socialism and anarcho-socialism for control of the Italian movement was an important, integral aspect of the broader conflict between the General Council and Bakuninists which, by the end of August 1871 was about to break through the surface of I.W.A. "solidarity."

[35] "Numero Saggio," July 2, 1871.
[36] Issue of Aug. 20, 1871. Mazzini immediately took to task "the young men who are writing imperturbably for a gazzette *dedicated to the sons of the people*," for not taking the trouble to acquaint themselves with his doctrines before criticizing them. "Gemiti, fremiti e ricapitulazione," *La Roma del Popolo*, Aug. 10, 17, 24, 31, 1871. The reference to *Il Proletario Italiano* was made in the Aug. 31 issue.
[37] Reprinted by *La Favilla*, Sept. 7; *L'Eguaglianza*, Sept. 10, 1871. See, also, Garibaldi's letter to Terzaghi of July 18, in *Il Proletario Italiano*, July 23; *La Favilla*, July 27, 1871.

INAUGURATION OF THE BAKUNIN-MAZZINI POLEMIC

By now the Bakuninist heresy had made considerable headway in France, Belgium, Switzerland, Spain, and—so the General Council believed— in Italy. Ever since the interregional congress of French sections, held in Lyon in March 1870, a conclave organized by Bakunin's friends and given over to resounding affirmations of apolitical, anti-statist, federalist, and libertarian socialism,[38] Bakunin had assumed the role of *pontifex maximus* of the anarcho-socialists. The main bulwark of the Russian, by the summer of 1871, was the so-called "collectivist and anti-authoritarian" faction of Swiss socialists concentrated in the Jura Mountains, the legitimacy of whose federal committee had been explicitly denied by the General Council in June 1870.[39] By late July 1871 Marx and Engels, determined to demolish Bakunin and his following once and for all, persuaded the London General Council to call a conference of I.W.A. chieftains, to be held in London on September 17, instead of a general congress of the association.[40] Marx and his "prime minister" immediately set about insuring a majority at the meeting that would give them the powers necessary to the execution of their plans. The outcome of this attempt was to have a decisive effect on Italian socialism throughout most of the ensuing decade.

Late in July, Bakunin came to the realization that the influence of the Paris Commune on Italian republicans had created a fertile field for his anarcho-socialist propaganda. In the months prior to his encountering Mazzini's first direct attack on the International ("Agli operai italiani," July 13), the Russian had kept in touch with a few key Italian friends, but nothing developed from these relations that contributed significantly to either the spread of socialist doctrines or the organizational growth of the International in Italy. After his *opéra bouffe* attempt in Lyon (September 1870) to "abolish the [French] state" and inaugurate the grand social revolution, a much chastened Bakunin spent a winter of isolation in his Locarno retreat, writing his *L'Empire knouto-germanique* and trying to realize his share of the family patrimony while living from hand to mouth on the personal loans he could solicit among his chronically purse-poor fellow revolutionaries in Switzerland and abroad. Gambuzzi, as

[38] "The political State no longer has any reason to exist; the artificial mechanism called government disappears in the economic organism, politics finds its basis in socialism." Bakunin's letter to the meeting speaks of "the liquidation of the State and bourgeois society, anarchy, that is, the true, honestly popular revolution, juridical and political anarchy, and the new economic organization from the bottom to the top and from the circumference to the centers." Guillaume, *I.D.S.*, II, 284-85.

[39] *Ibid.*, II, 55-56.

[40] *Ibid.*, II, 174-77.

noted above, contributed at least 1,310 francs to the Russian's upkeep.[41]

By the time Bakunin revisited Florence in the spring of 1871, his correspondents in the peninsula had dwindled to Gambuzzi, Fanelli, and possibly Friscia.[42] A commentary on the Russian's scant influence on this trio was their standing for election to the Chamber of Deputies in December, 1870. Gambuzzi alone failed to win a seat. The Russian, now describing himself as a "confirmed and impassioned [political] abstentionist," thus explained his friends' activity:

> Circumstances and times have changed. My friends . . . are so trained in our ideas and principles that there is no longer any danger of their forgetting, modifying, or sacrificing them, or of falling back into their old political habits. And then, the times have become so serious, the danger threatening liberty in every country so formidable, that men of good will everywhere must be in the breach, and our friends, most of all, must be in such a position that their influence becomes as effectively increased as possible.[43]

The Florentine visit of Bakunin, March 20 to April 2, the purpose of which is uncertain, had no visible effect, other than a renewal of the Russian's direct personal relations with old Florentine acquaintances such as Giuseppe Mazzoni, Berti-Calura, and Agostino Bertani.[44] Fanelli, Friscia, and Gambuzzi all put in an appearance, but their conversations with Bakunin had no ostensible issue. From early April through July, the Russian's laconic diary indicates correspondence with Berti-Calura in Florence and Gaspare Stampa in Abbiategrasso (near Milan). Stampa was apparently thought of primarily as a distributor of Bakunin's *L'Empire knouto-germanique*. On June 24, Bakunin wrote his first letter to Achille Bizzoni, director of *Il Gazzettino Rosa*, probably in the hope of developing a more effective north Italian outlet for his writings.[45] He

[41] *Ibid.*, II, 90-97, 132-33; Nettlau, *B.I.I.*, p. 190. It may well have been the Lyon fiasco that caused Bakunin to confess that "there was a capital defect in my nature: love of the fantastic, of extraordinary and unheard-of adventures, of undertakings revealing unlimited horizons . . . I suffocated in a calm and normal existence, I felt ill at ease. . . . My mind was in a continuous agitation, because it demanded action, life, movement." Kaminski, *Bakunin (una vita avventurosa)* (Milan: Istituto Editoriale Italiano, 1945), p. 28.

[42] Nettlau, *B.I.I.*, pp. 182-84, 187-90; Guillaume, *I.D.S.*, II, 132-33.

[43] Nettlau, *B.I.I.*, p. 189.

[44] *Ibid.*, pp. 190-91. Nettlau writes that Bakunin went to Florence to discuss a private affair with Luginin, a Russian refugee; Romano broadly implies Bakunin was directly involved in Gambuzzi's extortion activities in connection with the above-mentioned Neapolitan aqueduct contract. *Storia*, II, 87, 91 ff.

[45] Nettlau, *B.I.I.*, pp. 191, 246; Guillaume, *I.D.S.*, II, 164. On June 10, Bakunin asked Guillaume to "send . . . 210 or 200 copies [of *L'Empire knouto-germanique*] as quickly as possible, so that I can send them to Italy, where some friends are

continued, of course, his correspondence with Friscia, Gambuzzi, and Fanelli, and was twice visited in Locarno by the latter (April 16-19, June 19-25). Aside from these contacts, which, in relation to the attention Bakunin devoted to non-Italian matters in these months, can be interpreted as merely keeping open his lines of communication, the Russian agitator concerned himself very little with Italian affairs.[46]

The situation changed abruptly on July 24, when Bakunin read Mazzini's indictment of the International and its program in the July 13 issue of *La Roma del Popolo*.[47] Recognizing immediately that Mazzini's doctrinal criticism of the International's program was an attack on his own principles, Bakunin the very next day began the first article in a series directed against the apostle of Italian unity. He must have been pleased, indeed, by Mazzini's gratuitous publicizing of anarchist principles as the program of the socialist International. The advantages of polemicizing with Mazzini, from Bakunin's point of view, were irresistible. Through his contacts with Gambuzzi, Friscia, and Fanelli, he fully appreciated the impact of the Paris Commune on Italian republicans. He knew, even before he had confirmation from Italy, that Mazzini's war on the International would arouse indignation among those republicans who had identified the I.W.A. with the Commune. On the basis of his extensive first-hand contact with Italy and Italian radicals from 1864 to 1867, he also knew that the activist spirit pervading the *Risorgimento* was still vigorous, unappeased by either the attainment of national unity or the renewed interest of Mazzini in the social aspects of his program. Further, by answering Mazzini's specific ideological criticisms, Bakunin would compound, in effect, the misconception among Italian republicans that his own anarchist principles and those of the International were synonymous. Thus, under the guise of a polemic with Mazzini, the Russian would prosecute his feud with Marx, Engels, and the General Council in London. Finally, an attack on Mazzini, given the psychological aptness of the moment, promised to induce dissatisfied republicans to leave off their noisy protests of sympathy for the International and get down to the actual business of organizing I.W.A. sections.

The "Reply of an International to Giuseppe Mazzini by M. Bakunin, Member of the International Workingmen's Association," appearing as a

---

already waiting for them" (*ibid.*, II, 155). On July 19, the Russian sent fifty copies, along with the I.W.A. statutes, to Gaspare Stampa in Abbiategrasso (Nettlau, *B.I.I.*, p. 246). On the 22nd, *Il Gazzettino Rosa* offered Bakunin's pamphlet for sale; on the 25th, Enrico Bignami followed suit in the pages of *La Plebe*.

[46] For a picture of his primary preoccupations during the spring and early summer of 1871, Guillaume, *I.D.S.*, II, 130-33, 144-46, 148-56, 160-66.

[47] *Ibid.*, II, 173; Nettlau, *B.I.I.*, p. 247.

pamphlet supplement to the August 16 issue of *Il Gazzettino Rosa*,[48] was written in four days, testimony to the Russian's long experience in noting the weak points in the Mazzinian position. There was nothing original in this "Risposta"; its essential arguments had already been made by other critics of Mazzini years before. But, given the climate of republican opinion, given Bakunin's own cleverness as a polemicist, as a caricaturist, given his adeptness with colorful irony and sarcasm, his article of August 16—along with those that were to follow—had the effect of reducing the incoherent babble of protest among radical republicans to a few, simple, easily understood, easily remembered ideas. In the "Risposta" the Russian revealed his stature as a consummate propagandist, a *grand simplificateur*.[49] However unoriginal his arguments, however vulnerable Mazzini to the charge of ideological authoritarianism, the pamphlet of Bakunin contributed hugely to precipitating the internal crisis of the Italian republican party.

Fully aware of the reverence in which Mazzini was held by even those Italians who had attacked him for his anti-Communard position, Bakunin prefaced his rebuttal with a characterization of the Italian patriot as "one of the noblest and purest figures of our time; I would even say the greatest, if greatness were compatible with the obstinate cult of error." And again: "It is certainly not with a gay heart that one can decide to attack a man like Mazzini, a man whom one is forced to revere and love even while combatting him, . . . but piety, however legitimate, must never turn into idolatry."

The "cult" of which Mazzini is the last high priest is the system of thought based on religious idealism, authority, and the state. In accepting the principle of divine authority, Mazzini allies himself with reaction, allows "the mentality of the priest" to overcome his aspirations as a revolutionary. Mazzini, the worshipper of power, wants to substitute the power of the bourgeois republic for that of the monarchical state, the authority of the theologians for that of the Catholic Church. His trust in the bourgeoisie's potential willingness to help the workers is sheer

---

[48] *Il Gazzettino Rosa* announced the "Risposta" of Bakunin on Aug. 12: "Those who want to know what this bugbear really is, the International that gets on the nerves of the pure Mazzinians, will do well to read the reply of Bakunin; at least he excommunicates no one, no one is put under an interdict, and he does not want to impose—under pain of hell—abstruse metaphysical beliefs like the squaring of the circle."

[49] Bakunin himself was quite aware that his article was an oversimplification of the issues. In his letter to the editors of *La Liberté* (Brussels), thanking them for publishing his "Risposta," the Russian explained that "Italy is still at the ABC of socialism; it becomes necessary, therefore, to explain to [the Italians] many things that have already become banal for your public; I should not want to leave anything unexplained in addressing myself to the Italians . . ." Nettlau, *B.I.I.*, p. 252.

hypocrisy, for he knows that doing so would destroy the middle class, whose existence depends on exploitation of the proletariat.

Mazzini's accusations of atheism and materialism are more than welcome, for these are the "basis of all truth." The materialists, by "adjusting their social theories to the real developments of history, consider bestiality, anthropophagy, and slavery as the first points of departure of the progressive movement of society, while the idealists, in basing their speculations on the immortal soul and free will, inevitably end up in the cult of public order, . . . that is, in the consecration and organization of eternal slavery." Mazzini claims that materialists are incapable of dedicating themselves to the triumph of great causes, immune to stimulation by the ideals of liberty, justice, humanity, beauty, and truth, but— and here Bakunin's logic deteriorates into a specious play on words— theoretical materialism necessarily leads to practical idealism, while political idealism, the terrestrial application of religious idealism, is the root of all tyranny:

> Yesterday, under our very eyes, where stood the materialists and the atheists? In the Commune of Paris. And the idealists, the believers in God? In the National Assembly of Versailles. What did the men of Paris want? The final emancipation of humanity through the emancipation of labor. And what does the triumphant Versailles Assembly now want? The final degradation of humanity under the double yoke of spiritual and temporal power . . .

Mazzini, in good faith, spurred by a fanatical and sincere idealism, has committed two unpardonable crimes:

> At the very moment when the heroic population of Paris, . . . was being massacred by the tens of thousands, with their women and children, while defending . . . *the cause of the emancipation of the workers of the whole world;* when the frightening coalition of all the filthy reactions . . . heaped on them all the calumnies that only a limitless turpitude can imagine, Mazzini, the great, the pure democrat Mazzini, turning his back on the cause of the proletariat and remembering only his mission as a prophet and priest, likewise hurled his denunciations at them!

Mazzini promises proletarians glory, power, property, liberty, and equality if they become moral, if they adore God, accept the moral law Mazzini brings to them in His name, and if they help Mazzini create a republic "based on the marriage (impossible) of reason and faith, of divine authority and human liberty . . ." Socialism, on the other hand, offers the proletarian these dicta:

That the economic subjugation of the worker to the monopolist of raw materials and instruments of labor is the source of servitude in all its forms: social misery, moral degradation, political subjection, and

That, for this reason, the economic emancipation of the working classes is the great end to which every political movement ought to be subordinate as a *simple* means.[50]

Such, in its simplicity, is the fundamental thought of the International Workingmen's Association. It is understandable that Mazzini had to denounce it: and that is the second crime for which we reproach him.

Mazzini's social cooperativism results from his fear that the class struggle might destroy national unity. But, queried Bakunin, to which unity is Mazzini referring? There are at least five Italian nations: the clericals, the nobility and upper bourgeoisie, the middle and lower bourgeoisie, the city proletariat, and the peasantry. The last—the poorest, most numerous, and politically most naive class—are firmly in the hands of the priests, thanks to the superstition bred by their ignorance. Shaken out of their indifference and organized by socialism, the *contadini* could form, along with the urban workers, an "invincible army of social revolution." The city proletariat, though owning a patriotic past and still swearing in the names of Mazzini and Garibaldi, have not been entirely corrupted; in fact, the very poverty of this class ineluctably leads it to socialism. As for the middle and lower bourgeoisie, the class providing the backbone of the national unification, the tradition of abstract patriotism is dying hard. The continual economic difficulties besetting this segment of Italian society demoralizes it; it neither wants to turn back nor dares look ahead. Out of its ranks come the last disciples of Mazzini and Garibaldi, "poor young men full of generous aspirations, but incapable of orienting themselves." Yet, the Paris Commune opened the eyes of Italian youth; their intelligence and conscience counsels them to turn their backs on the bourgeois class from which they sprang. For their own spiritual salvation, they should be advised to turn into the path of popular social revolution. To find themselves, they must realize that "strength, life, intelligence, humanity, the whole future is in the proletariat."

That Bakunin's "Risposta" drew blood is attested to by the vigor of the Mazzinians' reaction. Vincenzo Brusco-Onnis, a veteran disciple of

---

[50] Italics mine. The original 1864 English text of the preamble to the I.W.A. statutes: "That the economical emancipation of the working classes is therefore the great end to which every political movement ought to be subordinate as a means." Guillaume, *I.D.S.*, I, 12. On June 11, 1870, the *Socialiste* (Paris) introduced the adjective "simple," probably in order to stress the anarchist argument that the statutes did not *require* socialist political activity. See, *ibid.*, II, 52, note 2; 58, note 1.

Mazzini, tried neutralizing the effects of the Russian's article in a series of three prolix pieces in *L'Unità Italiana,* under the heading, "Un Maestro dalla Russia." [51] He assured his readers that Bakunin's theories were neither new nor dangerous—after having devoted several thousand words to their analysis. Then, almost as if regretting the necessity of defending Mazzini, he extended the olive branch to the Russian: "We know very well that Mr. Bakunin and his followers abhor, as do we, the consequences of a foolish utopia; that they want the good of the people, as we want it." The "Risposta" of Bakunin, in addition to many such attacks by Mazzinian journals, provoked protests among numerous workers' and democratic societies.[52]

If these reactions were incoherent and often—as in the case of Brusco-Onnis' articles—not even based on a clear perception of the basic ideological differences separating the Mazzinian and Bakuninist positions, Mazzini himself never lost sight of his target. In a series of extremely lucid, tightly reasoned articles appearing in *La Roma del Popolo* during the month of August, Mazzini vigorously reaffirmed the ideas he had held for the preceding four decades and unerringly put his finger on the inaccuracies, contradictions, and arbitrary judgments contained in "the writing just published by a Russian, an influential member of the *International*," which makes "a systematic apology of *civil war* applied in the guise of a tonic for the nations." Still, there was no escaping the need for Mazzinians to deal more directly with the problem posed in the raw phrases of Bakunin, the social questions so dramatically underscored by the Paris Commune. *L'Unità Italiana* and *La Roma del Popolo,* beginning in September, were to be filled with references to the congress of Mazzinian workers' societies convoked by the Ligurian Permanent Commission on the very day Bakunin's "Risposta" appeared in *Il Gazzettino Rosa.* This, too, was the burden of Mazzini's correspondence for the next two months. Though completely aware of the devastation of his dreams by materialism and the materialist aspirations of the new generation, sensing the inequality of the struggle, Mazzini faced his last great organizational effort with a stout heart:

> I see only dissolution progressing around me. My war on materialism and the International has started a fire within the party. The young *freethinkers,* the *Gazzettino Rosa,* the *Favilla* of Mantua, the *Plebe* of Lodi, and the whole small republican press is beside itself with anger. Bakunin has published a periodical leaflet against me. I am now an apostate, a priest, a reactionary, the supporter of the men of Versailles: ambition, in the end, has possessed my soul; old age has made me superstitious and so on.

[51] Aug. 25, 28, 31, 1871.
[52] Rosselli, *Mazzini e Bakounine,* pp. 333, 335-36; Nettlau, *B.I.I.,* pp. 251-52.

It is a very sad dispute, but it had to break out, and I am not sorry to have initiated it. . . .[53]

For his part, Bakunin spent the month of August mustering his forces for the exploitation of the breach in the Party of Action he had so effectively helped to open. On the 5th, he wrote to Gaspare Stampa; on the 9th, Gambuzzi arrived in Locarno for a three-day conference; before he departed, Giuseppe Fanelli appeared on the Russian's doorstep; on the 13th, the cryptic diary carried the entry: "Riggio—Sicily—Girgenti" (the first Sicilian contact other than Friscia?); on the 14th Fanelli departed. On the 18th arrived a letter from Fanelli in Florence, while the Russian wrote to Enrico Bignami in Lodi (the first and only contact?) and to Stampa.[54] On the 20th, he received from Milan twenty-five copies of his "Reply," which he immediately sent back into Italy for distribution, not forgetting to include several copies for Friscia in Sicily. On the 21st, he plunged into an even lengthier attack on Mazzini,[55] probably stimulated by the appearance of Mazzini's "Gemiti, fremiti e ricapitulazione." To hasten the transition of Italian republicans from "the ABC of socialism" to a more "mature"—i.e., anarchist—conception, he urged La Liberté of Brussels, influential French-language organ of the "anti-authoritarians," to agree to an exchange with Italian socialist journals:

> There are some little newspapers founded by these young men in the North, for example, Il Gazzettino Rosa in Milan, La Plebe in Lodi, etc., etc., whom I have advised to propose an exchange with you. . . . [Il Gazzettino Rosa] is written by a small nucleus of very intelligent, lively, likable young men, full of generous aspirations, many freethinkers, but they have something, almost everything, to learn when it comes to socialism. The other paper, La Plebe, edited by Mr. Bignami, has declared itself very disposed to become the organ of the International sections being organized in and around Milan. It seems that [Bignami] is a young fellow full of good and serious will, but that he does not have all the intelligence and spirit of the writers for the Gazzettino Rosa.[56]

[53] Letter to Emilie Venturi, Aug. 29, 1871, S.E.I., XCI, 165 ff.
[54] See Bakunin's diary entries for August in Nettlau, B.I.I., pp. 247, 253; Guillaume, I.D.S., II, 173. Guillaume, visiting Bakunin "in August or . . . September," encountered a "young worker of Florence, named Gaetano Grassi," as a house guest of Bakunin. Ibid., II, 190-91.
[55] The work, consuming forty-nine days, was finished on November 16 and appeared under the title: La théologie politique de Mazzini e l'Association Internationale des Travailleurs (Neuchâtel: Commission de Propaganda socialiste, [Dec.] 1871), 111 pp. Cf., Nettlau, B.I.I., p. 250; Guillaume, I.D.S., II, 227.
[56] Nettlau, B.I.I., pp. 252-53. La Plebe, on Aug. 1, copied from La Favilla (July 26) a short biographical sketch of "Carlo Max," described as a man of astuteness, courage, energy, and spirit. On Aug. 17, the newspaper announced for the first time the sale of I.W.A. general statutes and regulations.

CONCLUSION

By early September 1871, the struggle for control of the radical republican group had found four protagonists: Mazzini, Garibaldi, the London General Council, and Michael Bakunin. Mazzini, through a workers' congress, would attempt to steer the Italian workers' movement into the safe haven of his antimaterialistic, cooperativistic formula for social transformation. He had issued his most eloquent appeal to Italian youth to spurn the materialist programs of the Commune and the socialist International, yet failed to realize that in directing his fire against the regenerated Proudhonism of Bakunin, he was only helping the Russian establish himself and his ideas as the symbol of Internationalist socialism in the eyes of Italian republicans. The error was substantially irrelevant from Mazzini's point of view, since the principles of both Marx and Bakunin, as materialist expressions, were proper targets for Mazzini's shafts.

Mazzini's error was irrelevant, too, in that most of the sympathetic reaction of Italian republicans to the Commune and the I.W.A. derived from the vigorous sense of frustration engendered by the monarchy's drawing the curtain on the unity process with the capture of Rome on September 20, 1870. One kind of *patria* had been realized, but the Paris Commune suggested that another had yet to be won: a fatherland, not only geographically and politically united, but one uniting the Italian nation with the bonds of social justice.[57] Precisely because he combined an obvious loyalty to this humanitarian aspiration and a legendary reputation as a man of action *par excellence,* Garibaldi seemed the logical leader of the "second revolution," the concept of which had been so stimulated by the emotional impact of the battle waged on the barricades of Paris.

Prior to August 1871 neither the General Council in London nor Bakunin seems to have appreciated the opportunity to channel this state of mind into the path of socialism. The former, through Cafiero, had confined its attention for all practical purposes to Naples, and even this organizational nucleus was suppressed almost at birth. The Sicilian

[57] In effect, Vincenzo Pezza was insisting that his was a higher type of patriotism when he wrote: "Only the Paris revolution of March 18 gave the initiative of a great idea, destined . . . to redeem the peoples from all economic and political tyrannies. No one more than we hopes that Italy will initiate that great political and social transformation toward which humanity is moving. But in conscience we can not repudiate the initiative that comes to us from others because it is foreign, taking refuge behind a niggardly national pride. We do not imitate, but we accept everything that conforms to the universal principles of liberty, without enrolling ourselves in this or that school. This we do, and the Mazzinians themselves must do to be logical." *Il Gazzettino Rosa,* Aug. 14, 1871.

sections were as yet isolated. Bakunin had allowed his contacts to dwindle to no more than three correspondents.

At this point, both Marx and Bakunin began to see Italy as one of the potential battlefields in a showdown struggle for domination of the international socialist movement. Engels, as the General Council's corresponding secretary for Italy, was about to assume the generalship in the Italian theater, while Marx mustered his friends as a "stacked jury" to pass the death sentence on the "anti-authoritarians" at the London Conference. Bakunin, under no illusions as to the outcome, sought to deny the Italian field to his London foes by taking up the cudgels against Mazzini, opposing to his principles, in the name of the socialist International, those of the anarchist heresy.

If Mazzini's failure to recapture the loyalties of radical republicans could already be prophesied, there was certainly no possibility of anticipating their choice between anarchism and "authoritarian" socialism. Though they had left Mazzini behind in adducing the class struggle from the episode of the Commune, they had yet to be convinced that the war of class against class could not be reconciled with what both Marx and Bakunin termed "bourgeois patriotism." In September 1871, *Garibaldinismo* represented their hope of squaring the circle.

IX

Bakunin versus Mazzini (September to November 1871)

CONFLICTING CONGRESS PROJECTS

THE Italian radicals to whom Bakunin addressed his propaganda in the fall of 1871 were completely unaware that Marx was the unnamed target of the Russian's polemic with Mazzini. Prior to mid-November, Bakunin neither attacked Marx openly nor challenged the authority of the General Council as the central administrative organ of the socialist International. Bakunin's attacks on Mazzini posed only the generic issue of choosing, as a guide to practical action, between the materialist doctrine of socialism, with its class-struggle hypothesis, its assertion of proletarian rights, its atheism, its internationalism, its thinly disguised hostility toward private property, and Mazzini's political idealism, his religiosity, his cult of *la patria*, his social cooperativism, his emphasis on duty. "German communist authoritarianism" versus "anti-authoritarian" socialism, the antithesis exercising the Swiss Bakuninists, meant nothing to Italian radicals, who were trying to digest the fact that the man who had captained Italian republicanism for almost four decades now appeared to have allied himself with the forces of social conservatism. Thus the socialist International was benefited by the adherence of the Italian dissidents, even though the new recruits cared nothing and knew nothing of the Marx-Bakunin controversy.

Bakunin's every attack on Mazzini, therefore, was a blow struck for the socialist International. Even while undermining Marx, the Russian was helping the organizational growth of the I.W.A. In this sense, his polemic with Mazzini, his defense of the International, his urging Italian radicals to organize themselves into socialist sections and apply for official recognition from the General Council, facilitated the work of Engels, the I.W.A.'s corresponding secretary for Italy.

Between August 21 and November 16, Bakunin devoted almost fifty days to the writing of his second brochure against Mazzini, "The Political Theology of Mazzini and the International Workingmen's Association." [1] To his friend Ogarev, he wrote on November 3: "Several reasons, my spleen, my indisposition, my empty purse, and, above all, a war that I have waged on *Ossip Ivanovich* [Mazzini], have . . . paralyzed me to the point where I have suspended all correspondence with my intimates." [2] Brusco-Onnis' attack on him in *L'Unità Italiana* caused Bakunin to interrupt his pamphlet against Mazzini long enough to pen a lengthy retort, published in the October 10, 11, 12, issues of *Il Gazzettino Rosa*. Late in October, the Russian's anti-Mazzinian polemic reached its apogee with a long propaganda effort entitled: "To my Friends of Italy on the occasion of the workers' congress convoked in Rome for November 1 by the Mazzinian party." [3] The Russian could not have chosen a more apt psychological moment to address himself to the Italian workers' societies, for every circumstance conspired to heighten the effect of his arguments against the workers falling in with Mazzini's ambitions for the Rome Congress.

Mazzini's general intent in urging a national congress of workers' societies was to fend off socialist penetration of the Italian labor movement; concretely, he wanted to revive the Pact of Fraternity adopted at Naples in 1864 and to create a strong organization under centralized control. He suggested that the delegates to the Rome Congress elect a "central directive commission," composed of five workers, and a council of thirty or more representatives of the workers' societies to act as a watchdog committee over the activity of the central organ. The "collective life" of the Italian workers could then begin; the social question, "today left to the arbitration of every local nucleus, will then be defined before the country, strong . . . in the indirect consensus of almost twelve million workers." Most important of all, it would frustrate the International, for the workers of Italy could then create, "with your brothers of other Nations, bonds of alliance that we all understand and desire, not submerging individuals or small nuclei in vast and ill-ordered Foreign Societies that begin by speaking to you of liberty, only to conclude inevitably in anarchy or the despotism of a Center [I.W.A. General Council] or of the city [London] in which that center is located." [4]

[1] Guillaume, *I.D.S.*, II, 187, 227, 280; Nettlau, *B.I.I.*, p. 250.

[2] Dragomanov, *Correspondence*, p. 352.

[3] Published in Italian translation by the anarchist organ, *Il Piccone* (Naples), June 24, 1885 ff.; *Il Paria* (Ancona), Aug. 17, 1885 ff.; as a pamphlet, *Il socialismo e Mazzini. Lettera agli amici d'Italia* (Ancona, 1885), 103 pp.; (Rome, Florence, 1905), 64 pp.; (5th ed., Rome, 1910).

[4] "Ai rappresentanti gli artigiani nel congresso di Roma," *La Roma del Popolo*, Oct. 12, 1871.

Wanting to attract the moderate workers' societies and to allay any middle-class alarm at the prospect of a unified labor movement, Mazzini recommended that delegates avoid discussion of "religious, political, or social doctrines, which a Congress today can not decide except with irresponsible declarations, ridiculous for their impotence." [5] It was a serious reversal by the man who, in the early 1860's, had urged political discussions and action on the workers as the indispensable condition of their social emancipation. Only a sense of desperation could have led him to anticipate winning over workers' societies of every political persuasion by the mere expedient of promising to avoid political discussion at the congress.

Nothing could have been more improbable, in fact, than a Mazzinian gathering abjuring political discussion; neither the government authorities nor the moderate societies were deceived in the least. The Minister of Interior secretly instructed his prefects to discourage local societies from accepting the invitation of "the revolutionary party which . . . seeks to propagate its pernicious doctrines and foment disorders." The Artisans' Brotherhood of Livorno refused to participate in the congress, fearing, among other things, a discussion of religious matters; the Neapolitan Workers' Society spurned the invitation on the grounds that the congress would probably degenerate into a political debate.[6] In Rome, the local workers' association used the excuse that the Ligurian Permanent Commission, in convoking the congress, had exceeded its authority, since the *Regolamento* of 1855 gave that power to the senior society of the city previously designated as the seat of the next convention. Since the Naples Congress had designated their city as such in 1864, the Romans informed the Ligurian Commission they would convoke a "legal" convention in the near future.[7] The recent dissolution by the authorities of the Sampierdarena and Oggiono-Como workers' associations for concerning themselves with political matters also gave immediacy to the prefects' advice to stay away from the Rome gathering.[8]

The Garibaldian opposition to the Mazzinian project posed an even more serious threat. The movement for a national congress of all Italian

---

[5] *La Roma del Popolo*, Oct. 12, 1871.

[6] Rosselli, *Mazzini e Bakounine*, pp. 362-63; *La Roma del Popolo*, Sept. 28, 1871. Like the Roman society, however, the Livorno association reversed its decision and delegated D. G. De Montel to the congress.

[7] *Ibid.*, Oct. 26, 1871. On the day before the Rome Congress convened, the rank and file membership of the society repudiated their leaders' ban on the congress and delegated Salvatore Battaglia and a certain Sterbini to represent them. Alessandro Bottero, *Dibattimenti nel processo per cospirazione e internazionalismo innanzi alla Assise di Firenze* (Rome, 1875), pp. 280-81 (cited hereafter as Bottero, *Dibattimenti*); *La Favilla*, Nov. 2, 1871.

[8] *Il Congresso di Roma e le società italiane* (Rome, 1871), pp. 2, 5, 7, 15, 54.

democratic societies initiated in August by Celso Ceretti and the Garibaldian societies of Mirandola, Mantua, and Verona by now frankly aimed at undermining the Rome convention, though Ceretti and his friends originally intended the initiative as a gesture of conciliation with the Mazzinians. Acceptances of Ceretti's invitation to a democratic congress poured in from all over the peninsula; even a society in Genoa, the Mazzinian stronghold, agreed to send a delegate.[9] In Florence, the Social Democratic Union named Battaglia, Grassi, and Piccioli-Poggiali as its representatives to the gathering and recommended for discussion abolition of the wage system, profit-sharing by the workers, abolition of indirect taxes, and the adoption of a single, progressive income tax. This they called socialism, "a rigorous application of the science of political economy, liberated . . . from the fetters binding the official economists of the monarchy." [10]

The Garibaldian congress was to be held in either Rome or Bologna in October, but Luigi Castellazzo, after having agreed to represent Garibaldi at the convention, persuaded his idol to approve a postponement until the following spring.[11] Though Ceretti, Castellazzo, and the other promoters of the scheme persisted in billing their project as a congress of democratic societies, the rank and file of the Garibaldian faithful very likely thought it was the first step in the organization of a nation-wide socialist movement, socialist, that is, in the broadly humanitarian sense understood by the general. On October 21, La Favilla of Mantua referred to the forthcoming meeting as the "socialist congress of the Italian democratic societies." And if a more explicit distinction between the Garibaldians' and Mazzinians' orientations was needed, Garibaldi provided it when he wrote Giuseppe Petroni, editor of La Roma del Popolo, disapproving the Mazzinian congress and justifying his declared adherence to the socialist International on the grounds that it represented "the continuation of the emancipation of human right." [12] On October 24, the general inferred from Mazzini's hostility toward the democratic congress movement that "conciliation with the infallibilities of the Roma del Popolo is a dream." [13]

<hr />

[9] La Favilla, Sept. 23, 27, Oct. 8. Enrico Bignami lent his full support. La Plebe, Sept. 23. Riggio and the Girgenti section approved the initiative on Oct. 10. La Favilla, Oct. 29, 1871.

[10] Conti, O.S.F., pp. 121-22.

[11] For the Garibaldi correspondence with Castellazzo, Ceretti, and Filopanti concerning the congress project, La Favilla, Oct. 15, 17, 24, Nov. 1; L'Eguaglianza, Oct. 12, 1871; Ciampoli, op. cit., pp. 587-88.

[12] Letter of Oct. 21, La Favilla, Oct. 31, 1871.

[13] Letter to Castellazzo, La Plebe, Nov. 9, supplement; La Favilla, Nov. 1; La Perseveranza, Nov. 2, 1871. See also, Garibaldi's letter of Nov. 9 to Gaetano Tallinucci, in Ximenes, comp., Epistolario, I, 392.

Given Garibaldi's identification with the socialist International, Mazzini's continuing public diatribes against socialism and the I.W.A.[14] had as their logical corollary his private ridicule of the whole notion of a congress of democratic organizations. If the Garibaldians wanted a national unity of democratic societies, why, asked Mazzini, did they simply not join his Republican Alliance? The Garibaldians were aiming at "a triumph of communistic and international follies." Garibaldi would probably not follow through with the scheme, but if he did, "it will be unique to see the man who dares not proffer the word 'republic' to Italy directing the discussion on collective property or some such matter." [15] On the eve of the Rome Congress, the Genoese patriot accepted the challenge in the terms posed by Garibaldi. On October 31 he wrote his friend, Harriet Hamilton King: "I want the Congress to draw a strong division line between our own Italian movement and the aim and method of the International Society. I hope I shall succeed: still, now especially that Garibaldi has chosen to side openly against me, there are many difficulties to be confronted." [16]

BAKUNIN'S "TO MY FRIENDS OF ITALY"

When Bakunin read Mazzini's address "To the Representatives of the Artisans in the Congress of Rome" in the October 12 issue of *La Roma del Popolo,* he immediately sensed the vulnerability of the apostle of republicanism as the sponsor of a workers' congress eschewing religious, political, and social questions. This, along with the fact that the Rome Congress was supposed to erect a *cordon sanitaire* between Italian workers and the socialist virus, was more than enough to cause Bakunin to drop his labors on the "political theology" of Mazzini and, between October 19 and 29, dash off a rousing propaganda circular entitled, "To my Friends of Italy" (*Ai miei amici d'Italia*). The manuscript was sent to Pezza in Milan, presumably for publication in *Il Gazzettino Rosa,* but Bakunin's new lieutenant, for reasons not revealed by the record, sent it on to the Neapolitan socialist nucleus of Cafiero, Palladino, Malatesta, Tucci, Leoncavallo, and their friends. Of this group, only Cafiero and Tucci had favored participation in the Mazzinian congress, but the arrival of the Bakunin manuscript, in Cafiero's words, "caused our opposers to make up their minds and to recognize the utility of going to Rome." [17] On the last page, Bakunin had written:

---

[14] "L'Internazionale svizzera," "L'Internazionale, cenno storico," *La Roma del Popolo,* Sept. 14, 21, 28, 1871.

[15] *S.E.I.,* XCI, 191, 222.

[16] *Ibid.,* XCI, 238.

[17] Nettlau, *B.I.I.,* pp. 256 ff.; Guillaume, *I.D.S.,* II, 227. Cafiero had already written to Turin, Milan, and Girgenti, urging attendance at the Rome Congress.

And even today, at the congress of Rome, if it is possible and if there is time, you should give the first battle. To the proposals of Mazzini you should ardently oppose your counterproposals. You shall probably be in a minority, but this should not frighten you, provided this minority be convinced, compact, and, precisely for this reason, respectable. You will certainly not find a better occasion to announce your program to Italy and Europe.[18]

The Neapolitans were so impressed by the Bakunin manuscript that they immediately translated the first twenty-five pages of it (the critique of Mazzini's "Ai rappresentanti . . ."), Cafiero—or one of his collaborators—added a conclusion of his own and the abbreviated version, under the title, "To the workers delegated to the Congress of Rome," was printed in time for Cafiero and Tucci to circulate the leaflet among the delegates at the Rome Congress.[19]

The Bakuninist part of the leaflet appearing at the congress contained a vigorously ironic analysis of Mazzini's "Ai rappresentanti . . . ," accusing him of seeking to establish a dictatorship over the Italian workers' movement, of wanting to build a "theological Chinese wall" around Italy. In attacking Mazzini's statement that the International leads to anarchy or the despotism of London and the General Council, Bakunin had written:

> *Anarchy* is the partisans of the abolition of the State in the International—Mazzini loves despotism; . . . only as a concession to the modern spirit does he call it *Liberty*. Mazzini wants the despotism of Rome, not that of London; but *we who have no religion, who detest despotism in general, reject that of Rome, as we would reject that of London, if there were any*. . . . [Italics mine.]
>
> Here is the last word: Mazzini, inspired and inspiring, dictator, and in his hands the whole working class of Italy, conveniently gagged, paralyzed, annihilated, to the advantage of the [Central Directive] Commission, itself directed by Mazzini, having become an instrument of theocratic republican reaction.[20]

The eagerness with which these young radicals adopted Bakunin's argument, the fact that they punished themselves so severely in turning

[18] Bakunin, *Oeuvres,* VI, 422; Nettlau, *B.I.I.,* p. 257.

[19] *Ibid.,* pp. 263-64, for the Cafiero contribution to the leaflet; Romano, *Storia,* II, 331-41, for the complete text of the "Agli operai delegati al congresso di Roma," by "Un gruppo di Internazionali."

[20] The charge that the directive commission was intended as a puppet of Mazzini was well founded. Before the congress he instructed his lieutenants that all questions for discussion brought by the delegates should be left to the central directive commission, "with the obligation to come to an understanding with me, through the intermediary of my friends in Rome." *S.E.I.,* XCI, 257.

it into a printed propaganda leaflet in Italian in something under forty-eight hours, suggests that the Russian's central theme of anti-authoritarianism struck a responsive chord. The guiding principle of local autonomy finds clear expression, too, in one of the paragraphs Cafiero (Tucci? Palladino?) appended to Bakunin's indictment of Mazzini. The workers were called upon to abjure:

> . . . Authorities or Central and Directive Commissions; instead, establish local and regional congresses, every three, every six months, in which . . . all the most important economic, political and religious questions are fully discussed, and thus prepare the material for discussions by an annual general congress, in which the workers are represented by delegates bound by an imperative mandate.

Though the short version of Bakunin's anti-Mazzinian piece used at the Rome Congress by Cafiero and Tucci had a clamorous effect, the unpublished portion of the Russian's address "To my Friends of Italy" was the first direct contact of the Neapolitan nucleus—save Tucci and Palladino[21]—with the revolutionary philosophy of the paladin of the International's anarchist wing. In it, Bakunin had formulated a social revolutionary program in far more immediate and concrete language than that used by Engels in his correspondence with Cafiero. Moreover, where Engels' letters were shot through with personal vituperation of Bakunin, with charges of sinister hypocrisy, the Russian's address "To my Friends of Italy" made no mention of his doctrinal differences with Marx and the General Council. Cafiero and his intimates may well have assumed that Engels was far more interested in crucifying Bakunin than in responding to Mazzini's challenge to the International. Cafiero, no less than Palladino, Malatesta, Leoncavallo, and Tucci, saw Mazzinianism as the immediate threat—as proved by their ready adoption of Bakunin's propaganda piece. That the ideas they accepted from it were clearly opposed to those of Marx and Engels proves no more than their belief that the I.W.A. permitted doctrinal differences as to method among its members. In fact, as Cafiero was later to point out to Engels, there were several good reasons why Bakunin could expect a sympathetic audience:

> *Bakounine* has many personal friends in Italy, having lived in this country, and he is in correspondence with some of them. Because of his past and the continuous work he performs for our cause, he is loved even by many who do not know him personally. The various replies of Bakounine to Mazzini which appeared in the *Gazzettino Rosa* in the form of pamphlets, the

[21] Bakunin's diary shows letters received from Palladino on Sept. 26 and Oct. 9; Bakunin wrote him on Sept. 28 and Oct. 16. Nettlau, *B.I.I.*, pp. 254-56.

writing he sent for the Congress of Rome and a work which he is currently completing on the *Mazzinian Theology*, a complete exposition of the International, could not fail to arouse a lively interest among the Italian internationalists.[22]

The failure of Cafiero and his friends to publish three-fourths of Bakunin's "Ai miei amici d'Italia" probably meant that they deemed these principles unsuited to their propaganda needs of the moment, or simply that they lacked the time to incorporate them in the piece they prepared for the Rome Congress. In any case, one can not rule out the possibility that this part of the Russian's address also had a powerful influence on the thinking of the young Neapolitan militants, so eager to oppose an action program of their own to the congress scheme of Mazzini.

Gone now was the Russian's once firm faith in the power of the Italian peasants, "the proletariat of rags," to overthrow bourgeois society.[23] The experience of the Paris Commune had underscored for Bakunin the peasants' need of help from the city proletariat, as it had taught Marx the urban workers' need of help from their country cousins. To his Italian friends, Bakunin recommended the alliance of city and country proletarians as the *sine qua non* of an effective assault on the capitalist state:

> In the name of revolutionary socialism, organize the proletariat of the cities; having done this, unite it in the same preparatory organization with the people of the countryside. The uprising of the city proletariat no longer suffices; with it one would have only a political revolution, which would necessarily have against it the natural, legitimate reaction of the people of the countryside, and this reaction, or merely the indifference of the peasants, would suffocate the revolution of the cities, as recently happened in France. Only the universal revolution is strong enough to overthrow, to shatter, the organized power of the State, sustained by all the means of the rich classes. But the universal revolution is the social revolution, . . . the simultaneous revolution of the people of the countryside and of the cities. Here is what needs to be organized, since without a preparatory organization the most potent elements are ineffective and mean nothing.[24]

[22] *Ibid.*, p. 273.

[23] ". . . only this ragged [rural Italian] proletariat is pervaded by the spirit and strength of the imminent social revolution." Dragomanov, *Correspondence*, p. 27. "Arouse the profoundly socialist instinct dormant in the heart of every Italian peasant." The *macinato* revolts of 1869 had "given the measure of the natural revolutionary socialism of the Italian peasants." From "Lo Stato e l'Anarchia," (1870) *Oeuvres*, IV, 32-37.

[24] Nettlau, *B.I.I.*, p. 259.

Bakunin then brought his anti-statist principle into the context of the immediate problem confronting the Italian socialists:

> Today, dear friends, it is your duty to organize an intelligent, honest, attractive and, above all, persevering propaganda in order to make [the mass of Mazzinian and Garibaldian workers] understand. To accomplish this, you need only to explain to them the program of the International. . . . And if, in doing this, you will organize yourselves throughout Italy and do it harmoniously, fraternally, without recognizing any leadership but your own young collectivity, I swear to you that in one year's time there will no longer be any Mazzinian or Garibaldian workers; that all shall have become revolutionary socialists, patriots, that is, and internationalists at the same time. Thus you shall have created the unshakable basis for an imminent social revolution.
>
> . . . Yes, these youths must have the courage today to recognize and proclaim aloud their *full and definitive separation from politics*, from conspiracy and from the republican enterprises of Mazzini, under pain of seeing themselves annihilated and of condemning themselves to inertia and shameful impotence. They must inaugurate their own policy.
>
> What can this policy be? Outside of the Mazzinian system, . . . that of the Republic-State, there is only one, that of the Republic-Commune, of the Republic-Federation, of the socialist Republic, frankly popular, that of *Anarchy*. It is the same as the policy of the social revolution, that puts first *the abolition of the State*, the economic and completely free order of the people, an order [constructed] *from the bottom to the top* by means of federation.[25]

THE CONGRESS OF ROME

Under the most inauspicious circumstances, the long heralded Mazzinian congress of workers' societies met in Rome on November 1: the overwhelming majority of moderate societies stayed away (out of more than 900 workers' societies in the country, only 135 sent representatives to the congress); the authorities kept the gathering under direct police surveillance; Garibaldi and his followers had refused their blessing; Alberto Tucci, representing a legally nonexistent Neapolitan section of the I.W.A., and Carlo Cafiero, mandated by the Girgenti section, attended as observers but immediately began trying to subvert the meeting by distributing copies of the leaflet, "To the workers delegates to the Congress

---

[25] Nettlau, *B.I.I.*, p. 260. Italics mine.

of Rome," dedicated to the proposition that Mazzini was the Italian workingman's worst enemy.[26]

The congress spent five days slightly retouching the 1864 text of the Pact of Fraternity, in the hope of giving it a more radical tone. Following Mazzini's instructions, the delegates replaced the central council created in 1864, dormant since birth, with a directive commission of five, resident in Rome, assisted by a twenty-one-member watchdog committee. The affiliated societies maintained their independence in strictly local affairs, but all decisions and execution of policy in national and international matters were reserved to the directive commission, thus establishing a greater degree of centralized control than that provided by the Neapolitan decision of 1864.[27] The executive group, in addition to numerous administrative functions, was instructed to found "a weekly newspaper, the official organ of the works and views of the working classes" (the first issue appeared on Feb. 1, 1872, under the title, *L'Emancipazione*). Aside from these accomplishments, however, the congress could not have more effectively sabotaged Mazzini's goal of avoiding the appearance of a republican propaganda meeting.[28]

Without a protest, a declaration of republicanism was voted on the first day of the convention, proof of the absence of moderate societies of monarchist persuasion. When the preamble of the Pact of Fraternity was brought under discussion, one delegate wanted to include a declaration of adherence, not merely to republican but specifically to "Mazzinian" principles. Mauro Macchi dryly suggested that the congress refrain from identifying itself with any individual and Francesco Pais, an ex-colonel on Garibaldi's general staff during the Vosges campaign and sympathizer of the International since the Commune, offered an equally sober admonition: "Do not be more Mazzinian than Mazzini!"

Warned away from identifying the Pact of Fraternity with Mazzini, the extremists, through the delegates Marini and Turchi, introduced

---

[26] For the proceedings, *Atti del dodicesimo congresso generale delle società operaie italiane tenutosi in Roma, li 1, 2, 3, 4, 5, 6 novembre 1871* (Rome, 1871); *Resoconto del XII Congresso operaio. Pubblicazione straordinaria della Roma del Popolo*, No. 3 (Rome, Nov. 4, 1871); *La Favilla*, Nov. 4, 7, 8, 9, 1871. Nettlau, *B.I.I.*, pp. 265-66, contains excerpts from the eight-page MS report of the proceedings signed by Cafiero and Tucci, *Resoconto del Congresso Operaio di Roma alle Sezioni di Napoli e di Girgenti dell'Associazione Internazionale degli Operai*. This report is summarized in *L'Eguaglianza*, Dec. 27, 1871. For secondary treatments, see the above-cited general works of Manacorda, Rosselli, and Romano.

[27] For the revised Pact of Fraternity, *La Roma del Popolo*, Nov. 9, 16, 1871; *Atti . . . congresso . . . Roma*, p. 57, cited above.

[28] The many questions submitted bearing on the immediate, practical, day-to-day problems confronting Italian workers (wages, hours, profit-sharing, strikes, etc.) were referred to the directive commission for study and recommendations for action.

resolutions affirming Mazzini's social and political principles. Still another delegate, seeking to clarify Marini's proposal, violently excoriated the International Workingmen's Association. Tucci and Cafiero, the only Internationalists present, could no longer confine themselves to observing and passing out subversive leaflets. In a speech echoing the lines he had written five years earlier for *La Situazione Italiana,* Tucci revealed himself still very much the libertarian:

> The *patria* is a fact, nor are the facts denied. However, if it is desired to make of these facts a religion with prophets who, in its name, evoke the laws of duty and aspire to establish a primacy over other peoples, we, the enemies of all religion, reject this religion of the fatherland and in the name of the solidarity of peoples we renounce any idea of prevalence or primacy. In our opinion, the fatherland is founded on the inevitable and indispensable bond which the solidarity of well-being and liberty imposes between peoples who have the same customs and language. However, in our view, *the fatherland is created spontaneously, once the present state of violence has ceased, from the bottom to the top* [italics mine], and it excludes every idea of conquest and forced annexation.

Tucci offered his own order of the day: "that the economic emancipation of the working classes—the great end to which every political movement must be subordinated—can be accomplished only by themselves." Cafiero immediately—and fully—subscribed to his friend's sentiments and warned that if a pro-Mazzinian resolution were passed, he would walk out of the congress.[29]

The Turchi proposal—to proclaim "solemnly the political and social principles proposed for forty years by Mazzini, as those that will lead more readily and effectively to the true emancipation of the worker"—was accepted by a vote of 34-19, with 6 abstentions. Cafiero, Tucci, and D. G. De Montel, delegate of the Livorno Artisans' Brotherhood, forthwith presented a written protest condemning Mazzini's principles as "contrary to the true interests of the working class and the progress of humanity," and left the meeting. Mauro Macchi, who had voted against the pro-Mazzinian resolution, also deserted the congress after the votes were counted.[30]

---

[29] Rosselli, *Mazzini e Bakounine,* p. 380. Tucci's proposal was excluded from the official *compte-rendu* of the Congress, but Rosselli found it in the MS report the two Internationalists sent to the Girgenti and Neapolitan sections. For Cafiero's brief speech, *L'Eguaglianza,* Dec. 27, 1871.

[30] *Ibid.,* Nov. 19, 1871; *cf.,* also, Bottero, *Dibattimenti,* pp. 128, 281 ff. Among the six abstentionists was Osvaldo Gnocchi-Viani, who was pro-socialist as early as September, 1865 (see above, p. 85, note 61). His experience in the Vosges with

Mazzini, in exile, drew scant comfort from the proceedings. He was pleased, of course, that he had an anti-Internationalist majority, but "I feel disillusioned in other respects." The first three days had been wasted in idle discussion, "only words, words," and, thanks to Garibaldi and the Internationalists, many societies had not been represented. The congress was full of "endless chatter, deviations, imprudences of friends who pushed my name forward, petty reactions of friends full of self-esteem, . . . uncertainty on the Central Commission." [31] Everything depended on the effectiveness of the Commission, and on this score he was hopeful, even though one of its members had yet to be coaxed out of his socialist tendencies. To Federico Campanella he wrote on November 16:

> The Congress went badly in one sense, but the important result remains. The Commission is elected. . . . Much . . . depends on the Commission itself. . . . Four are our men; the fifth is Battaglia, whom I know very well, but he is wavering a little under the influence of him who seeks to make him see the Dictator in me, the Pope, and I do not know what else. . . . Use your influence to make him feel the importance of the organization and the necessity of not going astray. I have written to him.[32]

Throughout the few months of life left to him, Mazzini was to continue his campaign against the International and his efforts to control the Italian workers' movement, indefatigably, uncompromisingly, without the slightest inconsistency of principle, but there could be no masking his defeat on the basic issue. With the Congress of Rome he had failed to lead the organized workers into a united antisocialist front.

The propaganda of a Bakunin and the foggy Internationalism of a Garibaldi aside, Mazzini owed much of his failure to his own refusal to recognize that the radical press, in depicting the Communard episode

---

Garibaldi, as in the case of so many Italian volunteers, induced him to move further toward the left, and Mazzini's condemnation of the Commune made him a socialist in all but name. Though a member of the Ligurian Permanent Commission that convoked the Rome Congress, Gnocchi-Viani was reported to Mazzini as "an Internationalist, Communist, everything that is evil" (*S.E.I.*, XCI, 255). In his memoirs, Gnocchi-Viani wrote that "the things exposed by [Cafiero and Tucci at the Rome Congress] seconded my own inclinations, and I should have liked to affirm my solidarity openly with them—but was it legitimate and honest to do so, when I held a mandate from an association that could not have associated itself with the protestants? I did not leave the Congress and I abstained from the vote." *Ricordi di un Internazionalista*, p. 126. Cf., also, Felice Anzi, "Dal mazzinianismo al socialismo (Osvaldo Gnocchi-Viani)," *Critica Sociale*, XXXIX, No. 7 (Apr. 1, 1947), 125-26.

[31] *S.E.I.*, XCI, 260, 266-67.

[32] *Ibid.*, XCI, 272 ff. Campanella's personal appeals failed to restore Battaglia's Mazzinian orthodoxy, to judge from Mazzini's subsequent complaints. See Mazzini's letters of Feb., 1872, to Campanella and Giannelli, in *ibid.*, XCI, 349, 371.

as proof of the secular egotism of the bourgeoisie, had irreparably discredited, among the more radical workers' societies, the Mazzinian dogma that proletarian salvation lay in collaboration with the middle class.[33] On the other hand, the great bulk of workers' associations, far more concerned with the immediate problems of syndical activity than with the institutional question, were not to be convinced that a unified labor movement under Mazzini's direction could be anything more than a political instrument for the attainment of a republic. Their absence at the Rome Congress was a silent testimonial to this fact.

Mazzini's lack of success in mustering Italian workers behind his republican banner has been attributed to his not perceiving "that the political-social problem, once the Risorgimento was completed, entered a new phase also in Italy, ... and that our country could not remain immune or extraneous to the European rise of socialism." [34] Actually, Mazzini was keenly alive to this new element in Italian social development and did not hesitate to admit that "the International is a tremendous symptom of a condition of things that overwhelmingly and rapidly demands a remedy." [35] Significant, in this connection, is the fact that even he tried to capitalize on the popularity of the I.W.A. In appealing to the workers, he ruled out only those socialist principles—chiefly the class-struggle doctrine—that did not and could not be squared with his own; for the rest—the rights of proletarians, the selfishness of the possessing classes, the international fraternity of peoples, the economic progress of the proletariat, liberal tax reforms, the workers' right to a just share of the product, free education, universal suffrage—he claimed a priority in propagating:

> All the truths contained in the programs and manifestations of the first period of the International [i.e., prior to 1868] belong to the Republican party in Italy and elsewhere, proposed long before the International arose. . . . The alliance of Fatherlands, emancipated and created according to the needs, nature, and desires of the peoples, was our ideal ever since the first republican teachings were initiated in Italy in 1832. The expression, *United States of Europe*, issued from the lips of an Italian republican, Carlo Cattaneo. The International only dismembered

[33] Mazzini, a week after the congress: ". . . to give oneself to the International is to place oneself against the entire bourgeoisie, with part of which, at least, it is necessary to proceed in accord to succeed." *S.E.I.*, XCVII, 416. A few days later: ". . . the workers must . . . come to an understanding with the republican bourgeois, just as the republican bourgeois must undertake the obligation to make of the republic a lever for the social transformation." *Ibid.*, XCVII, 420.

[34] Carlo Morandi, *I partiti politici nella storia d'Italia* (Florence: Le Monnier, 1945), p. 28.

[35] "L'Internazionale. Cenno storico," *La Roma del Popolo*, Sept. 28, 1871.

the program, on the one hand, and added fearsome and harmful errors to it, on the other.[36]

Not obtuseness to social realities, but the irremovable and consumately sincere conviction that social justice was impossible outside his republic, that a materialist system precludes development of the sense of morality needed to give substance to any concept of equity, be it political, economic, or social—here lay the basic obstacle to any effective effort by Mazzini to block the infiltration of the socialist idea. If Mazzini misread the signs of his time in any respect, it was that, in respect to the moderate workers' societies, he underestimated their indifference to the institutional question, while overestimating the sympathy of a whole generation of young radicals for his argument that realizing the republic was the shortest path to a just society.

INTERNATIONALIST STRENGTH (AUTUMN 1871)

For Italy's handful of bona fide Internationalists, Mazzini's losing battle to organize the labor movement for his own ends, to maintain the discipline and integrity of the Party of Action, had only one meaning: that the International was about to acquire wide support for the socialist idea. Even before the Rome Congress, Antonio Riggio promised Engels that "in one more year the destinies of the peninsula will be in our hands. Mazzini is alone." [37] Two days later, Cafiero wrote the General Council that there was not an important city in Italy where the I.W.A. had not put down "more or less deep roots" and that no force could eradicate them. "The International has possessed itself of the whole of Italy, from the Alps to the farthest reef of Sicily, in Turin, as in Catania, our glorious banner waves." [38] At the Rome Congress, reported Cafiero and Tucci, "we found fanaticism and dogma; but we found ourselves at the side of all men of good faith present at the Congress, so that we are sure that a new impulse shall have been given to the development of our ideas. And the great Association [I.W.A.] will shortly count new and numerous adherents." [39] If Mazzini had realized how the Rome Congress would help spread socialist ideas, he never would have summoned it. "Rome is ours,

---

[36] *Loc. cit.* The Mazzinian newspaper, *L'Unità Italiana*, in polemicizing with *La Favilla*, used the same argument, essentially, on Sept. 28, 1871: "At least by seniority, if not for other reasons, we were socialists long before the *Favilla*." Some socialists were willing to grant the priority but insisted that the I.W.A. was the logical development of Mazzinianism. See, for example, the Ferrara Workers' Society's address to the Bologna Mazzinian organ, *L'Alleanza*, as quoted by Rosselli, *Mazzini e Bakounine*, p. 394.

[37] Letter of Oct. 16, Nettlau, *B.I.I.*, pp. 237-38. See also, Riggio's glowing estimate of I.W.A. strength in Italy, in *L'Eguaglianza*, Oct. 15, 1871.

[38] Nettlau, *B.I.I.*, p. 262; Rosselli, *Mazzini e Bakounine*, p. 314.

[39] *L'Eguaglianza*, Dec. 27, 1871.

and not a few delegates, in this very hour, have already carried the sacred fire of the International into their respective societies"—thus Cafiero.[40] Nor did Engels' agent hesitate, in reporting to London, to credit Bakunin with the pamphlet he and Tucci had put into the hands of the Rome Congress delegates: "You offer me congratulations for the address . . . , which you find an excellent production, etc., which you would subscribe to in all its parts. But it is Bakunin you should congratulate and not I." [41]

In his letter to Engels of October 18, Cafiero recited a formidable list of Internationalist centers: Girgenti, Catania, Naples and environs, Sciacca, "many other small towns" in Sicily, Florence, Parma, Ravenna, Pisa, "many other less important cities" in Tuscany, the larger cities of the Romagna, Turin, Milan, and Rome.[42] How much was fact, how much the product of unchecked rumor, or of a conscious or unconscious desire to impress the men of London? There were doubtless many groups in the smaller cities and towns which, by a single manifesto or clandestine resolution, declared themselves sections of the International, some on the basis of a first-hand acquaintance with the statutes and principles of the Association, but most, in all probability, on the basis of little more than the sensation that the "International" was, in some vague way, synonymous with virtue. The existing evidence indicates only that, in terms of organizational strength, the Internationalism of even the chief urban centers of the country was more nominal than real. Engels was deluding his associates on the General Council—if not himself—when he told them on October 17 that in Italy the International was "fully established from one end of the country to the other." [43]

The Turinese "section" was a good example of much smoke and no fire. At its meeting on August 29, the London General Council was informed that "the International has been constituted in Turin," [44] an intelligence probably based on the notion that the Turinese "Republican League," whose imminent founding was announced in August, was to be an Internationalist organization. On September 24, Terzaghi and Carlo Laplace founded the Turin Workers' Federation, not inconceivably on instructions

[40] Letter to Riggio, L'Eguaglianza, Nov. 19, 1871.
[41] Letter of Nov. 29, 1871, Nettlau, B.I.I., pp. 256-57. After his months-long effort to convince Cafiero of Bakunin's personal and ideological deviationism, Engels must have been jarred by this evidence of his Neapolitan agent's mésalliance, tactical though it may have been, with the anarchist pope of Locarno; no less must it have embarrassed Marx's alter ego that he had given such an unqualified imprimatur to his foe's writing without knowing it.
[42] Ibid., p. 262.
[43] Il Gazzettino Rosa, Nov. 18, 1871. The General Council meeting of Nov. 7 was also given an enthusiastic report of I.W.A. progress in Italy. L'Eguaglianza, Nov. 26, 1871.
[44] Nettlau, B.I.I., p. 231.

from Bakunin,[45] an hypothesis not at all destroyed by Terzaghi's letter two days later, in which he asked the General Council to subsidize his newspaper, *Il Proletario Italiano,* and to authorize the creation of "a circle to be named the Emancipation of the Proletariat." [46] The Workers' Federation, formally constituted on October 8, never got around to translating its cheers for socialist principles into an official affiliation with the International. The constituent meeting of October 8 was thus reported by *L'Eguaglianza*:[47]

> Our friends, Terzaghi and Laplace, . . . proffered very noble words on the importance and purposes of the International Association of the workers. Unanimous and resounding *evviva* to the International showed that the assembly fully adhered to the principles of the great society. . . . With the meeting adjourned to the cry of "Long live Garibaldi, long live the International," its president sent General Garibaldi the following telegram . . . : "Today Turinese workers . . . founded . . . Workers' Federation adhering [to] International principles, unanimously send greetings . . ."

Two days later Terzaghi informed London that this group constituted a section of the International but betrayed his real doubts as to its bona fide Internationalism when he asked Engels to send an official representative to Turin "to give a truly International form" to the organization. Then, possibly in the naive hope that it would better his prospects for a subsidy from the General Council, he advised Engels that a workers' association in Ravenna, which had just declared itself a section of the I.W.A., would communicate with him "through the medium of Bakunin." [48]

The first political problem confronted by the Turin Federation opened a rift between the Mazzinian and "socialist" members. Over the objections of Terzaghi and Giuseppe Abello, the majority sent a delegate to the Rome Congress of workers' societies. The delegate, Giuseppe Beghelli, editor of *Il Ficcanaso* ("The Kibitzer"), voted with Cafiero and Tucci

[45] *Ibid.,* p. 232. Bakunin's contacts with Turin had begun on Sept. 6, when he received a letter from Terzaghi. Perruca, another Turinese, had closeted himself with Bakunin, Sept. 7-11, during which period the Russian's diary refers to a "contract made—collective letter to Turin." On the 18th, Bakunin received still another letter from Terzaghi but did not reply until the 28th. On Oct. 5, Perruca again visited Bakunin. *Ibid.,* pp. 253-54.

[46] For the letter, Romano, *Storia,* II, 116-17. This appears to have been Terzaghi's second request for General Council authorization of a Turinese section, since the Council, in its Sept. 26 session, was told that a letter from Turin had been received "which asked for the powers to create a new section in that city." Nettlau, *B.I.I.,* p. 231. Rosselli reports such a letter under date of Aug. 26, *Mazzini e Bakounine,* p. 310.

[47] Oct. 22, 1871.

[48] Nettlau, *B.I.I.,* p. 232.

against the pro-Mazzinian resolution adopted at Rome,[49] but on his return to Turin he proposed that the Federation accept the Mazzinian Pact of Fraternity and took a stand against the International in the columns of his newspaper, seconded by Laplace, who also chose this time to begin losing his socialist coloration.[50] Terzaghi mustered all available help to give him an edge in the polemic that now opened between him and Beghelli in the columns of *Il Proletario* and *Il Ficcanaso*. In addition to eliciting the support of *Il Motto d'Ordine* (Naples) and Carlo Cafiero,[51] he persuaded Bakunin, during a nocturnal session in Locarno on November 9, to get busy with an article for *Il Proletario*, to be used against his Mazzinian foes in the Federation.[52] As of mid-November 1871, it was an entirely open question whether the Turin Workers' Federation represented a Mazzinian redoubt or a socialist nucleus. Terzaghi's efforts to perpetuate the confusion were to continue.

As for Milan, Engels admitted in mid-November that "as of this moment we do not have any relations . . . except with the *Gazzettino Rosa*, to which we send some documents for publication, but which has not made any other offers to us for the organization of sections, etc." [53] Actually, the work of developing a Milanese section of the I.W.A. was well under way by this time, thanks to the fact that two of Bakunin's closest Italian collaborators were on the scene. Testini, a young agricultural student and friend of Vincenzo Pezza, the socialist writer for *Il Gazzettino Rosa*, was visiting Bakunin on September 7-11, a period in which the Russian's diary indicates the conclusion of a "contract" with his guests from Milan and Turin. Bakunin wrote Testini on September 28; on October 8 he received his first letter from Pezza; on the 15th of the same month, Pezza arrived in Locarno and, after a twenty-four-hour

---

[49] *L'Eguaglianza*, Nov. 26, 1871. Beghelli had been warned by the Society's membership that in view of the Federation's profession of loyalty to I.W.A. principles, he would have to assume an opposition position in many discussions at the Rome Congress. *La Favilla*, Nov. 1, 1871.

[50] See Terzaghi's letter to Engels, Dec. 4, 1871, Nettlau, *B.I.I.*, p. 232. Laplace's defection may have been induced by Dr. Giuseppe Ferrero-Gola, a Turinese republican whom Mazzini, on Nov. 17, asked to undertake the salvation of Beghelli and Laplace. *S.E.I.*, XCVII, 415-18. For further details on the Terzaghi-Beghelli dispute, *Il Gazzettino Rosa*, Nov. 24, 1871.

[51] See the article in *Il Motto d'Ordine*, written probably by Cafiero, reprinted in *Il Gazzettino Rosa*, Nov. 24, 1871, and dedicated to ridicule of Beghelli's role at the Rome Congress. To Engels, Cafiero reported on Dec. 18 that "Terzaghi and Abello are *bravissimi* Internationalists, and they are working very well in Turin . . ." Nettlau, *B.I.I.*, p. 273.

[52] *Ibid.*, p. 282.

[53] *Ibid.*, p. 235. Engels' relationship with *Il Gazzettino Rosa* proves no priority over Bakunin's contacts with Milan, since the Russian had written Bizzoni as early as June 24, and the latter had published Bakunin's *L'Empire knouto-germanique et la révolution sociale* on July 22 and his "Risposta" to Mazzini on Aug. 16.

session with Bakunin, the two reached a "complete accord"; finally, Bakunin followed up the contact late in October by sending Pezza his circular against the Mazzinian Rome Congress.[54]

In themselves, these relations prove nothing more than a certain intimacy between Bakunin and the two Milanese and agreement on undefined matters, perhaps ideological, perhaps having to do with socialist organization in Milan—perhaps both. Yet, when to this evidence is added the report of an interested and competent observer of the progress of the Internationalists' propaganda and organization in Milan during these weeks, Bakunin's directive function in the relationship is strongly suggested. In September 1871, a Workers' Society of Mutual Aid and Instruction was founded in Milan, a society which, though including many Mazzinians, accepted a program surreptitiously prepared by Pezza and Testini and intended to exercise a moral influence over the membership. Bakunin's two friends headed a socialist minority within the association and at every meeting urged adherence to the International.[55] Thus, while Bakunin was cementing his relations with Testini and Pezza, this pair not only persuaded the group to accept a presumably socialist program (given Pezza's conversion to socialism some months before) but also labored for the creation of an official I.W.A. section. If not cause and effect, the chronological parallel proves that friends of Bakunin initiated the effort to establish the International in Milan well before Engels and the General Council established contact with this effort.

The General Council's contribution to the rooting of the International in Milan dates from November 13, 1871, when, for the first time, Engels responded to the letter of the only socialist in the city who could be considered an agent of the General Council in the ensuing months of open struggle between London and Bakunin for control of the Italian movement: Theodor Cuno, none other than the witness to the priority of Testini and Pezza's organizational activity on behalf of the International.

Cuno, a German socialist militant, was a mechanical engineer who, after his expulsion from Austria, found employment with a Milanese firm in the fall of 1871. With another Milanese German, one Morf, and Johann Stocker, a Swiss, he wanted to organize an I.W.A. section in the city, probably because he had been told by Bizzoni, editor of *Il Gazzettino Rosa*, that there were many Internationalists in Milan. Though he had a low opinion of the socialist potentialities of Bizzoni (Engels' only previous Milan contact), Cuno lost no time in striking up an acquaintance with Bizzoni's collaborator, Pezza, under whose auspices he was introduced to

[54] *Ibid.*, pp. 253-55.
[55] Cuno to Engels, Nov. 30, 1871, *ibid.*, p. 236.

the recently organized workers' society.[56] It was Cuno's initial letter to
Engels on November 1 that elicited Engels' rather tardy and—as it de-
veloped—unavailing effort to exorcise the Bakuninist influence in the
Milanese socialist nucleus.

In the Emilia-Romagna region, Engels picked up a correspondent early
in November in the person of Lodovico Nabruzzi,[57] editor of *Il Romagnolo* (Ravenna), but again the contact was established too late for
Engels to acquire any real influence in the decisive crisis shaping up in
the ranks of Italian republicanism. Here, the actual organization of Internationalist sections got under way with no help from either Engels or
Bakunin. On September 3, 1871, six republican organizations in Ravenna
proposed fusion with the local republican *Consociazione,* if the latter
would agree that the I.W.A. "is the only means that can unite world
Democracy and lead the peoples to the triumph of Justice and the attainment of the general well-being," a proposal immediately rejected by the
Consociazione.[58] It was not until early October that these societies, joined
by the local Society of Brotherly Assistance (which had declared for
the International on September 24),[59] made a public declaration of adherence to the I.W.A.[60] Engels' reply of November 8 to Nabruzzi's
announcement of this development constituted the first contact of the
General Council with the most important region in Italy from the revolutionary point of view. Nabruzzi's newspaper reported in October the
imminent creation of three I.W.A. sections in the upper Romagna; "we
are receiving, moreover, reassuring news from the surrounding areas."
In Imola, local radicals declared for the principles of the International
in September.[61]

The "socialism" of radical republicans in the Emilia and the Romagna,

[56] Nettlau, *B.I.I.,* pp. 234-36. Cuno described Bizzoni as an ex-officer, duelist, a dapper
dresser and quite removed from thinking and living as a proletarian. "Satana," writing
in *L'Anticristo* (Turin), Mar. 31, 1872, referred to Bizzoni as a "rogue" who had
"more loves than colds" (*più amori che raffredori*). . . . Men call him handsome;
imagine what the women say! . . . He is a big clown (*pazzerellone*). More than
once he was seen, after having written an article on the International, running for
[his] office like a ten-year-old boy. . . . He is a dreamer of the first order . . ."
[57] Nettlau, *B.I.I.,* pp. 238-39.
[58] For the text of the deliberation, *Il Proletario Italiano,* Sept. 14; *La Plebe,* Sept.
12; *Il Romagnolo,* Sept. 9, 1871.
[59] *Il Romagnolo,* Oct. 1; *La Plebe,* Oct. 5, 1871.
[60] Nettlau, *B.I.I.,* p. 238; *cf.,* also, Engels' report to the Oct. 17 sitting of the General
Council (*Il Gazzettino Rosa,* Nov. 18, 1871). It appears that the formal constitution
of the Ravenna section was delayed until Jan. 1, 1872, when a Pact of Fraternity was
published under the title, "International Association of the Workers. Ravenna Section.
Pact of Fraternity." The document was signed by the delegates of five workers' societies and 478 members. *L'Eguaglianza,* Jan. 14; *La Campana* (Naples), Jan. 14,
1872. On Jan. 5, 1872, *La Plebe* reported a membership of about two hundred.
[61] Rosselli, *Mazzini e Bakounine,* p. 313, and note; Nettlau, *B.I.I.,* p. 240.

unlike that of Internationalists in Turin, Milan, Naples, and Sicily, was peculiarly the product of a desire to establish a national political organization under the aegis of Garibaldi. In this stronghold of *Garibaldinismo*, the democratic congress movement, fervent declarations of "Internationalism," and clamorous proclamations of "socialist sections" had a predominantly political purpose. The radicals of the Emilia-Romagna region, though about to spark the creation of a nationally organized socialist movement, moved toward regional federation in the fall of 1871 and began laying the network of relations with socialists in the rest of the peninsula, not in the hope of inaugurating a socialist regime on the Marxist or Bakuninist pattern, but substantially because they believed a national association under Garibaldi's leadership would somehow prove the springboard to achieve what Mazzini's forty-year apostolate had failed to realize: a democratic republic through popular revolution.[62] As for the goals of social revolution, these would-be emulators of the Parisian Communards were as hazy as their leader.[63] It is doubtful that Engels appreciated these implications when he read the following lines in Nabruzzi's letter of November 25:

> The work of the International in the Romagna is proceeding marvelously; every city of any importance already has its own section under way, modeled in the main on the Statutes of that of Bologna, and a provisional regional council for the Romagna is already functioning with optimum results and in complete accord with the internationalists of the Veneto, Lombardy, Piedmont, Tuscany, Naples, and Sicily. We believe that after the Democratic Congress of Bologna, the creation of a national Council will be the easiest thing in the world. . . .
>
> In general, for Italy, and particularly for the Romagna, the International will develop as an essentially revolutionary organization. Our youth has inherited in great part the rebellious aspirations of our fathers, who were conspirators throughout their lives, and desires struggle in the public thoroughfares to appear on the barricades, like the heroic defenders of the Paris Commune.[64]

[62] Garibaldi himself seemed to be promising precisely that in his famous letter to Giorgio Pallavicino of Nov. 14, 1871, when he spoke of forsaking his "habitual meekness" in order to "eradicate the cancers of this corrupt society." See below, p. 217.

[63] Witness Suzzara-Verdi's insistence, for example, that socialism is "the negation of all extrinsic authority, principally of divine authority, ... [it is] order without authority, a liberty regulated and guaranteed by atheism . . ." *La Favilla*, Oct. 5, 1871.

[64] Nettlau, *B.I.I.*, pp. 238-39. This passage suggests why the young Romagnol socialists were soon to choose Bakuninism, "the propaganda of deeds," over the Marxist formula of proletarian political action, by definition, in the historical context of the moment, gradualistic and pacific.

If the movement toward regional federation among the democratic societies of the Emilia-Romagna was well under way by mid-November 1871, it is clear that Engels' and Bakunin's relations with the movement, coming as late as they did, were extraneous to its origins. Engels' contact with Nabruzzi, beginning on November 4, was almost immediately neutralized, for all practical purposes, by Bakunin's relationship, initiated on November 7, with Celso Ceretti, the militant leader of the federation movement. Fully appreciating the opportunity to sow his ideas in a hitherto neglected but fertile field, Bakunin responded four days later with a letter which, though probably nothing more than a simple acknowledgment, dashed off in the midst of very trying circumstances, inaugurated an epistolary contact that was to give the Romagnol radicals' conception of socialism a far different content than the amorphous generalizations of Garibaldi.[65]

Elsewhere in the peninsula, there was plentiful evidence of a rapidly spreading pro-Internationalist sentiment, apparent in the markedly socialist tenor of many small newspapers that persisted in spite of police repression, but the existence of I.W.A. sections prior to mid-November is more to be inferred than documented. In his letter to Engels of October 18, Cafiero specifically mentioned Florence and Pisa as centers of Internationalism; Bakunin, on December 15, also referred to Livorno.[66] In Pisa a section may have been "in process of formation"—as the socialists of the time were prone to say—but it was not until January, 1872, that the activity of any such section appears in the record.[67] Neither Engels' nor Bakunin's letters indicate that either had a correspondent in the city. In Livorno, the local Artisans' Brotherhood may have been at least philo-Internationalist, if its sentiments were the reason for the fact that its delegate to the Rome Congress, De Montel, had joined Tucci and Cafiero in their walkout protest against the Turchi resolution. There is no clear evidence, however, arguing the existence of an officially constituted I.W.A. section in the Tuscan port city.

In Florence, the Social Democratic Union, the only radical society of any importance, had its socialist-tending members in Gaetano Grassi, Salvatore Battaglia, Ettore Socci, Luigi Castellazzo, Lorenzo Piccioli-Poggiali, and Francesco Natta, who carried on their propaganda inside the organization, but none of it prompted the S.D.U. to make a formal

[65] Nettlau, B.I.I., p. 282. Bakunin's wife was prostrated by news of her brother's death; the landlord, the grocer, and the butcher were closing in to collect long-overdue bills, and the Herzen family had just sent Mazzini a copy of Herzen's criticism of Bakunin's attitude toward the Polish insurrection of 1863. Bakunin's reaction: "Let the dogs bark at will." Letter to Ogarev, Nov. 14, 1871, Guillaume, I.D.S., II, 230-31.
[66] Letter to Ceretti, Dec. 15, 1871, Romano, Storia, II, 200.
[67] Nettlau, B.I.I., p. 241; L'Eguaglianza, Feb. 11, 1872.

declaration of adherence to the International, in part because the members feared the police would clamp down as they had in June in the case of the International Democratic Society, in part—and probably the greater part—because the S.D.U. itself, as noted above, had a strong, perhaps even prevalent, Mazzinian faction that continued strongly until at least the end of 1871. The Union's statute, announced in October, omitted all mention of the I.W.A., and the group sent its delegate to the Mazzinian congress in Rome with instructions to urge "national unity, with the broadest administrative decentralization and the autonomy of the Communes," hardly an expression of socialist intentions.[68]

Cafiero had held high hopes that Castellazzo would bring the Florentine republicans into the International as an officially constituted section, but after July 1871, all mention of Castellazzo disappeared from the Cafiero-Engels correspondence.[69] Very probably, this worshipper of Garibaldi was too taken up with promoting a "democratic congress" in the name of his hero to bother with the work of socialist organization in the restricted ambient of Florence. He wrote to Cafiero on November 8, but Cafiero's reply of December 26 reveals: (a) that the Neapolitan socialist by now considered himself far too busy with his socialist activities to give Castellazzo and the S.D.U. much attention; (b) that few letters passed between the two men after July ("Has the Union of Florence made formal adhesion to the International? If not, is it thinking of doing so?"); and (c) that Castellazzo, still seeking reconciliation with the Mazzinians, had written "a letter with greetings to Petroni and Mazzini" so shocking to Neapolitan socialist circles that Cafiero was asked to justify his previous classification of Castellazzo as "one of our men completely." [70] On what basis, then, Cafiero and Riggio reported in mid-October a remarkable progress of the International in Florence is not clear. The record indicates only that Castellazzo's socialist activity in the fall of 1871 was limited to joining his friends, the Socci brothers and others, in a local *trattoria* and urging socialist ideas on some uniformed customers from a nearby cavalry barracks.[71]

In Rome, the city Cafiero described on October 18 as "the last zone remaining to the defeated and completely discomfited Mazzinian army," a handful of ex-Mazzinians was spreading the doctrines of the Inter-

---

[68] Bottero, *Dibattimenti*, pp. 289-91. Federico Campanella, Mazzinian *par excellence*, told a Florentine court in 1875 that he had been a member of the Social Democratic Union and that, "far from accepting international theories, that society combatted them." *Ibid.*, p. 191.

[69] For the references to Castellazzo contained in the Cafiero-Engels correspondence, none of which delineate the Florentine as an effective socialist organizer, see Nettlau, *B.I.I.*, pp. 196-97, 221, 296; Romano, *Storia*, II, 308, 311-12.

[70] For the letter in full, Conti, *O.S.F.*, pp. 258-59.

[71] *Ibid.*, p. 125.

national late in 1871, with what effect is not apparent. Osvaldo Gnocchi-Viani, whose abstention from the vote on the Turchi resolution at the Rome Congress marked another step in his personal evolution toward socialism, certainly must have been more successful as a propagandist than a figure like Salvatore Battaglia, who, from his perch in the Directive Commission elected at the Rome Congress, was apparently still trying to make up his mind whether to legitimize his position there by reverting to his once unadulterated Mazzinianism, or to resolve his crisis of conscience by declaring unreservedly for the International. In any case, Cafiero's reference to Rome as an Internationalist center no more proves the existence of an I.W.A. nucleus in the Eternal City than does the same reference, two months later, coming from Bakunin.[72] Even less do these allusions necessarily imply that Engels or Bakunin was in direct touch with the first stirrings of Roman socialism.[73]

Given the many years of Saverio Friscia's preliminary apostolate, there is no need to discount entirely Antonio Riggio's statement of October 16 that "In Sicily we are in command. In the province of Girgenti alone, we shall have ten sections within a few days." The press run of his *L'Eguaglianza* now amounted to a thousand copies, "a rare phenomenon in Italy for a weekly sheet." [74] Friscia and Riggio were almost certainly responsible for much of the pro-International sentiment pervading the island radicals, though there is no way of determining, with even a semblance of accuracy, the influence, if any, of Engels and Bakunin, each of whom was in touch with the situation.

The Russian carried forward his correspondence with Friscia, though on a diminished scale.[75] His diary entry of August 13, 1871 ("Riggio—Sicily—Girgenti"), if it referred to a letter to or from Riggio, signified a

[72] Letter to Ceretti, Dec. 15, 1871, Romano, *Storia,* II, 200.

[73] For a discussion of the origins of Internationalism in Rome, Franco Della Peruta, "L'Internazionale a Roma dal 1872 al 1877," *Movimento Operaio,* Yr. IV (new series), No. 1 (Jan.-Feb., 1952), 12-13.

[74] Letter to Engels, Nettlau, *B.I.I.,* pp. 237-38. Lucarelli (*Giuseppe Fanelli,* p. 133) lists, for the period 1869-72, I.W.A. sections in Girgenti, Catania, Sciacca, Acireale, Porto Empedocle, Giarre, Messina, and Palermo. The present writer believes that Girgenti, Sciacca, and Catania were probably the chief Internationalist centers of Sicily, the last two cities on the basis of Friscia's earlier activity, of Engels' report on Oct. 17 of an unnamed Internationalist newspaper in Catania (*Il Gazzettino Rosa,* Nov. 18), of Cafiero's reference of Oct. 18 (letter to Engels, Nettlau, *B.I.I.,* p. 262; Rosselli, *Mazzini e Bakounine,* p. 314) and of *La Plebe's* reference (Sept. 27) to the founding of a Catania section, the Society of Bakers, under the presidency of a lawyer, one Condorelli, editor of the local *Apostolato.* On the basis of Antonio Riggio's activity, Girgenti was very probably an important socialist center.

As late as Feb., 1872, Mazzini refused to credit reports that Internationalism had made significant progress in Sicily: "If there is any zone that is with me, . . . it is Sicily." Giannelli, *Cenni autobiografici,* p. 548.

[75] Nettlau, *B.I.I.,* pp. 255-56.

contact remaining undeveloped in September and October.[76] A degree of influence on Riggio by Cafiero and Engels seems implied by Cafiero's assurance to Engels of late November that "I know Riggio intimately . . . ," by Riggio's publication of Cafiero's translation of Marx's "The Civil War in France," by Riggio's exchange of letters with Engels in October, and by Cafiero's representation of the Girgenti section at the Rome Congress. For his part, Engels apparently neglected Riggio in November, for Cafiero had to remind his London friend that "you will do well to maintain a regular correspondence with him." [77]

In Naples, the original stronghold of socialist Internationalism, Engels' only reliable agent, Cafiero, was compelled to carry on his propaganda without benefit of a local I.W.A. section or an official newspaper outlet. Cafiero himself chose to consider this no particular disadvantage from the broader perspective of a national development of socialism: "The section in Naples is dissolved," he wrote Engels on September 10, "but, if apparent damage has come from it in Naples, I find in it an advantage with respect to the whole of Italy; at various points . . . other sections have been formed and some suppressed sections flourish under another name." [78] Though the local authorities never did get around to putting Cafiero and his friends on trial for the subversion charged to their account in August, they made it impossible for the comrades to meet, even clandestinely. Cafiero, Palladino, and their friends had already begun to plan, nonetheless, the re-creation of the section under another name.[79] *Il Motto d'Ordine*, founded as a "liberal and antigovernment" semi-weekly in September 1871, provided an outlet for occasional articles by the Neapolitan socialists, thanks to Leone Leoncavallo, who assumed the editorship of the paper on November 10, but even this channel was denied them a month later, when the paper folded, presumably under the double pressure of police and lack of funds.[80]

Cafiero himself continued in full loyalty to Engels and the General Council in the period prior to mid-November, though the correspondence

[76] As late as Dec. 17, 1871, Riggio was referring to Bakunin as "Bakonnine" and "Battonnine," which hardly bespeaks direct epistolary contact with the Russian. See *L'Eguaglianza*, Dec. 17, 1871.

[77] Nettlau, *B.I.I.*, pp. 237-38, 270.

[78] *Ibid.*, p. 226. Later Cafiero wrote Engels: "Yes, my dear friend, the government has done us a good turn with its persecutions; *my arrest has been a real treasure.*" Rosselli, *Mazzini e Bakounine*, pp. 309-10.

[79] Nettlau, *B.I.I.*, pp. 228, 267.

[80] *Ibid.*, pp. 270-72; Rosselli, *Mazzini e Bakounine*, pp. 292-93. Cafiero called Engels' attention to the "uneven quality" of the articles, "but you know how the staff of that journal is composed." In any case, it "does not fully belong to us," and Cafiero's group was using it to the extent permitted by a management that refused to abdicate its authority to the Internationalists. *Cf.*, Cafiero's letter to Engels, Nov. 28-Dec. 19, 1871, in *ibid.*, p. 403.

between London and Naples became much more infrequent than the exchange of June and July.[81] On the other hand, Cafiero's lieutenant, Carmelo Palladino, to whom Engels had written on July 28, did not reply until November 13; in the meantime (late September), he opened up a steady correspondence with Bakunin.[82]

CONCLUSION

Beginning in mid-November 1871, the terms of the socialist polemic in Italy shifted radically in favor of the International. The reasons for this transformation were implicit in the pattern formed by the developments of the period just described. The essential components of the pattern were these:

1. From the Italian radicals' point of view, Bakunin's polemic aimed at destroying Mazzini's influence among Italian republicans. The wide publicity given the Russian's propaganda pieces, cleverly designed to dovetail with the basic reasons for radical dissatisfaction with Mazzini, appreciably augmented the chorus of protest. Their effectiveness is attested by their attractiveness, as anti-Mazzinian weapons, to none other than Cafiero, the one Italian socialist who, after digesting Engels' personal and doctrinal criticism of Bakunin, should have been convinced that no "true" socialist would associate himself with the Russian on any level. Further, the Russian was in touch with Milan (Pezza, Testini), Turin (Terzaghi, Perruca), Naples (Palladino), Sciacca (Friscia), and kept in contact with his roving disciples, Fanelli and Gambuzzi. The contact with Bologna (Ceretti) was just beginning. He had written to Girgenti (Riggio) and Lodi (Bignami) but apparently received no replies. The content of these letters and conversations is reasonably inferred from the concurrent activity of the Russian's correspondents, namely, preparing the establishment of I.W.A. sections. That most of these men failed to get in touch with the Association's corresponding secretary for Italy is no proof that Bakunin was responsible for the omission, since he never denied, and even emphasized, the function of the London General Council as a "correspondence center" for all sections of the International.

2. Engels had one fully committed Italian representative in Cafiero and two possibly committed supporters in Riggio and Bignami.[83] Cuno, in Milan, was no pillar of Marxian influence, as shown by his ready col-

---

[81] Cafiero to Engels, Sept. 10; Engels to Cafiero, Oct. 10; Cafiero to Engels, Oct. 18, 1871. Nettlau, B.I.I., pp. 225-26, 262, 267-68.

[82] Romano, Storia, II, 318; Nettlau, B.I.I., pp. 225, 254-56, 266-67, 282.

[83] Engels first heard of Bignami and La Plebe through Cafiero's letter of July 12-16, 1871. The newspaper, according to Cafiero, was the only one in Italy that "truly represents our party" (Nettlau, B.I.I., p. 224). La Plebe was founded in 1868, but Bignami did not become a socialist until 1871. Bignami first wrote to Engels in October, again on Nov. 6, 1871. Failing to get a response, he wrote again on Nov. 14, complaining of Engels' silence [Gianni Bosio, ed., Karl Marx, Friedrich Engels, Scritti

laboration with Bakunin's agent, Pezza. In Turin, Terzaghi, soon to be unmasked as a police spy, was of as little real support to Engels as he was to Bakunin. Contact with Ravenna (Nabruzzi) was still undeveloped. In the anti-Mazzinian campaign, the essential concern of Italian radicals during this period, the General Council's contribution amounted to one unpublished manuscript gathering dust in the Neapolitan police archives and the dispatch of I.W.A. statutes and general congress resolutions, the latter activity pursued by Bakunin as well.[84]

3. Italian socialists and socialist sympathizers, with the exception of Cafiero, Palladino, and Bakunin's network of correspondents, were indifferent—perhaps oblivious—to the anarchist-Marxist dispute, soon to split the International. The rapid diffusion of pro-Internationalist sentiment in this period derived almost exclusively from an internal crisis within the Party of Action, of which the decisive external stimulus was the life and death of the Paris Commune, not the labors of the General Council or Bakunin. The work of establishing bona fide I.W.A. sections in the peninsula had just begun, though relative to the number of sections existing prior to the Paris Commune, a startling advance had been registered.

4. The movement toward regional and national federation of socialist nuclei, implicit in the Garibaldians' "democratic congress" project, was gaining momentum, thanks to the initiative of radicals in the Emilia-Romagna region where, in fact, lay the key to control of the future national organization of Italian socialism.[85]

---

italiani (Milan, Rome: Ediz. Avanti!, 1955), p. 65]. Engels replied only on Nov. 30, without acknowledging Bignami's three previous epistles but merely admitting one Giuseppe Boriani to the I.W.A. (Nettlau, *B.I.I.*, p. 230). Despite a protracted, though fitful, correspondence between Engels and Bignami after 1871, the dominant socialist influence on Bignami was the Communard, Benoît Malon, whose ideas, by the canons of Marxist orthodoxy, were almost as heretical as those of Bakunin.

[84] The section of Engels' letter of July 28 to Cafiero dealing with Mazzini's charges contained in his "Agli Operai Italiani" was published, though anonymously, in *Il Libero Pensiero*, Aug. 31; *La Favilla*, Sept. 7, 1871. The lines devoted to Mazzini's attempt, through Major Wolff, to incorporate his "Act of Brotherhood" into the I.W.A. statutes in 1864 were published in *Il Romagnolo*, Sept. 9; *Il Gazzettino Rosa*, Sept. 13; *Il Motto d'Ordine*, Nov. 20, 1871. Here again, however, Engels ignored the ideological issues raised by Mazzini's criticism of the Commune, preferring to concern himself with a purely contingent and personal question.

[85] Bakunin seems to have appreciated this much sooner than Engels. The latter, in his Nov. 13 letter to Cuno, reasoned: "Milan, as . . . a great industrial city, is especially important to us . . . , since, with Milan, the silk industry districts in Lombardy must fall automatically into our hands." (Rosselli, *Mazzini e Bakounine*, p. 403, note 3) Bakunin, conversely, centered his fire on the Romagna from the moment he acquired a correspondent there in the person of Ceretti. The Romagnols' susceptibility to anarchist doctrines, according to Francesco Saverio Merlino, writing in 1889-90, was due, "not so much to economic unease as to hatred of the government that has treated the Romagna, like Sicily, as a conquered country and has made of both . . . the two Irelands of Italy." *Questa è l'Italia* (Milan: Cooperativa del Libro Popolare, 1953), pp. 216-17.

X

Italian Socialism and the "Authoritarian-Libertarian" Dispute (November to December 1871)

THE LONDON CONFERENCE AND THE SONVILLIERS CIRCULAR

THE Marxist-Bakuninist polemic broke into the consciousness of Italian socialists during the second fortnight of November 1871, when they learned of the decisions of a carefully selected group of I.W.A. chieftains meeting in London two months earlier. The London Conference of September 17-23 was a conclave of the thirteen members of the General Council, six Belgian socialists, two delegates from Switzerland (both unequivocal anti-Bakuninists), and a representative of the Spanish Federal Committee, Anselmo Lorenzo, the only delegate present with a *mandat impératif*.[1] The general congress of the I.W.A., scheduled for Paris in September 1870 had been called off with the outbreak of the Franco-Prussian War, but in 1871 the decision of Marx and his friends on the General Council to avoid a general congress in September had no such obvious justification.

---

[1] For the details on the London Conference, Guillaume, *I.D.S.*, II, 192-214. Noting Engels' suggestion to Cafiero (July 28, 1871) that Gambuzzi, during a projected business trip to London in September, be mandated to the Conference by the Neapolitan section, the Minister of Interior, through the Italian Foreign Office, tried to arrange for surveillance of Gambuzzi in London. Apparently, however, the Neapolitan called off his trip, for there is no evidence that he ever left Italy. For the relevant documents, see, Ministero dell'Interno, *Gabinetto, No. 3413, Sept. 7, 1871. Riservatissimo;* Maffei (Italian Minister to London) to Visconti-Venosta, Sept. 25, 1871, Ministero degli Affari Esteri, *N. Gab. 695, Politico 248. Riservato;* Lanza to Visconti-Venosta, Oct. 2, 1871, Ministero dell'Interno, *Gabinetto, N. 3762.*

Marx's preference for a highly restricted conference, whatever the other reasons advanced by his apologists, was based primarily on his determination to end, once and for all, the anarchist threat to what he considered officially established Internationalist orthodoxy, which, not surprisingly, coincided in every detail with his own doctrinal convictions. Given the composition of the group attending the London Conference, the anarchists naturally drew the conclusion that, failing all other measures, Marx had finally decided to play the game for ideological and political supremacy in the I.W.A. with a stacked deck. The decisions of the Conference, considered in the light of Marx's conviction that Bakunin's libertarian socialist ideas constituted a potent and dangerous heresy, speak for themselves.

Resolution IX sought to establish the last word on the question of political action by the proletariat, the cardinal point of difference with the anarchists. The London group held that the economic and political movements of the working classes are "indissolubly united," a conclusion based, among other reasons adduced, on Marx's Inaugural Address of 1864 [2] and a resolution of the Lausanne Congress of 1867.[3] Resolution XV gave the General Council authority to set the time and place of the next general congress—a move, in the Bakuninist view, designed to allow the General Council to postpone a general congress indefinitely and rule through secret conferences such as the London meeting. Resolution XVI, a masterpiece of casuistry, pretended to accept in good faith the self-dissolution of the Bakuninist Alliance of Socialist Democracy on August 10, 1871, but revealed Marx's doubts on this score by using as an argument against its right to affiliate with the I.W.A. nothing less than a resolution of the Conference itself. To lend an appearance of legitimacy based on a broader consensus than that of the little group of London conferees, the Council declared it would have to interpret in the light of its own opinion of the Alliance the administrative resolution of the Basel Congress of 1869, to wit: "The General Council has the right to admit or to refuse admission to any new society or group, save an appeal to the congress." It was a neat coupling, indeed, of a general *congress decision* with a General *Council opinion* to arrive at the desired conclusion. Substantially, the argument amounted to this: Bakuninism is heresy until a congress decides otherwise; the Council determines when a congress convenes; therefore, Bakuninism is heresy until the Council decides otherwise. Little wonder Resolution XVI ended with the sentence: "The Conference declares the

[2] "The conquest of political power has become . . . the first duty of the working class."
[3] "The social emancipation of the workers is inseparable from their political emancipation."

incident of the *Alliance of Socialist Democracy* closed." With such logic, Marx could not have closed the "incident" more hermetically.

The Swiss Bakuninists immediately reacted against what one of their sympathizers termed the "unitarian and authoritarian" resolutions of London and Karl Marx, "the evil genius, the Bismarck of the international Association." [4] At a congress in Sonvilliers, they issued a circular to all I.W.A. federations denouncing the London General Council as authoritarian, the decisions of the Conference as illegal, and called for a general congress of the Association at the earliest possible date.[5] The Sonvilliers Circular of November 2, 1871, was an act of open defiance of the authority of the General Council and, in addition to its charge of Council dictatorship, it set the question of proletarian participation in politics as the primary issue dividing Bakuninists from Marx and his London clique. Thus was the Marx-Bakunin controversy finally, publicly, and unequivocally announced.[6] Italian socialists, *for the first time,* had the necessary elements to make a considered choice between the two sets of ideas. Though they did not make that choice during the next six weeks, most of them opted clearly for the spirit of the Sonvilliers Circular.

PROTAGONISTS: BAKUNIN, THE LONDON COUNCIL, GARIBALDI

It was precisely at the beginning of this period that the primary target of Bakunin's propaganda barrage shifted from Mazzini to the General Council, or, more accurately, to the decisions of the London Conference. He had learned of the London resolutions for the first time on October 29,[7] but until November 16, he was still writing the final pages of "The Political Theology of Mazzini," and heavily burdened with domestic difficulties. Though he was completely extraneous to the preparation and proceedings of the Sonvilliers congress and the formulation of the circular demanding a general congress, of which he learned on November 20 from his lieutenant, Guillaume,[8] he promptly realized, no doubt, that his whole dispute with Marx and Engels could now be brought down to a single, immediate, and concrete issue in such a way that he could be assured in advance of widespread support, not only in the anarchist-ridden Jura region of Switzerland, but in Italy, Spain, France, and Belgium as well.

[4] Mme André Léo (wife of Benoît Malon) to Mathilde Roederer, Nov. 12, 1871, as quoted by Guillaume, *I.D.S.,* II, 222.

[5] For the Sonvilliers Congress proceedings and the text of the Circular, *ibid.,* II, 232-41.

[6] The Sonvilliers Circular coincided very closely with the diffusion in Italy of Resolution IX, published in full by *Il Motto d'Ordine* on Nov. 15, and in part by *La Plebe,* Nov. 23, 1871.

[7] Guillaume, *I.D.S.,* II, 229.

[8] *Loc. cit.*

The London Conference's Resolution IX could be easily represented as ideological authoritarianism, Resolution XV as organizational authoritarianism, while the Sonvilliers Circular, in his opinion "a magnificent and entirely legitimate protest," [9] offered itself as the symbol of a struggle for freedom, both doctrinal and organizational. He could now lay at the door of the General Council charges embodying the very principle inspiring his indictments of Mazzini, a fact in itself that probably convinced his Italian audience that his forthcoming polemic with the General Council was more a matter of principle than of personal rivalry. Bakunin immediately sensed the necessity of keeping his propaganda campaign against London on an impersonal plane. To a Russian friend he confided that he preferred to fight the General Council anonymously and to keep himself out of the picture entirely.[10] This was his tactic, then, when, after receiving a supply of printed copies of the Sonvilliers Circular from Guillaume late in November, he sent large quantities of them into the peninsula and, at the same time, began "to write a mass of letters to all parts of Italy to explain to friends the true sense of our struggle with London and to dispose in our favor the half-friends and quarter-friends." [11]

In the propaganda battle now joined between Engels and Bakunin on the Italian terrain, the former made a fatal choice of method, a choice the more difficult to understand in view of the adequate warnings against it received from Cafiero, the one Italian socialist whose constructive intentions were beyond question, the one friend of the General Council who, through his extensive correspondence relations with socialist groups, individuals, and newspapers in the peninsula, was in a position to make a sound assessment of their reaction to the London Conference resolutions and the Sonvilliers Circular. Despite Cafiero's implicit—and then explicit—pleas to the contrary, Engels chose to promote publicly the personal charges against Bakunin which for months he had confined to his private correspondence with Cafiero, instead of concentrating his attention on rectifying Marx's mistake of using the London Conference method of torpedoing Bakunin and his anarchist coterie.

This was the probable meaning of Cafiero's characterization as "eminently impolitic" an article Engels managed to have published in the December 21 issue of *La Roma del Popolo*, the Mazzinian organ, an article in which Engels accused Bakunin of seeking to substitute his "narrow and sectarian program" for the "broad program" of the Inter-

---

[9] Guillaume, *I.D.S.*, II, 250, note 2.
[10] "I remain behind the curtains and am doing all I can so that I am not even thought of." Letter to Joukovsky, Dec. 18, 1871, Nettlau, *B.I.I.*, pp. 227-88.
[11] *Loc. cit.*

national.[12] In the article that had stimulated Engels' letter of protest, Mazzini had cited certain doctrinal pronouncements of Bakunin, made prior to his admission to the International. Engels' objections to Mazzini's identification of these pronouncements with the official program of the I.W.A., though entirely justified vis-à-vis Mazzini, contributed nothing to Italian understanding of why, from the General Council's point of view, Bakuninism, *in its 1871* version, was to be considered a dangerous heresy. In the wake of the London Conference and the Sonvilliers Circular, it was the least promising method of discrediting Bakunin and his ideas among Italian radicals, who saw the Marx-Bakunin conflict almost entirely in terms of the London Council's "authoritarianism" versus the "anti-authoritarian" plea of the Sonvilliers Congress. The effects of Engels' mistaken tactic and of Bakunin's "inundating" Italy with the Sonvilliers Circular and the "mass of letters" to his Italian friends were clearly revealed by the end of 1871.

That these effects were delayed at all was due to the one factor prohibiting a description of the situation of late 1871 solely in terms of the General Council—Bakunin dispute: the question of where Garibaldi, from whom thousands of socialist-tending republicans took their cue, stood with respect to the two foreign contenders for control of the Italian movement. In his famous letter of November 14, 1871, to Giorgio Pallavicino, the Red Shirt hero's viceroy in Naples in 1860, Garibaldi was clear about only one thing: he was not taking sides.

> I belonged to the International . . . long before this Society had been created in Europe. . . . I do not tolerate . . . its anthropophagous tendencies . . . and I would jail . . . the archimandrites of the society in question should they persist in the precepts: *War on Capital—property is theft—inheritance another theft.* I do not interfere in the International and, because they know I do not approve their whole program, the chiefs would be justified in considering me excluded from it. But if the International, as I understand it, proves a continuation of the moral and material betterment of the working class, . . . I shall be with the International . . .
>
> I believe [the I.W.A.] will finally prevail. And will it not be better, in this case, to guide the powerful Association toward good, without leaving it to the mercy of people who would lead

---

[12] Also published, in part, by *La Plebe*, Dec. 12; *La Favilla*, Dec 16, *Il Gazzettino Rosa*, Dec. 21, 1871. Because Cafiero, on Dec. 19, commented on the letter of Engels published in *La Roma del Popolo* on Dec. 21, Romano (*Storia*, II, 204, note 123) questions Nettlau's assertion that Cafiero had called Engels' letter "impolitic." There is nothing strange at all in Cafiero's Dec. 19 comment on a document sent him from London on the 7th, and published by *La Plebe* and *La Favilla* several days prior to its appearance in *La Roma del Popolo*.

it astray and bring it to excesses, were they not restrained by enlightened and honest men?

You speak to me of being imprudent. But . . . prestige no longer matters to me. If I have exalted the people at times, I did it to compel them to do good, not to adulate them. . . . And if you once saw me as the gentle and humane dictator, *I am still in favor of honest Dictatorship*, which I consider the only antidote for eradicating the cancers of this corrupt society, and perhaps you shall soon see me forsake the habitual meekness to obtain a gratifying result.[13]

Obviously the rubric, "archimandrites" who preached "War on Capital," covered both Marx and Bakunin, but when Garibaldi added "property is theft" and "inheritance another theft," he was identifying Bakunin's ideas with the International. It is a significant commentary on Engels' respect for the general's prestige among Italian radicals that he did not complain when Garibaldi committed the same error Mazzini had permitted himself in his "Documents on the International" article. As yet, Bakunin too refrained, for transparent reasons, from attacking Garibaldi, despite his long-held opinion that the idol of Italian radical youth was a potential military dictator with a dangerously unclear set of social principles.

REPERCUSSIONS IN NAPLES

As Engels' established *longa manus* in Italy, Carlo Cafiero was probably the first Italian socialist to receive the news of the London Conference resolutions, very likely through a letter from Engels of October 10. After having been primed by Engels' earlier correspondence on the necessity of taking action against the Bakuninists, Cafiero registered no objections to the London Conference in his letter of October 18.[14] But a month later, reporting on the reaction of his Neapolitan associates to the London decisions, he waved a warning flag even while assuring Engels that he was confident the Council would maintain "our fundamental pact" inviolate and avoid arguments and schisms. Wrote Cafiero: "The idea of a

[13] Second set of italics mine. For the letter in full, Fonterossi, *Garibaldi e l'Internazionale*, p. 9. The sentence referring to "honest dictatorship" was apparently expunged by Pallavicino prior to releasing the letter for publication. The edited version was printed by many newspapers of the time (among others, by *Il Gazzettino Rosa*, Dec. 11, 1871). The autograph is in the Museo del Risorgimento of Turin. For Pallavicino's correspondence with Garibaldi in regard to the I.W.A., see B. E. Maineri, *ed., Su le quistioni del giorno. Alcune lettere di Giorgio Pallavicino* (Milan, 1874), 47 ff., 79; *La Favilla*, Dec. 9, 1871. It was by no means the first time Garibaldi had expressed his preference for "honest dictatorship." See his letter to Bignami, in *La Plebe*, Apr. 8, 1871; and to Lazzarini, editor of the *Corriere di Sardegna*, Apr. 11, 1871, in *La Favilla*, Apr. 27, 1871.

[14] Nettlau, *B.I.I.*, p. 262.

political party, even if it be opposed to any other bourgeois [party], scandalized: there were cries of treason [directed against] the bourgeois who, once inside the International, had managed to work their way up to the Conference itself." [15] On November 28, Cafiero introduced his first personal objection:

> . . . Resolution IX is creating confusion of every kind among us, since it confuses a position very clearly defined by the General Statutes. The constitution of the International into a political party . . . has been very poorly understood and, on the positive side, . . . it ties us to the feet of the Mazzinians. Read our report [sent by Palladino on Nov. 13] and then put yourself in our position and give us a reply.[16]

On the following day Cafiero began a long letter to Engels, completed on December 19, that constituted a complete rejection of Engels' monthslong argument that Bakunin had sinister designs on the integrity of the International and a vicious personal animosity toward Marx. He had noted, Cafiero wrote, that Bakunin had "words of profound esteem and respect for Marx" in his pamphlet, *L'Empire knouto-germanique;* that an unimpeachable witness had told him Bakunin had no interest whatsoever in supplanting anyone on the General Council; that Bakunin's anti-Mazzinian propaganda had very naturally won him a following in Italy, even among those who disliked the Russian personally. Cafiero was convinced that if Bakunin at times hurt the International by "some act ill advised by his . . . dissolvent nature," such acts derived not from an *animus criminis,* but from "the perfect conviction . . . of advancing the common cause." Probably because he had been warned that Marx and Engels intended to mount further attacks on Bakunin, Cafiero counseled the path of reconciliation and harmony. "I hope this letter of mine can reach you before you have cast the die. . . . Is there no way to make [Bakunin] see the evil he might do to an association in which he has at least demonstrated so much interest?" Attacks on Bakunin contribute nothing to furthering the International. "Was it really necessary to wash your dirty linen in public?" The real damage to the International, in Cafiero's opinion, derived not from Bakunin, but from Resolution IX, which "was and will continue to be our most vulnerable point, because all your comments will never succeed in completely correcting the spirit originally pervading it." [17]

In this letter, which helps explain Cafiero's imminent emergence as the paladin of libertarian socialism in Italy, is to be found also the evidence

---

[15] Nettlau, *B.I.I.,* p. 268.
[16] Cafiero to Engels, *ibid.,* p. 270.
[17] For the letter in full, *ibid.,* pp. 271-75.

that Engels was seeking to convince Cafiero that Resolution IX of the London Conference did not really require the organization of a workers' political party, at least in the commonly accepted sense. On December 3, a writer for the Spanish socialist newspaper, *La Emancipación* (Barcelona), very probably inspired by Engels (corresponding secretary for Spain as well as for Italy), published an article interpreting Resolution IX in a highly ambiguous sense, rejecting political collaboration with the established republican parties, without, however, closing the door on an independent socialist policy, the policy of a "workers' party." [18] Engels, in his letter of December 7 to Cafiero, either included a copy of this article or described its contents, adding that the Spaniard's interpretation of Resolution IX was in "perfect harmony" with the views of the General Council. This reconstruction of the background is confirmed by Cafiero's remark, in his letter of November 29—December 19: "I assure you that I was happier than ever to find in that letter of yours *an unexpected assistance*" (italics mine). Thus inspired, Cafiero wrote a commentary on Resolution IX in full agreement with the interpretation given by *La Emancipación*. This editorial effort, which he described to Engels as a compendium of his thinking in regard to the question of socialist political activity, appeared in *Il Gazzettino Rosa* on December 20.

Cafiero's article reveals that Engels had, in fact, convinced Cafiero, for the moment at least, that Resolution IX was consistent with the principle of political abstentionism in precisely the sense recommended by Bakunin! Cafiero had apparently never asked himself why Engels waited until *after* the London Conference decisions had raised such a storm of protest to advance such a remarkable interpretation of what Marx meant by his hoary dictum that "the first duty of the working class is the conquest of political power." If he had, he could not have written the following lines in good faith:

> The Italian internationalist agitators, in preaching complete political abstention to their comrades, were in perfect accord with resolution IX . . . , because they said that the proletariat, engaged in the struggle for its complete economic emancipation, could not have anything in common with the politics of the bourgeois, against precisely whom they were aligned. *Between the political state sustained by the bourgeois and the "economic organization" desired by the proletarians, there can be no point of contact.*
>
> It was well understood, however [and here lay Engels' escape clause], that the proletarians, in organizing themselves against

[18] Guillaume, *I.D.S.*, II, 244-46, for details.

their eternal exploiters, must have a policy entirely of their own, which would be *as different and opposed to that of the bourgeoisie as "economic organization"* [of the proletariat] *is to that of the political state.*[19]

Though Cafiero's explicit intent was to represent "the views of the General Council," the logical implications of this passage are clearly Bakuninist, whether its author realized it or not. If the existing political state and the "economic organization" of the workers had "no point of contact," such economic organization certainly involved no electoral or parliamentary action by the workers, no "running to the [electoral] urns," as the Spanish writer had put it. Yet, to deny this function was to deny the very *raison d'être* of a working-class "political party"—unless Cafiero meant that a workers' party should be, in fact, nothing other than an "economic organization" of the proletariat for the sole purpose of overthrowing the state by forceful subversion of its economic foundations; in short, revolutionary syndicalism, a far cry from Marxism. In this case, Cafiero implicitly accepted Bakunin's central argument and the definitive proof lies in the Russian's immediate approval of both the *Emancipación* interpretation and Cafiero's addenda:

> It is . . . a very remarkable article, to which I would subscribe with pleasure, except for one sentence, the one where [Cafiero] speaks of the *views* of the General Council as if these *views* had both a dogmatic and governmental importance. . . . I accept completely, and all my friends will accept, I am sure, both the spirit and the letter of the article . . .[20]

As for Cafiero's passage concerning the separation of proletarian "economic organization" and the "political state," Bakunin, in a completely ironic vein, observed:

> . . . If [Cafiero] expressed not his own opinion, but really that of the General Council, then we have only to rejoice in the immense progress the latter has just achieved. In this case, theoretically there would be no longer any disagreement between us.

Engels' Neapolitan agent, in fact, consciously sought to put himself above the specific doctrinal disagreement, a sure sign that for all practical purposes Engels would henceforth get no more than lip service from the young man who had carried Marx and Engels' hopes into the peninsula only seven months earlier. Engels must have realized this, too, when, in Cafiero's letter of December 19, he read this gem of ambiguity:

[19] Italics mine.
[20] Unfinished letter to Pezza and Testini, Dec. 23, 1871, Guillaume, *I.D.S.*, II, 251-52; *cf.*, also, Nettlau, *B.I.I.*, pp. 291-92.

I do not know if you are aware of it, but, as for me, I am only a materialist rationalist. My materialism and socialism, revolutionism, anarchism, and everything that the continuous development of thought can bring us in the future, and which will be rationally accepted by me, can only be, so far as I am concerned, modalities eminently suggestive to rational development. I am and shall remain a rationalist; that is the sum of the matter.[21]

In the same letter Cafiero notified Engels that Carmelo Palladino, his close collaborator in propagating socialism in Naples, had already made his choice—against the London General Council. "I must tell you . . . that Palladino is one of our staunchest friends [sic], but he would follow Bakunin even against us and anyone else, so blind is he for [Bakunin]." Six letters had passed between Palladino and the Russian from September 26 to November 11;[22] two days later—on receiving Bakunin's letter of the 11th?—Palladino sent Engels a brief history of the Neapolitan section since 1869, a report he had promised in July: "I believe that I have thus fulfilled my obligation and kept a promise that I tacitly made to the General Council." Then followed the substantive defection:

I have read, in part, the decisions taken by the last Conference; and I must frankly tell you that I do not accept them at all, be it for the manner in which the Conference was convoked, certainly not in line with the prescriptions of our General Statutes; be it for the scarcity of delegates, who arrogated to themselves the rights belonging to a General Congress; be it, finally, for the very tenor of these decisions, which, in my opinion, are in open contradiction with the principles of our Association, fixed in our General Statutes. I truly do not know how the General Council could have assumed the responsibility of publishing them and recommending them to the different internationalist federations as legitimate and legitimately issued norms of the Association. It seems to me a really very serious task that [the Conference] has assumed.[23]

Neither Palladino's qualified promise to write again after acquainting himself with the entire proceedings of the London Conference nor his "regret that with the first letter I send to you I bring an opinion opposed to that of the General Council," sufficed to hide the fact that Palladino, "believing that it should displease no one to want free discussion," had found in Bakunin's libertarian counsels a point of view with respect to

[21] *Ibid.*, p. 275. Engels wrote to Cafiero again on Feb. 29-Mar. 9, 1872 (*ibid.*, p. 276), but Cafiero did not reply until June, when he formally announced his defection.
[22] Sept. 26, 28; Oct. 9, 16, 30-31; Nov. 11. *Ibid.*, pp. 254-56, 282.
[23] *Ibid.*, pp. 266-67.

doctrinal authoritarianism more to his liking than that implied in the actions of the London Conference.

Engels wrote Palladino on November 23 in courteous but formal terms,[24] choosing to consider Palladino's opinion a purely personal one on the grounds that no I.W.A. section existed at the moment in Naples, strange logic in view of Palladino's assertion in his November 13 letter that many of the workers of the dissolved section were thinking of founding another. On December 19, Cafiero formally notified Engels of the formation of the Neapolitan Workers' Federation and the imminent appearance of the section's official organ, La Campana, to be edited by Alberto Tucci with Cafiero's assistance.[25]

By the end of 1871, then, the fortunes of international socialism in Naples were in the hands of three men: Cafiero, the political guide and liaison with other Italian sections, with no firm intellectual commitment to either side in the Marx-Bakunin controversy, but convinced that political action by the proletariat, in the commonly understood sense of the term, would never accomplish a social revolution; Tucci, editor of La Campana (first issue, January 7, 1872), still out of touch with Bakunin, but, as his speech at the Rome Congress demonstrated ("the fatherland is created spontaneously . . . from the bottom to the top"), still sharing a primary anarchist principle with the Russian; Errico Malatesta, secretary of the new Federation and thus far unidentified with either a Marxist or Bakuninist orientation. Palladino momentarily dropped out of the picture when he returned to his native village, Cagnano-Verano, a few weeks after the new section was organized.[26]

REPERCUSSIONS IN TURIN AND MILAN

In Turin the indefatigable intriguer Terzaghi welcomed Resolution IX as another opportunity to sow confusion and dissension among the members of the local Workers' Federation. In the pages of his nearly moribund Proletario Italiano he informed them of the resolution and interpreted it as "the postponement of socialism to politics," which brought a letter of denial from Engels, obligingly published by Terzaghi on November 29.[27] A probable motive for doing so appeared in his request, five days

[24] Nettlau, B.I.I., p. 268.

[25] Ibid., p. 273. Cafiero was probably anticipating the new section, for L'Eguaglianza did not announce its constitution until Jan. 21, 1872.

[26] Ibid., p. 279. On May 11, 1872, the Neapolitan questore reported that Palladino's father was confining the young socialist to Cagnano to keep him out of trouble, though Palladino continued to carry on a vigorous propaganda (Lucarelli, Palladino, p. 6). Apparently Palladino did not keep in touch with his former comrades in Naples, for in the Feb. 4, 1872, issue of La Campana, under the "Piccola Posta," was the plea: "C. P., Cagnano.—Document your existence. Many here doubt it. Per Cristo."

[27] For the letter in full, Romano, Storia, II, 188; Nettlau reprints excerpts, B.I.I., pp. 269-70.

later, that the General Council send him a subsidy to keep *Il Proletario Italiano* afloat.[28] Meanwhile, Terzaghi's former collaborator, Carlo Laplace, now back in the Mazzinian camp, was elected president of the Federation, thus exacerbating the conflict between Mazzinians and socialists within the organization to the point where Terzaghi was expelled on December 13. About 270 members seceded in protest and, as the year ended, mustered under the leadership of Giuseppe Abello, Cesare Bert, and Terzaghi to declare themselves a section of the International, the "Emancipation of the Proletariat." [29] On January 14 Terzaghi informed Engels that the group numbered four hundred, but five days later he sent dues for only half that number. His newspaper resumed publication on January 1, 1872, under the title of *Il Proletario; Periodico Socialista.* In relation to the Marx-Bakunin controversy, Terzaghi's position was to continue in a cloud of equivocation, but there was no doubt about the sentiment of the section members. On December 26 the Emancipation of the Proletarian group decided to send a representative to the future international congress demanded by the Sonvilliers Circular.[30]

In Milan, the pro-Sonvilliers position assumed by the local socialists was clearly presaged by Vincenzo Pezza's editorial in *Il Gazzettino Rosa* on November 20: "The International does not and must not have chiefs. . . . On the day when despotic and dictatorial tendencies manifest themselves in the men directing the Association, we shall repudiate them as we have repudiated the dogmatic tyranny of Mazzini." To channel these sentiments against the London Resolution, Bakunin wrote Pezza a long letter four days after he learned of the Sonvilliers appeal for a general congress and, after receiving a supply from Guillaume, sent copies of the circular to Milan.[31]

Engels' man, Cuno, got no such assistance from London in trying to counteract Pezza's influence in favor of the anarchist appeal. Engels had mailed him a full bill of particulars on Bakunin on December 16, but the communication never reached Cuno, with the result that the latter, as late as December 27, was still floundering for the proper attitude to

---

[28] Marx, "L'Alleanza della Democrazia Socialista . . ."

[29] For details, *Il Gazzettino Rosa*, Dec. 15, 17, 18, 21, 28, 1871; *La Favilla*, Jan. 14, 1872; Rosselli, *Mazzini e Bakounine*, p. 404.

[30] *Il Gazzettino Rosa*, Dec. 28, 1871. When this news reached London, the General Council decided, "in view of this hostile attitude," not to send the subsidy requested by Terzaghi on Dec. 4. Marx, "L'Alleanza della Democrazia Socialista . . ."; cf., also, Nettlau, *B.I.I.*, p. 234. The only hint that Bakunin may have influenced the Turinese declaration in favor of the Sonvilliers Circular is that on Dec. 15 he wrote letters to Perruca and Jacobi, on the 20th to Terzaghi. Since it was the period in which he was sending copies of the circular into Italy, these letters probably explained the circular from Bakunin's point of view. *Ibid.*, p. 290.

[31] *Ibid.*, pp. 236-37, 282.

assume toward the Sonvilliers Circular.[32] On the very day that Engels' agent was pleading for instructions from London, a personal emissary of Bakunin was persuading the Milanese socialists to declare for the Sonvilliers Circular. A few days before, thirty-two members of the Workers' Society had seceded, at the suggestion of Cuno, and, under the guidance of Pezza, Testini, and Cuno, set about establishing an I.W.A. section. In the midst of these discussions, Victor Cyrille, a young French Communard refugee, arrived with instructions from Bakunin. The Russian was worried by Il Gazzettino Rosa's publication of Cafiero's ambiguous interpretation of Resolution IX,[33] and its failure to publish the Sonvilliers Circular. "Brothers, what is happening among you? Your silence, accompanied by the obstinate silence of the Gazzettino Rosa, makes me wonder, afflicts me, worries me." [34] On December 28, Cyrille was back in Locarno reporting a mission accomplished,[35] as well he might, for he had left behind him in Milan "Un gruppo di internazionalisti" who had signed this public declaration:

> Convinced that the principle of the autonomy of the sections and of the regional and national federations constitutes the real strength of the International; that the development of the great Association, especially in the Latin countries, is due to this vivifying principle, which is in the spirit and the letter of its fundamental statutes; more confident than ever of the future of the International, which can not be enfeoffed to the will and authority of any individuals, but must be the work of collective activity and liberty; [we] adhere to the invitation of the Jura federation for the convocation of a general congress for the purpose of arresting the authoritarian tendencies manifested in the General Council and to make it withdraw into the limits of its powers.[36]

Hostility toward authoritarianism in London did not, however, entail the Milanese organization's acceptance of a Bakuninist position on the question of socialist political activity, for in its initial manifesto the signers insisted:

[32] Nettlau, B.I.I., pp. 236-37.

[33] In addition to publishing Cafiero's letter, Il Gazzettino Rosa reproduced the Emancipación article on Dec. 20 and, like La Roma del Popolo, published Engels' letter of Dec. 5 refuting Mazzini's "Documenti sull'Internazionale."

[34] Letter of Dec. 23, 1871, Guillaume, I.D.S., II, 251-52. Two letters to Pezza on Dec. 10, 18, and one to Testini on the 15th remained unanswered. Nettlau, B.I.I., p. 290.

[35] Bakunin's diary entry for Dec. 28: "Cyrille returned; he has succeeded." Guillaume, I.D.S., II, 252.

[36] Il Gazzettino Rosa, Dec. 29, 1871. Bizzoni added, in the name of his editorial staff: "We associate ourselves with this document and congratulate the Italian sections that have already adhered to the proposal of the Jurassian Federation."

. . . Political activity is the natural and necessary consequence of economic emancipation; that is, the social question is inseparable from the political question, and the solution of the first is the condition for the solution of the second; therefore, we recognize no other party than the democratic socialist party of the workers.[37]

Apparently Engels' man Cuno had succeeded in exacting a price for his signature on the manifesto.

THE BOLOGNA FASCIO OPERAIO

In the Emilia-Romagna region, the fact that Engels and Bakunin had both established contact with outstanding radical militants prior to mid-November had no visible effects on the "socialist" movement in that part of the peninsula. Nabruzzi, in boasting to Engels that the International was progressing "marvelously" in the region, had omitted saying that this progress had no stimulus from either London or Locarno; any incipient regional federation of "socialist" societies, such as Nabruzzi described, was obviously an outgrowth of the democratic congress movement initiated by Celso Ceretti and the Mirandola, Mantuan, and Verona societies in August, whereas Engels and Bakunin had no contacts with the Romagnol radicals until November. The "provisional regional council" for the Romagna, reported to Engels by Nabruzzi on November 25, probably originated in a November 19 meeting of the Garibaldian republican societies of Bologna, Imola, Ravenna, Forlì, Faenza, Lugo, Rimini, etc., which decided to send representatives to the "democratic Congress," to be held in the spring of 1872 and to hold a preliminary meeting of Romagnol societies in Bologna.[38] The decision clearly establishes the associative movement of these socialist-sympathizing groups in the context of the essentially political movement that Garibaldi's followers were trying to launch during these months.

This is the context, too, in which occurred the creation, on November 27, of the particular Romagnol society destined to spearhead the Bakuninist movement in Italy, the *Fascio Operaio* of Bologna, whose elected chief, or "consul," was Erminio Pescatori, prominent Garibaldian of the region.[39] The first manifesto of the group was published by most of the Internationalist organs of the peninsula,[40] though the declaration was

---

[37] For the full text of the program, dated Jan. 1, 1872, *L'Eguaglianza*, Jan. 21; *Il Martello* (Milan), Feb. 4, 1872. The group declared its adherence to the I.W.A. and sent dues to London for a hundred members. Nettlau, *B.I.I.*, p. 237; Rosselli, *Mazzini e Bakounine*, p. 407.

[38] *Il Gazzettino Rosa*, Nov. 22; *La Plebe*, Nov. 23; *L'Eguaglianza*, Dec. 10, 1871.

[39] *Il Gazzettino Rosa*, Dec. 6; *Il Fascio Operaio* (Bologna), Dec. 27, 1871.

[40] Among others, by *L'Eguaglianza*, Dec. 10, 1871.

only generically socialist and Internationalist in the humanitarian sense reflected in Garibaldi's pro-I.W.A. pronouncements:

> We ask only that our rights as men and citizens be respected. . . . *We care for neither abstruse doctrines nor meddling doctrinaires.* Freethinkers, we adore no idol. We do not expect our well-being from a God, but from ourselves, from our own poor forces; we want to do everything by ourselves. We recognize only truth, justice, and morality. Lovers of light, we do not conspire in the shadows: what we want to say we shall say publicly. We want *Liberty* with order, *Equality* with right, *Fraternity* with labor. We have no political questions, and we hope to emancipate ourselves from the double servitude of ignorance and poverty. . . . Since we believe . . . that the social question of the proletariat is not a national question, but a world question, we wish to unite with the Workers . . . of all nations in a solemn bond of solidarity and cooperation, because they are all our brothers.[41]

Entirely consistent with this kind of "socialism" was Garibaldi's immediate acceptance "with pride, [of] the precious title of member of the *Fascio Operaio* of Bologna." [42]

Nor is there the slightest hint, in the first issue (December 27) of the *Fascio Operaio*'s official organ, that the founding spirits of the new society were acquainted or concerned with the doctrinal distinctions between Marx's "scientific" and Bakunin's "anti-authoritarian" socialism. The purpose of the organizational meeting held on November 27, declared *Il Fascio Operaio*, was to create a workers' society which, "by excluding political and religious rivalries, would correspond better than existing [societies] to the urgent needs of the working class and advise as to the way to make possible union and solidarity among all the workers of Italy and other Nations, in order to develop the strength and power capable of solving the world social question, that is, of the emancipation of the most generous and unfortunate part of society: that of the proletariat."

In Ferrara, a workers' society, born in November, declared itself Internationalist, accepting the I.W.A. program, but without sacrificing its autonomy. On November 30 Engels accepted a local socialist, one

---

[41] *Il Gazzettino Rosa,* Dec. 6, 1871. Italics mine. The anti-doctrinaire attitude of the Romagnols accurately reflected Garibaldi's remark to Petroni in October: that he did not want to see the I.W.A. be "overcome by the spreaders of doctrines and thereby be pushed into exaggerations and . . . the ridiculous." *La Plebe,* Nov. 9, supplement; *La Favilla,* Oct. 31, 1871.

[42] Letter to Erminio Pescatori, Dec. 5, 1871, in *Il Gazzettino Rosa,* Dec. 10; *La Favilla,* Dec. 15; *Il Fascio Operaio,* Dec. 27, 1871.

Giuseppe Boriani, as an I.W.A. member, authorized to "admit new members and to form new sections." [43]

INAUGURATION OF BAKUNIN'S CAMPAIGN
TO WIN THE ROMAGNA

If the Bologna *Fascio Operaio,* along with the many other *fasci* inspired by it,[44] were "socialist" in the Garibaldian sense, if—as is certain—their leaders were devoted to the general, Bakunin had a delicate job on his hands in propagandizing the Romagnols. They had already been warned against the Russian by Garibaldi. To Ceretti, on December 19, the general had written:

> About Silvio [Bakunin's code name] and the General Council
> . . . we shall follow them in that which is comprised in human
> fraternity. In regard to certain ideas not agreed to by most, we
> shall maintain ourselves in our autonomy. In a few words, we are
> a branch of the International, the banner that was ours all our
> life. This must not deny us the right, however, to regulate our-
> selves internally as we like.[45]

Bakunin's first objective was to persuade the Romagnols to declare for the Sonvilliers Circular, but, since their movement might evolve into an organization under Garibaldi's sponsorship, he had to "sell" his own antipolitical formula without alienating his audience by obvious criticism of the general. His strategy was to block General Council influence first, that of Garibaldi later, but without compromising himself in shifting from one target to the next. He was entirely conscious of the danger, for despite the Bologna *Fascio Operaio's* resounding protestations of concern for the solidarity of the international proletariat, Bakunin could not have been unaware of the widespread diffidence toward foreign ideological influence reflected in Garibaldi's disdain for "spreaders of doctrines" that lead to "exaggerations" and the "ridiculous," in his insistence on maintaining independence toward "certain ideas not agreed to by

[43] *La Plebe,* Dec. 12, 1871; *La Favilla,* Jan. 19; *L'Eguaglianza,* Feb. 11, 1872; Nettlau, *B.I.I.,* p. 230.
[44] "The *Fascio Operaio* of Bologna is about to become a *fascione* [i.e., an outsize *fascio*], in which Ravenna, Imola, Lugo, Rimini, Sinigallia, etc., are united." *La Plebe,* Jan. 19, 1872. See, also, *L'Eguaglianza,* Dec. 3, 1871. "In Bologna the *Fascio Operaio* gives indications of becoming a formidable power that puts together in a vast network the former pontifical provinces." The organization started with 185 members on Nov. 27; by early Jan., 1872, it counted over 500. *Ibid.,* Dec. 27, 1871; Jan. 7, 1872.
[45] *La Favilla,* Dec. 27, 1871; *Il Fascio Operaio,* Jan. 3; *La Plebe,* Jan. 4, 1872.

most," and in the Bologna society's opposition to "abstruse doctrines" and "meddling doctrinaires."

Skillfully, Bakunin drew the tactical inferences relevant to gaining his objective: the attack on Marx and Engels must avoid the appearance of personal rivalry and be hinged on the question of the General Council's "authoritarian" actions, not on underlying doctrinal differences. If Garibaldi's current popularity advised against direct assault at the moment, gentle insinuations in favor of keeping the Romagnol movement out of politics might serve, in the meantime, to create the dialectical premises for a subsequent effort to cancel the threat to socialist development Bakunin saw in the Hero of the Thousand: the potential military dictator at the head of a really popular political movement. Finally, in view of Garibaldi's professed predilection for an "honest dictatorship," [46] any authoritarianism charged to the account of the General Council would constitute indirect propaganda against Garibaldi in the same way that Bakunin's polemic against the ideological authoritarianism of Mazzini had served his feud with Marx and Engels.

Though Bakunin's initial letter to Celso Ceretti on November 11 was only one of several Italian epistles written on a particularly busy day, the Russian, once apprised of the Sonvilliers Circular, wasted little time in concentrating his fire on the vital Romagna. On November 26, in the midst of penning another lengthy anti-Mazzinian article, which he was sending in installments to Pezza in Milan, Bakunin began a long letter to Ceretti. On the 30th his diary records, for the first time, a letter from Pescatori in Bologna. This contact with the newly elected consul of the Bologna *Fascio Operaio,* probably inspired by Ceretti, was an intimate one, for Bakunin's first major propaganda epistle to the Romagna (December 2-8) was addressed to *Luca* (Ceretti) and *Lupo* (Pescatori). The use of a *nom de guerre* for Pescatori suggests that Bakunin's acceptance of the Bolognese as a trusted member of his small circle of Italian intimates antedated the letter he received from Pescatori on November 30. The Ceretti contact, in any case, seems to have been Bakunin's opening wedge in penetrating the Romagna, for on December 1 a communication from Nabruzzi arrived. The fact that it was written —as it must have been—only three or four days after Nabruzzi had written to Engels (November 25), permits the inference that the editor of *Il Romagnolo* was ignorant of the issue posed by the Sonvilliers Circular or simply indisposed to declaring for either London or Locarno.[47]

[46] The motif appeared again in a letter (Dec. 30, 1871) to Ceretti: "I believe that in order to conquer the Byzantinism that afflicts world democracy, the only remedy is honest and temporary dictatorship." Nettlau, *B.I.I.,* p. 319.

[47] For the references to Bakunin's letters to and from the Romagna, see *ibid.,* pp. 282, 288, 290-91.

However momentarily undecided these Romagnol correspondents, the Russian's propaganda barrage of December, accompanied by copies of the Sonvilliers Circular, quickly spurred them into taking a stand with respect to the battle now joined between Bakunin and the London Council. In his letter of December 2-8 to Ceretti and Pescatori, subsequently characterized by its author as "a declaration of war on the General Council," Bakunin used his own previous criticism of Mazzini as a point of departure for his attack on Marx. In the comparison, the author of *Das Kapital* came off second best to the apostle of *italianità*. Both men, wrote Bakunin, are inspired by political vanity, "religious in one and scientific and doctrinaire in the other." But where Mazzini's vanity is disinterested, seeking only the victory of his ideas and party, Marx also seeks to impose his own personality. "The evil is hidden in the lust for power, the love of command, and the thirst for authority. And Marx is profoundly infected by this evil." From this, his political system is logically derived:

> As an authoritarian communist, he favors the liberation and reorganization of the proletariat through the State, i.e., from the top to the bottom, by virtue of the intelligence and education of a cultured minority that is naturally turning toward socialism, and, for the sake of the welfare of the ignorant and stupid masses, [Marx] influences them with his own legitimate authority.

The system is virtually that of Mazzini, for both men are seeking a world state. Where the Italian hopes to realize it through the primacy of Italy, Marx, "a Pan-German to the marrow of his bones," sees the German race as the hope of regenerating the world.

In identifying Marx with Mazzini, the Russian was cutting his cloth to fit the Romagnol republicans, whose adoration of Garibaldi far outweighed any attachment to the Genoese. In touching on theory, he established the premise of his own doctrines, not by adducing positive arguments that would call attention to himself, but by describing Marx's program in terms that would insure its rejection by any self-respecting Romagnol radical. With the dice thus loaded against Marx on a personal level, Bakunin, on December 15, blueprinted a positive plan of action for his Romagnol friends, not, however, without broadening his charges to include the General Council—probably to blunt any suspicion that the dispute was a strictly personal one between himself and Marx.[48]

In sending the Sonvilliers Circular, Bakunin described it as "a solemn protest in the name of liberty, the true principle of the International, against the dogmatic and governing claims of the general Council in London, whose whole task, according to the spirit and letter of our

---

[48] For the Dec. 15 letter to Ceretti, see Romano, *Storia*, II, 198-200. Excerpts are contained in Nettlau, *B.I.I.*, pp. 288-89; *La Favilla*, Jan. 3, 1872.

General Statutes, must be limited to that of a simple *Central Office of Statistics and Correspondence.*" In justification of this remarkable thesis, Bakunin argued:

> The International admits no orthodox dogma, official theory, or central government. It is entirely founded on autonomy, spontaneous development, and liberty of opinions and on the free federation of the workers' associations. . . . Since opinions are absolutely free, every section and every individual can profess his opinions, with the right of propagandizing them, but not of imposing them on anyone; even Mazzini, with his benevolent God and his custodian angels, if he wished, could become a member of the International on the sole condition that he accept, with all its consequences, the supreme Law, the only obligatory law of the International, that of *practical international solidarity.*
>
> The unity of the International . . . is founded, on the one hand, solely on the identity of the present poverty, economic servitude, needs, instincts, and aspirations of the proletariat of all countries; on the other hand, on the perfectly free organization of this *practical international solidarity* from the bottom to the top, and not from the top to the bottom, according to a spontaneous federation, crossing the frontiers of communes, regions, and states.

Bakunin meant by "practical" international solidarity neither structural cohesion nor doctrinal uniformity, but mutual assistance and support in direct action, whether it be a strike in a single city or revolution in an entire country. Here was the true measure of the contrast between the Russian's essential activism and Marx's concept of educating the masses to class action on whatever plane opportunity offered:

> If the workers of another trade, commune, region, or foreign country go out on strike, all internationalists are obliged to succor them to the limit of their ability. If [the former] make a revolution, there is even greater reason why [the latter] owe, in addition to their sympathy, their support; and there is no better way for them to support the revolution of their brothers in a foreign country than by staging an indigenous revolution. . . . Here are the bases of the International: all else must be the action of liberty.

By this definition, the resolutions of the I.W.A. congresses were not binding on the sections; even less obligatory, therefore, were the decisions of a "secret Conference, irregularly composed, arbitrarily selected and convoked by the General Council." The "illegal" London Conference had passed resolutions which, were they to prevail, would wreck the International by transforming it into "an instrument of Pan-German thought and ambition."

Bakunin's specific recommendations to Ceretti of December 15 may well have been the master source of the declarations in favor of the Sonvilliers Circular in other cities of the peninsula, given the Romagnols' "complete accord with the internationalists of the Veneto, Lombardy, Piedmont, Tuscany, Naples, and Sicily" mentioned by Nabruzzi in his November 25 letter to Engels:

1. Send a copy of the Sonvilliers Circular to Garibaldi, "*not in my name,* since I am here only as a simple go-between, but in the name of the Jura Federation's Committee."

2. Send the manuscript Circular to Pescatori, to whom "I am sending four more of them" for distribution, along with the printed Circular, to the Romagnol sections, "not forgetting *Il Romagnolo* of citizen Nabruzzi."

3. Ask the Romagnol sections "*to adhere publicly to the protest of the Congress of Sonvilliers and to the request for the immediate convocation of a general congress.*" Sympathetic sections should manifest their adherence (*a*) by informing the Committee of the Jura Federation, (*b*) by informing all Italian sections of the I.W.A. and sympathizing associations of their adherence and inviting them to do the same, and (*c*) by notifying all pro-socialist newspapers of Italy, asking them to publish the Sonvilliers Circular with a statement of approval—"beginning with the *Romagnolo.*" [49]

Then, since he could not appeal in the name of the national principle he had decried for years, Bakunin used the next best—or worst?—platform: "racial" solidarity—and here he convicted himself as either a complete opportunist, willing to violate his own principles to gain his immediate objective, or a consummate hypocrite in preaching "practical international solidarity" of the workers: [50]

> You will learn with pleasure that the whole of socialist and revolutionary France is with us, that the Spaniards declared themselves for us, that the Belgians are swinging to our side, that the groups of Turin, Milan, and Naples have already declared for us.

[49] Note Bakunin's emphasis on persuading Nabruzzi, the only Romagnol in direct correspondence with Engels. The Russian also wrote directly to Nabruzzi on Dec. 16. Nettlau, *B.I.I.*, p. 290.

[50] For an anarchist "justification" of Bakunin's references to "Pangermanism," *ibid.*, p. 289, note 1.

> *It is the Latin world that is federating, organizing and rising in the name of liberty against the dictatorship of the Pangermans of London.*[51]

Less than two weeks after Ceretti received this call to muster the Romagnols against the London General Council, the key society of the region, the Bologna *Fascio Operaio*, adhered to the Jura socialists' demand for the convocation of an I.W.A. general congress.[52]

CONCLUSION

The situation at the end of 1871 stood in startling contrast with that of little more than six weeks before. For Bakunin, Mazzini no longer constituted an important threat. Bologna, Milan, Turin, and Girgenti had joined in the demand for a general congress to review the work of the General Council and the London Conference.[53] In each of these cities, as well as in Naples, Bakunin had established promising contacts with radical leaders who, if not greatly concerned with the doctrinal points at issue between Bakunin and the General Council, had committed themselves to the position that the latter represented a menace to the continued health and integrity of the socialist International. Many of them owed what Bakunin considered a dangerous loyalty to Garibaldi, and in consolidating his own position, this factor would urge extreme caution, the same kind of obtuse approach with which he began in joining battle, first with Mazzini and then with the General Council. His entire tactic had been simplicity itself: avoid a war on two—or three—fronts; use victory over one adversary as the premise in attacking the next.

For his part, Engels, though clear as to his targets, was guilty of poor timing, doubly important in fighting a two-front war against Bakunin and Mazzini. Distance from, and lack of first-hand experience with, the

[51] Italics mine. Bakunin's theme was echoed by *La Favilla* on Jan. 13, 1872, when the Mantuan organ referred to the "Germanic Council of London," composed of "German elements."

[52] *Il Gazzettino Rosa*, Dec. 28, 1871. The Sonvilliers Circular was formally approved on Jan. 14, 1872. *La Favilla*, Jan. 23, 1872.

[53] The Girgenti section, in announcing its support of the Sonvilliers Circular, made the same charges of authoritarianism as had the Milanese, and also repeated Bakunin's argument that the General Council was "a simple central office of correspondence and statistics," to which function it must be compelled to return by a general congress. *L'Eguaglianza*, Jan. 7; *La Plebe*, Jan. 22, 1872. Antonio Riggio, who in July had considered political abstention "a very serious error," now devoted several columns of *L'Eguaglianza* (Jan. 14) to reprinting a chapter from *Parti socialiste*, a volume by A. Vermorel, martyr of the Commune, urging the rejection of parliamentarism as a social revolutionary tactic.

The Pisa section joined the protest movement on Jan. 7. *Cf.*, the section's letter to Engels, in Nettlau, *B.I.I.*, p. 241; *L'Eguaglianza*, Feb. 11, 1872. Sciacca (Sicily) followed suit early in January, *ibid.*, Jan. 14, 1872.

Italian terrain may account for the mistake, but Cafiero's letters should have constituted sufficient warning—if Engels had been less dedicated to discrediting Bakunin personally and more concerned with well-timed and constructive debate on the doctrinal level, geared to the peculiarities of the Italian republican environment. He missed the crucial element in the Italian situation of these months: that socialism's opportunity lay in exploiting the fact that Mazzini was alienating a large segment of republican opinion for reasons quite extraneous to his political objectives. But to Engels, the anarchists' political abstentionism guaranteed their failure in Italy—and this at a time when even Mazzini was compelled by the force of events to give a higher priority to the social question in his propaganda. Only sectarian dogmatism can account for Engels' remarkable statement of January 24, 1872, that "not many people are behind [the Bakuninists], because in the final analysis, the overwhelming majority of Italians are Mazzinians and will remain so as long as the International is identified with political abstention." [54]

Mazzini's political error of making an issue of the Paris Commune is understandable, since his lifelong commitment to a philosophy of idealism permitted him no other reaction. For him, the Commune offered nothing essentially revolutionary in the realm of ideas; it only reaffirmed the evil of materialism he had identified and attacked almost two decades earlier. To a generation arisen during the interval, however, the Commune heralded a decisive turn in human affairs, calling for a new orientation, and it was this difference in perspective that denied Mazzini an understanding of Italian radical youth's reaction. In the recollection of an anonymous contributor to *La Plebe*, that reaction inevitably entailed both a break with Mazzini and acceptance of Bakuninism:

> We can not recall those days [of the Commune] without, in a certain way, being moved, for it was really a *revolution* that occurred in our minds. It was felt that the Mazzinian Republic was no system that could satisfy the needs of the century. . . . When the Commune of Paris finally gave us an opportunity to study new phenomena, it was like the beginning of the new path on which we had put ourselves. What had been up to then a *presentiment* in us (I speak of us, the generation matured after the creation of the kingdom of Italy) became an *idea*—a rudimentary idea, if you like, but one which, to come to full maturity, needed elements that were bound to appear. Thus it was that, since we had already accepted the negation of *divine authority* (the great foundation of Mazzinian theory), we came necessarily and by degrees to the negation of *human authority*, that is,

[54] Letter to Cuno, Rosselli, *Mazzini e Bakounine*, p. 409, note 2.

anarchy. From Anarchy to Collectivism was an easy step, and when we learned of the [Sonvilliers] circular . . . , we all applauded . . .[55]

More was involved than mere rebellion against authority. The movement stimulated by the Paris Commune posed a positive goal: social justice for the working class. In effect, republican patriotism, as a *revolutionary* motif, had been displaced, robbed of its vitality by the consummation of political unity. In this moment, the Commune seemed a dramatic proof that within the context of national unity another revolution was still to be accomplished—but only by creating an active role for the masses. To cling to the traditional republican program, to continue considering proletarian material wants as an essentially irrelevant factor in revolution, now appeared unrealistic and fruitful of nothing but further frustration. Vincenzo Pezza, by no means the first to move from Mazzinianism to socialism, probably spoke for a whole segment of young Italian republicans when he wrote these lines:

> Italian youth, let us confess it to ourselves, up to now has not had the feeling of the reality in the midst of which it lives and wants to act. Habituated to seek its thought only in that of Mazzini and its will only in the heroic initiative of Garibaldi, it has become rather a youth without heart, without heroism, but it has also unconsciously accustomed itself to consider the popular masses with a kind of disdain because of their ignorance. Trained to an abstract patriotism, we lent ourselves readily to enthusiasm and faith, but at the same time we lost the cult of reason, and when the masses did not stir and remained indifferent and inert, we cursed the apathy of people who did not share our revolutionary exaltation.
>
> We must be tired of going around uselessly in a vicious circle, of thinking without creating anything, of crying to the wind in repeating the same thing to a public that no longer listens to us, of acting continually without accomplishing anything.
>
> Let us embrace the cause of the worker, not with words alone, but with deeds; let us fraternize with the sons of labor; there we shall hear the heartbeat of a new life.[56]

Rendering Pezza's suggestion more attractive was the existence of an international organization that insisted on its own social revolutionary potential, pointing to the Commune as an example of its power. When Bakunin defined the function of the I.W.A., not as the slow, educative task of inculcating class consciousness (after all, Mazzini's forty-year

[55] *La Plebe*, Jan. 15, 1872.
[56] *Il Gazzettino Rosa*, Nov. 26, 1871.

apostolato educatrice—though posing a quite different goal—had proved unavailing), but as international support of revolution *now*, he struck a responsive chord in discontented young radicals who, like Pezza, were searching for a revolutionary formula comprehending an active role for the masses.

Quantitatively, the malcontents represented but a small fraction of Italian republicanism. Antonio Riggio, whose penchant for exaggeration has already been noted, claimed there were more than a hundred groups in Italy either directly or indirectly affiliated with, or adhering to the principles of the International,[57] but Enrico Bignami, with no compelling reason to err on the side of conservatism, estimated the strength of the I.W.A. in the peninsula, at the year's end, as approximately six thousand members, divided among about twenty sections.[58] But even Bignami's estimate bears witness to the fact that Italian socialism had finally become a true political movement.

[57] *L'Eguaglianza,* Jan. 21, 1872.
[58] *La Plebe,* Dec. 30, 1871.

XI

Anarcho-Socialism Penetrates the Romagna (January to March 1872)

APPROVAL of the Sonvilliers Circular by the socialist nuclei of Bologna, Milan, Turin, and Girgenti reflected their hostility toward authoritarianism in general and the arbitrary implications of the London Conference decisions in particular. Once the issue was presented to the Italian socialists in these terms—as Bakunin so adroitly contrived—this reaction was to be expected. After having convinced themselves that Mazzini's authoritarianism potently threatened their intellectual independence, they were easily convinced by Bakunin that the London General Council represented the same peril in another form. Still, the Russian's propaganda success of December, 1871, did not achieve his strategic objective: that of a solid phalanx of Italian I.W.A. sections committed, along with the dissident federations of Spain, France, Belgium, and the Swiss Jura, to supporting his defiance of the General Council and establishing the legitimacy of anarcho-socialism as an Internationalist credo.

Such a commitment on the part of the Italian sections, as of the beginning of 1872, would have presupposed the neutralization, if not the elimination, of the influence of Giuseppe Garibaldi, who wanted the organizational unity of radical republicans as ardently as Bakunin, but for quite different reasons. If, from Marx's angle of vision, Bakunin was an element of confusion, a "diversionist," in the General Council's plans to bring the Italians into loyalty to London, so, from the Russian's point of view, Garibaldi, with his ambiguous "internationalism," posed a real obstacle to Bakunin's schemes. The difference lay in this: that

236

Bakunin, by incessant propaganda, had to create his own capital among Italian radicals; Garibaldi, by virtue of his stature as an authentic folk hero, already had an immense fund of prestige on which he could draw at will. The success of the Russian, by mid-1872, owed much to the general's unwillingness—or incapacity—to exploit his resources effectively.

By early January 1872, Garibaldi was convinced that the time had come to form a coalition of democratic forces in the peninsula, to include "Freemasons, Rationalists, Democrats, Mutual Aid Societies, Artisans' Brotherhoods, etc.," all of whom, according to the general, have their "tendencies toward good." [1] The scheme, no less unrealistic than ambitious, presupposed the possibility of agreement among all shades of republican opinion. Garibaldi's mention of Federico Campanella, die-hard Mazzinian, as one of the potential backers of the coalition movement attests to the general's willingness to work out a political compromise with the Mazzinian party; at the other end of the spectrum appears the name of Carlo Cafiero as a probable member of the "Provisional Central Office," to be created as the administrative agency of the organization proposed by Garibaldi.[2] On January 24, four of the general's Florentine admirers, Mario Aldisio Sammito, Luigi Stefanoni, Salvatore Battaglia, Luigi Castellazzo, and the moving spirit of the Romagnol democratic movement, Celso Ceretti, invited the "various Italian and foreign Associations—Humanitarian, Workers', Mutual Aid, Democratic, Internationalist, Freethinking, Veterans' . . . and editorial staffs of Democratic Newspapers" to support a general congress.[3] Garibaldi proposed "the aggregation of all existing societies aiming at the moral and material improvement of the Italian family. . . . A Workers' Congress took place under the inspiration of Mazzini. A Masonic one was proposed by Campanella, a Democratic one by Ceretti, and a Rationalist one by Stefanoni. Is not human betterment, perhaps, the goal of all these associations? Why march divided?" A general congress should dispense with political questions, since "all of us are adherents of the government of honest people—the republican—and since we can not bring it into being at this time" the delegates should confine their attention to "Rational and Social questions, the solution of which is practicable." Such a congress should act as the constituent assembly for a national organization

---

[1] Il Libero Pensiero, Feb. 1, 1872. See, also, Garibaldi's letter to Pescatori, Jan. 13, 1872, in Ximenes, comp., Epistolario, II, 7.

[2] Il Libero Pensiero, Feb. 1, 1872. For the "Proposta" and the "Statuto della Ragione," loc. cit.; La Favilla, Jan. 24, 1872; Ciampoli, Scritti [di Garibaldi], pp. 613-14. In view of Cafiero's vigorous opposition to compromise with the Mazzinians —the implicit goal of the democratic congress—the appearance of his name among the members of the "Provisional Central Office" of Garibaldi's fascio of "Reason" can only be understood as occurring without Cafiero's approval.

[3] La Favilla, Jan. 28; La Roma del Popolo, Feb. 1, 1872.

to be named "Reason," the chief purpose of which should be "the binding together, as brothers, of all good-hearted men [*uomini di cuore*] in mutual assistance, with the goal of consecrating their lives to the actuation of the great principles of truth and justice." [4]

Almost fifty democratic societies of various types (workers', war veterans', artisans' brotherhoods, republican leagues, socialist sections, etc.), as well as various newspapers (*La Favilla* of Mantua, *La Libertà* of Pavia, *La Plebe* of Lodi, *La Capitale* of Rome, *Il Fascio Operaio*, and *Lo Staffile* of Bologna), adhered to the congress initiative.[5] Only two prominent I.W.A. sections did not join in support of the scheme: Naples and Milan, from their inception supersensitive about bourgeois subversion of their socialist purity. Since the signers of the January 24 manifesto had announced their intention of fixing the time and place of the projected congress, it appeared, for the moment, that Garibaldi had only to let matters take their course in order to find himself the acknowledged unifier and leader of Italian democracy except for intransigent Mazzinians and radical Internationalists. The opposition of both these extremes, however, was immediate, militant, and, in the end, fatal to the general's dreams of a Rule of Reason.

In Naples, the socialist nucleus of Carlo Cafiero, Errico Malatesta, and their friends, blasted the Garibaldian congress movement in the columns of their newly founded organ, *La Campana*.[6] Any attempt at reconciliation with the Mazzinians was treason to socialism. The Mazzinian party, with the unification of Italy, had exhausted its historical function. Cafiero, considering himself the tutelary numen of socialist orthodoxy in Italy, ranted against both the "bourgeois" tendencies of Stefanoni, one of the democratic congress promoters, and the Romagnol socialists of the *Fasci Operai* for their support of Garibaldi and the congress movement. The Romagnols should dispense with the support of "professors, proprietors, bourgeois journalists, rationalist priests, and other reactionaries"; they

---

[4] *Il Libero Pensiero*, Feb. 1; *La Plebe*, Jan. 27; *La Favilla*, Jan. 27, 1872. The original suggestion for a "Universal Society of Rationalists" had been advanced by Stefanoni in Oct., 1871 (*Il Libero Pensiero*, Nov. 2, 23; *La Favilla*, Nov. 10, 1871) and Garibaldi had accepted the *statuto* proposed by Stefanoni (letter of Oct. 19, 1871, *loc. cit.*). A month later, however, Garibaldi proposed his own formula (letter to Sammito, Nov. 19, 1871, Ciampoli, *op. cit.*, pp. 601-02), which represented a modification of Stefanoni's text (letter to Pescatori, Jan. 10, 1872, in *La Favilla*, Jan. 19, 1872) but asked that it not be published until there was full agreement with Castellazzo and others. Castellazzo had nothing to add or change, apparently, for the *Proposta* of late January is identical with that suggested two months earlier by Garibaldi. For the original Stefanoni draft *Statuto*, *La Favilla*, Nov. 14, 15, 17, 1871. For Bizzoni's condemnation of the scheme, *Il Gazzettino Rosa*, Nov. 10, 23, 1871.

[5] *Il Libero Pensiero*, Feb. 15, 1872.

[6] *La Campana*, Jan. 7, 14, 21, 28, 1872.

should be "more prudent in their affirmation of the means suitable to bring the triumph of the people's cause"; they should not become "slaves and followers, at any cost, of any individual, no matter how illustrious." Appreciating the importance of the Romagna region to the success of the International in Italy, Cafiero did not attack Garibaldi directly. His diatribes against Mazzini carried the broad implication, instead, that the general represented an equal threat of bourgeois infiltration and ultimate control of the Italian socialist movement:

> You, dear friends, have involuntarily become instruments of equivocation and have offered a terrain to bourgeois politicians who are daily advancing and organizing to our harm. You have declared yourselves Internationalists, you have adhered to the International; but have you thought that this adherence puts a bottomless abyss between you and Mazzini, puts you in discord, not with the heart, but with the ideas formulated up to now in the mind of Garibaldi? [7]

Since Garibaldi's congress movement clearly anticipated reconciliation with the Mazzinians, La Campana's thunders against such compromise implicitly condemned the condottiero himself. "Why," Cafiero asked the Romagnols, "do you greet . . . projects of conciliation that would be ridiculous if they were not an attempt on the social revolution, a bloody injury to the Italian proletariat, wronged, betrayed by the hundreds of insignificant political revolutions?" [8]

Consistently enough, Cafiero had felt from the beginning that any democratic congress movement should aim, not at a union of democratic forces under the banner of Truth, Justice, and Reason, under the patronage of Garibaldi, the captain of "revolutionary militarism," but at socialist federation on a national level.[9] When the socialist section of Turin, the Emancipation of the Proletarian Society, proposed on January 28 a congress of I.W.A. sections in the peninsula, La Campana immediately published the Turin circular and, in the next issue, Cafiero clearly sealed off all hopes the Garibaldians might have entertained that the Neapolitan socialists could be enticed into seeking a modus vivendi with the Mazzinians.[10] In Turin, too, Cafiero's intransigence was abetted by the editor of L'Anticristo, Giovanni Eandi, certain that socialism could

---

[7] Ibid., Feb. 18, 1872.
[8] Loc. cit.
[9] See his letter to Castellazzo, Dec. 26, 1871, Conti, O.S.F., pp. 258-59.
[10] For the circular, La Campana, Feb. 4; La Favilla, Feb. 3; L'Eguaglianza, Feb. 11, 1872. For Cafiero's refusal to cooperate with the Mazzinians, La Campana, Feb. 11, 1872.

no more be harmonized with Mazzinianism than fire with water.[11] For Antonio Riggio, in Girgenti, the Garibaldian project represented "too many reservations, too much gallantry, too much docility" toward the privileged classes. "Why do we not openly raise [the standard] of a radical and profound revolution?" Between true socialists and Mazzinians reconciliation is impossible, "so long as we want liberty and the Mazzinians want authority; so long as we are for the abolition of slaves and the Mazzinians for the retention of the masters." [12] In Milan, the reaction of the newly founded I.W.A. section, the *Circolo Operaio*, to the idea of reconciliation with the Mazzinians was doubtless negative, too, since the section does not appear among those societies adhering to the Florentine appeal of January 24, nor was the section's outstanding militant, Vincenzo Pezza, less intolerant of compromise than Cafiero in Naples.[13]

Mazzinian hostility toward the democratic congress movement and its implicitly distensive tenor was fully as stubborn as that of Cafiero. In January and early February, Francesco Pais, left-wing Mazzinian editor of *L'Alleanza* (Bologna), preached collaboration with the "Internationalists *alla Garibaldi*," but by mid-February Mazzini's Romagnol captains replaced him with Luigi Rangoni, a far more faithful mirror of the master's sentiments.[14] In the opinion of Mazzini himself, Garibaldi's whole congress initiative was both absurd and dangerous to the cause of republicanism. On January 26 he lamented that Garibaldi, hypnotized by Reason, the I.W.A., and his own anticlericalism, was trying, through no provocation by Mazzini, to ruin the party and lead Italian youth down a false path.[15] On February 1, *La Roma del Popolo* published the Florentine circular of January 24, not as a welcome overture from the Garibaldians, but as a butt of criticism. Garibaldi's suggestion that the projected congress not deal with the political question, wrote Mazzini, missed the essential point: not to discuss the republican program because it is incapable of realization today "is not the best way to make it so

---

[11] *L'Anticristo: Cronaca grigia*, Feb. 11, 1872, pp. 1-3. *Cf.*, also, Eandi's article, "I Mazziniani e l'Associazione Internazionale," in the Mar. 3 (pp. 1-4), Mar. 10 (pp. 3-5), and Mar. 24 (pp. 1-5) issues of *L'Anticristo*. For the Neapolitans' appreciation of the assist from Milan, *La Campana*, Feb. 18, 1872. *L'Anticristo* lived only from Jan. 1 to May 13, 1872. For a brief description of Eandi and his activity, see Giuseppe Cita Mazzini, "Giovanni Eandi," *Movimento Operaio*, Yr. I, No. 2 (Nov. 1, 1949), 55-56.

[12] *L'Eguaglianza*, Feb. 11, 1872.

[13] See his "Ai nemici ed agli amici," *Il Martello*, Feb. 1, 1872.

[14] Rosselli, *Mazzini e Bakounine*, pp. 400-02. Under Rangoni's direction, *L'Alleanza* became the official organ of the Mazzinian *Società repubblicane consociate delle Romagne*, a transition, of course, prompting a venomous attack by Cafiero. *Il Fascio Operaio*, Mar. 2; *La Campana*, Feb. 25, 1872.

[15] Letter to Campanella, Jan. 26, 1872, *S.E.I.*, XCI, 322-23.

tomorrow." Garibaldi's idea—"holy in itself"—of creating a single organization of all republican and democratic societies is really utopian:

> They all have different goals or radically different methods to achieve a common goal. . . . To extinguish these radical differences, cherished by habit and sanctioned by long-accepted programs, is a work impossible to a Congress. To found an order on some phrase of brotherhood, torn from a moment of enthusiasm and forgotten the next day, is the same . . . as systematizing, not *strength,* but *weakness,* frustrating precisely that concentration which alone can bring success to the enterprise.[16]

When the editor of *Il Gazzettino Rosa* asked him to pronounce himself on "the Garibaldian question," Mazzini denied that he had ever attacked Garibaldi or even responded to the general's attacks on himself. "Even today I am ready to conclude some pact with him"—but only on the basis of Mazzini's republican program, to which Garibaldi had never openly adhered.

> If he does not wish to do so, Garibaldi does not have to shake my hand or any other. But [he] must say to the Italians: "Within twenty days or twenty years, you shall have well-being only from . . ." Then the country will know that we are united. An occasion will arise. Let us prepare ourselves to accept it with a practical, united effort. As for our sharing action with him, once the circumstance has arisen, a few days will suffice.
>
> Obtain this [commitment] from him. Leave off calling yourselves members of the International. Let us treat the religious question with respect. And the dissidence will disappear in a short time.[17]

Taking Mazzini's words as a challenge to him "to declare openly that I am a republican, . . . to deny that I belong to the International [and] to treat the religious question . . . with philosophic respect," Garibaldi was outraged. "The Mazzinians call these words conciliatory. I thought I was occupying my time with useful things." [18] Giving up all idea of reconciliation with the Mazzinians entailed, of course, renunciation of a democratic congress:

[16] *La Roma del Popolo,* Feb. 1, 1872. See, also, Mazzini's reply of a week later, when several societies in Livorno, Viareggio, Savona, Macerata, and Bologna asked him to bless the overture of the Garibaldians. *Ibid.,* Feb. 8, 1872.

[17] *Ibid.,* Jan. 25; *La Favilla,* Jan. 27, 1872.

[18] Mazzini's retort: "I do not know whether I do or write many useless things; but I would not do the most useless [thing] of all, that of giving advice to General Garibaldi." *La Roma del Popolo,* Mar. 7; *Il Gazzettino Rosa,* Mar. 5, 1872.

I am of the opinion that it should be indefinitely postponed; and before fixing the date for it we should come to a clear understanding with the majority of the Italian Associations . . . through correspondence, thus avoiding the tumultuous tempests that multiform doctrinarism—which is making a *bordello* of our country—would arouse. . . . I believe that it is convenient to let pass this period of anarchy that afflicts our country before undertaking anything serious.[19]

THE BOLOGNA CONGRESS
(MARCH 17-19, 1872)

Garibaldi's pronouncement left the Romagnol Internationalists in a peculiarly equivocal position. Cooperation with the Mazzinians under the general's patronage had proved impossible; without the Red Shirt hero's blessing and support, such a *rapprochement* became even more unthinkable. The Romagnols found themselves caught between two fires: the Mazzinians damned them for their socialism, the intransigents in Naples decried their lack of it. The time had come for a clarification of their political orientation. Their decision to move left, rather than right, was as much the result of the Mazzinians' inflexibility—compounded after the death of Mazzini on March 10—as of any of the other external pressures conducive to that decision.

Even before Garibaldi lost interest in a democratic congress on February 20, the socialists of the lower Romagna, captained by Lodovico Nabruzzi, clearly indicated that the stubbornness of the Mazzinians was forcing them into a more revolutionary attitude. On February 18 the socialists of Ravenna, Lugo, Forlì, and other sections of the area met in Villa Gambellera and there proclaimed their allegiance to the I.W.A., extolled Garibaldi, and enunciated a program smacking of anarcho-socialism: liberty of thought and conscience (including the freedom to be an atheist); emancipation of the Fourth Estate through the abolition of all existing privileges; autonomy of the communes of all nations, bound together only by common proletarian interests, which transcend the "chimeric demarcations of national confines"; and the direct rule of the communes by all citizens "without distinction of wealth, education, or sex."[20] If this program was only tendentially anarchist, the Romagnols' break with Mazzinian principles was definitive, and, in declaring the rupture, they gratuitously—and significantly—identified themselves with

[19] Letter to Ceretti, Feb. 20, *La Plebe*, Mar. 2; *Il Gazzettino Rosa*, Mar. 6, 1872. The same letter went to Stefanoni, *Il Fascio Operaio*, Mar. 2; *Il Martello* (Milan), Mar. 3, 1872.

[20] *Il Fascio Operaio*, Feb. 15, 1872, supplement, for the report on the proceedings, written by Nabruzzi. For further details, *Il Martello*, Feb. 25; *La Campana*, Mar. 3; *L'Eguaglianza*, Mar. 10, 1872.

the Neapolitan intransigents: "Like our brothers of Naples at the Workers' Congress of Rome, we shall intervene and discuss wherever it is convenient to the search for truth, but, like them, we shall never accept a Program which, in departing from God, inhibits individual liberty, sanctions the principle of authority, and maintains many of the privileges of the possessing classes." [21] Nor would they be deterred from this orientation by "the voice of old patriots from whom we separate ourselves, while in our hearts preserving a deep sense of gratitude for the good they have done to the Cause of Liberty!" [22] One notes that the "old patriots" had served the "Cause of Liberty," not that of *la patria*, the latter a bourgeois concept in the credo of the anarcho-socialists.

The congress of all the sections of the Romagna held on March 17-19 in Bologna revealed ambiguities in the Romagnols' political attitudes, but, compared to the confused ideological babel and schizoid tendencies characterizing the preceding months, the deliberations of the gathering amounted to a notable clarification. Fourteen sections of the Romagna and the socialists of Mantua, Mirandola, Genoa, and Naples—invited at the last minute—were represented, a geographical coverage giving far greater weight to the proceedings than any previous socialist meeting.[23] Alberto Tucci, Bakunin's ex-disciple, had been sent by the Neapolitans; Carlo Terzaghi, though expelled from the Turin section a month earlier, represented only himself—and/or the police.[24] The effective movers of the congress, however, were all Romagnols: Celso Ceretti, Pescatori, Nabruzzi, and Andrea Costa, a twenty-one-year-old Imolese who, while attending the University of Bologna as a promising student of Italy's premier poet, Giosuè Carducci, had been caught up in the general enthusiasm of republican youth for the Paris Commune.[25] From that time forward, he had given himself completely to the socialist cause, helping in the organization of the original *Fascio Operaio* of Bologna. By the time the

---

[21] Manacorda, *Il movimento operaio italiano*, pp. 80-81.
[22] Valiani, *Storia del movimento socialista*, I, 208-09.
[23] For the congress proceedings, *Il Fascio Operaio*, Mar. 24, 1872. See also, Romano, *Storia*, II, 244-47; Manacorda, *op. cit.*, p. 81; Valiani, *op. cit.*, I, 209-10; Nettlau, *B.I.I.*, pp. 347-48; Guillaume, *I.D.S.*, II, 268-69; Rosselli, *Mazzini e Bakounine*, pp. 423-25. The Romagnol sections attending: Bologna, Ravenna, Rimini, Fano (Marches), Massignano, Lugo, Montelparo, San Potito, Fusignano, Forlì, Faenza, Senigallia (Marches), Sant'Arcangelo, and Imola. The original decision to hold a Bologna meeting of Romagnol societies dated back to Nov. 19, 1871, but at that time it was projected—as noted above—as a preparation for the presumably imminent national democratic congress. The Fano section was founded in February, the Lugo section early in March (*La Plebe*, Feb. 24, Mar. 9); the Senigallia section probably early in February (*La Campana*, Feb. 18); the Montelparo section on Feb. 26 (*Il Fascio Operaio*, Mar. 2, 1872).
[24] Nettlau, *B.I.I.*, pp. 349-50, note.
[25] For his eulogy of the Commune, see above, p. 146.

Bologna Congress convened, the oratorical and dialectical skills of Andrea Costa, along with the ardor—unleavened by Mazzinian antecedents—of his socialist convictions, were already portending his future as one of Italy's most popular and influential socialists.[26]

The Bologna delegates officially affirmed their sections' adherence to the I.W.A. and associated the sections as a regional organization: "*Fascio Operaio,* International Workingmen's Association, Italian Federation, Bologna Region," a title clearly anticipating a national organization. The Bologna Regional Council was commissioned to arrange a national constituent congress of all Italian sections in May 1872.

On what principles might such a national organization of socialists be based? The Romagnols' answer showed that, of the four ideological currents competing for the loyalty of the Italian non-constitutional Left: the Mazzinian (class harmony and cooperation under a republic), the Garibaldian (universal fraternity under the Rule of Reason), the Marxian ("scientific" socialism) and the Bakuninist (anarcho-socialism), the *Fascio Operaio* was closest to the last-named. Against the cardinal principle of Mazzini that the social question must be subordinated to the political problem (i.e., the creation of a republic), the Romagnols, though recognizing "the just importance of the political question," affirmed the preeminence of the social problem and its solution. Against Marx's conviction that the path to socialist victory lay through political action, they abjured participation in political elections on the ground that "any authoritarian government is the work of the privileged to the detriment of the disinherited classes"; therefore, in addition to opposing the state, socialists should, by abstention from politics, deprive it of the means of sustaining itself.

The Bologna Congress voted a eulogistic address to Garibaldi and Andrea Costa, in transmitting it to the Red Shirt hero, invited him, "father and captain of the people," to the projected national congress.[27] Though the congress opposed a "partial insurrection," i.e., purely political and republican, and considered only a "general and collective" uprising, limited to the emancipation of the proletariat, as possible and useful, Garibaldi—probably without realizing that such a view condemned his own ideas of republican revolution quite as much as those of Mazzini— gave his stamp of approval to the Bologna resolution. There is no hint

[26] On Costa's ideological development, see Alessandro Schiavi, "La formazione del pensiero politico di Andrea Costa (da carte inedite)," *Nuova Antologia,* Yr. 83, Vol. 443, Fasc. 1769 (May, 1948), 11-38. For the most complete bibliography of writings by and about Costa, *Movimento Operaio,* Yr. IV, No. 2 (Mar.-Apr., 1952), 36-98, compiled by Renato Zangheri and others. The latest biography, distressingly romanticized, is by Lilla Lipparimi, *Andrea Costa* (Milan: Longanesi, 1952).

[27] Valiani, *op. cit.,* I, 209.

of an awareness that the Romagnols had embraced many of the anarchist ideas he had so long decried when Garibaldi assured Nabruzzi, in connection with the Bologna Congress' intention of setting up a national organization guided by the principles just approved, that "I certainly agree to cooperate in the Undertaking which everyone wants hurried up." [28]

As a step in ideological development, then, the Bologna deliberations brought the Romagnol socialists very close to the extremist—i.e., essentially anarchist—positions of the dominant socialist leaders in Milan and Naples. Such a unity of doctrinal approach between the latter and the numerous sections of the Romagna certainly presaged the imminent emergence of a national association of Italian socialists with a common program.[29] Still, if all signs pointed in mid-March to full-blown anarchism as the official doctrine of such a national federation, the Bologna conferees refused to identify themselves on an international level with the anarchist position in the current feud between the London General Council and the Bakuninist Jura Committee in Berne. The Bologna *Fascio Operaio*'s demand in December, 1871, for the convocation of a general congress of the I.W.A. to review the work of the London Conference of the preceding September was quickly followed by a clear insistence on the *Fascio*'s independence. On January 4 the group declared itself "an international society, conserving, however, its own autonomy and liberty." [30] Garibaldi, too, had counseled in favor of avoiding any organizational control from abroad. With these precedents, it is not surprising that the Bologna Congress recognized in the London Council and the Jura Committee "merely offices of correspondence and statistics" and instructed the Bologna Regional Council to initiate correspondence with both of them.

To Marx this was a revelation of "the mysterious existence of the secret center of the [Bakuninist] Alliance," to Engels, the Romagnols had "unmasked themselves as pure Bakuninists." [31] Both judgments exaggerated, for both Bakunin and the Jura anarchists immediately scolded the Romagnols for the damage they had done to the anarchist cause by implying that the General Council and the Jura Committee were rivals.[32] Marx, in fact,

---

[28] Nabruzzi and Trombetti had carried to Caprera a greeting from the Bologna conferees. Nettlau, *B.I.I.*, pp. 326, 348. For Garibaldi's acknowledgment, *Il Popolino* (Turin), Apr. 22, 1872.

[29] Pescatori had already asked the Turin section to declare its solidarity with the Bologna *Fascio Operaio*. Vitale Regis to Engels, Feb. 16, 1872, Nettlau, *B.I.I.*, p. 314.

[30] *Il Gazzettino Rosa*, Jan. 11, 1872.

[31] Marx, "L'Alleanza della Democrazia Socialista . . . ," p. 42; Engels to Cuno, Apr. 22, 1872, Nettlau, *B.I.I.*, p. 316.

[32] Bakunin, in writing to Ceretti, diplomatically attributed the mistake to a "misunderstanding." Letter of Mar. 13-27, 1872, Romano, *Storia*, II, 392. For the Jura Committee's clarification "To our friends of the Fascio Operaio," Jura *Bulletin*, Mar. 20, 1872.

had been trying for months to prove precisely such a point in order to muster backing for the expulsion of Bakunin and his followers from the I.W.A. The conclusion appears inescapable that the Romagnol socialists were simply unready to take sides in the Marx-Bakunin dispute, even though, from a purely doctrinal point of view, they had already moved far along the path to anarchism.

BAKUNIN'S LETTERS TO THE ROMAGNA (JANUARY TO MARCH, 1872)

To the extent that the Romagnols accepted anarcho-socialist principles and were sufficiently conscious of the Marx-Bakunin controversy to declare themselves neutral on the issue, the propaganda activity of Bakunin was decisive. From the inauguration of his contacts with Ceretti, Nabruzzi, and Pescatori late in 1871, the Russian realized that the impetus for a national union of socialists could best be imparted by the Romagnols. Their rapidly burgeoning *fasci operai* demonstrated an organizing capacity far beyond that manifested in any other socialist center in the peninsula. In his correspondence with Lodovico Nabruzzi prior to the Bologna Congress, Bakunin had one purpose in mind: to insure that the national federation of Italian socialist sections, if and when it came into being, would serve his own ambition to strip the London General Council of its powers and entrench anarchist dogma as the dominant doctrinal position of the I.W.A. The delicacy of the task required all the circumlocution the Russian could muster.

In his letter to Nabruzzi of January 3,[33] sent via Vincenzo Pezza in Milan, Bakunin defined the goals and methods of anarchism as "the true program of the International." If the *Fascio Operaio* program is the same, then "give us your hand and let us begin to work together." The first step is to declare openly for the I.W.A., since "you are all internationalists at heart" anyway. Garibaldi, unfortunately, hinders complete cooperation. Here Bakunin reverted to his favorite method of dealing with his opponents: first a feint in the guise of praise for the antagonist's nobility of character, then the body blow:

> No one more than I bows so sincerely and deeply to Garibaldi, the popular hero. His march into France, his entire comportment there, were truly noble in their greatness, generosity, simplicity, self-control, and heroism. His deep and instinctive understanding of the popular cause . . .
> But . . . he does not, in fact, know or understand [the International]. Garibaldi *is a fact, not an idea,* or more exactly, when his work concerns deeds, he is with us; where [it] concerns

[33] For the letter in full, Romano, *Storia,* II, 347-51.

theory he is against us. His *idée fixe* is dictatorship, and there is nothing more contrary to the social revolution than dictatorship. All his political ideas—and he is too old and stubborn to change them—all his political habits, chain him to the old world that we want to demolish. . . . If you have the misfortune to follow the political and socialistic guidance of Garibaldi, you will lose yourselves in a labyrinth of contradictions, because his policy is a continuous contradiction, as worthless as the socialism of Mazzini.

Has not the time come, perhaps, for the masses, with all the gratitude and respect due the great men of the past, to free themselves once and for all from their dictatorship, from all dictatorship? . . . .

Let us finish with the past. . . . Come without shame, without dissimulations, openly, into the International. . . . And since you call yourself Rubicon [Nabruzzi's *nom de-plume*], cross the Rubicon, give us your hand, join us openly, . . . declare yourselves a section of the International.

The letter should be shown to Ceretti and Pescatori, but "as much as possible, avoid speaking of me, or even mentioning my name openly," since ideas, not the individual, are important. Besides, "no one must say that a Russian, a barbarian, a Kalmuk, is trying to create a party for himself in your country," which would make ineffective propaganda and advantage the Mazzinians. Then, to clinch the point, Bakunin urged the Romagnols to "accept what suits you, throwing away the unnecessary; from the moment you accept an idea, it is no longer mine, it is yours."

Pezza, with whom Bakunin had already established an intimate working relationship, added a postscript to the letter in which he cautioned the Romagnols to limit knowledge of Bakunin's program to only "the most intimate" socialists and assured them they could join the I.W.A. without "abdicating to any system"—presumably the Bakuninist, since, despite the fact that "Silvio is a revolutionary phenomenon, . . . individual teaching must not become a dogma for us." Was Pezza trying to further Bakunin's argument for the impersonality of ideas or to prove his own independence of the master?[34]

[34] Nettlau (*B.I.I.*, p. 298) thinks Pezza was warning Nabruzzi not to be too impressed by the personality of Bakunin. Romano (*Storia*, II, 249-50) argues that Pezza's plea for secrecy as to the program "reveals the first moves of the secret [Bakuninist] Alliance," the existence of which Romano accepts on the basis of the "evidence" Marx presented in his polemical pamphlet of 1873, "The Alliance of Socialist Democracy and the International Workingmen's Association." The reader interested in this unrewarding series of charges and countercharges is referred, for the anarchist side of the question, to Guillaume, *I.D.S.*, Vol. II, *passim*. That Bakunin was engaged in a "conspiracy" to establish the supremacy of the I.W.A. general congresses over Marx and the General Council is no more true than that Marx and the

Perhaps because he feared his criticism of Garibaldi had offended the sensibilities of his Romagnol correspondents, perhaps because he was impatient to turn his fire against his principal opponent, Bakunin, in his next letter to Nabruzzi of January 23-26,[35] concentrated on indicting Marx and the General Council. In either case, the earlier attack on Garibaldi's tendencies toward dictatorship served as a natural springboard for the Russian's charge that Marx was an authoritarian. Again the condemnation was preceded by eulogy, a technique probably intended to establish the objectivity of the writer.

> Marx is the premier scholar of economics and socialism of our time. . . . I have never known any as gifted and profound as he. . . . [Marx and Engels] founded the party of the German communists and never ceased being active in this sense. Marx wrote that wonderful and profound preamble of the general Statutes and gave substance to the instinctive and unanimous aspirations of almost all the countries of Europe; he conceived the idea of the International . . . and proposed its realization. . . . These are very great and good services and we would be very ungrateful if we did not prize their significance.
>
> [But] Marx is an authoritarian and centralist communist. He wants what we want: the complete triumph of economic and social equality, but in the State and by means of the power of the State, by means of the dictatorship of a very strong provisional and—one might say—despotic government. . . . He is as absolute in theory as . . . in practice, and his truly extraordinary intelligence is accompanied by two ugly defects: he is vain and jealous. He had a horror of Proudhon only because the great name and fame of the latter was harmful to him. And there is nothing hateful that he has not written against [Proudhon]. Marx is egocentric to the point of madness. He says my ideas and does not want to understand that ideas belong to no one; . . . . [he] does not want to understand that as soon as an idea, even when he himself has expressed it, is understood and accepted by others, it becomes as much their property as his.
>
> Marx, already inclined toward self-adoration, was completely

General Council, in staging the London Conference of Sept., 1871, were "conspiring" to achieve by their own fiat what they feared no general congress would permit: the expulsion of all dissidents who did not accept Marx's interpretation of the I.W.A. statutes. The present writer believes that a history of the Italian socialist movement during this period has the principal task of explaining how and why the great majority of Italian Internationalists opted for the "anti-authoritarian" position of the Bakuninists. To insist that this choice was a "mistake," as does Romano, means assuming that Marx's revolutionary methodology alone can lead to socialism—an as yet untested assumption, in my opinion.

[35] For the letter in full, Romano, *Storia*, II, 352-71; excerpts in Nettlau, *B.I.I.*, pp. 300-02.

ruined by the idolatry of his scholars, who made a kind of doctrinal pope of him; and nothing is more fatal to the spiritual and
moral health of a man, even a very intelligent one, than being
. . . considered infallible. All this leads Marx to be even more
egocentric, so much so that he is beginning to abhor all who do
not bow their heads before him.

After lecturing the Romagnols on what he considered the obligations
and prerogatives of I.W.A. sections, Bakunin related his own version of
the history of the International, reserving his most venomous barbs, of
course, for the General Council, not neglecting to imply that much of the
Council's "authoritarian" attitude was really due to the influence of a
German-Jewish conspiracy.

Today it is evident that the German-Jewish group of Marx, still
lording it over the General Council, always plotted the ambitious
program of transforming the International into a kind of well-
regulated and disciplined state that obeys a unitary government
centralized in Marx's hands.

Bakunin's positive plan of action was very specific. A few weeks
earlier, the Belgian Federation of the I.W.A., fearing the General Council
had arrogated too much authority to itself, had decided to present a
draft revision of the International's statutes at the next general congress
and called on the other I.W.A. federations to do the same, "so that the
forthcoming international congress can conclude the final pact of federation." [36] The Italian sections, advised Bakunin, should gain formal
recognition from the General Council, accept the Belgian draft statute
as a basis for study and present the result for approval by "the great
Italian Democratic Congress that you intend to hold early in the year."
The important task was for the Italian delegates to the next general
congress to "appear . . . with a full acquaintance with what they must
represent, do and say there." At the general congress, the Italians must
have "a large and intelligent representation." Bakunin did not intend to
be outnumbered or outmaneuvered on that occasion. The Italian delegates must be furnished with "precise instructions, . . . an *imperative
mandate* on the principal questions, . . . they must be up to their task,
with a full knowledge of the bases, the duties, the situation, and the
function of this great international association of ours."

His own generalship of such a campaign was, of course, to be con-
cealed from the General Council. Bakunin cleverly associated his request
for anonymity with his general thesis on the impersonality of ideas and
principles. If the General Council sought to justify its conduct and atti-

[36] For the Belgian resolution of Dec. 24-25, 1871, Guillaume, *I.D.S.*, II, 255.

tude, the Italians, thanks to Bakunin's didactic letter, could reply "with full knowledge of the case, *but without mentioning my name, this I warmly pray you.*" If they found themselves incapable of replying to Engels on a specific point, "I am always at your disposal." If the Council sends a communiqué to be published, "do so if you agree with its contents—and expressly say that you publish it because it pleases you—and if you do not like it, do not publish it." If the Council sends a plenipotentiary, "greet him fraternally, as you would certainly do for any other member of the International, but not as the extraordinary delegate of a government, which does not exist in the International." Above all, Bakunin cautioned, the Italians should avoid direct polemics with the Council in their public utterances and writings and stay "in the sphere of principles." If they had to write against the Council, "always do it in the manner and with expressions that are most fraternal and measured."

Thus Bakunin spelled out the Italian socialists' role in the anticipated showdown with his London enemies. Certainly the persuasiveness of these January letters to Nabruzzi—also passed to Pezza in Milan, as well as to Ceretti and Pescatori—is reflected in the resolutions of the Bologna Congress of mid-March. On the other hand, Bakunin's instructions in the mechanics of conspiracy were ill reflected in the Romagnols' declaration of neutrality between the London Council and the Jura Committee, the more so in that, by mid-March, they were no longer committed to promoting a democratic congress under the Garibaldian slogan of Reason and Universal Brotherhood. Nor did the Romagnol sections take even the first tactical step recommended by Bakunin: securing the General Council's recognition as I.W.A. sections.[37]

However sesquipedalian, the letters to Nabruzzi are no true measure of Bakunin's efforts to woo the Romagnols into his camp. Giuseppe Fanelli, whose relations with Bakunin had gone sour as a result of his mission to Madrid in 1868-69, had only gradually resumed his contacts with the Russian agitator. After a visit to Bakunin's Locarno lair on January 19, however, Fanelli seems to have decided once again to devote the prestige of his revolutionary past to the anarchist cause, and from this point forward he was constantly on the move between the Italian sections and Locarno as a carrier of messages, as a propagandist and organizer.[38] It was to Fanelli, in all probability, that Bakunin referred in

[37] "The section of Ravenna has written us, announcing its adherence, but keeping its own autonomy. I simply asked them if they accept the Statutes or not." Engels to Cuno, Apr. 22, 1872, Nettlau, *B.I.I.*, p. 316.

[38] *Ibid.*, pp. 294, 304. Bakunin's diary: Jan. 19, "with Fanelli all day— . . . plan of campaign established in the evening"; Jan. 20: "With Beppe [Fanelli] . . ."; Jan. 21: "did not sleep all night—worked with Beppe and alone— . . . evening with Beppe . . ."; Jan. 22: "worked until 5 in the morning—aroused Beppe, who was late—I to bed at 6:30 in the morning—Beppe departed."

a letter to Ceretti on February 11, when he told the Romagnol that "one of these days, an intimate friend of mine will probably come to find you with a note from me. His name is undoubtedly known to you . . ." [39]

The anarchist dean, in his work of persuasion in the Romagna, was careful not to offend Ceretti's sympathy for the freethinking societies that Ceretti and the Florentine Garibaldians, prior to the general's renunciation of the democratic congress, were hoping would lend strength to their movement. In reply to Ceretti's query, Bakunin wrote: "Like you, I think that the movement of the freethinkers is very useful, and that it can not be discounted. They were the first to raise the standard of revolt against the theological authority of Mazzini and, like you, I think that any sincere freethinker must logically become a socialist. If he does not, it means that his thinking is only half emancipated." [40] And as for the democratic congress itself, Bakunin dared not voice a shade of disdain, even while trying to capitalize on its apparent inevitability. "I expect some very good results from your Congress, which will provide the means for the sincere socialist-democrats of Italy to know and understand one another."

By the time Ceretti received his next letter from Locarno,[41] three intervening events required a quite different tone in the Russian's approach to the Romagnols: Garibaldi postponed the democratic congress indefinitely, Mazzini died, and the Bologna Congress revealed how much Bakunin had yet to exert himself before the Romagnols fitted Engels' description of them as "pure Bakuninists."

He had been "very afflicted," wrote Bakunin, to learn that Garibaldi had postponed the democratic congress project, simply because he was "bored with the discordance of democratic and socialist opinions." Harmony of viewpoint is both unrealizable and undesirable; in politics, it spells despotism. Bakunin had never hoped that the democratic congress would reconcile socialism with the other elements of opinion on the Italian Left: the Free Masons, the Mazzinian republicans, the Free-thinkers, and the rest. The real utility of such a congress would be, not an impossible harmony, but the opportunity provided for the launching of a social revolutionary, conspiratorial organization. Bakunin's advice was a remarkable anticipation of Lenin's subsequent argument for revolutionary activity under the guidance of disciplined, militant, and convinced activists, organized by cells:

[39] *Ibid.*, p. 304.

[40] Feb. 11, 1872, *loc. cit.*

[41] Mar. 13-27, reproduced by Jacques Mesnil, in *La Société Nouvelle* (Brussels), CXXXIV (Feb., 1896), 175-99; Romano, *Storia*, II, 372-92; and, in part, by Nettlau, *B.I.I.*, pp. 319-26.

For all the socialist democrats, for all the revolutionary socialists of Italy, [the congress] would be . . . a magnificent occasion to know each other, to come to an understanding and to ally themselves on the basis of a common program. Naturally, this secret alliance would accept into its bosom only a very small number of individuals, the most trustworthy, the most devoted, the most intelligent, the best, for in these kinds of organizations, it is not quantity, but quality, that one must seek. . . .

These nuclei, intimately bound together with similar nuclei presently being organized, or that will be organized, in other regions of Italy and abroad, will have a double mission: first, they will form the inspiring and vivifying soul of [the I.W.A.] in Italy and elsewhere, and later they will concern themselves with questions that can not be discussed publicly. They will form the necessary bridge between the propaganda of socialist theories and revolutionary practice. . . .

Your congress, like all congresses, will be a kind of tower of Babel, but it will give you the possibility of recognizing your own, that is, the revolutionary socialists . . . of Italy, and of forming with them a serious minority, well organized and . . . powerful . . .

Even the death of Mazzini on March 10 proved so much grist for the anarchist propagandist's mill. No foreigner more than he knew the Italian republican's veneration of the apostle of nationality. With a keen intuition of his correspondents' state of mind, Bakunin lavishly eulogized the great Genoese: "Italy has just lost one of her most illustrious children. . . . An eminent intelligence, an ardent heart, an invincible will, an unwavering devotion, sublime. . . . The new Joshua, Mazzini tried to arrest the course of the sun. He has succumbed to the task. His great soul, fatigued, tortured, has finally found the repose which, alive, it never knew. The great mystic patriot, the last prophet of God, is dead. . . ."

But Mazzini's death presented perils to the socialist cause in Italy. His followers will probably split into "little foyers of political intrigue," and the "most vital, the most sincere, the youngest" will want to move into the socialist camp. They should be fraternally received. "Open wide the door to them, *but receive them only on the condition that they all frankly accept the program of the International.*" In the present moment of mourning for the Great Departed, there is the danger that "Mazzinians and Italian internationalists, the bourgeois revolutionaries and the socialist revolutionaries, momentarily forgetting their past disagreements, will extend a fraternal hand to each other." But in this "patriotic embrace" the socialists should not ignore the differences between the Mazzinian program and their own.

Do not let them involve you—and they certainly will not fail to
try it—in a common, practical enterprise, conforming to their
plans and modes of action, not to yours. Call them to join you on
your own terrain, but do not follow them on theirs, which you
could not accept without sacrificing and betraying [the] great
cause of the proletariat. . . . Do not forget that, between the
bourgeois revolution of which they dream and the social revolution demanding your services today, there is really an abyss,
not only as to ends . . . , but also in relation to means. . . .
By accepting their plans of action, you would not only ruin all
your socialist work . . . , but you would condemn yourselves
. . . to a sure defeat, to a bloody and complete fiasco.

Sound Leninist doctrine, too, was the advice given the Romagnol socialists as the criterion governing their attitude in the event Agostino
Bertani, whose aim was "an exclusively bourgeois republic," became the
"chief and occult director" of Mazzinian enterprises:

To ignore him would be a mistake, to ally oneself with him
would be . . . a still greater one. You are not utopian theo-
reticians, you want to form an active and powerful party, capable
of transforming, as quickly as possible, your beautiful Italy into a
country of liberty, equality, justice, happiness, and honor for all.
You will organize yourselves for action; consequently, you can
not afford to ignore any of the elements constituting the present
reality. You must be well acquainted with the strength of the
errors you will have to combat, as well as that of the elements
which . . . are forced to become, up to a certain point and
during the whole period of transition, your allies in some way,
. . . having the same adversaries. . . . The Mazzinians . . . are
the implacable enemies of that government which, fearing you
much more than it fears them, is beginning to persecute you
throughout Italy and will soon persecute you . . . with an even
more furious animosity. Up to a certain point, therefore, you will
be forced to march parallel with them, to keep yourselves informed of their enterprises, and not only to let them act, but at
times . . . even seconding them *indirectly*, inasmuch as, in doing so, you can hope to weaken and demoralize the present government. . . . In all the struggles . . . of the bourgeois republicans against the government, you will abstain . . . as much as
possible without committing moral and material suicide; but
every time you feel yourselves forced to emerge from this apparent passivity, you will do so, of course, only to take their part
against the government.
You will therefore be forced to . . . march parallel with them
in order to profit for the realization of your own ends . . . But

> you will be on your guard . . . against allying with them to the point of confounding yourselves, you will never allow them to penetrate your Organization. . . . It seems to me . . . absolutely necessary that all your organizations, public as well as secret, remain completely outside all the Mazzinian . . . organizations.

With the desired position of Italian socialists vis-à-vis the Mazzinians thus defined, with the techniques of revolutionary action clearly stated, Bakunin eloquently delineated the key anarchist principles he had failed to develop in his January letters to Nabruzzi. Italian socialists must prepare for a social revolution that seeks, on the negative side, the abolition of the state and the end of economic exploitation of labor by monopoly capital; on the positive side: "the absolutely free and spontaneous federation of the communes and workers' societies" (the political organization) and "the collective expropriation of capital and land by the workers' associations" (the social organization). To achieve such a revolution, all classes interested in the maintenance of the existing state—the financial, commercial, and industrial upper bourgeoisie, the great proprietors of land and capital, and most of the middle bourgeoisie, "a slothful and stupid class"—must be mercilessly liquidated. The petty bourgeoisie and the small rural proprietors have no program and are disoriented; their traditions and social vanity cause them to cling to the privileged classes. They still have some interests apart from the aspirations of the masses, but the Italian socialists must "reconcile those interests with these aspirations, without, however, sacrificing the latter."

With or without these two segments of capitalist society, however, the revolution depends principally on the urban and rural proletarians, "the real basis of the nation." Both are "necessarily, eminently, and instinctively socialist." The city workers have a newly awakened sense of revolutionary kinship with those of other countries; they are ready for revolution. Yet, under the influence of "bourgeois doctrines," they are "not too averse to the centralization of the State," a dangerous attitude, in that "the State means domination, and human nature is so constructed that any domination is inevitably and always transformed into exploitation."

Thus Bakunin cleared the ground for his pet thesis: that "the whole question of the revolutionary triumph reduces itself to that of *how to arouse, how to revolutionize the peasants.*" The decadence of Italy is due, in great part, to the nonparticipation of the peasants in the civilizing work of the cities. Up to the present they have remained passive, accepting, almost without resistance, the governments imposed on them by the cities. Thus the rural masses have become the sole *point d'appui* of the reaction. In this sense, revolutionizing the peasants is crucial. Even more important, the peasant, unlike the city proletarian, is a "natural federalist, passionately attached to the land and detesting . . . the domination of the cities and all external government that imposes its ideas and will on him." The city worker is better educated, has more of a revolutionary conscience, but the peasant is "naturally revolutionary," despite the influence of priests, which is only superficial. In Piedmont, Lombardy, and the former Kingdom of the Two Sicilies, the peasants' economic distress is such that a *jacquerie* is inevitable, even without leaders. Italian socialists have the obvious responsibility of providing that leadership.

"Practice," as Bakunin wrote with reference to the limits of social revolution, "always remains behind theory, because it is subject to a mass of social conditions, the whole of which constitutes the real situation of a country." So, too, while Bakunin was pinning his faith to the social revolutionism of the Italian peasantry, the Romagnol socialists were limiting themselves at the Bologna Congress to planning the creation of section committees to spread "the liberating idea of the International into the countryside, thus hastening the moment in which the sinister clerical and bourgeois influences shall have finished stupefying and tyrannizing those brothers of ours." [42]

CONCLUSION

Whatever the lag between the preachments of Bakunin and the practice of the Romagnol socialists, the direction of the latter was determined, in great part, by the sheer clarity, force, and coherence of the Russian's propaganda. To a large extent, he had the field to himself. Garibaldi, involved in his personal feud with Mazzini and paying lip service to an internationalism so generic as to defy definition, offered no real competition other than his reputation as a military captain. Engels, carrying the war for the General Council in the Italian theater, failed to exploit Mazzini's opposition to the Paris Commune and, with colossal shortsightedness, tried to influence the Italian radicals with more or less sporadic personal attacks on the anarchist chieftain. The Mazzinian dogma remained, of course, as an obstacle to the penetration of Bakuninism, but even here the Russian succeeded in his main objective: not that of converting the mass of Mazzini's followers—no foreigner could hope to undo the result of Mazzini's forty-year apostolate—but to propagandize the generation of Italian radicals that had come to maturity after the national unity of 1860-61 had neutralized the central appeal of the champion of Italian nationality. Mazzini's condemnation of the Commune facilitated Bakunin's labors to the point where he could eventually suggest to the Romagnol socialists that they accept Mazzinians into their ranks only

[42] *Il Fascio Operaio,* Mar. 24, 1872.

on their own terms, a far cry, indeed, from his earlier policy of direct criticism of Mazzini's principles, tacitly admitting their strength and appeal.

Bakunin's letters to the Romagnols in the first quarter of 1872, aside from their importance as an eloquent exposition of the matured anarchist dogma that was to dominate the Italian socialist movement for the next several years, are a clear commentary on the waning influence of Mazzini's ideas on the Romagna's radical youth. Gone now are the destructive analyses of Mazzini's ideological premises and conclusions; the issue is now one of how to capitalize, tactically, on the disintegration of the master's once formidable party. More important, Bakunin sees his principal work as the positive one of filling with his own doctrines the void created, in part, by his previous work of demolition. Some of his Romagnol correspondents, notably Ceretti and Pescatori,[43] were still to hesitate, to question the Russian's methods and objectives, but the confident tone of Bakunin's letters, the tone of a man sure of his audience, the smooth identification of his own ideas with the aspirations of his correspondents—these, indeed, are the measure of his success among Romagnol radicals who, once convinced, could be counted upon—more than any other radical concentration in the peninsula—to give a coherent impulse to the work of socialist organization and propaganda.

[43] Ceretti's reluctance to assume the extremist position urged by Bakunin was reflected at the Bologna Congress in his order of the day, rejected by the majority, favoring alliance with the Mazzinians, "should they ever decide to pass from the apostolate to action." *Il Fascio Operaio*, Mar. 24, 1872.

XII

Anarchist Triumph (March to August 1872)

SOCIALISM IN TURIN, MILAN, FLORENCE, AND NAPLES (JANUARY TO JULY 1872)

NOTHING more lucidly demonstrates Bakunin's sagacity in centering his efforts on the Romagna than the lack of unity among the I.W.A. sections in the other regions of Italy. By March 1872, dozens of sections were scattered throughout the peninsula,[1] and though practically all of them were not technically sections of the International, having neglected to meet the formal conditions set out in the statutes of the International,[2] the sudden proliferation of small self-proclaimed groups of "Internation-

---

[1] Romano, Storia, II, 210-16. By combining the sections indicated by Romano and Rosselli (Mazzini e Bakounine, p. 432) with those represented at the Rimini Congress of Aug. 1872, the midyear strength of Italian Internationalism consisted of less than half the generally accepted figure of approximately a hundred sections: Ancona, Bologna, Catania, Empoli, Faenza, Fano, Fermo, Ferrara, Fiesole, Florence, Forlì, Fusignano, Genoa, Girgenti, Grotte, Imola, Jesi, Lecco, Livorno, Lodi, Lugo, Macerata, Mantua, Massignano, Menfi, Messina, Milan, Mirandola, Modena, Montel-paro, Naples, Palermo, Pescia, Pisa, Pistoia, Porto Empedocle, Ravenna, Rimini, Rome, San Giovanni in Persiceto, San Potito, Sant-Arcangelo, Sciacca, Siena, Senigallia, Trapani, Turin, Velletri, Venice, and Verona. Of these, about two-fifths were located in the Emilia-Romagna region and the neighboring Marches. I exclude, for reasons indicated in the following chapter, the existence of a section in Lodi prior to Sept. 29, 1872.

[2] To gain official recognition by the General Council, a section had to fulfill the four conditions Bakunin urged the Romagnols to observe: (1) accept the I.W.A. general statutes as its fundamental law; (2) notify the London General Council of this acceptance; (3) draw up its own constitution in conformity with the I.W.A. statutes and send a copy to the General Council; (4) advise the General Council of its membership and send ten cents dues per member. Engels was to claim that only the Neapolitan section had been officially recognized by the Council (La Plebe, Aug. 28, 1872). For Terzaghi's challenge of this assertion, see the article by "Ateo" in La Favilla, Sept. 4; for Andrea Costa's rejoinder, ibid., Oct. 10, 1872.

257

alists" certainly testified to a commonly held notion among politically conscious workers and petty bourgeois intellectuals of radical persuasion that identification with the I.W.A. somehow promised fulfillment of their political and social objectives. Still, the sense of a common purpose, the feverish proclamations of loyalty to the socialist idea—understood in a very generic sense—could not of themselves give practical effect to these hopes. Outside of the Romagna, the work of binding together the many individual sections had not even begun. There were obviously many capable propagandists, but the lack of a federative tendency underlined the fact that Bakunin, in wooing the Romagnols, was directing his propaganda efforts to the right quarter. In the other principal socialist centers of the peninsula—Turin, Milan, Florence, and Naples—the conflict of ideas and personalities was such as to make impossible a federative movement in the manner of the Romagnols.

In Turin the new I.W.A. section, the Emancipation of the Proletarian, was kept in a state of constant turmoil by Carlo Terzaghi, not only one of its founders, but a police spy as well. The section had a membership of about seven hundred by late February,[3] which made it one of the largest Internationalist concentrations in Italy, but, in the hands of Terzaghi, little could be expected from it in terms of developing a north Italian, or even a Piedmontese, federation along the lines of the *Fasci Operai* of the Romagna. Terzaghi's attempt to launch a national congress of I.W.A. sections—perhaps to uncover the country's socialist groups for the benefit of the authorities—with his circular of January 28, only four days after the Florentine Garibaldians issued their call for a democratic congress, was doomed from inception, for neither the Florentines nor the Milanese were interested.[4] In February he was expelled from the section, not because his police connection had come to light, but for misappropriating the section's funds, for his "authoritarian and capricious way of acting, and his formal refusal to give any . . . explanation to the [section's] Federal Council."[5]

Terzaghi's loss of control did not in the least slow up his intriguing —in fact, he redoubled his efforts to put himself at the center of the local socialist movement, using his relations with both Bakunin and the General Council to advance his personal stock. The net effect of his contacts

[3] Nettlau, *B.I.I.*, p. 313.
[4] *Ibid.*, pp. 303, 310; Romano, *Storia*, II, 259, note 151. The Florentine *Fascio Operaio* on Feb. 26 rejected the Terzaghi proposal. Since his Turinese rivals welcomed the Florentine proposal, Terzaghi, to keep a hand in the business, sent his own adherence to the democratic congress initiative. *Il Libero Pensiero*, Feb. 15, 1872.
[5] Nettlau, *B.I.I.*, p. 313. Terzaghi had been inexplicably friendly with the local *questore*, one Bignami, who, curiously enough, was eventually arrested (Nov., 1875) on the same charge as Terzaghi: malversation of funds. *La Plebe*, Nov. 28-29, Dec. 1, 1875.

with Bakunin late in 1871 seems to have been nothing more than the publication of the Sonvilliers Circular in Terzaghi's newspaper on December 26. Bakunin wrote to him on January 22 and February 9,[6] but apparently this was the effective end of the contact, for in late March Bakunin informed Ceretti that "I have had no news from Turin for a long time; Terzaghi appeared to me too indiscreet, too much of a chatterer, for intimate relations, and outside of him I knew no one there." [7] Yet, when Engels' agent, one Vitale Regis, appeared in Turin in late February, Terzaghi, presumably to increase his own importance in the eyes of the General Council, sought to give the impression that he and the Russian were indeed on the most intimate of terms.[8]

Engels too was taken in by Terzaghi. The latter's publication of the Sonvilliers Circular brought only a mild reproach from London,[9] probably because the General Council's need of support in Italy was too great to sacrifice any contact, however equivocal. In fact, Terzaghi seems to have been considered by Bakunin's London foes as a valuable ally in trying to swing the Italian sections into the Marxist camp. On the eve of his clandestine mission into northern Italy during the last ten days of February, Vitale Regis thus outlined his strategy to Engels:

> If one delays any longer, the Italian sections will be so entangled in the intrigues of the dissidents that it would be vain and almost impossible to attempt to distract them. It may still be possible to distract the *Emancipation of the Proletariat,* and once I arrive in Turin, I hope, with the help of Terzaghi and good and convincing arguments, to succeed in doing so. The *Emancipation* is the most numerous and influential section . . . : once [it] is convinced, all the others will follow its example.[10]

On the scene of operations, Regis soon came to other conclusions.[11] Terzaghi promised that in return for General Council support, he would form a new I.W.A. section and declare openly for the International, but, after talking to some of the members of the section, Regis wrote off the ousted secretary as a friend of the General Council. The present section leaders had been persuaded by Terzaghi that political abstention was

[6] Nettlau, *B.I.I.*, pp. 284-85.
[7] Letter of Mar. 13-27, Romano, *Storia*, II, 390. Bakunin, like the Milanese and Romagnols, gave Terzaghi's congress initiative no support, expecting, instead, "great results" from the projected democratic congress. See his Feb. 11 letter to Ceretti, Nettlau, *B.I.I.*, pp. 303-04.
[8] *Ibid.*, p. 283.
[9] "You, a very new section, have adhered to the convocation of an extraordinary Congress, whose sole object is to accuse the General Council of authoritarianism and to abolish the powers given to the G.C. by the Congress of Basel." *Ibid.*, p. 309.
[10] *Ibid.*, p. 312.
[11] For the Regis mission to Italy, *ibid.*, pp. 311 ff.; Romano, *Storia*, II, 255-58.

official I.W.A. doctrine; they were "very happy," reported Regis, when they learned from him that this was not the case. According to Regis, too, some of the Milanese socialists favored more, not less, power for the General Council.

Under the circumstances, it was obvious to Terzaghi that Regis could not be deluded as easily as some of the Turinese socialists, with the result that the General Council's agent found himself crossing into Switzerland with the Italian police not far behind. The resourceful Terzaghi had adopted the simple expedient of using a protest meeting against his own expulsion from the local section to publicly announce to his friends— including the police—the presence of a fully mandated plenipotentiary of the General Council, who favored Terzaghi over the directive council of the section. Even this did not stop him from trying to ingratiate himself with Engels and asking for assistance. The Emancipation of the Proletarian section, he reported, was composed of hypocrites, Mazzinians, monarchists, and government spies! His support of the Sonvilliers Circular was "not to make war on you, dear friends, but one followed the current and our purpose was to bring a word of calm into the conflict." In answer to his plea for a subsidy of 150 *lire* to keep his *Il Proletario* afloat, Engels, now warned against Terzaghi by Regis, promptly assured him that the General Council had other uses for its money than subsidizing a newspaper guilty of publishing the Sonvilliers Circular.[12] It was an effective termination of Terzaghi's relations with the General Council, but not—unfortunately, from the Italian socialists' point of view—with the socialist movement in the peninsula.

The Emancipation of the Proletarian section appears to have maintained cordial relations with the General Council until at least July, 1872, for its governing committee then wrote Engels that it would be "very grateful" for any advice Engels might dispense in connection with the imminent Rimini Congress. Turin sent no delegate to Rimini, but the decisions of that gathering caused the Turinese to break off relations with London, for by November 2, 1872, Engels was complaining that from

[12] For the Terzaghi-Engels correspondence of Mar. 5, 10, 21, 29, see Romano, *Storia*, II, 258-60, notes 150, 151, 152; Nettlau, *B.I.I.*, p. 310; Marx, "L'Alleanza della Democrazia Socialista . . . ," p. 41. Terzaghi's newspaper ceased publication in April, but he found another outlet for his writings in Stefanoni's *Il Libero Pensiero* in Florence. See the issues of Apr. 23 (pp. 271 ff.), June 23 (pp. 380 ff.) and July 21 (pp. 66 ff.). In the latter issue, Terzaghi hoped "this is the last year that the Great Council [of London] has to function. In a society such as the International, it is not fitting to have such important teachers."—the result, probably, of his decision to attend the Rimini Congress a few days hence, at which friends of the General Council would obviously not be welcome.

With the demise of Terzaghi's *Il Proletario*, the Turin section founded another organ, *Il Popolino, monitore dei lavoratori*, edited by Eugenio Bosio. The paper, published from early April to Oct. 6 (No. 21), was both socialist and anti-Terzaghi.

Turin he received no news.[13] Whatever the nature of the section's relations with London prior to Rimini, the Emancipation of the Proletarian neither harmed nor contributed to the federative movement sponsored by the Romagnols and Bakunin.[14] The latter accurately identified the reason for the section's isolation when he wrote to Ceretti in March: "That poor section . . . seems to remain without any direction, oscillating between the vain and the intriguers, ... and it seems there is no one in Turin to put an end to this disgusting anarchy." [15]

If Turin lacked leadership, Milan's I.W.A. section suffered from an overdose of it. Running the group's affairs were Theodor Cuno, devoting his energies to advancing the General Council's point of view, and two intimates of Bakunin, Vincenzo Pezza and Testini. All three helped found the *Circolo Operaio*, a group of about thirty men who had split away from the Milanese Workers' Federation in late December 1871 to declare themselves a section of the International.[16] The organization tripled in size during the next several weeks, but there seems to have been no expansion of its influence beyond the limits of Milan itself.[17] During Regis' brief stay in Milan in February, the section impressed him as "tepid," which very probably indicates that in the battle of ideas being waged by Pezza and Testini on the one side and Cuno on the other, the friends of Bakunin were having the better of it. Engels wrote Cuno a lengthy refutation of Bakunin's anarchist theories in January, presumably in the hope of bolstering his sole Milanese correspondent against the blandishments of the Bakuninists, and a month later Regis, after being "greeted very well" by Cuno, consigned to the German engineer another

[13] Nettlau, *B.I.I.*, pp. 311, 366.

[14] The one and only attempt by the section to foster Internationalism outside its own closed circle was at the May 5, 1872, congress of Piedmontese workers' societies (Mazzinian), when two members of the section, Giovanni Eandi, editor of *L'Anticristo*, and a certain Perino, called for the congress to declare its adherence to the I.W.A. The proposal was voted down, and the Internationalists left the meeting. *L'Avvenire* (Modena), June 15, 1878; *cf.*, also, Rosselli, *Mazzini e Bakounine*, pp. 429-30; Cita Mazzini, "Giovanni Eandi," p. 56; Bertolini, "Cenno sul socialismo in Italia," in Rae, *Socialismo contemporaneo*, xcix.

[15] Romano, *Storia*, II, 390. Giovanni Eandi, member of the directive committee of the section who had founded *L'Anticristo* on Jan. 1, 1872, as an anticlerical, anti-monarchical, anti-Mazzinian organ, published the last issue on May 12, 1872, and went into French exile. Cita Mazzini, "Giovanni Eandi," p. 56.

[16] The section adhered to the I.W.A. on Jan. 7, and on Jan. 30 Engels formally reported its affiliation to the General Council. *Il Gazzettino Rosa*, Jan. 13; *L'Eguaglianza*, Jan. 21, 1872.

[17] On Jan. 11, the section reported a membership of about a hundred (Rosselli, *Mazzini e Bakounine*, p. 407), and on Mar. 1 Vitale Regis put the figure at about ninety, consisting of students and workers, the latter almost all employees of the Helvetica firm, where Cuno worked. There were some "very good" students, instructed by Cuno, but also others, like Testini, "affected by the theories of Bakunin." Cuno to Engels, Mar. 1, 1872, Nettlau, *B.I.I.*, p. 284.

letter from Engels and the General Council's official recognition of the *Circolo Operaio* statutes—which made it, as consistently recommended by Bakunin, a bona fide affiliate of the First International.[18]

Cuno's apostolate in the name of Marxian socialism was as unhappy as it was short-lived. As Marx himself heard the story, Cuno, "because of his Germanic origin," was ostracized by the friends of Bakunin.[19] Only a few days after Regis' departure for Turin, Cuno was arrested and on March 29 escorted by the Italian police to the Austrian frontier.[20]

Even without this "help from heaven," as Marx described the arrest and expulsion of Cuno, the Bakuninist grip on the section was never seriously threatened, thanks to the Russian's flood of correspondence with Pezza, Testini, and Gaspare Stampa.[21] Though Pezza, as a co-addressee for Bakunin's long letters to Nabruzzi of January 3 and 23, was privy to Bakunin's encouragement of the democratic congress movement, his own extremism—less adaptable and less perceptive than that of his friend in Locarno—did not permit him to share the Romagnol socialists' enthusiasm for the prospect of reconciliation with Mazzinians,[22] nor, of course, did it net the Milan section an invitation to attend the Romagnol congress of Bologna in mid-March. Perhaps even Achille Bizzoni, editor-in-chief of *Il Gazzettino Rosa,* found Pezza's militant anti-Mazzinian writings too venomous, for several successive January issues of his newspaper carried no articles by "Burbero" (Pezza's pen-name).[23]

Bizzoni's inconsistent entertainment of socialist pieces in the columns

[18] Nettlau, *B.I.I.*, pp. 313, 316; Romano, *Storia*, II, 254-55.

[19] "L'Alleanza della Democrazia Socialista . . . ," p. 39.

[20] *La Plebe*, Mar. 9; *La Campana*, Mar. 10; *L'Anticristo*, Apr. 28; *Il Gazzettino Rosa*, Apr. 23, 27, May 7, 1872. Cuno was discharged by the Helvetica firm for refusing to renounce his affiliation with the I.W.A. The police expulsion was based on Cuno's "lack of means of subsistence." Engels promised to publicize the affair in the European socialist press: "Those *Schweinhunde* [the police] must learn . . . that the arm of the internationalists is always longer than that of the King of Italy." Rosselli, *Mazzini e Bakounine*, p. 407, note 3.

[21] Bakunin's diary for the first six months of 1872 shows that his epistolary contact with these three men was only slightly less frequent than that maintained with the Romagnols. Nettlau, *B.I.I.*, pp. 290, 295, 306, 327-29, 350.

[22] Romano suggests that Cafiero made agreements with the Turinese and Milanese socialists to oppose the democratic congress in favor of a socialist congress to create an Italian national federation of the I.W.A., and introduces, in this connection, Terzaghi's socialist congress initiative of Jan. 28, *Storia*, II, 227-28. This hypothesis is contradicted by Terzaghi's assertion, in his Mar. 10 letter to Engels, that his attempt to launch an "International Italian Regional Congress" was "greeted with enthusiasm except by the Sections of Milan and Florence." *Ibid.*, II, 259. Actually, the Milanese, unlike Cafiero, considered Terzaghi's proposal as "premature." *Il Martello*, Feb. 17, 1872.

[23] Mazzini interpreted the interruption as evidence of "a conciliatory tendency on the part of Bizz[oni] and others" (*S.E.I.*, XCI, 309). But the truce did not last. After "five or six days of generous silence, the *Gazzettino Rosa* declares war and says that concord is impossible." Mazzini to Campanella, Jan. 24, 1872, *ibid.*, p. 319.

of his influential journal may have helped prompt the birth of two very militant organs in late January and early February. *La Lega Rossa,* a weekly edited by Giuseppe Cozzi, proclaimed itself "the little sheet of the workers who belong to the republican party and who are affiliated, out of conviction and sentiment, with the goal of the International."[24] Pezza founded *Il Martello* on February 4 as an organ of the *Circolo Operaio,* but the violence of its articles—or the sensitivity of the authorities— made it the shortest-lived socialist newspaper of the year. Only four issues were published from February 4 to March 3, and all but the first were confiscated by the police. The Milan *questore* justified his action against the last number on the grounds that one of its articles, "Modern Ideas," proposed socialism, and another, "Letter from Lugo," advocated a different form of government.[25] In late March Pezza was arrested, along with two other former staff members of *Il Martello,* and in May he began serving a jail sentence that may well have contributed to his premature demise of consumption in January, 1873. Testini, too, was arrested but escaped a jail term.[26] With the removal of Pezza, in any case, the *Circolo Operaio* became inactive, and the strict vigilance of the local police kept it so for the next several months.[27] Pezza continued in correspondence with Bakunin, but it was not until his discharge from prison in the early summer that he resumed his role as key promoter of Bakunin's plans for the unification of Italian socialists under the banner of anarchism.[28]

In Florence during the first half of 1872, the radical republicans were in a constant fever of activity, but none of it added up to a clear stand on either the issue of whether socialism could be harmonized with Mazzinian principles or that of whether Marxian socialism or Bakunin's anarcho-socialism better represented the aspirations of Italian radicals. The Social Democratic Union founded in the summer of 1871 joined in the effort to convene a democratic congress for the spring of the following year, but even before Garibaldi called off the project, the chronic bickering between republicans and "socialists" in the organization nullified any con-

---

[24] Rosselli, *Mazzini e Bakounine,* pp. 397-98, for a sample article, the gist of which is that Mazzini's stratospheric doctrines did not put any "meat in the stomach on Sunday." On May 15, 1872, Cozzi was fined £. 100 and given a two-month jail term. *Il Gazzettino Rosa,* May 16, 1872.

[25] Valiani, *Storia del movimento socialista,* I, 197.

[26] *Il Gazzettino Rosa,* Mar. 27, Apr. 10, May 15; *La Plebe,* Apr. 4, 1872. He was arrested on Mar. 26 and freed on £. 4,000 bail fifteen days later.

[27] Visiting Milan in June, Cafiero was "very satisfied" with the city's Internationalist movement, but, considering the alertness of the Milan police, his optimism may have reflected no more than Cafiero's gratification that the section was managing to survive at all. *Cf.,* the Neapolitan *questore's* report of July 9, 1872, quoted by Romano, *Storia,* II, 293-94, note 73.

[28] Nettlau, *B.I.I.,* pp. 327, 329, 350; Valiani, *op. cit.,* I, 198.

structive effort. Luigi Castellazzo, the guiding spirit of the S.D.U., moved to Rome in May, and from there on the organization, deserted by the socialist-sympathizing members, moved toward an orthodox Mazzinian republicanism. By July 1872, the local *questore* noted the "almost total decadence of the Social Democratic Union," thanks to the fact that a new association, the *Fascio Operaio*, had attracted a large proportion of the S.D.U. membership.[29]

Very probably it was the phenomenal growth of the Romagnol *fasci operai* in late 1871 that prompted a group of Florentine radicals, under the aegis of the local Freethinkers' Society, to meet in January with the representatives of several workers' organizations and establish the first Tuscan association in which socialist and proletarian elements were in a majority.[30] The leadership of the Florentine *Fascio Operaio* was composed of both workers (e.g., Gaetano Grassi, tailor; Francesco Natta, mechanic; Oreste Lovari, shoemaker) and petty bourgeois intellectuals (e.g., Antonio Martinati, Tito Strocchi, Lorenzo Piccioli-Poggiali, Ettore and Giovanni Socci, Salvatore Battaglia, Guido Corsi, and Luigi Stefanoni). The manifesto issued on January 10 omitted any reference to political issues and posed as the objective of the organization: emancipation from the "double servitude of ignorance and poverty."[31] The goal enunciated in its constitution was equally vague: "to arrange for a central point of communication and cooperation between the workers of the various nations tending toward the same objective, that is: the complete emancipation of the worker." Another article affiliated the *Fascio Operaio* with the First International in principle, if not formally (which would only have invited dissolution by the authorities): "The Society adheres generally to the Statute of the International Workingmen's Association of London."[32]

The abjuration of politics by the *Fascio Operaio* almost certainly re-

[29] Conti, *O.S.F.*, pp. 122-23. The new organization started with about two hundred members, mostly *braccianti* (*La Campana*, Feb. 11), and, in two months, had over five hundred (*L'Eguaglianza*, Mar. 10, 1872).

[30] The present discussion of the Florentine *Fascio Operaio* is based on the material presented by Conti, *O.S.F.*, pp. 128-41. *Cf.*, also, Romano, *Storia*, II, 213-14; Rosselli, *Mazzini e Bakounine*, p. 405; Nettlau, *B.I.I.*, pp. 194, 244; Francesco Pezzi, *Un errore giudiziario ovvero un po' di luce sul processo della bomba di Via Nazionale* (Florence, 1882), pp. 39-47 (this volume is cited below as Pezzi, *Un errore giudiziario*).

[31] For the manifesto, Pezzi, *Un errore giudiziario*, pp. 40-42. The signers: Oreste Lovari, Giuseppe Mazzini (copyist), Gaetano Grassi, Francesco Natta, Antonio Casini, and Giulio Baracchi.

[32] The minutes of the London General Council record no communication with Florence during the first half of 1872, and only on Aug. 15 did the *Eastern Post* report that the I.W.A. "is making progress in Italy, especially in Florence and Naples." Nettlau, *B.I.I.*, p. 195.

flected no Bakuninist influence, for there is no evidence that the Russian was in correspondence with any of the society's directive group. In all probability the evidently exclusive concern for the economic problems of the worker was due to both a desire to attract the greatest number of workers' societies and awareness, thanks to long experience, that a non-political initiative invited less surveillance by the police. Whatever the cause, the important fact is that for the first time in Florence, a group of radicals had emerged with a very clear conception of class struggle as the means of emancipating the workers. "Those who, by their social position, find themselves in permanent opposition to the principles of the Society" were excluded from membership by the constitution.

If the *Fascio Operaio* was definitely inspired by socialist principles, it is not so clear whether, prior to the Rimini Congress of early August, 1872, it was also a *de facto* section of the First International. Professor Romano treats it as such but claims it was quite distinct from a Florentine section reported to Engels by Regis on March 5 as having been founded by one Angelo Dalmasso.[33] Elio Conti, the historian of the Florentine movement during this period, implies that the *Fascio Operaio* was not an Internationalist section and divorces it from a section founded early in March 1872 by none other than several members of the *Fascio Operaio's* directive group, including Grassi, Martinati, and Stefanoni.[34] Conti mentions no Dalmasso in this connection. If Dalmasso founded the section, it is curious that the *questore* reports cited by Conti do not mention him as such. If the section was founded in early March, Conti fails to explain why Terzaghi referred to the Florentine "section" as one of two that spurned his proposal of January 28 for a socialist national congress.[35]

[33] *Storia*, II, 213-14, and note 15; 258, note 149. Romano refers to the launching of the *Fascio Operaio* in January as "the foundation of the International in Florence." Regis had written: "In Florence alone has there been formed, under the auspices of Dalmasso, who must have written to you, a section that recognized the authority of the General Council." Nettlau, *B.I.I.*, pp. 314-15. Romano, like Nettlau, urges the distinction but sheds no light on the creation of the "Dalmasso section." Nettlau produces some data on the section, but all of it applies to the period after the Rimini Congress of Aug., 1872. Romano follows suit.

Angelo Dalmasso, a Piedmontese and employee of the Ministry of Finance, was a friend of Terzaghi. Conti (*O.S.F.*, pp. 118, 148-49) identifies him as a "moderate socialist" who, in early Nov., 1872, founded, along with Giuseppe Campetti, Giuseppe Mazzini, Michele Facini, and Fortunato Serantoni—a pro-General Council I.W.A. section in protest against the decisions of the Rimini Congress in August.

[34] *Ibid.*, pp. 124-28.

[35] Terzaghi to Engels, Mar. 10, 1872, Romano, *Storia*, II, 259-60. Terzaghi claimed the Florentine socialists made him an honorary member of their section "in recognition of my merits" after he was ostracized by the Emancipation of the Proletarian group in Turin. Nettlau (*B.I.I.*, p. 315, note 1) avers that the "Dalmasso section" mandated Terzaghi to the Rimini Congress, but the *Fascio Operaio* was officially the only Florentine organization represented at Rimini, and, ostensibly at least, Piccioli-Poggiali and Grassi were its representatives (Conti, *O.S.F.*, p. 147).

The *Fascio Operaio*, the "Dalmasso section," and the section founded in March were probably all manifestations of the same socialist core in Florence. A reasonable hypothesis is that shortly after—perhaps even concurrently with—the launching of the *Fascio Operaio*, some of its members, including Dalmasso, decided to establish an I.W.A. section *within* the *Fascio Operaio* to provide a link between the parent public organization and the First International.[36] The *questore's* claim that the section was definitely constituted early in March does not rule out a period of incubation during which Castellazzo, Socci, Martinati, Piccioli-Poggiali, Grassi, Stefanoni, and Dalmasso planned the creation of an I.W.A. section. Dalmasso had already distinguished himself as a socialist, and if a section was being planned, there is no reason to suppose he was extraneous to the preparatory discussions, even though his role was probably not visible—or important—enough to elicit the attention of the *questore's* agents. Dalmasso doubtless communicated these plans to his Turinese friend, Terzaghi, who, in turn, described the "Florentine section" to Regis as an accomplished fact, gratuitously assuring him that the group was favorable to the General Council in the hope of increasing his own stature as a man of connections and influence. Nor was it out of character for Terzaghi, in mentioning the "Florentine section's" rejection of his socialist congress initiative, to have been referring, not to the action of an I.W.A. section, but to the unfavorable decision of the *Fascio Operaio* of February 26.

Whatever the intricacies of their organizational forms, the Florentine radicals, prior to August, 1872, made no appreciable contribution to the

---

Terzaghi, nonetheless, attended the Rimini Congress. One hypothesis might explain his representation there of a "Florentine section." Since Piccioli-Poggiali and Grassi, both of the extremist minority of the *Fascio Operaio*, went to Rimini over the protests of the majority of the members (*ibid.*, p. 141), the latter group—presumably moderate, perhaps pro-General Council and probably including Terzaghi's friend, Dalmasso—chose Terzaghi, on Dalmasso's recommendation, as its *unofficial* representative at Rimini. In the sense that the *Fascio Operaio* and the Internationalist section in Florence were probably but two manifestations—overt and clandestine—of the same organization, Terzaghi may not only have represented the Florentine section, as he claimed, but his mandate may actually have been a more legitimate one than that of Piccioli-Poggiali and Grassi, representing only a minority of the *Fascio Operaio*. It may also be significant, in this connection, that Terzaghi, after his Turinese newspaper folded in April, found an outlet for his writings in *Il Libero Pensiero* of Stefanoni, a member of the moderate majority in both the I.W.A. section and the *Fascio Operaio*.

[36] At the 1875 Florentine trial of Tuscan Internationalists, Natta admitted belonging to the I.W.A. and to "the *Fascio Operaio* that was a section of it . . . ," and when asked how long he had been a member of the I.W.A., he replied, "From the establishment of the *Fascio Operaio*." Bottero, *Dibattimenti*, p. 47. Pezzi (*Un errore giudiziario*, p. 42) writes that the *Fascio Operaio*, "without at first openly adhering to the International, accepted its program completely." *L'Eguaglianza*, Feb. 18, 1872, referred to the association as an I.W.A. section.

work of uniting Italian socialists then being pursued by their Romagnol cousins. The chief reason probably lay in their disagreement as to the kind of "internationalism" they wished to propagate. All called themselves Internationalists, but the majority—men like Castellazzo, Martinati, and Stefanoni—were impregnated with the Garibaldian notion that socialism was to be equated with abstract principles of Justice and the slow, un-hurried march of Reason, leading eventually to the triumph of "modern science." [37] Like that of their warrior hero, theirs was a "socialism" so broad in scope as to embrace the concept of an alliance with the Maz-zinians, since "they, too, tend toward the emancipation of the proletariat." Stefanoni alone objected to what he termed "a puerile spirit of con-ciliation between irreconcilable principles," but such criticism did not bring him any closer to an extremist position; it was only the intransigence of Mazzinian faithfuls like Campanella and Maurizio Quadrio, not that of Stefanoni, that torpedoed an alliance project launched by Martinati and Castellazzo early in March.[38]

The minority, led by Piccioli-Poggiali, Natta, Grassi, Strocchi, Oreste Lovari, Corsi, and Berni, was far less interested in the political action that union with Mazzinians implied than in the immediate economic problems of the workers banded together in the *Fascio Operaio*. There is no hint of political objectives in the argument used by Piccioli-Poggiali to justify representation of the *Fascio Operaio* at the Rimini Congress in August: "only from the meeting of all the workers' representatives of Italy can a common and practical action be deliberated for the advantage of the working people against the tyranny of capital." [39] The problem of these men was immediate and concrete, requiring *class* unity, not the distant universal brotherhood of man the Garibaldian intellectuals saw as the product of natural social evolution helped along by the propaganda of rationalism.[40] It was the work of this minority during the next eighteen months that was to make Tuscany the strongest socialist concentration—in point of numbers—in Italy. Before August 1872, however, these men wielded far less influence in Florence than did the Garibaldian "inter-nationalists." Until external developments increased the prestige of their ideas and program, their minority status compelled them to limit their efforts to organizing and propagandizing Tuscan workers' nuclei and to look to the Romagnol radicals, enormously aided by Bakunin's assiduous tutelage, to set the pace toward unification of Italian socialists.

Unlike the majority of Florentine Internationalists, the Neapolitan

---

[37] For illustrative excerpts from their writings, Conti, *O.S.F.*, p. 127.
[38] On the alliance initiative, *ibid.*, p. 128.
[39] *Ibid.*, p. 141.
[40] See "La Questione razionale e la sociale," *Il Libero Pensiero*, Feb. 15, 1872.

champions of the I.W.A. understood the primary problem of socialism as
that of "the abolition of privileged capital." [41] Within the framework of
this authentically socialist principle, the Neapolitans moved gradually
toward a clear affirmation of Bakuninism, even while refusing, prior to
late May, to side openly with the Russian against the London General
Council. The Neapolitan Workers' Federation, organized in late December under the leadership of Carlo Cafiero, Alberto Tucci, and Errico
Malatesta, had a program that combined Bakunin's egalitarianism and his
well-worn motto, "From the bottom to the top," with borrowings from
the preamble of the I.W.A. statute and—for obvious reasons of prudence
—gave tacit adherence to the International, without ever mentioning the
words "socialist" and "internationalist." [42] The association's official organ,
La Campana, first issued on January 7 under the editorship of Tucci, was
militantly socialist in tone and, in its brief life span extending only to
March 17, the gradual infiltration of Bakuninism is evident. In the first
issue, the "complete political abstention" of the Spanish workers is
favorably noted; in the second number (January 14) the writer of the
lead article—Tucci?—rejects Marx's notion of proletarian class domination and argues an extreme egalitarianism; in the fifth issue (February 4)
an article entitled "Dal basso all'alto" insists that the hierarchical structure of society, born of religion, is an affirmation of outmoded violence.
Equality must be substituted for authority:

> *From the bottom to the top,* that is, from the individual, his
> needs, from his rights, we see arising the free association of
> free forces, and we wish thus to create the equality of individuals
> and the permanent destruction of classes, that is, of inequality.
>
> *La patria* and liberty shall be achieved when we create the
> autonomy of individuals and collectivities; and this autonomy
> can issue only from spontaneous organizations, made from the
> bottom to the top . . .[43]

In regard to the dispute between the Jura anarchists and the London
Council, *La Campana* moved toward a pro-anarchist position. On January

[41] *La Campana,* Jan. 14, 1872. Stefanoni's insistence on religious emancipation
as the first step toward liberation of the proletariat was but one of several social
democratic theses that prompted Cafiero to attack him in *La Campana.* For Stefanoni's
side of the debate, in the course of which he vigorously condemned Marx and the
General Council, *Il Libero Pensiero,* Jan. 4, 25, Feb. 8, 22, Mar. 28, Apr. 18, May
23, Aug. 1; for Cafiero's defense of the I.W.A., *La Campana,* Jan. 14, 28, Feb. 11;
Il Gazzettino Rosa, Apr. 20, May 27, 1872. For Engels' reply to Stefanoni's article of
Jan. 4, *Il Gazzettino Rosa,* Feb. 20; for Marx's rebuttal of Stefanoni, *ibid.,* May 28,
1872.
[42] Reproduced in full by *L'Eguaglianza,* Mar. 24; *La Campana,* Mar. 10, 1872.
[43] The piece so closely parallels Tucci's speech at the Rome Congress of Nov., 1871,
that there can be little doubt as to its authorship. *Cf.,* also, the articles, "La patria"
and "Nazionalismo" in the Feb. 18 and Mar. 3, 1872, issues.

28 the editors regarded the Jura initiative for a general congress "with interest, but without preoccupation," and hoped to provide a "calm and fraternal word" in the conflict. On February 4 Saverio Friscia, with whom Bakunin had been in steady correspondence during the preceding two months,[44] urged the newspaper to take a firmer stand toward the General Council and in the same issue the Sonvilliers Circular was tardily published. By mid-February the staff was convinced that "some deliberations taken [at London] are harmful and that the system inaugurated by the General Council is dangerous." [45]

The trend evident in *La Campana* could not but please Bakunin, but the newspaper's blunt and fervid language, especially that directed against the Romagnol socialists for their support of a democratic congress and reconciliation with the Mazzinians, posed something of a problem for the anarchist chief, since it contrasted with the understanding and tolerant line he was using on the Romagnols to bring them around to what Cafiero had been driving for ever since his apostolate in Italy began in the spring of 1871: the federation of Italian socialist sections. Celso Ceretti, unenthusiastic about divorcing the socialist movement from all contact with the Mazzinians, apparently shared Garibaldi's distrust of doctrinaire socialists, especially when they sounded thirsty for bourgeois blood. When Ceretti asked Bakunin for his opinion of *La Campana,* the Russian performed the remarkable feat of condoning, in the name of doctrinal freedom, nothing less than Cafiero's dogmatism. In *La Campana* he had found:

> . . . some very remarkable articles, written with much talent and spirit. It is evident that the young people who direct it are ardently and sincerely convinced. No doubt, they put much passion into it. . . . But, *Santo Diavolo!*, as they say in Naples, since when has passionate and burning zeal become unpleasing; well then, fight them, oppose them with other ideas, but . . . leave to them that holy liberty of thought, which must not be a monopoly in the hands of our friend Mr. Stefanoni . . .[46]

Regardless of how close to Bakunin's principles the Neapolitan socialists moved, the fact is that until the Romagnols clarified their own thinking as to what kind of socialism they stood for, Cafiero's dream of a union of Italy's Internationalists would remain unrealized. Unlike the Russian

---

[44] As well as with Palladino and Gambuzzi. Even Attanasio Dramis' name appears in the Russian's diary on Jan. 21. Nettlau, *B.I.I.*, pp. 290, 294, 306. To this must be added the probable influence of Fanelli, who, in the course of his incessant travels in the peninsula, doubtless had some advice for his former colleagues in Naples, especially after he and Bakunin "established [their] plan of campaign" during Fanelli's visit to Locarno on Jan. 19-22.

[45] *La Campana,* Feb. 18, 1872.

[46] Letter of Mar. 13-27, Romano, *Storia,* II, 390; Nettlau, *B.I.I.*, p. 278.

agitator, Cafiero had neither the experience nor the temperament—nor, perhaps, the insight—to refrain from frontal attacks on the Romagnol's reluctance to forego *their* vision of a democratic front broad enough to encompass the two extremes of completely orthodox Mazzinians and Internationalists who, like Cafiero, insisted on proletarian emancipation as *the* goal and class conflict as *the* means. Bakunin inserted his doctrinal principles as the logical expression of the Romagnols' own aspirations, with the result that when, on their own initiative, they held their congress in Bologna in mid-March, they found themselves projecting a national congress of socialist sections on the basis of a fairly clear anarchist program. In that Cafiero, in his heated dialogue with the Romagnols in January and February, shrilly insisted that they themselves break a commitment from which only Garibaldi could release them, he probably contributed not at all to the initiative for a socialist national congress that emerged from the Bologna deliberations. It was Garibaldi's renunciation of the democratic congress project that cleared the way for that decision; it was Bakunin's propaganda, in large measure, that insured the socialist alternative.

ENGELS CONCEDES DEFEAT

After the Bologna Congress of March the cause of the London General Council was hopelessly compromised. With Cafiero slowly succumbing to the influence of anarchist ideas,[47] with Cuno and Regis unable to re-enter Italy, with Terzaghi now revealed as a correspondent of no real value, isolated in any case from the socialist section of Turin, Engels' contacts with the Italian movement were limited to Enrico Bignami in Lodi.[48] If, as Regis felt certain, Dalmasso in Florence had communicated with London, no trace of such correspondence has come to light, and, as noted, there was nothing about the development of the Florentine Inter-

[47] He had not written to Engels since mid-December, and he did not answer Engels' letter of Feb. 29—Mar. 9 (Nettlau, *B.I.I.*, p. 276, 332) until June 12, by which time it was beyond Engels' power to recapture his loyalty to London.

[48] The first correspondence from Engels appeared in *La Plebe* on Apr. 24, 1872, the second on June 8. On July 11, *La Plebe* summarized the General Council's dispositions for the forthcoming international congress at The Hague, and on Aug. 3 the newspaper carried them *in extenso*. Bignami's organizational activity seems to have been limited to scraping up individual I.W.A. affiliations and forwarding them to London. On Mar. 12, Bignami sent Engels the adherence of a section formed in Ferrara nine days earlier (Nettlau, *B.I.I.*, p. 309). This section, though not represented at the Rimini Congress of Aug., 1872, adhered to its resolutions and agreed to become a part of the Italian anarchist federation there constituted. In view of Bakunin's urging all Italian sections to join the International by contacting the General Council, Engels was desperately groping at straws when on May 7 he wrote Cuno: "The Ferrarese have submitted, they have recognized the Statutes and administrative Regulations, and they have sent their Statutes to be approved, which is completely contrary [*sic*.] to the motto of the Bakuninists . . ." *Ibid.*, pp. 316-17.

nationalist movement to suggest that it represented an effective support of the General Council in its war with the Bakuninists.

In Rome, socialist propaganda had been initiated by Salvatore Battaglia, Sterbini, Coen, and others as early as January, and the Social Democratic Union that sprang from their efforts increased its membership rapidly, but it was not affiliated with the International.[49] In early April, Jules Guesde, French Communard refugee, settled in Rome, and the minds and hearts of the Roman socialists—as Gnocchi-Viani recalled the event in later years—"opened as under the friendly kiss of a new spring sun," thanks to Guesde's "stringent and impassioned Marxist dialectic."[50] Guesde's influence and Gnocchi-Viani's contacts with Bignami and *La Plebe* in Lodi probably made the Roman socialist nucleus, early in 1872, more sympathetic to the cause of the General Council than to that of Bakunin—to the extent they understood the issues at all. Yet, these men did not officially declare their Workers' League of Arts and Crafts, organized in June, a section of the International until July 28, and then only after having been pressed to do so by Andrea Costa.[51] The section mandated its delegate to the Rimini Congress of August to support a limitation of the General Council's powers, yet within less than two weeks after that gathering had broken all ties with London, Gnocchi-Viani, the section's secretary, opened correspondence with Engels as if the Rimini deliberations had never occurred.[52] In short, the Roman section did not break completely with London, though it certainly constituted no focal point of General Council strength in Italy.

Vitale Regis' summary of the Italian situation in early March justified no optimism in London: "In Italy the terrain is completely gained to the dissidents." And several weeks later: "The news from Italy is infrequent and sad. You know what a deplorable condition the Romagnol regions are in and what influence the *Fascio Operaio* of Bologna has acquired, now won over completely to the cause of the Jurassians. . . . The energy and activity [they] put out are incredible, and their work has not remained without fruit."[53] In the midst of this depressing intelligence, Engels, far

[49] *L'Eguaglianza*, Jan. 7, 1872; Romano, *Storia*, II, 215.

[50] *Ricordi di un Internazionalista*, p. 121.

[51] *Il Gazzettino Rosa*, June 29; *La Plebe*, July 6, 1872; Nettlau, *B.I.I.*, pp. 309, 352. For details on the League, Franco Della Peruta, "L'Internazionale a Roma dal 1872 al 1877," *Movimento Operaio*, Yr. IV, No. 1 (Jan.-Feb., 1952), 13-17.

[52] *Ibid.*, pp. 39-40; Nettlau, *B.I.I.*, p. 352. Della Peruta claims that prior to March, 1873 (Congress of Mirandola), perhaps none of the members of the Workers' League were conscious of the real meaning of the "anti-authoritarian" resolutions of Rimini, being too involved in their own organizational problems. Such a conclusion ignores Guesde's affirmation that the section wanted the Council's authority reduced.

[53] Letters to Engels, Mar. 5, May 13, 1872, Nettlau, *B.I.I.*, pp. 314-15; Rosselli, *Mazzini e Bakounine*, pp. 430-31.

from regarding his own tactics as a partial cause of this condition, sought to convince the General Council—and perhaps himself as well—that it was all the fault of "representatives of the middle class." On March 5 he told his colleagues of the Council:

> . . . the authentic workers [in Italy] are completely favorable to the principles of the International as they are explained in the deliberations of the [London] Conference. The Doctrine preached by the representatives of the middle class that the working class must abstain from politics, has had no success.[54]

A week later the Manchester factory owner, who doubled as the I.W.A's corresponding secretary for Italy, reported:

> Up to now the correspondence as well as the newspapers have been in the hands, certainly not of the workers themselves, but of men of the middle class, lawyers, doctors, journalists, etc. In fact, the great difficulty for the Council has been to enter into direct relations with the Italian workers. This has now been done in one or two localities, and it has been found that these workers, far from being enthusiasts of political abstention, were instead very satisfied to learn that the General Council and the great mass of the International do not in fact adhere to that doctrine.[55]

By midsummer, when the proof of Regis' assessment of the Italian situation became all too evident, Engels said nothing more of bourgeois lawyers, doctors, and journalists hoodwinking Italian workers. Now he sought to rationalize his failure:

> The Italians must still attend the school of experience a little more to learn that a backward nation of peasants such as they only make themselves ridiculous when they want to prescribe to the workers of the big industrial nations how they must conduct themselves in order to arrive at emancipation.[56]

If it were true that Marxian socialism registered its initial failure in Italy because the country's economy was still predominantly agrarian, Engels might have explained why, while the issue of his duel with Bakunin was still in the balance, he had insisted that his Italian propaganda was both vital and promising. The institution of "autocriticism" as

---

[54] Nettlau, *B.I.I.*, pp. 308, 339, note 2.

[55] *Ibid.*, p. 309. On May 7 Engels again lamented the "impossibility" of direct contacts with the Italian workers: "everywhere those damned Bakuninist doctrinaires, lawyers, doctors, etc., have intervened, and they give themselves the airs of authentic representatives of the workers." *Ibid.*, p. 317.

[56] Engels to Cuno, July 10, 1872, Rosselli, *Mazzini e Bakounine*, p. 431.

an acceptable alternative technique of explaining mistakes not convincingly encompassed by the dialectic had yet to be invented.

THE "DEFECTION" OF CARLO CAFIERO

Nothing said or done by Engels could now stop the swift passage of Italian socialists into the anarchist camp. In the Romagna the extremist counsels of Nabruzzi and Costa, under the impetus given by the Bologna Congress decisions, were beginning to take precedence over the more moderate views of Ceretti and Pescatori. The death of Mazzini signaled open clashes between his followers and the Romagnol socialists. Only nine days after his death Internationalists and Mazzinians brawled in the streets of Ravenna; later in the month, a prominent Mazzinian, one Antonio Fratti, engaged in a duel with a young Internationalist in Bologna.[57] Garibaldi, alarmed by the "discords . . . that afflict those generous populations of the Romagna," appealed to Eugenio Valzania, famed republican insurrectional chief of the region, "to bind together once more the *fascio* of the honest . . . so that the energy of Italian youth not be dissipated."[58] On the night of May 2-3, Francesco Piccinini, a fervid Romagnol socialist propagandist and head of the Lugo *Fascio Operaio*, was shot and stabbed in that city. His assassins were not immediately identified, but public opinion held the Mazzinians responsible, and, so far as the Romagnol socialists were concerned, the episode erected an insurmountable barrier between themselves and the followers of the departed Mazzini.[59] Nor did Bakunin, from Locarno, neglect his incitement of the Romagnols, so vigorously launched in his earlier correspondence with Nabruzzi and Ceretti. The Russian's diary shows continued epistolary contacts with both men, but it seems that Pescatori was dropped by the anarchist agitator as an uncertain recruit.[60] Ceretti's

---

[57] *Ibid.*, p. 427.

[58] Letter of Apr. 3, 1872, *L'Anticristo*, Apr. 21, pp. 5-7; *Il Gazzettino Rosa*, Apr. 17, 1872.

[59] On the Piccinini affair, *Il Gazzettino Rosa*, May 11; *La Plebe*, May 8, 11; *L'Unità Italiana*, May 8; *Il Dovere*, May 8, 1872. One of the killers, Luigi Gavelli, was never apprehended, but his accomplice, Giuseppe Liverani, was tried and condemned to life at hard labor by a Ravenna court in Dec., 1876. Liverani confessed belonging to a Lugo Mazzinian society, the *Ciceruacchio*. *La Plebe*, Nov. 25, Dec. 16, 22, 1876; Nov. 18, 1877.

[60] Nettlau, *B.I.I.*, p. 327. Shortly after the Bologna Congress, Pescatori, already prey to misgivings about the trend toward radical socialism, resigned as head of the *Fascio Operaio* of Bologna as a result of a quarrel with the editor of the local Mazzinian organ, *L'Alleanza*. Romano, *Storia*, II, 274. On Mar. 1, Vitale Regis wrote Engels that he regretted not visiting Bologna during his Italian sojourn: "in the position in which Pescatori found himself, he certainly could have been convinced to march openly with us: he would have adhered in order to have a support." Nettlau, *B.I.I.*, p. 314.

vacillations Bakunin had to pretend to ignore, given his immense personal prestige in the Romagna; of Nabruzzi, Bakunin had no reason to despair —for the time being.

The Russian's key objective, an anarchist Italian federation amenable to his guidance, was, nonetheless, no nearer realization, unless he contrived an active collaboration between the three centers—the Romagna, Naples, and Milan—where, through Nabruzzi, Cafiero, and Pezza, the "anti-authoritarian" spirit was in the ascendant. Though Fanelli provided a link between these areas, though in Naples the ex-members of Bakunin's International Fraternity, Tucci and Gambuzzi,[61] seconded by Palladino and Malatesta, may have pressed in favor of taking a first stand against London, the fact remained that Cafiero, notwithstanding that he had betrayed sufficiently anarchist tendencies in *La Campana* to elicit a *bravo* from the Russian, persisted in defending the General Council.

Bakunin's worries on this score, however, were of short duration, lasting probably no longer than mid-April, despite the appearance of two articles by Cafiero in *Il Gazzettino Rosa* on April 20 and May 27 that used attacks on Stefanoni's "socialism" as a vehicle for the defense of the General Council.[62] What happened to relieve Bakunin's mind as to the personal orientation of the one prominent Italian socialist agitator still outside the Russian's web of collaborators? Three apparently disjointed developments provide the answer: (1) on April 15-19, Fanelli visited Bakunin in Locarno; (2) on May 10 the anarchist *Bulletin de la Fédération Jurassienne* carried the item: "We have received some letters written last autumn by M. Engels . . . to Italian friends, [in which he] abandons himself to the most odious slanders against honorable citizens belonging to the Jurassian Federation and against the spirit of our federation in general"; (3) on May 21 Bakunin wrote in his diary: "The whole day with Fanelli and Cafiero; *alliance perfectly accomplished.*" [63]

Cafiero's own explanation of his decision to ally with Bakunin is convincing enough: irritated by the "pungent questions" dividing the I.W.A. and wishing to resolve them to his own satisfaction before the imminent general congress, he decided to study the issue in order "to form an accurate judgment." Engels' letters of the year before, correlated with what others had told him in the interval, had brought him to ideological conclusions opposed to those of Marx and Engels.[64] What was more

---

[61] Bakunin's letters to Gambuzzi were not so frequent during the winter of 1871-72, but the correspondence continued at fairly regular intervals. Nettlau, *B.I.I.*, pp. 255, 290, 294, 327.

[62] Cafiero was forced to transfer his anti-Stefanoni polemic to the Milanese newspaper after the discontinuance of *La Campana*.

[63] *Ibid.*, pp. 327-28.

[64] *Ibid.*, pp. 335-36.

natural than journeying to Locarno to test his new-found conclusions against those of the anarchist mogul himself? His conversion to anarchist principles, in short, was an act of intellectual honesty.[65]

Cafiero's method of announcing his break with London, however, merits little charity of judgment. His visit to Locarno did not mark a sudden conversion, but a confirmation—as Cafiero attests—of previously held conclusions. The turning point came before mid-April, if the Engels correspondence mentioned by the Jura *Bulletin* was turned over to Bakunin on April 15 by Fanelli.[66] On this assumption, Cafiero's April 20 and May 27 articles in *Il Gazzettino Rosa*, proclaiming his solidarity with the General Council, can only mean that he was engaged in deliberate deception or—as one close student of the affair concludes—that he deemed it perfectly consistent and normal to defend the General Council vis-à-vis its external bourgeois enemies (read Stefanoni *et al.*), even after having chosen an anti-General Council position in the internal conflict wracking the First International.[67]

Whatever the motivation, Cafiero's betrayal of the Engels correspondence to the declared enemies of the Council fully rates the condemnation dispensed by even Bakunin's apologist.[68] Nor did Engels have the slightest advance warning, for it was Vitale Regis, not Cafiero, who informed him of the Jurassian *Bulletin*'s announcement: "I frankly warn you so that you be not too surprised by some unexpected defection." [69] Not until June 10, one month after the *Bulletin*'s revelation, did

[65] Alberto Tucci, in 1899, told Bakunin's biographer, Nettlau, that he had advised Cafiero to visit Bakunin in order to check on the charges Engels and Marx were hurling at the Russian, and that Malatesta had seconded this counsel. *Ibid.*, p. 279. As noted earlier, Cafiero's letter to Engels of Nov. 29—Dec. 19, 1871, was the first clear evidence that Cafiero's viewpoint was shifting in favor of Bakunin. Carmelo Palladino's testimony unfortunately does not establish precisely when the change occurred: "Believing him an agent of the General Council and an emissary of Marx, we put him in quarantine. All of us were suspicious of him. But I was the first to put an end to such a state of affairs, since, by affronting him openly, I took to opposing his principles. He was in good faith and it was not long before we came to an understanding; so that after several days of discussion, he accepted fully the principles of the anarchist school." Lucarelli, *Palladino*, p. 8.

[66] Guillaume (*I.D.S.*, II, 286) claims Cafiero sent the letters directly to Bakunin, after establishing epistolary contact, and, with Cafiero's authorization, the Russian sent them to Guillaume for publication in the *Bulletin*. On the other hand, Nettlau found no trace of a direct Bakunin-Cafiero contact prior to May 20 and, though he admits this does not disprove Guillaume's account, believes the letters were carried to Locarno by Fanelli, a natural liaison between the two men (*B.I.I.*, p. 331). Romano concurs (*Storia*, II, 279).

[67] *Ibid.*, II, 278.

[68] "They are not things to be done; . . . he comported himself in an irresponsible manner, . . . without taking into account the customs current among men." Nettlau, *B.I.I.*, p. 332.

[69] Letter of May 13, 1872, *ibid.*, p. 330.

Engels identify Cafiero as a responsible party: "Cafiero in Naples and some one else—I still do not know who—from Turin have transmitted my letters to the Jurassians."[70] Engels' demand for an explanation from Cafiero four days later was as vain as it was justified, for by this time Cafiero had irrevocably entered upon his hectic and short-lived career as the Galahad of Italian anarchism.[71]

Cafiero remained with Bakunin in Locarno from May 20 to June 18, except for a two- or three-day break for a quick trip to Milan.[72] On May 31 he read to an approving host the beginning of a long letter to Engels; by June 3 the epistle was completed; on the 19th, from Milan, Cafiero backdated it to the 12th, added a postscript dated the 19th and mailed it off to London.[73] If deception was involved in this juggling of dates—as Romano insists[74]—the substance of the letter was supremely unequivocal. More than a revelation of Cafiero's personal conversion, the document constituted a searing critique of Engels' Italian propaganda tactics, a testimonial to the success of Bakunin's campaign, and it marked the disappearance of the last roadblock to the national federation of Italian socialists.[75]

In that part of his letter discussing the current conflict of principles, Cafiero devoted more invective than logical analysis to what he termed the "German communist program." He had apparently read the Com-

[70] Letter to Cuno, June 10, 1872, ibid., pp. 317, 331, note 1; Romano, Storia, II, 288. Precisely which Engels letters were involved is none too clear, since the Bulletin announcement of May 10 identified them only as having been written "last autumn." From Oct. 1 to the end of Dec., 1871, the record shows only the following letters to Italy from Engels: to Riggio (Girgenti), Oct. 10; to Cafiero, Oct. 10; to Nabruzzi, Nov. 8; to Cuno (Milan), Nov. 13; to Palladino (Naples), Nov. 23; to Cafiero, Dec. 7; to Cuno, Dec. 16. The Oct. 10 letter to Cafiero informed him of the London Conference decisions; the Dec. 7 epistle contained Engels' rationalization of Resolution IX. These, then, were probably the Engels-Cafiero letters turned over to the Jurassians. Engels himself was under the impression for several weeks that only one letter was involved and that Terzaghi was the likely culprit (fragment of Engels' letter of late May to an unknown correspondent, reproduced by Romano [Storia, II, 287], who believes it was intended for Cafiero).

[71] "I have written to no one in Italy other than you, so the [Bulletin] must be referring to my letters to you. You must give me an explanation of this point and I should like to hope that you will do so. . . . I am not afraid of the publication of my letters, but it is a question of honor for you to inform me whether my letters were transmitted to my enemies with or without your consent. . . . If my supposition is correct, I must congratulate you for having fully renounced your fictitious autonomy, delivering it entirely and forever into the hands of the pope Bakunin." Romano, Storia, II, 288; Nettlau, B.I.I., pp. 331-32.

[72] Neapolitan questore report, June 8, 1872, Romano, Storia, II, 281.

[73] Nettlau, B.I.I., pp. 328-29, 333, 343.

[74] Storia, II, 285-86, note 54.

[75] For the letter in full, Nettlau, B.I.I., pp. 333-44; Bosio, ed., "Carteggio da e per l'Italia di Marx-Engels (1871-1875)," Movimento Operaio, Yr. II, Nos. 7-8 (Apr.-May, 1950), 207-11.

munist Manifesto but recently, and claimed that it provided the key to his understanding of the London Conference's controversial Resolution IX (the economic and political movements of the working class are "indissolubly united"). By an arbitrary interpretation of the Resolution of 1871 in the light of Marx and Engels' propaganda leaflet of twenty-three years before, Cafiero had satisfied himself that Marx's method of liberating the workers involved:

> . . . the creation of a new State that . . . apparently will have to be very *strong*, that will begin . . . by teaching the illiterate to read, by *fighting brigandage* and the *camorra* and by *educating* the people who, through the years, will then *gradually* obtain the use of that longed-for *capital;* while the State, having thus accomplished the great work of liberation, will be slowly dissolved in a new State *sui generis:* an *economic* State with all its *unitary centralization* and its *industrial armies, especially agricultural.* (On the first social uprising of our populations, I suggest that you come with Marx and propose *agricultural armies* to our peasants in the Calabria and the Abruzzi).[76]

The entire difference between Marxian socialists and anarchists was simply one of method, and the new recruit to anarchism simplified the difference out of all but the faintest resemblance to the complexities of the problem that Marx and Bakunin had been trying to crystallize for years:

> All [of us] want to . . . reclaim *capital* for the collectivity and for this purpose two different methods are proposed. Some advise a *coup de main* against the principal stronghold—the State— and once it has fallen into the hands of our people, the door of *capital* will be open to all; while the others advise overcoming all obstacles at the same time and *taking possession collectively, in fact,* of that *capital* which it is desired to make collective property forever. I lined up with the latter from the moment when, thanks to your *communist manifesto,* I was enabled to understand the position clearly.

[76] This passage indicates the substance of Engels' letter to Cafiero of Feb. 29—Mar. 9, 1872, for Cafiero, further on in the letter now under consideration, wrote: "I needed the whole *communist manifesto* with [its] entire construction of the *State of the future,* . . . ; I needed *your whole letter* [italics mine] proclaiming Italy's great need of a *really strong State* in order to be instructed, educated, *liberated from the camorra and brigandage* (!!!) before I could understand the deception." At still another point in his letter of defection, Cafiero refers to "the order of ideas developed in the *German communist Manifesto,* . . . so clearly commented on in your last letter . . ." In all probability, this was the letter referred to by Bakunin's June 11 diary entry: "Letter to Guillaume, with letter of Engels to Cafiero," thus completing the Jura Federation's dossier on Engels' Italian campaign. Nettlau, *B.I.I.,* p. 329.

Just how clearly Cafiero understood the doctrinal issues involved may best be left to the polemicists; much more significant is that part of the letter beginning with the line: "Once enlightened on the question of principle, and having chosen my side, I turned my attention to the question of the persons [involved]." The objective truth or falsity of Cafiero's exposition is far less relevant than the fact that it accurately describes the view of the Bakunin-General Council feud that guaranteed Italian acceptance of anarcho-socialism at the expense of initiating an open rupture of the First International.

After a few minutes of conversation with Bakunin, reported Cafiero, "we both realized we were in complete agreement on principles. Yet, they were the very principles I have been propagating in Italy during the [past] year, without knowing that they were different from yours." On the face of it, the assertion seems incredible, yet, Engels himself, in trying to soften the indignation aroused by Resolution IX, had deliberately encouraged Cafiero in this misconception when he assured him that the ambiguous interpretation of that decision given by the Spanish writer for *La Emancipación* (December 3, 1871) was "in perfect harmony" with the views of the General Council, an encouragement that had led Cafiero, in turn, to conclude that Resolution IX was consistent with the principle of political abstention in precisely the sense Bakunin himself had always urged.[77] Nor did Cafiero fail now to remind Engels of that costly deception:

> And I consider it a real equivocation the one created in one of
> your letters, which assured me that the General Council under-

[77] See above, pp. 219-20. In this connection, too, Engels' approval of the anti-Mazzinian pamphlet circulated at the Rome Congress by Cafiero and Tucci in Nov., 1871 ("The International does not reject politics in general; it might very well be forced to use it to the extent that it will be compelled to fight the bourgeois class . . ."), practically all of which was written by Bakunin, helps justify Cafiero's statement that he had believed Bakunin's ideas consistent with those of the General Council. Whether or not this passage, assuming it was written by Bakunin rather than by Cafiero, was due to one of Bakunin's "usual opportunistic and suggestive (*suggestionatrici*) conceptions toward Cafiero," as Romano claims (*Storia*, II, 283), the fact that Engels considered the Bakunin pamphlet "an excellent production" contributed to Cafiero's confusion. The present writer suspects that Cafiero, honestly seeking enlightenment, was simply caught in the crossfire of both Engels' and Bakunin's doctrinal pronouncements, which, given the bitter jockeying for position and adherents, often reflected a compromise of basic principles. No more than Bakunin can Engels be exempted from the charge of "opportunism" that Romano levels against the Russian. As for Cafiero's conduct, Romano seems unable to come to a firm assessment; in the same brief paragraph, we find these opposed conclusions: "The ambiguous, *insincere* conduct of [Cafiero] is, in my opinion, the major cause of the original deviation of Italian socialism. . . . Bakunin won . . . because the Italian socialist movement had the misfortune to find in its front ranks men like Terzaghi and Cafiero, the former in bad faith, *the latter in good faith*, but equally harmful." *Ibid.*, II, 208 (italics mine).

stood Resolution IX in the sense of the Spanish declaration.
And I, in the ardor of the cause, happy to have discovered how
. . . to prevent a schism in the International, hastened to publish
an article on Resolution IX, an article that came to constitute
nothing more than a very solemn ambiguity.[78]

Nor did this charge exhaust Cafiero's identification of Engels' mistakes
in performing his duties as the Council's corresponding secretary for
Italy. What basis in truth was there for Engels' complaint to the General
Council in March that "the great difficulty for the Council has been to
enter into direct relations with the Italian workers"? On this point,
Cafiero waxed ironic:

When have you asked me to put you in correspondence with
workers? When you asked my opinion on how to establish
relations with the different regions of Italy, did I not advise
corresponding directly with the various localities? Anyone reading [Engels' complaint] that knew me as the correspondent of
the Council could not help but conclude that I am one of those
plotting to keep the Italian proletariat separated from its beloved
(!) General Council.[79]

In direct defense of Bakunin, Cafiero was certain that the Russian and
the Jura dissidents "never intended to substitute their ideas for the
broad program of the International." They had always felt that the I.W.A.
was alone capable of organizing the world proletariat for the "*economic
struggle for its complete emancipation.*" The choice of means and tactics
resided in the federations and sections, but Resolution IX sought to
impose a "uniform tactic" on the whole International. The reaction of the
socialists in Spain, Belgium, Italy, the Jura, and part of France demonstrated "the absurdity of such a system."

Cafiero's letter was completed on June 3 and concluded with his promise
to continue writing to Engels, if the latter so desired. On June 1, Bakunin
had received a copy of Marx's famous "Private Circular" indicting all
Internationalists holding opinions opposed to his own—a "pile of filth,"
in the Russian's unusually laconic phrase.[80] On the reasonable assumption
that Bakunin showed the Marx pamphlet to Cafiero, the juxtaposition
of these two facts suggests that the anarchist chief did not wish to use

---

[78] Cafiero was referring to his *Gazzettino Rosa* article of Dec. 20, 1871.

[79] Nor was Engels' lack of direct contacts with Italian workers the fault of Bakunin,
for, as Cafiero pointed out, the Russian had always advised the Italian sections to
initiate correspondence with the General Council.

[80] Guillaume, *I.D.S.*, II, 296; Nettlau, *B.I.I.*, p. 328. The full title of the Marx
pamphlet: *Les prétendues scissions dans l'Internationale, circulaire privée du
Conseil général de l'Association internationale des travailleurs.* For Bakunin's response,
Jura *Bulletin*, June 15, 1872.

it as an excuse to break with the General Council—a conclusion confirmed by his advice to the Italians later in the summer.[81] For the moment, too, Cafiero seemed to agree, since his letter made no mention of the *Circular*. Yet, in the postscript he added in Milan on June 19, the day *after* he left Locarno, Cafiero referred for the first time to the *Circular*, and in unmistakable language broke off all personal relations with the London Council:

> I have read the private circular of the General Council. . . .
> Nothing of what is said in it is new to me. I now know all the
> facts and their entire meaning. *Consummatum est*, your work is
> finished! It is not I who say it, but the Belgian congress . . .
> and the mountains of the Jura, and Spain repeat it: *Consum-*
> *matum est!*—and Italy?—Italy will greet with joy the death of
> the General Council, which . . . has given all the evidences
> of a *strong government* in replying, to those who attacked its
> principles, with insinuation, slander, and the whole system of
> personal intrigues which form the quintessence of the strong
> policy of a model State.—Italy, jeering, will repeat: *Consum-*
> *matum est!*

Bakunin's opinion that the time was not ripe for an open break with London had apparently carried weight with the new recruit only while he was under the direct influence of Bakunin's uncommon powers of persuasion. Once free of "the coils of the great serpent"—as another young neophyte had phrased it several years earlier—Cafiero took it upon himself to initiate the schism between Italian socialism and the General Council.

ITALIAN SOCIALISM VERSUS
THE GENERAL COUNCIL

From the day Bakunin and Cafiero sealed their alliance, the Russian's relations with the Italian socialists assumed the character of a well-coordinated conspiracy, geared to a single objective: creation of an Italian federation before the general congress of the I.W.A. expected in September, a federation whose delegates—as Bakunin had told Nabruzzi late in January—would appear at the international congress "with a full acquaintance with what they must represent, do, and say there." On May 23 Bakunin informed Nabruzzi and Ceretti of his "perfectly ac-

---

[81] It is true that Bakunin declared for an open break with the General Council in mid-July, but only in case the Council refused to change the locale of the next general congress from The Hague to Switzerland (letter to Nabruzzi, July 16, 1872, Nettlau, *B.I.I.*, p. 354). In any case, such a decision could not have come before July 10, when the Council first announced The Hague as the scene of the general congress. Guillaume, *I.D.S.*, II, 301.

complished alliance" with Cafiero; on the 28th, Friscia and Palladino were advised; on June 8, Pezza in Milan was notified by telegram; on the 11th, letters were written to Nabruzzi, Ceretti, and Gambuzzi, along with Cafiero's doubtlessly enthusiastic endorsements.[82]

On June 14 the Bologna *Fascio Operaio* decided to convoke a national congress, but it was only after Bakunin had put direct pressure on Nabruzzi during the latter's visit to Locarno on June 25-26 and after Fanelli and Cafiero, now in Bologna, had talked Ceretti out of an apparent hesitancy, that the Romagnols released the circular of convocation, inviting the Italian sections to propose a host city for the gathering.[83] Whether the news of the General Council's June 18 decision to convoke the I.W.A. general congress for September 2 at The Hague reached Bologna in time to contribute to the release of the *Fascio Operaio's* circular is not certain,[84] but the Londoners' selection of The Hague certainly threw a wrench into Bakunin's plans. He and his Jura lieutenants now had the problem of insuring a strong anarchist representation at a congress held in a city too distant for their Spanish, Italian, and Swiss supporters to reach without incurring major travel expenses. The Jura Federation immediately called foul, and Bakunin hastened to Neuchâtel to concert strategy with James Guillaume and August Spichinger.[85] Precisely what agreement was reached is in some doubt, but so far as the Italian socialists were concerned, the line was laid down in instructions Bakunin must have imparted to Pezza, Ceretti, Gambuzzi, Nabruzzi, and Cafiero in his letter of July 15-16, i.e., immediately after the Russian, according to the testimony of his diary, had arrived at *"projets établis"* with his friends of the Jurassian federation.[86] A fragment of his letter to Gambuzzi indicates the tactic that Bakunin—if not the Jurassians— wanted to follow:

> . . . the Jurassian federal Council has decided to send a protest to the General Council, very moderate in form, but quite firm in content. . . . At the same time, [it] will ask the friendly federa-

[82] Nettlau, *B.I.I.*, pp. 328-29. Cafiero also wrote directly to Malatesta in Naples on June 1. Bakunin included Testini, in Milan, with a letter of June 10. *Loc. cit.*

[83] *Il Libero Pensiero*, July 11, 1872; Nettlau, *B.I.I.*, pp. 350-51. Bakunin to Ceretti, June 21: *"Carissimo,* I say nothing to you today, because at this very moment you have with you [Fanelli and Cafiero], who will tell you about it much better than I can through a letter. I await with great impatience the results of your conversation." *Ibid.*, p. 350; Romano, *Storia*, II, 290.

[84] *La Plebe* did not carry the announcement of the General Council decision until July 11.

[85] Nettlau, *B.I.I.*, p. 354. For the Jurassians' protest, Guillaume, *I.D.S.*, II, 301-04.

[86] Nettlau, *B.I.I.*, pp. 354-55. Thirty-two years later Guillaume denied that he had agreed to a separate anarchist congress if the General Council refused to shift the I.W.A. congress from The Hague to Switzerland. *Loc. cit.*

tions of Spain and Italy to support its protest and its [request that the general congress be held in Switzerland]. If London refuses this, the Italians and Spaniards will be invited to do as the Jurassians, that is, not to send any delegate to this Congress, but to send one instead to the Conference of the dissident and free sections in Switzerland, in order to assert and maintain their own independence and to organize their separate federation, the federation of the autonomous sections and federations of the International. Warn all the friends of this. . . . We have now received some letters from Spain and one of the regional Council (national) of Spain—an official letter—which advises us that all the Spanish sections and federations will pronounce themselves in our favor against London and will proceed solidly with us against the latter, requesting, as we are doing today, the abolition of the General Council . . .[87]

Two days later the Bologna *Fascio Operaio* announced Rimini as the seat of the Italian congress to be held on August 4.[88] The wavering Ceretti, again worried about the effects of such drastic Italian socialist action on his never really forsaken dream of a unity pact of action with the Mazzinians, had to be bolstered once more by Bakunin, but by now it really did not matter.[89] Well catechized, Bakunin's corps of agitators—Fanelli, Cafiero, Gambuzzi, Friscia, Palladino, and Malatesta in the *Mezzogiorno;* Nabruzzi, seconded by Costa, in the Romagna; Pezza, Testini, and Stampa in Milan—were preparing a different kind of unity pact.

THE RIMINI, HAGUE, AND ST. IMIER CONGRESSES

When the first national congress of Italian socialism convened in Rimini on the afternoon of August 4, the geographical distribution of the Bakuninist heresy was fairly accurately indicated.[90] Twenty-five delegates

[87] Nettlau, *B.I.I.*, pp. 354-55.
[88] *Ibid.*, p. 352.
[89] Romano, *Storia*, II, 393; Nettlau, *B.I.I.*, pp. 355-56. Bakunin was trying, in this letter, to soothe Ceretti's ire, aroused by a criticism Pezza had made—in all probability, a charge that Ceretti was too "soft" on the Mazzinians. At the same time, Garibaldi was still pressing Ceretti toward championing the idea of uniting "all our Italian Associations, to whatever party they belong . . ." Letter of Aug. 1, 1872, Ciampoli, *op. cit.*, pp. 629-30.
[90] A summary *resoconto* of the proceedings, signed by Cafiero and Costa, was printed as a single-page document entitled, *Associazione Internazionale dei Lavoratori. Prima conferenza delle sezioni italiane* (Rimini, 1872); reproduced by *Bollettino de' Lavoratori. Organo della Federazione operaia napoletana*, Aug. 31, 1872; and by *La Rivoluzione Sociale*, Sept., 1872 (only two issues published, the Sept. number in Neuchâtel, Switzerland, the second in Florence). Romano reproduces the entire document, *Storia*, II, 395-97; Nettlau quotes the bulk of it, *B.I.I.*, pp. 357-60. *Cf.*,

represented twenty-one sections: ten from the Romagna (Bologna, Ravenna, Rimini, Imola, Lugo, San Potito, Fusignano, San Giovanni in Persiceto, Forlì, Sant-Arcangelo di Romagna), three from the Marches (Fano, Fermo, Senigallia), Umbria (provincial representation), Emilia (Mirandola), Sicily (Sciacca), Naples, two from Tuscany (Siena, Florence), Rome, and Mantua. Of the delegates, only eleven can be identified: Ceretti (Bologna); Nabruzzi (Ravenna); Costa (Imola); Friscia (Sciacca); Cafiero, Malatesta, Fanelli (Naples); Tito Zanardelli (Rome?); Piccioli-Poggiali, Grassi, and Terzaghi (Florence).[91] Vincenzo Pezza, Milan's chief anarchist, was out of jail but too ill to join the Rimini conferees. The Milan section, however, sent a message advising the congress to abolish or at least limit the powers of the General Council.

With Cafiero presiding and Costa acting as secretary, the Rimini Congress voted a constitution for the "Italian Federation of the International Workingmen's Association," a *regolamento* coupling the preamble of the I.W.A. program (including the controversial line: "the economic emancipation of the workers is . . . the great goal to which every political movement must be subordinated as a method") with explicitly anarchist provisions drawn from the constitution of the Neapolitan section. Anti-authoritarianism and sectional autonomy found expression in the official definition of the Italian Federation as a simple pact between the various autonomous sections and in the decisions to limit the Federation's national organs to a correspondence commission, whose *sole* function was the collection and dissemination of news regarding the workers' movement, and a statistical commission, charged with collecting data on the workers' organization and living conditions.[92]

On the third and last day of the conference, the delegates unanimously voted the resolution marking the beginning of the end of the First

also, Bottero, *Dibattimenti* . . . , pp. 311-12; Jura *Bulletin*, Aug. 15—Sept. 1, 1872. For secondary treatments of the congress, Manacorda, *Il movimento operaio italiano*, pp. 82-86; Romano, *Storia*, II, 295-98; Pietro Vigo, *Storia degli ultimi trent'anni del secolo XIX* (Milan, 1908), I, 196-97.

[91] Circumstantial evidence suggests but does not prove, that the Roman section was represented by Tito Zanardelli, a twenty-four-year-old ex-actor from Vittorio Veneto. Zanardelli had worked for both *Il Motto d'Ordine* and *La Campana* in Naples in the fall of 1871 and the ensuing winter (Romano, *Storia*, II, 216, note 49). On Jan. 7, 1872, *La Campana* announced that soon one of the Neapolitan Internationalists would go to Rome to establish direct contacts with the socialists of that city. Though Zanardelli does not appear in the record as an active collaborator with Gnocchi-Viani in the founding of the Workers' League of Arts and Crafts, he represented that I.W.A. section at the Congress of Bologna in Mar., 1873. Della Peruta, "L'Internazionale a Roma," p. 21.

[92] *Programma e Regolamento della Federazione Italiana della Associazione Internazionale dei Lavoratori* (Rimini, 1872), reproduced by Nettlau, *B.I.I.*, pp. 362-64; *cf.*, also, Pezzi, *Un errore giudiziario*, pp. 13-14. Composing the statistical commission: Ceretti, Malatesta, Terzaghi.

International. In the preamble of the document,[93] all the charges made by Cafiero in his letter of defection to Engels are repeated—the attempt of the London Conference to impose "a special authoritarian doctrine" with Resolution IX, the "slander and mystification" of the Council, the "indignity" of the *Private Circular* of March 5, 1872, all of which revealed the Council's "lust for authority." The Council's decision to hold the next general congress in Holland is implied to have been a deliberate move to exclude the delegates of the "revolutionary countries." Therefore:

> . . . from this moment the Italian Federation of the International Workingmen's Association breaks all solidarity with the General Council of London . . . and proposes to all those sections who do not share the authoritarian principles of the General Council to send their representatives on September 2, 1872, not to The Hague, but to Neuchâtel in Switzerland, for the purpose of opening . . . the general anti-authoritarian Congress.[94]

What had prompted the Italians, of all the anarchist federations, to make the first formal break with the executive body of the First International, to call for a schismatic congress to be held on the very day set for the I.W.A. general congress at The Hague? The Rimini Congress was advised by the Spanish Federation "to hold high the banner of Anarchy and Collectivism" *and* to send as many delegates as possible to The Hague Congress; the Jura Swiss recommended that the Italians urge the General Council to shift that congress from Holland to Switzerland—but neither federation suggested a counter-congress and the rupture such a meeting would imply. Bakunin's July 16 letter to Gambuzzi seems the obvious explanation, but the fact is that Bakunin himself, at the August 18 Jura congress of La Chaux-de-Fonds, approved the Swiss anarchists' decision to send representatives to The Hague and to urge the Italians to do likewise, arguing that a counter-congress risked compromising the issue. Bakunin, too, is reported to have been both "surprised and unhappy" when he read the Rimini resolution.[95] Since the content of his last-minute correspondence with Cafiero and Nabruzzi prior to Rimini is not known, only two hypotheses are tenable: either the Russian changed his mind between mid-July and mid-August, in which case he had only himself to blame if he found the Italian resolution displeasing; or his talk of a counter-congress was simply a trial balloon, requiring discussion and

[93] Nettlau, *B.I.I.*, pp. 360-62; Pezzi, *Un errore giudiziario*, pp. 14-16; Romano, *Storia*, II, 398-99.

[94] Before the month was out, the Milanese and Ferrarese sections notified Costa of their approval of this resolution and adhered to the new Italian Federation. Nettlau, *B.I.I.*, p. 366; Guillaume, *I.D.S.*, II, 311, note 1.

[95] Guillaume, *I.D.S.*, II, 319, note 1. For the Chaux-de-Fonds congress, Jura *Bulletin*, Aug. 15—Sept. 1, 1872.

decision by the various anarchist federations before it could be assumed as a general tactic, in which case the Italians misunderstood the intent, or simply—through an excess of zeal not surprising in the new and youthful converts—talked themselves into the decision in an effort to prove their militancy and intransigence. Under the gavel of a fiery fanatic like Cafiero—who had not hesitated, despite the influence of Bakunin, to proclaim his own excommunication of the General Council —and under the spell of Andrea Costa's exuberant but frequently irresponsible eloquence, the Rimini delegates were very probably expressing their own sentiments, not the wishes of their Russian mentor, in breaking with London and convoking a counter-congress at Neuchâtel.[96]

More important than the question of whether Bakunin was responsible for the Rimini Resolution is the fact that the Italians, in setting the preamble of the I.W.A. program (written by Marx) as the basis of their program, could not have more clearly demonstrated that to them anarchist principles were a logical deduction from Marxian premises. Whether this denotes an objective gap in their logic—as the Marxist historian would insist—matters little; the fact is they believed their creed consistent with the goals and methods of the First International, as defined by its original program and the general congresses.[97] It was Resolution IX and Marx and Engels' attempt to challenge the right of a large segment of the International to draw its own conclusions as to revolutionary method that brought the Italian Federation into being.

The action of the Rimini Congress merely anticipated by less than a month, as it developed, the inevitable schism in the International. At the Hague Congress, held on September 2-7, only twenty-five of the sixty-five delegates present were of the anarchist current. Cafiero attended as an

[96] See, also, the evidence on this question presented by Leo Valiani, "Dalla prima alla seconda Internazionale (1872-1889)," *Movimento Operaio*, Yr. VI, No. 2 (Mar.-Apr., 1954), p. 235, note 12. Nabruzzi, twenty-seven years later, denied that Bakunin had written the resolution and insisted that it expressed the general sentiment of the delegates. Nettlau, *B.I.I.*, p. 364. Costa, in a letter to Bignami of Aug. 16, 1872, implicitly denied that Bakunin had anything to do with the Rimini resolution against the General Council: "You know of the acts of Rimini, but I want to tell you something of the spirit animating the Italian representatives, [a spirit] which— and the resolution relative to the General Council is an excellent proof of it—was one of absolute independence and complete autonomy. . . . The *International* . . . is not Karl Marx or Michael Bakunin; it has no idols of any kind . . . ; it is not a sect and has no dogmas . . ." *La Plebe*, Aug. 17, 1872. For his part, Engels was certain Bakunin was directly responsible for the Rimini resolution. See his letter to E. Glaser, Aug. 19, 1872, Guillaume, *I.D.S.*, II, 319.

[97] This is implicit in the Rimini Congress' decision that "the attributions of this Conference should be limited to matters of administrative organization, *since the program of the* [I.W.A.] *has already been formulated, discussed and approved by the general congresses*" (italics mine).

observer.[98] From the beginning there was no doubt about the tenor of the congress' final decisions. The General Council was given more, not less, power; Resolution IX was incorporated into the general statutes of the International; a committee of inquiry, headed by Engels' ex-Italian operative, Theodor Cuno, reported that Bakunin had headed a secret organization violating the principles and rules of the I.W.A.[99] Putting the logical capstone to the committee's report, the congress forthwith expelled Bakunin and his Swiss lieutenant, James Guillaume. The decision, in Marxist historiography, is rated a victory for Marx and Engels,[100] but the Hague Congress was the last international convention of the I.W.A. under the aegis of the General Council, and the seat of the Council itself was shortly transferred to New York, where it could exercise no real influence or control over European socialists. For their part, the Bakuninists, far from feeling ostracized, claimed the role of heirs of the socialist International.

The "anti-authoritarians" held their congress at St. Imier, Switzerland, on September 15 and there proclaimed their definitive rupture with the London Council.[101] Of the fifteen delegates present, five were Italians (Costa, Malatesta, Cafiero, Nabruzzi, and Fanelli), and Bakunin himself sat as a representative of the Italian Federation. The delegates at St. Imier, denying the legislative powers of general or regional congresses, rejected the decisions of the Hague gathering. The powers of the General Council were decreed incompatible with the autonomy of the federations and sections. "To safeguard their respective Federations against the governmental pretensions of this General Council, as well as to save and strengthen the unity of the International," the St. Imier delegates established a "Pact of Friendship, Solidarity, and Mutual Defense" between the anti-authoritarian sections and federations. There would be no central governing body; the federations and sections were to maintain direct contact with each other, without any intermediary.

[98] Proceedings in Guillaume, I.D.S., II, 319-56; Jura Bulletin, Sept. 15—Oct. 1, 1872. Thanks to his fat patrimony, Cafiero was probably the only Italian socialist who could meet the cost of the journey. Both he and Vincenzo Pezza attended the Jura Federation's Aug. 18 meeting at La Chaux-de-Fonds, which delineated the strategy to be followed by the Swiss anarchists going to the Hague Congress. Guillaume, I.D.S., II, 316-17. The Neapolitan police suspected that Fanelli also attended the Hague Congress. Lucarelli, Giuseppe Fanelli, p. 148, note 2.

[99] For the report, Guillaume, I.D.S., II, 345-47.

[100] See Manacorda, Il movimento operaio italiano, p. 87.

[101] For the St. Imier Congress, Zoccoli, L'Anarchia, pp. 389-92; Jura Bulletin, Sept. 15—Oct. 1, 1872; Guillaume, I.D.S., III, 4-11. When it became apparent that the other anarchist federations were resolved to send delegates to The Hague on Sept. 2, Costa, after an exchange of letters with the Jura Federation, agreed to shift the date of the "anti-authoritarian" congress to Sept. 15. Ibid., II, 318; Jura Bulletin, Aug. 15—Sept. 1, 1872.

Resolution III of the St. Imier Congress contained the essential statement of anarchist opposition to the Marxian tenet that a political party of the workers is the indispensable instrument of organization and struggle in annihilating capitalism:

1. . . . The destruction of all political power is the first duty of the proletariat; . . .

2. . . . All organization of a so-called provisional and revolutionary power to lead to this destruction can only be another deception and it would be as dangerous for the proletariat as all governments existing today; . . .

3. . . . Rejecting all compromise in arriving at the accomplishment of the social Revolution, the proletarians of all countries must establish, outside of any bourgeois policy, the solidarity of revolutionary action.

Not to a political party, then, but to the "spontaneous" action of the proletarians was the workers' movement to be entrusted.

CONCLUSION

The Congress of Rimini was the first organized expression of the Italian socialist movement on a national scale. As a fairly coherent social protest, the movement dated back to the summer of 1871, when the example and the extinction of the Paris Commune brought into focus, for the first time, a whole congeries of dissatisfactions among the younger and more radical generation of Italian republicans: dissatisfaction with Mazzini, with the existing government and society, even dissatisfaction with Garibaldi, who, by the summer of 1872, had found himself unable to activate a program which, when combined with his unquestionable prestige as a revolutionary leader, as a man of action, might have molded Italian republican youth into an effective and possibly revolutionary political force.[102]

Whether these dissatisfactions could be rationally justified in the existing historical context is very much open to question, but this does not deny their existence, nor their motive power among the malcontents. If these young men, in suggesting drastic social change, were unaware of the practical limits of reform, *at the time,* if, indeed, theirs were demands for an unrealizable utopia, their idealism was a natural enough legacy of that which had sustained their fathers and grandfathers during the preceding decades, when the vision of a united Italy, with all the hopes for social justice that the vision involved, had so frequently

---

[102] The revolutionary image of himself was one Garibaldi persisted in perpetuating. To Ceretti on July 1, 1872, he wrote: "When the hour of action comes, I hope to be at my post," *La Plebe,* July 25, 1872.

appeared a dream, condemned to perpetual frustration by the harsh realities of Austrian, Spanish Bourbon, and Papal opposition.

The young Italian socialists—and the overwhelming majority of them in the early 1870's were barely out of their 'teens—were quite confused in their thinking about the meaning of socialism, but phrases like "the emancipation of the proletariat," "class struggle," "abolition of the bourgeois state," and breaking the hold of institutionalized religion—these must have had one completely clear connotation: a call to *action now*. And in 1872, it was action, above all, that was wanted by young radicals unable or unwilling to adjust to the society into which maturity had brought them. In this respect, too, they were carrying on a venerable tradition, since for almost half a century the Italian republican movement had encouraged and even bred political activism as a virtue. The careers of both Mazzini and Garibaldi—to say nothing of lesser *Risorgimento* heroes like Pisacane, Orsini, and the Cairoli brothers—stood as testimonials to the sacredness of action.[103]

To summarize the appearance of anarcho-socialism in Italy in terms of the frustration of Marxian socialist doctrines distorts the actual meaning of the events described in the preceding five chapters. Time and time again, the articulate socialists of Italy demonstrated that they were unconcerned with—or perhaps ignorant of—the doctrinal issues Marx and Bakunin were contesting. Cafiero, the one Italian socialist Engels had consistently tried to educate in a Marxist direction, showed an appalling disorientation with respect to both Marxism and Bakuninism in the letter announcing his apostasy. Tucci, in the columns of *La Campana*, touched on anarchist themes, but his discussions hardly measured up, in terms of theoretical completeness and consistency, to the well-rounded and integrally anarchist exposition of Bakunin in his pamphlet-sized letter to Ceretti in March. Neither a clear-cut Marxian viewpoint nor an equally distinct anarchist doctrine is to be found in the propaganda literature of Italian socialists during this period. From the suppression of the Paris Commune to mid-November 1871 (Sonvilliers Circular), the polemic, strictly speaking, was not even concerned with a

---

[103] "The idea of violence . . . was inherited by the anarchists from democracy. Up to 1870, democracy in Europe, compelled to fight autocratic powers, moved on the terrain of conspiracy and armed struggle. Even if we had not become anarchists with the First International, it would have sufficed to be democrats to use revolt, even armed, against oppression. . . . Before accepting Bakunin's preaching, the Italian anarchists . . . had admired and exalted Agesilao Milano, Felice Orsini, and the *coups de main* of Mazzini. When they passed into the International, they learned nothing, in this respect, that they had not already learned from Mazzini and Garibaldi."—thus Malatesta, looking back from the twentieth century, as quoted by Armando Borghi, *Mezzo secolo di anarchia (1898-1945)* (Naples: Ediz. Scientifiche, 1954), p. 267.

socialist issue, per se, but with expressing indignation at Mazzini's negative reaction to the Commune. Certainly the Commune was interpreted
—or, more exactly, misinterpreted—in Italy as a manifestation of popular
democracy, political and economic, but the anti-Mazzinian polemicists,
in their writings, did not go beyond a merely negative criticism of Mazzini's unexpected condemnation of the Commune. In doing so, they
formulated neither a specifically socialist defense of the Commune nor
a specifically socialist critique of Mazzini's doctrines. This was done for
them by Bakunin, with his biting assaults on Mazzini, reducing the
polemic to a few easily remembered slogans and catch phrases, thus
encouraging the disaffection of many young republicans from the Mazzinian camp, without, at the same time, edifying them, to any great
extent, as to the principles of anarchism.

From mid-November, 1871, to the Congress of Rimini, the polemic
of Italian extremists was chiefly concerned—once the dream of a national
union of the republican Left was dispelled—with the question of the
General Council's "authoritarianism." A clarification occurred, certainly,
in that a more or less definitive rupture with Mazzinianism had been
achieved and the argument was now confined within the International.
Every Italian socialist, it seemed, had few doubts about his Internationalism, but there were evidently very few familiar enough with the
terms of the Marx-Bakunin dispute to arrive at a decision as to the
intrinsic merits of either formulation. The basic issue, in the minds of
Italian socialists in the late winter and spring of 1872, was, in fact,
almost completely extraneous to the all-important question of method,
of *how* the working class might liberate itself. The London Conference's
Resolution IX, to them, was not a point of departure for a reasoned choice
of anarchism as the more apt revolutionary methodology, but simply proof
that the General Council was trying to inhibit the organizational and
doctrinal autonomy of their sections. Again, it was Bakunin who gave
ideological content to what threatened to become another sterile nega-
tivism. In his letters to the Romagnols he began the process—not without
some casualties, like Pescatori—and with his conquest of Cafiero the
process was complete, or at least complete enough that the handful
of men he had indoctrinated were able, at Rimini, to produce not only
a national federation of socialists, but a clear and consequent doctrinal
platform as well. In brief, it was not until Rimini that social revolutionary
ideology, per se, assumed any real importance to the Italians.

It is only begging the historical question, too, to attempt to identify
Italy's relative lack of industrialization as the reason for the failure
of Marxian socialism, as a system of thought, to recommend itself to the
Italian radicals. The plain fact is that in Italy during the decisive year

following the fall of the Paris Commune, they were simply not well enough informed on "scientific" socialist doctrine for there to have been any real battle of ideas. Italy's lack of large concentrations of industrial workers explains the General Council's failure to establish Marxian socialism in the country no more than it accounts for the success of what one Marxist historian calls "the original deviation of Italian socialism."

In 1872 Italian extremists of the republican Left found themselves in an ideological void: they had turned their backs on Mazzini, Garibaldi offered only his name and sententious platitudes about human brotherhood, Engels confined himself almost exclusively to personal denigration of Bakunin.[104] For these radicals, Bakunin filled the void. Rimini was the proof of it.

[104] Engels, "in his malicious polemics, excited by rancors of personal hegemony more than by doctrinal differences and jealous of the Bakuninist hegemony in Italy, pointed to his formidable competitor as a vulgar 'intriguer.'" Roberto Michels, *Storia del marxismo in Italia. Compendio critico con annessa bibliografia* (Rome, 1909), p. 43.

XIII

Anarcho-Socialism versus the Italian State and Society (September 1872 to September 1873)

THE national organization of Italian socialism at Rimini made the government's attitude toward its activity an important conditioning factor in its development. With the authoritarian-libertarian issue resolved in favor of the anarchists, with the Mazzinian cause compromised in the eyes of radical youth by monarchical consolidation, with Garibaldi isolating himself from a movement whose program he disapproved, Cafiero, Malatesta, Costa, and their comrades could now try to actuate their program, no longer constrained to expend the bulk of their energies defending themselves against these republican foes. Opposition persisted after the summer of 1872, but the anarchist chieftains considered it weakened sufficiently that they no longer needed to extend themselves in decrying the authoritarianism of Marx and the General Council, the "political theology" of Mazzini, and Garibaldi's confusion of socialism with the brotherhood of man. By the fall of 1872, the ground was cleared for a new battle and a new enemy, the *bête noire* indicated by their central tenet: the state. The policy of the government in handling a movement intent on subverting the political and social foundations of the state constituted, so long as the movement retained its ideological and organizational integrity, the determining external element affecting Italian anarchism's growth and development.

To keep the matter in proper perspective, it must be remembered that from the government's point of view—even from that of the Italian middle

291

class—the challenge of the International, to the extent it was considered a challenge at all, was a relatively minor one during the decade of the 1870's. Bourgeois public opinion, like that of the men in government, saw in the Internationalist phenomenon a symptom of discontent deriving from poverty, a discontent susceptible, by the same token, to the curative powers of enlightened paternalism. The threat warranted no exceptional measures. Not until the late 1870's did Italian industrialization and the worker unrest it brought in its wake arouse concern, not in the middle class as a whole, but among those productive groups with economic interests directly affected. By then, however, the problem no longer presented itself as a socialist or Internationalist one, for the Italian International was already being rent by the centrifugal force of defection in its own ranks. In a broad sense, the ruling classes did not take the socialist challenge seriously until, in the 1880's, they began to identify it with the workers' movement. During most of the preceding decade, the absence of an industrial proletariat in a country just emerging from an artisan production system kept Italy's political class from attributing any real political importance to the socialist International. Hence, any discussion of the government's attitude toward the movement in the early and mid-1870's must depart from the premise that however vital to the existence of the International the government's point of view, the attitude itself reflected no sense of serious peril to bourgeois class interests.

The period extending from September 1872 to July 1876 featured, in succession, the planning and organizing of an armed insurrection, its attempted execution in August 1874, and a subsequent series of Internationalist trials. As the representative, defendant, and executive arm of bourgeois class interests, the government, by all the canons of Marxist historiography, should have immediately extirpated the Italian International by the simple expedient of exceptional laws. The anarchists' program flatly challenged every ideal of middle-class society. Moreover, the constitutional Right, not the Left, was in power during this period. Government reaction to the attempted subversion should have reflected —and did, according to contemporary historians of the Marxist Left— the dynamics of class conflict, hinged on fear and unalloyed bourgeois class egotism. Yet, by July 1876 all the Internationalists implicated in the 1874 attempt, having faced judges and juries drawn from the ranks of the possessing classes, found themselves free to reorganize their association on the same platform adopted at Rimini four years before, free to repeat their attempt to subvert the state and society by conspiracy and violence.

Several contingent reasons partially explain this outcome. Juries were influenced to leniency by appreciation of the existing social inequities the defendants claimed had motivated their actions. The prosecution mounted woefully inept cases. There were too many instances of third-degree tactics by the police to extract confessions, of the use of *agents-provocateurs*, of flimsy, irrelevant, and distorted evidence. Clever defense lawyers easily proved that their clients' actions did not fit the rigorous requirements of Italian laws defining conspiracy and attempted subversion of state security. Some of the leading defendants, in addressing the juries, proved exceedingly eloquent, masters of sentimental rhetoric, *simpatici* in their persons. Generally, they depicted themselves as the voice of popular conscience, protesting social injustice, as martyrs under the rod of reaction.[1] By 1875-76, moreover, the government of the Right reached the pinnacle of its unpopularity, for reasons that went far beyond its social policy.[2] Finally, the whole *Risorgimento* tradition of Mazzinian *coups de main*, of Garibaldian enterprises, of Agesilao Milano, of Felice Orsini, of Carlo Pisacane, sanctified, in the eyes of many, the actions of these latter-day paladins of the crusade against tyranny.[3]

Still, if one goes beyond these immediate reasons for the exoneration of Internationalists who, if they did not quite qualify as culprits under the specific charges brought against them, were certainly guilty of attempted insurrection in point of fact, it becomes clear that the favorable verdicts derived from a climate of public opinion—i.e., informed, bourgeois opinion—that was contrary to any departure from strict legality in handling the anarcho-socialist phenomenon, regardless of how unequivocally the Internationalists stated their challenge to bourgeois society. Any government action against a political faction could not avoid close scrutiny by public opinion; any suspicion that such action violated the principle of liberty under law meant that no Italian government, under normal circumstances, could hope to win approval of repressive measures. So long as the Right was in power, i.e., until March 1876, the prevailing spirit among Moderates was legalitarian and liberal, and what an Italian statesman told the French Ambassador in the summer of 1872 was generally true, even after 1876, of public opinion as well: "We have suffered so much because of arbitrary action when we lived according to the caprices of our many governments, that we want to believe in legality, now that we feel ourselves sufficiently strong to be a nation, one

---

[1] "We shall make of the court a people's platform"—thus Andrea Costa at the 1876 Bologna trial. Schiavi, "La formazione del pensiero politico di Andrea Costa," p. 14.

[2] "The discontent of the country against the moderates was due essentially to the tax policy they had followed since 1861." Giampiero Carocci, *Agostino Depretis e la politica italiana dal 1876 al 1887* (Turin: Einaudi, 1956), p. 24.

[3] ". . . the prestige of the political crime was still so great in Italy that the jurors unfailingly absolved them . . ." Merlino, *Questa è l'Italia*, p. 222.

and free; and we are clear-sighted enough to believe in liberty only under law." [4]

To what degree was the government of the Right, between 1872 and 1876, responsive to this spirit? The reader may judge from the ensuing record of the Italian International's experience, but certainly the meaning of that experience, in relation to the question at issue, is by no means clear except in the context of certain basic articles of faith prevalent among the men who ruled Italy. A summary of their attitude toward the social question, the International, and the general problem of how to deal with a socially subversive movement, points to the conclusion that the government reaction aroused by the insurrectional attempt of the anarchists was more maladroit than vicious, more the product of bewilderment than of class interest, certainly not aimed at the suppression of any political-economic program, not even—as Giovanni Lanza, a man of the parliamentary Right, told one of his colleagues—that "inspired by the most absurd sophisms of the socialist school." [5]

As viewed by the government, there was no real problem, in fact, as long as the propagation of these "sophisms" involved no organized attempt to overthrow the government by violence. When the anarchists actually tried "social liquidation," however, the terms of the conflict became more complex, not because suppression was technically impossible, but because men deeply attached to classical liberal principles would not adopt the only effective method of eliminating the International in Italy: exceptional laws, frankly violating constitutional liberties. The anarchists' exploitation of the government's dilemma proved only a temporary advantage, for it merely hastened the day when the government, no longer bound by liberal scruples, would treat them, not as political opponents, but as "an association of malefactors," legally in the category of common thieves and ruffians. That this development was delayed until the fall of the Right from power in 1876 attests, in itself, to the strength of the liberal idea among Moderates, such as Marco Minghetti, Giovanni Lanza, and Quintino Sella. The Italian International's war on the state from the Congress of Rimini to the summer of 1876 constituted—always within the limits indicated at the beginning of this chapter—a challenge to the liberal premises of Italy's ruling class. To what extent could that class tolerate direct attack on the principles of property, *patria* and—in the classical sense—liberty?

Prior to the summer of 1872 the necessity of finding an answer to such a question had probably not even occurred to the men responsible for the

---

[4] Fournier report, Aug. 12, 1872, Federico Chabod, *Storia della politica estera italiana dal 1870 al 1896*, Vol. I: *Le Premesse* (Bari: Laterza, 1951), p. 437.

[5] *Ibid.*, p. 436.

government of the Italian state. The reasons were several.[6] In the first place, they had no comprehension of the objective realities of the social problem, and even the term, "social question," left them perplexed.[7] Liberalism was their religion, but it remained a moral and juridical abstraction, only vaguely related to the framework of objective facts in which liberty might become the possession of all.[8] That freedom of thought, of association, of meeting, of speech, etc., might be less than sacred to a man with an empty stomach was a notion extraneous to their thinking. This did not mean they were blind to the need of ameliorating the lot of the poor. The matter was the source of lively discussion in the pages of the *Giornale di Modena* in the spring of 1871; Marco Minghetti, convinced that the redemption of the plebes was the supreme objective of the century, worried about the low estate of the peasants and the political implications of widely diffused poverty;[9] Francesco De Sanctis underlined the social question as the most serious problem confronting the rulers of Italy, arguing that its solution was the only means of overcoming the public indifference and apathy implicit in parties and formulas no longer corresponding to the realities of the situation.[10] These exceptions, however, only underscored the fact that the great majority of Italy's ruling class reposed their faith in paternalism and charity as the best technique of solving the social problem.[11] That their ideas and prejudices in regard to the relations between capital and labor needed

[6] The following discussion is based on the superb chapter of Chabod's previously cited work, "L'Ordine e la Libertà," pp. 325-454.

[7] See Rodolfo De Mattei, "La prima coscienza in Italia d'una 'questione sociale,'" *Storia e Politica Internazionale*, XXI, Fasc. 1 (Mar., 1943), 97-109.

[8] "With respect to [the] socio-economic problem, there frequently occurs in the moderates the juridical mentality, that does not take a broad enough view of the problem, that does not see it truly political aspect . . ." Paolo Alatri, "Ruggero Bonghi e la vita politica italiana," *Nuova Antologia*, Yr. 81, Fasc. 1750 (Oct., 1946), 172. More succinctly, G. De Ruggiero sums up this basic weakness of the Italian liberals' mentality, when, with reference to Silvio Spaventa, he writes: "only in the last years of his life was he to convince himself of the existence of a democratic problem within liberalism." *Storia del liberalismo europeo* (Bari, 1925), p. 341. All the Moderates, writes Carlo Morandi, "lacked a little the Cavourian courage to entrust themselves without reservation to liberty: the conquered treasure of national unity appeared too precious and the perils still too recent for them to have proceeded with greater ardor . . ." *I partiti politici nella storia d'Italia*, p. 32.

[9] Lilla Lipparini, *Minghetti* (Bologna, 1942), I, 11; D. Petrini, *Motivi del Risorgimento* (Rieti, 1929), p. 73.

[10] Edmondo Cione, *Francesco de Sanctis* (Messina, Milan: Principato, 1938), pp. 269-70.

[11] Mazzini's faith in the moral and cultural education of the masses as a means of enabling them to participate in the political life of the country found little echo among the Italian bourgeoisie; the few liberals who believed in popular education were unwilling to concede, because of the existing gap between proletarian and upper-class education, that the time was ripe for political collaboration with the masses. Chabod, *op. cit.*, pp. 354 ff.

serious revision, that charity, as a method of dealing with material poverty, belonged to an outmoded era—"morally inferior to ours," as Mazzini would have it[12]—these were concepts tenaciously clung to, destined to find expression throughout the next several decades.

Social conservatism, defense of the existing social order, was no less a hallmark of the constitutional Left than of the Right. The differences were only in tone, stemming mostly from the Left's eagerness to present itself as the vade mecum of the country's democratic forces. Substantially, all the parliamentary representatives of the Italian bourgeoisie agreed that property was sacred, that the middle class was the legitimate bulwark of the nation's political and social life. It was an organ of the Left, in fact, that sustained "the legitimate and merited influence of the bourgeoisie and the propertied class" in the newly created state, pointing out that in its contribution to the making of the fatherland, it did not form a class apart but actually "opened the way to complete emancipation for the worker and the rural class."[13] If the poor man worked hard, if he showed diligence, if he saved, if he demonstrated good will and capacity, he, too, could enter the ranks of the possessing classes— and not far beneath the surface lay the implication that poverty stemmed from vice, or at least from a lack of initiative and/or ability.[14] If the bourgeois class was open to the economically successful workers, the distinction between *borghesia* and *popolo* was merely semantic. It was argued that if there were two opposed classes in Italian society, they consisted of those who worked and those who agitated, those who minded their own business and the professional subversives. Actually, the social problem was not one of opposed classes, but of the relations between individuals; individually, the worker was free to improve his material status, to become bourgeois.[15]

Secondly, along with this social conservatism and the lack of understanding of the social problem that contributed to it, there was considerable bewilderment—perhaps inevitable—on the part of Italian liberal politicians as to what might be done to counteract the threatened rupture of the nexus between liberty and *patria*, their abiding article of

[12] *S.E.I.*, VII, 339.

[13] *Il Diritto*, Mar. 31, 1871.

[14] See, for examples, the spate of such preachments in the volumes of G. Martelli, Ignazio Scarabelli, Cesare Mosca, E. Strini, Leone Paladini, and C. Revel. In reviewing the Paladini volume, *Gli scioperi e la questione sociale in Italia* (Milan, 1873), *La Perseveranza* (Aug. 28, 1873) recommends it as "a little treatise in political economy for the use of the popular classes, in which the facility of the exposition is coupled with the sureness and orthodoxy of the doctrines. They are words of gold which the workers, to whom they are especially directed, should learn by heart."

[15] Chabod, *op. cit.*, pp. 347-48; see, also, *Il Diritto*, Mar. 30, 1871.

faith in the making of Italy. Socialism had emerged as an international movement, understanding liberty as the right to ignore the principle of private property in the name of the majority's well-being. In creating Italy, the liberals thought they had demonstrated, beyond all question, the indissoluble tie between *their* liberal ideas and a free, united fatherland. Yet, the masses seemed not to have noticed; many, without any urging by the socialists, even considered the unification a hoax perpetrated on the common people for the benefit of the *signori*, that unity had actually worsened the plight of the masses—and in some regions of the peninsula there was more than a grain of truth to the assertion.

National unity did not satisfy the material aspirations of Italian workers and peasants—for that matter, they probably expected no such change in their fortunes, given their unconcern with the essentially political ideals of the *Risorgimento*.[16] The cost of living climbed steadily in the post-unity years, and, so far as inadequate statistics indicate, the index of real wages in industry between 1870 and 1876 was generally downward.[17] Ever since the unification, there had been strikes and peasant disturbances, all reflecting economic distress, and in the summer of 1872, between the beginning of July and the end of August, thirty-one strikes occurred in twenty-five different localities, including a nine-day general strike in Turin and a three-day general strike in Milan that took the combined efforts of the police and troops to quell.[18]

Though the authorities concluded that the International was not the prime mover behind the strikes, there was evidence that the I.W.A. had favored them. There was concern, too, about a possible connection between the Italian strikes and contemporaneous disturbances in France. The Italian Foreign Office wanted its representative in Paris to sound out

[16] See the description of popular reaction to the completion of national unity in the novel by Riccardo Bacchelli, *Il Diavolo al Pontelungo* (3d ed.; Milan: Ceschina, 1939), pp. 258-62. For documentation, Nello Rosselli, *Saggi sul Risorgimento e altri scritti* (Turin, 1946), p. 262.

[17] Reliable statistics on real wages in industry during this period are unavailable, but there is no question that they fluctuated drastically and, by 1874, had reached a low point. The index of real wages decreased from 117 in 1870 to 96 in 1871, 84 in 1872, 91 in 1873, 82 in 1874, and then went up to 119 in 1875, 142 in 1876. A. Geisser and E. Magrini, "Contribuzione alla storia e statistica dei salari industriali in Italia nella seconda metà del sec. XIX," *La Riforma Sociale*, Yr. XI, Fasc. 10-11 (1904).

[18] Leo Valiani, "Le prime grandi agitazioni operaie a Milano e a Torino," *Movimento Operaio*, Yr. II, No. 13 (Oct.-Nov., 1950), 362-67; —, *Storia del movimento socialista*, I, 198 ff. The workers had given Italy "the first painful example of extended strikes." *Il Diritto*, Aug. 8, 1872. *Cf.*, also, *Il Gazzettino Rosa*, July 27, Aug. 1, 2, 6, 7, 8; *La Perseveranza*, Aug. 1, 2, 3, 10; *La Plebe*, Aug. 3, 7, 14, 1872; Vigo, *Storia degli ultimi trent' anni del secolo XIX*, I, 195-96.

the *Quai d'Orsay* on whether the French and Italian strikes had derived from common instructions originating with the socialist International.[19] An official of the *Pubblica Sicurezza*, in reporting on the outbreaks, concluded that they had demonstrated "anything but a subversive temper among our working classes" but cautioned that "a simple password . . . emanating from secret conventicles of obscure persons . . . can, from one moment to the next, throw thousands and thousands of deluded [people] into the piazzas." [20]

There was no disguising the fact that insurrectionism, nonetheless, was again becoming identified with social unrest and upheaval—a disturbing reminder of an aspect of the 1848 movement that Italian liberals preferred to forget. "The fact alone," writes Chabod, "that [1848] remained in the popular tradition as synonymous with disorder and anarchy, and that a '48 became a very common expression for designating great tumult, [rioting] peoples in the piazzas and the plundering of houses, sufficiently proves how profound the impression had been." [21] In the context of 1872, with the Italian national revolution completed, no patriotic objective remained to hallow disorder with social revolutionary overtones. Quite to the contrary, for the socialist International, the suspected inspiration of this latter-day plebeian unrest, was seen as a mortal enemy of not only private property, but of the sacred principle of *patria* as well. Where Pisacane's socialism had been patriotic and national, that of the international association cut across national boundaries, appealing to the classes against the nations.

This situation *sui generis* had no precedent in the experience of the men who had made the new Italy. But given their long-held conviction that patriotism and liberty were sufficiently impelling aspirations among all Italians to absorb any conceivable social longings of the multitudes, their reticence to draw any inference from the situation that might suggest measures inconsistent with their faith in classical liberal principles is understandable. National unity, guaranteed constitutional liberties, economic freedom, with these blessings, it was felt, no Italian could find fault with the new society. Of course, there would always be poverty, but every citizen also had the right to work out his own economic salvation in a liberal economy; his newly won political freedom guaranteed his immunity to extremist doctrines. The irreducible minimum of material suffering could be dealt with by private charity. Besides, as the constitutionalists of both Right and Left were fond of believing, Italy, with

---

[19] Chabod, *op. cit.*, p. 440.

[20] Valiani, "Le prime grandi agitazioni operaie a Milano e a Torino," p. 367. *L'Opinione* agreed with the police that the subversive spirit was missing. Issues of Aug. 12, 20, 1872.

[21] Chabod, *op. cit.*, p. 341.

its predominantly agricultural economy, lacked the "combustible material" for a social conflagration.[22]

More concretely, the men in government had no compelling reason to interpret economically motivated disturbances of the workers and peasants as symptoms of a social problem dangerous to the stability and security of the state. For one thing, the Italian Internationalists made no real effort to exploit the strikes of 1872 by organizing the workers for the cause of socialism. Cafiero, Malatesta, Costa, and the rest were far too involved in their feud with the London General Council to see the opportunity under their noses, a failing that Benoît Malon recalled to their chagrin several years later:

> . . . in Italy, while thousands of workers were wandering around the public squares, the chiefs were concerning themselves with discussions about the merits of *Anarchy* and about the proximity of the *Social Revolution;* instead of acting, they philosophized, instead of throwing themselves into the fray, they conspired.[23]

Secondly, the over-all picture of the new nation's economic health was reassuring. Private wealth, after severe downward fluctuations during the decade 1860-70, appreciably increased from 1871 to 1875; in the same period, average income increased by more than 7½ per cent over the average for 1866-70.[24] Besides, in terms of dissatisfaction with the status quo, the low-income segment of Italian society was only one of several lamenting the economic and financial policies of the government. If, as a modern student of that epoch insists, the men of the Right, with social roots firmly imbedded in the agrarian proprietor class of the north-central region of Italy, were "substantially blind to the demands and appetites of the bourgeois fractions most advanced in a capitalistic sense,"[25] how much less were they prepared to interpret sporadic peasant and worker disturbances, however severe, as symptomatic of a "social problem" in the modern sense?

It is true that proletarian unrest, if channeled by the International, could conceivably develop into a real challenge to the political structure of the Italian state, whereas the opposition of bourgeois financiers and industrial pressure groups was premised on its continued existence. But even eliminating from consideration the Right's foes within the ranks of

[22] The expression was Francesco Crispi's, used in a speech to the Chamber of Deputies on Jan. 25, 1875. Chorused *La Perseveranza,* two days later: "Italy gives the world an example of calm, concord, and good sense."

[23] *La Plebe,* Feb. 26, 1878.

[24] Francesco Coppola D'Anna, *Popolazione reddito e finanze pubbliche dell' Italia dal 1860 ad oggi* (Rome: Partemia, 1946), pp. 49, 57.

[25] Carocci, *op. cit.,* p. 23. See Carocci's discussion (pp. 32-46) of the opposition of Italy's high financiers and larger industrialists to the government of the Right.

those accepting the existing political system does not bring the workers and peasants into focus as a *class* threat to the status quo. The men of the Right, with their high sense of the state, judged their opponents in essentially political terms, and the use of this criterion, in the early 1870's, led them to see a far greater threat in republicans and clericals than in the embryonic socialist movement.[26] Significantly, the Right's discounting of the "red menace" was partly due to the clerical charge that socialism was not only the logical consequence of liberal doctrines but about to inherit the earth—unless, of course, all antisocialist forces mustered under the wing of Christ's Vicar.[27]

Though very clear about the threat of republicanism per se, the government could not always discern exactly where republican propaganda left off and that of the socialists began. The difficulty was inescapable, since practically all Italian socialists were ex-republicans, while many republicans were in the process of making the transition to the socialist camp. As late as the summer of 1872, many of the prominent socialists—thanks, in part, to Garibaldi's equivocal stand on the International—had still not broken with the Party of Action. Men like Celso Ceretti, Pescatori, Piccioli-Poggiali, Tito Zanardelli, and Salvatore Battaglia probably never accepted the premises that impelled Costa, Malatesta, and Cafiero to argue a dialectical incompatibility between their vision of a future society and that envisaged by a Mazzini or a Garibaldi.

In the sphere of action, as in that of propaganda, the socialist and republican currents were often intermingled, frequently causing the authorities to see the hand of the International in republican manifestations and vice versa. The purely republican disorders in Milan on July 24, 1870, and those of the following month in Genoa caused *La Perseveranza* (Milan) to remark the "strange concomitance" of a political with a social movement, of a republican effort against property.[28] Or,

[26] See, for example, *La Perseveranza*'s evaluation (Sept. 8, 1871) of the relative peril represented by the clericals and the Internationalists.

[27] See Chabod's extensive discussion of clerical reaction to the Commune and the socialist peril, *op. cit.*, pp. 403-18. The black, not the red, International was considered by far, the more potent threat to Italian liberty and unity. As Chabod points out, it was a logical conclusion, since the Italian clericals could count on strong foreign support in France, Austria-Hungary, and—with the Carlist resurgence of 1873-74—Spain, whereas the socialists, in Italy as elsewhere, lacked material support on an international level and, at the same time, consisted of an heretical minority. *Op. cit.*, p. 361. Besides, in Italy the clericals could count on mass peasant support, especially among the *sanfedisti* (ardent Catholics) of the south, while the socialists could not hope for a mass following until Italy reached a far more advanced stage of industrialization than that of the early 1870's.

[28] See the issues of July 26, 28, 31; Aug. 6, 8, 1870. For the repercussions of the disorders, *S.E.I.*, XC, 13 ff; *Il Dovere*, Aug. 4, 5, 1870.

again, when practically all but a handful of socialists lent their support to the Garibaldian congress project in the winter of 1871-72, it is not surprising that the authorities could not persuade themselves that the movement was essentially republican in inspiration and intent. Such confusion inhibited any clear appreciation of the socialist movement as a distinct challenge in itself; if anything, it tended to suggest that republicanism was acquiring further strength by identifying itself more closely with the economic aspirations of the humbler classes.

A more compelling reason for the Moderates of the government to see republicanism as the only conceivably serious danger on the Left was implicit in the circumstances surrounding the completion of national unity with the capture of Rome. Given the demonstrable fascination of French ideas and political developments for the Italians, the creation of the Third French Republic on September 4, 1870, suggested the possibility that the Italian republican movement would be spurred to greater and more effective efforts. The overthrow of Napoleon III was no cause for rejoicing by the Italian bourgeois press. The Florentine liberal daily, *La Nazione,* spoke for a huge segment of ruling-class opinion when, three days after the proclamation of the Third Republic, it insisted that Italy was now essentially a conservative nation and that, to be such, meant saving Italian unity, independence, and society from those who once more wanted to "Frenchify" Italy in the name of the republic; that now republicans must be fought in the name of national freedom, they must be opposed as traitors to *la patria.* The monarchy was equated with Italian patriotism; only the monarchy could guarantee national liberty, independence, and unity. In fact, a primary consideration motivating the government's decision to occupy Rome was precisely the fear that the republicans would take the initiative if the monarchy did not.[29] Victor Emmanuel and his ministers were under no illusions, furthermore, that conservative, monarchical Europe would tolerate a revolutionary republican solution of the Italian question, given Italy's unsavory reputation —thanks to the way in which unity had been accomplished—as a focal point of revolutionism in the European body politic.

Superficially viewed, the capture of Rome seemed to remove the republican peril: Mazzini's followers deserted his cause in increasing numbers; many of the former republican conspirators, from Francesco Crispi to Benedetto Cairoli, accepted the Sabauda monarchy; Garibaldi, for all his republican—and even socialist—pronunciamentos, was no longer a serious enemy. Mazzini's tirades against the Paris Commune, his

[29] Chabod, *op. cit.,* p. 331, note 5; 336; 568, note 3. "The monarchy of Savoy, forced to it by the rumbling revolution, took possession, *suo buono e malgrado,* of Rome." Thus Andrea Giannelli, *Cenni autobiografici,* p. 516.

implicit alliance with the forces of conservatism against the reds, did not go unnoticed by the ruling classes. Still, they could not fail to notice that it was precisely this alliance that alienated many of his followers without noticeably dampening their republican convictions and ambitions. Mazzini's personal prestige was no safe barometer of the republican potential, in any case, since the very existence of the Third French Republic and portentous republican rumblings in Carlist Spain promised to feed the republican spirit in the peninsula far more than a tired Mazzini, now giving his last energies to defending Italian youth against the inroads of corrupting materialism. Republican sentiment was plainly declining nowhere nearly as fast as the Genoese's personal influence among his once numerous band. But it was declining. And considering that socialism was rated far below republicanism as a danger to the regime, the slight degree of the Moderates' worry about the former becomes apparent.

The most revealing test of the government's attitude toward the so-called "specter of socialism" was its net reaction to the Paris Commune, viewed by Italian, as well as European, bourgeois opinion as a supreme effort of the socialist International. "There is no doubt," reported the Italian Ambassador to Paris on March 22, 1871, ". . . that the Parisian movement is the exclusive work of the *International* and that its most distinctive and even determining characteristic is social and communist and nothing else." [30] The bourgeois press of Italy fully concurred in this judgment.[31] Nor did the government see the phenomenon of class warfare in Paris as extraneous to Italian interests. In March 1871 it was informed by one of its consuls in France that a Garibaldian legion was being organized clandestinely in Paris, which, backed by the International, aspired to proclaim a republic in Italy and Spain and subsequently join the French Communards in a war of revenge against Germany. The Italian Foreign Minister, Visconti-Venosta, never an alarmist, was convinced that the strength of Communard resistance testified to "a real danger for Europe," especially for Italy, so close to the conflagration, with "numerous socialist elements within her borders." His conclusion, the true measure of his inquietude: that "in the presence of the common enemy, the Powers should . . . come to an understanding as to the means of reducing and disarming it." [32]

Significantly, Visconti-Venosti's private opinion never became public policy. However initially serious their concern, whatever their fears, the misgivings of Italy's rulers entailed no extraordinary government measures

---

[30] Chabod, *op. cit.*, p. 396.

[31] For examples: *Il Diritto*, Mar. 21, 30, May 29; *La Riforma*, Mar. 24, May 10, Aug. 24; *La Perseveranza*, Mar. 26, June 2, 7; *La Nazione*, Mar. 31, Apr. 18, May 21, 26; *L'Opinione*, Apr. 5, May 25, 26, 30, 1871.

[32] Chabod, *op. cit.*, p. 400, and note 5; p. 401.

against socialism. Like Cavour, they, too, put no faith in force as an antidote to a dangerous idea. The socialist school, Cavour had assured them, could not be fought effectively except by "opposing other principles to its principles. In the economic order, as in the political order, . . . ideas are combatted effectively only with ideas, principles with principles; material repression avails little. There is no doubt that, for a time, cannon and bayonets can repress theories and maintain material order, but if these theories are forced into the intellectual sphere, . . . sooner or later [they] . . . will gain the victory in the political and economic order." [33]

Once the Commune was liquidated, the Moderates were not far behind the parliamentary Left in proclaiming Italy beyond the reach of socialist subversion and the International. The bourgeois press unanimously opined that however much the International was to be damned, it still did not concern Italy. A Communard uprising was out of the question in Italy, declared *L'Opinione* on June 1, for the internal situation was too good to admit an effective subversion of society. *La Perseveranza* counted on the "uncorrupted" mentality of Italian workers:

> Here are lacking almost all the elements that concur to create the morbid conditions of other countries; here the threatening agglomerations of a worker population still do not exist in any city; here the corruption of customs has not yet reached that extreme limit met elsewhere; here living is cheaper and consequently needs are fewer; here the people are still not infected with that leprosy which for so long has insinuated itself among the working classes of the great European centers; here, in brief, instead of a corrupted people to be cured, we have a virginal people to be educated.[34]

Il Diritto, organ of the Left, was certain that proletarian sufferings in France and England had no parallel in Italy; not an overabundance, but a shortage of labor was Italy's problem. Fear of social war, therefore, was unfounded.[35]

In July, when Bismarck wanted the Italian government to join in a common action by the powers against the members of the I.W.A., the same Italian Foreign Minister who had thought well of the general idea in April was now convinced that in predominantly agrarian Italy there

[33] Speech of Apr. 15, 1851, in *Discorsi parlamentari,* ed. by A. Omodeo and L. Russo (Florence: La Nuova Italia, 1932 ff.), III, 268-69.

[34] Aug. 26, 1871; *cf.,* also, issue of Mar. 18, 1872.

[35] Mar. 31, 1871. The social question is to be solved by each person doing his duty and by giving a greater impulse toward individual initiative. Issue of Oct. 28, 1871. The perils deriving from the socialist International are "very distant" for Italy. Issue of Apr. 19, 1872.

were only insignificant traces of the International.[36] The only danger might arise, thought he, from a unification of the malcontents of the regime, including the Mazzinians, with the socialist nuclei, but even this was a relative peril, since the general tranquillity prevailing in Italy and diffused dynastic sentiment would frustrate any Mazzinian or socialist effort.[37]

The Minister of Interior, too, was no less convinced, on the basis of his subordinates' investigations, that the I.W.A. was having sparse success in establishing itself in Italy. As late as November 18, 1871, exactly one month after Carlo Cafiero assured Engels that "the International has possessed itself of the whole of Italy," Giovanni Lanza informed Visconti-Venosta that the socialist sect had but "a few dispersed adherents and little influence," and on May 31, 1872, he told the French Ambassador that he was perfectly informed on the activity of the socialist International in Italy, numbering no more than three to four thousand adherents. Mazzinians and socialists were at odds, and Garibaldi, aspiring to unite them, lacked the necessary organizing capacity: "He is only a name and a banner whose role has been played out in Italy." The only danger, in the Minister's view, lay in a *rapprochement* between freemasonry and the International. "The International association, especially in Italy, is . . . in a state of very rudimentary formation and is still seeking to decide on how . . . to manifest its action." [38]

The government was more than vaguely interested, of course, in the conspiratorial activity of individual agitators. Police surveillance reports on Carlo Cafiero in 1871-72 made a fat file, representing the expenditure of considerable time, energy, and money. The British government was unsuccessfully importuned to cooperate with Rome authorities in keeping track of Italian agitators arriving in London. Paris and London sent alarming reports on the comings and goings of real or presumed agents of the I.W.A.; Italian diplomats in European capitals busied themselves making inquiries of a police nature concerning the activities of those of their compatriots abroad whom the Minister of Interior, frequently unjustifiably, claimed were anything but simple tourists.[39]

Yet, during the pre-Rimini period, there was a definite lack of consistency in the way the government reacted to socialist activity. Cafiero

---

[36] Chabod, *op. cit.*, pp. 423-24. The Spanish government, in a circular of Feb. 9, 1872, also tried to promote an intergovernmental defense against the red peril, but the notion found no support in Italian parliamentary opinion. See *Il Diritto*, Feb. 26; *La Perseveranza*, Feb. 26; *L'Opinione*, Mar. 17, 1872.

[37] Chabod, *op. cit.*, p. 424.

[38] *Ibid.*, pp. 425-26, 437.

[39] *Ibid.*, pp. 426-27, 438-39, 448.

was arrested when the Neapolitan section was dissolved in August 1871, but never brought to trial. Vincenzo Pezza, arrested in late March, tried in May, and sentenced to five months in jail, was free before the end of July to conspire with Bakunin and agitate in the columns of *Il Gazzettino Rosa*. Socialist sections and newspapers proliferated during the year following the Commune; congresses were held and resolutions publicized. Arbitrary actions by the police were frequent, but more often the product of an excessive zeal on the part of prefects and local *questori* than of any pressure from Rome. The liberals running the central government had no intention of significantly abridging the right of association or political expression on the sole grounds of membership in or sympathy with the principles of the socialist International.

Basically, it was the strength of liberal ideals, however unrelated to social realities, that accounted for halfhearted repressive measures against socialists, for the token incarcerations, for the growth, not decline, of socialist newspapers, for the willingness to allow known conspirators like Cafiero, Malatesta, and Costa to unite Italian socialists at Rimini and enunciate a program calling for open war on bourgeois society. The Moderates' spirit of legality—inherent in their liberal creed—that prompted the French Ambassador to assure Paris that the Rome government would take no extraordinary measures against the Jesuits,[40] was the same spirit animating those leaders when they undertook action—more maladroit than malign—against the anarchists only when the latter adopted violence as the primary means of propagating their doctrines.

When the Italian International took up arms, the men in government, whose liberal system had permitted socialists to organize for violent ends, tried to apply the only formula consistent with their legalitarian convictions: formal prosecution of Internationalists on charges of conspiracy and attempted subversion of state security. The net result: they found themselves held guilty by public opinion of arbitrary action, illegal suppression of ideas, and sacrificing their own liberal principles. It was an ironic turn of affairs, for the charge derived, not from any arbitrary campaign of government repression, but from the incidental features, already noted, of the trial themselves and, above all, from the unpopularity the government had brought on itself for reasons unrelated to its treatment of Internationalists. In brief, interpretation of the Italian International's experience in the four years following Rimini as the product of a bourgeois government's fear-ridden reaction to the specter of socialism simplifies the telling but ignores the facts.

[40] *Ibid.*, p. 437.

THE ECLIPSE OF MARXIAN INFLUENCE

After the Rimini Congress the term "Internationalist" in Italy was synonymous with "Bakuninist"—or "anti-authoritarian collectivist," to use the anarchists' own label. Marxist penetration was practically non-existent. In early November 1872, Engels considered Enrico Bignami, editor of *La Plebe,* as the "only individual who has taken our part in Italy" but admitted that the Lodi publicist's support was something less than energetic: "he has printed my report on the Hague Congress and a letter that I wrote him." Bignami's tepid performance was excused on the ground that "he finds himself right in the middle of the 'autonomists' and must still take certain precautions." [41] Two weeks later Engels was asking Sorge, the new secretary-general of the Council (now in New York), for full powers for Italy, lest the Marxist cause be completely lost. Letters to Bignami and occasional pieces in *La Plebe* were not enough. [42]

For that matter, neither were polemical contributions, in the opinion of Bignami, who apparently wanted to give the Marxist view a fair hearing in the battle of ideas, without committing himself in the dispute. He made a distinction between personal invective and name-calling, on the one hand, and discussion of principles, on the other. Engels had sent him the anti-anarchist "Les prétendues scissions" ("The so-called schisms") early in June, but Bignami acknowledged receipt of the diatribe in a way that clearly announced he was hardly enthusiastic about its sub-

[41] Letter to Sorge, Nov. 2, 1872, Guillaume, *I.D.S.,* III, 21-22. Engels' presumption of Bignami's pro-General Council orientation is not supported by Bignami's selection of material for publication in *La Plebe.* Though the newspaper limited its coverage of the Rimini Congress to mentioning that the delegates had voted an address to Garibaldi and the purchase of a plaque for the murdered Piccinini's grave (Aug. 10), and though Bignami ran a generally sympathetic editorial (Sept. 19) on the authoritarians' Hague Congress, he also published (Sept. 4) Costa's invitation to the Italian sections to send representatives to the libertarians' St. Imier Congress. As an organizer, Bignami could not have been very active, for in his own home town of Lodi, an I.W.A. section, the "Association of Workers and Agriculturists of Lower Lombardy," did not appear until Sept. 29, 1872. Its declaration of principles favored neither the London nor the Bakuninist position, *La Plebe,* Oct. 2, 5. For Engels' acknowledgment of the new section, *ibid.,* Nov. 17; for Costa's acknowledgment, via the Imola section, *ibid.,* Oct. 16, 1872.

[42] Letter to Sorge, Nov. 16, 1872, Guillaume, *I.D.S.,* III, 22; *Correspondance Fr. Engels—K. Marx et divers, publiée par F. A. Sorge* (Paris: Costes, 1950), I, 112-13. Engels received "full powers" for Italy in Jan., 1873, *ibid.,* I, 131; *La Plebe,* May 15, 1873. *La Plebe's* support of the General Council had been limited to publishing the proceedings of the Hague Congress in the Oct. 5 issue; excerpts from an Engels letter in which he gave his version of the anarchists' reactions to the Hague deliberations (Oct. 8); an Engels letter of Nov. 11 describing freedom of assembly and association in England (Dec. 14); and another of Nov. 13, addressed to the Lodi section (issue of Nov. 17), in which also appeared an article by Engels describing Irish Internationalist agitation in favor of political prisoners and the right of assembly).

stance.[43] Bignami made the warning explicit on November 17, when he urged Engels to "speak as you please about the International but do not engage in polemics with the friends of Rimini." [44] This time, Engels took the hint, for late in October he sent Bignami an article entitled "On Authority," which, as a friendly analyst admits, examined anarchism, *for the first time*, on the plane of principle, going beyond "personal and contingent polemics." [45] Marx soon followed suit with "Indifference in Political Matters," but by the time these two essays appeared in print, it was far too late for them to have any real influence on Italian socialists.[46]

After this lone contribution to enlightening Italians on the dialectical superiority of "scientific" socialism, Engels quickly reverted to the "personal and the contingent." When Bignami was jailed for publishing a General Council circular in *La Plebe* on November 17, Engels saw the police action as proof that the Italian government considered the General Council and its supporters far more dangerous than the Bakuninists: "Nothing happier could have happened to us in Italy." [47] In early January 1873, he was reduced to thinking of the success of Marxian socialism in Italy in bargain-counter terms: a "colossal" success might be had for the sum of $30-$50. To Sorge he wrote on January 4:

> Bignami [still in jail] bombards me with letters demanding help for him and three other prisoners. . . . In America something should be done. It is *of the highest importance* that Lodi be sustained from the outside: it is our most solid post in Italy, and, now that Turin no longer gives any sign of life, the only one on which we can count. In Lodi a much more important result can be obtained, and *with less money*, than with the jewelry workers' strike in Geneva. . . . With half of what would be uselessly sacrificed for Geneva, or even less, one might obtain a colossal success in Italy. Think of the rage of the [Bakuninists] if they could read in *La Plebe: Subscription for the families, etc.: Received from the General Council of the Int*[ernational], *New York,* so many *lire,* and if the General

---

[43] Nettlau, *B.I.I.,* pp. 205, 337; Bosio, *ed.,* "Marx-Engels. Carteggio da e per l'Italia (1871-1895)," *Movimento Operaio,* Yr. II, Nos. 7-8, 9-10 (Apr.-May, June-July, 1950), 205, 267.

[44] Bosio, *ed., Marx, Engels. Scritti italiani,* p. 70, note 1.

[45] *Ibid.,* p. 71.

[46] Marx sent his article early in Jan., 1873, after repeated requests from Bignami (*ibid.,* pp. 70-71). The articles were not published until late 1873, thanks to Bignami's many troubles with the police and the courts. They appeared in his *Almanacco Repubblicano per l'anno 1874* (Lodi, Milan, 1873), pp. 88-95, for the Engels piece; pp. 141-48 for Marx's article.

[47] Letter to Sorge, Dec. 14, 1872, Guillaume, *I.D.S.,* III, 22. On Bignami's arrest and the sympathy it aroused among Italian Internationalists, *Il Gazzettino Rosa,* Nov. 26, Dec. 2, 1872, Apr. 12, 1873; *La Plebe,* Dec. 4, 1872.

Council . . . suddenly proved its existence in this manner! . . .
Certainly you should be able to get together 30 or 50 dollars;
but, little or much, send *something* and *right away*, promising,
if *possible*, still further donations. If we were to lose Lodi and
La Plebe, we should no longer have a single foothold in
Italy . . .[48]

When the Marxist plenipotentiary for Italy felt constrained to seek the
affirmation of Marxism and the existence of the General Council through
such petty and inconsequential needling of the Bakuninists, it should
have surprised no one—including Engels himself, if he had faced the
facts of the situation—that Lodi and *La Plebe* were Marxism's sole
point d'appui in the peninsula.[49]

Bignami himself was anything but a convinced Marxist. He dickered
with Marx to translate and publish *Das Kapital* in the winter of 1872-73,[50]
he accepted money from Engels to sustain him in his quarrels with the
local authorities, he continued to publish news and proclamations of the
General Council, but when *La Plebe* resumed publication on May 15,
1873, Engels decided against contributing further to its columns, no doubt
convinced that the eclecticism displayed by Bignami in his choice of
socialist writings for *La Plebe* made the newspaper an unsuitable medium
for the divulgation of Marxian texts.[51] One contemporary historian of the

---

[48] Guillaume, *I.D.S.*, III, 22.

[49] On Oct. 28, 1872, Bignami informed Engels that two newly founded sections
in Lodi and Aquila adhered to the I.W.A. and asked that their affiliation be communicated to the General Council (Bosio, *ed.*, *Marx, Engels. Scritti italiani*, p. 70).
The public prosecutor at the 1875 Florentine trial of Internationalists claimed that
the "dissident" section of Aquila and that of Lodi were represented at the
"authoritarian" (*i.e.*, Marxist) Congress of Geneva, Sept. 8-12, 1873 (Bottero,
Dibattimenti, p. 315). In fact, Lodi was not represented at the 1873 authoritarian
congress. Engels tried to insure the support of Bignami, but the latter, "informed
[of the lack of support for the congress], preferred to abstain" (Guillaume, *I.D.S.*,
III, 134)—a statement confirmed by Marx's letter of Sept. 27, 1873, to Sorge: "The
Portuguese, Spanish, and Italians had announced they could not be represented"
(*ibid.*, III, 136). As for the Aquila section, it was represented at Geneva in 1873,
but at the libertarian, not the authoritarian, congress.

[50] For details, *Karl Marx. Kronik seines Lebens in einzeldaten vom Marx-Engels-
Lenin Institut* (Moscow, 1934), Bignami to Marx, 10/X, 28/X, 1872; Marx to
Danielson, Sept. 16, 1872, in Bosio, *ed.*, *Marx, Engels. Scritti italiani*, p. 70; Bosio,
ed., "Marx-Engels. Carteggio da e per l'Italia," p. 270.

[51] General Council matters are touched on in the May 26, June 1, Aug. 11, Oct.
11, 1873, issues of *La Plebe*. *Cf.*, also, for further relations with Marx and Engels, the
issues of Sept. 20, 1873, Apr. 19, 1874. In Sept., 1874, Engels pronounced the
obsequies of the Marxist International in Italy: "The old International had died and
at a good point, . . . [for] the Italians declare that since public organization was
harmful, . . . they now prefer to conspire." *Correspondance Fr. Engels—K. Marx
et divers . . .* , I, 205. Engels did not resume collaboration with *La Plebe* until
early 1877. *Cf.*, his letter of Feb. 23, 1877, to Marx, *Briefwechsel*, IV, 447-48.

Italian socialist movement interprets Bignami's entertainment of Engels' anti-anarchist pieces in La Plebe as merely the fruit of "an intelligent curiosity for the great and new movements of European culture," and doubts that the Lodi publicist had assimilated the ideas expressed by his London collaborators.[52]

Nor were Bignami's contributors to La Plebe an influence toward an understanding or acceptance of the doctrines exported from London. Benoît Malon, the French Communard exile who exercised a notably moderating influence on Italian socialism during the next two decades,[53] had already concluded that both Marxists and anarchists were too sectarian in spirit, too committed to pushing their own narrow interpretations of the I.W.A.'s basic principles, to give practical effect to the dictum that "the workers must accomplish their own emancipation." Though Malon vigorously criticized the anarchists and their insurrectionism, the reformist socialism he preached—"integral socialism," as he characterized it in later years—could never be squared with Marx's stress on the necessity of proletarian political action.[54]

Osvaldo Gnocchi-Viani, Bignami's other leading collaborator, also had little sympathy for Bakuninism, but his unlimited faith in the efficacy of proletarian action on a purely economic plane, in trade-unionist solidarity and resistance as the primary means of struggle, put him as far from the Marxist position as Malon.[55] His consuming interest during the period of anarchist fever in Italy was not opposing Marxist doctrine to the influence of Bakunin, but in advancing the cause of the Universal League of Workers' Corporations, founded in Geneva in November 1873 as a kind of "Third International" to supplant both the anarchist and "authoritarian" movements. Its program was almost purely syndicalist, especially in its rejection of Marx's contention that the first duty of the working class is the conquest of political power.[56] On this central point, Gnocchi-Viani

[52] Romano, Storia, III, 131.

[53] In the pages of Il Povero (Palermo), a newspaper he helped Salvatore Ingegneros Napoletano found in 1874, as well as in La Plebe. In 1875 Bignami also published, as a supplement to La Plebe, Malon's Il socialismo, suo passato, suo presente, suo avvenire (Lodi, Milan, Rome, 1875), 118 pp.

[54] See his Le socialisme intégral (Paris, 1890-92), 2 vols. As for Marx's anti-Bakuninist pamphlet of 1873, "The Alliance of Socialist Democracy," Malon termed it "defamatory and even calumnious." "L'Internationale," La Nouvelle Revue, XXVI (Jan.-Feb., 1884), 758.

[55] An example: his article in La Plebe (Sept. 27, 1873).

[56] The Manifesto Program appeared in L'Union des Travailleurs (Geneva) on Nov. 15, 1873. The group accepted the I.W.A.'s cardinal principle that economic emancipation must be won by the workers themselves and, from this, drew the conclusion that political action was largely irrelevant. See Osvaldo Gnocchi-Viani, Le Tre Internazionali (Lodi, Milan, Rome, 1875), pp. 21-24. In commenting on the League's program, Gnocchi-Viani clearly rejects Marx's categorical imperative of the

was clearly as "deviationist" as the anarchists, though for quite different reasons. As late as November 1875 he was to write: "When and where I can, I definitely eliminate Politics, and when I can not eliminate it, I not only subordinate it to the Economic Question, but, since I contemplate it from a certain scientific point of view, it happens that I always see it either in a sinister or at least a dubious light. . . ."[57]

In Rome, where Gnocchi-Viani exercised his greatest practical influence in the local I.W.A. section, his trade-unionist preferences were reflected in the fact that until the section was wrecked by the arrest of Gnocchi-Viani and his fellow organizers on May 15, 1873, the group concerned itself almost exclusively with problems of economic resistance and syndical organization.[58] Still, the section was formally affiliated with the anarchist Italian Federation and maintained fairly frequent contacts with the correspondence commission before the summer of 1873.[59] On the other hand, there is no trace of ties with Engels and/or the General Council after Gnocchi-Viani formally notified Engels on August 18, 1872, of the section's creation. In the summer of 1873, the leadership of the organization passed in the hands of a group of anarchist immigrants from the Romagna and the Marches—all disciples of "social liquidation," not trade-unionism.[60]

In Florence, the same process of ideological clarification, in a sense unfavorable to the General Council, occurred within the local Internationalist nucleus.[61] The Rimini decisions of August 1872 proved catalytic, for it was around them and the question of breaking with the General Council that heated discussions revolved during the ensuing weeks. Luigi Stefanoni resigned from the *Fascio Operaio* in late August, not because he had softened his hostility toward the Marxists he had condemned in

---

class political organization of the proletariat. The Marxists "not only inculcate a special political action, but they do so in an *authoritarian* fashion; . . . they make of it in an international axiom, . . . obligatory, dogmatic, for the proletariat of the whole world." *Ibid.*, pp. 27-28.

[57] *La Plebe*, Nov. 21-22, 1875.

[58] Della Peruta, "L'Internazionale a Roma del 1872 al 1877," pp. 17-23. It was precisely this primary interest in organizing workers, as workers, that led Gnocchi-Viani and some of his Roman Internationalist collaborators, on Mar. 26, 1873, to appeal to the Mazzinian workers' societies for support of a projected Internationalist newspaper in Rome, an appeal thinly disguising their hope of penetrating the Mazzinian associations. Anzi, "Dal mazzinianismo al socialismo (Gnocchi-Viani)," p. 126.

[59] For examples, Della Peruta, "Nuovi documenti sull'Internazionale a Roma," *Movimento Operaio*, Yr. I, No. 2 (Nov. 1, 1949), 38-40; –, "L'Internazionale a Roma dal 1872 al 1877," pp. 40 ff.; Romano, *Storia*, III, 409-10, 413, 419.

[60] Della Peruta, "L'Internazionale a Roma dal 1872 al 1877," p. 24.

[61] For details on socialist developments in Florence from the Rimini Congress to late 1873, see Conti, *O.S.F.*, pp. 141-59; Pezzi, *Un errore guidiziario*, p. 46—from which the present summary is drawn.

the spring, but because he had no taste for the insurrectional implications of the now dominant brand of Italian socialism. Antonio Martinati also resigned and briefly entertained the notion of founding a new section, loyal to the General Council, but it was Angelo Dalmasso, close friend of the unsavory Terzaghi, who gave practical effect to Martinati's project early in November. After Dalmasso left Florence for Turin, however, the pro-General Council section soon lost its ardor for supporting a lost cause.[62]

The *Fascio Operaio* itself was dissolved by the police on December 1, 1872, but—true to time-sanctioned practice—it was reconstituted three days later as the Florentine Workers' Federation,[63] an organization notably successful in 1873 in organizing and propagandizing the workers of Florence and its neighboring *paesi*. No trace of a connection with the Marxist faction is to be found, but in February 1873 the governing council of the Federation sent a declaration of solidarity to the anarchist Jura Federation, approving its conduct vis-à-vis the New York General Council. By midsummer, the most influential figures in the Tuscan association were activists of the anarchist Italian Federation, Lorenzo Piccioli-Poggiali, Gaetano Grassi, and Francesco Natta. The only conceivable threat to their supremacy, the influence of moderates of the Stefanoni-Martinati persuasion, was about overcome.[64] So far as the local *questore* could determine, the Florentine anarchists had nothing to fear from Martinati, for "he has lost all influence among the Internationalists, as among the republicans . . ."[65] The Florentine socialist movement was securely tied to the anarchist cause.

Probably the most telling evidence that the Marxists, in the post-Rimini period, had lost their foothold in Italy is the fact that they were reduced, by the end of 1873, to speculating on the possibility of making an ally of none other than Carlo Terzaghi, notwithstanding that Marx

---

[62] Conti (*O.S.F.*, p. 148, note 5) assumes, on the basis of a May 12 *questore* report, that Dalmasso left Florence for Turin early in 1873. Actually, he removed to Turin either in the second half of April or early May, 1873, for he is indicated as the Florentine correspondent of Terzaghi's new journal, *La Discussione*, in a notice published by Terzaghi on Apr. 10, 1873. Until he left Florence, Dalmasso was constantly at war, apparently, with the leaders of the *Fascio Operaio* and the anarchist organization that took its place. See Terzaghi's article in the July 16, 1873, issue of *La Discussione*. A so-called "independent" section was re-created in Florence in June, 1873, and its leaders (Giuseppe Mazzini, Alfredo Mari, Fortunato Serantoni, Leopoldo Innocenti, and Giovanni Mazzini) insisted that Terzaghi and Dalmasso were "two of the best champions of true socialism." *Ibid.*, June 15, 21, 1873.

[63] Pezzi, *Un errore giudiziario*, p. 47. The *questore* described it as the "Tuscan Workers' Federation." Conti, *O.S.F.*, p. 141, and note 6.

[64] See Piccioli-Poggiali's report to Costa on the Tuscan section. Romano, *Storia*, III, 421-23.

[65] Report of June 20, 1873, Conti, *O.S.F.*, p. 152.

himself had made some serious charges against the Turinese in his "Alliance of Socialist Democracy," that in mid-March 1873, the anarchists, at their Bologna Congress, expelled him as a police agent after hearing a well-documented indictment presented by Andrea Costa.[66] Even the charitable—if not gullible—Garibaldi, long flattered by Terzaghi, had complimented Celso Ceretti on his condemnation of Terzaghi as an *agent-provocateur* in police employ.[67] In his newly founded newspaper, *La Discussione*, Terzaghi announced in September, 1873, that he had moved "bag and baggage" into the Marxist camp. Only a few weeks later, John Becker, now a Marxist luminary, urged the secretary-general of the I.W.A. to get in touch with Terzaghi without delay, "for I have reason to believe that something can be done in Italy with this fellow." [68]

THE CONSOLIDATION OF BAKUNINISM

With respect to propaganda and organizational activity in Italy, practically all the energy expended in the name of socialism was that of the anarchists. It was their efforts, not those of the few lukewarm supporters of the General Council, that had the government worried, Engels' wishful thinking to the contrary. In the months following the St. Imier Congress, the key organizer and propagandist of the anarchist International in Italy was Andrea Costa.[69] Fanelli, Malatesta, Cafiero, Nabruzzi, and Pezza left Switzerland for Italy after the St. Imier meeting, but Costa remained behind, planning the transformation of the Italian sections into a revolutionary *Apparat* and elaborating, with Bakunin, a thoroughgoing anarchist program as a guide for revolutionary action.[70] "Since we have full confidence in the instincts of the popular multitudes," the document stated, "our revolutionary method consists of unleashing what are called the *brutal passions* and the destruction of what, in the same bourgeois language, is called *public order*." [71] By early October, Bakunin and Costa had put together the first issue of *La Rivoluzione Sociale*, a newspaper

[66] See below, pp. 315-16.
[67] Robert Michels, *Il proletariato e la borghesia nel movimento socialista italiano*, pp. 41-43.
[68] Guillaume, *I.D.S.*, III, 138.
[69] ". . . indefatigable in organizing local and regional sections and federations, in deciding indifferent workers' societies to adhere to [I.W.A.] principles, in eliminating doubts and difficulties, in moving the uncertain, in exciting the timid, in combatting the resisters and riotous with every art, [Costa's correspondence] . . . reveals his prodigious activity, the predominant influence he exercised, and how, in a short time, he succeeded in giving the Federation an organization and a vigorous and promising order."—thus the public prosecutor at the Florence trial of 1875. Bottero, *Dibattimenti*, p. 319.
[70] Guillaume, *I.D.S.*, III, 43.
[71] For the *Programma oggetto della Federazione italiana*, Bottero, *Dibattimenti*, pp. 334-35. The line quoted above also appears in the program of the *Fratellanza Socialista Rivoluzionaria*, which, in 1875, claimed to "have been, as it had to be, the true center, the soul and the invisible guide of the revolutionary organization of

intended for clandestine distribution in Italy. The warning that violence was to be the fruit of Italian socialist unification again appeared: "Today, propaganda no longer suffices, now we need to organize ourselves for the struggle." [72] And when the Italian sections were asked to support a republican mass meeting in favor of universal suffrage, to be held in the Roman Colosseum in November 1872, it was Costa who spoke for the Italian Federation, as well as his home-town section of Imola, when he signed a rebuff stating that the anarchist policy was "negative," and that "the emancipation of the workers can be obtained only through the spontaneous federation of the workers' forces, freely constituted, and not by means of a government or a constitution hierarchically organized [dall'alto al basso]." [73]

From his retreat in Locarno, Bakunin spurred his Italian disciples to prepare for the day of social redemption, which, to judge from his diary entries of the period, was to coincide with the outbreak of several simultaneous uprisings in western Europe. The Swiss, Spanish, Belgian, and Italian anarchists, his most convinced followers, received lengthy collective letters from the Russian in November. [74] Cafiero conferred with Bakunin for a week early in November; Fanelli called again on November 25-27; from December 25-28, Cafiero, Fanelli, and Carmelo Palladino (the latter's first personal contact with the Russian), "approved a decision of a very secret character," which Bakunin's biographer concludes was a project for Cafiero to buy a large Swiss residence near the Italian border to serve as a conspiratorial headquarters for the Italian anarchists and as a rent-free home for the chronically penurious Bakunin, who would appear as the nominal owner of the property and provide a front of bourgeois respectability vis-à-vis the Swiss authorities. For the first time, two other Italian socialists' names appear in Bakunin's diary entry of the 30th: Chiarini and Orsone, "Romagnols of Faenza," with whom Bakunin had "fraternization." [75]

---

the workers in Italy." The document was found by Professor Della Peruta—to whom I am indebted for calling it to my attention—in the documentation presented against Malatesta and Francesco Saverio Merlino by a Roman prosecutor in 1884 (*Archivio di Stato di Roma*, Processo n. 29969, foglio 97, n. 135). The appearance of this passage in the program of the "Revolutionary Socialist Brotherhood" suggests that the revival of Bakunin's secret Alliance of Socialist Democracy—at least for Italy—was the intimate purpose of Bakunin and Costa's planning after the St. Imier Congress. Apparently, however, the project was not brought to fruition until late in 1873—see below, pp. 330-31.

[72] Romano, *Storia*, III, 370.
[73] Guillaume, *I.D.S.*, III, 43-44.
[74] Nettlau, *Errico Malatesta*, p. 105.
[75] Guillaume, *I.D.S.*, III, 54, 96-97; Nettlau, *Malatesta*, p. 105. Francesco Orsone was one of the co-signers, with Costa and Nabruzzi, of the Bologna *Fascio Operaio*'s circular convoking the Rimini Congress of Aug., 1872. *Il Libero Pensiero*, July 11, 1872.

On January 8 the anarchists lost one of their most vigorous propagandists when Vincenzo Pezza died of consumption in Naples. The authorities refused burial in the local Catholic cemetery, but, under pressure from Pezza's friends, agreed to allow interment in a peripheral area reserved for stillborn infants, justifying the decision, it was said, on the grounds that "he who has no religion is like one who has never lived." [76]

As decided at Rimini, the Italian Federation's correspondence commission, early in January, 1873, convoked a second national congress in Mirandola "to affirm once more truth, justice, and revolutionary morality, to tighten even more the bonds of solidarity with the sister [foreign] federations, . . . to propose . . . the spontaneous union of the workers' forces in anarchy and collectivism." [77] Since the congress was to convene on March 15, the police had more than enough time to make their own arrangements to forestall any such gathering of subversives. The Mirandola section was dissolved on March 12, as it was completing final arrangements. Celso Ceretti, member of the statistical commission, was hauled off to the police station, along with the revealing documents he had compiled concerning the Italian Federation. Most of the delegates to the projected congress were diverted in time from Mirandola by the members of the correspondence commission, so on the scheduled opening day, 53 delegates, representing about 150 sections, met in Bologna. [78] On the night of the 16th, the second day of the scheduled three-day meeting, the Bologna police broke in and arrested Cafiero, Costa, Malatesta, and several others. Again the conferees moved their meeting to another locale and continued their deliberations. The Bologna, San Giovanni in Persiceto, Modena, Parma, and Imola sections were immediately dissolved by the police, and the arrested members imprisoned for several weeks. From the Ministry of Interior all provincial authorities received an order to extirpate the Italian Federation at the roots. [79]

From this point on, Giuseppe Fanelli dropped out of the picture as an active Internationalist, due, according to his biographer, to his disapproval of insurrectional ideas. He finally lost his parliamentary seat in the fall of 1874, gradually lost his sanity, and died in a rest home for the mentally ill at Capodichino, near Naples, on Jan. 5, 1877, while a member of the Neapolitan City Council. Lucarelli, *Fanelli*, pp. 150, 155-56, note 2. For an appreciation, Jura *Bulletin*, Jan. 21, 1877.

[76] Jura *Bulletin*, Feb. 1, 1873; Guillaume, *I.D.S.*, III, 55. For a socialist appreciation of Pezza's contribution to the movement, *La Plebe*, Jan. 22, Feb. 27, 1873.

[77] *La Plebe*, Jan. 13, 19; *La Favilla*, Jan. 15, 1873; Bottero, *Dibattimenti*, p. 313.

[78] Bottero, *Dibattimenti*, p. 314; Jura *Bulletin*, Apr. 1, 1873.

[79] For the Congress of Bologna and the police measures, *La Plebe*, Mar. 23, 1873; Angiolini, *Cinquant'anni di socialismo in Italia*, pp. 99-103; Romano, *Storia*, III, 117-20; Manacorda, *Il movimento operaio italiano*, pp. 89-93; Costa, *Bagliori di socialismo*, p. 20; Nettlau, *Malatesta*, p. 100; Bottero, *Dibattimenti*, pp. 248-52, 314-15. So far as the present writer can determine, the Bologna arrests provided the single occasion, during the Right's tenure in power, when the charge of membership in an

Government repression had little dampening effect on the Bologna delegates. They declared:

> It is logical that the State persecutes us, . . . the consciousness of its imminent disappearance causes it to see an enemy in every worker. . . . we are not disturbed by this recrudescence of persecution, and we calmly wait for the work of the bourgeoisie to hasten our turn. . . . The arrogance of which our [arrested] comrades are victims shows once more how legitimate is the struggle for social emancipation; [the congress] sends a fraternal salute to the imprisoned friends but does not lament for them, since they are undergoing the consequences of their convictions, consequences that none of the members of the Congress fear to affront.[80]

The Rimini and St. Imier congresses of the preceding summer had slammed the door in the face of Marx and his friends, but the Bologna conferees locked it securely. The perennial charges of authoritarianism against the General Council were renewed, the Rimini and St. Imier resolutions reconfirmed, and the formal excommunication pronounced by the Hague Congress of September, 1872, declared invalid, so far as the Italian Federation was concerned. In harmony with their oft-repeated principle of sectional autonomy and their insistence that general congress decisions not bind member sections and federations, the Bologna meeting submitted its resolutions to the approval of all member sections of the peninsula. In defining their anarchist principles, the delegates called themselves atheist, materialist, antistatist, federalist, collectivist, and antipolitical. No political action has merit, "other than that which . . . directly conduces to the actuation of [anarchist] principles." It followed that "any cooperation or complicity with the political intrigues of the bourgeoisie, even though called democratic and revolutionary," is to be rejected.[81]

Bakunin's recurrent theme of enlisting the aid of the peasants was repeated in Resolution IX, which insisted that proletarian emancipation is impossible without "the complete fraternization" of city and country workers. The peasants should be propagandized by their city cousins, since "fourteen million peasants in Lombardy and the southern provinces are in agony because of fever and hunger and anxiously wait the hour of emancipation."

Finally, in a secret session, the Congress heard the charges against

---

"association of malefactors" was used, a charge thrown out by the court when it rendered a decision of *non farsi luogo a procedere*. See, Giuseppe Ceneri, *Opere* (Bologna, 1891), I, 161.

[80] Angiolini, *op. cit.*, pp. 99-100, 103.

[81] *Ibid.*, pp. 100-02; Bottero, *Dibattimenti*, pp. 314-15; Guillaume, *I.D.S.*, III, 66.

Terzaghi and decreed his expulsion from the Italian International and the post he had held since Rimini on the statistical commission, a vantage point unequalled for purposes of keeping the police informed on the spread of Internationalism in the peninsula. He managed to organize a small group of dissident socialists in Turin during the following months, but the Bologna Congress truncated his effective interference in the development of Italian socialism.[82]

In addition to confirming the Italian socialists in their anarchist orientation, the Bologna Congress, by engendering government reprisals, focused popular attention on the Italian Federation as an outlet for dissatisfaction with a deteriorating economic situation. Released from jail, Bakunin's corps of agitators gave their all to maintaining that focus. Cafiero, though not contributing directly to this effort, spent most of the summer in Barletta, fighting for his share of the legacy left by his wealthy father, recently deceased. The money, of course, he intended to put at the disposal of the social revolution. When the Spanish insurrection broke out on July 9, Bakunin, anxious to show himself on the barricades, sent Malatesta to Barletta to ask Cafiero for traveling expenses, but the local police picked up the Russian's emissary the day after his arrival and started him on a six-months' jail term.[83]

Cafiero, advised of Bakunin's intentions, wrote the Russian immediately, begging him—according to Bakunin's account—not to risk his "precious person" in the Spanish enterprise. In August, when Cafiero finally arrived back in Locarno with money in hand, the Spanish affair no longer looked promising, but by this time Bakunin had another use for the Pugliese's wealth: he had contracted for the purchase of a dilapidated villa called the Baronata, situated on a rocky hillside at the northern tip of Lake Verbano, just inside the Swiss border. Cafiero's dream of a revolutionary nerve center and hideout for Italian anarchists had at last become a reality. As agreed by Cafiero, Bakunin moved in as the nominal proprietor, to give the appearance of "a tired and disgusted revolutionary who, . . . after having lost his illusions, throws himself with passion into the material interests of property and family." The threadbare Russian agitator was to play the role with a vengeance. For his part, Cafiero made an initial payment of 14,000 francs on the property—only the first of many expenditures to establish headquarters for the social revolution.[84]

Once out of jail, Andrea Costa resumed a feverish correspondence with

---

[82] In announcing the imminent publication of his new organ, *La Discussione*, on Apr. 10, 1873, Terzaghi wrote that he would welcome the collaboration of all socialists, provided they did not "idolize the so-called great ones." Romano, *Storia*, III, 414-15.

[83] The charge: conspiracy against the state. Jura *Bulletin*, Dec. 7, 1873.

[84] Guillaume, *I.D.S.*, III, 96-102; Zoccoli, *L'Anarchia*, pp. 128-32.

sections all over the peninsula, advising, scolding, and urging the spread of anarchist principles and the organization of new sections.[85] The revolutionary appeal to the Italian peasants and the history of police persecution of the International that appeared in the *Bollettino della Federazione Italiana* (May 1873) may well have come from Costa's prolific pen.[86] On July 4 he wrote the Jura anarchists:

> The Italian Federation, it is true, does not have the formidable organization of the Spanish Federation; but our principles are extremely diffused among the people and the revolutionary instincts of the Italian proletarians are better. . . . Our people are more mature than is thought, and secular servitude has not enervated revolutionary instincts among the manual workers, particularly in the small localities and . . . in the countryside.[87]

On the organizational level, regional propaganda commissions were established throughout the country, spurring new sections into being, grouping them into local and regional federations. On June 26 the Italian correspondence commission notified the Swiss anarchists of twenty new sections and a new socialist newspaper, *Il Risveglio* of Siena.[88] On July 26 at San Pietro in Vincoli, the Romagnol Federation was formed; on August 10, in a congress at Pietra la Croce, the Marchigian-Umbrian Federation was launched.[89] Costa was on hand for both occasions.[90] A few days after he advised the Florentine socialists to take a similar initiative, the local Section of Socialist Propaganda issued a circular convoking a congress to unite all Tuscan sections into a regional federation.[91] When the anarchist international congress convened in a Geneva beer

---

[85] See the correspondence covering the period May-Aug., 1873, in Romano, *Storia*, III, 418-59. Costa was released on May 9, 1873. See the letter of A. Dondi, of the Roman I.W.A. section, to Tito Zanardelli, May 16, 1873. Della Peruta, "L'Internazionale a Roma dal 1872 al 1877," p. 44.

[86] Guillaume, *I.D.S.*, III, 96.

[87] Jura *Bulletin*, July 13, 1873. For a propaganda piece aimed at the Sicilian peasants, see Costa's "Il lamento del povero," *Il Povero* (Palermo), Aug. 31, 1873.

[88] Guillaume, *I.D.S.*, III, 96. Among the new sections: Aquila and Perugia, *Il Risveglio*, July 6, 1873.

[89] Guillaume, *I.D.S.*, III, 96; Jura *Bulletin*, July 27, Aug. 31; *Il Risveglio*, Aug. 24, 1873. The Marchigian-Umbrian Federation was promoted by the Ancona section (*ibid.*, July 6); the Romagnol-Emilian Federation by the Italian Federation's propaganda commission elected at the Mirandola-Bologna Congress of mid-March—see the commission's circular of Mar. 30 in Romano, *Storia*, III, 412-13. The final decision was made in late June, and the Romagnols urged other regions to follow suit. *La Plebe*, June 29, 1873.

[90] Lipparini, "Cronologia della vita di Andrea Costa," p. 185.

[91] Circular of Sept. 20, 1873, *Il Risveglio*, Sept. 28, 1873. The federative movement seems to have been touched off by the Italian correspondence commission's announcement, in mid-July, of the international anarchist congress, scheduled for September. *La Perseveranza*, July 17, 1873.

hall on September 1, 1873, Costa, Cesare Bert, Victor Cyrille, and Francesco Mattei represented Italy. England, France, Belgium, Holland, the Swiss Jura, and Spain had a total of nineteen delegates on hand—a formidable showing, in terms of geographical coverage, that contrasted sharply with the poorly attended and unrepresentative Marxist congress held in the same city a few days later—a "fiasco," as Marx admitted.[92] Calling their meeting the "Sixth General Congress of the International," the anarchists revised the general statutes of the I.W.A. by giving the sections and federations full autonomy, abolished the General Council and denied general congresses the right to legislate in matters of principle.

In reporting on the development of the Italian International, Costa said it owed its existence to Mazzini's anti-Communard campaign. Despite the elimination of the Marxist opposition, enemies were still plentiful: the government, priests, "intransigents" (moderate socialists), Mazzinians ("believers in the emancipation of the workers by means of the social republic"), and Garibaldians (partisans of equivocation who "tend to substitute the prestige of one man for the strength of the Association," promoters of military dictatorship). The progress of the Italian International depended on acting revolutionarily; Italian workers wanted struggle, not theories.[93]

With experience, Costa was to alter radically his faith in violence and insurrectionism, but for the rest of his life he was to support—often under

[92] Letter to Sorge, Nov. 27, 1873, Guillaume, *I.D.S.*, III, 136. For the circular convoking the anarchist Geneva Congress, Romano, *Storia*, III, 443. For the proceedings of this congress, Association Internationale des Travailleurs, *Compte-rendu officiel du Sixième Congrès Général de l'Association Internationale des Travailleurs, tenu à Génève du 1er au 6 septembre 1873* (Locle, 1874), 119 pp.; Jura *Bulletin*, Sept. 7, 14, 1873; *La Perseveranza*, Sept. 11, 12, 13, 14, 1873; Guillaume, *I.D.S.*, III, 108-34. For Costa's report on the congress, see the articles by "Italo" in *Il Risveglio*, Sept. 7, 21, 1873. The ubiquitous Terzaghi put in an appearance, claiming to hold mandates from "intransigent" sections in Turin and Treia and a butchers' mutual aid society in Catania, but the congress showed him the door. For his report on the congress, *La Discussione*, Sept. 11, 1873.

[93] *Compte-rendu officiel* . . . , p. 32. *La Perseveranza*'s Genevan correspondent gave a curiously contrary rendition of Costa's speech: "Costa said that . . . the Garibaldians 'gave a good account of themselves at the time of the national revolution, but for a social revolution they are entirely inept. They know nothing of theory or science; they only know how to fight! fight! fight!' Costa concluded that the propaganda of the socialist movement needs men of theory and discussion, not soldiers. There is a bitter struggle to be sustained against the revolutionary 'soldiers' of the school" (Issue of Sept. 11, 1873). On the basis of this version, plus Costa's opposition to the general strike and to making the I.W.A. a purely workingmen's association, *La Perseveranza* ran a lead editorial (Sept. 14) congratulating "this unknown young man who has been seized by a madness, but *all'italiana;* that is, by tempering it with the larger doses of good sense that can make wisdom out of madness."

heavy pressure—the view he expressed when the delegates asked themselves whether a distinction should be made, for purposes of admission to the International, between manual workers and "workers of the mind," i.e., bourgeois intellectuals sympathetic to the cause of the social revolution:

> . . . I believe that one would restrain enormously the forces of revolution by eliminating what are called the workers of thought. When one wishes to make revolution, no force must be rejected. And I would add that if you refuse to accept all revolutionary forces, you risk seeing turn against you, at a certain moment, the forces that you have repelled. . . .
>
> The goal of the International is the abolition of classes and the establishment of human fraternity. Would it be consistent with our goal to consecrate in the very bosom of our association this distinction between classes that we wish to abolish? How can the bourgeois be expected to learn to sympathize with the workers and to share their aspirations, if the workers reject them? For me, there are only two categories of men, those who want the revolution and those who do not; [and] there are some bourgeois who want the revolution much more energetically and seriously than certain workers.[94]

Costa's premise that the bourgeois could be taught "to sympathize with the workers and to share their aspirations" might have been a page taken from Mazzini. But where Mazzini had suggested that the teachers "express [their] needs and ideas . . . without anger, without aggressiveness, without threatening," [95] we find Costa speaking of "the immediate struggle" and "the spontaneous uprising of the popular multitudes, revolting to overthrow all bourgeois institutions." The idea was echoed in Costa's report on the Geneva Congress, directed to his Italian comrades: "While our adversaries of all shades believe themselves more secure than ever in their positions of privilege, the Italian proletariat musters its forces, closes its ranks and awaits the first occasion to be able to show the bourgeoisie that it knows how to do something." [96]

In the winter of 1873-74, Costa and his fellow Italian anarchists were completely wedded to the notion of the inevitability of imminent social revolution, regardless of the illogicality of coupling Costa's essentially

---

[94] *Compte-rendu officiel* . . . , pp. 73, 100. Almost three decades later, Costa, in reviewing the history of the Italian International (*Bagliori di socialismo*, pp. 9-10), insisted that it was never considered a purely workers' association, but one intended for "the emancipation of man, to whatever class he belonged." Thus, too, wrote Errico Malatesta in 1928. See his preface to Nettlau, *B.I.I.*, xxv-xxvi.

[95] *S.E.I.*, LXIX, 22.

[96] Jura *Bulletin*, Dec. 7, 1873.

anticlassista orientation with the preaching of class warfare. The contradiction on a theoretical plane, however, mirrored a certain incapacity to square thought and action, to realize that effective revolutionary action depends, in a large measure, on a certain indispensable minimum of consistency in revolutionary theory. Costa and his friends denied the need of any theory at all: "the Italian workers are not greatly concerned with theories, . . . they desire struggle." And if the anarchists excluded proletarian political action as a compromise with the principle of authority, embodied in the state, they spurned, with equal vigor, trade-unionism as a method of struggle. To Costa, the Italian proletariat's lack of economic organization, far from being a disadvantage, was actually a virtue from the social revolutionary point of view. On this score, Costa revealed the full measure of the anarchist *mystique*, the essential romanticism of the faith in the revolutionary spontaneity of the economically oppressed. In Italy, he wrote in November 1873:

> . . . we do not have . . . great industrial centers, where life in common is a necessity, where association is the indispensable condition of labor. In Italy, except in some localities, each one works in his own home and on his own account; . . . there exist among [the workers] no relations except physical proximity, community of interests, the desire to be emancipated, revolutionary passion. In such a state of affairs, economic organization is very difficult; but the revolutionaries lose nothing by it; on the contrary, in this economic isolation of the worker, needs make themselves felt all the more, for him the realization of our ideas is an imperious necessity, which we will be forced to obey. For the Italian proletarian, solidarity consists precisely in this sharing of woes, hopes, defeats, victories, in harmony and in the spontaneous uprising of all the living forces of social revolution, and not in a more or less mechanical assembling of all the forces of production.[97]

On this set of assumptions was based the anarchist attempt at "social liquidation" in the summer of 1874.

[97] Guillaume, *I.D.S.*, III, 159.

XIV

The Propaganda of Deeds: I.
The Insurrectional Attempt of 1874
(October 1873 to June 1876)

ANARCHIST RESOURCES, INTERNAL
AND EXTERNAL

In the summer of 1874 the Italian anarchists tried to translate their articles of faith, their conviction that hungry and oppressed workers would obey the "imperious necessity" of revolting against their exploiters, into an armed insurrection. Against the repressive power of the bourgeois state, they pitted a few hundred rifles and an intense belief in the justice of their cause. In part, it was an action for the sake of action, but it was also an act of generosity intended to open the path to terrestrial felicity for Italian workers. They honestly thought they could succeed in their enterprise.

The optimism of Costa, Cafiero, Malatesta, and their brothers in the faith, was founded on more than their own subjective belief in the spontaneous revolutionism of the proletariat. In addition to an attractive animating idea (social justice), there was the conviction that two other elements essential to their purpose were present in the situation of 1874. The numerical and organizational strength of the Italian International now seemed to promise sufficient battalions for breaching the ramparts of bourgeois society. Secondly, proletarian economic unrest had reached the point where Costa and his friends, given their assumptions, concluded that the plebes, incited by an anarchist initiative, would express their solidarity "in the spontaneous uprising of all the living forces of social revolution." A closer look at both these factors denies the conclusion that the insurrectional attempt of 1874 derived only from the superheated imagination of young utopians, blind to all but their revolutionary objective.

In early 1874 the Italian Federation, in numbers and organization, bore very little resemblance to the association created at Rimini eighteen months earlier. By now, the I.W.A. membership was more heavily concentrated in Tuscany than in the Romagna, a development implicitly recognized by the transfer, in November 1873, of the national correspondence commission headquarters from Bologna to Florence. The move involved the election of a new commission, composed of Francesco Natta, Gaetano Grassi, and other Tuscan militants.[1] The work of grouping the sections into regional federations that began on the eve of the Geneva Congress of September, 1873, was carried forward at a secret meeting of nineteen Tuscan sections in Pisa on December 7, when a Tuscan Regional Federation, with headquarters in Livorno, was established.[2]

By the early months of 1874, ten regional federations of the anarchist International blanketed the peninsula and the islands. In order of descending numerical strength, they consisted of the Tuscan, Romagnol, Neapolitan (southern Italy), Siculian (Sicilian), Marchigian, Venetian, Lombard, Piedmontese, Ligurian, and Sardinian. On February 4, the Roman *questore* reported an official anarchist claim of 26,704 members. Two months later, the same official put I.W.A. strength in the peninsula at 32,450.[3]

The anarchists' insurrectional plan of 1874 envisaged using no more

[1] Bottero, *Dibattimenti*, p. 337; Conti, *O.S.F.*, p. 159. Natta, Grassi, and Piccioli-Poggiali had been members of the correspondence commission since the Bologna Congress of Mar., 1873, according to Natta's 1875 testimony. Piccioli-Poggiali resigned in Oct., 1873. Bottero, *Dibattimenti*, pp. 47, 84, and correction following p. 528. Costa resigned from the commission to devote himself to liaison work between the Italian Federation and the Federal Committee of the anarchist International, to which he had been elected at the Geneva Congress of Sept., 1873. Guillaume, *I.D.S.*, III, 111; Bottero, *Dibattimenti*, p. 337. Giuseppe Campetti, one of the new members of the correspondence commission, was later discovered to be a *confidante* of the police. Pezzi, *Un errore guidiziario*, p. 59.

[2] *Il Risveglio*, Dec. 14, 28, 1873; Pezzi, *Un errore giudiziario*, p. 48; Bottero, *Dibattimenti*, pp. 320-21. The secrecy was imposed, apparently, by police objections to a public congress, for on Nov. 23, 1873, the Jura *Bulletin* reported that the Tuscan congress had been indefinitely postponed "for reasons of *force majeure*." The Federation had a total of sixty-four sections (three local federations of at least twelve each in Florence, Livorno, and Pisa, plus twenty-eight unattached sections in the rest of the region), Bottero, *Dibattimenti*, pp. 320-21. For the *Regolamento* of the new federation, Conti, *O.S.F.*, pp. 267-68.

[3] Della Peruta, "La consistenza numerica dell'Internazionale in Italia nel 1874," *Movimento Operaio*, Yr. II, Nos. 3-4 (Dec. 1949-Jan., 1950), 104-06; Conti, *O.S.F.*, p. 146. The Apr. 3 report divided the membership as follows: Tuscan Federation: 36 sections, 8,000 members; Romagnol: 30, 6,000; Neapolitan: 17, 4,500; Sicilian: 15, 4,000; Marchigian: 18, 4,000; Venetian: 9, 1,800; Lombard: 11, 1,650; Piedmontese: 8, 2,000; Ligurian: 6, 500; Sardinian: 1 [250 members indicated in the Feb. report].

than a small fraction of this membership in initiating the projected uprising, but the conspiratorial leadership depended on sections everywhere in Italy to provide the backbone of a mass uprising, once a few local successes were registered.[4] This hope, during the event, was disappointed, since the plan went awry at the moment of its attempted actuation. Whether the sections would have acted revolutionarily, in case the initial effort had succeeded, is unimportant. The relevant point, so far as explaining why the anarchists made the attempt is concerned, was the existence, in fact as well as in the opinion of the leaders, of a potential revolutionary *Apparat* numbering approximately 30,000 Italians, professing allegiance to a common program and held together by a fairly efficient clandestine communication system.

From the anarchists' point of view, the nexus between their decision to try insurrection and the economic situation of the Italian workers in the months preceding the attempt is readily documented by a passage from Costa's letter to his comrades of November 28, 1873:

> The poverty that is growing with the approach of winter, the faults and arbitrary acts of the government, the culpable indifference of the happy people of the world, are increasing the discontent and revolutionary passions of the hungry plebes. Ask the workers of the countryside, ask those of the cities: all will tell you that this can not go on, that it is necessary to have done with the *signori* and that when the poor die of hunger, while the granaries of the rich are gorged with wheat, the people know what they must do to get themselves out of the difficulty.[5]

The implication that spontaneous revolution was just around the corner reflected a basic article of Costa's anarchist faith, but the reference to growing poverty and hunger was inspired by a situation of objective fact. Italy was, indeed, under peculiarly severe economic strain; for a significantly large proportion of the country's humblest classes, the effect was uncommon hardship.

The crisis of 1873-74 was but one symptom among many that the Italian economy was shifting from an artisan to a modern industrial base.[6] As in other western European countries that had already undergone the same transition, the temporary rupture of production relations meant technological unemployment and privation for an artisan class meeting large-scale machine competition for the first time. In the case of Italy, however, neither the government nor private enterprise was in a position

---

[4] Bottero, *Dibattimenti*, p. 346, following the Bologna *questore*'s report of Aug. 17, 1874, reproduced in full by Romano, *Storia*, III, 497-506.
[5] Guillaume, *I.D.S.*, III, 159.
[6] Corbino, *Annali dell'economia italiana*, II, 103 ff.

to soften the effects of such a brusque collapse of the old equilibrium. Northern Italy, particularly Lombardy, was most afflicted, but even in Tuscany, still predominantly agrarian, the phenomenon made itself felt, the more so since the characteristic and centuries-old share-cropping system was in an advanced state of decay.[7] Only southern Italy, still virtually devoid of factories and commercially significant artisan production, stood outside the play of this progression.

Another underlying weakness in the Italian economy during the fifteen-year period following the unification of 1860 was the almost chronic financial crisis under which the state labored. Notwithstanding extraordinary tax measures and officially enforced circulation of an ever increasing flow of paper money, government expenditures exceeded revenue every year until 1875.[8] In 1866 the government inaugurated the much debated *corso forzoso* (compulsory paper money circulation), compelling acceptance of the *Banca Nazionale's* notes as nonconvertible legal tender, in return for a loan to the state of 25,000,000 *lire*. In preparation for the war with Austria, the government levied a compulsory national loan of 350,000,000.[9] The sale of Church property, beginning in 1867, meant the enrichment of private speculators but failed to take the government out of the red. Since the land for sale exceeded the capital available for its purchase, prices fell far below the level the government had hoped to maintain.[10] In 1869 a new milling tax (*tassa sul macinato*) not only aroused an angry peasantry against the government but failed to deliver the anticipated revenue because of technical difficulties of application. By 1872 the functioning of the system was greatly improved, returning a revenue of almost 60,000,000 *lire* in that year, but the annual budget deficit still amounted to more than 80,000,000.[11] For the period 1869-83, the government sold its tobacco monopoly to a private concern, provoking stormy protests against the state's assumption of a debt of 237,000,000 to realize a return of 171,000,000.[12] In 1870 the government

---

[7] Conti, *O.S.F.*, p. 129; *cf.*, also, Romano, *Storia*, III, 194-97.

[8] Plebano, *Storia della Finanza Italiana*, I, 495. In millions of *lire*, the budget deficit for 1866 was 721.44; in 1867: 214.15; 1868: 265.8; 1869: 148.87; 1870: 214.76; 1871: 47.1; 1872: 83.57; 1873: 89; 1874: 13.38. In 1875 revenue exceeded outlay by 13,870,000 *lire*. *Loc. cit.*

[9] For details, Plebano, *op. cit.*, I, 201 ff.; Camillo Supino, *Storia della circolazione cartacea in Italia dal 1860 al 1928* (2d ed.; Milan, 1929), pp. 25 ff.; Francesco Ferrara, "Il corso forzato dei biglietti di banco in *Italia,*" *Nuova Antologia* (May-June, 1866), 21 ff., 343 ff.; *Atti della Commissione d'inchiesta sul corso forzoso* (Rome, 1869).

[10] Corbino, *op. cit.*, I, 266 ff.

[11] Plebano, *op. cit.*, I, 495. For a contemporary examination of the *macinato* tax, E. Morpurgo, "Le nuove imposte in Italia: il dazio sulla macinazione dei cereali," *Il Politecnico* (Mar., 1868), 254-70.

[12] Plebano, *op. cit.*, I, 290.

borrowed again from the *Banca Nazionale,* which had the effect of pushing the quantity of paper money in circulation from 650,000,000 to 800,000,000 *lire.* A few days later another loan raised the figure to 850, 000,000; in March, 1871, it went up to 1,000,000,000; a year later to 1,300,000,000.[13]

The new nation's financial problem in these years, as Chabod points out, was essentially political. Extraordinary fiscal measures were required to cut down the deficit, for Italy's rulers saw in balancing the budget a test of whether the country could prove to Europe and the world that national unity was here to stay.[14] Still, however heroic and necessary this succession of heavy tax levies and enforced paper circulation, government expenditures exceeded the nation's economic capacities, and no amount of compulsory currency circulation and unusual taxation would bring real economic stability and health unless, and until, expenses were brought into line with the wealth-producing capacity of the nation.[15]

The fantastic increase in the issuance and circulation of paper money, encouraging a wild, speculative activity, meant official favoring of the possessors of liquid capital and a consequent further aggravation of social imbalances. The fiscal policy of Quintino Sella in the early 1870's, especially his tax on liquid wealth, taking 13.2 per cent of all incomes, bore hardest on the working classes and the petty bourgeoisie.[16] It was distinctly a class policy, only slightly attenuated by the fact that for the

[13] *Ibid.,* I, 340 ff., 362 ff.; Supino, *op. cit.,* p. 47. After 1866 the banknotes of the five banks of issue (six, after 1870, with the *Banca Romana*) were made nonconvertible. The *Banca Nazionale* was given a distinct advantage, however, since the activity of the others was strictly limited, and the holders of their notes were allowed to convert them only for the paper issued by the *Banca Nazionale.* Gino Luzzatto, *Storia economica dell' età moderna e contemporanea* (3d ed.; Padua: CEDAM, 1955), II, 381. Francesco Ferrara, Finance Minister in the Rattazzi government that assumed power in April, 1867, said the *corso forzoso* was inaugurated in the interest of the *Banca Nazionale,* but a year later he withdrew this charge and admitted the necessity of measures against convertibility. *Ibid.,* II, 388-89.

[14] *Storia della politica estera italiana,* I, 485-501. "To have understood this imperative, to have perceived its terrible importance, constitutes the Right's great claim to glory in its last years of government . . ." *ibid.,* p. 499.

[15] For development of this theme, E. Scalfari, "La politica finanziaria della Destra nel periodo delle origini (1860-64)," *Nuova Antologia* (July, 1947), 283-99. After 1870, Italy was trying to play the role of a first-class power with second-class economic resources—an illusion dispelled only by the fall of Mussolini's regime and military defeat. The self-deception was perhaps inevitable, after the long trials and tribulation of the *Risorgimento,* but the hard fact was that in the period 1870-76 the average national income was only 40 per cent that of France, 48 per cent that of Germany and only 32 per cent of Great Britain's. Coppola D'Anna, *Popolazione reddito e finanze pubbliche dell'Italia dal 1860 ad oggi,* p. 49.

[16] Morandi, *La sinistra al potere e altri saggi,* pp. 64-65. The tax on liquid wealth, though arousing the protests of bourgeois producers' groups, weighed most on small incomes, on the shopkeepers, artisans, and skilled workers, thanks to the ease with which high income groups could evade the impost. Carocci, *Agostino Depretis,* p. 29.

period 1871-75, direct taxes (income, inheritance, etc.) provided the highest proportion (49.67 per cent) of national revenue in modern Italian history, while consumer taxes, notwithstanding the income from the *tassa sul macinato*, furnished the lowest (44.37 per cent).[17] Even this boast of the Right was vitiated by the fact that the government's preference for direct taxes was due, not to considerations of fiscal equity, but to the economic depression that imposed the necessity of getting tax money by the quickest and most drastic method.[18] The fiscal policy of the Right during the first sixteen years of Italian unity almost perfectly illustrated the contemporary socialist historian's judgment that the state and the capitalist class were allied, in effect, against the economically unfavored segments of society, that the government's policy entailed increasing poverty for rural and urban workers and an accelerated "proletarianization" of the petty bourgeoisie.[19]

A more immediate factor in producing what Costa thought was a general revolutionary temper among the nation's poor was the effect of the financial crash of 1873, the focal point of which was in Austria-Hungary and Germany, but which soon reverberated in all those European countries maintaining commercial relations with the two Germanic empires.[20] Italy was peculiarly vulnerable to the shock, thanks to its unhealthily expanded credit structure and the frenetic stock market speculation that characterized the period 1870-73.[21] The *Mezzogiorno*, with little liquid wealth, was least affected, but here a low point had been reached independently of external pressures. After making two on-the-spot surveys in 1873-74, an acute observer of the time noted that the economic strengthening of the southern bourgeoisie accomplished in fourteen years of national unity had entailed an incredible pauperization of the *contadini* and city poor.[22] For quite other reasons, Lombardy, too,

[17] Coppola D'Anna, *op. cit.*, p. 102; *cf.*, also, Scalfari, "La politica finanziaria della Destra," p. 299.

[18] Carocci, *op. cit.*, p. 28.

[19] For an eloquent argument in favor of this thesis, Aldo Romano's introduction to his third volume of *Storia del movimento socialista in Italia*, "Il capitalismo e lo stato agli inizi della vita unitaria," pp. 11-105. The author concedes, however, that other than class-interest imperatives motivated the men governing Italy. For an extended defense of the sixteen-year rule of the Right, see Nello Rosselli's essay, "L'Opera della Destra," in his volume, *Saggi sul Risorgimento e altri scritti*, pp. 217-60.

[20] For the effect on Italy, A. Errara, "Il krach nel 1873-74," *Nuova Antologia* (Feb., 1874), 416 ff.; Emilio Sereni, *Il capitalismo nelle campagne (1860-1900)* (Turin: Einaudi, 1947), pp. 49 ff.

[21] T. Canovai, *Le banche di emissione in Italia. Saggio storico critico* (Rome, 1912), pp. 43 ff.

[22] Leopoldo Franchetti, *Condizioni economiche e amministrative delle Province Napoletane. Abruzzi e Molise. Calabria e Basilicata. Appunti di Viaggio* (Florence, 1875), *cf.*, especially, pp. 24 ff., 96 ff. For Sicilian conditions, Leopoldo Franchetti and Sidney Sonnino, *La Sicilia nel 1876* (2d ed.; Florence, 1925).

escaped the worst consequences of the financial crisis of 1873: here, a solid economic base of agricultural production was reinforced by rich complementary industries; the equilibrium achieved through multiple forms of enterprise made the region better able to resist market fluctuations, both domestic and foreign. In Lombardy, too, most industrial enterprises were the product of a gradual, healthy growth, strictly integrated with the region's capabilities, not, as elsewhere, the creation of small groups of speculators more concerned with fast, fat profits than with long-range exploitation of an area's resources. In short, the effects of the crash of 1873 varied considerably from region to region, but speculative activity, taking the form of get-rich-quick maneuvers, rather than the financing of increased production and trade, suffered a hard shock, the effects of which were felt all over the peninsula.

The poorer classes of Italian society, least equipped to withstand these pressures, had manifested their unease in sporadic disorders ever since the unification,[23] but beginning with the seventies, popular discontent was more frequently and vigorously expressed. In the period 1860-69, the country had averaged only thirteen industrial strikes per year, but in 1871 there were twenty-six.[24] In 1871-72, the number, intensity, and spread of proletarian protests, frequently in violent forms, strikingly increased.[25] By 1873-74, popular discontent and poverty reached an acute phase,[26] aggravated by a poor harvest for two years running. When to the unemployment and under-employment implicit in the general economic lag was added the prohibitive price of cereal products—the staple of the Italian poor—strikes for wage increases, as well as outright hunger demonstrations, swept the peninsula. It was these frequent manifestations of vehement rebelliousness that convinced the anarchists that the hour of "social liquidation" was at hand.

In Tuscany particularly, strikes and agitations in 1873 ominously underlined the social peril implicit in the deteriorating economic situation.[27] In February the Florentine bread supply was threatened when unemployed bakers were denied a shift at the ovens. To avert catastrophe, the authorities had to man the ovens with soldiers drawn from the army commissary service. In May the Florentine bakers again went out on strike, this time in support of their Livorno colleagues; in Pisa, masons left

---

[23] Examples: the peasant agitations in southern Italy in 1860; the Palermo rising of 1866 [see Paolo Alatri, *Lotte Politiche in Sicilia sotto il governo della Destra (1866-1874)* (Turin: Einaudi, 1954), pp. 105-50]; the *macinato* revolt of 1869 (see above, pp. 128-30).

[24] Luzzatto, *Storia economica*, II, 398.

[25] For details, Romano, *Storia*, II, 217 ff., III, 95-98.

[26] See above, p. 297, note 17.

[27] The following data concerning Tuscan agitation are taken from Conti, *O.S.F.*, pp. 130 ff.

their work, and hundreds of striking textile workers, with a red flag at the head of their procession, stoned a factory still in operation and forced its employees to join their strike. Street-sweepers in Florence struck in May and agitated for a pay raise again in July; in December, the public taxi service of the city was paralyzed when the carriage drivers went out on strike.

The *questore* of Florence indicated the prime mover of these agitations when he warned his superiors that "the economic state of the country leaves much to be desired. The high cost of basic foods is such that the proletariat today buys a living with much difficulty." [28] It was almost an understatement when a kilogram (2.2 lbs.) of bread took anywhere from 17 per cent to 33 per cent of a Florentine worker's daily wage.[29] For the pro-government newspaper, *L'Opinione Nazionale,* such conditions increased the masses' susceptibility to subversive ideas: ". . . the very difficult condition of the poor man greatly contributes to augmenting the ranks of those who see in the social disorders [the possibility] of a new organization of the human family." [30]

Popular discontent was not limited to Tuscany. In the Neapolitan provinces of the south, in the central Lazio area, the agitations continued.[31] By the early months of 1874, the *benpensanti* began to take an apocalyptic view of the situation: "Hunger has fraternized with the people. The general poverty of our time is one of those infallible symptoms of certain and imminent catastrophe"—thus *La Rivista Indipendente* on March 10.[32] Roman and Turinese cigar workers struck in February; their Florentine colleagues followed suit in June and July. When the Florentine nobility set up soup kitchens for the hungry, wall posters, put up under cover of darkness, shrilly pointed the moral: "People! Not the pap of the economic kitchens, but work! Down with the economic kitchens . . . they are created to f—— the people!" [33] On March 1, a hungry mob

[28] Report for the second quarter of 1873, Conti, *O.S.F.,* p. 130.

[29] A skilled worker's maximum wage was 3 *lire* per day, but the price of bread in this period frequently went above 50 *centesimi* per kilogram. *Ibid.,* pp. 129-30, note 3. In Jan., 1874, bread in Florence retailed for 57-63 *centesimi* per kilogram; in Venice, 60; Mantua, 62; Brescia, 60; Genoa, 62; Rome, 47-65 (depending on quality); Naples, ditto; Turin, 50-55; Milan, 58-62. *La Perseveranza,* Jan. 22, 1874.

[30] Sept. 22, 1873, as quoted by Conti, *O.S.F.,* p. 130. See also the reaction of *La Perseveranza,* Apr. 17, May 12, July 1, 3, 11, 12, 1873.

[31] Romano, *Storia,* III, 197-98 Vigo, *Storia degli ultimi trent'anni,* I: 329. In Rome, "economic kitchens" and public ovens were instituted in Mar., 1874. *Ibid.,* I, 330. See also, the Jura *Bulletin,* Mar. 15, 1874, for details on the misery in Rome and nearby Velletri.

[32] As quoted by Conti, *O.S.F.,* p. 169. *La Perseveranza* remarked the "contagious character" of the strikes. Mar. 3, 1874.

[33] Conti, *O.S.F.,* pp. 169-70. *Cf.,* also, the article entitled, "The economic kitchens and legalized vagabondage," which argued that only professional panhandlers would accept the charity; the *vero povero* ("true poor man") was too proud to do so, in

forced food vendors at a public market in Dicomano, near Florence, to sell their merchandise at prices set by the crowd. In April, the masons, woodworkers and ironworkers of Mantua struck; in Parma, as well as in Mantua, barricades appeared in the streets. On May 17, troops were called in to suppress a seditious uprising in Padua's central *piazza*.

In late June and early July, the disorders suddenly multiplied like weeds; the common motif was hunger, writ large. On June 29 a crowd of mostly women and children sacked bread shops in Forlimpopoli; on July 1 a mob demanded price cuts from poultry and vegetable dealers in Forlì and, when refused, threw the produce into the street. On July 2 Florence's public security forces and *carabinieri* had to quell a demonstration by striking tobacco workers and unemployed sympathizers. In Predappio, a crowd of forty forced several grain dealers to sell them wheat at thirty *centesimi* a sack, had it milled, and sold it to the bakers at the same price, with instructions to keep the price in proportion. In Rimini on July 4, women and children gathered in Piazza Cavour, demanded that the price of bread be lowered and broke into the bread shops, carrying off their contents. On the 6th, rioting citizens in Pisa threw a bakery proprietor into one of his own ovens, while other enraged demonstrators sacked shops and beat their owners. Other tumults quickly followed in Lucca, Cervia, Cesena, Pescia, Monte San Sevino, Montevarchi, Pistoia, Bologna, and Massa. On the 7th, the grain dealers of Arezzo were beaten and their wheat sold by their attackers for three to four *lire* per bushel less than the going price; in Livorno, bands of women paraded the streets shouting "We want bread at fifteen *centesimi*, we want work!"; in Pietrasanta the cry was "Down with the thieves! Lower the price of bread!" Next day in Florence mounted police broke up a crowd in the *Piazza della Signoria*, but when eight hundred tobacco workers struck again on the 16th, the army had to be called in to maintain order. In Imola, a frenzied mob of women tried to sack a trainload of wheat guarded by a cordon of *carabinieri* and soldiers with fixed bayonets.[34] By the summer of 1874, the Italian social situation seemed, indeed, on the point of exploding.

Il Ladro Primo (Florence), June 28; and the sarcastic editorial in *Il Risveglio*, Feb. 15, 1874. The soup kitchens did not pass out free food but charged very low prices. In Imola, for example, the local "economic kitchen" sold a bowl of vegetable soup for ten *centesimi*, of *pasta* in broth for fifteen. A. Tabanelli, ed., "La vita sociale e politica imolese dalla Cronaca Cerchiari, 1865-1901," *Movimento Operaio*, Yr. III, Nos. 15-16 (Mar.-Apr.-May, 1951), 561-62.

[34] Andrea Costa was on hand to harangue the crowd, but order was restored when the Imolese subprefect cancelled the train's departure. For details of this incident, Anselmo Marabini, *Prime lotte socialiste. Lontani ricordi di un vecchio militante* (Rome: Ediz. Rinascita, 1949), pp. 25-28. For the other incidents here summarized, see Romano, *Storia*, III, 198-201; Conti, *O.S.F.*, pp. 169-72; Bertolini, "Cenno sul

INSURRECTIONAL PRELIMINARIES

Twenty-four years after the event, Andrea Costa explained the anarchists' 1874 decision to try insurrection in these terms:

> Violent action . . . was considered . . . a necessity. Having no other means at hand, [we needed one] corresponding to the Garibaldian, Mazzinian, revolutionary Italian traditions of the people, just emerged from the recent revolutionary period; [we needed] an affirmation, the propaganda of the deed, to pose the problem, to show the new ideal above the old ones. . . . It was necessary to act, to do something.[35]

Errico Malatesta's explanation, offered in 1876, was less abstract. At a congress in Bern he told his fellow anarchists that "the International [in Italy] found itself having to disown these popular acts entirely or to declare its solidarity with them" and that the second alternative was adopted out of fear of losing "all the practical partisans of revolution." [36] What he failed to mention was that the International did its best to promote the "spontaneous" tumults of 1873-74. Anarchist headquarters in Brussels urged Italian socialists in January 1874 to organize limited strikes and to lay the groundwork for a general strike.[37] Costa recommended socialist support of striking workers, and the hunger demonstrations of 1874 were accompanied by inflammatory editorials in the socialist press.[38]

Such incitement was only part of the larger program of preparing the ground for a nation-wide social war. Late in 1873 the Italian Federation's leadership transformed itself into an underground organization called "The Italian Committee for the Social Revolution," complete with passwords, clandestine communication channels, code names, cyphers, and all the other conspiratorial paraphernalia so dear to Bakunin.[39] In the *Mezzogiorno*, the Romagna, and Tuscany, a hard core of trusted conspirators—Costa, Malatesta, Grassi, Natta, Lovari, and others—provided

---

socialismo in Italia," lii; Bottero, *Dibattimenti,* pp. 344-45. For particulars, *Il Ladro Primo,* July 2, 3, 9, 12; *La Perseveranza,* July 3, 9, 10, 13, 1874; Pezzi, *Un errore giudiziario,* pp. 51-54; Vigo, *op. cit.,* I, 355, 372-73.

[35] Prison diary notes, May 25-June 2, June 8-July 7, 1898, Schiavi, "La formazione del pensiero politico di Andrea Costa," pp. 13-14.

[36] Guillaume, *I.D.S.,* III, 189; IV: 95. Malatesta's argument was incorporated in a history of the Italian movement that appeared in *L'Avvenire* (Modena) in 1878. See, specifically, the issue of July 6, 1878. Francesco Pezzi adduces the least likely explanation: that the insurrection was attempted "in order to show the government that it alone is responsible for the violent manifestations of the people . . ." *Un errore giudiziario,* p. 17.

[37] Florentine *questore* report, Jan. 4, 1874, Conti, *O.S.F.,* p. 170.

[38] Bottero, *Dibattimenti,* pp. 325, 344.

[39] Guillaume, *I.D.S.,* III, 169; Bottero, *Dibattimenti,* pp. 338, 344.

liaison and coordination of the Italian sections with Locarno.[40] Conferences with Bakunin at the Baronata, writing propaganda pieces, eluding the police, clandestine contacts with section leaders—thus, in the winter and spring of 1874, they prepared for the day of social redemption.[41]

In January 1874 a clandestinely distributed proclamation by the Italian Committee for the Social Revolution exhorted "the plebes who are dying of hunger, the miserable, the exploited, all those who work and suffer," to organize and arise against their oppressors. Written by Costa,[42] the document was conceived in the most violent terms:

> We declare war on reaction . . . , divine-right monarchy, the bourgeois republic, Capital, the church, the State, all the manifestations of contemporary life. . . . We are few, we are weak, we are poor, we have neither a penny nor a name; they imprison us, they exile us, they shoot us, they slander us; we are ill regarded and misunderstood; but we want . . . the destruction of the State in all its economic, political, and religious manifestations, . . . the abolition of armies, banks, cults. We want [raw] materials, tools, and the product to him who labors; . . . [we want] the individual, the family, the corporation, the commune, to be free; . . . [we want] to be a society of men and not a society of beasts. . . . Convinced that the pacific propaganda of revolutionary ideas has seen its day and that the clamorous and solemn propaganda of insurrection and the barricades must take its place, we shall neglect no means to inaugurate the struggle between the multitudes and the privileged. . . . If we can manage that not one stone remains above another of the present society, then woe to you, victors, exploiters, the triumphant of today! [43]

[40] Lodovico Nabruzzi found the delights of existence at the Baronata too attractive to devote any time and energy to conspiratorial activity in Italy. Bakunin relates that when he returned to the villa in Oct., 1873, he found the place *"en pleine debauche."* Nabruzzi had moved in with his mother and a *"demoiselle* very difficult to classify." The two women were invited to leave and in the spring of 1874, Nabruzzi, too, left the Baronata to take up residence in Lugano. Guillaume, *I.D.S.,* III, 181.

[41] For Malatesta's conspiratorial contacts, in preparation for the insurrection, see Lucarelli, *Carlo Cafiero,* pp. 45-46; Giulio Trevisani, "Il processo di Trani contro gli internazionalisti," *Movimento Operaio,* Yr. VIII, No. 5 (Sept.-Oct., 1956), 639-62.

[42] Costa admitted his authorship during the Bologna internationalist trial of 1876. Ceneri, *Opere,* I, 84.

[43] The entire document is reprinted by Bottero, *Dibattimenti,* pp. 252-53; Lucarelli, *Carlo Cafiero,* pp. 42-45; Romano, *Storia,* III, 479-81. For Costa's instructions to the correspondence commission in Florence, detailing the method of printing and distributing the piece in a manner to insure against police discovery of its origin, see his letter of mid-Dec., 1873, in Bottero, *Dibattimenti,* pp. 340-41; Romano, *Storia,* III, 470-71.

In the same month, the Italian Federation's correspondence commission in Florence, according to the local *questore,* asked the financial and moral support of the international anarchist headquarters in Brussels for the organization of armed bands in the Romagna, to be put into action during the spring. Brussels hedged about approving the project, asking for further details on the strength of the Italian movement and for more information on the specific goal of the scheme. The plan was apparently hatched in Locarno by Costa and Bakunin, for we find Costa in mid-February advising the Florentine center that he and the Russian, assisted by three non-Italian anarchist chieftains (Cyrille, Pindy, Verry), were in the midst of preparing an insurrectional plan for Italy, to be presented for approval by a Locarno anarchist conclave scheduled for March 18. After consulting with Celso Ceretti, Costa told his Florentine comrades that the insurrection would definitely occur. The whole affair was called off in mid-March, according to Costa, because the non-Italian delegates to the Locarno meeting of March 18 doubted that the "socialist spirit in Italy was . . . very extensive or understood." [44]

Whether this postponement—or Costa's foreknowledge of it—accounted for the changed tone of the second "Revolutionary Bulletin" of the Committee for the Social Revolution, issued in March, is not clear, but the document had a far less urgent tenor than that of the January proclamation. Now the tone was almost completely didactic: to an anarchist analysis of the ills besetting Italian society was added a detailed critique of the clerical faction, the parliamentary parties, and the Mazzinian republicans. The sharpest barbs, however, were directed against the Garibaldians' party, "self-styled socialists and revolutionaries," who, by exploiting the general's prestige, "seek to divide the Workers' forces, sowing equivocation and misunderstanding" and thereby becoming unconscious allies of the bourgeoisie. If let alone by his friends, the generous-hearted Garibaldi would far prefer to "fight as a simple soldier for the popular Revolution," but, instead, he has allowed himself to support an "illogical, absurd, and impossible confusion of parties." The people must liberate themselves by a collective effort, since:

> . . . no general's sword, no lawyer's code, no priest's evangelism, can do it for them; as we were against Mazzini and the Mazzinians, so, too, we shall oppose, if need be, Garibaldi and the Garibaldians if they want to sacrifice the real emancipation of the people to their personal ideas and sentiments.
>
> The Garibaldians have no program; . . . they want Military Dictatorship. . . . Socialism, as Garibaldi conceives it, is an

[44] Florentine *questore* reports, Jan. 21, Feb. 11, 22, 27, 1874; Costa report to the correspondence commission, Apr. 16, 1874, in Conti, *O.S.F.*, pp. 173-74.

equivocation: what he calls the exaggerations of the socialists are the fundamental principles. . . .

The manifesto's only constructive suggestion to the Italian people was to organize a party "independent of those who come to you to speak of a republican state or a popular government." [45]

On the face of it, the anti-Garibaldian tenor of the March manifesto indicated the unwillingness of anarchists to accept assistance from the general's followers in preparing and executing their revolutionary project. This may well have been, in fact, the personal view of Costa, the author of the document.[46] Though the situation in the spring and summer of 1874 was extremely confused, it seems that the other anarchist leaders in Italy, especially Ceretti, were ready to recognize the ideological chasm between Garibaldi's convictions and the anarcho-socialist program but could not resist the fascinating prospect of republican assistance—Garibaldian and/or Mazzinian—on the barricades. In a February circular to the Italian sections, the correspondence commission affirmed that the struggle to which the International had dedicated itself must be anti-republican and anti-Garibaldian, but the cooperation of elements "of the irreconcilable and social fraction" of the republican camp must not be disdained "at the moment of action," provided accounts were settled later over the smoking ruins of the existing regime.[47]

On the doctrinal level, certainly, Garibaldi's support was inconceivable, for there is no reason to suppose that he had changed the opinion he held in October 1872 when, after ruminating on the principles codified by the anarchist congress in Rimini, he penned this critique in a letter to Andrea Costa:

> 1. You say war on capital by labor; and when labor possesses capital it must pass to the side of the enemy. Therefore, continuous defections and wars.
> 2. I understand abolition of the priest, since he is an impostor; but the abolition of matrimony is a serious affair that merits much pondering.
> 3. Collective [ownership] of land, instruments of labor, etc. The ancient Romans, certainly our superiors, fought for centuries without achieving it. Finally, in not admitting the authoritarian principle, you fall into the anarchy that no one must desire. The

---

[45] For the manifesto in full, Romano, *Storia*, III, 481-92. Costa also subsequently admitted his authorship of the March "Bulletin." Ceneri, *Opere*, II, 84.

[46] The anti-Garibaldian section of the March manifesto was substantially nothing more than an elaboration of the charge Costa made against the general's followers in his above-mentioned speech at the Geneva anarchist congress in the preceding September.

[47] Bottero, *Dibattimenti*, p. 346.

above-mentioned [principles] and others are the exaggerations to which I refer, and I am sorry that I lack the time to worry about them.[48]

On the tactical level, i.e., cooperation with the anarchists in the preparation of an insurrection, the general's role is by no means as clear. Celso Ceretti, twenty-three years later, claimed he had brought Garibaldi around to promising support, and there was at least a rumor that the Red Shirt hero had talked Eugenio Valzania, prominent Romagnol republican chieftain, into going along.[49] Whatever the truth of these reports, the fact is that Costa, the leading militant among the anarchists, reposed no faith in Garibaldi's support, if one is to judge by the March manifesto, far more a declaration of incompatibility with the Garibaldians than a condemnation of the Mazzinians and the constitutional parties. Most significant, Garibaldi's personal intervention was completely lacking when anarchist plans were actuated in August.

So far as the Mazzinian leadership was concerned, there was room for compromise with the anarchists on neither the ideological nor practical terrain.[50] Maurizio Quadrio was certain that "any uprising provoked only by class interests, not only produces disorders and civil wars but is destined to end in compounding misery and becoming the prey of tyranny. The cult of brutal instincts and interests does not inspire sacrifice and is not destined to impress its tendencies and laws on the multitudes."[51] Aurelio Saffi, the most imposing Mazzinian of them all, sneered at "the proclaimers of material action, the deprecators of moral action, who believe they can mount the breach at any moment, without worrying about the changed situation, about means, about preparation, about the moral cooperation of the country." This was doubtless the reason Saffi, as well as Quadrio, objected that "the times are still not ripe" when Andrea Giannelli, at a secret republican meeting in Genoa on the first anniversary of Mazzini's death, urged republican action to exploit

---

[48] Letter of Oct. 28, 1872, Marabini, op. cit., pp. 30-31. See his letter, in the same vein, in La Plebe, Oct. 8, 1872. Garibaldi kept up a constant criticism of the "doctrinaires and exaggerators" in his correspondence with Ceretti and others after the Rimini Congress. See, Ciampoli, op. cit., pp. 637-39. Subsequently he shifted to attacking the anarchist International's opposition to the principle of authority. Ibid., pp. 661, 668.

[49] Guillaume, I.D.S., III, 204; Romano, Storia, III, 153. Valiani gives a slightly different version. "Dalla prima alla seconda Internazionale," p. 235. Ceretti, too, sounded out Valzania. Consociazione Romagnola e gli arresti di Villa Ruffi, Lettera di Aurelio Saffi ad Alberto Mario con aggiunta di note e documenti (Forlì, 1875), p. 79.

[50] Even La Perseveranza (Oct. 9, 1873) recognized that agreement between Mazzinians and Internationalists would contravene "common sense and logic."

[51] Letter to Raffaele Pepe, June 28, 1874, Antonio Lucarelli, "Internazionalisti e Mazziniani in un autografo di Maurizio Quadrio," Movimento Operaio, Yr. I, No. 1 (Oct., 1949), 9-11.

current poverty and discontent. Federico Campanella, though believing in the need of "shaking the people out of their lethargy" in anticipation of "the opportune moment to bring about the triumph of their ideas," saw no possibility of an alliance of republicans and socialists so long as the latter clung to "the savage theories of the abolition of property, the family, the fatherland, and such." [52] Saffi made the argument official when, speaking for the Republican *Consociazione* of the Romagna, he told the Italian republican societies:

> . . . recourse to violence to heal the economic ills of Italy would only spread and exacerbate them; . . . the confusions of social pressure, made an instrument of disorders and bloodshed, would render the solution of the social question more difficult . . . , and a division between the bourgeoisie and the artisan classes, in addition to being contrary to the historical traditions and current attitude of the Italian [republican] societies, would be harmful to *la patria* and liberty.[53]

A few republican figures of lesser stature—men like Luigi Castellazzo, Antonio Martinati, and even Andrea Giannelli—were flirting with the notion of temporary alliance with the anarchists to further their plans for the overthrow of the monarchy.[54] It was probably to put an end to such talk and to curb defection of the activist elements of the republican party to the socialist cause that prompted Saffi and other nationally known republican leaders to meet secretly on August 2 in Villa Ruffi, on the outskirts of Rimini.[55] But the police surrounded the villa, let them talk, and then jailed the lot of them. The charges:

> . . . conspiracy, tending to change and destroy the form of Government, concerted and concluded between them in the years, 1873-74, in the territory of the State; for having organized in various provinces and districts, in the above-mentioned period and especially from March, 1873, to August, 1874, a vast Republican Association, called *universal;* for having prepared plans, arms, munitions, and means; for having issued instructions and circulars, negotiating with the International Society [i.e., I.W.A.] for the purpose of overthrowing the Government; and for having

---

[52] Conti, *O.S.F.*, pp. 163, note 7; 176-177; 178, note 1.
[53] Saffi, *Ricordi e scritti* (Florence, 1901-04), XI, 127 ff.; Bottero, *Dibattimenti*, p. 346.
[54] See the evidence presented by Conti, *O.S.F.*, pp. 176 ff.
[55] Jessie White Mario wrote that the Villa Ruffi conclave was called for the purpose, among others, of finding "the most suitable way for the democratic party to have nothing in common with the International." *Agostino Bertani e i suoi tempi* (Florence, 1888), II, 361.

resolved among themselves to act and to have their members act to put the Republic in its stead.[56]

While the twenty-eight arrestees insisted that the sole purpose of their conclave was to define their party's line of conduct in the imminent administrative elections, the Romagnol anarchists, who had dreamed of eliciting republican support for their revolutionary enterprise, found themselves almost completely isolated—precisely the effect the police were seeking in rounding up the Villa Ruffi republicans.

RUPTURE OF THE BAKUNIN-CAFIERO ALLIANCE

While Italian socialists vainly tried to enlist the aid of republicans in doing away with Victor Emmanuel's government, while Andrea Costa and Errico Malatesta indefatigably spun the web of conspiracy in central and southern Italy, their movements assiduously watched by the police,[57] the spiritual godfather of the projected social revolution, aided and abetted by Carlo Cafiero, was working hard—and quite successfully— at dissipating the only funds available for financing the redemption of Italy's disinherited.[58] Because the Baronata was proving too small to house Bakunin, his indigent exile friends, and their many relatives, to say nothing of visiting Italian anarchists, and because—to hear Bakunin tell it—Cafiero was worried about the effect of the Baronata's damp masonry on Bakunin's health, the construction of another house on the property was projected, complete with a promenade where Bakunin might "breathe the balsamed air of the flowers." To get the stones for the new construction, the garden was dug up, but when Bakunin contemplated the resultant expanse of raw earth, nothing would do but to turn it into a small but expensive artificial lake. To reach the site of the new house, up the mountainside from the Baronata, a road had to be carved out of the stony soil. Our revolutionaries had neglected to check the water

---

[56] On Dec. 23, 1874, the *Sezione d'Accusa* of the Bologna Court of Appeal declared there were insufficient grounds for prosecution of the Villa Ruffi arrestees on these charges. *La Perseveranza*, Jan. 2, 1875. On the Villa Ruffi affair, see, *La Consociazione Romagnola e gli arresti di Villa Ruffi*, and the above-cited biography of Bertani by Jessie White Mario, II, 359 ff.

[57] For the extent of police coverage of the conspiracy, see the *questore* and prefect reports reproduced by Romano, *Storia*, III, 146-53, notes; *cf.*, also, Conti, *O.S.F.*, pp. 172-79. On Apr. 24, the Roman *questore*, noting Costa's presence in the capital, asked his opposite number in Bologna to help him find an excuse to immobilize the agitator: ". . . inform me as soon as possible as to the moral, as well as political, antecedents of Costa, his condition and profession, and his means of subsistence, indicating to me whether he might be considered an idler and vagabond." Ceneri, *Opere*, I, 107.

[58] The following description of life at the Baronata is based on the detailed account of Guillaume, *I.D.S.*, III, 181-83, 187, 198-99; see, also, Zoccoli, *L'Anarchia*, pp. 131-34; Lucarelli, *Carlo Cafiero*, pp. 35 ff.

supply when the villa was bought, so a reservoir had to be provided. To wrest some income from the rocky terrain, fruit trees were planted, and Bakunin projected a vegetable garden in the hope of cutting down the fantastic outlays for food, necessitated by the cosmopolitan gustatory preferences of his "free-loading" house guests of all nationalities. Cafiero, footing the bills, was getting a painful education in the maintenance of a model revolutionary center.

One expense led to another. Two cows were purchased, but since the conspirators knew nothing of bucolic routines, a local peasant woman had to be hired to milk them. Cafiero thought Bakunin, in his new role as a bourgeois squire, should have a carriage and horses, but when these were bought, Cafiero found himself having to hire a coachman-groom, repair the stable, and build a shelter for the carriage itself. Then, too, there were the cash outlays for the rifles, ammunition, and Orsini bombs to be smuggled into Italy for the day of reckoning with Victor Emmanuel's armed minions. One of the boarders, a certain Cerutti, was put to fabricating bombs, but when Bakunin wanted to entertain visiting revolutionaries, the Baronata's ordnance expert provided nightly pyrotechnic displays, making a dazzling splash of color over the placid waters of Lake Verbano and, of course, a still further dent in Cafiero's fast dwindling patrimony.[59]

The pain of meeting the Baronata's incredible expenses was eased for Cafiero by his presumably amorous relationship with one of the villa's female inhabitants, young Olympia Kutusov, the sister-in-law of a Russian friend of Bakunin. In February or March 1874, she went to Russia to see her ailing mother, but when, after the mother's death, she tried to return to the Baronata and Cafiero, the tsarist police refused her a passport. Handing Bakunin fifty thousand francs to tide the household over during his absence, Cafiero left for St. Petersburg, legalized his union with Miss Kutusov on June 27 in the office of the local Italian consul, and brought her back to Locarno as Mrs. Cafiero, Italian citizen.[60] Bakunin greeted the newlyweds with the intelligence that he had just purchased an adjoining piece of property, well wooded, "to increase the value" of the Baronata and that his wife, his three children, and his father-in-law who

---

[59] Concurrently, the Swiss anarchists were trying to persuade Cafiero to finance the construction, at an estimated cost of fifty thousand francs, of an engravers' cooperative workshop in Chaux-de-Fonds. Cafiero, at first sympathetic, decided that his money was "better destined to other uses than that of creating some new bourgeois." Guillaume, *I.D.S.*, III, 184-85.

[60] Lucarelli cites the marriage as proof of Cafiero's "goodness and heroism," since it was motivated, "not so much by love as by [the desire] to rescue her, with Italian citizenship, from deportation to Siberia." *La Puglia nel secolo XIX; con particolare riferimento alla città di Acquaviva in Terra di Bari* (Bari, 1926), pp. 226-28.

had been living in Russia, were to move in permanently within a few days.[61]

Putting his bride up in a rented room in the neighborhood, Cafiero dashed off to Barletta to convert the remainder of his inheritance into cash. On July 14 Bakunin's family arrived, and that night Cafiero got back from Italy. It was an unhappy conjunction, from Bakunin's point of view, for Cafiero chose this moment to inform him that he believed those who accused the Russian of exploiting Cafiero's confidence and inexperience, of abusing his friendship to ruin him financially. Henceforth, ordained Cafiero, "not a *sou*, not a thought, not a particle of his energy," for the Baronata, for these now belonged to the revolution. Bakunin's reaction, in his own words:

> I swear that this discourse threw me into consternation and struck me like a club. . . . If I had been alone, at the first word I would have left to him that damned Baronata with all its contents. . . . But the thought of the despair and abyss into which I was going to plunge Antonia [Mrs. Bakunin] and her father made me fainthearted. Instead of thinking of my honor, unfairly insulted by one from whom I least should have expected it, I thought of how I might save, not myself . . . , but my dear ones. As for me, my resolution was made, I had decided to die. But, before dying, I believed it necessary to assure the fate of my family.
>
> All those days after the 15th were a veritable hell for me. . . . After many vain efforts, I made the supreme decision that I should have made at the first moment. I signed the agreement whereby I abandoned the Baronata to him, with all that it contained, including the cows and the sick horses. But I still had the weakness to accept from him the promise to assure, in one way or another, the lot of my family after my death, which, I hope, is not far off.[62]

The Italian anarchist leaders, for their part, were convinced that the social revolution could not wait for their Nestor's broken heart to heal. While the Russian, in the fortnight following the dispute, was "paralyzed completely," Cafiero made good on his vow to devote his money and energy to the revolution—a decision suggested to him, perhaps, by his first direct contact, after many months, with the deteriorating Italian social situation during his clandestine trip to Barletta. The last remnants

[61] This was no surprise to Cafiero, for he had provided the money to get them out of Russia. Guillaume, *I.D.S.*, III, 203.

[62] From Bakunin's *Mémoire justificatif*, July 28-29, 1874, Guillaume, *I.D.S.*, III 199-200. His wife and father-in-law were ignorant of the true source of Bakunin's income, believing it derived from a favorable turn in his years'-long effort to realize something from his father's estate.

of the young Pugliese's once imposing patrimony now went for rifles, ammunition, and dynamite. A Russian revolutionary of the Baronata entourage, who called himself "Ross," purchased dynamite at a nearby factory; Cafiero's bride was sent to Bologna with a load of it wrapped in a napkin knotted around her waist. Costa showed up briefly for last-minute consultations, returned to Italy to alert the comrades for imminent action. Ross, in Milan, trying to convert thirty thousand Swiss francs Cafiero had given him to help finance the uprising, met trouble when the bank to which he applied refused to do business with an unvouched-for stranger. Costa, summoned by telegram, cleared the bottleneck by persuading a local lawyer friend to act as intermediary, whereupon Costa departed for Bologna with the cash.[63]

Bakunin, having deeded the Baronata to Cafiero, now thought better of risking his person in an enterprise he realized could not succeed, but, rather than renege on his well-advertised—except to his wife—vow to seek death on the barricades in Italy, he left Locarno on July 27, taking a circuitous route through Switzerland. On the eve of descending into Italy to ignite the "combustible material" his propaganda had always insisted was there, he penned a justification of his financial relations with Cafiero in the form of a last will and testament ("And now, dear friends, I have only to die, *adieu*"). Behind him at the Baronata was a wife who had been told that her husband was making a short visit to Zürich.[64]

THE ATTEMPTED "SOCIAL LIQUIDATION"

Anarchist plans called for revolt in Bologna on the night of August 7-8, to be followed in rapid succession by uprisings in Tuscany, the Marches, in Rome, and in the Puglia.[65] Since Bologna was to spark the insurrection, it was here that Bakunin repaired on July 30. Hidden away in rented quarters, described by his Romagnol comrades as one "Tamburini," a rich, ill, and deaf *rentier*, he prepared to mastermind the overthrow of Italian society. Costa conferred with him immediately, hurried

[63] Guillaume, *I.D.S.*, III, 200-01. Costa's itinerary during the second fortnight of July, 1874: Aquila, Naples, Pescara, Arezzo, Pontassieve, Rome, Milan, Imola, and Bologna. Lipparini, "Cronologia della vita di A. Costa," p. 186.

[64] Guillaume, *I.D.S.*, III, 201-04.

[65] *Ibid.*, III, 205; Angiolini, *op. cit.*, p. 115. The Bologna *questore* had heard that the anarchists of Florence, Livorno, Palermo, and Ravenna had "thousands" of Orsini bombs on hand, that four thousand Vetterly rifles were being sent to the Romagna and Tuscany (Romano, *Storia*, III, 500). At the same time, *i.e.*, early August, five cases of rifles, labelled as scrap iron, were on their way to Naples from Taranto, dispatched by Malatesta (Nettlau, *Errico Malatesta*, pp. 12 ff.). Lucarelli claims the shipment originated in Gardone and Brescia and that the conspirators had some fifteen thousand bayonets on hand (*Carlo Cafiero*, pp. 39, 47). For further details on the southern arms, see Ceneri, *Opere*, I, 69-70; Trevisani, "Il processo di Trani . . . ," pp. 642-45, 656.

off to Rome to make final arrangements for the uprising in the capital, and returned on August 3.[66] But now the government's long and careful tracking of the revolutionary movement began to pay off. The Villa Ruffi arrests warned that the police were on the *qui vive*, but this did not keep Costa from being picked up by the police on the night of August 5.[67] Thus, at the very outset, the insurrection was denied its chief organizer; thus, too, began a series of setbacks that made the long heralded "social liquidation" fit material for an *opéra bouffe*.

By now the die was cast: the arms were at hand, the revolutionary nuclei in Tuscany, the Romagna, the Marches, Rome, and the Puglia were awaiting the sound of the tocsin. It came on the morning of August 7, when the third "Bulletin" of the Italian Committee for the Social Revolution appeared in various cities of the peninsula and Sicily.[68] On buildings, on walls, even pinned to the back of an unsuspecting Neapolitan policeman,[69] the document called on the proletarians of Italy to "finish with an unsupportable state of affairs, . . . to fight to the death for the abolition of every privilege and the complete emancipation of human kind." The anarchist leadership had passed the point of no return:

> There is only one reality in the world—force. . . . Our enemies are strong only because of the strength we have given them; their union exists only because of our disunity; let us resolve to finish it, and we shall finish it. The future is in your hands: you can choose between liberty and slavery. . . .

But since it was to be an armed rebellion, the manifesto addressed itself to those who would be called upon to suppress it:

[66] Guillaume, *I.D.S.*, III, 205. Costa had been in close contact with the Roman Internationalists, having consulted with them, on Mar. 31, in mid-April and early June. Della Peruta, "L'Internazionale a Roma dal 1872 al 1877," pp. 26-27.

Accepting a Bologna *questore* report of Aug. 17, 1874, Conti (*O.S.F.*, pp. 175-76) and Lucarelli (*Carlo Cafiero*, pp. 80-81) state that Costa read a report on the revolutionary readiness of the Italian International to a secret anarchist congress in Brussels on Aug. 1-2. This was physically impossible, since Costa was with Bakunin on the night of July 30 and again on August 3, with a trip to Rome during the interval. Bakunin's diary is explicit in the matter (Guillaume, *I.D.S.*, III, 205). For the *questore* report in full, Romano, *Storia*, III, 497-506. Its unreliability was demonstrated at the Bologna Internationalist trial of 1876 (see Guillaume, *I.D.S.*, IV, 2-3; Ceneri, *Opere*, I, 93 ff.). Costa's defense lawyer claimed Costa was in Adria, in the Veneto, on August 1-2.

[67] Guillaume, *I.D.S.*, III, 205; Lipparini, *Andrea Costa*, pp. 77-78. Alceste Faggioli, organizer of the Modena and Reggio Emilia sections, was with Costa when the latter was arrested, but made good his escape, only to be caught on Aug. 9. Romano, *Storia*, III, 501-02.

[68] For the manifesto, *La Perseveranza*, Aug. 16, 1874; Bottero, *Dibattimenti*, pp. 258-59.

[69] Romano, *Storia*, III, 156.

To our brothers in the army, we say: Brothers, we are a part of you, your families are like ours. . . . We shall not be the first to turn our arms against you:—*Mark you:*—they are your brothers that you kill for the glory of your executioners and for your eternal infamy:—you do not want us to damn you, to be forced to lacerate our own limbs in you; you do not want the blood you spill to fall upon you.

Discipline is a vain nightmare invented to brutalize you, poor human ghosts; the glory, of which your masters make so much show, is your infamy; the fatherland is their never sated belly.

The first duty of the slave is to revolt. The first duty of the soldier is to desert. Proletarians, revolt. Soldiers, desert: turn the rifles against the masters who put them in your hands to kill us: only in this way will we be brothers; and you shall have deserved well of the Social Revolution.

This is our last word: and very soon events will confirm it. Meanwhile, we salute you, oh dawn of our redemption.

The plan for the Bologna uprising envisaged an attack on the local arsenal by several thousand Bologna Internationalists mustering in two bands outside the city. The assault was to begin when several thousand more Romagnol insurrectionists, coming from Imola and other points in the region, joined the Bolognese. In Bologna itself, two noncommissioned officers attached to the city's arsenal had promised to open its doors to the insurgents; material for barricades had been collected and about a hundred local republicans had promised to cooperate—as individuals, not as a party.[70]

On schedule, the Bolognese insurgents gathered outside the city on the night of August 7-8.[71] In Imola, Antonio Cornacchia, captain of the local band, found he could not muster the several thousand followers he had hoped for, thanks to a police action in the wake of the Villa Ruffi arrests that had frightened off promised republican assistance.[72] Undeterred, Cornacchia gathered together about 150 men, armed with a few pistols, rifles, and knives, and headed for his rendezvous with the Bolognese. The column was only one third of the way to its destination when the authorities in Bologna received a telegraphic warning. Police,

[70] Guillaume, *I.D.S.*, III, 205.

[71] For details of the Bologna attempt, *L'Avvenire* (Modena), which reproduces a detailed account taken from the Aug. 8, 1874, issue of *Il Monitore di Bologna*; *La Perseveranza*, Aug. 13, 1874 (taking its story from the *Corriere delle Marche*); Costa, *Bagliori di socialismo*, pp. 16-17.

[72] Cornacchia, a mason, was a Romagnol active in the Rome conspiratorial nucleus. His role in the attempted insurrection of August was in the nature of detached duty, assigned by Costa. See Della Peruta, "L'Internazionale a Roma dal 1872 al 1877," pp. 27-28.

carabinieri, and a few army troops boarded a passenger train headed for Imola, arrested forty-three rebels on the spot and began scouring the hills for those who had escaped. After a vain several-hour wait, the insurgents waiting outside of Bologna disbanded. Their chiefs managed to bury their arms in the countryside but did not escape the efficient police roundup.

In Florence, the correspondence commission members, Natta and Grassi, had set August 15 for the uprising.[73] News of events in the Romagna dampened enthusiasm, but in order to "better paralyze the forces of the state, help the insurgents of Imola, and facilitate the insurrection of the provinces," D-Day was moved up to August 8, with the section of Pontassieve (eighteen kilometers east of Florence) assigned to "massacre the authorities and the few *carabinieri*" of the town. Warned in plenty of time, the police took the necessary precautions, and, for a moment, the affair seemed terminated. The revolutionary leaders were still at liberty, however, and on August 12, Francesco Natta, who had gone into the Romagna to scout the progress of the movement there—the setback of August 7-8 was considered only a temporary hitch—notified his comrades in Florence to initiate the insurrection. The plan was so fantastic that only with difficulty did the police persuade themselves the anarchists seriously intended to carry it out: a fire in the city's center to signal the opening of hostilities, seizure of the National Guard's rifles, organization of the workers into shock battalions for the barricades, cutting telegraph and rail communications, emptying the jails, and then a direct assault on the Palazzo Vecchio, the prefecture, the *questura,* the *Banca Nazionale,* the gas works, and the goldsmith's shops on Ponte Vecchio. The armed forces of the city were accordingly disposed, and, though for the next several days rumors of revolution held the solid citizenry in a state of nervous suspense, officials charged with maintaining public order were never seriously worried. As early as August 8, the Florentine prefect dissolved thirty-two Tuscan republican and Internationalist societies.[74] About a hundred individuals, fifty-seven of whom proved subsequently to have had nothing to do with the disturbance, were jailed, but two of the key conspirators, Gaetano Grassi and Guido Corsi, eluded the police and fled to Switzerland.

In Livorno and Rome, Internationalists were similarly frustrated by

[73] For details on the Florentine movement, *La Perseveranza,* Aug. 13, 14, 15, 16, 18, 1874; Angiolini, *op. cit.,* pp. 116-17; Conti, *O.S.F.,* pp. 178-82; Pezzi, *Un errore giudiziario,* p. 56; Bottero, *Dibattimenti,* passim, but see, especially, the "Atto d'Accusa," pp. 6-18, and the "Fatti speciali della Causa," pp. 347 ff.

[74] *La Perseveranza,* Aug. 13, 1874; the Pisa prefect followed suit, *ibid.,* Aug. 26, 1874.

timely police measures.[75] In Palermo some republicans got as far as distributing a manifesto intended to arouse the masses to fighting pitch, but there was not a sign of revolt.[76] In the Puglia, Errico Malatesta had settled on Castel del Monte, a hamlet about thirty kilometers inland from the Adriatic coast, as the springboard for launching the liberation of the south's rural proletariat.[77] The epic, in Malatesta's terse description, thus unfolded—or, more accurately, folded:

> Several hundred confederates had promised to be at Castel del Monte. I arrived there, but of all those who had sworn to come, we found we were only six in number. It does not matter, the case of arms is opened: it is full of old muzzle-loaders; *non fa niente*, we arm ourselves and declare war on the Italian army. We fight the campaign for several days, seeking to involve the peasants on our side, but without getting a response. The second day, we have a fight with eight *carabinieri*, who fired on us and imagined that we were very numerous. Three days later we saw that we were surrounded by soldiers; there was but one thing to do: we buried the guns and decided to disperse; I hid myself in a hay wagon and thus succeeded in getting out of the danger zone.

After hiding a few days in Naples, Malatesta headed for Switzerland, but the police dragnet caught him in Pesaro.[78]

How had Michael Bakunin fared in his quest "to die in the midst of a great revolutionary torment?" He spent the night of the insurrectional attempt in Bologna, hidden in his room, revolver in hand, and by 3:40 A.M., hearing no shooting and certain that no news meant bad news,

[75] Bottero, *Dibattimenti*, p. 350; Angiolini, *op. cit.*, pp. 117-18; Della Peruta, "L'Internazionale a Roma dal 1872 al 1877," pp. 27-28.

[76] On events in Sicily, Bottero, *Dibattimenti*, p. 350; Romano, *Storia*, III, 161; Trevisani, "Il processo di Trani . . . ," pp. 655-56; Alatri, *Lotte politiche in Sicilia*, pp. 573-78.

[77] For Malatesta's adventure, *La Perseveranza*, Aug. 18, 23, 1874; Bottero, *Dibattimenti*, p. 350; Guillaume, *I.D.S.*, III, 207; Lucarelli, *Carlo Cafiero*, pp. 47-49; Nettlau, *Errico Malatesta*, pp. 121 ff.; Francesco Sarri, *La Internazionale innanzi alla sezione d'accusa di Trani* (Barletta [1875]), 29 pp.; Trevisani, "Il processo di Trani . . . ," pp. 640-46. Carmelo Palladino met secretly with Malatesta on Aug. 3, but refused to join the Castel del Monte venture. Lucarelli, *Palladino*, pp. 6-7.

[78] For further details, Romano, *Storia*, III, 163 and notes 92-94. The Pesaro authorities had been warned by telegraph to expect him. Result, according to Cafiero's letter of Oct. 11, 1874, to the Jura *Bulletin:* "Gathered at the station [was] a big crowd of bourgeois, come to be present at the arrival and arrest of a 'capobrigante.' " As quoted by Borghi, *Errico Malatesta*, p. 49. When arrested on Aug. 18, Malatesta had in his possession: 1,200 *lire*, a revolver, a code, and some letters. Under questioning, he denied everything: "In fact, I am extraneous to politics and I was going to Milan to buy books . . ." Lucarelli, *Carlo Cafiero*, pp. 50-51,

would have used the weapon on himself had not one of his comrades, who happened in at that moment, deterred him from doing so—thus wrote Bakunin several days later. On the 12th, disguised as a priest, shorn of his magnificent beard, wearing green glasses, a cane in one hand and a basket of eggs in the other, he departed from Bologna by train, headed for Swiss soil. In entering the carriage that was to take him from his hideout to the Bologna railway station, we are told, the burly Russian mounted the conveyance so impetuously that he wedged himself into the doorway, unable to move in or out. Only after much tugging and heaving by his companions—who had a double reason for nervous perspiration— was he finally stuffed in and sent on his way—fitting finale to that whole ludicrous comedy, played out in the name of "social liquidation." [79]

THE TRIALS OF 1875: ROME, FLORENCE, TRANI

Incarceration of several hundred Internationalists and government dissolution of republican and socialist societies diminished not at all the ebullience of the few anarchist leaders still at large in the country. Quite to the contrary, for on August 29 appeared a fourth "Bulletin" of the Committee for the Social Revolution, which made no reference to the frustrated insurrection and shrilly urged Italian proletarians to man the barricades and wage war on the monarchy, the priests, and the rich.[80] From the security of the Baronata, Carlo Cafiero took another view of the whole matter.[81] In an address to the I.W.A. congress held in Brussels on

[79] Guillaume, I.D.S., III, 205-06; Zoccoli, L'Anarchia, p. 136, notes 1, 2; Angiolini, op. cit., p. 116.

[80] For the manifesto, Bottero, Dibattimenti, pp. 350-51; Romano, Storia, III, 493-95. The manifesto was sent to La Stampa (Venice), which published parts of it. The sender(s) signed themselves "The Italian Committee for the Social Revolution." The manifesto was also circulated in Padua on the night of Sept. 2, ibid., Sept. 4, 1874; it may have been the same circular distributed in Rome, in the Emilia and in the Veneto on the night of Oct. 1-2, 1874. Jura Bulletin, Oct. 25, 1874.

Who authored the manifesto? Costa could not have written it before his arrest on Aug. 5, for the third "Bulletin" of early August began with the words: "This is the last time we address you." Cafiero is an improbable author, for he had sent word from Locarno on Aug. 21 that "there was nothing further to be done in Italy (Guillaume, I.D.S., III, 207). Natta and Oreste Lovari seem the more likely responsibles, for Natta, during the week of Aug. 14-21, still thought with Bakunin that revolt was possible ("plan of action complete, code and signals established"—loc. cit.). He returned to Italy about Aug. 21 and remained at large until Nov. 2, Lovari until Sept. 27 (Bottero, Dibattimenti, pp. 47, 66; Vigo, op. cit., I, 398; Jura Bulletin, Nov. 15, 1874). Thus, of the Florentine group that had distributed the first three Revolutionary Bulletins, Natta and Lovari were the only men at liberty in late August.

[81] Lucarelli states, but does not document, that Cafiero was in Italy during the August attempt (Carlo Cafiero, p. 51). I have seen no proof that Cafiero ever left Switzerland between his return from Barletta on July 14, 1874, and October, 1875, when he moved to Milan, except for a quick trip into Italy in April, 1875.

September 7-13, 1874, he wrote—also in the name of the Italian Committee for the Social Revolution—that the August attempt failed to win popular support because the Italian people, "fundamentally disposed to conspiracy," distrusted the legal and public system of I.W.A. organization in Italy. Merely defining the Italian International for what it was, "a vast conspiracy prepared in the full light of day," sufficed to show the "absurdity" of the system.[82] Ergo, the International in the peninsula would transform itself into a "vast and solid revolutionary socialist conspiracy," operating clandestinely.[83] Only the form would change, not the program, for "the truth and justice" of anarchist principles had demonstrated their popular appeal:

> And since experience has shown us that [clandestine] organization was greatly superior to [public and legal] organization, were we not right in saying that the end of the legal International in Italy was a happy result that we all owe to our government? . . . Today the revolutionary forces are alive, better organized, and more numerous than ever before; they form a network that envelops the whole of Italy more and more. The era of congresses is definitely finished for us and the task of addressing you, as we now do, will be difficult to repeat on other similar occasions. Revolutionary Italy . . . will continue to follow the path chosen as the only one that can lead to its ultimate goal, the triumph of the social revolution.[84]

Cafiero's references to Italian revolutionary forces being "more alive, better organized, and more numerous than before" were sheer rhetoric, for in the months following the August fiasco, Italian police measures against subversion from any quarter were so severe that even the republicans were driven to extreme circumspection in trying to rebuild their shattered organization.[85] Internationalist federations and sections existed only in name—it could not have been otherwise, with all the militant anarchist leaders in jail or in Swiss exile, with the sympathy of the masses fast ebbing before the workers' fear of compromising them-

---

[82] The "intransigent" (i.e., pro-Terzaghi) organ, *Il Petrolio* (Ferrara) had drawn the same conclusion long *before* (Jan. 19, 1874) the fiasco of August.

[83] "Is it not very singular that an Association that wants to remain secret solemnly talks, before a Congress, about such a proposal and renders involuntary homage to publicity?" *La Perseveranza*, Sept. 14, 1874.

[84] For the address in full, Jura *Bulletin*, Sept. 13, 1874.

[85] In Florence, for example, the leaders of a newly founded republican "Popular Education Circle" thought that instead of "forming . . . a new association, exclusively political and therefore susceptible to finishing like those of the past," the society should concern itself with "instruction, brotherhood, progress, civilization, and the moral and material interest of the people." Conti, *O.S.F.*, pp. 189-90. For a description of police repression after the August attempt, Jura *Bulletin*, Oct. 25, 1874.

selves by identification with the International. Until anarchist propagandists could once again circulate freely in the peninsula, until the
Internationalist press could function without constant government interference,[86] the movement simply did not exist as such and the wishful
thinking of Cafiero and his friends could alter the reality not at all.

This is not to say that Cafiero limited himself, during those months
at the Baronata, to living the "anchorite's existence"—milking cows,
carrying manure, and cutting wood—described by Guillaume.[87] It is true
that relations with Bakunin, who now lived in Lugano, remained cool,[88]
but Cafiero maintained his interest in the revolutionary cause in Italy.
In October he began contributing to the *Bulletin* of the Jurassian Federation "news of our arrested friends, a chronicle of government persecutions, accounts of the misery of the Italian proletarians, and, at times,
considerations of general policy." [89] Though the documentation is too
sparse to permit a description of Cafiero's conspiratorial relations with
the Italian movement and the other Italian anarchist exiles during the
year following the August insurrectional try, contacts were maintained,
and some kind of armed subversion was projected in the spring of 1875.
Cafiero, Francesco Pezzi, Tito Zanardelli, Lodovico Nabruzzi, and Benoît Malon seem to have constituted the links in the conspiratorial chain.
In a letter intercepted by the police, Cafiero had written: "For the moment I do not move from Locarno, where I await the organization of
the armed bands with Zanardelli and Nabruzzi. In a few days, Leo
[Malon] will leave for . . . Italy to stimulate the prompt and ample
organization of the faithful." [90] It was presumably in connection with

[86] *Il Vero Satana*, a socialist newspaper, appeared in Florence on Feb. 24, 1875, but
the police forced its demise after a few issues. Pezzi, *Un errore guidiziario*, pp. 60-61;
Conti, *O.S.F.*, p. 307.

[87] *I.D.S.*, III, 287.

[88] While the Russian was in Italy, Cafiero informed Mrs. Bakunin that he was the
real owner of the Baronata and asked her and her family to leave. Safely back in
Switzerland, Bakunin told Cafiero he intended to retire completely from political activity and refused a monthly pension of three hundred francs offered him by Cafiero and the
Swiss anarchist leaders but continued to negotiate with Cafiero, through intermediaries, for small loans. On Feb. 15, 1875, he wrote Elisée Reclus: ". . . the hour of
revolution is past, not because of the frightful disasters we have witnessed and the
terrible defeats of which we have been more or less guilty victims, but because . . .
revolutionary hope and passion are absolutely not to be found in the masses. . . . As
for me . . . , I have become too old, too sick and . . . too disabused to . . . participate in this work. I have definitely retired from the struggle and I shall spend the rest
of my days in contemplation, not idle, but . . . intellectually very active." *Ibid.*,
III, 209, 235-38, 254-56, 283-85.

[89] *Ibid.*, III, 240. See Cafiero's criticism of Garibaldi and Aurelio Saffi, "two
coryphées of bourgeois republicanism," when they were elected to the Chamber of
Deputies in Nov., 1874, in *loc. cit.*; and his anti-Garibaldian article in the Mar. 21,
1875, issue of the Jura *Bulletin*.

[90] Romano, *Storia*, III, 182, note 10. On Pezzi, *ibid.*, note 11; Pezzi, *Un errore
giudiziario*, pp. 22-23.

this project that Cafiero, in April 1875, made a short trip to Italy. Whatever the scheme, nothing came of it. Transparently, the anarchist movement, in order to survive at all, needed the guidance of men like Costa, Malatesta, and Natta, active organizers and indefatigable propagandists incapable of trying to superimpose a "rural and pastoral existence" on a social revolutionary career.[91]

In 1875 all but the Bologna Internationalists were brought to trial on charges of conspiracy. Except for a few, the accused were guilty as charged, but this had little influence on the juries' verdicts. The prosecution presented a mountain of evidence collected by the police in many months of tracking the development of the conspiracy, and even after eliminating unsubstantiated information, there was still more than enough to warrant verdicts against the accused. The latter perjured themselves time and again, their defense attorneys made long and impassioned—but technically irrelevant—speeches about the iniquities of Italian society and government; public dissatisfaction with the policies of the Right was exploited to the advantage of the defendants. Juries were asked to believe that men who collected rifles, who distributed "Revolutionary Bulletins" advising proletarians to man the barricades and soldiers to desert, were but simple proletarians with no subversive political intent, devoted only to helping their fellow proletarians find a pacific way to improve their standard of living. The acquittal of the defendants represented, certainly, a condemnation of Italian economic and social conditions but also underscored the gap between the law of popular conscience and the law of Victor Emmanuel's government. The prosecuting attorney at the trial in Florence, though making an impeccably logical plea for the inseparability of law and liberty, was ignoring the real criterion by which the defendants were judged when he told the jury:

> It is quite true that in Italy liberty is very extensive in the speculative order, because there is no opinion, however absurd, that can not be publicly sustained and defended.
>
> But liberty of opinion can not, must not, be . . . liberty of conspiracy, nor can one ever confuse the thinker and seer of the farthest political and social horizons with the *agent provocateur* and the agitator of the *piazza*.
>
> Now the International does not simply make theories; it intends to apply its doctrines, it moves the will to action and proposes to reach its goal even with barricades and armed insurrection—therefore, it has the *animus hostilis*, that is, the

[91] Guillaume, *I.D.S.*, III, 256, 259, 287. Nabruzzi had apparently overcome his rancor at being ousted from the Baronata the year before. When Bakunin moved to Lugano in Oct., 1874, Nabruzzi resumed cordial relations with the Russian (*ibid.*, p. 254). Gaetano Grassi was still at large and was probably a party to the vague scheme of the spring of 1875.

intention of achieving that goal through an unjust, unconstitutional, violent, criminal path.

If this kind of liberty were permitted, one would have
permanent revolution and the negation of every idea of government, so all liberals, to whatever party they belong, must . . .
agree that the Government would betray the nation if it permitted everyone to act as he liked and to raise the banner
of revolt in the hope of applying political and social theories
contrary to the institutions that guarantee national unity and
liberty.[92]

In the winter of 1874-75 the government's "grand offensive" against
the International—as the socialist historian would have it—began with
the freeing, "for lack of evidence," of seventeen of the twenty-seven
arrestees in Rome, practically all of those in Ancona, Macerata and
Pesaro, thirty-six out of seventy in Florence and three out of eighteen in
Trani (Puglia), where the Malatesta group was held.[93] The Rome trial
got under way on May 5, featuring intemperate harangues by the
prosecuting attorney, evidence of police mistreatment of the prisoners,
protests of injured innocence on the part of the accused. By May 8 a
verdict of guilty as charged (conspiracy and incitement to commit
crimes) was returned. The prosecution, perhaps inspired by the scenes of
public sympathy for the accused played out in the courtroom, asked for
the minimum penalty; the defense, probably under the same stimulus,
demanded the maximum for all but one of the ten accused. Result:
sentences ranging from three months' confinement to ten years at hard
labor.[94]

The Florentine *mise-en-scène* lasted from June 30 to August 31.[95] Here
the chief mistake of the prosecution was to indict, along with the

[92] Bottero, *Dibattimenti*, p. 357.

[93] Guillaume, *I.D.S.*, III, 259; Pezzi, *Un errore giudiziario*, p. 60; Sarri, *op. cit.*,
p. 11; *La Perseveranza*, Mar. 12; *Jura Bulletin*, Mar. 28, 1875. Of the ninety-nine
arrestees in the Bologna and Marches area, twenty-nine were freed before the trial,
leaving seventy-nine defendants, nine of whom, on the opening day of the trial, were
still at large. Guillaume, *I.D.S.*, III, 314; IV, 2.

[94] For the Rome trial, Filandro Colacito, *L'Internazionale a Roma. Considerazioni
Politiche di F. Colacito. Colla relazione estesa del dibattimento per la causa di
cospirazione* (Rome, 1875), pp. 37-126; Guillaume, *I.D.S.*, III, 259; *Jura Bulletin*,
May 23; *La Plebe*, May 16, July 13, 1875. Romano asserts that "not one [of the
accused at the Rome trial] could be considered a true and proper director of the movement" (*Storia*, III, 174), yet practically all of them are painstakingly identified by
Franco Della Peruta as *capi-squadra* (squad leaders) and "principal members, the
most active and dangerous" of the Roman would-be insurrectionists ("L'Internazionale
a Roma dal 1872 al 1877," pp. 26-27).

[95] For the Florence trial, Bottero, *Dibattimenti; La Plebe*, Sept. 5, 1875. For secondary treatments, Pezzi, *Un errore giudiziario*, pp. 60-61; Conti, *O.S.F.*, pp. 186-87;
Angiolini, *op. cit.*, pp. 121-23; Guillaume, *I.D.S.*, III, 288; Romano, *Storia*, III, 176-78.

authentic Internationalist conspirators, several persons completely extraneous to the affair of 1874 (Salvatore Battaglia, Ettore Socci, and even
a monarchist, one Count Grifoni). This allowed important figures of
republicanism like Saffi, Campanella, Andrea Giannelli, and Maurizio
Quadrio to take the stand as character witnesses. By discrediting the
prosecution's case against republicans in the dock, they managed to
weaken the argument against the Internationalists as well. Garibaldi
contributed immensely to swinging public opinion behind the defendants
when, in a deposition read in court, he rendered one of his quaint
definitions of Internationalism:

> Unlike Mazzini and Battaglia, I am an internationalist and [if
> they were] consistent with the principles of common sense, I
> believe they, too, might be such. To explain [!]: what difference
> is there between an American and an Italian? They are the same
> men and morally they must be brothers. I had the good fortune
> to fight for the American people, as for my people; therefore, I
> am for the fraternity of the human race. Thus, if by interna-
> tionalist is meant he who, having a hundred *scudi* in his pocket,
> the fruit of his own labor, is obliged to share it with another
> who demands to live slothfully on his shoulders, the latter is a
> thief; such is my internationalism.[96]

Of the three dozen defendants, only Francesco Natta admitted membership in the International, which represented, said he, "the heart-rending
voice of thousands of honest workers who, lacking work or poorly paid,
arise to protest against him who is the cause of it all . . ."[97]

Already softened up by press sympathy for the accused, by the unsavory character of some of the prosecution witnesses, by a battery of
simpaticissimi defense lawyers, by the news that a Court of Cassation in
Rome had annulled the May verdict against the capital's Internationalists
and ordered a retrial,[98] by the acquittal of the Trani Internationalists, the
jury was understandably vulnerable to the sentimentalism that spilled
out of the final statement of Natta, the "simple, honest" worker:

> Now, oh gentlemen of the jury, as free citizens of a materially
> comfortable class of society, if you consider these facts in rela-
> tion to a famished multitude of unemployed workers, with
> helpless old people and emaciated babies in the arms of mothers
> made desolate and exhausted by poverty, who arise, motivated

---

[96] Bottero, *Dibattimenti*, p. 265. Garibaldi's definition of Mazzini as an "internationalist" echoed an argument the general had used in 1872: "In his whole life,
Mazzini never denied his cult of humanity, so that he, too, was an International." In
Il Gazzettino Rosa, Nov. 7, 1872.
[97] For Natta's final declaration, Bottero, *Dibattimenti*, pp. 503-06.
[98] *Jura Bulletin*, Aug. 8, 1875; for the retrial, *ibid.*, May 28, 1876.

> not by the manipulations of a party, but by a much more
> powerful cause, poverty, who arise to demonstrate against those
> who, though able, . . . do not provide a remedy, but imagine,
> instead, an impossible conspiracy; if you believe that these
> unhappy but honest workers, who ask for bread and work,
> deserve imprisonment, then I can only submit calmly to my fate,
> convinced that I have nothing to reprove myself for. But if . . .
> in your conscience you have penetrated that heart-rending cry,
> then I do not doubt finding an act of justice in you and for me it
> will be a day of joy, in embracing my children, to be able
> to say: Not all the bourgeois are insensitive.

Three successive salvos of applause, we are told, greeted the jury's decision that all but three of the accused were innocent.[99]

As for the trial of the Puglian Internationalists, held in Trani on
August 1-5, an anonymous local sympathizer described its culmination
far more eloquently than its objective import:

> Never as on this occasion had the city of Trani presented a more
> beautiful and moving aspect. The whole population followed the
> trial, not only the more educated classes, but also that which
> used to be called the "low people," the suffering and oppressed
> class. . . . The jury was composed of the richest proprietors of
> the province and a big body of troops had been arrayed. . . .
> The presentation of the public prosecutor was what it always
> is, a tissue of insults and atrocious slanders. Addressing the
> jurors, the representative of the prosecution uttered these precise
> words: "If you do not condemn these men, they will come one
> day to take your women, violate your daughters, steal your
> property, destroy the fruit of your perspiration, and you will be
> left ruined and poor, with dishonor on your brow." Well then,
> despite this ridiculous tirade, with which he tried to frighten
> them, the jury rendered a verdict of acquittal, and after the
> judgment, the jurors went to shake the hands of the accused
> and mixed with the crowd that gave a real ovation to the
> socialists as they were leaving prison. In the whole city, in the
> public as well as in the private meetings, our friends were
> the object of the most cordial demonstrations. To judge from
> the innumerable attestations of adherence given to our principles
> on that occasion, we must conclude that in the Puglia Interna-
> tionalist propaganda has made giant strides. Oh, if only the

___

[99] Not one of the three was a major figure in the preparation of the conspiracy. One
was given nine years for violent theft; another, six months for illegal possession of
firearms; the third, eight months for manufacturing arms. Bottero, *Dibattimenti*, p.
527. Gaetano Grassi, still at large in Switzerland, was found in contempt on Apr. 11,
1876, and sentenced to eleven years at hard labor. Conti, *O.S.F.*, p. 187.

government would multiply these trials! They will cost some of us some years in prison, but they will immensely benefit our cause . . .[100]

Aside from the fact that sympathy for anarchist principles among rich Puglian landowners was highly improbable, the sober truth behind the trials of 1875 was that they represented anything but a stimulus to the diffusion of anarchist doctrines. The anarchist press was thoroughly muzzled,[101] and the liberation of the Puglian and Florentine leaders facilitated no serious reorganization of the Italian International. Malatesta left Italy immediately, visited Cafiero briefly at the Baronata, stopped in Lugano to see Bakunin—whom he found in a state of "decomposition"—and then, mistaking the current anti-Turkish rebellion of the populations of Bosnia and Herzegovina for the birth of a European-wide revolution, dashed off to fight the minions of Abdul Aziz.[102] Francesco Natta presumably reverted to propagandizing his fellow Florentine workers after his acquittal on August 31, but the historian of the local movement finds no traces of his activity during the winter of 1875-76, other than his attending a few secret meetings in the home of one of the comrades. A "Socialist Circle," in which Natta probably held a key position, found it impossible to break down the diffidence of the workers and the "passive resistance" of the city's democratic societies.[103]

Carlo Cafiero hardly represented a vigorous force in bringing the anarchist International out of its post-1874 slump. He remained at the Baronata until October, 1875, continuing his collaboration with the Jurassian *Bulletin*. Now reduced to real poverty, he made his peace with

---

[100] *La Plebe*, Aug. 26, 1875. For the indictment, Sarri, *op. cit.*, pp. 8-11, 16-18, 20-22. On the trial itself, see the just cited issue of *La Plebe*, and Lucarelli, *Carlo Cafiero*, pp. 51-53. Sarri, in defending the accused, argued that a real revolution, one aiming at I.W.A. objectives "can not be entrusted to the disorganized movement of a few silly persons." The defendants were guilty only of "bombastic words, . . . frenetic phrases, and today they lack faith in their purposes, the courage of their opinions," *op. cit.*, pp. 22-24.
The above-quoted description of the Trani trial was not written by Cafiero, as Romano avers (*Storia*, III, 180), but by an anonymous Trani correspondent of *La Plebe*, which published it on Aug. 26, 1875. The Jura *Bulletin* did not publish the account until Sept. 5, 1875.
[101] Giuseppe Scarlatti, for example, began publishing an anarchist weekly in Florence, *L'Internazionale*, on Oct. 24, 1875, but gave up after the third issue. Conti, *O.S.F.*, p. 304.
[102] Guillaume, *I.D.S.*, III, 300. He was joined by Celso Ceretti, Achille Bizzoni, editor of *Il Gazzettino Rosa*, and Giuseppe Barbanti-Brodano, who returned in time to defend Costa at the 1876 Bologna trial. See Barbanti-Brodano's record of the Balkan adventure, *Serbia. Ricordi e studi slavi* (Bologna, 1877), pp. 192-95, 197, 225-27.
[103] Conti, *O.S.F.*, p. 190. *Cf.*, also, Pezzi, *Un errore giudiziario*, pp. 61-66, for Florentine socialist activity during the first half of 1876.

the ailing Bakunin, bade his wife farewell as she entrained for Russia and a revolutionary propagandist's career, and then settled in Milan to work as a photographer's assistant.[104] In January, 1876, he transferred to Rome, where, with the help of Emilio Borghetti and Errico Malatesta (now returned, disillusioned, from the Balkan adventure), he reorganized the local section as the "Workers' Circle." Acquittal of the Roman Internationalists (Giuseppe Bertolani, Giuseppe Berni, etc.) in mid-May momentarily encouraged the work begun, but Borghetti was arrested on May 30 and jailed for three months, Cafiero was told to get out of town, and in mid-June the police sent Malatesta off to Naples, where he was put under surveillance.[105] What the Florentine *questore* wrote of Tuscan socialists on April 26, 1876, very likely also applied to their comrades in the rest of the peninsula: "The more practical and less idealistic of them see in Costa the mind suited to directing, with stable norms, the International association scattered throughout central Italy." [106]

GENESIS OF A LEGALITARIAN CURRENT

Costa's talents were sorely missed indeed. By December, 1875, Tito Zanardelli and Lodovico Nabruzzi had come a long way in their thinking since their vague cooperation with Cafiero in the spring of that year. In Lugano, encouraged from Milan by Benoît Malon, they published an *Almanacco del Proletario per l'anno 1876*, highly critical of the insurrectional attempts of 1874. The Swiss anarchists called it a "war machine directed against the present organization of the International in Italy," inspired by "miserable rancors." [107] In the same month, Zanardelli and Nabruzzi founded a dissident Ceresio section in Lugano—under the very nose of Bakunin—which proposed the reorganization of Swiss and Italian workers "in the most realistic and certain way," i.e., by nonrevolutionary methods.[108] At Christmas, Zanardelli wrote the congress of the Belgian Federation in Verviers that "the International in Italy will never be a secret conspiracy, but vigorously proclaims the principles of anarchy

[104] Guillaume, *I.D.S.*, III, 301-02. Cafiero to Bakunin, Oct. 10, 1875: "I embrace you, Michael, I warmly embrace you, I embrace you again." Lucarelli (*Carlo Cafiero*, p. 54) errs in imputing Cafiero's transfer from Switzerland to Milan to "the amnesty promulgated by the new government of the Left," since that government did not assume power until Mar., 1876.

[105] *La Plebe*, July 6; Jura *Bulletin*, July 2, 1876; Della Peruta, "L'Internazionale a Roma dal 1872 al 1877," pp. 30-31. If Cafiero left Rome on May 30, he did not stay away very long, for on about June 20 he was once more sending reports from Rome to the Jura *Bulletin*. Guillaume, *I.D.S.*, IV, 29. For his correspondence from Milan and Rome, *ibid.*, III, 314, IV, 1, 4, 29.

[106] Conti, *O.S.F.*, p. 190.

[107] Guillaume, *I.D.S.*, III, 303.

[108] Romano, *Storia*, III, 507-09.

and collectivism and does not recognize the mysterious authority called the Italian Committee for the Social Revolution." [109] What he meant by "proclaiming the principles of anarchy and collectivism" soon became clear.

The separatist movement of the two Italians in Lugano was given an impetus with the arrival on January 8, 1876, of Benoît Malon,[110] who had been urging the Bignami group in Milan and the Ingegneros nucleus in Palermo toward an anti-Bakuninist orientation, indirectly abetted by Osvaldo Gnocchi-Viani, who, even before the 1874 insurrectional attempt, had been trying to shift the emphasis from conspiracy for armed uprisings to a trade-unionist approach. On February 7, the Ceresio group circularized Italian sections in an attempt to arrange a congress of the Italian Federation,[111] but the action resulted in nothing more than a twelve-man meeting in Lugano on April 14, in the course of which Malon denounced the "defects, errors, and deformed, incomplete results" deriving from anarchist theory. The anarchists, said he, were "the principal cause of the present divisions in the International, proponents of disagreements and promoters of the unfruitful agitation that for the past three or four years have disorganized and thinned out the forces of the socialist party, wasting its energy with unfecund conflicts of personalities and interests . . ." Reorganization of the I.W.A. should be based on a return to the original program of the International, with special emphasis on the necessity of educating the workers to their responsibility to emancipate themselves.

Even Malon, however, was still unprepared to reverse completely the anarchists' antipolitical principle. "Without entering immediately into the field of politics and exercising a direct action," every section should be advised "to favor and support electoral reform in the peninsula and have its members registered as voters." [112] Among those present was Enrico Bignami, who pledged support of these principles in his newspaper, *La Plebe,* now a Milan daily.[113] True to his word, he published an editorial on May 19 calling for abandonment of the insurrectional tactic:

> In the period of crisis that Socialism is going through, after having undergone many bloody defeats, after having repudiated

[109] Franco Della Peruta, "La Banda del Matese e il fallimento della teoria anarchica della moderna 'Jacquerie' in Italia," *Movimento Operaio,* Yr. VI, No. 3 (May-June, 1954), 348-49.

[110] Malon, arrested on Jan. 5 in Milan, was expelled from Italy without explanation. *La Plebe* (now in Milan), Jan. 6; Jura *Bulletin,* Jan. 16, 1876; Guillaume, *I.D.S.,* III, 314.

[111] For the circular, Romano, *Storia,* III, 510. *Cf.,* also, Della Peruta, "La Banda del Matese," p. 349, note 32.

[112] For the *compte-rendu* of the Apr. 14 proceedings, Romano, *Storia,* III, 510-13.

[113] Della Peruta, "La Banda del Matese," p. 350, note 34; see, also, note 36.

certain errors that contributed so much to its early failures, after having appealed to science and experimentalism, we say Socialism needs to change its method of action to acquire new strength. And the period of revolutionary attempts—necessarily impotent in the present condition of Europe—must be succeeded by the period of propaganda, which we might call demonstrative.[114]

On the organizational level, the initiative now passed from the Ceresio group to Milan, where in mid-May the local socialist circle, the Sons of Labor, closely tied to the staff of La Plebe, came to life as the promoter of a Lombard Federation of the I.W.A. A month later, a commission of socialist statistics and propaganda, arisen from within the staff of La Plebe, gave birth to a Circle of Economico-Social Studies, the very title of which implied a repudiation of the "propaganda of deeds." [115] Cardinal principle of the Circle was exclusive acceptance of "an active and illuminated propaganda" as the means of proletarian emancipation, a conclusion deriving from "the examination of the natural laws that regulate the constitution and progress of society, their mode of being, and their economic development." [116] It was only a matter of time before the anti-Bakuninist forces of Bignami in Milan, Gnocchi-Viani in Rome, and Ingegneros in Palermo would back up their doctrinal opposition to Bakuninism with schismatic efforts on a concrete plane. Italian anarchism stood in dire need of a stronger and more effective defense than that provided by Cafiero and Malatesta in the winter and spring of 1876.

THE BOLOGNA TRIAL OF 1876

Fortunately for the anarchist cause, Andrea Costa was about to re-emerge as the animating spirit of the movement. The Bologna trial opened on March 15, 1876, with seventy internationalists in the prisoners' dock and nine at large, to be tried in absentia. The pattern was the now familiar

---

[114] This position marked the end of Bignami's long-standing policy of exposing all sides of the socialist question, typified by his publication on Nov. 26-27, 1875, of an article by James Guillaume, lambasting the gradualist socialists as the greatest enemies of progress. Worth noting, too, is that in justifying his new orientation as the result of an appeal to "science and experimentalism," Bignami was very probably alluding to the Malonian thesis of evolutionary social development, based on the scientific positivism of Auguste Comte, not the "scientific" materialism of Marx. Bignami's contacts with Marx and Engels from Apr. 19, 1874, to early 1877, were limited to Bignami's Oct. 5, 1875, request that they contribute to his projected "Biblioteca Socialista." Bosio, ed., "Marx-Engels. Carteggio da e per l'Italia," Movimento Operaio, Yr. II, Nos. 9-10 (June-July, 1950), 270.

[115] La Plebe, May 19, 28, June 4, 1876.

[116] For the Statuto-Regolamento, ibid., Aug. 6, 1876.

one, with several new touches added.[117] As Costa promised, in the course
of his three-day interrogation, the "tribunal was turned into a tribune."
Unlike their comrades in the trials of the year before, the majority of
the accused readily admitted their membership in the International—
testimonial to their confidence of acquittal in any case. Costa not only
professed his affiliation but saved the prosecution the trouble of reciting
the history of the organization by doing it himself—an easy task, said he,
for up to that moment it had been done so poorly. Summing up his
reply to the prosecution's charge, he managed to muster primitive
Christianity, the French Revolution, and the judgment of history as allies
of anarcho-socialism:

> My comrades and I are not concerned with the names of male-
> factors. The bourgeoisie, . . . who were called *straccioni* [the
> ragged ones] and *sans culottes* a century ago, forget their former
> allies, now that they are in power, and . . . call us malefactors
> and worse. Very well, we accept this title, just as the bourgeoisie
> once did. And who knows but that some day, just as the cross,
> from an instrument of infamy, became a symbol of redemption,
> this name of malefactors, given to and accepted by us, may
> indicate the precursors of a new generation. . . . If, despite this,
> you must condemn us, we shall not appeal to a Court of Cassa-
> tion . . . ; we shall appeal, instead, to a much more severe and
> formidable tribunal, a tribunal, oh citizens, that must one day
> judge us, the accused, and you, the judges. We will appeal to the
> future and to history.[118]

The courtroom, packed with substantial citizens, their wives and even
school children playing hooky to hear such molten eloquence, rang with
"*Bene!*," "*Bravo!*" and other manifestations of high endorsement. One
of Costa's lawyers gratuitously professed affiliation with the International
and declaimed that he would far prefer to entrust any daughter of his to
a "malefactor" like Costa than to "one of your perfumed fops, supporters
of the throne and altar." This gambit, the record relates, also brought
"irresistible and prolonged applause." Giosuè Carducci, poet laureate of
Italy and quondam mentor of Costa at the University of Bologna, said
he regretted the young Imolese's decision to forsake his studies, since

[117] For the indictment, *La Plebe*, Jan. 31; *Jura Bulletin*, Sept. 12, 1875; for the
Bologna trial proceedings, *ibid.*, Apr. 2, 9, May, 7, 28, June 4, 18, 25, 1876; *Lo
Scarafaggio* (Trapani), Apr. 9, 23, May 7, 1876; Ceneri, *Opere*, I, 41-118 (Ceneri's
defense of Costa in the sessions of May 18, 19, 1876); Lucarelli, *Carlo Cafiero, passim*;
Romano, *Storia*, III, 185-90.
[118] For the entire discourse, *Processo degli Internazionalisti. Parole di Andrea Costa
ai Giurati della Corte di Assise di Bologna, nell'udienza del 16 giugno 1876*
(Bologna, 1876).

he had been a very promising student. Still, said Carducci, when the old society is receding before a new, though as yet undefined, order of things and when the choice is between "utilitarian scepticism" and "generous utopianism," it is entirely natural that "young people of intelligence and heart are entirely attracted by the ideas of the International," which contain "the germs of the solution of many social problems."

Eloquence alone did not, of course, determine the outcome of the Bologna trial. Influencing the jurors were the acquittals of the Internationalists in Livorno and Massa-Carrara, as well as those of Rome, Trani, and Florence.[119] During the trial, too, the Right had fallen from power, and, for the moment at least, the climate of political opinion favored the accused Internationalists, in that it was the general but erroneous impression that the new government would reverse its predecessor's policy toward socialist and republican associations. The press also helped by giving the widest publicity to the propaganda speeches delivered by the Bologna defendants from the witness stand, to say nothing of the prosecution's attempt to use unreliable police reports, so transparently inaccurate that the formidable dialectical capacities of the battery of defense lawyers were almost wasted in ridiculing their substance.

Though it constituted no endorsement of anarchist principles or the socialist International, the verdict of "not guilty" rendered shortly after midnight on June 17 testified, in effect, to public disapproval of a government policy that seemed to violate the moral conscience of the nation—or at least a big segment of it. The question of whether, in the name of freedom, a minority had the right to seek to impose, by violence, its brand of liberty on the majority was never really confronted. Until the principles of socialism were to penetrate the nation, conceived as the majority, the momentary victory of the anarcho-socialists, the affirmation of the individual's civil rights, was an essentially hollow one, and all the evidence of government infringement of those rights did not alter the fact.

With the freeing of the Romagnol Internationalists, Andrea Costa threw himself into the task of reconstituting the Italian Federation. "The work of reorganization," he wrote his Swiss friends a few days after his liberation, "has already begun. The Roman and Neapolitan federations are already reconstituted; just today the Imola section was reorganized; tomorrow the Bologna federation will reorganize; and in a few days we shall celebrate the second congress of the Romagnol sections and federations, which will precede, by a short time, the third congress of the

[119] The Livorno Internationalists had been acquitted on Dec. 18, 1875. *La Plebe,* Dec. 20, 1875.

Italian Federation." [120] In itself, the message denied Cafiero's assertion of September, 1874, that "the era of congresses is definitely finished for us," that the Italian International would transform itself into a clandestine, illegal, conspiratorial *Apparat*. Reorganization "in the full light of day" implied, in fact, a recognition on the part of many Italian Internationalists that the experience of August 1874 and its aftermath suggested a change of tactics. On July 1, the old correspondence commission, now consisting of Francesco Natta and Gaetano Grassi, issued a circular convoking a national congress, clearly presaging a new orientation:

> After the events of 1874, the Italian International felt the need of a period of peaceful contemplation and calm [*sic!*]. It has tested its forces, it has strengthened itself in the study of its failures, it has prepared itself for a new period of struggle, to take a new step toward the accomplishment of its program. Full of life, it once again descends into the public arena and prepares to show that it exists, as always, to fight for the cause of the human race, trampled underfoot . . .[121]

On the very day that Natta and Grassi issued this call for the resurgence of the anarchist International in Italy, a manifesto was launched in Milan announcing the creation of the Lombard Federation of the I.W.A.[122] The document, challenging anarchist tactics and opposition to trade-unionism, constituted the first coherent, programmatic affirmation of the anti-Bakuninist current and clearly portended an imminent and decisive differentiation among Italian socialists in the sphere of organization as well.

Nor can we leave the date of July 1, 1876, without noting it as the day on which Italian anarchists lost their original source of inspiration. Michael Bakunin died in Bern. His lifelong philosophical commitment was aptly embodied in his famous aphorism: "The will to destroy is, at the same time, a creative will." [123] But, on the practical plane, he had recognized a qualification when, after pondering the failure of popular revolution in France and Spain, he had written: "We have made our calculations without taking into account the adherence of the masses, who did not want to interest themselves in their own emancipation, and because of the lack of this popular support, we were powerless in spite

---

[120] Guillaume, *I.D.S.*, IV, 21-22.

[121] For the circular, Jura *Bulletin*, July 23, 1876.

[122] Program manifesto, "Agli Operai, alle Operaie, alla gioventù d'Italia," *La Plebe*, July 6, 1876.

[123] *Die Lust der Zerstörung ist zugleich eine schaffende Lust*. Guillaume, *I.D.S.*, III, 312.

of being right theoretically." [124] That the qualification was not only important, but determining, had yet to be appreciated by the fanatical wing of the Italian International, still dedicated to the proposition that the success of a political movement depends only on the nobility of its intentions and the ardor put into professing them.

[124] Guillaume, *I.D.S.*, III, 202. For the Italian socialist press reaction to Bakunin's death, Pier Carlo Masini, "Echi della morte di Bakunin in Italia," *Movimento Operaio*, Yr. V, Nos. 5-6 (Sept.-Dec., 1953), 808-16.

XV

The Propaganda of Deeds: II.
San Lupo (July 1876 to April 1877)

ITALIAN SOCIALISM AND THE GOVERNMENT
OF THE LEFT

THE acquittal of Internationalists in the trials of 1875-76 and the public sympathy for the defendants that had contributed so heavily to the verdicts of absolution very logically produced a euphoric state of mind in the leaders of the Italian socialist movement. Nothing more was heard, as in the fall of 1874, of the virtues of clandestine conspiracy as a means of forwarding the cause; the Italian International, as the correspondence commission's circular of July 1, 1876, promised, was to "descend into the public arena." Presumably too, nothing of the anarchist program would be sacrificed in the resumption of public activity; anarchy and collectivism were to remain the goals, insurrection the means.

The decision to reorganize the International publicly was apparently premised on the notion that a public opinion that had caused the downfall of the Right in March 1876, at least partly because of that government's obtuseness with regard to the constitutional guarantees of both republicans and socialists, would certainly force the new government of the Left into moderating, if not reversing, this aspect of its predecessor's policy.[1] As the new Minister of Interior, Giovanni Nicotera, quondam brother-in-arms of Carlo Pisacane during the Sapri expedition of 1857, seemed a guarantee that public socialist organization and propaganda were reasonable possibilities. As it developed, Nicotera had no compunction about contradicting his own revolutionary past and, in

---

[1] In an appeal "To all the Workers of Italy" of June 26, 1876, by the Imola I.W.A. section, the hope was made explicit. *Cf.*, Gianni Bosio, Franco Della Peruta, "La 'svolta' di A. Costa, con documenti sul soggiorno in Francia," *Movimento Operaio*, Yr. IV, No. 2 (Mar.-Apr., 1952), 287-88, note 2; Jura *Bulletin*, July 9, 1876.

promising to maintain public order "with energy and vigor," drastically understated the character of the program of suppression he was to inaugurate against the socialists. He preferred, too, to deny the anti-socialist intent of his Draconian police-state measures: true Internationalists did not exist in Italy, he told the Chamber of Deputies; the victims of his campaign of repression were actually common miscreants, Romagnol knife-wielders, Neapolitan Camorrists, and Sicilians of the Mafia, using the name to cover their misdeeds.[2] It was a real change in government tactics in handling the Internationalist problem, far from the change hoped for by the socialists, and Andrea Costa identified it as a peril far greater than the policy of the Right:

> The Right . . . had a certain interest in leaving a shadow of life to the International, the name of which it used as a scarecrow to keep itself in power. The Left, on the other hand, having declared that the International did not exist in Italy, that it was an invention of the moderates, had every interest in causing people to believe that, if certain harebrains were preaching Emancipation and social Revolution, there was no serious organization in Italy. Hence the difference in the conduct of the two parties toward us. The Right tried to strike us especially as a party and as an organization; the Left has particularly tried to strike us as individuals. The first dissolved our associations and decreed mass arrests; the second, though of late it has come to ape the Right, at first attacked each one of us, admonished him, put him under trial, tried, in short, to deny him the possibility of movement. The Right treated us as political enemies, the Left has tried to defame us and have us considered vulgar malefactors, as bums and vagabonds who, neither wanting nor having anything else to do, were waiting to assault other people's lives and property.[3]

Such a policy was to have a drastic effect on the physical structure of the anarchist International in Italy, for no organization whose leaders were kept in jail or under *ammonizione* could long survive.[4] When to

[2] *Il Risveglio*, Feb. 11, 1877. For Costa's reply, see the special supplement to the Jan. 25, 1877, issue of *Il Martello* (Bologna). Most of the piece was also printed by *Il Risveglio*, Feb. 17, 25, 1877. *La Perseveranza*, now an opposition organ, charged (Dec. 18, 1876), that Nicotera's refusal to consider the Italian internationalists as political opponents was irresponsible, given the danger implicit in their program.

[3] Costa report to Verviers Congress, *L'Anarchia* (Naples), Oct. 6, 1877.

[4] The person admonished was required:
  1. Never to give occasion for adverse comment on his conduct;
  2. To go to the local police station between 9 and 11 A.M. every Sunday and there have his residence papers stamped;
  3. To remain in his home town and not change domicile without prior consent of the police;

this were added suppression of socialist newspapers, interception of correspondence between socialist chiefs, unrelenting police surveillance, the use of spies and informers, and all the other techniques available to a modern government intent on destroying a subversive organization, the plight of the Italian International in the post-1876 period became unbearable.

It was no consolation to the socialists that the government was simply going along with the spirit of the times. These were the years when the German socialist movement fell under the ruthless regime of Bismarck's anti-socialist laws, when Marshal MacMahon governed France as if the Communards he had suppressed in 1871 were scheming another uprising in Paris, instead of shriveling away in New Caledonian prisons or evading police surveillance in exile. Among Italy's rulers, the respect for constitutional liberties, the confidence that the social question posed no political problem, the faith that "ideas can be fought only with other ideas," these precepts, that had helped create the climate in which the Italian International had developed, were now in great part overpowered by fear of the socialist idea. The government very probably construed the acquittal of Internationalists in 1875-76 as an indication of increasing public recognition of the legitimacy of socialist demands for ameliorating the material condition of the lower classes, even if not as a sign of sympathy for the specific program of the absolved Internationalists.

Violation of constitutional guarantees by the government was to finish off the Italian International as an organization, but, as Cavour had warned, material suppression can not indefinitely contain the spread of an idea. Nor did it, so far as the essential socialist idea was concerned. This, however, was not the issue in the Italian socialist movement of the late 1870's. Not the general question of the validity of socialism's ultimate objectives was at stake, but that of method, that of whether the insur-

---

4. To stay out of hotels, cafés, and other public gathering places;
5. To stay in his own house from one hour after sunset to dawn and to be on hand for police interrogation at any time of the day or night;
6. Not to carry any kind of arms or any object capable of wounding;
7. To have a regular job or profession and to notify the police of same within eight days after being admonished;
8. Not to associate with, or speak to, persons suspected of real or imaginary crimes or misdemeanors.

The *ammonizione* was originally intended to apply to highway robbers, members of the Mafia and the Camorra, to bandits arrested, but subsequently freed for lack of evidence, and to recaptured escapees. The first violation of *ammonizione* was to be punished with a prison term, the third with deportation to a penal island in the Mediterranean (*domicilio coatto*). Jura *Bulletin*, Sept. 3, 24, 1876. The regulation, termed "a kind of juridical degradation. . . . in strident contrast with the constitutional precept that denies the administrative authorities the power of issuing regulations restrictive of personal liberty," was declared unconstitutional by the Italian Constitutional Court on July 3, 1956. *Il Messaggero* (Rome), July 4, 1956.

rectional *rationale* of the anarchists was sound in its premises and susceptible of effective application to the objective social and political situation of the time. This was an issue even more relevant to the diffusion of anarchist ideas than the material repression of the forces of law and order. The failure of the insurrectional movement of 1874 seemed an obvious portent of serious questioning, from within the ranks of the movement, of the wisdom of too thorough a commitment to the "propaganda of deeds," and doubtless heavy casualties were counted among the International's rank and file between August 1874 and July 1876. Still, as of the latter date, the spirit among the organization's leaders was one of optimism in regard to rebuilding the numerical and structural strength of the Italian International and, in most of them, of even more intense faith in violent revolution as the only effective method of destroying bourgeois society. Less than three years later, this optimism and this faith were shattered. The elimination of the former by the government and the liquidation of the latter under the impact of criticism stemming from within the movement itself constitute the twin threads of development after the Bologna jurors of 1876, in acquitting Andrea Costa and his fellow revolutionaries, opened the curtain on the final act of what has been described as the "romantic jag" of the Italian socialist movement.

THE CONGRESSES OF FLORENCE-TOSI AND BERN (OCTOBER 1876)

In the summer of 1876 the keynote among Italy's socialists was reorganization. As the Natta-Grassi circular of July 1 attests, the correspondence commission in Florence was once more in business. On July 16, the Emilian sections of the I.W.A. joined the Romagnol sections and federations in their second regional congress, held in Bologna.[5] Out of the deliberations came the foundation of the Romagnol-Emilian Federation, a decision to entrust Andrea Costa with the writing of a popular biography of the recently-deceased Bakunin,[6] and a solemn promise "to fight for the actuation of the ideas that Michael Bakunin . . . professed." Costa, acting as president, defined those ideas as "*anarchy* (the negation of all authority, that is, of any power which, by means of laws or force, imposes itself from above on [those] below) and *collectivism* (possession, by him who works, of the material and instruments of labor)." Since

[5] For the proceedings, *Atti del Congresso delle sezioni e federazioni della Romagna e dell'Emilia tenuto a Bologna il 16 di luglio del 1876* (Bologna, 1876), 20 pp.; *La Plebe* (Milan), July 23; Jura *Bulletin*, July 29, Aug. 6; *Il Martello*, July 29, 1876.

[6] Costa never finished the job, writing only forty-eight pages, covering Bakunin's career up to 1869. This effort appeared as *Vita di Michele Bakunin* (Bologna, 1877), Vol. I of the "Biblioteca del Martello" (Bologna). *Cf.*, also, Masini, "Echi della morte di Bakunin in Italia," p. 813,

neither a "workers' state" nor a "communist authoritarian" state was desired, anarchists necessarily abstained from politics. The insurrectional principle of Bakunin, though not explicitly stated, was implicit in Costa's reference to the goal of "the direct emancipation of the people."

On July 23 the Tuscan Federation came to life with its second regional congress in Florence. The delegates approved a federal pact for the region, fixed the seat of the correspondence commission at Siena, of the statistical and propaganda commission at Livorno, and decided to publish an official newspaper in Livorno, *Il Nuovo Risveglio*. Not at all consistent with Costa's ideal of "direct emancipation of the people" was the congress' approval of an initiative for the creation of trade-unions and workers' mutual aid societies, with resistance funds. The delegates favored strikes as "a means of protest of labor against the tyranny of capital." [7]

The regional congress of the Marchigian-Umbrian anarchists in Jesi on August 20 reiterated the orthodox anarchist line of the Bologna congress, elected a new federal commission, and adopted the Fabriano socialist newspaper, *Il Martello*, as the federation's official organ.[8] Yet, less than two weeks after the congress' affirmation of anarchist orthodoxy, *Il Martello* published (September 2) a piece on anarchist collectivism which, in effect, significantly expanded Costa's definition at Bologna. "And as we support the collective ownership of [raw] materials and the instruments of labor, we support the collective ownership of the products of labor; any individual who gives to society according to his capacities must receive from it according to his needs." The logical, though unstated, consequence of this position was a tacit repudiation of the Bakuninist formula, since any collective ownership of the "products of labor" implied a common authority with the power to assess their value and decree the method of their distribution—*communist* collectivism, not *anarchist* collectivism. Even such intransigent anarchists as Cafiero and Malatesta were soon to accept the communist principle,

[7] For the congress, *Il Martello*, July 29; *La Plebe*, July 30; *Jura Bulletin*, Aug. 6; *Lo Scarafaggio (Trapani)*, Aug. 7, 1876; Pezzi, *Un errore giudiziario*, p. 66; Guillaume, *I.D.S.*, IV, 48.

[8] For the congress proceedings, *La Plebe*, Aug. 28; supplement to *Il Martello*, Aug. 23; *Jura Bulletin*, Sept. 10, 1876; Guillaume, *I.D.S.*, IV, 66; Zoccoli, *L'Anarchia*, p. 345.

Il Martello had been founded on Apr. 22, 1876, with the program of educating the workers and reconciling Mazzinians and socialists. It began publication on Apr. 28 and broke off on July 1. When it resumed publication on July 29, 1876, under the editorship of Napoleone Papini, the paper dropped the plea for harmony and became uncompromisingly Internationalist. Enzo Santarelli, "Una fonte per la storia del movimento operaio marchigiano, 'Il Martello' di Fabriano-Jesi," *Movimento Operaio*, Yr. V, Nos. 5-6 (Sept.-Dec., 1953), 817-24.

though without drawing the logical inference with respect to the need for authority.

For the moment, such notes of doctrinal discrepancy went unnoticed. The Tuscan, Romagnol, and Marchigian-Umbrian reorganizations by no means constituted the full extent of the socialist resurgence in the summer of 1876. In the Veneto, in Lombardy, Piedmont, Sardinia, the Abruzzi, and Sicily, the work of rebuilding the International was well under way.[9] In Rome, the local Socialist Propaganda Circle, early in September, issued a call for a regional congress of the Lazio and Comarca sections; in Naples, the Workers' Federation invited all sections of the *Mezzogiorno* to organize; from Bari, the local section announced its reconstitution and urged the rebuilding of the Puglian Federation.[10] In Florence, Francesco Pezzi's wife spurred an all-female section into being, and in October the Florentine section of the I.W.A. was reconstituted.[11]

In September, 1876, the correspondence commission publicly convoked the third congress of the Italian International, to be held in Florence on October 22.[12] According to Pezzi, the purpose of the congress was the reorganization of the International and fixing its "line of conduct with respect to the agitation of the various political parties," [13] but Giovanni Nicotera and his police advisers believed—or pretended to believe— otherwise. Andrea Costa, who had been arrested less than two months before for leaving Imola to attend the Marchigian-Umbrian congress,[14] was again nabbed by the police, on the same excuse, as he arrived at the Florence railway station on the evening of October 19. He, Natta, and Grassi were jailed in the *Murate,* where they were joined the following evening by Massimo Innocenti, Giovanni Talchi, and other would-be delegates to the projected congress.[15] With the meeting hall and the

[9] *La Plebe,* July 6, 15, 19; *Lo Scarafaggio,* July 23; *Il Martello* (Fabriano), Aug. 19, 1876; Guillaume, *I.D.S.,* IV, 48, 66.

[10] *La Plebe,* Sept. 4; *Il Martello,* Sept. 16; Jura *Bulletin,* Sept. 24, 1876. According to Della Peruta, the Roman appeal never resulted in an actual regional federation. "L'Internazionale a Roma dal 1872 al 1877," p. 31.

[11] *Il Martello,* Aug. 19; Jura *Bulletin,* Oct. 15, 1876; Pezzi, *Un errore giudiziario,* pp. 66, 68. Women's sections were subsequently created in Aquila, Perugia, Carrara, and Prato. *Il Risveglio,* Dec. 24, 1876; Feb. 17, 1877.

[12] For the circular announcing the congress, *Il Martello,* Sept. 16, 23; *La Plebe,* Oct. 1, 1876. According to Pezzi, the decision to convoke a general congress for Oct., 1876, was taken by a group of Internationalists meeting in Rome some time earlier that year. Pezzi identifies them only as "different from those at large in Switzerland, different from those [exonerated at] the trials, and others . . . still not known to the police." *Un errore giudiziario,* p. 26.

[13] *Ibid.,* p. 68.

[14] Costa had been sentenced to a month in jail and six months' surveillance, but a Bologna court, on appeal, reversed the sentence. Jura *Bulletin,* Sept. 3, 1876.

[15] *La Perseveranza,* Oct. 21; *La Plebe,* Oct. 22, Nov. 5; Jura *Bulletin,* Oct. 29; *Il Martello* (Jesi), Nov. 19, 1876. Costa was acquitted on Nov. 22, 1876. *La Plebe,* Nov. 25; *Il Risveglio,* Nov. 26; *La Perseveranza,* Dec. 3, 1876.

delegates' hotel occupied by the police, the forty-odd delegates who managed to escape arrest repaired to Pontassieve, outside Florence, but here, too, the deployment of *carabinieri*, public security agents, and a company of infantry drove them to seek another meeting place, the village of Tosi, well up in the Appenines, reached only after a nine-hour march in a driving rain. The police denied them the local inn, so the soggy troop convened its congress in a nearby wood, the downpour continuing. "As you might imagine," Cafiero related, "there were no long speeches."

Practically all Italian regions were represented at the congress that opened on October 21, but the presence of Cafiero, Malatesta, Tommaso Schettino, and Emilio Covelli from Naples, of Francesco Pezzi and his wife, of Fortunato Serantoni and Alfredo Mari (Florence), guaranteed a strong support for anarchist extremism.[16] Enrico Bignami, mandated by the newly founded Federation of Upper Italy, arrived too late to add his moderating councils to the discussion. Still, the nature of the questions submitted for debate suggests that many segments of the Italian International had begun to reconsider the tactics of the past. A Neapolitan section queried whether the International should be organized by trade-unions; Bari asked whether it might not be useful for the I.W.A. to participate in political elections (to allow "pure socialists" to affirm socialist principles in a bourgeois parliament); Florence asked whether socialists should help in establishing a republic.[17]

On all questions of tactics, the delegates reaffirmed an intransigently anarchist line: only by revolution can the social question be resolved; revolutionary agitation is the only effective way to educate the workers to socialism and to bring them into the struggle against privilege; socialist participation in elections would make the proletariat "an unconscious instrument of bourgeois political parties"; socialist assistance in a republic or any other form of government would constitute a "real betrayal of the cause of Humanity."

The break with the past came when the congress made official the

---

[16] For the proceedings and background details, *La Plebe*, Nov. 5; *Il Risveglio*, Nov. 9; *Il Martello*, Nov. 19, 1876; Pezzi, *Un errore giudiziario*, pp. 27-29, 68-70; Guillaume, *I.D.S.*, IV, 66-68.

Emilio Covelli (1846-1915) was a childhood friend of Cafiero. Born of a wealthy, noble family of Trani, he had studied law in Florence, Turin, and Heidelberg. Thanks chiefly to Gaetano Grassi, he had been brought into the Neapolitan socialist group after the Bologna insurrectional attempt of 1874. See Lucarelli, *Carlo Cafiero*, pp. 85-90, 103-10. Cf., also, Angiolini, *op. cit.*, p. 166; Romano, *Storia*, III, 299, note 9; Schiavi, "La formazione del pensiero politico di Andrea Costa," p. 29, note 2.

[17] *La Plebe*, Oct. 16; *Il Martello*, Nov. 19, 1876; Guillaume, *I.D.S.*, IV, 66. One of the delegates later complained to Bignami that many questions were not fully discussed and that the resolutions voted did not correspond to the views of many sections. *La Plebe*, Nov. 15, 1876.

communist principle enunciated by *Il Martello* several weeks earlier: "Each must do for society all that his abilities allow him to do, and he has the right to demand from society the satisfaction of all his needs, in the measure conceded by the state of production and social capacities." [18] The traditional anarchist slogan, "from each according to his ability, to each according to his productivity," had given way to the communist one, "from each according to his ability, to each according to his needs." The old formula, Malatesta explained many years later, was abandoned because "the only solution that can realize the ideal of human fraternity and eliminate all the insoluble difficulties of measuring the effort made and the value of the products obtained is a communist organization, in which each voluntarily gives his contribution to production and freely consumes that which is required for his needs." [19] More specifically, he indicated on another occasion, if the individual's share of the product depends on his productive capacity, the resulting competition to possess the most efficient means of production would disadvantage the less able and perpetuate "bourgeois morality," thus preventing man from reaching that moral condition in which he neither does nor wishes to do anything that harms others.[20]

The fact that the International moved from a collectivist to a communist theory of future society mattered little in itself, but it was evident that even the extremists were beginning to subject their articles of faith to the test of logic and common sense. The congress' reiteration of the insurrectional and antipolitical method showed that the same critical analysis had not yet affected tactical formulas, but these were soon to be subjected to the test of experience, far more rigorous than that of theoretical discussions in a rain-soaked forest.

The Tosi delegates wound up their labors by electing Francesco Pezzi, Carlo Cafiero, and Gaetano Grassi to the correspondence commission, the seat of which was transferred to Naples from Florence, and mandating Cafiero and Maltesta to represent the Italian Federation at the imminent international anarchist congress, scheduled to convene in Bern on October 26.

At the Bern conclave,[21] Malatesta recited the history of the Italian Federation since 1874 and, for the first time, defined his concept of the organization in the same *anticlassista* sense expressed by Andrea Costa at Geneva three years earlier:

[18] Conti, *O.S.F.*, p. 194.
[19] *Pensiero e Volontà* (Rome), Aug. 29, 1926.
[20] Errico Malatesta, *Scritti scelti*, ed. by Cesare Zaccaria and Giovanna Berneri (Naples: Edizioni RL, 1947), pp. 275 ff.
[21] For the proceedings, Guillaume, *I.D.S.*, IV, 91-111; Jura *Bulletin*, Oct. 29, Nov. 5, 12; *La Plebe*, Dec. 4, 1876.

From our point of view, . . . the International must not be an exclusively workers' organization; the goal of the social revolution, in effect, is not only the emancipation of the working class, but the emancipation of the whole of humanity; and the International, which is the army of the revolution, must group under its banner all revolutionaries, without distinction of class. In Italy, it is not trade-unionism that can ever give a serious result; the economic conditions of Italy and the temperament of the Italian workers are opposed to it.

By Marxist canons, Malatesta's refusal to identify the cause of social revolution with a single class was a negation based on "an absolute incomprehension of the objective historical inevitability of the function of [the working] class." [22] The Marxian premise aside, however, the most to be said is that Malatesta's condemnation of trade-unionism as "reactionary" revealed a blindness to the social revolutionary potential of organized labor. But, saddled with the premise that "the masses" are inherently and spontaneously revolutionary, Malatesta could have come to no other conclusion. [23]

The same spirit of intransigence was manifested in Malatesta's comments on the proposal to hold an international congress the following year to resolve the differences between the various tendencies of European socialism. "The International"—meaning the anarchist organization—"is the sole existing association that really represents the socialist aspirations of the people. Consequently, we believe that our association must be represented at the socialist congress, not to be absorbed by a new organization, but only to defend its principles and methods of action and to seek to attract to itself those workers' organizations that still have not entered its ranks."

Malatesta's historical summary of the Italian International's activities after 1874 prompted two Swiss social-democratic newspapers to insinuate that the organization was split by two widely divergent currents of opinion. In issuing a *démenti,* he and Cafiero included a precise definition of their anarchist position:

---

[22] Thus, Romano, *Storia,* III, 258. "The substance of Marxism consists in the affirmation of the necessity of the *hegemony of the proletariat in the revolution* and in demonstrating the historic inevitability of this hegemony, being based on the very laws that regulate the objective development of capitalist society." Thus, Palmiro Togliatti, writing under the pseudonym of *Ercoli,* "Marxismo e bakuninismo," *Stato Operaio,* Paris (Nov., 1934), 823.

[23] With the experience of half a century behind him, Malatesta was to write: ". . . we had a mystic faith in the virtue of the people, in their capacity, in their egalitarian and libertarian instincts. The facts showed . . . how far from the truth we were." Preface to Nettlau's volume, *B.I.I.,* xxvii-xxviii.

. . . 2. The Italian Federation believes that the *insurrectional fact*, destined to affirm socialist principles by deeds, is the most effective means of propaganda and the only one which, without tricking and corrupting the masses, can penetrate the deepest social layers and draw the living forces of humanity into the struggle sustained by the International;

3. The Italian Federation considers the collective ownership *of the products of labor* as the necessary complement of the collectivist program, *the cooperation of all for the satisfaction of the needs of each* being the only rule of production and consumption that corresponds to the principle of solidarity . . .[24]

With this reiteration of the communist formula covering the distribution of consumer goods in a hypothetical socialist society, we may take leave of the matter, for by now, European anarchists, no less than the Italian, were agreed on the principle.[25]

With respect to the insurrectional principle, however, insistence at this late date belied the confident note of Cafiero and Malatesta's affirmation, in the same document, that the only Italian socialists not adhering—or in the process of adhering—to the anarchist program were "a little group which, inspired by personal interests and reactionary objectives, is trying to make a propaganda that it calls 'gradual and pacific.'" By this group was meant, as Malatesta's allusions in his historical report to the Bern congress indicate, Tito Zanardelli and Lodovico Nabruzzi, who, according to Malatesta, were seeking to exploit the Italian workers' movement for their own advantage out of spite for having been excluded from the secret Committee for the Social Revolution that had prepared the 1874 insurrectional project. The plain fact was that the two disgruntled Italians in Lugano, by the fall of 1876, represented neither the core nor the extent of the schismatic current developing in the ranks of Italian socialism. Milan, not Lugano, was the focal point of the dissension; Enrico Bignami and Gnocchi-Viani, not Zanardelli and Nabruzzi, were its effective animators.

CONSOLIDATION OF THE LEGALITARIAN CURRENT

Though the original impetus to an anti-anarchist orientation came from the Ceresio section of Lugano, the founding of the Lombard Federation on July 1, 1876, marked the beginning of a fairly coherent revisionist movement on Italian soil. The manifesto issued by the Milan nucleus

[24] Jura *Bulletin*, Dec. 3, 1876.

[25] According to Malatesta, the Italian resolution was immediately and enthusiastically endorsed by Peter Kropotkin, Elisée Reclus, and the Swiss anarchists. *Scritti scelti* (1947 ed.), pp. 275 ff.

centered around Bignami and *La Plebe* very precisely defined the areas
of disagreement with the anarchists, even while indicating those points
of the anarchist program from which the "legalitarians" were still reluctant to detach themselves.[26] On the conspiratorial and insurrectional
tactic, the Milanese were emphatically hostile, but insisted on calling
themselves "revolutionary."

> . . . In the present state of affairs, conspiracy and certain
> revolutionary attempts can generally serve only as a pretext for
> an implacable repression. If, because of these words, someone
> were to accuse us of being too *opportunistic* and too *pacific*, we
> would reply to the impatient ones that we are even more
> impatient than they, but that we can not delude ourselves about
> attempts always destined to have an unhappy outcome and that,
> knowing nothing can be done now if not on the condition that
> we have *numbers and organization,* we are waiting to become
> numerous and organized. And it is precisely for this reason that
> we, *revolutionaries* as much as they and even more *revolutionary,*
> in the scientific sense of the word, than those who urge these
> proofs, are reorganizing ourselves.[27]

On the question of syndical organization, the manifesto challenged
both the anarchists' neglect of trade-unions as a social revolutionary
medium and their hostility toward the general principle of class organization. Bignami and his friends were obviously not alluding to the
Bakuninist International when they wrote:

> The International, . . . with its *arts and crafts Associations,*
> with its *Societies of resistance,* with its *workers' Chambers of
> labor,* with its *workers' Federations,* with its *credit, consumers'
> and producers' Societies* and with the innumerable *Strikes* it has
> supported, . . . has intervened everywhere to defend the in-
> terests of the workers.

This is the kind of activity to be intensified, the manifesto continued,
and ultimate separation from the anarchist International was implicit in
the proposal for the creation of a "Workers' Party of Italy," which, in a
national congress, should lay the bases for "a powerful International
Federation." Such an appeal, though clearly superseding the anarchist
position against syndical organization of the workers, did not at all imply
that a "Workers' Party" should concern itself with political struggle, for
the Milanese legalitarians, remembering Malon's advice against precipitate entry into political activity, were still not ready to break with the
anarchist view of the state. They rationalized their hesitancy on this point,

[26] For the July 1, 1876, manifesto, *La Plebe,* July 6, 1876.
[27] *La Plebe* reiterated the motif on Sept. 10 and Dec. 31, 1876.

however, by producing a definition of anarchy based on their peculiar understanding of federalism:

> The *federalists* want the regional and communal groups, political as well as economic, to preserve the free disposition of themselves and to cooperate freely in supporting social burdens of a general interest. ANARCHY, which literally means *no government, no authority,* is nothing but *federalism* carried to its ultimate political and social consequences. It is the substitution of popular inspiration for *raison d'État.*

It was this watering down of the anarchists' total opposition to the state and politics that permitted Enrico Bignami, in the pages of *La Plebe,* to characterize electoral activity as "merely a question of tactics" to be resolved in different ways, according to the country and circumstances concerned. In the Italy of 1876, political abstention was called for.[28] Here again, the practical conclusion harmonized with the anarchist position, but admitting the criterion of relativity was a clear repudiation of the anarchists' absolute hostility toward political action.

Such pronouncements brought their challenge in the anarchist press. Throughout the fall and winter of 1876-77 the debate roared on, beginning on the plane of principle, but soon degenerating into mere invective. On the one side were *Il Martello,* which came under Costa's direct personal control early in January, 1877, when it was transferred from Jesi to Bologna; the *Nuovo Risveglio* of Siena, appearing in November, 1876; and the *Bulletin* of the Swiss Jurassian Federation. In Florence, the local extremists announced a December 5 publication date for a new journal, *L'Anarchia,* promising to make it a weapon against the "new charlatans of socialism, . . . the most dangerous enemies of the working class." [29] On the legalitarian side were *La Plebe* and *Il Povero* (Palermo), the latter resuming publication on September 24, after a hiatus extending back to August, 1874. Each camp, of course, accused the other of betraying and corrupting the workers. Thus, *Il Povero,* in attacking the "vagabond missionaries and revolutionaries at any cost" for their lack of discipline and pride of program:

> Ours is not a banner of sterile, improvised agitations, nor the mark of individual impatience—it is the banner of the proletariat, not of any single faction or camarilla. The proletariat has no chiefs, no *condottieri,* no emissaries, no prophets, no martyrs, no altars. . . . Let us put ourselves on the true path and remain loyal to the only true program of the old International. He who

[28] Oct. 1, 1876.
[29] Jura *Bulletin,* Dec. 10, 1876. Publication had to be postponed, however, and the paper ultimately appeared in Naples on Aug. 25, 1877.

drags us elsewhere, he who wants to walk further than is possible, does not help his brother take one step forward, nor does he improve much or little the condition of the poor plebe.[30]

Thus, *Il Martello*, with an article entitled, "Little by Little," accused "the apostles of conciliation and equivocation" of "finding satisfaction of their own aspirations in the state of present poverty," which makes them "more dangerous than the avowed enemies of the popular cause."[31]

Concurrently with these press polemics regarding questions of principle, the legalitarians made significant progress on the organizational level. On the eve of the Florence-Tosi Congress, the Milanese Circle of Economic-Social Studies had announced its intended participation in the anarchist convention and convoked a preparatory meeting of the Lombard socialists, as well as those of Piedmont, the Veneto, Ferrara, and the neighboring Swiss canton of Ticino. The result was the formation on October 15 of the Federation of Upper Italy, composed of twelve sections, with a program based on the trade-unionist, evolutionary program of Bignami's Milanese study group. Bignami was subsequently elected to the Federation's propaganda commission, Osvaldo Gnocchi-Viani to its correspondence commission.[32] It was the voice of this rapidly expanding organization that failed to be heard—thanks to Bignami's late arrival— when the Italian International reaffirmed its anarchist orientation at Tosi on October 21-22.

While north Italian socialists, in mandating Bignami to the national congress, indicated that as yet they had no serious schismatic intent, Sicilian socialists were openly split on the question of continued adherence to the national organization, as currently constituted. Early in August 1876 the Trapani socialist newspaper, *Lo Scarafaggio*, in the name of the local Propaganda Circle and that of Palermo, proposed to the island's socialists a regional congress to organize a Sicilian Federation. In turn, the Palermo section, under the control of the legalitarian, Salvatore Ingegneros, and backed by the socialists of Girgenti and Trapani, urged all the country's socialists to abstain from any national congress until all regional federations were reconstituted.[33] The Catania section, however, announced its intention of attending the Florence-Tosi congress, and, after Enrico Bignami urged the other Sicilian groups to do the

[30] *Il Povero*, Oct. 23; reprinted by *La Plebe*, Dec. 10, 1876.

[31] Nov. 19, reprinted by the Jura *Bulletin*, Dec. 10, 1876. Guillaume, (*I.D.S.*, IV, 114) and Romano (*Storia, III*, 263) attribute the article to Costa; Francesco Pezzi, in 1882, attributed it to Cafiero. Letter of Apr. 7, 1882, Gianni Bosio, *comp.*, "Lettere ad Andrea Costa e ad Anna Kuliscioff di Francesco Pezzi," *Movimento Operaio*, Yr. II, Nos. 7-8 (Apr.-May, 1950), 199.

[32] *La Plebe*, Oct. 9, 22, Nov. 15, 1876. *Il Risveglio*, Dec. 24, 1876, reproduces the federal *Regolamento* adopted by the Federation.

[33] Aug. 7, 27; *La Plebe*, Aug. 20, Sept. 4, 1876.

same,[34] the Girgenti and Trapani associations, along with those of Cianciana and Santa Caterina, mandated Andrea Costa to represent them at the national congress, though they identified themselves as tendentially dissident by suggesting congress discussion of such questions as full autonomy for regional federations in choosing their revolutionary methods and socialist participation in municipal government.[35]

Even in Naples, the original stronghold of Bakuninism, an evolution-ist group had appeared, headed by Luigi Felicò, one of the veterans of the Neapolitan Workers' Federation who, in the columns of *Il Povero*, took Cafiero, Malatesta, and Emilio Covelli to task as "mystifiers of the International, . . . insensate little students, . . . bourgeois masked as proletarians, who advance themselves as teachers of the workers, but who are only slothful parasites who live without justifying their means of subsistence." [36] The characterization must, indeed, have rung strangely in the ears of the once wealthy Cafiero, who had pauperized himself, however unwisely, in the hope of redeeming, among others, the wretched *straccioni* of *la bella Napoli*.

By February 1877 the anti-anarchist movement in northern Italy had reached an ideological position that no longer permitted the fiction that the Federation of Upper Italy and the Italian anarchist International could collaborate on the organizational level. At the Federation's second congress, held in Milan on February 17-18,[37] less than two dozen dis-sident sections were represented, but their geographical distribution (Lombardy, Piedmont, and the Veneto) suggested the imminent ex-clusion of anarchist influence in northern Italy, at best never as extensive or intensive as in Tuscany and the Romagna.[38]

Osvaldo Gnocchi-Viani, reporting on socialist tactics, defined the anarchists' concept of "revolution" as "material force," as "synonymous with Insurrection." The legalitarians, said he, also accept this kind of revolution but, unlike the anarchists, regard it as "one among many methods." Even admitting it as "the most energetic or . . . the ultimate, definitive method," does not prejudice the adoption of others "suggested

[34] *La Plebe*, Oct. 1, 1876.

[35] *Ibid.*, Oct. 22, Dec. 10, 1876. For the subsequent sharp debate between the Sicilian sections attending the Florence-Tosi Congress and the Palermitan "absten-tionists," see *Il Martello*, Nov. 19, 1876; *La Plebe*, Dec. 31, 1876; *Il Povero*, Oct. 23, 1876.

[36] Apr. 18, 1877.

[37] For the proceedings, *Secondo Congresso della Federazione dell'Alta Italia e Nuclei Aderenti tenuto in Milano nei giorni 17-18 febbraio 1877* (Milan, 1877). *La Plebe*, Feb. 26; *Il Risveglio*, Mar. 4, 1877.

[38] For the member sections of the Federation, see Della Peruta, "La Banda de Matese," pp. 351, 353; *cf.*, also, *La Plebe*, July 15, Dec. 4, 1876; Jan. 21, 30, 1877.

by special considerations of time and place." Until the time is ripe for insurrection, it behooved socialists to find other ways to relieve proletarian suffering, otherwise, socialism "risks becoming torpid, distrusted, while leaving the way open for astute adversaries to hide themselves in the midst of the suffering classes, to delude them with this or that expedient, to win their sympathies and thus interfere with our work."

Joseph Favre, secretary of the Swiss Ceresio section, supported Gnocchi-Viani's point of view but extended the attack to political abstentionism:

> We believe that all methods are good and we accept them all. . . . I, too, say that hunger has no need of political eloquence, but it would be spurning the most evident truth to reject the process of the permanent evolution of human beings.
>
> We are told that "the goal will be reached only by revolution," We, too, believe that an ultimate, violent effort will have to be made; but one must prepare for it with all possible means and by making propaganda. Therefore, there is no need to repeat [that] *there is no salvation outside of the church*. It is not by crying: *Anarchy! Revolution!* that we shall persuade the masses, but rather by demonstrating that a great economic-social reform is necessary. To demonstrate and persuade today, one must speak and write. . . . If all the workers were to form an independent *socio-political* party and move frankly toward the goal, I, too, would go to the urn to name *worker-socialist* deputies, if for no other reason than to have socialism present in the Parliaments. . . . To the comrade who sympathizes almost exclusively with the ideas of martyrdom and propaganda made with prisons and trials, I will respond that we already have enough martyrs of the revolution and that it is not worth the trouble to create more of them to give pleasure to the bourgeoisie.

It was a commentary on the doctrinal chasm separating the legalitarians from the anarchists that the delegates debated, not whether syndical organization of the workers was desirable, but whether organization by crafts was preferable to mixed associations. The Mantuan delegates favored the latter as "less alarming to the capitalists and industrialists" and not likely to provoke employer coalitions. Precisely herein, retorted Gnocchi-Viani, lay the proof that general associations offered little hope for the workers. Struggle is inevitable, so the substantial question is which form of organization produces the greater class solidarity. Gnocchi-Viani's definition was a repudiation of the anarchist conception that assigned only a pre-insurrectional value to any economic agitation and a rejection of the Mazzinian search for morality in class collaboration.[39]

On the basic question of revolutionary method, Florido Matteucci, delegate of the Pavia section, insisted that noninsurrectional methods "only deceive the proletariat, because they are palliatives." He proposed that the Federation adopt the constitution of the anarchist Romagnol-Emilian Federation and declare its immediate adherence to the Italian International.[40] On all scores the majority remained obdurate. The congress concluded that "for the development and triumph of socialism, no method should be neglected, from the simple word of the propagandist to the most energetic manifestation of the multitudes"—which, of course, left the door open for political activity. In its *Regolamento*—perhaps out of fear of being called "authoritarians" by the anarchists—the Federation of Upper Italy denied legislative power to general congresses in matters of doctrine, but otherwise ignored the constitutional pattern set by the Bologna Congress of the Romagna-Emilia Federation.[41] Though agreeable to participation in the universal socialist congress projected by the anarchist Bern Congress of October 1876 in the hope of reconciling authoritarians and anarchists, the Italian legalitarians rejected, in effect, the modifications of the original I.W.A. statutes by the anarchist Geneva Congress of 1873. Though continuing to consider themselves "part of the International," they affirmed the independence of the Federation of Upper Italy from the other federations of the peninsula.[42] The move was a logical consequence of conflicting tactical formulas, which in turn reflected the legalitarians' rejection of the anarchists' fundamental and erroneous premise: that the single fact of poverty determines the will and capacity to revolt.

Certainly the legalitarians' shifting the emphasis from the insurrectional method to that of trade-unionism as a resistance weapon, to say nothing of their justifying political action as one of several legitimate methods of struggle, brought them closer to Marxism than Italian socialists had ever been before. Marx noted, with gratification, the dissident federation's return to the original I.W.A. statutes of 1864—though

---

[39] Manacorda, *Il movimento operaio italiano*, p. 112.

[40] Matteucci was obeying his mandate from the Pavia section. Jura *Bulletin*, Feb. 25, 1877.

[41] For the *Regolamento Federale*, *La Plebe*, Apr. 3, 1877.

[42] *Il Martello's* reaction (Feb. 24, 1877): "We can not help but marvel . . . that the Federation of Upper Italy does not adhere to the Italian Federation 'so as not to be bound to anyone' and then, without batting an eyelid, accepts its future Program from nothing less than the . . . *Povero* [of Palermo]." Two decades later, however, Andrea Costa, viewing the programs of the Italian Federation and the Federation of Upper Italy, claimed there was no "essential difference" between them! *Bagliori di socialismo*, p. 21.

he failed to note, as well, that this also excluded recognition of the London Conference decison of September 1871, which *required* political action.[43] Engels, in an article in the German Social Democratic organ, *Vorwärts*, interpreted the Milan Congress deliberations as a sign that the Italian workers' movement was "preparing its own renewal" and joining the stream of European development.[44]

Actually, the Italian legalitarians had by no means accepted the conclusion that "the economic and political movements are indissolubly united" (London Conference) or that "the first duty of the working class is the conquest of political power" (*Inaugural Address* of 1864). To the extent that their principles derived from any single source, that source was Benoît Malon's scientific positivism, taken, in turn, from Auguste Comte.[45] Bignami, Gnocchi-Viani, and their friends, though manifesting a clear preference for trade-unionism, were still essentially eclectic, or "experimentalist," as they preferred to describe their approach. Their refusal to adopt the single method of insurrection was grounded on the fact that "it would exclude the great experimental method," [46] or again, as Bignami put it, "Experimentalism teaches us that the use of one method must not exclude others." [47] Just as their rejection of insurrection as the primary method of struggle separated them from Bakuninism, so, too, their unwillingness to accept political action as the essential tactic put a gulf between them and Marxism.[48] The anarchist position had been superseded; the Marxist position had yet to be reached.

[43] Letter to Engels, Mar. 3, 1877, *Briefwechsel,* IV, 449. Actually, the Milan Congress meant by the "original statutes" those voted by the Geneva Congress of 1866, as Bignami was careful to point out. *La Plebe,* Apr. 3, 1877.

[44] Mar. 16, 1877; reproduced in *Le Mouvement Socialiste,* XXXIV (Sept.-Oct., 1913), 147-53. True to form, Engels saw the Italian development as an occasion to voice his rancor toward the anarchists. "In Italy, therefore, the breach in the fortress of the lawyers, literati, and triflers has been made." Engels to Marx, Feb. 23, 1877, *Briefwechsel,* IV, 447-48. Engels added: "With this schism in Italy, the gentlemen dictators of anarchy are really darlings. From the little cry of alarm in . . . *La Plebe* in regard to the *narrow, anarchist,* and at the same time—monstrous contradiction— *dictatorial* spirits, it appears that Bignami has known at first hand the peculiar character of those people." Engels to Marx, Mar. 6, 1877, *ibid.,* IV, 451-52.

[45] See Valiani, *Storia del movimento socialista,* I, 226-27.

[46] Resolution adopted by the Milan Congress of Feb. 17-18, 1877.

[47] *La Plebe,* Mar. 13, 1877. For his part, Gnocchi-Viani could have given no clearer proof of his social Darwinism, than when he wrote: "If natural law, illustrated by the genius of Darwin, explains to us the anthropological process of organic nature, why shouldn't this same logic make us see unexpected phenomena in the infinite combinations of ideas?" *Ibid.,* Nov. 21-22, 1875.

[48] Non-Marxian, too, was the *anticlassismo* of Bignami, revealed in his articles in *La Plebe,* Dec. 31, 1876, Mar. 13, 1877, and Feb. 5, 1878, all denying Giulio Trevisani's judgment that "the reading of the collection of *La Plebe* makes us see in Enrico Bignami not only a fundamentally firm Marxist conception, but also an anticipatory vision of the functions of the party." "La Plebe di Lodi: marxismo contro anarchismo," *Nord-Sud,* Yr. II, No. 17 (Oct. 15-31, 1946), 11-14.

"SOCIAL LIQUIDATION," REVISED EDITION:
SAN LUPO

The Milan Congress provoked bitter invective in the anarchist camp. "Bourgeois disguised as socialists" was the epithet applied to Bignami and Gnocchi-Viani by the Jurassian *Bulletin*;[49] to Andrea Costa and his fellow propagandists of *Il Martello*, those who believed in the pacific liberation of the workers were "metaphysicians." But there was a defensive note in the anarchists' explanation that they did not want revolution because they were bloodthirsty, but because—since revolution was inevitable in any case—they felt the sooner it came the better.[50] By now, Costa himself was convinced that the best way to speed the day of reckoning was not conspiracy, but propaganda, if his famous open letter to the Minister of Interior is to be taken at face value:

> By means of conspiracy a change in the form of government can be obtained; a principle can be dispossessed or punctured and another put in its place, but it can not achieve social revolution, as the International understands and desires it. To do this is a matter of widely diffusing the new principles in the masses, or better, to awaken them in them, since they already have them instinctively, and to organize the workers of the whole world, so that the revolution occurs by itself, from the bottom to the top and not vice versa, either by means of laws and decrees or by force. And this necessarily involves publicity, since it is impossible to reconcile the idea of such a vast propaganda with the necessarily restricted circle of a conspiracy.[51]

It was not Costa, however, who determined the tactic of the Italian International in the spring of 1877, but Carlo Cafiero and Errico Malatesta, who had by no means forsaken the Bakuninist concept of permanent revolution as the shortest path to the ultimate destruction of bourgeois society. Since the fall of 1876, these two paladins of conspiracy had been hatching another insurrectional project. They had stayed in Switzerland for several weeks after the Bern Congress of late October, trying to dispose of the Baronata in order to raise the needed cash. Failing in this, they persuaded a Russian revolutionary socialist, one Mlle Smetskaia, to lend them four thousand francs and Cafiero managed to scrape up five to six thousand more from his family in Barletta as the

---

[49] Mar. 11, 1877. For the legalitarian counterattack of Malon and Bignami, *La Plebe*, Mar. 6, 13, 1877.

[50] *Il Martello*, Mar. 1, 1877.

[51] "Lettera aperta di un gruppo di Internazionalisti a G. Nicotera," special supplement, *ibid.*, Jan. 25, 1877.

final liquidation of his inheritance. Late in December 1876 they repaired to Naples, now the seat of the Italian correspondence commission. Here, in collaboration with Francesco Pezzi and Gaetano Grassi, the other members of the commission, they began a three-month period of intensive preparation for an armed uprising in the *Mezzogiorno*.[52]

The general plan called for creation of an armed band that would "move about in the countryside as long as possible, preaching war, exciting to social brigandage, occupying the small communes and then leaving them after having performed those revolutionary acts that were possible and advancing to those localities where our presence would be manifested most usefully." [53] In the calculations of the insurrectionists, the fate of their own enterprise was irrelevant, if it succeeded in sparking a mass conflagration. The conception was Bakuninism pure and simple.[54] Pietro Cesare Ceccarelli, who, with Cafiero and Malatesta, was to lead the effort, subsequently explained that the action was intended as purely provocatory:

> We could not hope to win, since we knew that a few tens of individuals armed with almost unserviceable rifles can not win battles against regiments armed with Vetterlys. Partisans of the propaganda of deeds, we wanted to commit an act of propaganda; persuaded that revolution must be provoked, we committed an act of provocation. . . . We were a band of rebels destined to provoke an insurrection, [a band] that can not and must not count on anything but the echo it might find in the populations.[55]

Bakuninist in inspiration, too, was the selection of the scene of operations, for here was to be found the "proletariat of rags," the landless peasants who, in the Russian's formula, were an essential factor in social revolution. Ceccarelli justified the conspirators' faith in the possibility of a modern *Jacquerie* in these terms:

---

[52] Pezzi, *Un errore giudiziario*, p. 30; Jura *Bulletin*, Dec. 24, 1876; *La Plebe*, Jan. 7, 1877; Guillaume, *I.D.S.*, IV, 116. Late in Jan., 1877, Cafiero informed the Federal Committee of the Jura that socialist reorganization was well advanced in Italy, so much so that the time was not very distant when "the socialist revolutionary movement will be imposed on the bourgeoisie." Lucarelli, *Carlo Cafiero*, p. 57.

[53] Letter of Pietro Cesare Ceccarelli to Amilcare Cipriani, Mar. or Apr., 1881, reproduced by Della Peruta, "La Banda del Matese," Documentary Appendix, pp. 377-84. This document is cited below as "Ceccarelli to Cipriani."

[54] "We must ceaselessly make revolutionary attempts, even if we were to be defeated and routed completely, one, two, ten, even twenty times; but if, on the twenty-first time, the people support us by taking part in our revolution, we shall have been repaid for all the sacrifices we supported." Dragomanov, *Correspondence de Michel Bakounine*, p. 85.

[55] Ceccarelli to Cipriani, p. 380.

Against the peasants, or also even without the peasants, a political change is possible, but not the social revolution, especially in a country like Italy, in which the rural element is in the great majority, and in which heavy industry and big workers' agglomerations are still the exception. . . . The Italian peasant, . . . the proletarian of the countryside, is in Italy a hundred times more revolutionary than the city dweller and the entire history of the century proves it. . . .

Naturally, it is not political transformations nor the empty phrases of liberalism that can excite the peasants, for whom "liberty" has always meant an increase of the tax in blood and money. The social revolution is needed to make the peasant arise, that which calls him to the expropriation of the *signori* and the sudden sweeping away of *carabinieri*, petty bureaucrats, and magistrates. . . .

If you had been able to follow the events of recent years in Italy, you would have seen that the thousand spontaneous movements occurring in the rural communes justify our resting our greatest hopes on the peasants. And besides, only a peasant revolution can securely guarantee us against a purely political transformation, which would only be the consolidation of the power of the bourgeoisie. . . .[56]

Selected as the specific site of operations was the rugged knot of mountains known as the Matese, sixty-odd kilometers northeast of Naples, offering maximum opportunity for guerrilla-type warfare and inhabited by "a warlike population that gave a very strong contingent to brigandage," believed ripe for revolution.[57] The area was close enough to Naples to afford ready contact with conspiratorial headquarters, and several members of the revolutionary groups were familiar with the countryside and its inhabitants.[58]

Costa was to deny that the Italian International, as such, had anything to do with the affair: it was "a purely individual act," involving only "voluntary participants"; the plan was known only to "a restricted number of individuals," and its actuation in no way compromised the national

[56] Ceccarelli to Cipriani, pp. 378-79.
[57] Costa later said that since the peasant's only channel of active protest against oppression was to become a brigand, the logical step was to make brigandage popular by identifying it with social revolution (*L'Anarchia,* Oct. 6, 1877). As Della Peruta observes, Costa was making "an Italian translation of the Bakuninist myth of Russian banditry as a revolutionary force" ("La Banda del Matese," p. 357). A police official admitted that the choice of the Matese was an excellent one: "If those descendants of the ancient Samnites had joined the rebellion, repression would not have been easy in that zone . . ." E. Sernicoli, *L'anarchia e gli anarchici. Studio storico e politico* (2d ed.; Milan; 1894), I, 150.
[58] Ceccarelli to Cipriani, p. 380.

organization.[59] The Imolese, who believed that "conspiracy . . . can not achieve social revolution" was naturally hesitant to admit the Italian International's identification with the plot brought to fruition in the spring of 1877, but the fact is that, even while predicting its failure without the preliminary persuasion of the southern *contadini* by press and oral propaganda, he promised to second the Matese movement with an action in the Romagna.[60] It was in their capacity as members of the Italian Federation's correspondence commission, moreover, that Cafiero, Pezzi, and Grassi, assisted by Malatesta, held their clandestine meetings with Internationalists, not only in Naples, but in Rome, Florence, Bologna, and other cities, and there is no reason to suppose they were engaged in anything but recruiting for their own band of revolutionaries and/or arranging for supporting action in the rest of the peninsula.[61] Since the Matese venture was nothing more than an attempted actuation of the anarchist insurrectional principles enunciated at the Italian International's Tosi Congress of October, 1876, nothing could have been more "official," however opposed Costa may have found himself. Costa's *ex post facto* claim that he had advised against the San Lupo undertaking appears rather lame, for only six weeks before the attempt he wrote in *Il Martello* an article that completely agreed with the insurrectional *rationale* used by Malatesta and Cafiero:

> In order for the popular masses to participate in the struggle for common emancipation, there is needed something much more potent than propaganda and organization, [something] that can jolt the viscera of society; something which, with the evidence of deeds, can be understood by all and which pulls everyone into the struggle. And this something . . . can only be popular, violent, destructive revolution, . . . civil war.
>
> The revolution must occur before the organized forces of the proletariat can be brought to believe seriously in the possibility of a pacific emancipation.
>
> Nor is it valid to say that the revolution can not occur before the masses have acquired a consciousness of their rights and

[59] *L'Anarchia*, Oct. 6, 1877; Costa, *Bagliori di socialismo*, pp. 23 ff.

[60] Lipparini, *Andrea Costa*, p. 108. Defending himself in 1881 against his ex-comrades' charges that he had opposed the enterprise, Costa explained: "I did not approve it because the moment seemed to me ill chosen and because the many [Internationalists] who were being counted upon existed, unfortunately, only in the heated fantasy of a few; and I said so . . ." *Ai miei amici ed ai miei avversari* (Cesena, 1881), published as a pamphlet supplement to the Sept. 18, 1881, issue of *Avanti!* (Cesena).

[61] On their movements in Jan., Feb., and Mar., 1877, see the police reports reproduced by Romano, *Storia*, III, 270 (note 53), 273 (note 56), 275 (note 59), 533-36. Grassi and Pezzi had reorganized the Tuscan societies at a Florentine congress held on Nov. 26-27, 1876. *Il Risveglio*, Dec. 3, 1876.

duties. The moral revolution can not be accomplished, so long as there is economic oppression, if not in the very act of the material revolution. . . .

It is not necessary . . . to create the socialist sentiment, but only to provoke its explosion; and for this a shock suffices. . . .

We believe that revolution is the only way to achieve the true and complete emancipation of humanity. Anything that leads away from this salutary path is lacking in strength, the game of children or madmen, which creates harmful illusions that must necessarily entail disillusionment and corruption.[62]

All of Costa's fire-and-brimstone revolutionism never got beyond the oral stage, never led him personally to the barricades. In 1877, as in 1874, the most vociferously revolutionary agitator of the Italian International was absent in the hour of action.

While Costa fretted, while the Neapolitan conspiratorial nucleus serenely wove its insurrectional design, the Italian police again prove the efficiency of their informant system by following every twist and turn of the developing scheme. The time, the place, the means, the persons, the strategy involved in the project were all accurately identified by the Neapolitan *questore* well in advance of D-Day.[63] Under the circumstances, the failure to jail the ringleaders, confiscate the arms being collected, and deny the Matese to the insurrectionists, was conceivably a consequence of the Minister of Interior's decision to catch them *in flagrante delicto,* thus finding a justification, before public opinion, for smashing the socialist movement once and for all.[64] In any case, the error of taking preventive measures, as in 1874, was not repeated.

So it was that in early March, Malatesta rented a seven-room house, part of the Taverna Jacobelli, situated a stone's throw from the little mountain hamlet of San Lupo.[65] Here, hard against the rocky sides of

[62] *Il Martello,* Feb. 24, 1877. The article, "Il Socialismo Legale ed il Socialismo Rivoluzionario," signed by "Italo" (Costa), was republished by *Il Risveglio,* Mar. 18, 25, 1877.

[63] For details, see the police reports, in Romano, *Storia,* III, 268-75, 533-41. These reports deal with an armed assault by Cafiero and Pezzi on Tommaso Schettino on the evening of Jan. 30, 1877, and Romano uses them to support his conclusion that the Neapolitan police—"in carrying out orders from Rome—did not arrest [Cafiero and Pezzi] because the government *wanted* the San Lupo . . . attempt undertaken." (*Ibid.,* III, 274-75). Thirty-four pages later, however, one reads that Pezzi was, in fact, arrested prior to the San Lupo affair (*Ibid.,* III, 309, note 41).

[64] The Minister of Interior, Giovanni Nicotera, was apparently defending himself against such an implication when he told the Chamber of Deputies that the negligence of Benevento police authorities was to blame for the attempt not having been truncated before any damage was done. *Il Povero,* Apr. 18, 1877.

[65] The following account is based on the previously cited letter of Ceccarelli to Cipriani; on Eugenio Forni's *requisitoria* against the Internationalists at the subsequent Benevento trial, *L'Internazionale e lo Stato* (Naples, 1878), pp. 394 ff.; Costa's

the Matese, approximately a hundred Internationalists from Naples, Rome, the Romagna, and the Marches, were scheduled to convene on May 5. By then, the snows would have melted, and the band would have the mobility essential to their plans. One Kravchinsky, former tsarist artillery officer encountered by Cafiero and Malatesta in Switzerland the previous fall, now residing in Naples for the sake of a consumptive Russian lady friend, had produced a handbook on guerrilla warfare for use in the coming venture, to which he promised his personal participation. A certain Salvatore Farina, ex-Garibaldian and experienced hunter of brigands in the Matese, knew the area and its people, so Malatesta enlisted him to recruit local peasant support. Farina, more avaricious than interested in emancipating the proletariat, forthwith milked the Internationalists of all he could, peddled his information to the police, and disappeared from the scene.[66] Unhappy omen this—like the arrest of Costa on the eve of the 1874 attempt, but again it was too late to draw back. Farina's treason, in the words of Ceccarelli, "confronted us with the alternatives of renouncing the attempt and seeking refuge abroad or precipitating things, if we did not want to be arrested without having done anything." [67] Things were precipitated—by moving the date of the insurrection up from May 5 to April 5.

On the morning of April 3 Cafiero, Malatesta, and a "blonde, green-eyed *signorina*," presented themselves at the Taverna Jacobelli as an English gentleman, his secretary, and his cousin, come to inspect the newly rented quarters destined for the *signore*'s sick wife in Naples. They had several heavy boxes unloaded from their carriage, and after a horse-back reconnaisance of the surrounding terrain, headed back toward Naples. By the evening of the 5th, two more cases of war equipment, sixteen Internationalists (including Cafiero, Malatesta, Cesare Ceccarelli, Antonio Cornacchia, and Napoleone Papini),[68] and four *carabinieri* had arrived at San Lupo, the latter hidden under a nearby bridge with orders to keep the Taverna Jacobelli under surveillance. Night

---

letters of Apr. 14, 21, 1877, to the Jura *Bulletin,* in Guillaume, *I.D.S.,* IV, 184-90; the correspondence commission's circular of June 8, 1877, written by Malatesta, in the Jura *Bulletin,* June 10, 1877, and *L'Anarchia* (Naples), Aug. 25, 1877; Costa's report of Sept. 8, 1877, to the Congress of Verviers, in *L'Anarchia,* Oct. 6, 1877, and Romano, *Storia,* III, 559-64; Neapolitan *questore* reports of Mar. and Apr., 1877, in *ibid.,* III, 533-43; and, finally, on detailed accounts in *Il Risveglio,* Apr. 15, 19; *Il Povero,* Apr. 18; Jura *Bulletin,* Apr. 22, 29, 1877.

[66] Guillaume, *I.D.S.,* IV, 116-17, 182.

[67] Ceccarelli to Cipriani, p. 381.

[68] Cornacchia, the reader may recall, led the Imola group during the 1874 attempt. Papini was the editor of *Il Martello* during its Internationalist phase in Fabriano-Jesi, July 29—Nov. 19, 1876. The great majority of the band was from the Romagna and the Marches. See the first twenty-six names on the list of thirty-seven defendants at the Benevento trial, Jura *Bulletin,* Dec. 2, 1877; Guillaume, *I.D.S.,* IV, 281-82.

settled, and while the *Arma Benemerita* mounted vigil, Internationalists bedded down to await the comrades with whom, on the morrow, they were to ignite the social revolution.

Several hours later, when the *carabinieri* left their hiding place to investigate a moving light they had interpreted as a signal for imminent action at the Jacobelli hostelry, trigger-happy Internationalists wounded two of them, one mortally. Believing themselves under heavy attack, Malatesta, Cafiero, and their followers loaded their supplies aboard three mules and took to the mountains, resolved to initiate their liberation of the countryside without waiting for reinforcements. It was just as well, for the police had already rounded up Grassi, Kravchinsky, and two companions at the Solapaca railway station; four others at Pontelandolfo.[69] The only reinforcements contacted were ten Internationalists, encountered by sheer chance after the band left San Lupo. They had escaped the police dragnet only by virtue of having missed the train they had intended to take from Rome.

Thus, the band of San Lupo, numbering twenty-six in all, spent two days threading its way through the mountains, headed for the Molise, where it was hoped the population would support their enterprise. On the morning of April 8, while the municipal council of Letino sat in Sunday morning session, the peasants of the tiny commune were stupefied by the appearance of twenty-six Internationalists, wearing red and black cocardes and carrying a flag of the same colors. Victor Emmanuel was declared deposed, the people sovereign, and the files of the municipal archives given to the flames.[70] As the records of their civic obligations went up in smoke, the now enthusiastic peasants applauded vociferously and quickly passed the word to their friends in the countryside that the day of their secular redemption had come indeed. From the center of the *piazza*, where the red and black banner of the International now fluttered, Carlo Cafiero explained the principles of the social revolution, greeted by the crowd—according to Malatesta's account—"with the greatest sympathy." When one of the village women demanded an immediate partition of the land, Cafiero, with admirable aplomb, assured her he could not spare the time at the moment, for other sections of the region were awaiting the revolutionary stimulus of the band. Referring to the collection of rusty rifles and axes he and his cohorts had found in the city hall and distributed to the crowd, Cafiero added, in the dialect

---

[69] Arrested at Solapaca: Kravchinsky, Grassi, Massimo Innocenti, and Leopoldo Ardinghi; at Pontelandolfo: Pietro Gagliardi, Florido Matteucci, Dionisio Ceccarelli, and Silvio Fruggeri. Della Peruta, "La Banda del Matese," p. 373; *cf.*, also, Guillaume, *I.D.S.*, IV, 187, notes 2, 3.

[70] The invaders spared the records of the Congregation of Charity, since it was considered "a thing of the people." *Ibid.*, IV, 184.

of the region: "The rifles and axes we have given you, the knives you have. If you wish, do something, and if not, the hell with you." [71] Caught up in the enthusiasm, even the local priest incited his flock to make common cause with the revolutionaries, "true apostles sent by the Lord to preach his divine laws." [72]

After wining and dining at the local *osteria,* the liberators formed up and marched off toward the neighboring village of Gallo, the *evviva* of the intoxicated Letinesi ringing in their ears. The lamentations of the local innkeeper, whose mercenary, petty bourgeois heart was apparently not touched by the apostolate of these hungry but penniless messengers of the Lord, were not stilled until Errico Malatesta signed and handed him a scrap of paper on which was written: "In the name of the Social Revolution, the Mayor of Letino is ordered to pay twenty-eight *lire* to Ferdinando Orsi for food furnished the band that entered Letino on April 8, 1877." [73]

As the revolutionaries neared Gallo, they were preceded by another cooperative ecclesiastic, who went from door to door assuring his parishioners they had nothing to fear, for the invasion meant only "a change of government and burning of papers." The Letino performance was repeated, with two elaborations: Cafiero and his companions rifled the till of the tax collector (the take: fifty *lire*) and made it a point to break the counting mechanism on the grain mills of the neighborhood,[74] assuring the transported peasants that their days of paying the hated *tassa sul macinato* were gone forever. Notwithstanding such bravado, the "combustible material" refused to ignite. Invited to collectivize property, the Gallo peasants replied that they had no inclination to risk their own massacre by the troops of Victor Emmanuel.

By now, a battalion of the 56th Infantry, two companies of the 55th, two squadrons of cavalry, and two companies of *bersaglieri* had begun to tighten a noose thrown around the area, while at Ponte Molle in Rome police arrested nine more Internationalists as they prepared to join the San Lupo band. For two days, April 9 and 10, the insurgents tramped the mountains, vainly seeking a village, free of troops, where their example might find emulators. Soldiers denied them every inhabited place.

On the night of the 10th, with food supplies gone, they decided to attempt piercing the military cordon by crossing Mount Casamara. Next day the climb was undertaken: freezing rain, knee-deep snow, empty

[71] "I fucili e le scuri ne li avimo dato, i cortelli li avite. Se volite facite, e se no vi fottite." Forni, *L'Internazionale e lo Stato,* pp. 410-11.
[72] *Ibid.,* p. 412.
[73] *Ibid.,* p. 413.
[74] The device counted the revolutions of the mill, thus determining the tax to be paid.

stomachs, rifles and ammunition so wet "they would not have taken fire in a furnace," [75] a guide who had lost his way and, as night drew near, an impenetrable fog. Retreat to Letino. A few kilometers from their goal, troops found twenty-three of them a few hours later, huddled in a farmhouse, too spent to resist and, by now, much too miserable to care. Two others were picked up in the vicinity, despite their protestations of utter innocence. The twenty-sixth member of the band, one Francesco Gastaldi, was arrested three weeks later in the house of his Neapolitan mistress. Nor did the police neglect rounding up the confused guide and the two priests of Letino and Gallo who, for a fleeting moment, had seen salvation for their parishioners this side of paradise.

[75] Thus, Malatesta, *L'Anarchia,* Aug. 25, 1877.

XVI

Disintegration of the Anarchist International as an Organization

THE INSURRECTIONAL PRINCIPLE ON THE DEFENSIVE

THE San Lupo affair gave the government an ideal excuse to clamp down on the Italian International: outlawing of the organization, dissolution of the sections, arrest of the leaders, surveillance of the lesser propagandists, and banning and confiscation of socialist newspapers—the whole repressive machinery of the state was mobilized to stamp out the socialist infection. In Bologna, Imola, Florence, Rome, and Naples, anarchists escaping the police dragnet either remained in hiding or fled abroad. Imola, having provided a heavy proportion of the San Lupo band, was put under virtual martial law, with soldiers bivouacked in the streets and *carabinieri* patrolling the city and its environs. The government even tried—according to Costa—to force socialists to sign a declaration that they either had never belonged to the International or had no intention of remaining in the Association.[1] *Il Martello* had to cease publication, and *Il Nuovo Risveglio* was sequestered when it printed a "Bulletin of the Insurrection" expressing sympathy for the San Lupo arrestees.[2] Costa himself was forced to flee from Forlì to Imola to Bologna, where he fruitlessly tried to maintain contact with other socialist nuclei, but by late April police pressure forced him into Swiss

---

[1] See Costa's letter of Apr. 21, 1877, in *Il Risveglio*, Apr. 22; Jura *Bulletin*, Apr. 29, 1877. The Moderates, unlike the Left, were still sceptical that the International should greatly worry the government, for one of their most authoritative organs, *L'Opinione Nazionale* (Apr. 10, 1877), not only minimized the importance of the San Lupo enterprise, but attributed it to Bourbon, not Internationalist, inspiration.

[2] Supplement (dated Apr. 19, 1877) to the Apr. 15, 1877, issue.

exile.[3] With Emilio Covelli under arrest in Naples, with Grassi held in the Benevento jail, with Cafiero, Malatesta, and Ceccarelli incarcerated at Santa Maria Capua Vetere, with Costa, Pezzi, and other anarchist chieftains reduced to impotence in Switzerland, the Italian International once again faced a period of calm and relative inertia.[4]

No less than the anarchists, the legalitarian socialists felt the repressive hand of the government. Ingegneros was jailed in Palermo, Bignami's "socialist study circle" was dissolved in Milan, and the Federation of Upper Italy was broken by prefectural decree.[5] *La Plebe,* however, continued its attacks on the anarchists, labeling the San Lupo fiasco as "a poorly corrected second edition" of the 1874 Bologna attempt,[6] while *Il Povero* publicized Benoît Malon's criticism of the anarchists as *agents provocateurs* and opined that the San Lupo affair had irreparably compromised the anarchist cause:

> To act in such a manner one must be downright insane. No one will question how much harm these parasites of labor masquerading as Internationalists, have done; the veil has fallen, . . . Their intentions are anything but disinterested and modest: let the people be on guard against them, and let us work assiduously at propagating those principles which alone can lead to the social revolution . . .[7]

The whole barrage of name-calling was swollen by the anti-anarchist press abroad: to the editors of the German social democratic organ, V*orwärts,* the San Lupo enterprise was a "highly stupid fraud"; to Jules Guesde, now writing in *Le Radical* (Paris) the ex-insurgents were cowards (*les fuyards de Cerreto*) and represented but an insignificant

[3] Costa's recollection, several years later, of his personal activity during the San Lupo affair: ". . . when I knew that the movement was set and that the friends wanted to move at any cost, I left . . . the hideout where I had been driven . . . and went to Forlì, . . . ready to emerge with the friends in case the movement in the southern provinces were to have any appearance of being capable of sustaining itself. . . . But everyone knows how things went. The newspapers had still not announced to us that the band had gone into action when they informed us that it was already captured. With the band taken, we renounced going into action . . ." *Ai miei amici ed ai miei avversari. Cf.,* also, Guillaume, *I.D.S.,* IV, 190, 197; Lipparini, "Cronologia della vita di A. Costa," p. 188.

[4] Covelli had been arrested, along with six other Neapolitan Internationalists, for complicity in the San Lupo enterprise. *La Plebe,* May 20; Jura *Bulletin,* June 3, 1877.

[5] *La Plebe,* Apr. 24, 1877, for the order dissolving the F.U.I. Bignami claimed the federation's membership at the moment of dissolution stood at more than 3,500. In place of the Milanese socialist study circle, there appeared, on July 10, 1877, the Milanese Socialist Circle, intended by its sponsors as the nucleus of "the great Italian Association of Socialist Circles." *Ibid.,* July 11, Aug. 30, 1877.

[6] Apr. 24, 1877. Bignami lifted the expression from the Apr. 18 issue of *Il Povero.*

[7] *Loc. cit.*

fraction of the Italian International; the *Tagwacht* of Zürich repeated the charge of *agents provocateurs*.[8] Retorting from his prison cell, Malatesta damned *La Plebe* as a "newspaper of mystification," Bignami, Malon, and their friends as "ambitious and evil," intent on convincing the workers that "the existing political administrative organs of the State offer infinite means of arriving at the solution of the social question, without the need of having themselves killed by poor simpletons of fanatics."[9] The Jura *Bulletin* implied that the staff of *Il Povero* was working for the police.[10]

Neither government repression nor the ridicule of the legalitarians had any immediately neutralizing effect on the anarchists' loyalty to the principle of direct action as the best revolutionary propaganda. Costa was probably not exaggerating, with reference to his own convictions, when he informed the Jurassian *Bulletin* a few days after the San Lupo affair that the attempt had had a constructive result:

> In effect, it is the first time that, without "decrees" and without the customary, revolutionary *mise-en-scène*, the anarchist revolution was affirmed on the terrain of action. . . . You can not imagine what hopes this event has aroused in our camp! what an ardent desire for struggle, and what fright in the bourgeoisie![11]

The Jura *Bulletin* came to practically the same conclusion. Since the peasants and workers had neither the time nor the inclination to read the socialist press, even if the socialists had the money to make propaganda through such a medium, the propaganda of the deed was needed "to awaken the popular conscience." And once aroused, it needed nourishment, the deed must carry a lesson. Thus, the San Lupo insurrectionists:

> . . . had taken two little communes, and there, by burning the archives, they had shown the people how much respect one must have for property. They gave the people the tax money, the arms that had been taken from them; and in doing that they had shown the people the disdain one must have for the

---

[8] *Il Povero*, Apr. 22, 29, June 3, 1877; Guillaume, *I.D.S.*, IV, 185, 188, 197, 214-15. *La Plebe*, May 20, 1877, carried a roundup of foreign press reaction.

[9] Letter to Masvero, June 6, 1877, Schiavi, "La formazione del pensiero politico di Andrea Costa," p. 27.

[10] Issue of May 6, 1877.

[11] Guillaume, *I.D.S.*, IV, 185. Little wonder the bourgeoisie were frightened, when their press told them that Malatesta, Cafiero, and their friends had marched towards the province of Benevento, "sacking, stealing, as usual, burning the villages through which they passed, [causing] great terror among the inhabitants, defenseless against those malefactors." Vigo, *Storia degli ultimi trent'anni*, II, 188.

government. It is impossible that the people did not say [to themselves], "We would be much happier if what these poor young men want were accomplished some day." From there to helping [the insurrectionists], there is only one easy step to take.[12]

Though the Italian International, as such, remained quiescent for the remainder of 1877, the "ardent desire for struggle" was evident in the numerous isolated manifestations of those socialists still at large in the country. In Naples an insurrectional scheme was projected for June 1877, but had to be abandoned under the alert surveillance of the police.[13] In Naples, too, Emilio Covelli, cleared in July of complicity in the San Lupo conspiracy, began reorganizing the local section in August and later that month brought out the long awaited anarchist newspaper, *L'Anarchia*.[14] In Bologna there were five reconstituted I.W.A. sections by the end of August; in Rome and Perugia, despite the police, Internationalists continued to meet.[15]

In Florence, police kept the local anarchists continually off balance with unrelenting harassment.[16] On the same Sunday that the San Lupo band was illustrating social revolution to the peasants of Letino and Gallo, Florentine socialists invaded a clerical-sponsored meeting against "blasphemy and obscene language" and found themselves arrested for insisting that the best cure for both ills was violent overthrow of the existing social system.[17] Two days later, all Tuscan Internationalist associations were dissolved by prefectural decree, all socialist meeting places shut down, and for the rest of the year socialists were under surveillance. They were stopped in the streets and searched on general principles, and their homes were subjected to search. Despite all, they managed to create what they called "workers' educational circles" in the more populous quarters of the city, which enabled them to continue making speeches and distributing propaganda pamphlets.[18]

As for the prisoners at Santa Maria Capua Vetere, the fact that they were being held officially incommunicado did not interrupt their relations

---

[12] Issue of Aug. 5, 1877.

[13] Romano, *Storia*, III, 298. The author does not identify the conspirators.

[14] Carmelo Palladino, also arrested in connection with the San Lupo affair, but liberated immediately, collaborated with Covelli on *L'Anarchia*. Lucarelli, *Palladino*, p. 7. After seven issues, of which six were confiscated by the police, the paper was transferred to Florence in October. Guillaume, *I.D.S.*, IV, 280; Romano, *Storia*, III, 299, note 10.

[15] Guillaume, *I.D.S.*, IV, 281.

[16] For details, Pezzi, *Un errore giudiziario*, pp. 74-79.

[17] *La Perseveranza*, Apr. 10, 1877; Pezzi, *Un errore giudiziario*, pp. 72-74; Vigo, *op. cit.*, II, 188-90.

[18] Angiolini, *op. cit.*, pp. 148-49; Conti, *O.S.F.*, pp. 198, 200.

with the comrades at large. Malatesta, in the name of the correspondence commission, composed his version of the San Lupo affair for publication in the Jurassian *Bulletin*, answered the attacks of Bignami and Malon, and even maintained conspiratorial relations with the Neapolitan anarchist nucleus.[19] Cafiero used his time in writing a summary of *Das Kapital*, intended as a popular guide to the iniquities of capitalism.[20] The prisoners formed an I.W.A. section and mandated Andrea Costa to represent them at the Ghent international congress scheduled for September 9, called to explore the possibility of reconciling the differences between legalitarian socialists and anarchists as to revolutionary tactics. Costa was instructed to uphold the intransigently anarchist line laid down at the third Italian congress of Florence-Tosi and the anarchist international congress of Bern of the year before.[21]

In the name of thirty-five Italian sections, Costa managed to establish himself as an extremist among extremists at the preparatory anarchist congress of Verviers (Belgium) on September 6-8, convened to define the attitude anarchists were to assume in dealing with the non-anarchist factions of European socialism at Ghent.[22] Against the now moderating influence of the Jurassian Federation, Costa advanced the thesis that Italian social and economic conditions made revolution more imperative there than elsewhere and secured congress approval of a resolution that a revolutionary movement in one country should be supported by the militants in other states. In all other matters of principle, too, the Verviers Congress rendered traditionally intransigent decisions. "The solidarity of fact in revolutionary method" was affirmed as the indispensable and most practical method of struggle. Trade-unionism would never lead to proletarian emancipation; unions had only one valid function: to abolish wages and wrest the tools of production from their owners. And on the all-important question of politics:

[19] See his letter to Vincenzo Pappagallo, one of the co-defendants of the 1875 Trani trial, reproduced by Romano, *Storia*, III, 300, note 14.

[20] Printed in 1879 as *Il Capitale di Carlo Marx, brevemente compendiato da Carlo Cafiero* (Milan, 1879), 128 pp. *Cf.*, also, Guillaume, *I.D.S.*, IV, 294-95; Gianni Bosio, "La diffusione degli scritti di Marx e di Engels in Italia dal 1871 al 1892," *Società*, Yr. VII, No. 2 (June, 1951), 280. In acknowledging a copy sent him by Cafiero, Marx described it as the best summary yet written. Gianni Bosio, comp., "Carteggio da e per l'Italia di Marx-Engels (1871-1895)," *Movimento Operaio*, Yr. II, Nos. 9-10 (June-July, 1950), 272.

[21] For the text of the Santa Maria mandate, Aug. 25, 1877, see the Jura *Bulletin*, Sept. 9; *L'Anarchia*, Sept. 22, 1877.

[22] For the Verviers Congress, *L'Anarchia* (Naples), Sept. 15, 22; Jura *Bulletin*, Sept. 23, 1877. In addition to Costa, Italy was represented by a certain Martini, possibly the Ranieri Martino, a Pisan worker, later to turn up as a co-defendant with Natta and Pezzi in the Florence conspiracy trial that began in Nov., 1879. Conti, *O.S.F.*, p. 233.

> The Congress declares that there is no difference between the various *political* parties, whether they call themselves socialist or not: all of these parties, without distinction, form . . . a reactionary mass, and [the Congress] believes it its duty to combat them all.
>
> It hopes that the workers who still march in the ranks of these various parties, instructed by the lessons of experience and by revolutionary propaganda, will open their eyes and abandon the political path in order to adopt that of revolutionary socialism.[23]

As for the "pact of solidarity" with the authoritarian socialists, discussed the year before at Bern, the Verviers delegates renounced the project on the grounds that the disparity in principles and tactics was so great as to make organizational unity impossible.

At Ghent,[24] the full depth of legalitarian-libertarian incompatibility was thoroughly documented, with Andrea Costa taking great pains to leave no doubt about the intransigence of the Italian International. The peninsula's legalitarians—the editorial staffs of *La Plebe, Il Povero,* and *Il Nuovo Paese* (Siena)—had mandated Tito Zanardelli, so both factions had a voice in the proceedings, but, given Costa's position and Zanardelli's often equivocal performance—almost as if he could not bring himself to break completely with his Bakuninist precedents—the delegates derived the very clear notion of Italian socialism as predominantly and decisively in the anarchist camp.

On the question of collectivizing land and the instruments of production, the anarchists favored ownership by workers' federations, the legalitarians insisted on ownership by the state or the commune, "representing the totality of the people." The statist resolution carried. Zanardelli voted for neither formula, but produced a resolution of his own, favoring collective ownership, but "without establishing its forms and conditions in advance." It is not the tendencies of modern production which are dangerous, said he, but the fact of individual property. The resolution mustered only the votes of its sponsor and one other delegate.

[23] Guillaume, *I.D.S.,* IV, 264.

[24] For the circular convening the Ghent Congress, Jura *Bulletin,* July 1, 1877. For the Ghent proceedings, *Congresso Socialista universale tenuto a Gand nel Belgio dal 6 al 9 settembre 1877* (Siena, 1877), 31 pp.; *La Plebe,* Sept. 23, 30; *Il Povero,* Oct. 27; *L'Anarchia* (Florence), Sept. 22, Oct. 10, 28, 1877; Guillaume, *I.D.S.,* IV, 265-80. For secondary treatments, Ludwig Brügel, *Geschichte der österreichischen Sozialdemokratie* (Vienna, 1922-25), II, 333 ff.; Manacorda, *op. cit.,* pp. 116-18; Romano, *Storia,* III, 302-05. For the significance of the congress with respect to the development of the European socialist movement, see Valiani, "Dalla prima alla seconda Internazionale," p. 192.

On the central question of proletarian political action, the traditional positions were taken: to combat the bourgeois parties, the legalitarians insisted that socialists should form their own political parties and win control of the state; the anarchists urged abstention from parliamentary politics and destruction of the state by social revolution. Again the legalitarian resolution carried.[25] Again, too, Zanardelli had unsuccessfully offered a compromise resolution recommending revolutionary propaganda both in the parliaments and on the barricades, though qualifying insurrection as more effective and determining in the case of "mature States."

Even on those issues where the anarchists and legalitarians generally agreed, Costa refused to compromise. The entire congress favored trade-unionism, but Costa withheld his vote on the grounds that trade-unions were not as important in industrially retarded Italy as in other countries, and that the existing Italian workers' societies were obstacles to socialism, not allies. When the congress agreed to establish an innocuous central bureau of correspondence and statistics as an external sign of socialist unity, Costa abstained. And as for the basic goal of the congress, exploring the possibility of a European socialist unity pact, Costa was flatly negative, declaring that the most to be hoped for was that the two camps would avoid mud-slinging in their polemics. To this proposition all the delegates adhered, which only served to underscore their disapproval of a report read by Zanardelli, in which he lambasted the San Lupo band as "intriguers." [26]

Ghent signified the effective end of the anarchist International as a European-wide movement, for by now two of the main bulwarks of the Bakuninist creed, the French and Belgian socialists, had opted for trade-union organization and political activity, while James Guillaume, representing the Swiss Jurassian Federation, had clearly enough shown his anti-conspiratorial and anti-insurrectional tendencies at Verviers, and his support of Brousse and Costa's intransigent attitude at Ghent was more a token of formal solidarity than of personal conviction. The Spanish and Italian anarchists now constituted a definite minority.[27]

[25] "Considering that social emancipation is inseparable from political emancipation, the congress declares that the proletariat, organized as a distinct party opposed to all the parties formed by the possessing classes, must employ all the political means tending toward the social emancipation of its members."

[26] Costa, Guillaume, and Brousse charged that Benoît Malon had written the Zanardelli report, a charge subsequently denied by Malon [Guillaume, I.D.S., IV, 271-72; Malon's letter to César De Paepe, in La Revue Socialiste, XLVIII (Oct., 1908), 445]. Zanardelli later handed Costa a written retraction, assuring him that his accusations were not directed against the San Lupo group and their friends, Guillaume, I.D.S., IV, 272.

[27] Marx to Sorge, Sept. 27, 1877: "Whatever the Congress of Ghent left to be desired in other respects, it as least had this virtue: that Guillaume and Co. have been

Though in Italy itself the anarchists still held a clear numerical superiority over the legalitarians, though Costa, far more than Zanardelli, was qualified to speak for Italian socialism as a whole, the fact remained that when Zanardelli adhered, at the conclusion of the Ghent proceedings, to a "pact of mutual assistance" between the socialist organizations of Belgium, Germany, Switzerland, and Denmark, he was, in effect, bringing Italian socialism into the current of European socialist thought that was to produce the Second International twelve years later, frankly Marxist in orientation. The immediate consequence of the congress, too, was a token of Marx's victory on the basic question of proletarian political action: the majority delegates, aiming at a general union of European socialists, issued a "Manifesto to the Workers' and Socialist Organizations of all Countries," exhorting socialists to participate in elections, to demand broadening of the suffrage, and to develop workers' organizations and bring them into the political arena.[28]

Entirely valid for Europe as a whole was *La Plebe*'s assertion that the Ghent Congress "signals the beginning of a new period of world socialism," that "once socialism was only the International, [but] now the International is only a fraction of socialism." [29] With the overwhelming majority of European socialists convinced that the anarchist position, in the existing historical context, was contradictory, illogical, and completely utopian, *La Plebe*'s generalization would soon apply to Italian socialism as well. The time was not yet, but only because the Italian government, notwithstanding the hardening of its policy toward the Internationalists after the San Lupo affair, had still not convinced them that there was really no practical alternative to seeking social change within the framework of the bourgeois politico-juridical system. Even the legalitarians—if we are to judge from Zanardelli's compromise position between anarchist and social democratic credos at Ghent—were still not entirely persuaded.[30] Notwithstanding this reticence to forsake the insurrectional principle, destined to give a peculiar stamp to Italian socialism for several decades to come, the experience of the years 1878 and 1879 was to result in both the destruction of the Italian International

totally abandoned by their former allies." *Briefe und Auszüge aus Briefen J. P. Becker, J. Dietzgen, F. Engels, K. Marx und Anderen an F. A. Sorge und Andere* (Stuttgart, 1906), p. 156; Guillaume, *I.D.S.*, IV, 279.

[28] For the manifesto, *Il Povero*, Oct. 27, Nov. 18; *La Plebe*, Nov. 6, 1877.

[29] Issue of Sept. 23, 1877.

[30] Bignami, as late as Feb., 1878, was still on the defensive when referring to the insurrectional method: ". . . if the energetic and public manifestation of a whole rebellious people can be revolutionary, the simple word of a propagandist can also be such. The timely efficacy of a popular explosion does not keep the word erupting from a public tribune or the agitation for the conquest of even a single human right from also having its timely efficacy." *La Plebe*, Feb. 5, 1878.

as an organization and the liquidation of anarchism as the movements's dominant ideology.

1878: DECAPITATION OF THE ITALIAN INTERNATIONAL

For most of 1878 Florence was the active center of Internationalist efforts, for it was here that the correspondence commission came during the winter and it was here that Natta, Grassi, and Pezzi, now fully seasoned propagandists of the anarchist movement, undertook the work of reorganization.[31] In its overt manifestations, the Tuscan International, aided by frequently hysterical police repression, gave the impression that the socialists were peaceful citizens demanding the right to propagate their ideas in the face of brutally gratuitous persecution by overzealous *questura* agents.

On February 9 a Florentine worker, one Emilio Cappellini, whom the Internationalists disclaimed as a comrade, threw an Orsini bomb into a parade commemorating the recently deceased Victor Emmanuel II. No one was killed. Cappellini, arrested on the spot, claimed he had had to hurl the bomb to save his own life—"unknown persons," said he, had put it in his pocket unbeknownst to him. He was held for three months and then freed for lack of evidence, but four Internationalists were arrested for the crime. A local newspaper, *La Vedetta* (sold to the police, according to the socialists), insinuated that the local Internationalists were responsible, a charge vigorously protested by the correspondence commission: Grassi, Natta, and Aurelio Vannini. *La Vedetta* retracted its remarks.[32]

Throughout the spring and summer of 1878, the Florentine Internationalists held public meetings and continued propagandizing and organizing the workers. By July, I.W.A. membership in the area, according to one of its chiefs, was up to 2,556, a formidable enough accomplishment, even though we can take *cum grano salis* his statement that the workers of Florence "raced each other" to join the International. On March 18— seventh anniversary of the Paris Commune—a big socialist rally voted an address of fraternal solidarity with the deportees of New Caledonia. In May, when some local socialists rented a boat for a joy ride on the

---

[31] Grassi, along with the seven other Internationalists arrested at Solapaca and Pontelandolfo on Apr. 5, 1877, had been freed under a political amnesty granted by King Humbert after the death of Victor Emmanuel on Jan. 9, 1878. Guillaume, *I.D.S.*, IV, 308. Pezzi, who had not taken part in the San Lupo enterprise because he was in jail for complicity in the Jan. 30, 1877, knifing of Tommaso Schettino, had been provisionally freed.

[32] *La Perseveranza*, Feb. 10; Jura *Bulletin*, Mar. 11, 1878; Pezzi, *Un errore giudiziario*, pp. 80-81; Guillaume, *I.D.S.*, IV, 313-14; Conti, *O.S.F.*, pp. 211-12.

Arno, they were immediately arrested, and the next day the police spent several hours trying to verify their suspicions that the arrestees had mined the Ponte Vecchio, much to the ribald amusement of onlooking citizens. In July, when a soldier was killed in a brawl by a pair of disreputable characters, La Vedetta's charge that the culprits belonged to the I.W.A. aroused loud disclaimers by the Internationalists, and, in the course of subsequent fisticuffs between friends of the killers and the socialists, the police stood aside in the hope the latter would compromise themselves enough to warrant a mass clean-up of the local International. Pezzi relates that public condemnation of this provocatory police inaction finally forced the questura to round up the anti-Internationalist faction, not neglecting to include socialists who had involved themselves in the brawling.[33]

Thus the public manifestations of the Florentine International: a cat-and-mouse game between the questura and the followers of Grassi, Pezzi, and Natta. Beneath the veneer of peaceful propagandists for the improvement of the workers' condition, these chieftains remained as adamantly insurrectionist as ever in their aims. In late January 1878, Natta told a secret meeting of local I.W.A. leaders that "now more than ever it is necessary to prepare the terrain for an imminent uprising" and agreed with them that the need was now for "trustworthy, ferocious men, capable of great deeds." [34] A month later, he advised his friends that a European war over the Near Eastern question was inevitable and that such a conflict would provide the conditions, given the existing unemployment, hunger, and poverty of city and country proletarians, for a general insurrection. The Internationalists must remain "compact and ready" for the occasion.[35] This kind of talk, diligently noted in the questore's records, of course, disquieted the police quite as much as their discovery on February 18 of almost half a hundred bombs in the home of a Livorno Internationalist.[36]

Early in March, too, the Florentine socialists set their minds to planning, for late April, "a simultaneous insurrectional movement in the most populous cities of the kingdom and the formation of armed bands in the countryside." To lay the groundwork, Pezzi and his wife made a trip to Carrara, where the action was to begin, with Florence, Lucca,

---

[33] Pezzi, Un errore giudiziario, pp. 83-85; Conti, O.S.F., p. 206.

[34] Ibid., pp. 201, 207. The Florentine meeting may well have inspired the secret congress of thirty-five Romagnol sections held in late Jan. or early Feb., 1878. Jura Bulletin, Feb. 11, 1878.

[35] Conti, O.S.F., p. 207; Romano, Storia, III, 308-09.

[36] Bertolini, "Cenno sul socialismo in Italia," cxv-cxvi; Guillaume, I.D.S., IV, 314. According to police information, the bombs were intended for use during the Livorno funeral ceremony for Victor Emmanuel. Conti, O.S.F., p. 212.

Pisa, Siena, and the Romagna to follow Carrara's lead. According to the Florentine *questore*, the whole scheme collapsed when the news arrived that Andrea Costa had been arrested on March 22 in Paris, a fact in itself that casts some doubt on the seriousness of the preparations.[37]

That the insurrectional intent, if not the means, existed is verified by the proceedings of a highly secret fourth congress of the Italian International, held in Pisa on April 11.[38] Here, thirteen Internationalists, mostly from Pisa and Florence, decided to initiate in the immediate future "a general insurrection of our whole [Italian] federation, and it was further decided that this insurrection would have to be made by [armed] bands." [39] The formal resolution was not so explicit:

> The Congress, in view of the reports received from the various sections and federations, invites all the Italian anarchist socialists to conduct revolutionary propaganda without heeding the sacrifices, since the day is not far distant when the armed proletariat will bring about the downfall of whatever remains of the bourgeoisie, throne, and altar.

Perhaps because police pressure was getting too heavy in Tuscany, a new correspondence commission, including Emilio Covelli, Florido Matteucci, and Giuseppe Foglia, was elected and its headquarters moved from Florence to Genoa.[40]

The Pisa Congress deliberation was approved by regional and local congresses held during the next three months, but the summer of 1878 passed without a trace of the insurrection projected for July.[41] According to the correspondence commission, adequate organizational strength for such an undertaking existed. On June 11, a circular addressed to *L'Avvenire* (Modena) boasted of swelling I.W.A. membership all over the peninsula, even in Lombardy and Liguria (despite the obstacles put

[37] *Ibid.*, pp. 207-08. On Costa's arrest, see below, p. 401.

[38] On the Pisa Congress, *La Plebe*, Apr. 16, 1878; Manacorda, *op. cit.*, pp. 118-19; Angiolini, *op. cit.*, pp. 151-52; Conti, *O.S.F.*, p. 208. Among those attending, according to the police, were Natta, Grassi, Pezzi, and Leopoldo Ardinghi. Manacorda, *op. cit.*, p. 119, note 83.

[39] Letter of Florido Matteucci, one of the delegates, to Anna Kulisciov, Sept., 1878, Conti, *O.S.F.*, pp. 273-74. The bulk of the Matteucci-Kulisciov correspondence of the summer of 1878 is also to be found in *La Perseveranza*, Nov. 18, 21, 1879.

[40] Covelli, arrested for complicity in the San Lupo affair, was freed for lack of evidence on July 7, 1877. Lucarelli, *Cafiero*, p. 65; Romano, *Storia*, III, 297, note 3. Matteucci, one of the four arrested at Pontelandolfo on Apr. 5, was freed by King Humbert's amnesty. Guillaume, *I.D.S.*, IV, 308. The Tuscan prefect assessed the correspondence commission's move to Genoa as an attempt to penetrate this Mazzinian stronghold, though "the true center [of the International] will always remain in Florence and in the Romagna." Conti, *O.S.F.*, p. 208, note 4.

[41] Angiolini, *op. cit.*, p. 152.

up by the "Mazzinian church").[42] Only in Naples was there definite proof that the boast was unfounded, for here Luigi Felicò, aided by several socialists sorely disillusioned by the failure of the San Lupo enterprise, had developed, by the summer of 1878, a strong anti-anarchist current among the Parthenopian socialists, at least strong enough to endure so long as the anarchist International made no special effort to counter this evolutionary, syndical trend.[43]

Nor was leadership lacking for the actuation of anarchist plans. Malatesta and Cafiero languished in jail at Santa Maria Capua Vetere, but Pezzi, Natta, Grassi, Covelli, Carmelo Palladino, Arturo Ceretti (editor of *L'Avvenire*), Matteucci, and two new recruits, Francesco Saverio Merlino and Giovanni Domanico, provided an adequate corps of elite conspirators, all profoundly permeated with the anarchist gospel, all anxious to implement their convictions. On June 23 Matteucci informed a friend in Switzerland that:

> . . . the movement we shall make this year will be very different from the movements we have made up to now; it will not be only one band or one province that will take part in this movement, but all the regions where our organization exists will arise; it will be . . . a general movement from which we hope much.[44]

By late August, too, Cafiero and Malatesta, the most prestigious and certainly the most faithful disciples of the anarchist dogma, were once more at liberty, thanks to a curiously favorable chain of legal developments. On September 21, 1877, the thirty-seven arrestees of April were charged with a formidable array of political and common-law crimes.[45] On December 30, the *Sezione d'Accusa* of Naples absolved the two priests and the guide involved in the San Lupo affair and remanded the remaining thirty-four defendants to the Court of Assises on charges of conspiracy, attempts against the security of the state and complicity in

---

[42] *L'Avvenire* (Modena), June 15, 1878. For the reconstruction of the Bologna International, Lipparini, *Andrea Costa*, p. 124.

[43] Romano, *Storia*, III, 318-19. The Neapolitan gradualists, writes Romano, were in touch with Ingegneros in Palermo and perhaps even with Guesde. The French Communard's other Italian contacts were Gnocchi-Viani and Zanardelli, who had agreed to act as correspondents for Guesde's Paris newspaper, *Egalité*, launched in Nov., 1877. Guillaume, *I.D.S.*, IV, 296. The Jurassian Federation in Switzerland, on the other hand, kept in touch with the Italian anarchist current through Natta or Covelli, but the contact, in view of Guillaume's stand at the Ghent Congress, represented no encouragement of Italian anarchism. *Ibid.*, IV, 312.

[44] Letter to Kulisciov, Conti, *O.S.F.*, p. 272.

[45] *La Plebe*, Oct. 14; Jura *Bulletin*, Dec. 2, 1877; Guillaume, *I.D.S.*, IV, 281. Among others, the charges: "incitement to civil war, armed rebellion against the forces of the State, conspiracy to overthrow and change the form of government, burning of public registers, qualified theft for having voluntarily opened the cash-box of the tax collectors of Gallo and taking out the sum of fifty *lire*."

the death of the *carabiniere* shot at San Lupo, thus rejecting the prosecution's charges of other common crimes (the invasion of Letino and Gallo, stealing public funds, burning public records, etc.). Frustrated, the prosecution appealed the decision before the Court of Cassation.[46] With the Umberto amnesty of January 1878, the eight arrestees of Solapaca and Pontelandolfo were cleared completely and the remaining twenty-six automatically found themselves cleared of the political charges. On February 15, the Neapolitan Court of Cassation rejected the prosecution's appeal against the judgment of the *Sezione d'Accusa*, so the twenty-six members of the San Lupo band wound up facing trial before a Benevento court on the single charge connected with the shooting of the *carabiniere*.[47] In absolving the accused, the jury, as an anarchist writer readily admits, "denied the existence of the fact," i.e., one dead *carabiniere*, whose doubtless proletarian family could hardly have appreciated the socialists' argument that *they* were the victims of bourgeois persecution.[48]

The release of Cafiero and Malatesta on August 25 brought Internationalist plans for insurrection no nearer realization. Malatesta, with the help of Palladino and Merlino, who had become an anarchist in the course of defending the San Lupo group, fought, with considerable success, the legalitarian, trade-unionist current in Naples and Sicily but then disappeared from the Italian scene completely for the next five

---

[46] Guillaume, *I.D.S.*, IV, 294.

[47] Jura *Bulletin*, Feb. 11, Mar. 4, 1878; Guillaume, *I.D.S.*, IV, 313. For the trial, Lucarelli, *Carlo Cafiero*, pp. 65-67; Nettlau, *Malatesta*, p. 163. Even had Humbert's amnesty not intervened, it is doubtful that the charge of an attempt against the security of the state could have been sustained, for, under Articles 156-60 of the Penal Code, such an attempt required: (1) a concrete, determined, concluded plan, arrived at by the participants in the attempt; (2) that *suitable* means be used to attain the goal; (3) that the attempt not remain in the preparatory stage, but have already entered the stage of execution. In an absolute sense, it would have been impossible to prove that the antique rifles of the twenty-six San Lupo Intenationalists constituted "suitable means" of harming the security of the Italian state. As for the argument of relativity, it could easily be argued—as it was by Giuseppe Ceneri when he defended Costa at the Bologna trial of 1876. *Opere*, I, 62-66—that since material force creates a peril only if it has the support of popular sentiment, the San Lupo band was in no position to jeopardize state security, given its all too evident lack of public favor. On the technical obstacles to establishing the existence of a conspiracy, see Cilibrizzi, *Storia parlamentare politica e diplomatica d'Italia*, II, 81-82.

[48] A commentary on the quaint quality of justice handed out is that Nicotera, the Minister of Interior who epitomized (for both the socialists of the time and some Italian socialist historians of today) the "reaction," consented when Carlo Gambuzzi appealed to him to remove the San Lupo defendants from the jurisdiction of martial law, an accommodation motivated by Gambuzzi's reminder that the San Lupo insurrectionists had been inspired by the same spirit animating Carlo Pisacane, the father of Nicotera's ward. Borghi, *Malatesta*, pp. 55-56; Monticelli, *Andrea Costa e l'Internazionale*, p. 21.

years.[49] As for Cafiero, his biographer asserts that he "turned again to propaganda work in the south, especially in his native Puglia," but fails to document such activity or to indicate precisely when Cafiero left Italy.[50] In any case, the young Pugliese disappeared from the ranks of Italian anarchist militants in the fall of 1878, and no further notice of him is found until the summer of 1879, when Guillaume reports having met him in Paris.[51]

If the Italian International, in the summer of 1878, had sufficiently determined leaders, adequate numerical following, and organizational cohesion, why was insurrection not tried? Why did two such convinced insurrectionists as Cafiero and Malatesta leave the scene of projected operations within a few weeks of their acquittal? What, if not serious revolutionary intentions, was the meaning of the violently worded manifestos circulated in June, in August, and again in September, inciting their readers to rebellion? [52] Police surveillance was close, but this alone, as demonstrated by past socialist performance, had never proved a sufficient deterrent to action.

The police knew the answer. On September 14 the Neapolitan *questore* reported that "the Internationalists recognize that the threatened insurrectional movement is still not ready," and on September 25 he advised that the insurrectionary manifestos by no means proved that the Internationalists were "really ready" for revolt but were primarily intended "to keep the government agitated." [53] The accuracy of this evaluation was attested to by a member of the Italian correspondence commission who, in a letter of this period, intercepted by the police, reduced the anarchists' problem to sheer lack of material means:

[49] The exact date of Malatesta's departure from Italy is not certain. He was still in the country on Sept. 23 (Romano, *Storia*, III, 320, note 82). Nettlau claims the old Bakuninist secret brotherhood was revived by Paul Brousse and Peter Kropotkin in Aug., 1877, and that Malatesta, once out of jail, joined the group. *Anarchisten und Sozialrevolutionäre* (Berlin, 1931), pp. 6, 266 ff. Whatever the accuracy of this statement, no reflections of such a reorganization were felt in Italy at the time. For the reorganization work of Malatesta, Merlino, and Palladino after the Benevento trial, see Romano, *Storia*, III, 320-21, and notes 82, 83.

[50] Lucarelli, *Carlo Cafiero*, p. 67. In his earlier volume (*La Puglia nel secolo XIX*, pp. 236-37), Lucarelli claims Cafiero left Italy for Switzerland with Emilio Covelli after the Passanante affair of Nov. 17, 1878, but Covelli was actually in jail from Oct., 1878, until early summer, 1879 (see below, pp. 403 and 409). Nettlau (*Malatesta*, p. 175) picks up Cafiero again when he went to Switzerland in "the second half of 1879, or 1880." Romano, of extraordinary bibliographical diligence, urges no Italian activity of Cafiero in the months following his acquittal: "After the trial of Benevento he had again gone abroad." *Storia*, III, 349.

[51] *I.D.S.*, IV, 325.

[52] Romano, *Storia*, III, 321-22; Conti, *O.S.F.*, p. 275. *Cf.*, also, Aristide Venturini, *Due opposte decisioni sulla Internazionale* (Bologna, 1879), p. 33.

[53] Romano, *Storia*, III, 320, note 82.

We were in such a condition that we could not go forward or backward . . . and . . . we can not go ahead for the sole reason that we have nothing to eat. It is an incredible situation; after having made a great and good organization, not to be able to do more, the necessary, because of lack of means. . . . We organized our whole association in secret, we made a big agitation among the people. . . . We absolutely must arise, since not maintaining [the Pisa Congress] deliberations would lead to the discouragement and disesteem that befell the Republican Party for promising to make a revolution and never doing anything. But . . . we must stop for lack of means; for this reason we can not complete our organization or arm the greater part of our friends.[54]

Matteucci referred, too, to "extreme remedies for extreme cases," which suggests the veracity of Florentine police charges that the local anarchists actually tried to raise the money for arms by writing threatening letters to a Marquis Panciatichi and a Russian prince, one Paul Demidov, well known as an open-handed supporter of local charitable organizations and sponsor of workers' mutual aid societies.[55]

The impasse was quickly, if not favorably, resolved for the Internationalists. On September 29, fourteenth anniversary of the founding of the I.W.A., several hundred Florentine socialists held a rally outside the city and then marched to the Piazza della Signoria, where they disbanded shouting "*Viva l'Internazionale!*"[56] No heads were bloodied, no arrests made, but the next day the Minister of Interior ordered his prefects to put the Internationalists under close surveillance.[57] The police action of the next few days in Florence is partly explained by the Matteucci letter of September:

It is necessary to get out of this situation, and this month we shall hold a meeting of the most intimate friends, in which we shall decide on what to do: we are determined to have recourse to truly extreme means. After this family meeting, another general meeting of all the comrades will be held, in which will be decided how to pass the months that separate us from the [coming] spring, since [revolutionary] bands in our mountains are not possible in the winter.[58]

[54] Matteucci to Kulisciov, Sept., 1878, Conti, *O.S.F.*, pp. 273-74.
[55] *Ibid.*, p. 209. Conti reports a rumor that Pezzi even tried to persuade the general of the Jesuits, Father Becks, to contribute funds for the revolution. *Ibid.*, p. 210.
[56] *La Perseveranza*'s correspondent avers he heard the crowd shouting: "Down with the Hebrews!" Issue of Oct. 2, 1878.
[57] Angiolini, *op. cit.*, p. 154.
[58] Letter to Kulisciov, Sept., 1878, Conti, *O.S.F.*, p. 274. *Cf.*, also, the *questore* report of Oct. 3, 1878, quoted in *ibid.*, p. 210.

To the "family meeting" in Florence, held September 30 to October 1, came Matteucci, two delegates from Pisa, one from Livorno, and representatives from Siena, the Romagna, Umbria, and the south Italian sections, as well as the Florentine leaders.[59] So far as the police knew, it was the first national meeting of Internationalists since the Florence-Tosi congress of October, 1876. And if the police were aware of anarchist unpreparedness for insurrection, they had no strong reason to believe that this exhausted the anarchist arsenal of revolutionary possibilities.

One type of action required neither numbers nor money: individual acts of violence. And in the police view, there was plenty of circumstantial evidence to support the hypothesis that the Italian International was contemplating recourse to such measures. Aside from the Orsini bombs discovered in Livorno the preceding February, there were other indications that European anarchists had decided on giving individual violence a trial. Spanish anarchists had organized terror squads to dynamite the homes of especially detested enemies of the working classes; in Russia the tsarist governor of St. Petersburg, in January 1878, fell victim to an armed attack by a certain Vera Zasulič; in Germany, Emperor William I, in May and June, escaped two attempts on his life in the space of less than a month. Italian police authorities were certain that Italian anarchists were part of an international conspiracy to rid the world of kings and emperors. On July 10, the Tuscan prefect advised the *questore* of Florence that "the Russian Committee resident in Geneva, the Correspondence Commission of Genoa, and the Committee of the French International in the Jura have decided to recommend to all socialists the abandonment of theoretical propaganda in order to dedicate themselves exclusively to that of deeds." Nor did the manifestos of the Romagnol Federation help dispel the notion that Italian anarchists were anxious to follow the assassination tactics of their comrades abroad: "Let us arise, Let us arise against the oppressors of Humanity: all kings, emperors, presidents of republics, priests of all religions, are the true enemies of the people; let us destroy, along with them, all juridical, political, civil, and religious institutions." [60]

Given the authorities' belief in the existence of an international conspiracy, of a "Russian Committee" in Geneva in touch with the Italian correspondence commission; given a conclave of Internationalists from the most vigorously anarchist areas in the peninsula; given the terrorist activity elsewhere in Europe, the Italian police very probably concluded that a reign of anarchist terror was at hand when there arrived in Florence on the evening of September 30—precisely in the middle of

[59] Conti, *O.S.F.*, p. 210.
[60] *Ibid.*, pp. 212-13. For the Romagnol manifesto, *La Perseveranza*, Aug. 10, 1878.

the "family meeting" of anarchist chieftains—a strikingly handsome young Russian blonde, freshly departed from Switzerland and a former co-militant of none other than Vera Zasulič.[61] The golden-haired newcomer called herself Anna Kulisciov.

Born Anna Rosenstein in 1854, Kulisciov—as she was known to Italian socialists—was already a veteran revolutionary when she arrived in Florence. Barred from tsarist Russian universities because of her sex, Anna had attended the Polytechnic Institute of Zürich in the early 1870's, made brilliant progress in her scientific studies but soon gave them up to throw herself completely into the verbal radicalism of the local Russian student and *émigré* circle. Anarchist insurrectionism held her loyalty through the next several years, during which she returned to Russia, married a fellow revolutionary (subsequently jailed by the tsarist police from 1876 until 1883), militated in Odessa and Kiev, tried unsuccessfully, during a trip to Switzerland in the summer of 1876, to enlist Bakunin's cooperation with the conspiratorial schemes of her comrades at home, and in April 1877 left Russia permanently when the Okhrana identified her as one of the mainsprings of a projected peasant rebellion in southern Russia.[62]

In the Lugano residence of Francesco Pezzi and his wife, Kulisciov met Andrea Costa in August 1877. A love affair quickly developed between the two, with the result that when Costa moved to Paris immediately after the Ghent Congress, Anna was not far behind. In the French capital, the couple passed the winter as militants in the Parisian anarchist colony, meeting living expenses with an occasional donation from Anna's father and the pittance Costa earned as a combination clerk-handyman in a flower shop situated above a cabaret run by a French anarchist. On March 22, along with Lodovico Nabruzzi and Tito Zanardelli, Costa and Kulisciov were arrested as Internationalists. Costa was handed a two-year jail sentence and a heavy fine; Kulisciov, never a member of the I.W.A., was conducted to the Franco-Swiss border.[63] In Switzerland, she met Benoît Malon, wrote occasional articles for Arturo Ceretti's *L'Avvenire* in Modena, and, to learn Italian, moved in with a Lugano friend of Costa, a barber from Faenza. In the meantime, she had been put in touch—probably by Costa—with Florido Matteucci, member

[61] Franco Venturi, "Anna Kuliscioff e la sua attività rivoluzionaria in Russia," *Movimento Operaio*, Yr. IV, No. 2 (Mar.-Apr., 1952), 282.

[62] For details on Kulisciov's pre-1877 activity, see the previously cited article of Venturi. For general bibliographical data, *Anna Kuliscioff, in memoria. A Lei, agli intimi, a me,* comp. by Filippo Turati (Milan, 1926); Alessandro Schiavi, "Anna Kuliscioff e Andrea Costa (da lettere inedite)," *Nuova Antologia*, CDXLI, Fasc. 1762 (Oct., 1947), 109-28; Lipparini, *Andrea Costa, passim;* Angiolini, *op. cit.,* p. 154.

[63] For the trial, *L'Avvenire*, May 18, June 29, 1878.

of the Italian correspondence commission in Genoa.[64] Her ostensible reason for coming to Florence at the end of September was to study medicine; Matteucci's letter of September, though suggesting that Kulisciov was not asked to attend the scheduled "family meeting" of September 30, certainly makes it clear that revolutionary activity in Italy, as much as the study of medicine, was her purpose in coming: "I advise you to remain in Switzerland until early October; I shall let you know our decisions, and I shall also tell you to which city you might come in order to be useful to us, it being understood that your existence in Italy must be known to only a very few friends, since our government is about to apply exceptional laws against us." [65]

It was not an "exceptional law," but a ministerial decree of October 2 that inaugurated the government's final campaign to wipe out the anarchist International in the peninsula.[66] The police moved first against the Florentine nucleus. On October 2, Kulisciov was arrested at Francesco Natta's house, along with Natta and "Gigia," the wife of Pezzi.[67] The charge: conspiracy against the security of the state. On the 10th, Pezzi and several other Florentine anarchists were sent to join their comrades in the *Murate*. Almost simultaneously, the police intercepted a large quantity of Internationalist manifestos in the Pisa post office, inviting the workers to join in the "Social Revolution that will soon break out, not as a *monotonous* and *platonic* insurrection," but as a revolt "that goes to the limit." [68] A month later, the Neapolitan Workers' Association, in a mass meeting, laughed down several Internationalists who were distributing manifestos calling on "the sons of Masaniello to arise," decided on a permanent committee to create an "Italian Workers' Federation," and concluded the proceedings with cheers for King Humbert, Garibaldi, and the Italian premier, Cairoli. For their pains, the Internationalist distributors of the incendiary manifestos were arrested and kept out of circulation for more than a year.[69] A similar fate befell the

[64] For Kulisciov and Costa's correspondence with Mazzotti, the Lugano host, see Schiavi, "Anna Kuliscioff e Andrea Costa," pp. 112-13. For further details, Lipparini, *Andrea Costa*, pp. 119-22; Angiolini, *op. cit.*, p. 154; Romano, *Storia*, III, 316-17; Schiavi, "La formazione del pensiero politico di Andrea Costa," p. 26.

[65] Conti, *O.S.F.*, p. 273.

[66] *La Perseveranza*, Oct. 14, 1878; Angiolini, *op. cit.*, p. 154.

[67] *La Plebe*, Aug. 3, 1879.

[68] *La Perseveranza*, Oct. 13, 1878.

[69] *Ibid.*, Nov. 13, 14, 1878. Arrested on the spot were Francesco Saverio Merlino, Pietro Cesare Ceccarelli, Francesco Gastaldi, Giovanni Maggi, and Saverio Salzano. The Giustiniani's, Antonio and Vincenzo, were arrested later in the month. *Ibid.*, Nov. 14, 30, 1878. The group was sent before the Court of Assises in Nov., 1879. *La Plebe*, Nov. 16; *Il Movimento Sociale*, Nov. 30, 1879. From the evidence here presented, it is apparent that the Neapolitan Workers' Federation was anything but sympathetic to the anarchist cause, as sustained by Romano, when he writes: "in

correspondence commission in Genoa, with the arrest of Emilio Covelli, Matteucci, and Foglia.[70]

The Neapolitan arrests were probably precautionary measures against the possibility of harm to King Humbert, his queen, and the crown prince, who had just begun a series of appearances in important Italian cities. Since they were due in Florence on November 7, the local police rounded up many Internationalists and kept them in jail during the royal visit. Nothing untoward happened, and the arrestees were released, but after a loud socialist protest meeting on November 13, Cesare Batacchi, one of the few Florentine I.W.A. chiefs still at liberty, was arrested on the 16th as a public security measure.[71] The following Sunday, November 17, a twenty-nine-year-old cook, wielding a knife bearing the inscription, "Long live the international republic," threw himself on Humbert as the king's carriage moved through the streets of Naples, inflicting a slight scratch on the royal arm and a minor leg wound on Benedetto Cairoli, the premier. Interrogation of the would-be assassin, one Giovanni Passanante, turned up no connection with the International, but it was only after a long detention that four Neapolitan members of the organization, Tommaso Schettino, Matteo Melillo, Elviro Ciccarese, and one D'Amato, arrested as accomplices, were finally liberated for lack of evidence.[72]

However unjustifiably, public opinion indicted the International for this, and a series of violent episodes that seemed to be touched off by the Neapolitan attempt. The day after Passanante's futile gesture, Florentine monarchists organized a parade to celebrate Humbert's narrow escape. In Via Nazionale someone threw a bomb into the crowd, killing four persons and wounding ten others. Instantly arose the cry—initiated

---

Naples on November 10 the movement of the International was so strong that an important meeting of workers—organized by [the I.W.A.]—was held . . ." *Storia*, III, 322.

[70] Angiolini, *op. cit.*, p. 154; Conti, *O.S.F.*, pp. 210-11. The Genoese police had arrested Matteucci, Covelli, and Foglia once before (late June or early July) but apparently had to free them for lack of evidence. *L'Avvenire*, July 6, 1878.

[71] Pezzi, *Un errore giudiziario*, pp. 88-89.

[72] For the official report on the Passanante affair, Vigo, *op. cit.*, II, 313-14; *La Perseveranza*, Nov. 18, 1878. For additional details, *ibid.*, Nov. 19, 20, 21, Dec. 6, 1878; *La Plebe*, Nov. 16, 1879. Passanante's death sentence (see *La Perseveranza*, Mar. 10, 1879) was confirmed by the Neapolitan Court of Cassation on Mar. 28, 1879, but the following day, on the initiative of King Humbert, the sentence was commuted to life at hard labor, and the King donated a life pension to the culprit's mother from his private patrimony. Vigo, *op. cit.*, III, 33-35; Cilibrizzi, *op. cit.*, II, 169, note 2. In view of the inhuman physical and mental tortures accorded Passanante by the prison administration, Humbert's commutation of the death sentence was, in effect, no act of mercy. For the brutal details, Merlino, *Questa è l'Italia*, pp. 106-09. Melillo, Schettino, and Ciccarese were absolved of the charges of complicity and conspiracy in Nov., 1879. *La Plebe*, Nov. 16, 1879.

by the police present, according to socialist sources—of "Death to the Internationalists!" and fifteen minutes later, as if by magic, appeared signs urging "Death to the Internationalists, assassins of the people." Cesare Batacchi, released from jail only two hours before the explosion, was re-arrested immediately, along with fifty-seven others, nine of whom denied belonging to the International. Not a single arrest had been made on the actual scene of the crime, and all those imprisoned had strong alibis to prove they had been neither on nor near the spot when the bomb was hurled.[73] Two days later, an Orsini bomb was thrown into a Pisan crowd celebrating the Queen's birthday; no one was killed, but this time some students grabbed the culprit. He and several other Internationalists were held for trial.[74] In the Romagna, a wave of arrests not only decapitated, but practically eliminated, the anarchist organization in the region, except for a handful of Internationalists rounded up the following spring.[75] Arturo Ceretti, editor of *L'Avvenire*, was arrested on December 21 in Mirandola; the charge: suspected Internationalism.[76] Of all the anarchist chieftains who had directed the Italian International in 1878, only Gaetano Grassi appears to have eluded the dragnet by going into exile.

From the socialists' point of view, it was a supreme irony that Giuseppe Zanardelli, the Minister of Interior who had adopted the principle of "repression, not prevention" as the keynote of his policy toward the International, the man designated by his parliamentary adversaries as the *teorico della libertà* (theoretician of liberty), was forced to resign on December 12 because his government's policy, in the words of Ruggiero Bonghi, had been too "limp and lazy in action, timid in [its] concepts, pleasing to and favored by the most mobile and subversive parties of the country."[77]

THE TRIALS OF 1879

Attempting to capitalize on the public indignation caused by the Passanante, Via Nazionale, and Pisa bomb-throwings, the Italian government

[73] For the Via Nazionale affair, *La Perseveranza*, Nov. 19, 21, 1879; Pezzi, *Un errore giudiziario*, pp. 89-94; Vigo, *op. cit.*, II, 315; Angiolini, *op. cit.*, pp. 155-56; Conti, *O.S.F.*, pp. 213-14; Romano, *Storia*, III, 323-24.

[74] *La Perseveranza*, Nov. 23, 1878; Vigo, *op. cit.*, II, 315-16.

[75] *La Perseveranza*, Dec. 7, 14, 1878; Venturini, *op. cit.*, pp. 3-7, 27-31.

[76] *La Perseveranza*, Dec. 25, 1878; *La Plebe*, Sept. 28, 1879. He, along with four other Internationalists, was tried by a Modena Court of Assises in Sept., 1879, on the charge of conspiracy against the internal security of the state. *La Perseveranza*, Sept. 19, 1879.

[77] Bonghi, *Discorsi parlamentari*, I, 647 ff., for his criticism of the Cairoli-Zanardelli government on Dec. 3, 1878. For Zanardelli's famous speech at Iseo of Nov. 3, 1878, in which he defined and defended his basic liberal concepts, see his *Discorsi parlamentari*, I, 92 ff.; *La Perseveranza*, Nov. 5, 1878.

issued a secret circular on January 20, 1879, to all prefects of the realm.[78] The "sect of the International" was to be destroyed and all its members put under *ammonizione*. The use of this weapon, normally applied only to habitual delinquents, implied that the Italian International was an association of common malefactors, not a political organization. The government's attempt to establish this principle, during the series of trials held in 1879, failed in almost every instance, thanks chiefly to magistrates who insisted that the law not be twisted to suit the political exigencies of the government in power and the current temper of public opinion. Where the charge involved a common crime, the Internationalists were punished as malefactors, not as members of the I.W.A. Where the charge was Internationalism per se, the defendants had very little to lament in the decisions of the courts.[79]

In the trials involving actual attempts against persons, sentences were severe, and, by the nature of the cases, the police were able to contrive "evidence" which, in view of outraged public opinion, gave the jurors no real alternative but to render affirmative verdicts. The first trial, concerned with the Florentine bomb attempt of February 9, 1878, was held in May, 1879. Cappellini, the actual hurler of the missile, was cleared after a preliminary hearing a few months after the event. Of the four Internationalists held as the real responsibles, one hanged himself in his cell when he learned of his indictment, and the other three, Giuseppe Franciolini, Raffaele Degl'Innocenti, and Francesco Colzi, were sentenced to twenty-year prison terms on the sole basis of a statement by a police agent that he knew, from "a confidential source," that the bomb "was thrown by Tommaso Lanfredini [the suicide], assisted in a special way" by the other three defendants.[80]

The trial for the Via Nazionale affair of November 18, 1878, saw nine Florentine Internationalists in the defendants' dock: Cesare Batacchi, Pietro Corsi, Giuseppe Scarlatti, Natale Nencioni, Agenore Natta (brother of Francesco), Aurelio Vannini, Lisandro Marchini, Natale Conti, and Sante Sicuteri—all workingmen.[81] The charge: "premeditated homicide,

[78] Conti, *O.S.F.*, pp. 225-26.

[79] Article 426 of the Italian Penal Code required proof that the purpose of the presumed "association of malefactors" was true malefaction, e.g., assassination, theft, sacking, arson, etc. If trying to change the economic and social order involved offenses against persons and property, the act remained a political, not a common, crime. Thus, defense lawyers could easily prove that their clients were members of no "association of malefactors." As an example, see Ceneri's defense of Domenico Francolini before a Forlì court on Oct. 6, 1879, in Ceneri's *Opere*, I, 147-66.

[80] Angiolini, *op. cit.*, p. 157; Conti, *O.S.F.*, pp. 214-15.

[81] For the proceedings, Pezzi, *Un errore giudiziario*, pp. 95-148; *La Plebe*, June 9; *La Perseveranza*, May 27, 28, 30, 1879. For secondary treatments, Conti, *O.S.F.*, pp. 215-16; Angiolini, *op. cit.*, pp. 157-58; Romano, *Storia*, III, 328-34.

consummated and unconsummated." The police had left no stone un-
turned to insure a verdict of guilty. Informants had been placed in the
same cells with the accused in order to provoke them into making compromising statements. Prosecution witnesses included habitual thieves
and paid police informers. Others were promised jobs in return for rigged
testimony, still others were threatened with *ammonizione* if they failed
to testify as ordered. Defense witnesses were actually put under *ammonizione* in the course of the trial, some even arrested in the courthouse
corridors.

The indictment charged that the defendants had decided on the
evening of November 15 to commit the crime of the 18th, but the
prosecution never explained how the accused could have anticipated a
demonstration that was a direct result of the November 17 Passanante
attempt on Humbert in Naples. Nor did the prosecution explain why
Cesare Batacchi, jailed as a precautionary measure during Humbert's
visit to Florence, released and then rearrested on November 16, had been
freed a mere two hours before the scheduled demonstration of November
18. No one explained, either, how signs urging "Death to the Internationalists" could have been produced in the space of fifteen minutes after
the bomb exploded. The only contradiction of the defendants' alibis was
furnished by persons paid or threatened by the police. Two of them, far
from the reach of police reprisals in 1881, signed affidavits admitting
that their testimony had been a tissue of lies dictated by the *questura*.[82]

In the spring of 1879, however, public opinion demanded retribution
for the November attempts, and the police, under pressure from Rome
to wipe out the International, obligingly furnished the scapegoats. Batacchi was handed a life sentence; Scarlatti and Natta sentenced to twenty
years' confinement; Corsi, Nencioni, Vannini, and Conti to nineteen;
Marchini and Sicuteri were acquitted. From his prison cell, Scarlatti
drew a clear distinction between the role of the police and that of the
magistracy: ". . . in our trial, justice was suffocated by partisan hatred,
the magistracy tricked by partisan police, who wanted to strike in us, not
the authors of the horrendous misdeed of Via Nazionale, but the
members of the International Workingmen's Association." [83]

Where membership in, or propaganda activity for, the International
was attributed to the dozens of other socialists gathered up in the winter

[82] For the statements of Francesco Alessi, May 19, 1881, and Narcisso Menocci,
July 7, 1881, Pezzi, *Un errore giudiziario,* pp. 161-68.
[83] Letter to Fortunato Serantoni, June 11, 1879, Pezzi, *Un errore giudiziario,* pp.
168-70, italics mine. A court of cassation turned down the defendants' appeal, and
Pezzi's publication of the perjured witnesses' statements in 1882 brought no retrial.
Only in 1899 did an organized demand for the defendants' liberation begin, resulting
in a full pardon on Mar. 16, 1900. Conti, *O.S.F.,* p. 216.

and spring of 1878-79, only one court held to the doctrine that Internationalism was illegal—a decision later reversed by a higher court. On September 7, 1879, a Bologna court handed down jail sentences ranging from thirty days to eighteen months for fourteen Internationalists charged with I.W.A. membership, distributing subversive pamphlets and manifestos, resisting arrest and inciting to treason. Four were completely exonerated.[84] Yet, exactly one month later, a Forlì court found I.W.A. membership insufficient grounds for prosecution of twenty Internationalists and, in the case of five others, charged with distributing manifestos without proper authorization, absolved two and fined the rest slightly over twenty-five *lire* each. In Modena, Arturo Ceretti was acquitted of the charge of conspiracy.[85] In Naples, Reggio Emilia, Genoa, Massa, Ancona, and other cities, the pattern was the same: I.W.A. membership, the courts held, was not a crime, common or political.[86]

If any further demonstration of the government's failure to establish such a principle were needed, it came with the eminently political trial that opened in Florence on November 9, 1879. The defendants were Francesco Pezzi and his wife, Francesco Natta, Anna Kulisciov, Florido Matteucci, and nine others involved in the "family meeting" in Florence. All were charged with conspiracy against the internal security of the state.[87] The gist of the prosecution's case revolved about the deliberations of the secret congress of Pisa in April, 1878, the Florence meeting of September 30—October 1, 1878, and the sequestered Matteucci-Kulisciov correspondence of the intervening summer. Debate established two facts: that the Italian Internationalists' plans for "armed bands" in 1878 never got beyond the talking stage and that more than clandestine planning of

[84] *Il Movimento Sociale* (Naples), Sept. 15; *La Plebe*, Sept. 14, 1879; Venturini, *op. cit.*, pp. 10-25. For the socialist protest against the Bologna decision, *La Plebe*, Sept. 21, 28, Oct. 9, 1879. A Bologna Court of Appeals reversed the sentence and freed the Internationalists in Dec., 1879. The following summer a Rome Court of Appeals did the same for Imola socialists sentenced for Internationalism. *Ibid.*, July 15, 1880.

[85] *Il Movimento Sociale*, Oct. 21; *La Plebe*, Sept. 28, Oct. 5; *La Perseveranza*, Oct. 9, 1879; Venturini, *op. cit.*, pp. 40-42.

[86] *La Plebe*, Aug. 3, 10, Sept. 14, Oct. 19; *La Perseveranza*, Oct. 11; *Il Movimento Sociale*, Sept. 21, 1879. The eleven Ancona Internationalists, tried in October, had been arrested for punctuating their commemoration of the Paris Commune with shouts of "Long Live the French Republic,—the Tuscan Republic,—the Republic of San Marino,—Anarchy,—the Paris Commune,—Passanante,—*il petrolio;* down with the Army!"
The Court of Cassation in Florence had on two previous occasions (Feb. 5, 22, 1879) rendered the decision that I.W.A. membership constituted insufficient grounds for putting an individual under *ammonizione*, a decision concurred in, though in less specific language, by the Italian Supreme Court. *La Perseveranza*, Mar. 26, 1879.

[87] For the trial proceedings, *La Plebe*, Dec. 14, 21; *La Perseveranza*, Dec. 14, 16, 28, 1879. For secondary treatments, Angiolini, *op. cit.*, pp. 163-65; Conti, *O.S.F.*, p. 233; Romano, *Storia*, III, 334-37.

an insurrection was required to qualify them legally as threats to internal state security. For her part, Anna Kulisciov established beyond any doubt that she had overcome the anarchist orientation of her revolutionary activity in Russia:

> I replied to Matteucci that the internationalists can not make revolutions at their own convenience, because individuals are incapable of making or provoking them; it is the people who make them. Therefore, it is useless to arise in armed bands; one must wait until those revolutions and armed bands are formed in order to guide them toward socialist principles. The socialists . . . must take part in popular movements, as in every other manifestation of popular life, in order to guide them, but they themselves can not create them. The revolution must issue from the people and can not be made despite them. . . . The movement is not created by Socialism; it is promoted by the abnormality in which existing society finds itself and by the poverty of the many. . . .
>
> In my opinion, Socialism does not order armed bands, but it is ready to direct those that social conditions cause to appear. To provoke armed bands, where they have not already arisen, would be to remain outside the people. . . .[88]

Natta, Pezzi, and the other defendants could not have had a more eloquent Portia—and certainly none more appealing to a male jury: "she . . . seemed like a Slav virgin. With the head of a madonna, a light complexion, roseate with health, long, luminous blonde tresses reaching to her shoulders, she made one think of the graceful women of the pre-Raffaelites."[89] On January 5, 1880, the jury returned a verdict of not guilty.

[88] For her discourse, Angiolini, *op. cit.*, pp. 164-65; Schiavi, "Anna Kulisciov ed Andrea Costa," pp. 116-17; Romano, *Storia*, III, 336-37.

[89] Thus, Angiolini, *op. cit.*, p. 163.

XVII

The Ideological Liquidation of the Italian International (1879-1882)

THE ANARCHIST DILEMMA

THE acquittal of Pezzi, Natta, Matteucci in Florence, of Covelli in Genoa, of Ceretti in Modena, and of Schettino in Naples marked the end of the Italian International's consistency as a revolutionary organization. Malatesta and Cafiero were in exile, Costa was being hounded by the police. Government persecution and zealous police use of the *ammonizione* to control the movements of individual anarchists continued to deny them an opportunity to practice the propaganda of action. As demonstrated by the attempts of 1874 and 1877, popular support, alone capable of justifying the insurrectional tactic, simply did not exist, and more important, the public reaction to the Passanante affair, the Florence and Pisa bomb episodes, guaranteed that such support was out of the question in the foreseeable future. Anarchists could tell themselves that, as individuals, they had the duty of propagating their doctrines of violent revolution, of antistatism, of antiparliamentarism, but none could pretend that the Italian association, per se, was any longer a force in either an insurrectional or propagandistic sense. What Emilio Covelli wrote of the international socialist movement, after his acquittal in Genoa, was equally true of the Italian movement: "The International . . . no longer exists, either as a Marxist association or as a Bakuninist sect. There are revolutionary and anarchist socialists in every part of the world, but there is no longer any *contract*, public or secret, between them." [1]

Nonetheless, the external pressures the authorities brought to bear on the Italian International, however heavy, were not the fundamental reason for its decline. Even without such pressure, the Bakuninist

---

[1] *La Plebe*, July 27, 1879.

program of the organization would not have permitted the slow, laborious effort needed to educate the masses to revolutionary readiness. In fact, the anarchist credo assumed that such an effort was unnecessary. Even Andrea Costa, while recognizing, in his open letter to Nicotera of January 1876 [2] the inescapability of a campaign of popular education, insisted that it was simply a problem of arousing the *instinctive* revolutionism of the masses. For their part, Cafiero and Malatesta, after the San Lupo enterprise, abandoned neither the insurrectional principle nor the unrealistic assumption that proletarians are instinctively revolutionary, but they could not reasonably argue the historical accuracy, after 1879, of Costa's conclusion that "insurrectionism, if practiced, leads to nothing if not the triumph of reaction and, if not practiced, it leads to the disesteem of him who preaches it and it remains merely verbal." [3] Here, indeed, was the kernel of the anarchists' dilemma: that the only conceivable way to avoid both merely verbal insurrectionism and the triumph of reaction, as they defined it, was denied them by their own principles. They could have escaped the dilemma, of course, by sacrificing the insurrectional tactic, but the only alternatives were trade-unionism and/or electoral activity, the adoption of which would have liquidated the anarchist credo entirely. A "reformist" anarchism, by definition, would lack the element of idealism that had drawn so many young recruits from the ranks of republicanism. In this insoluble contradiction, not in government persecution, lay the basic cause of the Italian International's demise.

Those anarchists unwilling to adopt the political or syndicalist alternatives had to resign themselves to immobility, ultimately as disastrous to their doctrine, in terms of its power to evoke concrete political action, as any effort to continue the insurrectional tactic. It was for this discouraged segment that Francesco Pezzi spoke when, in April, 1880, he informed Costa that "we no longer concern ourselves actively with anything . . . because we find that our fortunes are so changed . . . , rather than provoke schisms and frictions among the socialists, we think it better and more useful to remain simple observers." [4]

For those Italian anarchists ready to recognize the impasse into which their central tactical dogma had led them, unable and unwilling to resign themselves to the role of spectators, the ideological crisis of the movement could have but one outcome: dropping their unconditional hostility toward the state and seeking its conquest through electoral activity. Such a decision marked an acknowledgment of Marx's dictum that political action of the proletariat is essential to the triumph of socialism, and on

---

[2] See above, p. 376.
[3] Costa, in *Le Précurseur*, June 4, 1881, as quoted by Borghi, *Malatesta*, p. 62.
[4] Conti, *O.S.F.*, pp. 233-34.

this fundamental issue, Marx, not Bakunin, was vindicated. Still, the shift in tactic was a response, not so much to any serene assessment of the relative merits, *in vacuo*, of the old libertarian-legalitarian argument, but to a combination of historical circumstances which, several years earlier, were probably as unanticipated by Marx and Engels as they were by Bakunin and his Italian disciples. Only with the advent to power of the parliamentary Left did the prospect of universal suffrage begin to appear a concrete possibility. That this possibility was bound to affect the premises of the anarchist attitude toward the state was indicated by Costa less than five months after he sustained a rigidly Bakuninist position at the congresses of Verviers and Ghent. In the Parisian newspaper of Jules Guesde, *L'Egalité*, he admitted that if democratic liberties, including universal suffrage, had existed in Italy, the anarcho-socialists, too, would have had to participate in the elections.[5] In the late 1870's, the agitation and parliamentary discussion that were to produce a law quadrupling the electorate in January 1882 could not have failed to jar the in-transigence of anarchists who had adopted Bakuninism at a time when Italy's ruling classes firmly believed that extension of the suffrage would jeopardize private property and the bourgeois basis of the social order.[6]

Nor did Italian developments alone suggest a re-examination of the anti-political tenet. The French elections of October 1877, in frustrating the reactionary monarchist forces symbolized by Marshal MacMahon, certainly underlined the democratic potential of electoral action. In Bis-marckian Germany, the continued vigor of the Social Democratic Party in the face of political persecution that made the Italian authorities' cam-paign against socialists look like rank amateurism, must have pointed up the moral that electoral activity, given a sufficiently broad electorate, offered a practical way to breach the battlements of bourgeois conserva-tism.

From the beginning, anarchists had argued that parliamentary activity by socialists would corrupt their principles, that socialists in bourgeois legislatures, having accepted—even if temporarily—the existing political structure, could not sincerely and effectively work for its destruction. Still, prior to the early 1880's, there were not enough socialist deputies in Western European parliaments to support or disprove the contention. And at a time when alternative paths of socialist activity were so few,

---

[5] Valiani, *Storia del movimento socialista*, I, 239, note 39.

[6] Chabod, *Storia della politica estera italiana*, I, 357-58. The electoral law that went into effect on Jan. 22, 1882, increased the voting population from slightly over 600,000 to over 2,000,000, by lowering the voting age from 25 to 21, reducing the tax qualification from 40 to 19.8 *lire* per year, and establishing a minimum requirement of four years elementary schooling or two years military service. Cilibrizzi, *Storia parlamentare*, II, 217-24.

the anarchist argument constituted no real deterrent to socialist exploitation of a broadened suffrage to win legislative representation.

THE SHIFT TO LEGALITARIANISM:
ANDREA COSTA'S DEFECTION

The job of voicing, rationalizing, and formalizing the shift to legalitarian, reformist socialism that these conditions not only warranted, but demanded, fell to Andrea Costa. In redeeming the redeemable, Costa earned a solid niche for himself in the annals of the Italian socialist movement; extension of the suffrage and the appearance of a modern industrial proletariat during the 1880's unquestionably revealed the utter inadequacy of the anarchist formula as a guide to organizing proletarians for struggle as a class. It was high time, indeed, to pass from the romantic activism of Bakunin and Pisacane, from endemic insurrectionism, to the less spectacular but more enduring organization of a mass party.

But in recognizing the historical necessity of such a change, in developing a new formula to fit changed circumstances, Costa saddled the Italian socialist movement with a schizoid program that proved, in the long run, perhaps as damaging to the real progress of the movement as Bakuninism had been, even though his practical recommendations for immediate action undeniably corresponded to the needs of the time. He laid down the wholly undemonstrable proposition that economic and political reforms favoring the workers create the popular revolutionary temper needed for eventual *violent* social transformation. The fate of Italian socialist "maximalism"—and Costa's doctrine was its seed—between 1880 and 1922 lies outside the scope of the present volume, but Errico Malatesta, looking backward over that period and commenting on the historical consequences of the new doctrine, bitterly observed that the anarchists' "prophecies on the degeneration into which socialism would fall in becoming legalitarian and parliamentary have been justified, and even more than we thought." [7]

Precisely when and under what psychological stimuli Costa decided to abandon the anarchist positions he had put forward at the Congress of Ghent in September 1877 remains a mystery, thanks to the scarcity of direct documentation of his thinking during the twenty-month French sojourn that ended in June, 1879. As already noted, his hostility toward the conspiratorial method and his conviction that the essential problem of socialism was to educate the masses to revolutionary preparedness dated from January, 1876, when he wrote his open letter to Nicotera. Rejection of insurrectionism was implicit in his attempt to talk Cafiero and Mala-

[7] Preface to Nettlau, *B.I.I.*, xxx.

testa out of staging the San Lupo affair. Given these precedents, Costa's intransigent stance at Ghent may have represented, not so much a strong personal conviction, but a sense of obligation to obey his mandate from the San Lupo arrestees, and perhaps even to compensate for his refusal to join their undertaking and suffer its bitter consequences. At both the Verviers and Ghent congresses, moreover, Costa could not have failed to be struck by the moderation of Guillaume and the Jurassian Federation and the arguments used by such estimable figures of European socialism as Wilhelm Liebknecht and Leo Fränkel, men with a promisingly powerful German Social Democratic Party in being to lend weight to their arguments in favor of legalitarian socialism.

After the Ghent Congress, in a letter to Anna Kulisciov, Costa stressed the need for an "immense propaganda . . . [and] a government that would allow us to meet, to associate, and to publish something," an attitude that may well have stimulated the complaints about his ideas by some of the French anarchists with whom he associated after moving to Paris in late September, 1877. Aside from the anti-anarchist influence of Kulisciov, who arrived on November 11, contact with Jules Guesde, Lodovico Nabruzzi, and Tito Zanardelli, the latter heavily under the influence of Benoît Malon, may have contributed, too, to Costa's review of the positions he had supported at Ghent.[8]

At his trial before a Parisian court in late April and early May, 1878, Costa fixed one of the basic concepts of his subsequent "revolutionary" philosophy. In defining anarchism, he no longer spoke of a direct assault on the state. Collectivize capital, land, and the instruments of production and the state will disappear:

> We are *Anarchists.* . . . We think that once this economic transformation occurs, a transformation in the political relations of society must also take place, since a social phenomenon is never produced by itself; . . . in collective property the State necessarily disappears and in its place comes a new political order corresponding to the new economic principle—an order that is not and can not be the State, that we signify with the name of *Anarchy.*[9]

In effect, Costa had accepted the Marxian thesis that the state is simply the political expression of the prevailing system of production. Change the economic base, and the form of government necessarily changes. Like the Marxists, too, he had arrived at the notion that in a collectivist so-

[8] For Costa's letter of Sept. 18, 1877, to Kulisciov, see Bosio and Della Peruta, "La 'svolta' di Andrea Costa, con documenti sul soggiorno in Francia," *Movimento Operaio,* Yr. IV, No. 2 (Mar.-Apr., 1952), 300.

[9] *L'Avvenire,* June 29, 1878.

ciety the need of government is gradually reduced until the state vanishes entirely. No later than at this point, Costa ceased being a Bakuninist, for he was implicitly accepting the existing state as the political framework in which socialists should attempt to destroy its economic foundations. Where Bakunin had held destruction of the bourgeois state to be the *first* step in the emancipation of the workers, Costa now makes it a distant goal to be reached only *after* the overthrow of capitalism and the establishment of a collectivist society.

To the extent that European anarchists generally, by the late 1870's, had acknowledged that anarchism—or "anarchic communism," as they came to call it—was not immediately possible, Bakunin's doctrine had been left behind, so Costa's position was startling only in relation to his pre-1877 utterances. If his argument with Italian anarchist intransigents had been limited to the question of whether the goal of a stateless utopia is attainable later rather than sooner, the two positions might have been reconciled. But Costa, precisely because he denied the possibility of imminent violent revolution, was forced into recommending an immediate action program which, according to his ex-comrades, hopelessly compromised the chances of total social subversion at *any* time in the future. In brief, Costa refused to pay the price of theoretical consistency: to admit that a violent social revolution is not prepared with tactics premising its indefinite postponement. The proof that he was perfectly aware of the inconsistency lay in the manner in which he exposed his new orientation: two steps forward and one step backward, until the only remaining recommendation for concrete and imminent revolutionary action revealed itself as an ingenuous absurdity. The process began in the spring of 1879.

In a letter of May 24 to his Lugano friend, Mazzotti (Filippo Boschieri),[10] Costa justified his imminent defection from the anarchist camp by arguing that socialists should not miss the opportunity to exploit a popular demand for a republic that Costa was certain would succeed the present period of "brutal reaction." The anarchists must surmount their disdain of the workers' everyday problems, overcome their sectarian isolationism and their incapacity for practical action; otherwise, moderate and opportunist republicans alone would profit from a resurgence of republican sentiment among the masses. Costa proposed trying to remedy matters immediately on his release from his French prison. "Perhaps I shall be in disagreement with some of our people; but what of it? . . . willy-nilly, we are all marching toward the same goal."

[10] Reproduced, in full, by Bosio and Della Peruta, "La 'svolta' di Andrea Costa," pp. 310-11; in part, by Schiavi, "La formazione del pensiero politico di A. Costa," p. 29; Lipparini, *Andrea Costa*, pp. 131-32.

Amnestied and freed on June 5, 1879, Costa departed for Switzerland. In Lugano he was feted on July 13 by a solid phalanx of legalitarian socialists—Benoît Malon, Agostino Pistolesi, Enrico Bignami, Mazzotti, Pederzolli, Moneta, and others. Malon, according to Costa's biographer,[11] advised the Romagnol agitator to follow Marx, but not to neglect the idealistic factors in history. It was in this ambient that Costa, on July 27, wrote the famous open letter, "To my Friends of the Romagna," that constituted the new tactical and strategic directive of the Italian socialist movement.[12] If its author had been less concerned with arguing that his new orientation was as "revolutionary" as his former anarchist position —"substantially, we must remain where we were" [sic!]—the appeal would have been far less open to the charge of hypocrisy with which many of his former associates greeted it.

Taking a page from Bakunin's book, Costa prefaced his criticism of anarchist practice with praise of its positive achievements. In combatting the religious idealism of Mazzini and the "blind, ideologically amorphous" Garibaldian party that was moving toward military dictatorship, the anarchists had "energetically revealed and affirmed the vital force of the century—the working class"; they had welcomed the cooperation of those members of the bourgeoisie who, detesting the privileges of their class, had put their knowledge of science at the service of the proletariat; they had raised all the questions relating to the emancipation of the proletariat: property, family, state and religion; they had carried forward the revolutionary traditions of the Italian people, especially the Pisacanian principle that ideas are to be propagated through deeds. This promising start, however, had been neutralized by the anarchists' insurrectional program:

> . . . since the failure of revolutionary attempts deprived us of liberty for entire years, or condemned us to exile, we unfortunately lost touch with the daily struggles and practice of real life: we closed ourselves up too much and worried more about the logic of our ideas and the composition of a revolutionary program that we tried to actuate without delay, instead of studying the economic and moral conditions of the people and their sensed and immediate needs. Thus, we inevitably neglected many manifestations of life, we did not mix enough with the people; and when, impelled by a generous impulse, we tried to raise the banner of revolt, the people did not understand us, they let us alone.
>
> Let us profit from the lesson of experience. Let us complete

[11] Lipparini, *Andrea Costa,* p. 134.
[12] For the complete text of the letter, *La Plebe,* Aug. 3, 1879; reproduced by Manacorda, *Il movimento operaio italiano,* pp. 335-39.

what was interrupted. Let us throw ourselves once more among the people and strengthen ourselves in them.

Italian socialists had to remain a "party of action," for the question between proletariat and bourgeoisie required a violent solution, historically inevitable. "Every right and every human liberty was always bought and will always be bought . . . at the price of blood." Costa's persistent *anticlassismo* again appeared in his statement that the party should welcome the youth, thinkers, and women of the middle class who loath present conditions and want social justice. The object is to create a new spirit in people generally. "The people are idealistic by nature . . . and will not arise until socialistic ideas have the same prestige and force of attraction for them that religious faith once had"—Malon's advice had apparently taken root.

Though inevitable, the revolution will not occur tomorrow or next year. Meanwhile, the traditional program stands: *"Collectivism* as the means, *Anarchy* as the goal—the program of today, which was our program of yesterday." And here Costa repeated his argument that collectivization of land, tools, and products creates a situation in which:

> . . . every law that regulates the relations between men must necessarily disappear, since the abundance of production and the new education, which the new social conditions and the practice of human solidarity give man, will make them useless. Then can be actuated that *anarchic communism* that appears today as the most perfect social order.

Since his ideal society, in which the state would have no *raison d'être,* was a "distant ideal," Costa proposed, as an "immediately actuable program," collectivism as the economic foundation and federation of autonomous communes as the political organization of the post-capitalist society. As to how long this transitional regime between capitalism and anarchic communism was to endure, Costa hazarded no guess but said it had to be achieved gradually and without violence, that its development would be determined by the capacity of future generations to discover and adapt themselves to the laws governing human relations. Thus, in effect, Costa premised the disappearance of the state on the creation of an intermediate politico-economic system of unpredicted and unpredictable longevity.

Costa's letter was at once a negation of the insurrectional tactic, of "action at any cost," and an affirmation that his new program represented a reform, not an abdication, of the traditional anarchist platform. And it is worth noting that he even invoked Pisacane's revolutionary activism as a legitimate forebear of the views he now exposed. Still, all his emphasis on the revolutionary intent of his program, his tenacious styling himself an "anarchist," his recommendation that the "Italian Revolutionary Socialist Party" be reconstituted, could not hide the fact that, in all logic, his indefinite postponement of abolishing the state amounted to nothing less than a denial of anarchism's central dogma: that destruction of the state is the prerequisite, not the consequence, of emancipating the worker.[13] Costa had reversed the formula. His human desire to sweeten the pill of his defection for his comrades of yesterday is entirely understandable, but to take seriously his protestations that his "revolutionism" was rooted in anarchist premises is to ascribe to him an ingenuousness not at all consistent with his capacity to identify the impractical and unrealistic aspects of those doctrines. Costa still had to spell out his program for immediate action, to pronounce himself on the question of socialist political activity, but in his letter to his Romagnol friends he had publicly established the legalitarian, evolutionary premises—however disguised as revolutionary in nature—for recommending "the practical means . . . that must be used to put us more broadly among the people, . . . the conduct we must pursue toward the government, as well as the other political parties, and what importance we shall give to political reforms. . . ."

Costa's open letter may have come as a surprise to the uninitiated, but several of the more prominent anarchist chiefs were quite prepared to accept the Romagnol's plea for a new orientation—at least on a theoretical level. On the same day that Costa composed his letter to the Romagnol socialists, *La Plebe* carried a letter from Emilio Covelli in which he described the socialist ideal: "anarchic communism as the ultimate goal; as a transient necessity, that degree of collectivism that the economic and moral conditions of so-called civil society permit us." [14] This declaration, along with Costa's letter, proved to Benoît Malon's satisfaction, at least, that "the reconciliation movement among socialists on the terrain of science continues" and that the legalitarians and anarchists had been divided on the question of method more than that of goals. "We fought anarchic communism *considered as capable of immediate realization*, but we collectivists considered it the most splendid ideal that human genius has been able to conceive up to the present." [15] Costa's theme of renewing the party by conquering a broad popular base was echoed by Gaetano Grassi: "All our efforts must be applied to reorganizing our forces into a party that can expand into all social

[13] Bakunin in 1871: ". . . the policy of the social revolution . . . puts first the abolition of the state . . ." See above, p. 194.
[14] *La Plebe*, July 27, 1879.
[15] *Ibid.*, Aug. 3, 1879.

strata [and] open minds to new horizons, to a greater and more human ideal. . . ." [16] From the Veneto, Carlo Monticelli seconded Costa's sentiments in a letter to *La Plebe*. Socialists, wrote he, must "go to the plebe, live his existence, study his needs, make our aspirations his." The error of the past:

> . . . we put too much faith perhaps in the revolutionary spirit of the Italian people; poets more than thinkers, we preferred martyrdom to success; and today, when we must renew ourselves [and] again participate in the struggle, we feel the need of correcting ourselves, and we seek to give a broader development to our program of action. The revolution is inevitable! who does not know it? but, more than organizing the revolution, we must be prepared to receive it.[17]

Malon's assertion that these expressions demonstrated past disagreement on means, rather than ends, was a sophistry he himself would probably have denounced as such two years earlier. But in September 1879, the denunciation came in a circular of the Italian correspondence commission,[18] challenging the whole Costian orientation by adopting the simple logic that "methods and goals are reciprocal terms; the one is simultaneously the cause and the effect of the other." As Romano points out, the document was a plea for "the romantic schemes of the insurrectional tactic . . . . [and] it lacks, or underestimates, the need of mass organization as an instrument of struggle," [19] but it also unerringly identifies Costa's theoretical inconsistencies. The author of the Circular readily granted the need of renewing and reorganizing the party in a progressive sense, but Costa's formula amounted to *immobilismo:* the price of government tolerance was to become moderate, parliamentarian, and legalitarian, which would be regression, not progress. Costa's quoting of Pisacane's line that deeds produce ideas was implicitly branded as hypocrisy by the simple expedient of completing the quotation from the *Political Testament:*

> One can disagree with the method, the place, and the timing of a conspiracy, but to disagree with the principle is an absurdity, an hypocrisy, it is to hide a base egotism.

[16] *La Plebe*, Aug. 25, 1879. Grassi still believed, however, that Italian economic conditions promised the possibility of imminent armed insurrection: "The revolution in Italy will not be long in coming—it will be a *jacquerie*. Peasants and progressive workers, peasants and priests, all with arms in hand. . . . In any case, our revolution will be terrible. So let us study the morrow . . ." Letter from Lugano, Romano, *Storia*, III, 349, note 56.

[17] Issue of Aug. 30, 1879. But Monticelli did not accept Costa's premises. See his letter to *La Favilla*, Oct. 20, 1881.

[18] For the Circular, dated Sept. 27, 1879, Romano, *Storia*, III, 575-78.

[19] *Ibid.*, III, 348.

I respect him who approves conspiracy and does not himself conspire, but I feel only contempt for those who not only want to do nothing, but take pleasure in belittling and damning those who do want to act. . . .

Costa pleads for a party to include all socialists, but he anathematizes the revolutionaries because they compromise the possibilities, vis-à-vis the government, of pacific socialist propaganda. There are no objections to propaganda activity, per se, but without "a more or less immediate goal of action" it becomes useless:

Propaganda . . . is effective only when it is made in the name of a serious, vigorous party that continually affirms its existence; if not, propaganda leads us to utopias . . . , [it] does not put us among the people, but the bourgeoisie. The people do not understand us when we speak the language of science, . . . [but] when we, by interpreting their needs and aspirations, indicate to them in a practical manner the way to satisfy both immediately.

The Italian International's mistake, according to the Circular, was faulty party organization; the remedy: "establishing *serious and secret* bonds between all of us." As for the question of theoretical goals:

Let us put aside the dispute between Collectivism and Communism; it is said that Collectivism is easier to actuate than Communism and (though we think the contrary, though Collectivism is not understood by the people, who understand Communism very well, though Collectivism is a dangerous theory) let us not enlarge our divisions; let us be satisfied in calling ourselves—Communists and Collectivists—the *party of the social revolution;* let us try to make understood and to demonstrate with deeds that we and we alone want the true revolution, the one that means the *renewal* and not the *reform* of society.

Costa's retort to the Circular came in an article entitled, "Tribuna Aperta." [20] Violent revolution, he wrote, is necessary because the idea is "instinctive" in the people, but the popular revolutionary instinct must be elevated into a principle, "the revolution must be made *conscious* and capable of producing what is expected of it." To change the existing political conditions in such a way as to permit socialists "to apply all the living forces of the people to the resolution of the economic question" requires *no political party,* but "socialistic agitation," carried forward in

[20] *La Plebe,* Nov. 16, 1879.

alliance with city workers who believe—and Costa said he did not share their belief—reforms necessary to their emancipation. After having ruled out the anarchist insurrectional tactic in his July letter, Costa now voices the broadest eclecticism:

> If following . . . a certain program or using certain methods were to lead us to anarchy, one would only have to concern himself with executing to the letter the program itself; but neither the violent revolution nor the legal revolution by means of decrees (necessarily preceded by the violent revolution) can institute *anarchy*. Anarchy will be the natural consequence of an indefinite evolution of production and the new culture; never the social state of tomorrow. With respect to the *ultimate goal* we envisage, the use of this or that means is more or less a matter of indifference; therefore, while adopting the most appropriate and readily available means, let us not neglect the rest: let us seek to become a great social force capable of putting in motion all the instruments we have at hand: economic, political, moral forces.

For the benefit of anarchists who believed Costa's indefinite postpone-ment of the advent of anarchic communism meant his effective renunci-ation of the antistatist principle, Costa gave the assurance that in his intermediate collectivist society the political order would not be "the state in the present meaning of the word, but, in some places, . . . a popular and workers' State, in others, a Federation of communes." The only alternative transitional regime is authoritarian communism ("Ger-man communism" Costa called it, doubtless remembering the Circular's sarcastic reference to socialists beginning a *sinfonia alla tedesca*), which denies individual liberty.

From this point forward, Costa left off attempts to delineate his misty utopia and worried not at all about the gap between his professed "revo-lutionary" objectives and the methods forced on him by the realities of the objective situation. His ex-comrades' invocations of the ideal "make me sick at the stomach. The ideal, cabbage! For myself, I prefer the worker laboring one hour less per day and having one more dish on his table to all the aristocratic ideals in the world. One does not eat with the ideal." [21] At a Bologna meeting of Romagnol socialists on March 14, 1880, Costa's guidance produced a resolution that envisaged instituting eco-nomic collectivism while destroying all forms of authority, that proposed the use of all methods, including gradual social and political reforms,

[21] Letter to Kulisciov, in Lipparini, *Andrea Costa*, p. 165.

while indicating "violent struggle" as the only method that can guarantee the advent of a new social order.[22]

The Bologna gathering discussed the reconstruction of an Italian socialist party, to include "all the heretofore dispersed workers' forces," but it was the legalitarian nucleus of Bignami and Gnocchi-Viani in Milan that issued an appeal on April 4 "To all the Socialists of Italy" to meet in Milan on May 10 to create a national party that would include socialist and workers' organizations, unorganized workers, socialist sympathizers, and even republican youth and students.[23] But few socialist organizations adhered to the initiative—perhaps indicative of the fact that the legalitarian viewpoint had by no means conquered the peninsula. To hide the failure, Gnocchi-Viani and Bignami provoked the Milanese prefect into prohibiting the congress before it had a chance to meet.[24]

Costa's response to the abortive Milanese congress initiative was the issuance in Milan on May 15 of the *Rivista Internazionale del Socialismo,* apparently intended to orient the debate about a new party toward acceptance of Costa's hybrid revolutionary-evolutionary formula. To the effort, Anna Kulisciov, Benoît Malon, César De Paepe, Elisée Reclus, contributed articles, along with Italian socialists, including Bignami, Gnocchi-Viani, Luigi Castellazzo, and several of Costa's Romagnol friends, Antonio Cornacchia, Teobaldo Buggini, and Alfonso Leonesi. In an article entitled "The Congress of the Italian Socialists,"[25] Costa listed the practical reform measures needed to win the masses over to socialism: shorter working hours, new rules on factory working conditions, limitation or abolition of child and female labor, abolition of the *macinato* tax, of all indirect taxes, of the lottery, of preventive incarceration, regulation of prostitution, establishment of technical schools, abolition of conscription in favor of a national militia, and partitioning of unused lands among the peasants. But these reforms had no intrinsic value for Costa; they serve to arouse the people, to make them conscious of "the inevitability of the economic revolution, *because of the experience that will be had of the ineffectiveness of the political reforms obtained*" (italics supplied). Here Costa betrayed, despite all his protests to the contrary, his effective rejection of the principle of violent social subversion: his formula "en-

[22] Manacorda, *op. cit.,* p. 126; Lipparini, *Andrea Costa,* pp. 145-46; Bosio and Della Peruta, "La 'svolta' di Andrea Costa," p. 313. *La Plebe* (Mar. 18, 1880) eliminated the anarchist references in publishing the Bologna resolution.

[23] For the convocation manifesto, *La Plebe,* Apr. 4, 1880.

[24] On this affair, see Gnocchi-Viani, *Ricordi di un internazionalista,* pp. 129 ff.; Manacorda, *op. cit.,* pp. 126-28.

[25] Issue of May 15, 1880.

trusted the birth of the revolution to a nebulous process of popular delusion with the vanity of the reforms conquered at the price of so many gradual struggles." [26] And in trying to bring his theoretical revolutionism down to a practical level, to prove that he, too, had "a more or less immediate goal of action," Costa proved only that he was as ingenuous, in one respect, as he had been in 1874—or something less than sincere:

> . . . if we were able to mandate our friends to the Commune [i.e., elect representatives to city councils] and one fine day a Commune were to refuse to pay taxes to the government, and perhaps vote collective ownership of Communal lands, and declare war on the State, and incite surrounding Communes to do the same, would not the insurrection of this Commune, though suffocated in blood, perhaps be worth years of propaganda?

Accompanying this left-handed recommendation of socialist candidacies in administrative elections was an equally indirect suggestion that it was time to put socialists into the Chamber of Deputies, a broadening of the suffrage permitting:

> Do you believe . . . that when some one vigorously arises in Parliament and shames [the bourgeois deputies] . . . , and plants the red banner with a firm hand in the fortress of our adversaries, do you believe that . . . his words would not open the eyes of millions of suffering people, whom our voice does not reach, and hasten the final decomposition of that already half-dead organism that governs us?

Costa continued to insist, as he did at a conference held in Bologna on November 1, 1880, that his was the language of a revolutionary. Socialists, said he, have no faith in universal suffrage; its chief value lies in facilitating the "struggle against order." The real question is economic in nature:

> . . . it is the struggle between capital and labor. Nothing will be obtained with legal and juridical methods, but with force. Only a revolution that does not stop with appearances, but tears out the evil by the roots, . . . is really effective revolution.[27]

However succinct as a statement of maximalist theory, Costa could have been more laconic—and sincere—if he had dared to reduce his argument to its essentials: to arrive at revolution requires creating conditions that make it unnecessary—and highly improbable.

[26] Valiani, *Storia del movimento socialista*, I, 234.
[27] *La Plebe*, Dec. 12, 21, 1880; for the conference, Manacorda, *op. cit.*, pp. 129-32; Lipparini, *Andrea Costa*, pp. 151-52.

Costa's shift from his implicit recommendation that a socialist deputy plant the red flag in parliament to assuming that role for himself extended over the next two years. And though he manifested much hesitancy and uncertainty, the destination was predetermined by the fact that the trend of the times supported his tactical conclusions, if not the assumption on which they were based. On April 30, 1881, he founded in Imola the antecedent organ of today's Italian Socialist Party, *Avanti!*, which he used as a platform for urging socialist electoral activity. In August of the same year, he tried to initiate the Italian Revolutionary Socialist Party he had suggested in his open letter of 1879. At a secret Rimini conclave of about forty Romagnol socialists,[28] Costa, intent on underlining his break with anarchism while retaining the aura of the revolutionary, persuaded all but an exiguous cluster of anarchist delegates to "reconstitute" the "Revolutionary Socialist Party" of the Romagna and to project the creation of a national party with the same name. The statute revealed the extent of the departure from anarchist theory and practice. Though member organizations were allowed complete freedom in choosing their "special sociological theories," goals and practical courses of action, all had to accept the general program, under pain of disciplinary action by a party congress. Premising acceptance of the program, all trade-unions, workers' circles, social study circles, antireligious associations and popular educational societies were welcomed into the new party. The program itself conceived the party as an instrument of class struggle, rejected conspiratorial, terroristic, and insurrectional tactics, urged reforms through agitations that "hasten the revolution, fertilizing the spirit of opposition and revolt in the people."[29] The immediate goal is not anarchy, but the conquest and exercise of political power by a "temporary dictatorship of the working classes," an affirmation suggesting that Costa's condemnation of the authoritarianism of "German communism" only nine months earlier was either sheer rhetoric or the point of departure for a singularly rapid intellectual evolution, not to mention Costa's pre-Benevento view that it was useless to declaim on proletarian virtues and sense of justice: "proletarians are neither better nor worse than anyone else, and if they find themselves in a position identical with that of the bourgeoisie of [17]89, they would act as the bourgeois did."[30] Costa's personal views aside, the program of the

---

[28] For the congress proceedings, *La Favilla*, Aug. 25, 28, Sept. 4; *Avanti!*, Aug. 28, 1881. For an incisive analysis of the deliberations, Manacorda, *op. cit.*, pp. 135-40.

[29] For the *Programma* and *Regolamento*, *Avanti!* (supplement), Aug. 28; *La Favilla*, Sept. 11, 1881. Reproduced by Manacorda, *op. cit.*, pp. 340-48.

[30] "Il Socialismo Legale ed il Socialismo Rivoluzionario," *Il Risveglio*, Mar. 25, 1877. Gnocchi-Viani not only criticized the acceptance of the dictatorial principle but accused Costa of putting the dictatorship of the working class on the same level with

Romagnols, with its emphasis on class party organization, helped precipitate the discussion among Italian socialists that was to culminate in the foundation of the modern Italian socialist party at Genoa a little over a decade later. Its tactical formulas, as the vade mecum of Italian socialists, endured for the next several decades.

In commenting on the Romagnol program, *La Plebe* asked what reasonable objections could be raised to having socialist deputies in parliament if the Romagnols accepted the principle of socialist participation in city administrations and of protest candidates in national elections.[31] Costa, in effect, agreed on December 26,[32] but even after the new suffrage law went into effect (January 22, 1882), we find him once again talking in terms of socialist candidacies for parliament only as a protest, as a means of facilitating the propagation of socialist ideas among the masses.[33] And at a February meeting of Romagnol socialists in Imola, called to make a decision on socialist electoral activity, now that the question was no longer academic, participation in both local and national elections was sanctioned, but the congress affirmed the principle that any socialist elected to the Chamber of Deputies should refuse to take the oath of allegiance to the regime and await forcible expulsion from the body, thus underlining the need of abolishing the oath. The socialist deputy should then "return to the people to continue his work of social emancipation." [34] The position was, indeed, an awkward halfway house between anarchist abstentionism and legalitarianism.

Up to the very eve of the October 29 elections, Costa did not explicitly deny this position—which may well have facilitated his own election to

---

"the dictatorship of the aristocratic and clerical class in the past and of the bourgeois class in the present." *La Favilla*, Oct. 9, 1881; *cf.*, also, the discussion of the Romagnol program in *La Plebe* (now a monthly), Sept., 1881. For Costa's rebuttal, hinged on the thesis that proletarian dictatorship was justified by the fact that "force alone can eventually resolve the social question," *Avanti!*, Oct. 17, 1881.

[31] *La Plebe*, Sept., 1881. The Romagnol party's program "is of an exasperating eclecticism . . . in it is manifested the author's effort to hide his reformist tendencies and maneuver the revolutionary instincts of the mass of the party." Merlino, *Questa è l'Italia*, p. 221. *Avanti!* (Jan. 22, 1882) called for the selection of a committee to prepare the organization of a national socialist party, but Pezzi, claiming to speak for the Tuscan socialists, spurned the proposal on the grounds that the projected party would shift the emphasis from socialist internationalism to questions of nationality. "More interested in its existence in Italy than elsewhere, it will become . . . a self-centered party dealing with questions of *patria* at the expense of the international question," a development that necessarily implies forsaking the ideal of violent revolution. Letter to the Romagnols, Feb. 16, 1882, Bosio, *ed.*, "Lettere . . . di . . . Pezzi," p. 197.

[32] *Avanti!*, Dec. 26, 1881.

[33] "Decidiamoci," in *Avanti!*, Feb. 5, 1882.

[34] For the conference proceedings, *Avanti!*, Mar. 5, 1882. *Cf.*, also, Manacorda, *op. cit.*, pp. 145-47; Borghi, *Malatesta*, p. 62.

the Chamber of Deputies with the help of republican allies who thought they were voting for a protest candidate.[35] But once elected, Costa could no longer procrastinate, for the new legislature was soon to convene. Technically, the decision of whether he should take the oath belonged, not to Costa, but to the Ravenna socialists who had elected him, for the Romagnol party's program, almost surely written by Costa himself, was conveniently flexible: the provincial associations (not the party) had the authority to "*fix the conduct* of the comrades who might be elected deputies," whether their candidacies had been "positive" or protestant. Thus, on November 29, while the packed *aula* of Montecitorio still echoed the clamor aroused by the forcible ejection of a republican deputy refusing to take the oath, Andrea Costa replied to the ritual formula of the president, not with a firm "no," nor even with a "yes" qualified as only he could qualify it, but with a simple "*Giuro*" ("I swear"). Before the day was done, he sent off an "explanation" to the newspapers, in which he said he had entered parliament to "modify and abolish" laws harmful to the working class: "Only for this reason were we able, for one instant, to renounce our personality as free citizens and revolutionaries." [36] Whether Costa's subsequent political career proved his renunciation of his "revolutionary personality" to be momentary or permanent is still an open question.

OBSEQUIES OF THE ITALIAN ANARCHIST MOVEMENT

Whatever the discrepancy between Costa's new tactical formula and his professed social revolutionary objective, it was nowhere near as great as that existing between the anarchists' insurrectional principle and the practical chances of actuating it. And if Costa's theoretical inconsistency justifies scepticism about his ultimate intentions, the opposition of the hard-shell anarchists to socialist political action in the interest of the working classes, however honest an effort to keep means coherent with ends, bars accepting at face value their desire, clearly implied in the correspondence commission's Circular of September 1879, to attract a mass following. Their losing battle against socialist political action, conducted amidst growing enthusiasm for the prospects offered by a widely expanded suffrage, betrayed that they still valued theoretical integrity above effective political influence, even when it could no longer be said that the proletariat lacked interest in its own emancipation. Francesco

---

[35] For Costa's contribution to the Romagnol Democratic Electoral Union, which included a promise "to intervene in the struggle for the claims put forward by other [democratic] parties," see Lipparini, *Andrea Costa*, p. 198; Borghi, *Malatesta*, pp. 62-63.

[36] Lipparini, *Andrea Costa*, pp. 212-13.

Pezzi could attribute the Italian International's low estate to the anarchists' mistaken judgement of Costa,[37] Cafiero could lament that the Romagnol had shown a lack of character and sense of responsibility,[38] but the real explanation lay in their own failure to read aright the signs of the times.

The Milanese legalitarian nucleus headed by Bignami and Gnocchi-Viani gave the anarchists an opportunity to make a face-saving retreat from total intransigence when they convened on December 5, 1880, in Chiasso, just over the border in Switzerland, a congress to reconstitute the Federation of Upper Italy.[39] Though the legalitarians had hoped the meeting would establish a common formula between themselves and the now thinned out directive group of the Italian International, almost limited to the Lugano clique of Cafiero, Grassi, Matteucci, and Ergisto Marzoli, the most the reformist arguments of Gnocchi-Viani and Giuseppe De Franceschi could accomplish was a unanimous approval of the position sustained by Costa at Bologna only a month earlier: that agitation for universal suffrage was primarily useful as socialist propaganda.[40] Under Cafiero's chairmanship, which he used to argue political abstention, the Chiasso majority affirmed that "the only hope of the Italian proletariat" was the preparation of an armed insurrection. Even Tito Zanardelli and Lodovico Nabruzzi had apparently moved back into the anarchist camp, for they had helped to compose, and Zanardelli now read, a manifesto to the congress urging recourse to insurrection. The declaration's chief author was Amilcare Cipriani, whose long imprisonment on New Caledonia had by no means broken the spirit of activism that had led him to fight the Piedmontese at Aspromonte, the Turks on Crete, and the bourgeois enemies of the Paris Commune.

Though the Chiasso deliberations represented nothing more than a formal victory of the anarchist exiles in Lugano,[41] they seem to have begun planning immediately the implementation of the congress' insurrectional directive. For the next several weeks, Italian police were kept on

[37] Letter to Cafiero, Nov. 3, 1880, La Plebe, Dec. 12, 1880.
[38] Letter to Pezzi, Nov. 20, 1880, Conti, O.S.F., pp. 235-36.
[39] For the proceedings, La Plebe, Dec. 12; Grido del Popolo (Naples), Dec. 13, 24; Le Révolté (Geneva), Dec. 11, 1880, Jan. 8, 1881; Manacorda, op. cit., pp. 132-35; Zoccoli, L'Anarchia, p. 396; Michels, Storia del marxismo in Italia, p. 36; Conti, O.S.F., p. 236; Valiani, Storia del movimento socialista, I, 236.
[40] The Italian anarchist leadership in Italy, concentrated in Florence and Naples, had already declared itself "abstentionist with respect to the current movement for universal suffrage." La Plebe, July 18, 1880.
[41] Costa, on the Chiasso deliberations: "Fortunately, social and economic agitation will occur with or without those revolutionaries, who try to oppose the natural evolution of the century in the name of I-do-not-know-what absurd principles." Letter to Kulisciov, in Lipparini, Andrea Costa, p. 164.

the alert by reports that the Lugano group—Cafiero, Grassi, Marzoli, Matteucci, Zanardelli—had formed the "Italian Revolutionary Committee" which, with the help of Russian nihilists and a group of Communards organized by Cipriani in Paris, would descend on Italy in April to inaugurate revolution in the Romagna and Tuscany with arson and assassination of public officials.[42] If police information was correct, the presence of Cafiero and Cipriani in Rome in January, ostensibly to participate in a projected convention of all radical and republican militants favoring universal suffrage,[43] may have meant that the contacting of insurrectional elements was under way. In any case, when Cipriani made the mistake of visiting his father in Rimini at the end of the month, he was arrested, and the whole fantastic scheme collapsed. Cafiero once more disappeared into exile, the Lugano group dispersed, and Marzoli, writing to his fellow conspirators in Florence, said he and Grassi, now in Genoa, were penniless and hounded by the police.[44]

In Italy itself, only Florentine and Neapolitan anarchists held out against the current, but they were obviously on the verge of going under completely. By the end of 1880, according to the local *questore,* the Florentine International was without organization, discipline, or influence, and its sole activity consisted of naming a "secret committee," composed of Natta, Pezzi, Giovacchino Niccheri, and Eugenio Ringressi, who maintained contact with Lugano until that nucleus dissolved. Now, too, began that exodus to France, Egypt, and South America which, by 1885, was to denude Florence of its once numerous company of anarchists.[45]

In Naples, Francesco Saverio Merlino, though recognizing the need of anarchist penetration of the working classes, tried to convince the local anarchists that a successful struggle against the Italian state required the

---

[42] For details of this last anarchist attempt at "social liquidation" by insurrection, Conti, *O.S.F.,* p. 237, note 2. For Cafiero's last literary effort to defend "permanent revolution, by word, by writing, by the dagger, the rifle, dynamite," see his article in *Le Révolté* of Dec. 25, 1880, reproduced by Romano, *Storia,* III, 579-81.

[43] Nettlau, *Malatesta,* p. 182; Vigo, *Storia degli ultimi trent'anni,* III, 223-24; Valiani, *Storia del movimento socialista,* I, 236.

[44] Conti, *O.S.F.,* p. 237, note 2.

[45] *Ibid.,* pp. 236-38. In Nov., 1883, Malatesta came to Florence and, to propagate the anarchist dogma, founded *La Questione Sociale,* in the pages of which he waged a violent war on Costa and the Romagnol Revolutionary Socialist Party. In Feb., 1884, he and Merlino were tried for conspiracy in Rome. When fifty-eight Florentine Internationalists signed a manifesto of solidarity with the accused, they were heavily fined and handed thirty-month jail sentences. Early in 1885, after the sentences were reduced, fifteen of the group turned themselves in for imprisonment; the rest—including Natta, Malatesta, Francesco Pezzi, and his wife—expatriated clandestinely to Argentina. *Ibid.,* p. 239.

support of peasants and the *déclassés* of the petty bourgeoisie.[46] By May, 1882, he was completely discouraged, for he had found his fellow anarchists in the Parthenopian city "impossible people, . . . incapable of taking the least initiative, . . . invaded by a diabolical spirit of puerile envy, . . . [dedicated] to sowing discord, dividing and demolishing" every constructive organizational effort, even among the workers.[47] The most revealing commentary on the condition of the Neapolitan International was the *questore's* assertion in May 1883 that the local anarchists had committed "no criminal public deed" and had held no meetings after August 1881.[48]

Aside from these last paroxysms of the Italian International, the only other anarchist manifestation in the peninsula was a new spate of individual condemnations of Costa's "apostasy," occasioned by the formation of the Romagnol Revolutionary Socialist Party in August 1881 and by Costa's simultaneous call for a national legalitarian party. Carlo Cafiero called for his friends in the Romagna to "do justice to the perfidious charlatan, if you do not want the people to curse the revolution as a false and lying god." Vittorio Valbonesi labelled the Romagnol agitator a renegade and hypocrite who "deceives the people in the full consciousness of deceiving them, because his ambition and vanity do not allow him to declare firmly that he is no longer what he was." Merlino developed the same indictment in the pages of his newspaper, *Grido del Popolo*. From Cagnano-Verano, Carmelo Palladino accused Costa of exploiting the admiration of a handful of deluded persons for the purpose of satisfying his ambition to head a "so-called socialist party." His was "not evolution, but reaction and apostasy." [49]

---

[46] These, in any case, were the positions he upheld at the London international anarchist congress in July, 1881. See Valiani, "Dalla Prima alla Seconda Internazionale," p. 205. Several months earlier, he had posed the problem as simply the choice between demolishing the state or the economic system (by the abolition of private property), but, in either case, violent revolution must come—and soon, for "improvements in small doses, even when achieved with the help of legal agitation, are always pregnant with antidotes that neutralize their effects." Letter to Tancredi Liverani, Oct. 20, 1880, in Romano, *Storia*, III, 353, note 62.

[47] Letter to Antonio Murgo, May 19, 1882, in Franco Della Peruta's preface to Merlino's *Questa è l'Italia*, vi. Luigi Felicò, as one of the chief obstructionists, resigned his duties with Merlino's *Il Grido del Popolo* in 1882. *Ibid.*, vii.

[48] *Loc. cit.*

[49] For Cafiero's and Valbonesi's criticisms, *Il Grido del Popolo*, July 21, 1881; for that of Merlino, *ibid.*, Aug. 10; of Palladino, *ibid.*, Sept. 18. For Costa's rebuttal, see his letter "To my Friends and to my Enemies," in *Avanti!* (now in Cesena), supplement to Sept. 18, 1881, issue. Palladino had accepted Costa's invitation to contribute to the *Rivista Internazionale del Socialismo* but broke off personal relations with Costa after a quarrel over a German translation of a Palladino essay on "L'Astensione," Lucarelli, *Palladino*, p. 7. Malatesta, with Costa undoubtedly in mind,

Of all the anarchist militants who denounced Costa for his new orientation, only one reversed himself, but his was an "apostasy" most of his friends forgave as the malfunctioning of a seriously sick mind. After an abortive attempt, with Errico Malatesta and Vito Solieri, to launch a London anarchist newspaper, *Insurrezione,* in the summer of 1881,[50] Carlo Cafiero fell prey to delusions of persecution, seeing police spies in even his closest friends.[51] In March 1882 he returned to Milan "to advise his Italian comrades to follow henceforth . . . the parliamentary tactic in the German social democratic sense and to convince them to prepare themselves for the conquest of public powers." [52] After informing Bignami and Gnocchi-Viani of his change of mind, Cafiero offered this justification:

> Today the party has definitely taken this new path; those who, with me, disagreed with it, have adhered. Therefore, it seems to me that the question presents itself in a precise and decisive way: to submit or resign. I did not like to resign from the defense of popular right, so I submitted to the party, frankly and freely accepting its new line of conduct. Today's fact is a fact, and it is useless to lose oneself in vain investigations of the arguments of the former contending factions; it is much better to take a single step with all the comrades on the real path of life than to remain isolated and to cover hundreds of leagues in the abstract.[53]

Cafiero's friends refused to take his defection seriously. Pezzi assured the reformists that the Pugliese could not have accepted an evolutionary program unless "his brain has gone." [54] Palladino called the defection an "evolution," but a "true and dignified one, not false and Jesuitical like

---

was still bitter almost fifty years later about the "subtle way the new converts to parliamentarism conducted themselves, denying and affirming, attenuating or accenting the new tendency according to the . . . circumstances, and pulling in the more ingenuous with the sentimentalism of personal friendships, almost without their being aware of it." Introduction to Nettlau, *B.I.I.,* xxix.

[50] Nettlau, *Malatesta,* pp. 187-88, and note; Borghi, *Malatesta,* p. 62. The paper's title reflected the decision to persist in insurrectional activity that was affirmed by the anarchists' international congress of London, July 14-20, 1881. Malatesta here recognized the importance of anarchist contact with the masses but insisted that in Italy the struggle against the state was more urgent than the conflict on the economic plane. Valiani, "Dalla Prima alla Seconda Internazionale," pp. 204-05.

[51] Nettlau, *Malatesta,* pp. 189-90. For details on Cafiero's mental aberrations, see Gianni Bosio, "Carlo Cafiero dal soggiorno di Locarno al manicomio di S. Bonifacio," *Movimento Operaio,* Yr. I, No. 1 (Oct. 1, 1949), 21-25.

[52] Michels, *Storia del marxismo in Italia,* p. 39.

[53] Letter to Alcibiade Moneta, *La Favilla,* Apr. 9/10, 1882.

[54] Letter to Costa, Apr. 7, 1882, Bosio, *ed.,* "Lettere . . . di . . . Pezzi," p. 198.

that of Costa." [55] And as an answer to reformists who thought Cafiero's change of mind would eliminate the last objections to the new trend, Tuscan anarchists met in Poggibonsi on March 15 and reaffirmed the "absolute inefficacy of the political vote for the social redemption of the oppressed." Socialists were advised to use the electoral agitations for propaganda purposes and to insist that any socialist elected to the Chamber of Deputies refuse to take the required oath of allegiance.[56]

Arrested in Milan in April 1882, jailed as a delinquent for several months, despite his increasingly manifest insanity, and then set free in Switzerland, Cafiero promptly attempted suicide by slashing his throat and wrists with the lenses of his spectacles. After his old Locarno friend, Emilio Bellerio, had nursed him back to relative physical and mental health, he made his last effective contribution to the Italian socialist movement by supporting, in the fall of 1882, the parliamentary candidacies of Emilio Covelli and Barbanti-Brodano, though refusing the pleas of socialists in Florence, Forlì, Rimini, and Turin to present himself as at least a protest candidate.[57] His final recommendation, on the eve of the October 29 elections, unreservedly accepted the Marxian thesis he had spent his political career in denying:

> Today the party . . . has accomplished a radical mutation in our tactic. It wants a representation in Parliament because it wants laws tending toward the emancipation of the workers, to achieve which will require pushing our representatives into the conquest of power. Such is the new war that we are undertaking . . .[58]

[55] Lucarelli, *Palladino*, p. 7.

[56] Manacorda, *op. cit.*, p. 147. The new electoral law and the coming elections "interest us officially as a party; individually, each is free to act as he chooses. As private persons we have advised workers to get on the voting lists. . . . But the party, as such, will never run a candidate. . . . We shall use the vote principally as a potent means of agitation, ... we shall impose conditions, i.e., a strictly revolutionary conduct, . . . on the workers' candidate: if elected, [he must] go to the Chamber, refuse to take the oath and to leave the hall unless forcefully dragged out, ... thus inviting his electors to protest. . . . This . . . would be an excellent way to foment disorders and clamor, to open the road to something good." Pezzi letter of Feb. 16, 1882, Bosio, *ed.*, "Lettere . . . di . . . Pezzi," p. 198. The Florentines managed to get five hundred railway, gas, and Galileo optical firm workers inscribed on the voting lists. Conti, *O.S.F.*, p. 208.

[57] *La Plebe*, Oct. 8, 22, 27, 1882; Nettlau, *Malatesta*, pp. 189-90; Bosio, "Carlo Cafiero dal soggiorno di Locarno al manicomio di S. Bonifacio," pp. 22-23. Despite Cafiero's refusal, he was run as a protest candidate in several cities and won 183 votes in Florence, 169 in Turin, 113 in Corato, and 60 in La Spezia. *Loc. cit.* On the background of Cafiero's candidacy in Florence, where Natta received 212 votes as a "worker candidate," see Conti, *O.S.F.*, p. 238.

[58] *La Plebe*, Oct. 27, 1882.

And though conscious that his own condition forbade joining the parliamentary spearhead in the war on capitalist society, he accepted the logical alternative by urging Costa to "go to Parliament, frankly take your oath, and serve the common cause with the nobility of mind you are capable of using." [59]

The renunciation of anarchist principles and the acceptance of socialist political struggle, symbolized by Cafiero's final advice and Costa's prompt compliance with it, marked the opening of a new historic phase in the development of the Italian socialist movement. With anarchism effectively liquidated as the dominant ideology, the way was cleared for the transition from the necessarily restricted and sectarian movement to which the Italian International had been reduced to the organization of socialism on a mass and class basis. The shift was to be protracted over the ensuing decade, for it required the fusion of two distinct elements that in 1882 were only beginning to emerge: a political socialist movement, with its focal point in the traditionally revolutionary Romagna, and a workers' movement, equally eager to exploit the widened suffrage, with its base in Lombardy, by now the country's industrial stronghold. The appearance of an Italian socialist movement, in the contemporary sense, would depend on eliminating the distinction.

[59] Schiavi, "La formazione del pensiero politico di Andrea Costa," p. 31. In the spring of 1883 Cafiero returned to Italy, was found wandering naked in the hills of Fiesole (outside Florence). His sanity had not returned when he died, at the age of forty-seven, in a rest home in Nocera Inferiore on July 17, 1892. Emilio Covelli, who also died insane, may well have pronounced the most apt and accurate epitaph to Cafiero's political career: "Do you know why Cafiero is crazy? Because, in not knowing how to bend, he had to break." Pier Carlo Masini, "Carlo Cafiero ed una controversia intorno alla sua ultima posizione politica," *Volontà*, Yr. I, Nos. 8-9 (Mar. 1, 1947), 83. Pezzi committed suicide in 1917.

Index

(Newspapers and periodicals are italicized.)